Madhya Pradesh
Development Report

सत्यमेव जयते

Planning Commission
Government of India

Madhya Pradesh
Development Report

सत्यमेव जयते

PLANNING COMMISSION
GOVERNMENT OF INDIA
NEW DELHI

Published by

ACADEMIC FOUNDATION
NEW DELHI

First Published in 2011 by
Academic Foundation
4772-73 / 23 Bharat Ram Road, (23 Ansari Road), Darya Ganj, New Delhi - 110 002 (India).
Phones : 23245001 / 02 / 03 / 04. Fax : +91-11-23245005. E-mail : books@academicfoundation.com
www.academicfoundation.com

Published under arrangement with :
Planning Commission,
Government of India,
New Delhi.

Cataloging in Publication Data--DK
Courtesy: D.K. Agencies (P) Ltd. <docinfo@dkagencies.com>

Madhya Pradesh development report / Planning Commission, Government of India.
p. cm.
ISBN 13: 9788171888689
ISBN 10: 8171888682

1. Economic development--India--Madhya Pradesh. 2. Madhya Pradesh (India)--Economic policy. 3. Madhya Pradesh (India)--Social policy. 4. Human services--India--Madhya Pradesh. I. India. Planning Commission.

DDC 338.9543 22

Designed and typeset by Italics India, New Delhi
Printed and bound in India.

Core Committee

Dr. Bhalchandra L. Mungekar Member, Planning Commission	Chairman
Principal Adviser/Adviser (State Plan-Central)	Member
Principal Secretary (Planning), Government of Madhya Pradesh	Member
Representative, Partner Institution Sanket Information and Research Agency, Bhopal	

सत्यमेव जयते

एम. एस. आहलुवालिया

MONTEK SINGH AHLUWALIA

1857 1907 1947 2007

जय हिन्द

उपाध्यक्ष

योजना आयोग

भारत

DEPUTY CHAIRMAN

PLANNING COMMISSION

INDIA

FOREWORD

One of the important Tenth Plan initiatives of the Planning Commission was to sponsor preparation of the State Development Reports, assigning the exercise to reputed institutes, the independent exercise of Union and State Government has been undertaken in recognition of the fact that economic circumstances and performance of individual states have varied considerably. It was felt to examine the development challenges of each state in light of the state-specific opportunities, constraints and resources. The basic idea has been to produce a quality reference document on development profiles of individual states and devising appropriate strategy for accelerated development.

The Madhya Pradesh State Development Report reviews Madhya Pradesh's development experience and highlights critical inputs for the state's development in the years ahead. I hope this publication will stimulate debate on growth strategies appropriated for Madhya Pradesh. I am also sure the roadmap indicated in the Report will stimulate a broader awareness of the critical policy issues facing the state, and would enable the state to move to a higher growth path, securing welfare for all its citizens.

(Montek Singh Ahluwalia)

Yojana Bhawan, Parliament Street, New Delhi : 110001 Phones: 23096677, 20396688, 20396699 Fax : 23096699 E-mail : dch@yojana.nic.in

Shivraj Singh Chouhan
Chief Minister

Government of Madhya Pradesh
BHOPAL - 462 004

Dated: 15 October 2009

MESSAGE

Madhya Pradesh, the second largest state of India, is the 9th biggest state economy in the country. Blessed with vast natural resources and comparatively peaceful environment, the state still faces formidable challenge of removing historical constraints of development.

We have taken great strides in improving the infrastructure including roads, power and irrigation in the last few years. However, great deal of efforts are still required to bring the state at par with the other developed states. The recent initiatives to empower women and girl child have been appreciated across the country. Ladli Laxmi Yojana and Deendayal Antyodaya Upchar Yojana have been hailed at the national level. The state has done very well in terms of implementation of Centrally Sponsored Schemes including flagship programmes and Bharat Nirman Schemes. Meticulous fiscal management has given a thrust to the state economy.

I am happy to learn that the Planning Commission of India is bringing out the "State Development Report" for Madhya Pradesh. We have embarked upon an ambitious goal of placing Madhya Pradesh in the category of leading states in terms of development. I am sure that the State Development Report will not only capture the trends of various sectors of development, but also will help us in designing and strategising the future initiatives for faster development.

(Shivraj Singh Chouhan)

Contents

List of Tables, Boxes Figures and Annexures

Tables

Boxes

Figures

Annexures

Acknowledgements

Preparation of the State Development Report was quite a challenging considering the vast span of subject it deals with. At the same time is most crucial in the sense of reviewing the performance of different developmental sectors of the economy and its influence on the social and economic development of the citizens of the state. The report not only reflects upon the current status of state's performance but also provides references and guidelines for important policy decisions for future development. We are very grateful to the Planning Commission of India for giving us the opportunity of undertaking this endeavor; thus contributing in the development process of the state.

We are also appreciating efforts, patience and timely contribution of all our main chapter writer, subject matter specialist contributors in accomplishing this report.

Mr. Sandeep Dikshit, Expert, Rural and Human Development issues

Dr. P.D. Joshi, Former, Deputy Director, NSSO, GoI

Dr. Pradeep Bose, Expert and Development Practionar

Mr. Kiran P. Mali, Forest Resource Economist, Indian Institute of Forest Management, Bhopal

Mr. Devendra Singh Bhadoria, Principal Programme Co-ordinator, Lupin Human Welfare and Research Foundation, Bhopal

Mr. Manu Sinha, Development Consultant, Bhopal

Ms. Pallavi K. Mali, Programme Co-ordinator, Sanket, Bhopal

Mr. Manish Shankar, Vice President, Access Development Services, Bhopal

Mr. Ankur Singhal, Livelihood Specialist, Pradan, Bhopal

Sanket Team

We express our thanks to our team member Sanjay Shrivastava, Devkant Tripathi, Jitendra Shrivastav, Santosh Joshi for their kind support and assistance in undertaking research and analysis for this report.

State Government

Our sincere thanks are also due to

Mr. Devendra Singhai, Principal Secretary, State Planning Commission, Madhya Pradesh

Mr. Mangesh Tyagi, Additional Secretary, MP State Planning Board

Mr. D.P. Ahirwar, Deputy Secretary, Department of Planning, Economics and Statistics, MP

Mr. R.K. Zariya, Senior Research Officer, Department of Planning, Economics and Statistics, MP

Mr. Manoj Jhalani, Commissioner, Rajaya Shiksha Kendra, Bhopal

We are pleased to convey the thanks to all the state government officials of various departments including Health, Agriculture, Industry and Commerce, Village Industry, Forestry, Tourism, Finance, Energy.

We are highly obliged to Dr. B.L. Mungekar, Member, Planning Commission India for providing us the opportunity and trusting our efforts. Our special tanks to Mr. A.K. Panda, Director, State Planning Cell Planning commission India, for his constant support and valuable guidance in accomplishing the task.

Executive Summary

Centrally located, Madhya Pradesh (MP) is also known as the heart of India. Spread across an area of 308,000 sq km, MP is the second largest state of the country and ninth largest economy in India. The state is endowed with vast natural resources like forests, minerals, rare and valuable herbs and medicinal plants and eight important rivers flowing across the state. MP is the largest producer of oilseeds and pulses, garlic and coriander in the country. Low cost of basic infrastructure and availability of skilled manpower and cheap unskilled labour further paved the way for expanding existing industrial base to greater extent. Its rich cultural heritage and comparatively peaceful law and order situation, coupled with good connectivity with neighbouring states leverage the state as one of the emerging economy with high potential.

Trend analysis for the newly formed Madhya Pradesh indicates that the state is trying hard to lift its economy to more developing strides and to come out of the BIMARU bracket. Two distinct waves were noticed while preparing the State Development Report (SDR) for Madhya Pradesh. Fiscal scenario of the state has shown significant improvement on one hand, thereby transforming the state's economy from revenue deficit to revenue surplus state. Such fiscal discipline has multiplier effect on the various components of the economy to develop and expand further. Sectoral composition clearly shows that the economy of the state is gradually shifting from the primary sector to secondary and tertiary sectors. But one has to be cautious as the state's GDP is highly sensitive to growth in agriculture sector. Hence, proper attention must be given to this sector as it has the potential to boost both industry and service sector through direct and indirect ways. Also, the development objectives of income and employment generation, poverty alleviation, balanced regional development can be addressed through proper focus on agriculture and allied sectors.

Latest achievements of the state include infrastructure development in terms of physical connectivity and ICT, increased literacy, enrolment and access to schooling, promoting the thriving sectors like tourism and industry and initiating public-private partnership (PPP) for raising assets with minimum debt burden.

On the other hand, the state's performance on basic human development indicators and other developmental indicators is not impressive, and many a times fall far below the set standards or national average. The following key areas are still the cause of great concerns if the state has to pursue balanced and equitable socio-economic development which includes health and nutrition specifically for women and children, access to safe drinking water and sanitation, housing and availability of electricity, financial inclusion of marginalised sections and productivity of agricultural crops and high poverty ratio.

Thus, the state has to put forth the strategic efforts in improving the current pace of providing health services, quality of both primary education and higher education, non-farm income and employment generation opportunities, and reducing exploitation of natural resources for sustained growth. This is of an immense importance in light of the fact that nearly 35 per cent of the state's population belongs to Dalit and tribal communities, 38.3 per cent population is living below poverty line. Since these marginalised sections are highly dependent on the state government for survival, hence the responsibility of the upliftment of these sections lies primarily with the state government only.

It is essential for the state to have balanced development on the fronts of economic indicators and social indicators. Favour of any one side may result into large scale disparity in the overall development of the state and will have farthest consequences in the lives of its citizens.

The SDR in its analysis tried to cover different social and economic sectors of the economy through 13 chapters ranging from growth of economy, employment and livelihood status, governance, agriculture, health, education to infrastructure and industrial development in the state. The scheme of chapterisation is as follows:

1. Comparative Development Profile

The chapter deals with overall growth of the state's economy, interstate comparisons based on per capita GSDP, sectoral growth of the economy, sector-wise plan outlays in FYP, overview of budgetary performance, comparative profile of poverty in the country, ranking on human development, population growth and implications for the state.

2. Employment and Livelihood

This chapter covers trends in growth in employment situation in the state, size class holding, forest based livelihood, employment in enterprises and establishment including both agriculture and non-agriculture, rural non-farm employment, unemployment, underemployment, quality of employment, labour productivity, employment strategies and constraints and policy recommendations.

3. Agriculture

The chapter describes agro-climatic zones, land use classification, agriculture growth in the state, cropping pattern, share of MP in India's agriculture output, horticulture, allied services in agriculture, institutions and supporting services in agriculture, irrigation potential created and utilised in the state, crop-wise irrigation, and road ahead.

4. Finance

The chapter attempted trends in revenue receipts, analysis of both tax and non-tax revenues, trends in capital receipts, debt/GSDP ratio, trends of internal debt of the state government, expenditure side analysis including size of the budget, plan and non-plan expenditure, revenue and capital expenditure, analysis of various components of expenditure, developmental and non-developmental expenditure, adherence to FRBM, quality of expenditure, accurate budgeting, fiscal decentralisation, measures taken for financial discipline and way forward.

5. Governance

In this chapter, we tried to cover the topics like ranking of India on governance indicators, interstate comparisons based on quality of life, good governance, governance issues pertaining to Madhya Pradesh including human development, poverty and hunger, law and order situation and state of vulnerable communities, corruption, democratic institutions for governance, urbanisation, migration, social inequality, government initiatives for improving governance in the state.

6. Education

The chapter describes status of elementary education, secondary education, higher education, technical education, quality of education, equity in education, provisioning of teachers, decentralisation of academic support institutions, education budget, various partners in education.

7. Forest

This chapter deals with state of forest in MP, conservation of biosphere reserves, importance of forestry sector in state's economy, production of non-timber forest produce and minor forest produce, expenditure on forest sector, social forestry, joint forest management, state level initiatives and road ahead.

8. Status of Women and Children

Focus of this chapter is on status of women and child on key survival indicators, child mortality, maternal mortality, overall and child sex ratio, education profile, economic profile of women, child labour, political voice of women, crime against women and children in the state, gender budgeting and women's empowerment.

9. Tourism

The chapter covers tourism in India, importance of tourism, tourism in Madhya Pradesh including tourist destinations in the state, hospitality, tourist arrival in the state, growth of tourism sector, tourism policies, institutional mechanism for promoting tourism, achievements of tourism sector and strategies for tourism development.

10. Infrastructure

The chapter highlights some of the very pertinent issues related to major sub-sectors of infrastructure like physical connectivity through road, air and railways, telecom, power and water supply and sanitation.

11. Handloom

This chapter describes status of handloom sector in MP, performance of handloom on various indicators, handloom based textile clusters in MP, demand for handloom, market profiles for handloom products, supporting industries, key initiatives of state government and future strategy for growth of the sector.

12. Health

The chapter discusses about the indicators on the state of health, infant and child mortality, maternal health in the state, factors affecting basic health, health infrastructure in MP, expenditure on health, state policies and initiatives, medium term health sector strategy for the state and road ahead.

13. Industry

The last chapter covers role of industry in the state's economy, key industries, industrialisation in MP, comparative performance of factory sector in MP, industrial clusters, SEZs in the state and investment opportunities for promoting industrialisation.

Chapter 1

Comparative Development Profile of Madhya Pradesh

1. Introduction

Planned development in India made its beginning immediately after achieving independence in the year 1947 through successive Five Year Plans (FYPs). The economic policy makers of these FYPs have constantly sought to direct the developmental resources in to the parts of the country that are less developed for balanced regional development. However, the approach to the Tenth Plan addressed the issue of uneven growth and increase in the socio-economic and demographic standards in different states of the country. Development strategies in different states, therefore, need attention to make them consistent with twin objectives of growth and capacity building for achieving the desired level of socio-economic development and demographic goals. This report aims to provide dimensions of development for the state of erstwhile and newly formed Madhya Pradesh over a period of time and thereby emerging policy thrust for development.

The state of Madhya Pradesh was formed on November 1, 1956 by merging the then states of Madhya Bharat, Vindhya Pradesh and the princely state of Bhopal on the recommendation of State Reorganisation Committee. Further, with the enactment of Madhya Pradesh Re-organisation Act in the year 2000, it was bifurcated to carve out a new state Chhattisgarh. Before carving out Chhattisgarh, Madhya Pradesh was the state with the largest area in the country with natural beauty and abundant natural resources and economically useful minerals in large quantity namely, diamond (sole producer in the country), copper mining (80 per cent in the country), magnesium ore, limestone, coal and coalbed methane.

2. Economic Profile: Interstate Comparisons

There was a group of states in 1960-61 with per capita incomes (at current prices) fairly close to each other. These were: Himachal Pradesh with a per capita income of Rs. 236, Uttar Pradesh with Rs. 253, Madhya Pradesh with Rs. 254, Kerala Rs. 260, J&K Rs. 268, Andhra Pradesh Rs. 276 and Rajasthan Rs. 282. The all-India per capita income level was Rs. 331. Table 1.1 presents the index of per capita state domestic product (SDP) at constant prices.

TABLE 1.1

Index of Per Capita State Domestic Product (SDP) at Constant Prices (Three-Year Averages)

State	*1960-1963*	*1975-1978*	*1990-1993*	*1996-1999*	*1999-2001*	*2003-2006*
Andhra Pradesh	87.84	89.61	78.86	90.84	92.56	103.05
Himachal Pradesh	78.98	107.00	98.90	91.39	91.15	133.11
Kerala	79.95	89.23	84.98	99.53	96.14	132.81
Madhya Pradesh	74.59	72.60	74.20	73.20	74.70	62.52
Rajasthan	90.15	91.44	83.90	84.30	82.17	78.74
Uttar Pradesh	76.84	72.71	72.22	62.14	63.30	52.93
All-India	100.00	100.00	100.00	100.00	100.00	100.00

Note: The indices indicate the proportion of the per capita income of the then less developed states to the national average (represented by index value of 100).

Source: Directorate of Economics & Statistics of respective state governments, and for All-India — Central Statistical Organisation.

Over the period of 40 years' span, the development of the states based on per capita income index shows diverse trends. Andhra Pradesh, Himachal Pradesh and Kerala have done far better compared to situation in 1960s. One thing to be noticed here strikingly is that the index of per capita SDP of these states has not only improved but it has crossed the national average figures. On the other hand, performance of the states like Madhya Pradesh, Rajasthan and Uttar Pradesh has deteriorated over the same time period. Per capita SDP index of these states shows decline since 1960s and also the index is much below the national average.

In terms of per capita income, these peer group states of the sixties followed relatively different growth paths. As may be seen from Table 1.2, of these states, while the relative position of MP has improved in relation to national per capita income till mid-nineties but after bifurcation of the state, it has shown a drastic fall at 21 position among all the states. Performance of Uttar Pradesh has remained stable until mid-nineties, experiencing a continuous relative decline *vis-à-vis* the all-India level over the next four decades. However, two of the states in this peer group of the sixties experienced considerable improvement in their relative all-India position; these were Himachal Pradesh and Kerala.

Table 1.2 gives the ranking of states on the basis of per capita gross SDP at constant prices for major states of India.

TABLE 1.2

Ranking of States on the Basis of Per Capita SDP at Constant Prices

State	*1960-1963*	*1996-1999*	*2003-2006*
Andhra Pradesh	10	9	11
Assam	7	14	19
Bihar	17	17	23
Gujarat	3	3	8
Haryana	6	4	3
Himachal Pradesh	13	8	6
Karnataka	8	6	10
Kerala	12	7	7
Madhya Pradesh	16	12	21
Maharashtra	1	1	5
Orissa	15	16	20
Punjab	4	2	4
Rajasthan	9	11	17
Tamil Nadu	5	5	9
Uttar Pradesh	14	15	22
West Bengal	2	10	12

Source: Directorate of Economics & Statistics of respective state governments, and for All-India — Central Statistical Organisation and Office of Registrar General & Census Commissioner of India.

It may be seen that notable declines in relative all-India rankings have taken place in the major states of eastern India, most notably West Bengal, but also in the case of Bihar, Orissa and Assam. In the north, the state of Uttar Pradesh has shown a slight and continuous decline over four decades. Haryana has continuously improved its position and Punjab has remained more or less stable. However, ranking of the states in southern and western India has shown slight decline.

TABLE 1.3

GSDP-MP and GDP at 1999-2000 Constant Prices

(In Rs. Crore)

Year	*GSDP-MP*	*GDP-India*	*% Share of MP*
1999-2000	80132	1786525	4.49
2000-01	74582	1864773	4.00
2001-02	79891	1972912	4.05
2002-03	76765	2047733	3.75
2003-04	85530	2222591	3.85
2004-05	88254	2389660	3.69
2005-06 (Q)	94158	2604532	3.62
2006-07 (A)	99110	2844022	3.48

Note: Q: Quick Estimate; A: Advance Estimate.

Source: Estimates of state domestic product of Madhya Pradesh, 1999-2000 to 2006-07, Directorate of Economics & Statistics, GoMP.

TABLE 1.4

Recent Trend in Rate of Growth of Per Capita Income

States	*1993-94 to 1998-99 (Average)*	*2002-03 to 2005-06 (Average)*
Andhra Pradesh	3.52	4.97
Assam	1	3.10
Bihar	2.6	-0.09
Gujarat	6.2	8.00
Haryana	3.6	4.91
Himachal Pradesh	3.9	3.98
Karnataka	6.4	4.51
Kerala	4.2	5.49
Madhya Pradesh	2.3	3.67
Maharashtra	5.4	4.99
Orissa	2.9	6.46
Punjab	3	2.24
Rajasthan	5.3	4.75
Tamil Nadu	5.8	5.49
Uttar Pradesh	2.3	2.45
West Bengal	5	4.32
All-India	4.8	4.97

Source: Census data and mid year projections, Directorate of Economics & Statistics of respective state governments, and for All-India — Central Statistical Organisation and Office of Registrar General & Census Commissioner of India.

In 1993-94, the per capita income of Madhya Pradesh (base year: 1993-94) was Rs. 6584 and that of India was Rs. 7690. The per capita income of Madhya Pradesh as a proportion of all-India per capita income was 86 per cent. In the year 1999-2000, the per capita income of MP rose to Rs. 8248 but after the bifurcation, it fell to Rs. 7195 in year 2000-01. In year 2003-04, it was Rs. 8149 and in year 2004-05 the per capita income of MP is estimated to be Rs. 8238. The all-India per capita income for 2004-05 is Rs. 12416, which is 50 per cent higher than that of MP. Thus, in the last 10 years, the all-India per capita income increased at a greater rate than the per capita income of MP. The scenario has changed after the division of MP; in financial year 2001-02, MP's GSDP was 4.05 per cent of the GDP of India. The share shows continuous decline over the years and presently it is at 3.48 per cent in 2006-07.

To round off the picture of income growth, we take a look at the recent trend in rate of growth of per capita income for the years 1993-94 to 1998-99 and 2002-03 to 2005-06 indicated in Table 1.4.

TABLE 1.5

Growth in Per Capita Income of MP in Comparison with All-India

Year	*Per Capita Income, India*	*Percentage Increase*	*Per Capita Income in MP*	*Percentage Increase*
2004-05	22946	9.60	14471	1.14
2005-06	25956	13.12	15466	6.88
2006-07	29254	13.75	16875	9.11
2007-08	33283	12.73	18051	6.97
2008-09	38084	14.42	20256	12.22

Source: Department of Economics and Statistics, GoMP.

The average rate of growth of per capita income for MP has shown an increase from 2.3 in mid-nineties to 3.67 in the period of 2002-03 to 2005-06. It is worthy to note that states of Karnataka, Maharashtra, Punjab and Rajasthan have shown a decline in growth rate in the new millennium.

Public policy has consistently attempted to reduce regional disparities and bring about balanced regional development. The long-term trends seem to indicate that these efforts have not been particularly successful. The failure of poorer states to catch up with the better off states is often attributed to "initial conditions" and disabilities. In fact, it may be argued that the initial conditions prevailing in the early sixties indicated more balance, at least as far as levels of income were concerned, as compared to the situation prevailing today.

The saving grace is that faster growth in some states does not seem to have been achieved at the expense of growth in other states, particularly in the more recent period. Growth of all-India per capita income has accelerated in the eighties and nineties relative to earlier period, and growth rates of most of the states have risen, in inter-temporal terms. For example, in the case of MP, negative growth rates of per capita incomes in the sixties and seventies have been replaced by growth rates in the nineties and then in the early years of new millennium. But the all-India growth rate has shot up by more than proportionately from around 1 per cent per annum in the sixties and seventies to nearly 5 per cent per annum in the nineties and shows slight rise in the early years of next century. For all states, the range of growth rates has widened, and if this persists, then economic disparities between states will continue to widen.

However, the above analysis at the state level hides regional or district level disparities in per capita income. As evident from the recent report released by Department of Economics and Statistics on district level GSDP for 1999-2000 to 2007-08, 31 out of 45 districts in the state are not able to cope up with the pace of state level per capita income growth. These districts have low per capita income compared to state figures. In 15 districts, the situation is worse as average income is less than Rs. 40 per person per day. Tribal districts are dominating the list of poor performing districts. Reasons cited for such dismal performance are heavy dependency on agriculture, more extent of unirrigated agriculture, less or no industrialisation and poor expansion of service sector.

TABLE 1.6

List of Top and Worst Performing Districts in MP based on Per Capita Income

Sr. No.	*Top Ten Districts*		*Worst Performing Districts*	
	District	*Per Capita Income in Rs.*	*District*	*Per Capita Income in Rs.*
1	Indore	38830	Barwani	10915
2	Bhopal	34964	Tikamgarh	10947
3	Hoshangabad	25043	Shivpuri	11483
4	Jabalpur	24298	Bhind	11563
5	Gwalior	24039	Mandla	11619
6	Ujjain	23117	Jhabua	11621
7	Sidhi	22944	Rewa	12061
8	Ratlam	21221	Dindori	12125
9	Harda	20991	Sheopur	12209
10	Chhindwara	20220	Chattarpur	12384

Source: Department of Economics and Statistics, GoMP.

3. Growth in Economy of Madhya Pradesh

The first observation on the undivided state of Madhya Pradesh is the relative constancy in the share of its economy in the national economy, right from its formation as a state till very close to its division. Very shortly after the formation of the state in 1960-61, the economy of MP at constant prices (base 1993-94) represented a proportion of 5.6 per cent of the economy of India as a whole. Four decades later, the undivided MP in 1998-99, still represented a share of 5.6 per cent of the economy of India. After the division of MP, in financial year 2001-02, its GSDP was 4.05 per cent of the GDP of India. The share decreased to 3.480 per cent in financial year 2006-07.

TABLE 1.7

Break-up of NSDP in Rural and Urban at 1999-2000 Base Prices

Particulars	Rural	Urban	Combined
NSDP (in lakh)	3832156 (52.74)	3433380 (47.26)	7265536
Estimated population ('000)	43158 (73.56)	15511 (26.44)	58669
Per capita income	8879	22135	12384

Note: Figures in bracket are the percentages.
Source: Economic Survey of Madhya Pradesh (2007-08), Dept. of Economics & Statistics, Govt. of MP, Base Year 1999-2000.

Table 1.7 reveals that the per cent NSDP in rural MP is higher compared to urban areas, so also its population proportion. When comparison is made between per capita income of rural and urban areas, it is much lower than the urban areas owing to larger proportion of rural population.

TABLE 1.8

Gross and Net State Domestic Product at Current and Constant Prices (1999-2000)

Year	Gross State Domestic Product		Net State Domestic Product	
	Current Prices	Constant Prices	Current Prices	Constant Prices
1999-2000	8013210	8013210	7265536	7265536
2000-01	7920335	7458167	7101063	6675017
2001-02	8674496	7989110	7752185	7152534
2002-03	8683192	7676549	7666148	6779491
2003-04	10283864	8553048	9087059	7539985
2004-05	10728189	8862255	9368993	7810114
2005-06 (p)	11632222	9237128	10086706	8100570
2006-07 (q)	12820164	8625405	11122479	8437959

Note: p-provisional, q-quick.
Source: Economic Survey of Madhya Pradesh (2007-08), Dept. of Economics & Statistics, Govt. of MP, Base Year 1999-2000.

The trend of gross state domestic product (GSDP) and net state domestic product (NSDP) of MP in selected years after the division of the state has been presented in Table 1.8.

It is instructive to look at the trend in per capita income of the state. Table 1.9 presents the scenario.

TABLE 1.9

Per Capita Gross and Net Income at Current and Constant (1999-2000) Prices

Year	Per Capita Gross Income		Per Capita Net Income	
	Current Prices	Constant Prices	Current Prices	Constant Prices
1999-2000	13658	13658	12384	12384
2000-01	13231	12459	11862	11150
2001-02	14208	13085	12697	11715
2002-03	13935	12320	12303	10880
2003-04	16190	13465	14306	11870
2004-05	16576	13693	14476	12068
2005-06 (p)	17649	14015	15304	12290
2006-07 (q)	19108	14346	16578	12577

Note: p-provisional, q-quick.
Source: Economic Survey of Madhya Pradesh (2007-08), Dept. of Economics & Statistics, Govt. of MP, Base Year 1999-2000.

Annual growth in GSDP at constant prices between 1999-2000 and 2006-07 was 3.36 per cent. Compared to previous year, GSDP in 2006-07 at constant prices was estimated to be 4.20 per cent whereas the same in 2005-06 compared to its previous year recorded as 4.23 per cent. The growth has come down on account of continued drought in 2000-01 and 2002. As per quick estimate for 2006-07, the increase in GSDP at current and constant prices compared to year 2005-06 was 10.21 per cent and 4.21 per cent respectively. At constant prices, per capita net income increased from Rs. 12384 to 12577 in 2006-07, which means growth of 1.56 per cent. At current prices, it increased from Rs. 12384 to Rs. 16578 in 2006-07 resulting in growth of 33.87 per cent. Per cent change in GSDP and NSDP at current and constant prices compared to previous year may be seen in Table 1.10.

It is of interest to look into share of primary, secondary and tertiary sectors along with per cent change compared to previous year. Tables 1.11 and 1.12 present the scenario of GSDP and NSDP at current and constant prices in different years.

Agriculture along with forests form the major characteristics of the state of MP. Table 1.13 presents growth in agriculture sector compared to preceding year.

TABLE 1.10

Per cent Change Compared to Previous Year in Gross and Net Domestic Product at Current and Constant Prices

Year	Gross State Domestic Product		Net State Domestic Product		Per Capita Gross Income		Per Capita Net Income	
	Current Prices	Constant Prices	Current Prices	Constant Prices	Current Prices	Constant Prices	Current Prices	Constant Prices
2002-03	+0.10	-3.91	-1.11	-5.22	-1.92	-5.85	-3.10	-7.13
2003-04	+18.43	+1142	+18.53	+11.22	+16.18	+9.30	+16.28	+9.10
2004-05	+4.32	+3.62	+3.10	+3.58	+2.39	+1.70	+1.19	+1.66
2005-06(p)	+8.43	+4.23	+7.66	+3.72	+6.47	+2035	+5.72	+1.85
2006-07(q)	+10.21	+4.20	+10.27	+4.17	+8.27	+2.37	+8.32	+2.33

Note: p-provisional, q-quick.

Source: Economic Survey of Madhya Pradesh (2007-08), Dept. of Economics & Statistics, Govt. of MP, Base Year 1999-2000.

TABLE 1.11

Sector-wise GSDP at Current and Constant (1999-2000) Prices, Per cent Share of Sectors to all Sectors and Per cent Change Compared to Previous Year-MP

Sector	1999-2000	2000-01	2001-02	2002-03	2003-04	2004-05	2005-06	2006-07
GSDP at Current Prices								
Primary	2383910	1958170	2395991	2129823	3098254	2893998	3190202	3604691
Secondary	1941932	2041765	2135634	2157505	2449331	2782854	2972978	3212938
Tertiary	3687368	3920400	4142871	4395864	4736279	5051337	5469042	6002535
All groups	8013210	7920335	8674496	8683192	10283864	10728189	11632222	12820164
% share								
Primary	29.75	24.72	27.62	24.53	30.13	26.98	27.43	28.12
Secondary	24.23	25.78	24.62	24.85	23.82	25.94	25.56	25.06
Tertiary	46.02	49.50	47.76	50.62	46.06	47.08	47.02	46.82
All groups	100.00	100.00	100.00	100.00	100.00	100.00	100.00	100.00
% change								
Primary	-	-17.86	22.36	-11.11	45.47	-6.59	10.24	12.99
Secondary	-	5.14	4.60	1.02	13.53	13.62	6.83	8.07
Tertiary	-	6.32	5.67	6.11	7.74	6.65	8.27	9.75
All groups	-	-1.16	9.52	0.10	18.43	4.32	8.43	10.21
GSDP at Constant Prices								
Primary	2383910	1757729	2171516	1767789	2417398	2313266	2405050	2462285
Secondary	1941932	1923164	1947201	1931848	2035102	2186805	2270688	2345299
Tertiary	3687368	3777264	3870393	3976912	4100548	4362184	4561390	4817821
All groups	8013210	7458157	7989110	7676549	8553048	8862255	9237128	9625405
% share								
Primary	29.75	23.57	27.18	23.03	28.26	26.10	26.04	25.58
Secondary	24.23	25.79	24.37	25.17	23.79	24.68	24.58	24.37
Tertiary	46.02	50.65	48.45	51.81	47.94	49.22	49.38	50.05
All groups	100.00	100.00	100.00	100.00	100.00	100.00	100.00	100.00
% change								
Primary	-	-26.27	23.54	-18.59	36.75	-4.31	3.97	2.38
Secondary	-	-0.97	1.25	-0.79	5.34	7.45	3.84	3.29
Tertiary	-	2.44	2.47	2.75	3.11	6.38	4.57	5.62
All groups	-	-6.93	7.12	-3.91	11.42	3.62	4.23	4.20

Source: Economic Survey of Madhya Pradesh (2007-08), Dept. of Economics & Statistics, Govt. of MP, Base Year 1999-2000.

TABLE 1.12

Sector-wise NSDP at Current and Constant (1999-2000) Prices, Per cent Share of Sectors to all Sectors and Per cent Change Compared to Previous Year-MP

Sector	*1999-2000*	*2000-01*	*2001-02*	*2002-03*	*2003-04*	*2004-05*	*2005-06*	*2006-07*
NSDP at Current Prices								
Primary	2287843	1854144	2276599	1997106	2949696	2722373	2997789	3386555
Secondary	1562914	1622518	1670154	1645085	1817368	2101679	2193130	2365595
Tertiary	3414779	3624401	3805432	4023957	4319995	4544941	4895787	5370329
All groups	7265536	7101063	7752185	7666148	9087059	9368993	10086706	11122479
% share								
Primary	31.49	26.11	29.37	26.05	32.46	29.06	29.72	30.45
Secondary	21.51	22.85	21.54	21.46	20.00	22.43	21.74	21.27
Tertiary	47.00	51.04	49.09	52.49	47.54	48.51	48.54	48.28
All groups	100.00	100.00	100.00	100.00	100.00	100.00	100.00	100.00
% share								
Primary	-	-18.96	22.78	-12.28	47.70	-7.71	10.12	12.97
Secondary	-	3.81	2.94	-1.50	10.47	15.64	4.35	7.86
Tertiary	-	6.14	4.99	5.74	7.36	5.21	7.72	9.69
All groups	-	-2.26	9.17	-1.11	18.53	3.10	7.66	10.27
NSDP at Constant Prices								
Primary	2287843	1655681	2060585	1648147	2287630	2175480	2258962	2312255
Secondary	1562914	1522270	1524524	1475953	1491067	1641878	1680862	1738016
Tertiary	3414779	3497066	3567425	3655391	3761288	3992756	4160746	4387688
All groups	7265536	6675017	7152534	6779491	7539985	7810114	8100570	8437959
% share								
Primary	31.49	24.80	28.81	24.31	30.34	27.85	27.89	27.40
Secondary	21.51	22.81	21.31	21.77	19.78	21.02	20.75	20.60
Tertiary	47.00	52.39	49.88	53.92	49.88	51.12	51.36	52.00
All groups	100.00	100.00	100.00	100.00	100.00	100.00	100.00	100.00
% change								
Primary	-	-27.63	24.46	-20.02	38.80	-4.90	3.84	2.36
Secondary	-	-2.60	0.15	-3.19	1.02	10.11	2.37	3.40
Tertiary	-	2.41	2.01	2.47	2.90	6.15	4.21	5.45
All groups	-	-8.13	7.15	-5.22	11.22	3.58	3.72	4.17

Source: Economic Survey of Madhya Pradesh (2007-08), Dept. of Economics & Statistics, Govt. of MP, Base Year 1999-2000.

TABLE 1.13

Growth in Agriculture Sector Compared to Preceding Year

Year	*Per cent Growth*
1999-2000	-
2000-01	-28.29
2001-02	27.31
2002-03	-19.64
2003-04	40.14
2004-05	-4.71
2005-06	4.17
2006-07*	2.80

Note: *quick estimate.
Source: Economic Survey, GoMP, various years.

The growth in the different sectors of the state has been very uneven. The primary sector growth which employs about 70 per cent of state's population has had very wide fluctuations across the last 10 years. The principal reason for such wide variation is over dependence of agriculture on the monsoons. Growth in the secondary sector is also marked with varying fluctuations year after year, while tertiary sector growth has been more even and positive. It tends to move with the growth rate of the secondary sector. Sudden drops in sectoral performance tend to hit the poor the worst.

The prospects of increased growth exceeding 6 to 7 per cent at constant prices and climbing up to 8 per cent over a sustained period of time are critical for the state.

Stagnation in agriculture, slow rate of investment in industry and growing but not accelerating service industry are the major challenges for the state at present. If we take the long term SDP figures, agriculture growth in MP has been nearly stagnant. Between 1993-94 to 2005-06 while the state's overall income grew by 61 per cent at constant prices, the agricultural domestic product remained the same, a growth of 1 per cent, while the contributions of agriculture to the state's income falling from 40 per cent 12 years ago to 25 per cent today. Even in last 5 years or so, manufacturing (both registered and un-registered) has been actually been declining. The remaining sectors seem to be pulling up the state's economy.

3.1 Financial Inclusion

Financial inclusion is the delivery of the banking services at an affordable cost to vast sections of disadvantaged and low income groups. RBI report on the financial inclusion expressed serious concern on the fact that Madhya Pradesh and Chhattisgarh (CG) fall short of the national average, both in terms of inclusion and outreach of the banking services at a time when financial inclusion is the buzzword in Indian banking industry.

These two states are also behind the newly formed states like Uttarakhand and Jharkhand in terms of number of accounts per 100 of adult population. MP and CG have only 39 and 32 accounts while Uttarakhand and Jharkhand have 78 and 44 respectively. Similarly, on the parameter of percentage of exclusion in credit gap for rural and semi-urban category, MP and CG stands at 94 and 95, whereas the all-India figure is at 90. In the category of deposit gap for rural and semi-urban population, the percentage of exclusion in MP and CG is at 74 and 76 respectively, compared to the all-India figure of 69.

The above figures proved the claims of banks in MP and CG hollow. Even the claims made in Ratlam and Jhabua districts about 100 per cent financial inclusion is not true in reality. Lower inclusion rate is also due to the reluctance of banks in extending credit to the people in tribal region as pointed out by an official source of RBI.

4. Size of Five Year Plans

The total size of the Eleventh Plan for Madhya Pradesh is Rs. 69788 crore as against the Tenth Plan approved outlay of Rs. 33724.96 crore at current prices. Size of the 11th Plan is 2.07 times compared to the Tenth Five Year Plan. The sectoral outlays for the Tenth and Eleventh Plans are presented in Table 1.14.

TABLE 1.14

Sector-wise Per cent Distribution of Plan Outlays for Madhya Pradesh

Sr. No.	*Major Sectors*	*10th Plan (2002-2007)*	*11th Plan (2007-2012)*
1	Agriculture & allied activities	5.66	4.86
2	Rural development	14.12	16.61
3	Irrigation & flood control	21.53	21.64
4	Energy	14.88	13.46
5	Industry & mining	0.83	0.83
6	Transport	9.97	11.31
7	Science, technology & environment	0.36	0.25
8	General economic services	2.43	2.19
9	Social services	29.06	28.69
10	General services	1.16	0.16

Source: Planning Commission of India.

It is clear from the above table that share of agriculture and allied activities in 11th FYP have slightly reduced compared to 10th FYP. The two sectors namely, rural development and transport are under focus with greater weightage compared to rest of the sectors. The outlays mentioned above gives the sectoral distribution out of the state plan. But besides this, there are many public investments that took place in the state which do not get reflected in the above distribution. These are mainly of central support nature through centrally sponsored schemes like NREGS, SSA and NRHM. An outlay for NREGS is Rs. 22025.70 crore, which is more than double the size of state plan in the rural development sector.

5. Budgetary Performance

5.1 Deficit

From 2001-02 to 2003-04, Madhya Pradesh was a revenue deficit state but from 2004-05 onwards, its fiscal performance has improved significantly and it became a revenue surplus state with highest revenue surplus of Rs. 3356.37 crore in 2007-08. Over the years, fiscal deficit although showed a fluctuating trend has also come down from 4.2 per cent in 2001-02 to 3.0 per cent in 2008-09. This is quite within the suggested targets of FRBM and the credit definitely goes to the financial discipline adhered by the state government.

5.2 Receipts

Total receipts of the state government and the respective proportion of revenue receipts is presented in Table 1.16. Total receipts for the state has grown more than double from Rs. 17321.6 crore to Rs. 34602.5 crore in 2007-08 with recorded annual growth of 23.13 per cent in 2007-08. Over the years, proportion of revenue recipts in the total receipts has gone up from 2001-02 till latest estimates for 2008-09.

5.3 Plan and Non-Plan Expenditure

Average percentage growth presented in Table 1.17 shows that the average growth in plan and non-plan expenditure was 21.4 and 11.6 respectively. Plan expenditure indicated significant growth in two years particularly in 2006-07 and 2007-08 but the estimate for subsequent year shows a greater dip. Similarly, non-plan expenditure has come down drastically from 44.3 per cent in 2003-04 and has shown negative growth of 10.4 per cent in 2006-07. But the last two fiscal years show substantial rise in non-plan expenditure.

6. Comparative Profile of Poverty

Poverty is multidimensional in nature, the multiple dimensions being income poverty, hunger and malnutrition, vulnerability and insecurity, marginalisation and so on. According to the concept of income poverty in India, minimum level of income or consumption expenditure that ensures minimum level of calorie consumption is defined as poverty line.

The Planning Commission has been estimating the incidence of poverty at national and state level using the methodology contained in the report of the Expert Group on Estimation of Proportion and Number of Poor (Lakdawala Committee) and applying it to consumption expenditure data from the large sample surveys on consumer expenditure, conducted periodically by the National Sample Survey Organisation (NSSO). Official poverty estimates are accordingly available for the years 1973-74, 1977-78, 1983, 1987-88, 1993-94, 1999-2000 and 2004-05.

There are several problems with respect to the comparability of NSS data of 1993-94 with that of 1999-2000 data on account of change in survey methodology on reference period (uniform reference period and mixed reference period). Scholars have doubted for contamination of data. Several alternative estimates of poverty have been provided by scholars. It has been reported by Planning Commission (2007) that 1999-2000 estimates may be roughly and not strictly compared with 2004-05 estimates obtained under mixed reference period (MRP) and 1993-2004 estimates may be compared with 2004-05 estimates obtained under uniform reference period (URP). These official estimates may be considered to be the standard measure in mapping of state level poverty. Between two consecutive periods, there are often short-run fluctuations or variations in poverty estimates for particular states, which may not give a true picture of the overall trend, and may sometimes be due to changes in methodology. However, in considering this period as a whole, these variations tend to be ironed out and a better picture of the overall trend emerges. In the comparison of states, a long term trend of nearly three decades is available, if we consider the period from the first estimates for the years 1973-74, till the latest estimates in 1999-2000.

6.1 Interstate Comparison

The official estimates of poverty for the 16 major states in the rural and urban sectors for selected years is presented in Tables 1.18 and 1.19.

TABLE 1.15

Deficit Indicators

(In Rs. Crore)

Years	*2001-02*	*2002-03*	*2003-04*	*2004-05*	*2005-06*	*2006-07*	*2007-08 (RE)*	*2008-09 (BE)*
Revenue deficit/surplus	-3167.8	-1169.4	-4475.76	1716.87	33.32	3331.68	3356.37	2839.78
% GSDP at current prices	3.7	1.3	4.4	1.6	0.0	2.6	2.36	1.80
Fiscal deficit	-3646.41	-4062.29	-7322.92	-6491.77	-4572.42	-2814.23	-4499.75	-4741.00
% GSDP at current prices	4.2	4.7	7.1	6.0	3.9	2.2	3.16	3.0

TABLE 1.16

Year-wise Total Receipts, Revenue Receipts, Annual Per cent Growth and Revenue Receipts as Per cent of Total Receipts

Years	*2001-02*	*2002-03*	*2003-04*	*2004-05*	*2005-06*	*2006-07*	*2007-08 (RE)*	*2008-09 (BE)*
Total receipts	17321.6	17044.2	21863.9	26247.8	28048.6	28102.9	34602.5	39462.8
Annual % growth		-1.60	28.28	20.05	6.86	0.19	23.13	14.05
Revenue receipt as % of total receipts	64.7	78.6	65.4	75.2	73.4	91.4	86.2	87.2
Annual % growth		19.55	6.71	38.17	4.32	24.75	16.13	15.29

TABLE 1.17

Annual Growth in Plan and Non-Plan Expenditure

(In Rs. Crore)

Expenditure	*2001-02*	*2002-03*	*2003-04*	*2004-05*	*2005-06*	*2006-07*	*2007-08 (RE)*	*2008-09 (BE)*
Plan	4311.4	6433.2	5684.7	7269.4	7950.2	10571.7	14216.6	15351.8
Annual growth (%)		49.2	-11.6	27.9	9.4	33.0	34.5	8.0
Non-plan	12126.6	11062.2	15963.0	19018.8	20071.0	17975.2	20166.0	24090.5
Annual growth (%)		-8.8	44.3	19.1	5.5	-10.4	12.2	19.5

Source: Report on State Finances, Reserve Bank of India, various years and State Budget Books, GoMP, various years.

TABLE 1.18

State-wise Head Count Ratio in the Rural Sector

State	*1973-74*	*1977-78*	*1983*	*1987-88*	*1993-94*	*1999-2000**	*2004-05(URP)*	*2004-05* (MRP)*
Andhra Pradesh	48.41	38.11	26.53	20.92	15.92	11.05	11.2	7.5
Assam	52.67	59.82	42.6	39.35	45.01	40.04	22.3	17
Bihar	62.99	63.25	64.37	52.63	58.21	44.3	42.1	32.9
Gujarat	46.35	41.76	29.8	28.67	22.18	13.17	19.1	13.9
Haryana	34.23	27.73	20.56	16.22	28.02	8.27	13.6	9.2
Himachal Pradesh	27.42	33.49	17	16.28	30.34	7.94	10.7	7.2
Karnataka	55.14	48.18	36.33	32.82	29.88	17.38	20.8	12
Kerala	59.19	51.48	39.03	29.1	25.76	9.38	13.2	9.6
Madhya Pradesh	62.66	62.52	48.9	41.92	40.64	37.06	36.9	29.8*
Maharashtra	57.71	63.97	45.23	40.78	37.93	23.72	29.6	22.2
Orissa	67.28	72.38	67.53	57.64	49.72	48.01	46.8	39.8
Punjab	28.21	16.37	13.2	12.6	11.95	6.35	9.1	5.9
Rajasthan	44.76	35.89	33.5	33.21	26.46	13.74	18.7	14.3
Tamil Nadu	57.43	57.68	53.99	45.8	32.48	20.55	22.8	16.9
Uttar Pradesh	56.53	47.6	46.45	41.1	42.28	31.22	33.4	25.3
West Bengal	73.16	68.34	63.05	48.3	40.8	31.85	28.6	24.2
All-India	56.44	53.07	45.65	39.09	37.27	27.09	28.3	21.8

Note: • Comparable (not strictly) with 2004-05 under mixed reference period (MRP).
Source: Planning Commission of India.

TABLE 1.19

State-wise Head Count Ratio in the Urban Sector

States	*1973-74*	*1977-78*	*1983*	*1987-88*	*1993-94*	*1999-2000**	*2004-05 (URP)*	*2004-05* (MRP)*
Andhra Pradesh	50.61	43.55	36.3	40.11	38.33	26.63	28	20.7
Assam	36.92	32.71	21.73	9.94	7.73	7.47	3.3	2.4
Bihar	52.96	48.76	47.33	48.73	34.5	32.91	34.6	28.9
Gujarat	52.57	40.02	39.14	37.26	27.89	15.59	13	10.1
Haryana	40.18	36.57	24.15	17.99	16.38	9.99	15.1	11.3
Himachal Pradesh	13.17	19.44	9.43	6.29	9.18	4.63	3.4	2.6
Karnataka	52.53	50.36	42.82	48.42	40.14	25.25	32.6	27.2
Kerala	62.74	55.62	45.68	40.33	24.55	20.27	20.2	16.4
Madhya Pradesh	57.65	58.66	53.06	47.09	48.38	38.44	42.1	39.3
Maharashtra	43.87	40.09	40.26	39.78	35.154	26.81	32.2	29
Orissa	55.62	50.92	49.15	41.63	41.64	42.83	44.3	40.3
Punjab	27.96	27.32	23.79	14.67	11.35	5.75	7.1	3.6
Rajasthan	52.13	43.53	37.94	41.92	30.49	19.85	32.9	28.1
Tamil Nadu	49.4	48.69	46.96	38.64	39.77	22.11	22.2	18.8
Uttar Pradesh	60.09	56.23	49.82	42.96	35.39	30.89	30.6	26.3
West Bengal	34.67	38.2	32.32	35.08	22.41	14.86	14.8	11.2
All-India	49.01	45.24	40.79	38.2	32.36	23.62	25.7	21.7

Note: • Comparable (not strictly) with 2004-05 under mixed reference period (MRP).
Source: Planning Commission of India.

It may be seen that for the last two decades, of the less developed states, the states of Bihar and Orissa have been at the bottom of Table 1.18 in this group of major states (as well as all-India) in terms of percentage of persons living below the poverty line in rural areas. The overall decline in rural poverty ratio in these two states since 1973-74 has not been very large, it has been of an order less than 20 percentage points.

In the case of Madhya Pradesh and Uttar Pradesh, the drop in the rural poverty ratio since 1973-74 has been of the order of about 25 percentage points, which is better than for Bihar and Orissa, but not enough in relation to the achievement of other states. But in contrast to Uttar Pradesh, the difference between rural and urban poverty is very much significant in case of Madhya Pradesh and is definitely a cause of concern for the state from the angle of quality of life of the citizens. Other major states have recorded equivalent or better results in reducing the rural poverty ratio, with the result that the relative ranking of MP and UP in this group of 16 comparable states has been going up (which in this case represents a less desirable situation). From having a rural poverty ratio that was the fifth highest in the group through the seventies and eighties, the rural poverty ratio for undivided MP in 1999-2000 had risen to third position in this group, indicating that poverty reduction was taking place in the state at a slower pace than for the majority of comparable states. Similarly, UP slipped from eighth to fifth in the relative ranking of rural poverty. At the other end of this spectrum, both the states of Kerala and West Bengal recorded a dramatic decline in the rural poverty ratio of over 40 percentage points since 1973-74.

The percentage of population below poverty line (BPL) at national level was 21.8 per cent in 2004-05 under MRP, compared to 26.09 per cent in 1999-2000. In the same period, India's GDP grew at around 6 per cent, compared to the present GDP growth of over 8 per cent.

There are two schools of thought on the impact of economic growth on poverty reduction. One view is that growth *per se* has a poverty reducing impact, and accordingly one would expect to find poverty decline more rapidly in the faster growing states and less rapidly in the others. According to this view, only a substantial higher rate of growth can bring about the expansion in productive income earning opportunities needed to bring about a significant reduction in poverty.

The other view is that while economic growth has the potential to reduce poverty, equating growth with poverty reduction is too simplistic. Effective public policy interventions are needed for translating growth into reduction in poverty levels. These interventions should be such that they bring about improvements in physical and social infrastructure leading both to expansion of social opportunities as well as more equitable access to productive assets. Otherwise, growth *per se* would not have a trickle-down effect, and may instead, in all likelihood lead to worsening of inequalities.

In the long run trends of selected states above, there does appear to be a positive linkage between growth and poverty reduction in the case of some states. Significant declines of between 33 and 40 percentage points in rural poverty as a whole have been recorded in the period in question by the faster growing states of Maharashtra, Tamil Nadu, Karnataka, Gujarat and Andhra Pradesh. In the case of MP, moderate growth has been accompanied by moderate declines in poverty over a long period. Both Bihar and Orissa have recorded relatively poor economic growth, and there seems to have been correspondingly little impact on poverty reduction.

The growth-poverty reduction linkage does not have such a good fit in the case of West Bengal and Kerala. Both states have recorded significant declines in the rural poverty ratio over the last three decades. However, as we have seen in the analysis of growth performance, Kerala had a relatively weak to moderate growth performance till the eighties, with per capita income growth ranging from negative to less than 2 per cent per annum. However, in the nineties, its growth has been good, with per capita income growing at more than 4 per cent per annum (Table 1.4). However, the reduction in the rural poverty ratio of almost 50 percentage points in less than three decades is much more than for states that has been recording a strong growth performance. Kerala is widely acknowledged as a success story of human development. The priorities that have guided public policy in the state have led to expansion in social opportunities, and a high level of human development in relation to the rest of the country. These policies have been followed over a long period, and it may be argued that the achievements in human development created a conducive environment for a significant decline in rural poverty and eventually also an increase in growth rates.

In the case of West Bengal too, economic growth has been very weak in the first two decades, rising significantly only in the nineties to a per capita income increase of 5 per cent per annum. However, this could not have been a contributory factor to the significant decline of 41 percentage points in the rural poverty ratio, most of which seems to have occurred in the period before the nineties. What may have set apart West Bengal is the different direction of public policy that it has followed since the seventies. The policy of increasing the access of the rural poor to assets, i.e., agricultural land, through a programme of asset redistribution (land reforms) may have helped spread income earning opportunities more evenly and contributed to a major decline in rural poverty in this period without having a noticeable impact on the growth rate of the economy. It is a matter for examination whether the fact that during large parts of this period, left-leaning governments governed these states is merely a coincidence. There are lessons to be learnt from the experiences of these states.

As reported by Planning Commission, poverty has declined at a much slower rate in the past decade or so. Poverty declined by a mere 0.74 per cent during the 11-year period (1993-94/2004-05). The number of poor has remained more or less the same, despite rapid growth in the Indian economy, poised to become the third largest economy in GDP terms within the next five years.

The largest decline in percentage terms was witnessed in some of India's poorer states, and rural poverty has declined at a faster rate. The steepest decline in poverty was in India's poorer states. Leading them was Assam and the northeastern states, where the percentage of people below the poverty line decreased by nearly 4 per cent annually during the five-year period, followed by Jharkhand (2.51 per cent), Chhattisgarh (2.15 per cent) and Bihar (1.69 per cent).

6.2 Inter-Temporal Comparison of Poverty

In the rural areas of undivided Madhya Pradesh, the poverty level has come down from 62.66 per cent in 1973-74 to 40.64 per cent in 1993-94. However, in the newly formed state, the head count ratio in the year 2004-05 was 36.9 per cent (175.65 lakh persons were under BPL) compared to 28.3 per cent (2209.24 lakh persons) at the national level. The share of poor persons in all-India was around 8 per cent in the rural sector.

In the urban sector, 42.1 per cent in the year 2004-2005 were BPL; this amounted to 74.03 lakh persons and the share of urban poor in the state was therefore, around 11 per cent. Table 1.20 presents head count ratio in the rural and urban areas of Madhya Pradesh compared to all-India and per cent share of poor to all-India.

TABLE 1.20

Head Count Ratio in the Rural and Urban Areas of Madhya Pradesh Compared to All-India and Per cent Share of Poor to All-India

Year	*Head Count Ratio*				*% Share of Poor*	
	Rural		*Urban*		*All-India*	
	MP	*All-India*	*MP*	*All-India*	*Rural*	*Urban*
1973-74	62.66	56.44	57.65	49.01	8.85	7.51
1977-78	62.52	53.07	58.66	45.24	9.38	8.49
1983	48.9	45.65	53.06	40.79	8.55	8.81
1987-88	41.92	39.09	47.09	38.2	8.63	8.55
1993-94	40.64	37.27	48.38	32.36	8.86	10.79
1999-2000	37.06	27.09	38.44	23.62	11.25	12.12
2004-05	36.9	28.3	42.1	25.7	7.95	9.16
2004-05*	29.8	21.8	39.3	21.7	8.34	10.11

Note: Figures for 2004-05 are for MP after bifurcation.
* MRP.
Source: Planning Commission of India.

Urban poverty was below rural poverty during the seventies, as was the pattern at national level. It is in early eighties that urban poverty overtook rural poverty in the state and this continues to be the case at present. This is because rural poverty declined significantly during 1977-1983 and 1983-1987. Urban poverty, on the other hand, came down only marginally. Urban growth in the eighties and nineties and internal migration from rural to urban areas may be attributed to higher poverty in the urban sector compared to rural sector.

Poverty explicitly means scarcity and involves strategies for basic services. Hunger and malnutrition are often mooted in poverty. Recently, good number of child deaths on account of malnourishment has been reported in media. Further, India State Hunger Index (ISHI) obtained for 17 states in the context of Global Hunger Index (GHI 2008) reported by International Food Policy Research Institute, Washington Report 2008 has placed Madhya Pradesh at the bottom most (17th) position among 17 states. It is no surprise that, in terms of calorie consumption, MP presents an alarming picture. It is the only state reporting as high as 90 per cent calorie deficient population in 1999-2000 by NSS if, 2400 kcl is taken as the requirement in the rural sector. As per the data from NFHS-III (2005-06), malnourished children in urban areas of MP were 52.8 per cent, much higher than the national average of 36.4 per cent. The pace of reduction in child malnutrition during 1992-1998 in the state has been much slower than that at the national level. After the previous survey of NFHS-II in 1998, the rate of malnutrition has actually increased in MP, which is a major concern for the state.

Other critical indicators of human development continue to reinforce the "BIMARU" tag with which the less developed (undivided) heartland states of Bihar, Madhya Pradesh, Rajasthan and Uttar Pradesh have been labelled.

The low economic growth in the state, particularly in agriculture, forestry and non-form rural activities is responsible for high poverty, both in rural and urban areas of the state, way above the national average.

The growth is required to attain equity at desirable levels of quality of life. A comparison of per capita income in MP and India at constant prices (1993-94) reveals that the gap between national per capita income and that of MP is increasing. From 1993-1994 to 1999-2000 at constant prices, the per capita income in MP was on an average about 81 per cent of national average; from 2000-01 to 2004-05, this fell to an average of 68 per cent. In this period of last four years, the per capita income at constant prices in MP grew at a modest 3.32 per cent per annum. The relatively more developed states of course grew even faster. The income gap is increasing with the more developed states.

Growth is an essential prerequisite for the reduction of poverty. It also enables the state to generate increasing revenues which are essential for investments in anti-poverty measures, in infrastructure and in social sectors. Low per capita income has a negative impact on the purchasing power of people and hence their ability to access the necessary resources and goods for maintaining certain required and desired quality of life.

The efforts to counter poverty have increased significantly in the last few years with additional investments in poverty alleviation schemes in the rural sector—Backward Region Grant Fund (BRGF) and National Rural Employment Guarantee Scheme (NREGS).

7. Human Development

The basic purpose of development is to enlarge people's choice. Accordingly, human development means increased capabilities of people that enable them to access larger opportunities in life. Economic growth *per se* does not ensure human development. It regards economic growth as essential but emphasises the need to pay attention to its quality and distribution, analyses at length to link with human lives and questions its long term sustainability.

Average achievements on three basic aspects of human development: longevity, knowledge and a decent standard of living is provided by a composite index known as human development index (HDI) defined by UNDP. Accordingly, trend in HDI for 13 major states of India has been presented in Table 1.21.

TABLE 1.21

Trend in Human Development Index in Selected States of India

S.No.	State	1981		1991		2001	
		HDI	Rank	HDI	Rank	HDI	Rank
1	Gujarat	0.360	4	0.431	6	0.479	6
2	Kerala	0.500	1	0.591	1	0.638	1
3	Punjab	0.411	2	0.475	2	0.537	2
4	Tamil Nadu	0.343	7	0.466	3	0.531	3
5	Maharashtra	0.363	3	0.452	4	0.523	4
6	Haryana	0.360	5	0.443	5	0.509	5
7	Karnataka	0.346	6	0.412	7	0.478	7
8	West Bengal	0.305	8	0.404	8	0.472	8
9	Rajasthan	0.256	10	0.347	10	0.424	9
10	Andhra Pradesh	0.298	9	0.377	9	0.416	10
11	Uttar Pradesh	0.255	11	0.314	12	0.388	12
12	Bihar	0.237	13	0.308	13	0.367	13
13	Madhya Pradesh	0.245	12	0.328	11	0.394	11
	All-India	0.302		0.381		0.472	

Source: National Human Development Report, 2001.

The table reveals that the position of MP compared to the other 12 states has improved only by one step ahead of Uttar Pradesh and Bihar in the year 1991 and remained the same in 2001 which may be attributed to steps taken for progress in literacy level in education sector. Thus, Madhya Pradesh has to re-orient its development process to ensure that its economic growth improves the opportunities in the lives of all socio-economic groups in the state.

8. Growth of Population and Population Stabilisation

Population growth is the net effect of natural growth (resulting from births and deaths) and net migration. Higher population growth rate for a state reflects demographic transition in which death rates have declined but birth rates have yet to decline commensurately. The first comparison is therefore, of the growth rates of population, for which the most recent data is provided by 2001 Census. The census of 2001 has put the population of Madhya Pradesh at just over 6 crore, showing a growth rate of over 24 per cent over the decade. This puts the annual increase in population at 2.2 per cent or 13.3 lakh persons per annum. For the selected states and all-India, the scenario is shown in Table 1.22.

TABLE 1.22

Population, Growth Rate and Urban Population as Per cent of Total in Selected States and All-India Census 2001

States	*Population-2001 (in millions)*	*Decadal Growth Rate 1991-2001 (per cent)*	*Urban Population as Per cent of Total in 2001*
Madhya Pradesh	60.35	24.3	26.7
Bihar	83.00	28.6	10.5
Gujarat	50.67	22.7	37.3
Maharashtra	96.88	22.7	42.3
Rajasthan	56.51	28.4	23.4
Uttar Pradesh	166.20	25.8	20.8
All-India	1028.74	21.4	27.7

Source: Census of India, 2001.

It may be seen from the table that even today, the state of MP continues to be one of the states recording relatively high levels of population growth. This has its own problems, especially for a poorer state, in terms of providing essential services and adequate opportunities for its people.

A high rate of growth today also means that it will be a long time before the population of the state stabilises. The implication of this can be seen by the extrapolation of these growth rates into likely years by which the replacement level of the fertility rate of 2.1 would be achieved.

Table 1.23 presents the dimension of population in selected years (actual and projected) along with the growth rate.

TABLE 1.23

Population (Actual and Projected) and Growth Rate—Madhya Pradesh

Population	*1991*	*2001*	*2005*	*2010*	*2015*	*2020*
Population, actual and projected	48.56	60.38	69.0	78.4	88.7	99.9
Growth rate per annum projected for next five years		2.70%	2.60%	2.50%	2.40%	2.52%

Source: Census of India, 2001.

According to informal estimates made by the National Commission on Population, projected total fertility rates (TFR) will be 2.1 for major states, based on current trends as indicated in Table 1.24.

TABLE 1.24

Progress towards Population Stabilisation—Major States

States	*Est. TFR in 2001*	*Est. Year of TFR=2.1*
Gujarat	2.3	2006
Karnataka	2.6	2011
Maharashtra	2.6	2011
Andhra Pradesh	2.2	2006
Tamil Nadu	1.5	Achieved
Rajasthan	4.1	2040
Orissa	2.8	2011
West Bengal	2.2	2006
Madhya Pradesh	3.8	2030
Uttar Pradesh	4.6	2060
Bihar	3.9	2020
Kerala	1.5	Achieved

Source: National Commission of Population, New Delhi.

Madhya Pradesh will, therefore, achieve TFR of 2.1 not before 2031.

This brings out the urgency of the situation for MP, and portends widening of the gap in per capita income levels between MP and other states with earlier estimated dates for population stabilisation, even with all other factors and growth performance being the same. The targeted date as per Economic Survey 2008, Madhya Pradesh is 2011. It is true that 'development is the best contraceptive'. However, there is nothing to lose, and much to gain for the state by simultaneously pursuing an enlightened population stabilisation policy, along with more aggressive efforts at enhancing levels of human development.

Poor infrastructure has always been a handicap to growth. In the last decade, the importance of adequate infrastructure has been widely recognised and emphasised. Favourable infrastructure endowments are now seen as an important factor contributing to the attractiveness of the state for private investments. The most comprehensive recent exercise in mapping infrastructure levels of states was undertaken by the Eleventh Finance Commission (EFC) in its report. The EFC Report has measured infrastructure facilities available in different states in terms of eight major sectors of agriculture, banking, electricity, transport, communication, education, health and civil administration. Taking these components into account, EFC developed an index of social and economic infrastructure for states, which is indicated in Table 1.25.

TABLE 1.25

Index of Social and Economic Infrastructure

States	*Index*	*States*	*Index*
Goa	200.57	Mizoram	82.13
Punjab	187.57	Bihar	81.33
Kerala	176.68	Orissa	81.00
Tamil Nadu	149.10	Assam	77.72
Haryana	137.54	Madhya Pradesh	76.79
Gujarat	124.31	Nagaland	76.14
Maharashtra	112.80	Rajasthan	75.86
West Bengal	111.25	Meghalaya	75.49
Sikkim	108.99	Manipur	75.38
Karnataka	104.88	Tripura	74.87
Andhra Pradesh	103.30	Jammu & Kashmir	71.46
Uttar Pradesh	102.23	Arunachal Pradesh	69.71
Himachal Pradesh	95.03		

Source: Report of the Eleventh Finance Commission, Government of India.

Successive Five Year Plans aimed to reduce such infrastructure differentials through public policy regimes directing public and private investments to 'backward' areas. Nevertheless, as may be seen, there remain wide differentials in the infrastructure index even after many decades of planned development. The infrastructure index for Madhya Pradesh is amongst the poorest in the country, well below that of even other less developed major states like Bihar, Orissa and comparing only with the indices for north-eastern states, It is arguable that low levels of infrastructure endowments have been a factor in inability of the state to accelerate economic growth. Poor infrastructure would impact on the efforts to expand social opportunities as well as avenues for increasing incomes in productivity.

The trend presented above indicate, in sum, that the state of Madhya Pradesh recorded rising but moderate levels of growth during the period of its existence as an undivided state, neither increasing nor decreasing its share in the national economy. The proportion of rural poverty in the state has declined, but at a slower pace in relation to other states. The goal of population stabilisation is a long way ahead. In terms of human development indicators, while significant progress has been made on the literacy front in the last decade, the overall relative position continues to bracket the state in the group of heartland states with relatively poorer indicators. Wide infrastructure differentials remain between MP and most other states.

9. Implications for the State

The issue is, however, not that Madhya Pradesh is stagnating; it is that other comparable states seem to be progressing faster, and accordingly the gap between the leading states and Madhya Pradesh is growing. It would not be possible for the country as a whole to realise the high growth rates projected for the Tenth Plan and beyond, unless the relatively lower growth rates in major states like MP are stepped up. The Approach Paper to the Tenth Plan expresses this in the following words, "It is important to recognize that the sharp increase in the growth rate and improvement of social indicators that is being contemplated for the Tenth Plan is possible only if there is a significant improvement in the growth rates of the slow growing states. Indeed if the higher growth targets is sought to be achieved with a continuation of the low growth rates observed in some of the most populous states, it would necessarily imply a very large increase in inter-state inequality with serious consequences for regional balance and national harmony."

Increasing the rate of growth of the economy of the state is thus not only an imperative for the state but also for the country as a whole. There is a need to focus on ways and means to increase the rates of growth of the state significantly, aiming perhaps at a rate double the current one. It is essential for the state government to be honest in defining and setting the judicious targets to pursue sustainable growth in the economy. To lift the present GDP growth from 3.3 per cent per annum to the height of 7 per cent, it should allow the primary sector to grow by 4 per cent, secondary sector to grow at 8 per cent and tertiary sector to grow at 9 per cent per annum respectively.

While increased growth rate would by itself contribute to some extent to poverty reduction, as noted earlier, appropriate public policy initiatives for reduction in poverty by better land and water management would help broad-base the benefits of growth. The state would also need to concentrate on both improving infrastructure and the levels of social development, since both are interlinked in terms of delivery of services as well as providing access to income earning opportunities. These areas prioritise themselves precisely because the state lags far behind the rest of the country, and because these areas are amenable to public policy action.

However, public policy interventions need to be supported by adequate financial resources. These resources may be public or private. The aim should be for private investments to lead in the financing of the growth of economically productive activities in the state, whether in the industry, agriculture and services sectors. Industrial growth depends upon availability of infrastructure support in the form of power, transport, communications, while agricultural growth depends on rural infrastructure such as irrigation, rural electrification and rural roads. Public investments would need to be focused on social and livelihood development, to expand opportunities for the people, and also on strengthening of infrastructure. These alone would make the state attractive for private investment flows, much more than any incentives that the government may provide. Such productive activities in different sectors of the economy can potentially grow significantly, given the improvement in development and infrastructure (that ought to be the focus on public investment).

Ideally, both Central and state sector public investments should be directed as much as possible to build economic and social infrastructure in poorly endowed and less developed states like Madhya Pradesh, to help remove constraints on growth and leverage private investments. At the same time, there is a case for a focus by the Centre on these problems of developing infrastructure and human development in the poorer states. The Eleventh Finance Commission noted that, "States with good infrastructure are attracting private investments" and that "Central investments should be redirected taking this fact in view". Realistically though, the state should not sit back and await any spectacular action by the Centre in this regard. There is a lot that the state can and should do.

Chapter 2

Employment and Livelihoods

1. Introduction

The most defining and determining need for a human being is livelihood. By performing a set of activities on a regular basis, adequate cash and non-cash income is generated to maintain a desired standard of living, both on a day-to-day basis and over a large period of time. A livelihood in many ways therefore, almost covers the entire gamut of issues in human life. It is adequate when the income and quality of life it can support meets widely accepted standards, such as poverty line and allows the members of a household the required amenities to survive well. The Constitution of India recognises the right to livelihood. Article 39A of the Directive Principles of the Constitution enjoins the state to ensure that every citizen has adequate means of livelihood.

Gainful and sustainable employment ensures a basic level of remuneration for all human beings. Employment by itself is not a complete condition for a sustainable livelihood—it is the character of employment, its regularity and periodicity, level of income or benefits from it, and security of employment, and ensured basic rights of employment. Thus, analysis of livelihood involves lots of complexities of livelihood sector.

People need sustainable livelihoods to ensure that they and their dependents are able to have access to basic resources and basic needs to ensure a life of dignity, decent living, safe from disease, hunger, squalor, poverty, deprivation and denial of basic rights. This means that livelihoods ensure nutrition, lack of hunger, ability to access basic health, basic education to children, ability to afford a decent shelter, clothing, necessary resources for daily needs and social expenditures.

Livelihoods, in much way would then be a sum total of both the employment portfolio of a household and what it earns in monetary terms, or as services and goods, and what a household receives as entitlements being a citizen of the state or *gram panchayat*. Dealing with both these aspects, we will concentrate more on the status, trends, issues and action on livelihoods of people and lesser on the livelihoods provisioning by state, or other agencies.

The most crucial need for sustainable livelihoods for an individual or household is gainful employment over a period of time that ensures a level of remuneration satisfying basic needs and quality of life. There are few ways of assessing these. One of the most widely used measures is income poverty. Households subsisting below this level of income (calculated using expenditure estimates), would be the most vulnerable and deprived households. The other measures could be dimension of employment in different categories including households involved in labour, without possession of land, households with very little land (marginal farmers, or even small farmers owning poor quality or unirrigated lands), households with just one member employed (especially in rural areas, and employed as labour, or very small trading or wage employment), persons employed in activities facing crisis/shrinking/decline and so on.

Indications on the state of livelihoods are access to productive capital/assets, ownership or access to land, access to forest and forest produce, including access to natural resources (pond and lakes for fish folk, access to clay for the potters, access to dead carcass for leather flayers, etc.), access to water.

In the Indian context, reality is far different from one's ideal thoughts. Here is the bitter truth of income and employment conditions of Indian nationals. "For 836 million Indians, Rs. 20 per day or Rs. 600 per month is essentially buying them their sustenance," highlights the first authoritative study on the state of informal employment in India, complied by National Commission for Enterprises in the Unorganized Sector. The report further shows that the large chunk of these 836 million Indians or 77 per cent population of the country are above the poverty line at Rs. 12 per day. This group largely comprised SCs, STs, OBCs and Muslims. A staggering 394.9 million or 86 per cent of India's population works in unorganised sector without any social security cover. Nearly 80 per cent of these workers are living on less than Rs. 20 per day. Dr Arjun Sengupta said, "If people do not earn, how will they spend or save?" The Report suggested that promoting agriculture is the fertile ground for poverty reduction of small and marginal farmers, 84 per cent of whom spent more than they earned and were often caught in debt traps.

Madhya Pradesh has a very large population, nearly 71 per cent being dependent on agriculture. Large number of these persons are employed in the primary sector, which lack in high growth rate. The challenge of employment is therefore, not just new jobs, but to make existing livelihoods stronger and sustainable.

The last decade has seen many changes in Madhya Pradesh, including high rate of growth in the economy. Evidence, both from people's field experience and from studies based on data show that in spite of rapid growth, employment opportunities created in the state are inadequate. The general perception in the country is that although GDP growth has accelerated, it has not been accompanied by a commensurate increase in employment leading to worsening of the employment situation in the post-reform period. These considerations have led to demand for greater attention to the objective of employment. There is also a concern on educated youth unemployment as its increase will lead to waste of human resources and creation of social tensions.

Information on the level of employment in the state is derived from both census records and data based on National Sample Survey (NSS) on employment and unemployment conducted in the form of rounds having stabilised concepts and definitions. As there are conceptual differences in these data sets, we have made use of NSS data.

2. Employment Situation and Trends

2.1 Work Participation Rates (WPR)

Worker-population ratios provide an idea about the participation of population in economic activity.[1] Table 2.1 provides the worker-population ratios for the period 1983 to 2004-05. The worker-population rates for rural and urban Madhya Pradesh are higher than rural and urban sectors at all-India level. Sectoral difference in WPR in MP has come down from 14 percentage points in 1999-2000 to 11 percentage point in 2004-05. The WPR over the years show that many more people in households are required to be working to maintain themselves. The WPR in rural Madhya Pradesh has remained almost stagnant but has increased significantly in the urban areas.

TABLE 2.1

Work Participation Rates: MP and All-India

Year	*Madhya Pradesh*		*All-India*	
	Rural	*Urban*	*Rural*	*Urban*
1983	49.8	32.3	44.5	34.0
1987-88	47.9	32.3	43.4	33.7
1993-94	49.4	31.7	44.4	34.7
1999-2000	46.2	31.9	41.7	33.7
2004-05	45.9	34.7	43.9	33.7

Source: NSS Rounds on Employment and Unemployment (38th, 43rd, 50th, 55th and 61st Rounds).

Gender-specific difference over years separately for rural and urban areas of MP and India presented in Table 2.2 shows declining trend, except in the case of urban males. In the year 2004, participation rate of both males and females have increased in urban areas, as compared to 1999-2000.

1. In order to capture the complexities of the employment situation in a predominantly agrarian and unorganised economy like India, the estimates of employment and unemployment by NSSO are derived from three concepts: Usual Status (US); Current Weekly Status (CWS) and Current Daily Status (CDS). The three concepts are based on three different reference periods for ascertaining the activity status of a person. Under the US concept, the reference period is one year and the activity status of a person as employed, unemployed or out of labour force is determined on the basis of activity pursued by him for the major part of the year. On the CWS criterion, a person is considered as employed or unemployed if he has worked or has not worked though was available for work, respectively, even for one hour during the week. Under the CDS approach, the unit of classification is half day. Under this approach, the person days are distributed by activity category during an average week. A deficiency of the present time criterion based estimates of employment is that one gets to know little about how well employed (income etc.) are the persons who are seen as employed. They also do not provide the multiple activities by persons/households.

TABLE 2.2

Work Participation Rates for Males and Females: MP and All-India

Year	Madhya Pradesh		All-India	
	Rural	Urban	Rural	Urban
Male				
1993-94	57.2	47.1	55.3	52.1
1999-2000	53.6	48.8	53.1	51.8
2004	54.3	51.3	54.2	54.0
Female				
1993-94	41.0	14.2	32.8	15.5
1999-2000	38.2	13.4	29.8	13.9
2004	37.2	14.3	31.5	15.0

Source: NSS Rounds on Employment and Unemployment (50th, 55th and 60th Rounds). For 60th Round, statement 6.2 of report no. 506, pp. 73-78.

TABLE 2.3

Percentages of Child Labour among Children across States in the Rural Sector

State	1993-94		1999-2000		2004-05	
	5-9	10-14	5-9	10-14	5-9	10-14
Andhra Pradesh	3.6	34.4	2.7	25.1	0.7	14.6
Assam	0.3	4.9	0.4	4.6	0.2	3.6
Bihar	0.5	7.5	0.2	5	0.1	3.0
Gujarat	0.2	8.4	0.7	11.5	0.1	5.5
Haryana	0.2	5.1	0.1	2.6	0.0	3.9
Karnataka	3.6	25.1	1.1	15.2	0.3	11.1
Kerala	0.1	1.3	0	0.7	0.0	.3
Madhya Pradesh	1.1	17.3	0.3	10.6	0.2	6.5
Maharashtra	0.9	12.6	0.8	8.5	0.3	9.0
Orissa	1.2	14.4	0.4	9	0.6	10.0
Punjab	—	5.3	0.5	5.5	0.1	3.6
Rajasthan	5	25.4	2.5	16.7	0.5	10.4
Tamil Nadu	2.1	18.3	0.4	8.6	0.0	2.8
Uttar Pradesh	0.4	10.4	0.2	6.4	0.3	7.7
West Bengal	0.7	10.4	0.4	8.8	0.1	6.1
All-India	1.3	14.0	0.7	9.3	0.3	7.1

Source: NSSO 50th, 55th and 61st Rounds.

Estimates of incidence of child labour in Madhya Pradesh as available from NSS surveys reveal that approximately 17 per cent of children in the age group 10 to 14 years were working in 1993-94, occupying fifth highest position amongst the major states of India as may be seen in Table 2.3. In urban areas on the other hand, the rate of child labour is relatively much lower (2.3 per cent) in 1993-94. In 1999-2000, child labour in Madhya Pradesh has gone down significantly in rural areas and has increased slightly in urban areas compared to 1993-94 levels. Compared to all-India level, the percentage of child labour in urban Madhya Pradesh is low and is slightly higher in the rural area. In fact, the level of WPR in the rural and urban areas of MP has come down to the level of 6.5 per cent and 3.1 per cent respectively.

TABLE 2.4

Percentages of Child Labour among Children across States in the Urban Sector

State	1993-94		1999-2000		2004-05	
	5-9	10-14	5-9	10-14	5-9	10-14
Andhra Pradesh	1.3	12.9	0.7	7.1	0.0	5.8
Assam	0.2	6.5	0.3	7.8	0.2	1.7
Bihar	0.2	2.5	0.1	3.4	0.0	2.6
Gujarat	0.5	3.3	0.0	3.6	0.3	3.3
Haryana	0.6	4.1	0.0	2.4	0.0	1.6
Karnataka	0.8	8	0.1	5.9	0.0	2.0
Kerala	0	1.1	0	0.5	0.0	0.6
Madhya Pradesh	0.6	2.3	0.2	2.5	0.0	3.1
Maharashtra	0.1	4	0.0	2.3	0.0	1.7
Orissa	0.3	5.1	0.0	1.7	0.0	3.4
Punjab	—	3.4	1.8	3.5	0.0	2.0
Rajasthan	0.6	6.1	0.4	5.1	2.0	6.1
Tamil Nadu	0.5	8.8	0.1	4.7	0.0	2.9
Uttar Pradesh	0.4	6.2	0.3	5.5	0.8	8.0
West Bengal	0.6	6.7	0.2	6.2	1.3	7.9
All-India	0.5	5.6	0.3	4.3	0.3	4.1

Source: NSSO 50th, 55th and 61st Rounds.

2.2 *Employment Growth*

Table 2.5 shows that in rural Madhya Pradesh, rate of growth in employment declined from 1.82 per cent per annum (1983 to 1993-94) to 0.69 per cent per annum (1993-94 to 1999-2000). In the early years of next decade, the employment growth gone up, both in rural and urban areas. The rate of growth of employment (per annum) increased to 2.93 per cent in rural areas and 4.83 per cent in urban areas (1999-2000 to 2004).

TABLE 2.5

Employment Growth (per cent per annum): MP and All-India

Period	Rural		Urban	
	MP	All-India	MP	All-India
1983 to 1993-94	1.82	1.73	2.98	3.34
1993-94 to 1999-2000	0.69	0.67	2.94	1.34
1999-2000 to 2004	2.93		4.83	

Source: NSSO Rounds.

TABLE 2.6

Employment Growth (per cent per annum): Madhya Pradesh

Period	Rural Workers (in '000s)			Urban Workers (in '000s)			All Workers
	Male	Female	Total	Male	Female	Total	(In '000s)
Workers in 1983	11897	8803	20700	3108	825	3933	24633
Workers in 1987/88	12900	9200	22100	3600	1000	4600	26700
Workers in 1994	15788	10689	26477	4142	1120	5262	270039
Workers in 1999-2000	16463	11116	27579	5054	1100	6154	33733
Workers in 2004	18061	12893	30954	5953	1549	7502	38456
Rate of Change in Workers per Annum							
Between 1983 to 1987/88	1.63%	0.89%	1.32%	2.98%	3.93%	3.18%	1.62%
1987/88 to 94	4.12%	3.05%	3.71%	2.84%	2.29%	2.82%	3.56%
1993/94 to 2000	0.70%	0.65%	0.69%	3.37%	-0.30%	2.94%	1.08%
2000 to 2004	2.34%	3.78%	2.93%	4.18%	8.93%	4.83%	3.29%

Source: Computed by the author based on NSS and Census data. For absolute numbers, Census figures are used.

Employment and unemployment indicators along with GSDP/GDP for Madhya Pradesh and all-India presented in Table 2.7 reveal that except for unemployment rate in the state of Madhya Pradesh compared to all-India, the employment elasticity and GDP is poor, while employment growth shows little edge over all India figures.

TABLE 2.7

Employment and Unemployment Indicators

Item	Year	Madhya Pradesh	All-India
Employment	1999-2000	28725	336736
Employment growth	1993-94 and 1999-2000	1.28	1.07
Unemployment rate	1993-94	3.56	5.99
Employment elasticity	1999-2000	4.45	7.32
GDP growth rate	1993-94 and 1999-2000	4.7	6.7

Source: NSS Rounds.

Agriculture, manufacturing and services are the three important sectors for livelihood in the state of Madhya Pradesh. Accordingly, their share presented in Table 2.8 reveal that the share of agriculture in both MP and all-India has come down in 2004-05 compared to 1993-94. The share in manufacturing sector has increased in both Madhya Pradesh as well as at national level. However, in the services sector, the share has increased at the national level but not in Madhya Pradesh.

Type of household is an important indicator of livelihood. The per cent distribution of persons presented in Table 2.9 reveal that in the rural sector of MP as high as 47.9 per cent and 32.2 per cent belong to the category of self-employed in agriculture and agricultural labour respectively which is quite high compared to rural areas at the all-India level.

TABLE 2.8

Employment Share by Sector

Sector	1993-94		2004-05	
	Madhya Pradesh	All-India	Madhya Pradesh	All-India
Agriculture	77.7	64.5	69.1	57.0
Manufacturing	5.5	10.5	7.5	12.4
Services	13.4	20.7	8.2	24.1

Source: Directorate of Economics and Statistics, GoMP and Economic Survey for MP and India.

TABLE 2.9

Per cent Distribution of Persons by Type of Household, 2004-05

Household Type	Madhya Pradesh	All-India
Rural		
Self-employed in agriculture	47.9	38.4
Self-employed in non-agriculture	9.4	17.0
Agriculture labourer	32.2	23.6
Other labourer	6.3	11.8
Others	4.3	9.2
Urban		
Self-employed	40.8	41.8
Regular salaried	41.7	40.4
Casual labourer	11.8	12.4
Others	5.7	5.4

Source: NSS Rounds.

3. Proliferation of Marginal and Small Farmers

The data presented in Table 2.10 shows that the share of marginal and small farmers in area and number of holdings increased over time from 9.6 per cent in 1970-71 to 21.5 per cent in 1995-96, an increase of 75 per cent in terms of land under small and marginal farmers. Around 61 per cent of the landholdings belong to marginal and small farmers with 21.5 per cent share of total area.

There are 39.3 lakh small and marginal farmers in the state and they are mostly underemployed. The size of landholding of these farmers (average landholdings of small and marginal farmers was 0.91 hectares in 1995-96) is uneconomical and majority would also be working as agricultural or casual labourers to supplement their income from farming to sustain their livelihood. However, data from NSS report reveal that there is a gradual casualisation of the workforce, and the number of casual labourers in MP has gone up from 32 per cent male and 38 per cent female casual labourers in 1993-94 to 37 per cent male and 44 per cent female casual labourers in 1999-2000.

TABLE 2.10

Distribution of Operational Holdings and Area by Size Classes: 1970-71 and 1995-96

Year	*Marginal*	*Small*	*Semi-Medium*	*Medium*	*Large*
		No. of Holdings (in lakhs)			
1970-71	16.8	8.9	10.7	11.7	4.9
1995-96	22.8	16.5	13.8	9.5	2.0
2000-01	28.4	19.5	14.9	9.2	1.7
		No. of Holdings (%)			
1970-71	31.8	16.8	20.1	22.0	9.3
1995-96	35.2	25.5	21.4	14.7	3.1
2000-01	38.6	26.5	20.2	12.5	2.3
		Area (in lakh hectares)			
1970-71	7.2	13.2	30.9	73.5	87.2
1995-96	11.4	24.4	39.3	57.9	32.9
2000-01	14.0	27.3	41.2	54.4	25.5
		Area (%)			
1970-71	3.4	6.2	14.6	34.7	41.2
1995-96	6.8	14.7	23.7	34.9	19.8
2000-01	8.6	17.3	25.2	33.3	15.6

Note: Marginal (below 1 ha); Small (1.0 to 2.0 ha); Semi-medium (2.0 to 4.0 ha); Medium (4.0 to 10.0 ha); Large (above 10.0 ha)

Source: Commissioner of Land Records and Settlement, Gwalior, MP.

BOX 2.1

Subsistence (marginal and small) Farmers (landholding between one acre to five acres of land)—A Study of Households in Narsinghpur, Hoshangabad, Ujjain and Neemuch

Marginal and small farmers normally till their own land, their own *khudkasht* holdings and many amongst them also take land on lease, owning two to four acres of land, and on average lease two to three acres of land on *batai*. Every subsistence farmer wants to grow food for tiding over at least six months' worth of consumption needs for his/her family, and it was found that they were able to grow 12-15 quintals of food grains per annum. Produce grown by them include edible oils, like linseeds, sesame, rapeseeds, *taramira*, and also some coarse millets like tapioca (*kodo*), *sama* and pulses like *arhar*, *moong* and *urad*, and some vegetables in the kitchen garden. Most subsistence level farmers (about 90 per cent), reared one or two bullocks for tilling, renting them out and use dung for manuring the fields. The requirement of dung for one acre of land is about 10 cartloads and one buffalo/cow produces about 10 cartloads of dung per annum. A subsistence farming family (of seven members) needs about four acres worth of agricultural produce for meeting six months of domestic needs. This requires four heads of cattle, which generally consists of a cow, one or two calves and a pair of bullocks. However, the study team found that in most cases, the subsistence farmers had access to only two to three acres of land (either their own land or sharecropped land). They also do not own any other assets of significant monetary value like bullock carts, mechanical devices etc., though they do have implements like ploughs, levelling planks etc.

The subsistence farmers have to complement the agricultural yield with wage labour (local as well as migration), gathering residuals (from harvested fields) and other subsidiary non-farm occupations (e.g., service, pottery, hair-cutting, carpentry, fishing etc., depending on castes and available choices). Fishing is an important livelihood source for communities (especially *kevats* or *dhimars*) living near water reservoirs. Another activity undertaken by such farmers is collection and sale of non-timber forest produce and sale of head loads of fuel wood in the nearby markets.

Households belonging to this category (especially the SC/ST ones) are often bound in exploitative relationships (as reflected in low wage payments, harassment of women and harassment of school-going children) with the dominant segments i.e., the larger farmers. In Bundelkhand and Chambal regions, livelihoods of this category are subsistence livelihoods. In districts like Narsinghpur, Hoshangabad, Ujjain and Neemuch, some of the farmers with 4-5 acres of land might even belong to marginally surplus livelihoods, helped mainly by the black cotton soils of Malwa region and ample water for irrigation. One of the chief features of this group is its perpetual state of indebtedness to the local money-lenders. The debt burden on the small and marginal farmers is lesser than on the landless labourers provided: (i) the former have not faced any major health problems in which case they are compelled to avail loans from the local money-lenders, (ii) the family does not have more than one daughter to be married, and (iii) the family has at least four *bighas* of irrigated land which are dual cropped and the family grows vegetables and other cash crops on that irrigated land.

The small and marginal farmers stand a much better chance of getting some land to cultivate on sharecropping basis than the landless because they have wherewithal to undertake farming, whereas the landless would neither have bullocks and agricultural inputs nor much of prior experience in farming. The details of the agriculture labour and non-agriculture labour are more or less the same but for the fact that the small and marginal farmers remain fairly busy in their own fields and therefore, are unable to work as much in the field of others as agriculture labour as the landless in the village. This group is more likely to have cattle but the milk produced is invariably used more for self-consumption than for sale.

Source: Fieldwork by Project Team.

4. Forest-based Livelihoods

Nearly 40 per cent of the state's villages are either forest villages or are situated close to forests. Forests play a significant role in the livelihoods of people in such villages. It is difficult to estimate the exact number of people dependent to some extent on forests, since data captures by either the census operations or by NSS do not capture employment sources that give support for brief periods. In case of persons collecting non-timber forest produce (NTFP), the period of direct person days of employment is not very significant, say 10 to 15 days to a month or so at the maximum overall in a year. But the forest produce play a significant role in people's lives is very evident from the three brief case studies of villages presented here. A list of some of the main NTFPs collected in Madhya Pradesh is also presented in Table 2.11.

TABLE 2.11

List of Some of the Main NTFPs Collected in Madhya Pradesh

Name of NTFP	*Botanical Name*	*Uses*	*Month of Collection*
Mahua	*Madhuca indica*	Commercial, medicine, oil	June–July
Kanji	*Pongamia pinnata*	Non-edible oil	January–March
Mahua phool	*Madhuca latifolia*	Beverage	March–April
Areetha	*Sapindus emarginatus*	Soap	February–April
Aonla	*Embelica officinalis*	Medicine/trifala component, fruits very rich in Vitamin C	November–January
Baheda	*Terminalia bellerica*	Medicine	March–May
Gond dhawra	*Anogeissus latifolia*	Gum	February–June
Gond salar	*Baswellia serrata*	Gum	March–June
Gond karaya	*Sterculia urens*	Gum	March–June
Gond babul	*Acacia nilotica*	Gum, medicine	March–June
Gond khakra	*Butea monosperma*	Gum, dye	March–June
Kali musli	*Curculigo orchioides*	Medicine	September–October
Safed musli	*Cholrophytum tuberosum*	Medicine	September–October
Satavari	*Asparagus racemosus*	Medicine	September–October
Ghat bor	*Zizyphus xylopyra*	Edible fruits	March-April
Bel guda	*Aegle marmelos*	Diarrhoea, heat stroke	April–June
Gond godal	*Lannea cormandelica*	Gum	March–June
Shahad	*Apis dorsota*	Medicine/food	Throughout the year
Mom	*Apis dorsata*	Commercial	Throughout the year
Gond khair	*Acacia catechu*	Gum	March–June
Lac	*Tachardia lacca*	Jewellery, sealing	March–June
Baheda chhal	*Teminalia bellerica*	Medicine	March–May
Adusa	*Adhatoda vasica*	Medicine	January–June
Gokharu	*Tribulus terrestris*	Medicine	Sepember–October
Ratanjot	*Jetropha carcus*	Medicine, oil	September–November
Aswagandha	*Withania somnifera*	Medicine	Throughout the year
Marorphali	*Helicteres isora*	Medicine	October–December
Sankh pushpi	*Evolvlus aisiniodes*	Medicine	September–November
Tendu patta	*Diaspyros melanoxylon*	*Beedi* making	April–May
Chironji	*Buchanania lanjan*	Food/dry fruit/nuts	May-June
Bark of khakra	*Butea monosperma*	Fibre for ropes	June-July/Throughout the year
Kosa/tassar	*Terminalia tomentosa*	Cocoons for *tassar* silk	March-May
Mangoes	*Mangifera indica*	Edible fruits	June-July
Jamun	*Syzgium cumini*	Edible fruits	May-June
Head-loads of wood	Many species of trees	Fuel wood	Throughout the year

Source: Department of Forests, Government of Madhya Pradesh, Bhopal.

The regime governing forests and peoples' rights over forests is highly regulated and governed by national acts. In Madhya Pradesh, the large population that depends on forests for incomes and consumption has had to contend with such laws, but there has also been a gradual shift on part of the government to grant more rights to people with regard to basic needs from forests, and to bring people more and more into management of forests. Rights of *nistari* were granted to people way back in 1970s. Madhya Pradesh today also has a large programme under Joint Forest Management (JFM). The impact or the results of the JFM programme have certainly been beneficial as far as the forest cover in the state is concerned. The latest satellite imagery released by ISRO shows that the forest cover in the state has increased over the last five years by 376 sq kms. Much of the credit for this could go to the effective role played by JFM groups in the state.

The relation between people and the forest management and regulatory regime under the acts has led to a decrease in tension between villagers and forest authorities in the state.

BOX 2.2

Livelihoods of NTFP Collectors

Panna:

A study of 53 households living on the outskirts of the Panna Reserve Forest in Panna district revealed that the villagers earned a total annual income of Rs. 3.23 lakh approximately through collection of NTFPs. They plucked *tendu* leaves worth Rs. 1.5 lakh which were sold to *tendu patta* co-operatives, collected *mahua* leaves and nuts worth Rs. 98,000 which were either sold in *haats* or to traders in barter and sold fuel wood to the Majhgaon Diamond Mine Employees Colony worth Rs. 65,000 annually. While these households also had other income sources, the NTFP income of the households accounted for 85 per cent of the total income of 46 households in the village. On an average, 2.7 persons from 46 families were engaged in NTFP collection and marketing. Each family on an average earned Rs. 9450 from the forests and total incomes accruing to them annually was Rs. 11,000.

Jhabua:

In another village of 83 households in Jhabua district, there were two JFM committees. In this village, 68 households draw approximately 35 per cent of their total annual income from forest produce. This village is of mixed caste households. The nearby dry deciduous mixed teak forest has about 50 per cent vegetation density. All the big trees are below 30 years of age. It has about 60 per cent *tectona grandis* or *sagwan* population, besides, *khakra*, *sirish*, bamboo, *neem*, *tendu*, *pipal*, *dhawra*, mango, jamun and some *piloo* trees. There is big undergrowth of *bers*, *khakra*, small *khajoor*, *adhatoda* or *adusa*, *gobar-sungha* and *ratanjot* plants. In this village, details of NTFP quantity collected and value realised by villagers is presented below.

***Mahua* flowers**	***Mahua* seeds**	***Tendu* leaves (Bags)**	**Gums**
5261 Kg.	3916 Kg	163	1.5 Qt. For Rs. 2250
@ Rs. 8 per Kg.	@ Rs. 10 per Kg	@ Rs.400 per bag	Value realised per Kg.
= Rs. 42088	= Rs. 39160	= Rs. 65200	and amount in Rs. total income

realised annually from the NTFPs = Rs. 1.49 lakhs approx. Average family income = Rs. 2180. Besides the sales through village committees, each of the NTFP collectors sell some small amounts of NTFPs individually in *haats* for about Rs. 800 per annum. Hence, the total average income through the NTFPs is Rs. 2980 or Rs. 3000 per household per annum.

Mahakaushal:

Collection of NTFP includes food, fuel, fodder, *tendu* leaves, *mahua* flowers and seeds as well as *chironji* or *achar* seeds. Fruits like mangoes, custard apples, guavas and small berries are also abundant in this area. Some other forest produce gathered are the tuberous roots of indigenous trees which are used for eating/consumption, some green leaves of grasses and herbs used as vegetables and fodder and leaves of *khakhra* (*chevla/dhak*), used by the ginger cultivators to cover the tender plants of ginger and for making plates and bowls by sticking the leaves together with tiny wood pieces or scraping. For those people who have access to forest and NTFP, say, typically, a household of seven persons, with four of them engaged in NTFP collection, is able to collect *tendu* leaves worth 200 rupees per day for 7 to 10 days in a year i.e., an annual income of Rs. 1400-2000. Similarly, for *mahua* seeds and flowers, the collectors get about the same amount of money over 30-40 days in a year. On an average, they collect *mahua* flowers and seeds from about 4-5 trees and each *mahua* tree yields about Rs.500 worth of NTFPs per year. Hence, Rs. 2000-2500 is the average income from mahua. Other NTFPs and fuel wood, fodder and foods fetch a household with four collectors yield worth about Rs.1000 per year. Hence on an average, a household with four collectors collects NTFP worth Rs.4400 to 5500 per year.

It needs to be stressed that all households in a village do not collect NTFPs. It is the people at the subsistence level of livelihood (generally SCs and STs), who collect NTFPs.

Source: Fieldwork by Project Team.

TABLE 2.12

Number of Establishments (agricultural, non-agricultural) and Compound Annual Growth Rate

Indicators			*EC-1998*	*EC-2005*	*CAGR during 1998-2005*
No. of establishments	MP	Rural	844158	918701	1.22
		Urban	749185	816561	1.24
		Combined	1593343	1735262	1.23
	India		30348900	41826989	4.69
No. of agricultural establishments	MP	Rural	80570	72793	-1.44
		Urban	13793	11661	-2.37
		Combined	94363	84454	-1.57
	India		3474800	6079983	8.32
No. of non-agricultural establishments	MP	Rural	763588	845908	1.47
		Urban	735392	804900	1.30
		Combined	1498980	1650808	1.39
	India		26874100	35747006	4.16

Source: Economic Census, 2005.

5. Employment—Enterprises and Establishments

Non-agriculture establishments and enterprises carry out the large numbers of non-farm activities. The results of the 5th Economic Census conducted in Madhya Pradesh reveal that in the year 2005, there were 1,735262 establishments of which 84454 were agriculture establishments and 1650,808 were non-agriculture establishments. When compared with the results of the 4th Economic Census conducted in 1998, the compound annual growth of establishments during the period 1998-2005 was of the order of 1.23 per cent. Details of rural urban break-up both for the years 1998 and 2005 are presented Table 2.12.

The large number of enterprises and establishments form the bulk of the strength of rural non-farm employment. Table 2.13 presents per cent distribution of establishments in the rural and urban sectors of Madhya Pradesh and all-India. The table reveals that around 53 per cent of establishments in MP are located in rural areas. It is these units that hold the key to sustainable employment growth in rural Madhya Pradesh. Most of them are of a size that affords fund inputs and capacity to take risks, undertake technical and personnel changes. Such units must form a critical part of any employment strategy. The basic needs of such units are to remain technically relevant in their area, and to be able to access and use credit, appropriately and timely. For the former, a vibrant local apprenticeship system has evolved, but which often requires technical inputs; but for credit, scarce avenues are available and former credit institutions are not good at giving them required assistance.

The number of persons engaged in establishments was 3978566 in 2005. Employment grew at the rate of 0.19 per cent per annum during the period 1998-2005. Details of rural urban break-up both for the year 1998 and 2005 are presented in Table 2.14. In the rural sector of MP, employment grew at the rate of 1.09 per cent per annum whereas in the urban sector, negative growth that is, falling in employment (-0.51 per cent) has been noticed during 1998-2005.

TABLE 2.13

Sector-wise Per cent Distribution of Establishment, Economic Census-2005

Sector	*Madhya Pradesh*	*All-India*
Rural	53	61
Urban	47	39

Source: Economic Census, 2005.

TABLE 2.14

No. of Persons Employed, Economic Census-2005

Indicators			*EC-1998*	*EC-2005*	*CAGR during 1998-2005*
No. of persons employed	MP	Rural	1661160	1792130	1.09
		Urban	2265682	2186436	-0.51
		Combined	3926842	3978566	0.19
	India		83299500	100904121	2.78
Persons engaged in ag. est.			6748900	10913601	7.11
Persons engaged in non-ag. est.			76550600	89990520	2.34

Note: CAGR - Compound annual growth rate.

Source: Fact sheet of 5th Economic Census. MOSPI website, state report not yet available in published form.

6. Changes in Sectoral Distribution of Workers and Rural Non-Farm Employment

Diversification of rural livelihoods is important for several reasons. The demographic pressures on land have been increasing significantly in the state. With its share of around 35 per cent in GDP, agriculture and its allied activities has to bear the burden of 75 per cent of rural workers. Therefore, labour productivity has been low in agriculture. Urban areas have their own problems of demographic pressures. As a result, rural non-farm sector becomes an escape route for agricultural workers. In order to increase wages in agriculture and to shift the workers to more productive areas, the only open avenue is rural diversification.

Year 1987-88 was a period of severe drought affecting most parts of the country, though its impact on Madhya Pradesh was not so severe. Still the dip that is seen in rural workforce in the primary sector in this year is directly a result of drought and not of diversification of rural workforce. The per cent of workers in primary sector in rural Madhya Pradesh was much higher than that of all-India rural in 1983 and for all subsequent years for which data is presented. The gap between the share of primary sector workers in rural India to the share in rural Madhya Pradesh has also been higher in the 1990s compared to 1980s. This shows that the change in workforce diversification has been much faster in other parts of India compared to Madhya Pradesh.

There has been a gradual expansion of the tertiary or services sector in Madhya Pradesh, with manufacturing related activities growing gradually. In fact, share of employment in the secondary sector dropped between 1983 and 1993-94, and picked up in 1999-2000. The per cent of workers in secondary sector in rural Madhya Pradesh was 4.8 per cent in 1983 and 5.8 per cent in 1999-2000 compared to all-India increase from 9 per cent to 11.4 per cent during the same period. In 1983, the tertiary sector's share in the state was half. In 1999-2000, the share of tertiary sector in rural Madhya Pradesh came down. In 2004, the workers in secondary sector of rural Madhya Pradesh increased and the workers in primary sector decreased. In tertiary sector, a slight decrease in the share of rural workers was noticed.

Table 2.16 shows that the percentage of rural non-farm employment in Madhya Pradesh increased significantly from 7.2 per cent in 1983 to 12.7 per cent in 1987-88, and thereafter it stagnated and showed a decline for both males and females. In other words, jobs in the rural non-agricultural sector were created slowly. Since rural labour absorption in the non-farm sector is crucial for poverty reduction, what has happened in Madhya Pradesh in the 1990s with regard to non-farm employment creation is disturbing. Comparison of the non-farm employment of Madhya Pradesh with India reveals that one-fourth of employment in India is in this sector whereas half of employment is in Madhya Pradesh. The Census 1991 figures on rural non-farm employment supports this. In 1991, the share of rural non-farm employment to total employment was the lowest in Madhya Pradesh amongst rest of the states.

TABLE 2.15

Broad Sectoral Distribution of Workers in Rural MP and India

Year	*Rural MP*			*Rural All-India*		
	Primary	*Secondary*	*Tertiary*	*Primary*	*Secondary*	*Tertiary*
1983	90.7	4.8	4.6	81.5	9.0	9.4
1987-88	87.9	6.8	5.3	78.3	11.3	10.3
1993-94	90.4	4.5	5.1	78.2	10.2	11.5
1999-2000	87.5	5.8	6.9	76.1	11.3	12.5
2004	82.5	11.0	6.6	72.4	13.6	13.9

Source: NSS 38th, 43rd, 50th, 55th and 60th Rounds. For 60th Round, page No. 93 of report no. 506.

7. Trends at One-Digit Level

Table 2.17 provides the trend in employment in Madhya Pradesh at one-digit level of National Industrial Classification. As mentioned above, the increase in rural non-farm employment has been slow except a jump between 1993-94 and 1999-2000, when workers in this sector in rural areas went up by 25 per cent. In the period 2000-2005, the rural non-farm sector showed a remarkable increase in percentage of workers with all time high of 37.2 per cent, almost 11 per cent higher than in 2000. The increase is mainly concentrated in construction and trade sectors.

Table 2.18 provides gender-specific changes over the time in different industry groups. For males, marginal increases were noticed in non-farm employment such as trading, hotels and restaurant, construction and transport. In case of females, the rise was mainly in manufacturing, construction and trade.

TABLE 2.16

Percentage of Non-Farm Employment in Rural Madhya Pradesh and Rural All-India

Year	Males		Females		Total	
	MP	All-India	MP	All-India	MP	All-India
1983	12.6	22.4	6.2	12.2	7.2	18.4
1987-88	14.9	25.7	9.5	15.3	12.7	21.6
1993-94	12.7	26	6.2	13.9	10.9	21.7
1999-2000	15.8	28.7	8.6	14.6	12.9	23.8

Source: NSS data on Employment and Unemployment.

TABLE 2.17

Percentage Distribution of Workers by Industry at One-Digit Level in Madhya Pradesh

Rural Sector	*1983*	*1987-88*	*1993-94*	*1999-2000*	*2004-05*
Agriculture & allied	90.1	87.3	89.1	86.9	82.5
Mining and quarrying	0.6	0.6	1.3	0.4	0.7
Manufacturing	4.0	5.0	3.4	3.8	5.0
Electricity, water etc.	0.1	0.2	0.2	0.1	0.1
Construction	0.7	1.6	0.9	1.9	3.6
Trade, hotel & restaurant	1.6	2.1	1.7	2.8	4.0
Transport etc.	0.3	0.4	0.5	0.8	0.7
Services	2.7	2.8	2.9	3.3	3.4
Rural non-farm sector	9.9	12.7	10.9	13.1	17.5
Urban Sector	*1983*	*1987-88*	*1993-94*	*1999-2000*	*2004-05*
Agriculture & allied	11.4	13.7	15.1	15.2	12.1
Mining and quarrying	6.5	2.0	2.5	1.8	1.9
Manufacturing	22.2	23.0	17.1	17.9	20.1
Electricity, water etc.	1.6	0.7	1.3	0.5	0.6
Construction	7.2	5.2	5.6	8.0	7.3
Trade, hotel & restaurant	17.8	16.5	18.4	26.3	25.4
Transport etc.	10.8	8.1	8.8	8.3	6.9
Services	22.5	30.4	31.2	22.0	25.6
Combined Sector	*1983*	*1987-88*	*1993-94*	*1999-2000*	*2004-05*
Agriculture & allied	77.4	74.7	76.8	73.6	62.8
Mining and quarrying	1.5	0.8	1.5	0.7	1.0
Manufacturing	6.9	8.1	5.7	6.4	9.2
Electricity, water etc.	0.3	0.3	0.4	0.2	0.2
Construction	1.7	2.2	1.7	3.0	4.6
Trade, hotel & restaurant	4.2	4.6	4.5	7.2	10.0
Transport etc.	2.0	1.7	1.9	2.2	2.4
Services	5.9	7.6	7.6	6.8	9.6
Non-farm sector	22.6	25.3	23.2	26.4	37.2

Source: NSS Rounds.

8. Unemployment

Estimates of unemployment are based on assessment of people in the labour force, i.e., they are either working or are seeking for work or are not working for reasons other than not getting work (such as illness, holiday, festival etc.) and those amongst them who have not got employment. Unemployment rate is the ratio of unemployed to labour force. The unemployment rates under usual status are relatively high in urban are as compared to rural areas in Madhya Pradesh (Table 2.19). Further, the rates among males are higher than females in rural and urban areas, except in the drought years of 1987-88, when males must have found it more difficult to get employment as agriculture and allied sector would have dried up substantially.

The unemployment rates by usual status for males indicate no growth in unemployment since 1987-88, in both rural and urban areas of Madhya Pradesh. For females there has been a gradual decline in unemployment rates. As may be seen from Table 2.19, the unemployment rates according to CDS are higher than those of usual status. Except for females in urban Madhya Pradesh, the unemployment rates of males and females went up considerably between the period from 1987-88 to 1999-2000. In 2004-05, the trend continued except for slight decline in unemployment rate of female in urban Madhya Pradesh.

9. Underemployment

Underemployment is commonly defined as the under utilisation of labour time of the workers. Some of the workers classified as usually employed do not have work throughout the year due to seasonality in work or otherwise and their labour time is not fully utilised—they are therefore underemployed. The unemployed person days for rural males in Madhya Pradesh has increased from 1.8 per cent in 1993-94 to 3.2 per cent in 1999-2000 and 5.0 per cent in 2004-05 (Table 2.20). Similarly, it increased for rural females also. For the females, the percentage of employed increased significantly in 1999-2000 and came down to the extent of 65.7 per cent. Females 'not in the labour force' declined during the period 1993-94 and 1999-2000 and increased in 2004-05.

Field studies and the general condition of poor indicate that the poor in India cannot afford to remain without work for longer period of time. With low level of educational attainment, the poor do not have any qualms or constraints in taking up any kind of work whatever be the remuneration they receive for their work. Apart from unemployment, there is large scale under–utilisation of workforce.

TABLE 2.18

Distribution of Workers by Industry at One-Digit Level: Males and Females (%)

Sector	Rural Males			Rural Females		
	1993-94	1999-2000	2004-05	1993-94	1999-2000	2004-05
Agriculture & allied	87.2	84.2	79.0	93.9	91.6	87.6
Mining and quarrying	1.5	0.4	0.7	0.8	0.3	0.9
Manufacturing	3.2	3.9	4.5	3.2	4.2	5.7
Electricity, water etc.	0.2	0.1	0.2	0.1	0	0
Construction	1.2	2.2	4.6	0.4	1.2	2.4
Trade, hotel & restaurant	2.2	3.9	5.2	0.7	1	1.8
Transport etc.	0.7	1.2	1.2	0.1	0	0
Real estate business activities etc.	0.1	0.2	0.4	0	0	0
Services (public adm. etc.)	3.6	3.9	4.3	0.9	1.9	1.6
Total	100	100	100	100	100	100

Source: NSS Reports on Employment and Unemployment.

TABLE 2.19

Usual Status and Current Daily Status Unemployment Rates in MP and India

	Usual Status				Daily Status			
	MP		India		MP		India	
	M	F	M	F	M	F	M	F
Rural								
1983			2.1	1.4			7.5	9
1987-88	0.9	1.2	2.8	3.5	2.3	2.1	4.6	6.7
1993-94	0.8	0.2	2	1.3	2.6	2.6	5.6	5.6
1999-2000	0.7	0.2	2.1	1.5	4	3.5	7.2	7
2004-05	0.9	0.2	2.1	3.1	5.9	4.8	8	8.7
Urban								
1983			5.9	6.9			9.2	11
1987-88	4.3	5.6	6.1	8.5	6	7.8	8.8	12
1993-94	5.7	4.6	5.4	8.3	7	5.9	6.7	10.4
1999-2000	4.3	1.6	4.8	7.1	7.2	5.7	7.3	9.4
2004-05	3.3	2	4.4	9.1	6.7	5.2	7.5	11.6

Note: Usual status refers to principal status.
Source: Different rounds of NSS data.

10. Quality of Employment

Focusing on employment and unemployment fails to capture an aspect of the employment problem, which is extremely important, and this relates to what may be called the quality of employment. Income or wages is one of the variables reflecting quality. Many people are employed but they get low wages and income. The proportion of self-employment has been declining over time though it slightly increased in 2004-05. One of the reasons is the decline in farmers' cultivation on their own land owing to fragmentation of holdings. There has been sharp increase in percentage of casual labourers from 1983 to 1999-2000. However, it has come down in 2004-05.

As shown in Table 2.22, the percentage of casual labour increased for both males and females till 1999-2000 but showed a downward trend afterwards.

TABLE 2.20

Underemployment: Per 1000 Distribution of Person Days of Usually Employed (principal and subsidiary) by their Current Daily Status in Rural MP

Current Daily Status	Males			Females		
	1993-94	1999-2000	2004-05	1993-94	1999-2000	2004-05
Employed	926	917	909	672	703	657
Unemployed	18	32	50	17	24	32
Not in labour force	56	52	41	311	273	310
Total	1000	1001	1000	1000	1000	999

Source: NSS Rounds.

11. Labour Productivity

Gross state domestic product (GSDP) at constant prices per NSS worker provides one meaningful absolute measure of employment quality. Accordingly, worker productivity of Madhya Pradesh and India is provided in Table 2.23. The table reveals that labour productivity in agriculture remained more or less stagnant between 1983 and 1993/94, before rising in 1999-2000. In construction sector, there was a significant decline over this period, especially in 1999-2000. On the other hand, manufacturing sector recorded significant increase from 1987-88 onwards. Transport sector was another sector where per worker productivity rose to twice what it was in 1983. Comparison with all-India level up to 1993-94 shows that the levels of labour productivity in Madhya Pradesh in agriculture, construction and services were higher for all-India. The near stagnant or declining per worker output in agriculture and construction points to the crisis of productivity and the urgent need to take people out of these sectors into manufacturing, transport, services and even trading activities.

TABLE 2.21

Distribution of Usually Employed by Category of Employment

Year	Rural MP			Rural All-India		
	Self-Employed	Regular Employed	Casual Labourers	Self-Employed	Regular Employed	Casual Labourers
1987-88	64.9	7.3	27.8	59.4	7.7	32.9
1993-94	61.9	4.0	34.1	58.0	6.4	35.6
1999-2000	56.6	3.5	39.9	55.8	6.8	37.4
2004-05	60.3	5.3	34.4	57.3	7.8	35.0

Source: NSS Rounds.

TABLE 2.22

Percentage of Casual Labour in Rural Areas for Males and Females

Year	MP		All-India	
	Males	Females	Males	Females
1983			29.2	35.3
1987-88	25.5	31	31.4	35.5
1993-94	31.7	37.6	33.8	38.7
1999-2000	37.1	44.1	36.2	39.6
2004-05	32.1	37.7	32.9	32.6

Source: NSS Rounds.

TABLE 2.23

Labour Productivity (GSDP per UPSS worker) in Different Sectors (Rs. in constant 1980-81 prices) in MP and All-India

Year	Agriculture	Construction	Services	Manufacturing	Transport	Trade
MP (GSDP per person)						
1983	2306	6955	8261	7439	7619	7881
1987-88	2184	5716	8631	7049	10073	8540
1993-94	2387	7163	9142	12813	11300	10218
1999-2000	2571	5168	14093	15527	14520	8115
Average of 16 States GSDP Per Person						
1983	2491.65	9450.89	9196.60	7529.89	8761.21	8210.72
1987-88	2532.92	8160.88	10714.26	8453.60	10005.86	8359.71
1993-94	2870.87	9139.12	12326.58	10800.23	11468.26	9678.27

Source: For Madhya Pradesh calculated by MPHDR Team from NSS (various volumes) and Economic Survey, Government of Madhya Pradesh (various volumes) and figures for India from Bhalla (2000), Bhalla (2001).

Estimate on output per worker and worker productivity per annum are given in Tables 2.24 and 2.25 (based on GSDP at constant 1993/94 prices). These estimates show that manufacturing and services sector recorded the best per annum increase whereas agriculture sector's performance was in fact negative.

TABLE 2.24

Output per Worker in Madhya Pradesh (at GSDP at constant 1993/94 prices)

Industry	1993-94	1994-95	1995-96	1996-97	1997-98	1998-99	1999-2000	2000-01
Agriculture, forestry, fishing	12,226	11,920	11,783	12,119	11,340	12,039	11,966	11,893
Mining and quarrying	164,913	156,971	166,631	173,079	173,376	174,856	176,664	178,490
Unregistered manufacturing	53,319	61,368	63,879	70,881	72,811	76,806	81,611	86,717
Registered manufacturing	49,613	55,350	58,246	60,297	64,038	69,157	73,086	77,237
Electricity, gas and water supply	410,532	416,537	460,133	453,296	455,649	463,876	471,211	478,661
Construction	49,871	46,854	51,262	49,713	48,161	49,330	48,867	48,408
Trades, hotels, etc.	51,938	50,438	50,425	52,672	50,872	49,142	48,256	47,386
Transport, storage and communications	74,890	77,322	80,810	84,314	87,657	90,071	92,325	94,635
Finance, insurance, real estate & business services	388,092	400,503	429,745	460,271	483,253	505,702	527,106	549,415
Community, social & personal services	33,949	34,512	36,722	40,299	40,378	44,022	45,904	47,866
Average	25,093	25,269	26,027	27,105	26,764	27,918	28,339	28,774

Source: Various volumes of Economic Survey, Government of Madhya Pradesh and Sundaram (2001).

TABLE 2.25

Worker Productivity Increase per annum in Madhya Pradesh (at GSDP at constant 1993/94 prices)

Industry	1994-95	1995-96	1996-97	1997-98	1998-99	1999-2000	2000-01	Average Increase
Agriculture, forestry, fishing	-2.50%	-1.15%	2.85%	-6.43%	6.17%	-0.61%	-0.61%	-0.33%
Mining and quarrying	-4.82%	6.15%	3.87%	0.17%	0.85%	1.03%	1.03%	1.19%
Unregistered manufacturing	15.10%	4.09%	10.96%	2.72%	5.49%	6.26%	6.26%	7.27%
Registered manufacturing	11.56%	5.23%	3.52%	6.20%	7.99%	5.68%	5.68%	6.55%
Electricity, gas and water supply	1.46%	10.47%	-1.49%	0.52%	1.81%	1.58%	1.58%	2.28%
Construction	-6.05%	9.41%	-3.02%	-3.12%	2.43%	-0.94%	-0.94%	-0.32%
Trades, hotels, etc.	-2.89%	-0.03%	4.46%	-3.42%	-3.40%	-1.80%	-1.80%	-1.27%
Transport, storage and communications	3.25%	4.51%	4.34%	3.97%	2.75%	2.50%	2.50%	3.40%
Finance, insurance, real estate & business services	3.20%	7.30%	7.10%	4.99%	4.65%	4.23%	4.23%	5.10%
Community, social & personal services	1.66%	6.40%	9.74%	0.20%	9.02%	4.27%	4.27%	5.08%
Total	0.70%	3.00%	4.14%	-1.26%	4.31%	1.51%	1.53%	1.99%

Source: Various volumes of Economic Survey, Government of Madhya Pradesh and Sundaram (2001).

12. Strategic Options

12.1 Challenge

The above facts on macro scenario shows that the immediate challenge is to diversify the activities that include shifting of workers to non-agriculture sector for improving the livelihoods of poor workers. It may be noted that agricultural growth would not be sufficient to absorb the growing labour force. Poor people are too poor to be unemployed for a long time. We have the concept of "working poor". In other words, many people are working at low wages, low working conditions in agriculture and informal sector. Therefore, the challenge is to shift these workers to high productivity sectors and also to create new jobs in the non-agriculture sector. Thus, the real nature of the unemployment problem is not that people are not 'employed' in some activity but that large number of those classified as employed are engaged in low quality employment, which does not provide adequate income to keep a household above the poverty line. Besides, the employment opportunities available in the market too often do not come up to expectations of the new and increasingly educated entrants to the labour force. The employment strategy we need, therefore, is not a strategy which ensures an adequate growth in the volume of employment but one, which ensures a sufficient growth in high quality of employment opportunities.

Around 96 per cent of the Madhya Pradesh workers are in the unorganised sector. Therefore, policies have to take into account the unorganised sector. The options will also have to deal with equity and reduce the gap between per worker outputs and wages amongst different sectors, and ensure that sectors employing larger numbers provide better incomes.

12.2 Projections and Strategic Options[2]

In order to have macro strategies, we need to know the likely scenario of employment and investments needed in future. Therefore, we have made projections for the workers and investments in the 5-year period and 20-year period. Also, five scenarios of projections were made in order to know the impact of investments in different sectors on poverty and inequality. The procedure followed for projections is as under:

- Using employment data of Census 1981 and 1991 for 10 NIC (national industrial classification) categories (one-digit level) and state domestic product (SDP) data, we computed the CAGR of output per worker.
- Based on this, we projected employment and output in each category from 2005 to 2020.

TABLE 2.26

Projections of Workforce (in millions) in Madhya Pradesh

Industry	*1993-94*	*1994-95*	*1995-96*	*1996-97*	*1997-98*	*1998-99*	*1999-2000*	*2000-01*
Agriculture, forestry, fishing	15.66	16.00	16.35	16.70	17.06	17.43	17.81	18.20
Mining and quarrying	0.16	0.16	0.16	0.16	0.16	0.16	0.16	0.15
Unregistered manufacturing	0.52	0.52	0.53	0.53	0.53	0.53	0.53	0.53
Registered manufacturing	0.97	0.98	0.98	0.98	0.98	0.98	0.98	0.98
Electricity, gas and water supply	0.06	0.06	0.06	0.06	0.07	0.07	0.07	0.07
Construction	0.54	0.56	0.59	0.62	0.65	0.68	0.71	0.74
Trades, hotels, etc.	1.20	1.27	1.34	1.41	1.49	1.57	1.66	1.75
Transport, storage and communications	0.41	0.43	0.44	0.46	0.47	0.49	0.51	0.53
Finance, insurance, real estate & business services	0.11	0.11	0.11	0.11	0.12	0.12	0.12	0.12
Community, social & personal services	1.39	1.40	1.41	1.42	1.43	1.45	1.46	1.47
Total	21.02	21.49	21.97	22.45	22.96	23.48	24.01	24.54
Projections								
Population	*1981*	*1991*	*2001*	*2005*	*2010*	*2015*	*2020*	
Population, actual and projected		48.56	60.38	69.0	78.4	88.7	99.9	
Growth rate per annum projected for next five years			2.70%	2.60%	2.50%	2.40%	2.53%	
WPR %		50%	49%	48%	46%	45%	44%	
Workforce (in millions)		24.3	29.6	33.1	36.1	39.9	44.0	

Source: Mahendra Dev and Mahajan, 2000.

2. This sub-section is based on Mahendra Dev and Mahajan (2000).

TABLE 2.27

Incremental Capital Output Ratio in Madhya Pradesh, 1993-94

Industry	*1994-95*	*1995-96*	*1996-97*	*1997-98*	*1998-99*	*1999-2000*	*2000-01*	*Avg. ICOR*
Agriculture, forestry, fishing	-10.75	4.35	0.88	-0.92	0.55	2.83	2.86	1.76
Mining and quarrying	-6.17	5.94	9.70	-229.42	62.37	48.25	49.79	7.82
Unregistered manufacturing	0.45	1.53	0.60	2.27	1.19	1.05	1.04	1.16
Registered manufacturing	2.53	5.35	8.29	5.01	3.98	5.70	5.94	5.26
Electricity, gas and water supply	13.46	4.33	41.23	16.39	11.93	12.44	12.38	11.49
Construction	-2.82	0.38	3.33	3.57	0.74	1.41	1.43	1.81
Trades, hotels, etc.	1.02	0.49	0.29	1.43	1.42	0.79	0.81	0.89
Transport, storage and communications	4.48	3.77	3.76	3.93	4.62	4.77	4.73	4.30
Finance, insurance, real estate & business services	2.23	1.18	1.15	1.45	1.50	1.55	1.51	1.51
Community, social & personal services	2.96	1.04	0.68	6.13	0.73	1.32	1.30	2.02
Total	4.36	2.48	2.04	13.57	2.04	3.53	3.56	4.51

Source: Mahendra Dev and Mahajan, 2000.

TABLE 2.28

Annual Rate of Change in ICOR in Madhya Pradesh

Industry	*1995-96*	*1996-97*	*1997-98*	*1998-99*	*1999-2000*	*2000-01*	*Avg. ICOR Growth Rate*
Agriculture, forestry, fishing	-1.41	-0.80	-2.05	-1.60	4.19	0.01	-0.27
Mining and quarrying	-1.96	0.63	-24.66	-1.27	-0.23	0.03	-4.58
Unregistered manufacturing	2.40	-0.61	2.79	-0.48	-0.12	0.00	0.66
Registered manufacturing	1.12	0.55	-0.40	-0.20	0.43	0.04	0.26
Electricity, gas and water supply	-0.68	8.52	-0.60	-0.27	0.04	-0.01	1.17
Construction	-1.13	7.83	0.07	-0.79	0.91	0.01	1.15
Trades, hotels, etc.	-0.52	-0.40	3.92	-0.01	-0.44	0.02	0.43
Transport, storage and communications	-0.16	0.00	0.05	0.18	0.03	-0.01	0.01
Finance, insurance, real estate & business services	-0.47	-0.03	0.26	0.03	0.04	-0.03	-0.03
Community, social & personal services	-0.65	-0.35	8.02	-0.88	0.81	-0.02	1.16
Total	-0.43	-0.18	5.64	-0.85	0.73	0.01	0.82

Source: Mahendra Dev and Mahajan, 2000.

- The employment and output along with the incremental capital output ratio (ICOR) was used to estimate the investments needed and the CAGR of SDP from 2005 to 2020.

Following assumptions were made regarding ICOR:

- In general, productivity enhancement has been assumed to be coincidental with increase in ICOR.
- Accordingly, ICORs have been increased where they were low.
- However, ICORs have been reduced where efficiency gains are likely to set in due to private ownership, competition etc.

The projections show that employment would increase from 29.6 million in 2001 to 44 million in 2020 i.e., by 14 million. If we add the 3.7 million backlog of unemployed and severely underemployed in 2000, labour force increase by 2020 would be 18 million. These numbers in a sense, sum up the employment problem for the state in the coming decades. The ICOR in the state for our projections and evolving strategic options are presented in Tables 2.27 and 2.28.

13. Employment Strategies: Five Options

The next question is to examine the strategic options, which would give an idea of the likely impact on employment, poverty and inequality. Projections have been made for 10 major economic sectors covering agriculture, manufacturing and services, for growth in output (value added), livelihoods (employment) and the impact on income disparity (between agricultural workers and average workers). It has been assumed that in the selected sectors, investment will also lead to increase in productivity and reduction in ICOR. The projections of impact of investments on employment, workforce productivity, income disparities between agriculture wages and other wages would ensure that strategic choices lead to best input to output ratio for investments to employment, meanwhile ensuring sustainable livelihoods and better equity.

Growth requires investments, and to build projections, investment scenarios have been worked out. Projections were made for investments in natural resources (land, water, forests and livestock), in infrastructure (power, roads, warehouses, market yards, telecom etc.), human resource development services (nutrition, health, education, vocational training), and institutional development services (financial services, public administration, law and order, local government). Total investments were worked out in the range of Rs. 10,000 crore per year (10-15 per cent more than 2000-2001 estimates).

The following are the four options:

- *Status Quo:* No change from 1981-1991 trends and this is termed as base.
- *Agriculture and Allied (NR) and Services (HR) Sectors:* Productivity has been enhanced, as also employment in the latter two sectors. Here also, we are assuming that there is no increase in agricultural employment.
- *Infrastructure Services (IF) and Institutional Development (ID):* Infrastructure includes electricity, gas and water and transport and communications, and institutional development includes financial and business services.
- *Agriculture and Allied, Services, Infrastructure Services and Institutional Development:* In the service sectors, productivity and employment has been significantly enhanced.

In these four options, we make assumptions on investments, and corresponding growth rates in incomes, employment and sectoral change in employment etc.

14. Key Findings

Our estimates of the key indicators of different strategic options for employment generation are presented in the table below.

The results of projections and their impact based on the investments mentioned in Table 2.29 are shown in Table 2.30.

TABLE 2.29

Projections of Investments and CAGR of Output Per Worker

CAGR of GFCF in the Five Year Period		*1993-2000*	*2001-2005*	*2006-2010*	*2010-2015*	*2016-2020*
Agriculture, allied and forestry	NR	2.5%	5.0%	4.0%	4.0%	3.0%
Commerce and services	HR	3.5%	7.0%	6.0%	5.0%	5.0%
Electricity, gas and water	IF	3.9%	7.8%	7.8%	6.0%	6.0%
Transport and communications	IF	5.5%	8.0%	8.0%	6.0%	6.0%
Financial and business services	ID	3.1%	5.0%	5.0%	3.0%	3.0%
Average annual investment in five year period in Rs. crores	Base		11061	13249	15991	19454
Average annual investment in five year period in Rs. crores	NR+HR		11194	13496	16355	19913
Average annual investment in five year period in Rs. crores	IF+ID		11471	14229	17429	21468
Average annual investment in five year period in Rs. crores	NR+HR+IF+ID		11604	14475	17713	21748

CAGR of productivity and CARR of ICOR as proportion of CAGR of GFCF in that five year period is shown below:

Policy Scenario —>	*HR*	*ID*
GFCF CAGR to ICOR, CARR factor	0.20	0.20
GFCF CAGR to productivity, CAGR factor	0.40	0.10

Note: GFCF - Gross fixed capital formation; CAGR - Compound annual growth rate; CARR - Compound annual reduction rate; ICOR - Incremental capital output ratio; NR - Natural resources; HR - Human resources; IF - Infrastructure; ID - Institutional development.

Source: Mahendra Dev and Mahajan, 2000.

TABLE 2.30

Impact of Investments and Growth in Different Options on Key Indicators

Scenario	*Base*	*NR+HR*	*IF+ID*	*NR+HR+IF+ID*
Unemployment 2005 in millions	5.20	4.84	5.17	4.80
Unemployment 2010 in millions	4.41	3.36	4.31	3.26
Unemployment 2015 in millions	4.04	1.90	3.86	1.72
Unemployment 2020 in millions	3.28	-0.28	3.02	-0.41
GSDP growth 2005	4.27%	4.42%	4.45%	4.60%
GSDP growth 2010	4.09%	4.30%	4.41%	4.61%
GSDP growth 2015	3.96%	4.20%	4.35%	4.53%
GSDP growth 2020	3.89%	4.12%	4.25%	4.37%
Disparity ratio 2005	2.67	2.65	2.69	2.67
Disparity ratio 2010	2.92	2.88	2.98	2.94
Disparity ratio 2015	3.18	3.09	3.30	3.20
Disparity ratio 2020	3.45	3.31	3.64	3.47

Source: Mahendra Dev and Mahajan, 2000.

The projections have been made up to the year 2020. The detailed results of these investments are presented in earlier tables. The best scenario is enhanced investment in NR+HR. This will lead to highest employment, with moderate GSDP growth and least income disparity. Investments in agriculture and allied and services option seems to be the most desirable from the point of view of increasing employment, while reducing poverty and income disparity significantly

The second best scenario is enhanced investment in NR+HR+IF+ID. This leads to high employment with highest GSDP growth and moderate income disparity. This option including all sectors is better in terms of employment created, but requires more investment and does not reduce income disparity as much.

The scenario of enhanced investment in IF+ID will lead to moderate employment generation, with moderate GSDP growth and higher income disparity. The result of investment in industry generates lowest employment, with highest GSDP growth and highest income disparity.

Putting the strategic options in a box, the following matrix exhibits the projected positive impact on different groups by investing in different sectors.

Invest in → *Groups ↓*	*NR*	*HR*	*IF*	*ID*
Landless	High	Medium	Low	Medium
Tribals	High	Medium	Low	Medium
Urban unskilled	Low	High	Medium	Medium
Women	Medium	High	Medium	Medium

15. Constraints and Policy Recommendations

Public sector is not generating enough jobs and therefore, the future employment has to be created in organised and unorganised private sector. Government should act as a facilitator to increase private sector investment, which in turn increases employment. Livelihoods in Madhya Pradesh are very largely dependent on agriculture, or are forest based or lie in the urban unorganised sector. It may be mentioned here that there is no strict rural or urban livelihood region or sector. Within the wide range of livelihoods, there are those that exist at subsistence levels. The vulnerable groups amongst those employed are the landless labourers, the marginal farmers, the tribals, and the urban unskilled labourer.

Trend shows that approximately 10 lakh persons would be entering in to the workforce every year over the next two decades. The challenge for livelihoods promotion over the next 20 years is therefore, to ensure productive livelihoods for this number, as also for the existing 25 million workers and the 5 million unemployed. This requires a job-led growth of the economy, which in turn needs a specific investment pattern in different sectors.

Changes are required in the pattern of livelihoods in the state. Livelihoods need to be moved from primary sector to secondary and tertiary sectors. The change in employment pattern needs to be substantial enough to reduce workforce in agriculture from over 80 per cent to 40 per cent by 2020. So a large workforce would need to move out of agriculture to manufacturing, construction and infrastructure, but primarily and substantially to services. Not just this, even within agriculture, diversification is needed, from crop cultivation to horticulture, dairy, poultry, fishery and forest-based activities. Further, there is an urgent need to increase productivity and wages. This kind of change will require policy and institutional changes, and re-focusing and re-prioritising of investments and programme specifics.

15.1 Market Failure and Other Constraints

Market failure and other constraints prevent active private sector participation in promising sub-sectors. This in turn has a negative impact on employment. The direct control and access to natural resources such as land, water and forests, as well as on infrastructure such as power and roads, by the government has restricted action by private sector and civil society institutions. Some examples of market failure and other constraints are given.

Labour Market Failure: A large amount of seasonal unemployment in south central and south eastern districts co-exists with shortage of agricultural labour in the Malwa districts for urban manual activities. The abundance of labour in Mandla migrates to depressed agricultural wages even during peak demand season in agriculturally prosperous Narsinghpur, whereas in northern Malwa, competition from neighbouring districts and Kota in Rajasthan keeps agricultural wages comparatively higher all through the year.

The shortage of adequate labour, which is to say labour with required training or experience, is also missing in many sectors. In some places, this has also led to construction contractors to go in for mechanical equipment for digging, earthwork, road lying and so on. The problem is even more severe when one slightly moves up the skill ladder, such as for carpenters, masons, plumbers and electricians.

There is an absence of mechanisms for moving workers out of sub-sectors where demand is declining, such as *beedi* rolling or handlooms and into those sub-sectors where demand is increasing, such as construction, repairs and small engineering. This failure in the labour market can partly be explained by the lack of information, inadequate rural-urban transportation linkages and inadequate difference in wage rates to compensate for the risk of migration.

Natural Resource Regime: The forest laws and management regime has kept people away from forests. This regime is in place although the economic exploitation of forests, both wood and non-wood produce, is directly based on people, especially those who traditionally and at present work in forests and survive very substantially on forest, both as consumers of forest produce and as collectors of forest produce and workers in forests. The forest laws have kept people away from any direct control or any form of ownership or community partnership in preservation and sustainable exploitation of the vast wealth of the forests of Madhya Pradesh. The conflicting interface between forest dependent population and the forest laws has had negative impact on livelihoods of a very large number of people in the state.

In the last decade, there has been considerable work in involving people in managing forests through the joint forest management programme, and innovative strategies through the Lok Vaniki programme, and efforts to promote bamboo cultivation etc.

Credit Market Failure: There is a huge unmet demand for credit. As per the state focus paper of National Bank of Agriculture and Rural Development (NABARD), the potential plans prepared by NABARD for the undivided Madhya Pradesh was estimated to be Rs. 19,969 crore for the period 1997/98 to 2001/02, compared to Rs. 6,978 actually disbursed. The actual "ground level credit flow" according to NABARD for the new Madhya Pradesh during 1999/2000 was only 75 per cent of what has been estimated as potential in rural MP. At the same time, there is no constraint of funds, as is obvious from the credit-deposit ratio of the state at 57.8 per cent in March 2000.[3] In fact, the credit-deposit ratio in Madhya Pradesh has been declining over the years. The average credit per hectare of area cropped in Madhya Pradesh for the year 1999/2000 was just below Rs. 560. This shows the fairly low agriculture credit dispersed in the state. There is a huge network of banks, even in rural areas, with 2842 rural branches. There are even targets and priority sector lending obligations.

Yet, the availability of credit, both for fixed asset purchases and for working capital, have been a problem area both in terms of access and transaction costs. Due to the inadequacy of loan amount, time delay and excessive paper work in getting a loan from formal institutions, a majority of the producers rely on informal channels, such as traders for working capital. The SHG movement in the state testifies the extent to which the poor face credit constraints and the extent to which they are willing to invest their time in having access to flexible and friendly credit sources.

Apart from credit market failure, the newer rural sub-sectors fail to attract private investment as the private sector seeks opportunities with an assured return, considerably higher than the bank interest rates. If the return is higher but perceived risk is also higher, then private sector hesitates from investing. Thus, an attempt needs to be made to reduce risk perception through information sharing and appropriate regulatory frameworks. For example, investments in the forestry sector will not come as long as restrictions on felling and transport of timber are not rationalised.

Commodity/Product Market Failure: Lack of information about new market opportunities has restricted the participation of the private sector or constrained micro-entrepreneurs to continue catering to declining market segments. The example of soyabean

3. Lower credit-deposit ratio indicates not necessarily 'surplus' but utilisation of funds elsewhere. In general, credit-deposit ratio for rural areas in the country is lower than for urban areas indicating that rural areas are net savers whereas urban areas are net investors.

illustrates this the most. While there is a competitive squeeze in the edible oil market due to cheap palm oil imports, the market for protein-focused soyabean product markets has remained untapped. No one has responded to this. This is due to lack of information on new market segments.

Similarly while there is a large market, especially export market, for the *durram* variety of wheat grown in Madhya Pradesh (due to high protein content), no marketing arrangements have come about to take advantage of specific demand for this type of wheat.

Generally the role of middlemen in marketing is criticised as they siphon off a major share of the value added. However, the positive role of "middlemen" has to be recognised in marketing products that are produced by the unorganised sector. It includes their role in identifying the market demand pattern, transportation and taking risk of the product damage and price changes in between transporting it from the producer to the market. In several cases, members of self-help groups (SHGs) find it difficult to market their products. They could actually benefit by dealing with competitive middlemen. The move by state government to bring in private sector involvement in selling produce of self-help groups indicates a change in the marketing arrangements and could pave the way for an effective marketing intervention.

Infrastructure Constraints: In terms of infrastructure, the state of Madhya Pradesh has been lagging far behind the other parts of the state. The index of social and economic infrastructure constructed by the report of the Eleventh Finance Commission places Madhya Pradesh at 18 out of 25 states in the country.

Two sectors where the state has special problems are roads and power. The state's power situation has turned bad especially due to the bifurcation of the state, with many of the power units going off to Chhattisgarh.[4] Lack of power in rural areas is an important constraint for agriculture as well as some of the rural non-farm sub-sectors. Any of the medium sized non-farm units require electricity, such as small lathe machines, small wood units, large pottery units, handloom weavers, so that they can weave late in the night using electric light. Power is also necessary for any unit expanding from a household enterprise to employing 4-5 people or attempting to increase productivity. Lack of adequate and sustained power has also affected agriculture operations in the last two years due to drought conditions in the state. The recent changes in the state charging power supply to rural areas, and the attempts to streamline distribution and enhance production would hopefully help reduce uncertainties and shortfalls in power over the next three to four years.

The road network of Madhya Pradesh is poor, and the large landmass coupled with low population density makes it difficult to get good road connectivity. This problem is compounded by the state public works department's inability to keep roads in the black cotton area in proper shape. Recent efforts where private sector has already been partnered in about a dozen major roads in the state for construction and maintenance, the efforts in rural connectivity through the Pradhan Mantri Gram Sadak Yojana (PMGSY) and state government's own efforts from the *mandi* cess levied for better rural transport should help the rural road connectivity in the state. Road connectivity has very direct benefits such as marketability, push to the transport and rural tourism sectors, local horticulture production, etc.

The telecommunication network in the state has also been lagging far behind national achievements. However, the last few years have changed the situation in Madhya Pradesh. The public sector provider BSNL along with Touchtel, a private sector telecom provider have given the state a very good networking system, and the state can not only boast of being the first state to have private telephony, but also the largest fibre optic network in India.

The lack of training and infrastructure is also felt in almost all sectors, especially in rural non-farm sub-sectors. While there are funds and provisions available for both these schemes (there is a provision for up to 20 per cent expenditure on infrastructure and 10 per cent on training of borrowers (all as a grant) under Swarnjayanti Gram Swarozgar Yojna (SGSY), not all these funds are still being utilised. One of the main reasons for this "market failure" is the long chain of decision-making from the Government of India, to state government, to *zila parishad* to *janpad panchayats*, resulting in unrealistic norms and non-implementation.

15.2 National Rural Employment Guarantee Act, 2005

NREGA is one of the highly ambitious programme started by GoI in 2005 with the aim to provide enhancement of livelihood security, giving at least 100

4. Thirty-six per cent of the production of power has gone off to Chhattisgarh.

days of guaranteed wage employment in every financial year to every household, whose adult members volunteer to do unskilled manual work. *Panchayats* at districts, intermediate and village levels will be the principal authorities for planning and implementation of the scheme. No doubt the scheme has great potential to transform rural economy by curbing rural migration but the filed report claims several shortcomings in its implementation with true spirit. Here is the example of Madhya Pradesh revealing true stories.

TABLE 2.31

Latest NREGA Statistics for MP

Employment provided to households:	23.68012 lakh
Person days (in lakh):	
Total:	932.48
SCs:	167.71 (17.99%)
STs:	421.07 (45.16%)
Women:	379.39 (40.69%)
Others:	343.7 (36.86%)
Total fund:	2361.97 crore.
Expenditure:	1269.54 crore (53.75%)
Total works taken up:	367303
Works completed:	57427 (15%)
Works in progress:	309876 (84%)

Source: *http://nrega.nic.in/homestciti.asp?state_code=17&state_name=MADHYA%20PRADESH*

Madhya Pradesh has reportedly been performing better in implementation of NREGS, but is caught in the trap of high level of corruption and mismanagement on the part of state implementing agencies.

15.3 *Critique by Comptroller and Auditor General of India (CAG)*

1. On an average, the employment provided was 67 days only against the compulsory provision of 100 days.
2. During the period from 2005-2007, 38.49 per cent families have been never offered any kind of employment.
3. From April 2007 to January 2008, around 65.39 per cent families have not been provided employment for even a single day.
4. In 12 months period, average employment provided was for only 16 days, however, on paper it was recorded at 63 days.
5. There were observed fake entries on muster roll or job cards to the extent of 75 per cent.

16. Policy Suggestions and Recommendations

The government has to act as a facilitator and create favourable conditions for private sector participation, and identify and prioritise key sectors with employment potential and ensure successful implementation. The state has already ventured on three sets of initiatives in the state directed at promoting livelihoods. One initiative is the set of strategies employed at creating conditions for increasing productivity of assets and enhancing the productive potential of people and their productive assets, such as the watershed mission and joint forest management. The other initiative has been two major programmes, one the Indira Gandhi Garibi Hatao Pariyojana that covers 14 of the state's poorest districts, and another that is on the anvil is MP Rural Livelihoods Project in 17 districts. Both these programmes together could provide a platform for sustained and co-ordinated action on livelihoods.

The third set of initiatives is in the realm of policy and legal framework for livelihoods. The state has embarked upon bringing in changes in the land and natural resource (especially water) management and use regime through a proposed legislation that attempts to ensure equity in the use and exploitation of such resources. Simultaneously, there is also an attempt through advocacy to change certain provisions of national forest acts to give greater community control and participation in managing and using forests. These legal efforts will undoubtedly have a substantial impact on peoples' livelihoods. Related with the legal framework, are efforts at the policy level.

The state government has just released the Economic Development Policy of the state, which takes a look at and covers the entire spectrum of economic activities from agriculture to manufacturing, from energy to roads, from social sector development to biotechnology. It provides a comprehensive picture of where the state would like to go, and also comments on what should be the nature and thrust of private–public partnership, and the role of state and its supporting agencies.

Towards promoting livelihoods, the involvement of the state government, and through its direct and indirect incentives, private institutions and private organisations also have to play their part.

The role of the government should be to mainly invest in:

- Natural resource development (land, water, livestock, forests),
- Human development (nutrition, health, education, vocational training),
- Government should attract investment but not directly invest in infrastructure, industry, construction and trade sectors.

A major responsibility of the government will also be to improve productivity of capital through institutional development services. The investment of government, both financial and institutional building on such services as law and order, loan recoveries (strengthening Debt Recovery Tribunals), contract enforcement, regulation of markets etc. These will have a signal impact on investments.

In micro strategies, the issue is of where should investment be attracted and undertaken. Some important principles to be kept in mind are not to spread everywhere, but select and invest in clusters. Small towns are important engines of rural growth, so infrastructure and markets are important there. Also, there should be focus on one or two small towns other than the district headquarter in each district, making up around 100 growth clusters for Madhya Pradesh.

Based on the strengths of different employment sub-sectors and current trends, 100 growth engines have been identified for Madhya Pradesh. There are 30 in natural resources, 30 in rural and urban small industries, 20 in rural and urban small infrastructure, and 20 in rural and urban services. The reasons for selecting a large number are to ensure full employment and ensure regional coverage. The 100 growth engines and 100 growth clusters give a livelihood promotion strategy. It is a "guide to action" for development agencies. In practice, any district would have 3-5 growth engines and each engine would be spread over 5-7 districts.

A list of the possible growth engines for Madhya Pradesh is listed below.

Natural resource-based growth engines:

- For the landless and marginal farmers, concentrate on soyabean and mustard, cotton, wheat and paddy, pulses and *jowar*, fruits and vegetables, spices, cultivated medicinal and aromatic plants, and repair of agro equipment such as tractors, sprayers and pumpsets.
- For tribals, natural resource-based opportunities lie in NTFPs (*tendu, mahua, amla, harra*), gathered medicinal and aromatic plants, bamboo and grasses, timber (CP teak and others), eco-tourism based livelihoods, and natural resource-based handicrafts (wood, bamboo, metal).

A list of the possible human resource development based growth engines would be:

- For the landless and marginal farmers, primary and elementary education, and vocational skills.
- For tribals, this would mean investing in natural resource conservation skills and eco-tourism guides.
- For women, it will require investing in agricultural skills and livestock rearing skills.

The possible growth engines for the urban and unskilled would be in repairs and recycling services. These options also mean investing in conserving capital, the environment and generating jobs for the poor.

- In repairs, the potential lie in repairs of vehicles (which are growing at geometric rates), electrical equipment, electronic goods, and buildings.
- Recycling of organic solid waste, paper, cloth, glass, metals, and linking these with power generation if possible.

The promotion efforts for livelihoods would require specific and focused intervention. These will involve:

- Selection of those growth engines for focused intervention which affect thousands of people e.g., soyabean, dairy, NTFP, power.
- Getting professional agencies to draw up plans and implementing them. This does not call for report writing, but agencies involved in livelihood promotion and action.
- Selection of clusters for pilot intervention in each growth engine.
- Appointing agencies in-charge and empowering, monitoring and incentivising them.
- Review every six months and scaling up to more locations and more growth engines.

Livelihood promotion is a complex task, and needs "collaborative polygons". It means that different types of agencies, people and action are required. The state

BOX 2.3

Government-led Promotion of the Soyabean Sector

The promotion experience of soyabean in Madhya Pradesh is one of the major success stories of government-led promotion. The soyabean sector changed the lives of more than 30 lakh farmers, who shifted from *kharif* fallow, minor millets and cotton to soyabean cultivation. But the impact was not just on farmers, but it also affected 40 lakh farm labourers, about 50 thousand are involved in loading-unloading, 10 thousand involved in transportation, 6 thousand involved in 60 odd processing units, and many more in related and support industries, such as production and distribution of seed, *rhizobium*, fertiliser, gunnybags, transport support, and *dhabas*.

What went into making this happen? This was a concerted co-ordinated programme launched through the National Oilseeds Development Programme following the commitment of Government of India to become self-sufficient in edible oils. There was focused research of oilseeds, and simultaneously in Madhya Pradesh the Tawa dam project went into action, bringing large areas under perennial and assured irrigation.

The state played its role and:

- Established a co-operative network;
- Created processing facilities;
- Created warehousing facilities;
- Ensured that no barriers were imposed on movement of goods;

What went wrong?

- Failed to enter the human grade protein market effectively;
- Could not compete with oil from Malaysia;
- Productivity stagnated around a tonne per hectare.

What could be the way ahead?

- Enhance productivity of soyabean;
- Farmer is looking for a return per acre of land and not return per tonne;
- Even if we can push productivity to about half of world average production, return for farmers would double;
- But the market may induce shrinkage in area under soyabean.

What do we have?

- We have the agro-climatic condition: soil, rainfall, temperature, sunshine;
- We have infrastructure facilities to serve such a large area base;
- We have 30 lakh farmers in commercial cultivation;
- We have a forward looking state administration looking for solutions.

Possibly we can look at:

- Organic cultivation of crops, such as cotton, as;
  - There is experience of cotton cultivation;
  - Agro-climatically suitable;
  - With rejection of synthetic fabric, cotton is coming back, and
  - MP conditions are suitable for eco-friendly production: Maikal experience.
- Look for other similar commodity sub-sectors where we have a competitive advantage.

Source: Based on the discussions with researchers at National Research Centre on Soyabean, Indore, MP.

government has to be a leader in this field, but not the sole or dominant agency. The role of the state government is to ensure participation by all concerned organisations and people, and see to it that required initiatives are in place. Government must get into public-private partnerships—with corporate sector and private traders for the market side and NGOs for social mobilisation.

17. Selected Growth Engines

The growth sectors that should be focused for selected promotion are given in Box 2.4. The selection of these growth engines is based on their current strength, potential and expected growth track based on trends. The selection of which growth engine or sector to select and promote must be undertaken regionally and district-wise, depending on local field realities.

BOX 2.4

Sector-wise Growth Engines for Employment Opportunities in Madhya Pradesh

Natural Resource

- Watershed development—to enhance productivity and stabilise incomes of dryland farmers: soya, mustard, *arhar, chana, jowar*.
- Irrigated crops—to increase productivity and quality for local processing and export marketing: wheat, cotton, sugarcane, paddy.
- Horticulture development—citrus, peas, potato, vegetables, flowers, cultivable aromatics.
- Joint forest management—*tendu, mahua, amla*, myrobalans, other NTFPs, bamboo, timber.
- Livestock rearing—dairy, poultry, sheep/goat.
- Fishery, sericulture.
- Minor minerals—stone, sand, limestone.

Rural and Small Industries

- Agro-processing—wheat, soyabean, mustard, paddy, pulses, cotton, spices, vegetables.
- Crop inputs—bio-fertilisers, bio-pesticides.
- Livestock-based processing—dairy, poultry, fish, leather, meat.
- Timber and NTFP—aromatics, medicinal plants, bamboo, tendu (*beedi*), *mahua, amla* processing.
- Stone processing, cement building materials.
- Textiles—handloom (niche products), powerloom, apparel (low and high end).
- Metal, glass, ceramic and plastic products.

Rural and Small Infrastructure

- Power—decentralised generation, biomass.
- Power—local power distribution franchises.
- Irrigation—tanks, canals, borewells.
- Water—drinking water franchises.
- Roads—construction and repairs, toll collection.
- Road transport terminals; container depots.
- Warehouses and cold storages.
- Plant nurseries, tissue culture units.
- Market yards (*mandis*) and *haats*.
- Telecom, including voice and Internet.

Services

- Wholesale trading.
- Retailing-marketing agencies.
- Health care.
- Veterinary care.
- Education all levels.
- Vocational training.
- Rural tourism: hotels and restaurants.
- Entertainment services.
- Micro-finance—thrift, credit, insurance.
- Business and real estate services.

Urban Unskilled Services

- Transport of passengers and goods.
- Repairs—vehicles, electrical equipment, electronic goods, buildings.
- Recycling—solid waste, paper, cloth, glass, metals.
- Retailing (hawking)—food items, vegetables, cloth, other consumables.
- Household services—domestic help, child care, old-age care, housekeeping services, catering.
- Security services, plumbing/electrical repairs, office services.

Source: Economic Development Policy, GoMP.

18. Conclusion

Given the current share of employment in agriculture, it is not desirable to create more employment in this sector. Input to raise labour productivity and income is needed and not the employment. In fact, some of the unproductive labour from agriculture should be diverted to other sectors.

The nature of employment problem in Madhya Pradesh, therefore, can be summarised as follows:

- Employment in Madhya Pradesh is largely unorganised, rural and non-industrial. The work participation rates declined significantly in both rural and urban areas in the 1990s.

- The employment growth recorded a drastic decline during 1993-94 to 1999-2000 as compared to those for the period 1983-84 to 1993-94. Probably, the expectations of increasing employment opportunities due to economic reforms has not materialised at the aggregate level.
- There has been a proliferation of small and marginal farmers over time. The share of cultivators in the total declined while those of agricultural labourers increased.
- Only around 6 per cent of the total workforce is in the organised sector in Madhya Pradesh. The growth of employment in the organised sector has declined over time. In the post-reform period, the growth of public sector employment declined drastically while that of private sector employment increased. However, the growth of private sector employment has not been able to compensate for the loss of jobs in the public sector.
- The share of non-farm employment in rural areas has been stagnant since 1983. There has been some variation over the years, but the rural non-farm share has become more or less constant. According to Census 1991 estimates, Madhya Pradesh had the lowest share of rural non-farm employment to total rural employment.
- There is no sign of increase in the usual status unemployment rates. However, the daily status unemployment recorded significant increase in the 1990s. It is a matter of concern for the state. The problem of unemployment is more with the educated and youth.
- Casualisation has been increasing over time.
- Labour productivity showed high growth in agriculture and manufacturing in the 1990s. In spite of this, the growth of real wages in rural areas declined significantly in the 1990s.

Our macro projections show that focus on agriculture and allied and services option seems to be the most desirable from the point of view of increasing employment, while reducing poverty and income disparity significantly.

We have discussed about the constraints for private sector participation. Market failure in labour, credit and product are some of the constraints. Low infrastructure is another important constraint. Given the problem of unemployment and underemployment for the masses and unemployment for educated, there is a need to have twin strategies for improving the livelihoods. The first sub-strategy should aim at rural and urban masses who are illiterate/semi-literate, unskilled, semi-literate/skilled. The second sub-strategy has to address the educated unemployed. The policy goal should be to improve economic growth in rural areas with emphasis on employment for the poor, and to shift workers from agriculture to non-agriculture activities, particularly services in rural areas. To achieve this goal, it is necessary to focus on selected growth engines and clusters as suggested earlier.

In conclusion, we can say that the task of generating employment is an urgent one and needs a range of concerted actions from the government, donors, banks, the private sector and from civil society institutions.

Chapter 3

Agriculture in Madhya Pradesh

1. Introduction

Agriculture along with forests form the major characteristics of the state of Madhya Pradesh. A primarily agrarian and rural economy, with very little industrialisation and few modern sunrise sectors, the state depends very much on the primary sector. Although Madhya Pradesh has not been amongst the green revolution zones in the 1960s and 1970s, yet it has its own very successful ventures in agriculture that exist with large tracts of traditional low technology, and dryland farming areas. Major characteristics of agriculture in Madhya Pradesh are as follows:

1.1 Strengths

Excellent land–man ratio, good soil type, rich bio-diversity, good support system of 4500 primary agriculture co-operative societies, 240 agriculture *mandis*, 2 state agriculture universities and 11 agriculture colleges.

1.2 Weaknesses

Nearly three-fourth holdings of the state are small and marginal in nature and possessing only 26 per cent of the land area. Two-third of the gross cropped areas is rainfed showing great dependence on vagaries of the monsoon and frequent natural calamities. Large turn off and soil erosion in most parts of the state results into: (a) water congestion due to impeded drainage in early parts of the monsoon season and (b) inadequate moisture in latter part when needed the most. Further, agriculture of the state lacks diversification, high proportion of low value crops in cropping patterns (coarse cereals 20.6 per cent in *kharif* particularly), low use of HYV seeds, fertiliser and less mechanisation. The state has a large tribal population and marginal and small farmers having low investment capacity for adoption of high technology. Rural credit system in the state is also weak and there are infrastructure bottlenecks in terms of power and transport facilities. The state has high proportions of in descript animals and fodder shortage in spite of large proportion of fallows and wastelands.

There are crucial links between agriculture and rest of the state's economy as it is more of agrarian in nature. The performance of the economy is dependent on the performance of agriculture since it supplies the major food items and raw materials to the state, and on the demand side, it provides a market for non-agricultural goods and services. As per Census 2001, agricultural activities in Madhya Pradesh engage 72 per cent of the workforce although its contribution to the gross state domestic product (GSDP) has declined from 36 per cent in 1993-94 to 31 per cent in 1999-2000 and reduced further to 23.88 per cent in 2006-07. The much needed push factors in the economy are emerging from agriculture, and the poor quality of agriculture has kept many areas in the economic scenario at a depressing position.

2. Agro-Climatic Zones of MP

The district composition of the 11 agro-climatic zones of Madhya Pradesh is shown in Table 3.1.

3. Land Use Classification

Reorganised Madhya Pradesh has a total geographical area of 307.56 lakh hectares. Figure 3.1 shows the land use classification of Madhya Pradesh in 2005-06.

TABLE 3.1

Agro-Climatic Zones of Madhya Pradesh

Agro-Climatic Zones	*Districts*
Chhattisgarh plains	Balaghat
Northern hill region of Chhattisgarh	Shahdol, Sidhi, parts of Mandla
Kymore plateau and Satpura hills	Rewa, Satna, Panna (partly), Seoni and Katni *tehsil* of Katni
Central Narmada valley	Jabalpur, Katni (except Katni *tehsil*), Narsinghpur, Hoshangabad and Harda
Vindhya plateau	Bhopal, Sehore, Raisen, Vidisha, Guna, Sagar and Damoh
Gird region	Gwalior, Bhind, Shivpuri (except Picchore and Karera *tehsil*), Morena and Sheopur Kalan
Bundelkhand region	Chhattarpur, Datia, Tikamgarh, part of Panna, *tehsil* Karera and Pichhore of Shivpuri
Satpura plateau	Betul and Chhindwara
Malwa plateau	Mandsaur, Ratlam, Ujjain, Dewas, Indore, Shajapur, Rajgarh and Dhar (except Kukshi and Manawar *tehsils*) and Petlawad *tehsil* of Jhabua
Nimar plains	Khandwa, Khargone, Barwani, Kukshi and Manawar *tehsils* of Dhar
Jhabua hills	Jhabua district (except Petlawad *tehsil*)

Source: Department of Agriculture, GoMP.

FIGURE 3.1

Land Use Classifications in Madhya Pradesh, 2005-06

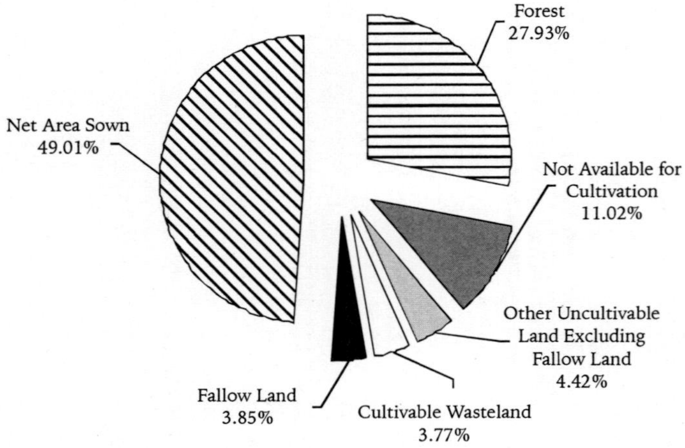

Source: Compendium of Agriculture Statistics, GoMP, 2006-07.

The net sown area in the state is just 49 per cent, and 28 per cent has been under forest reserve in the state. Another 8 per cent of the land area is classified as fallow land and cultivable wastelands etc., and would form a productive potential for the future.

According to data from remote sensing, 19 per cent of the total land area of the state was wastelands. Ten per cent of the total state's land area is classified by remote sensing as wasteland with or without scrub, and another 6 per cent as degraded forest lands, plus 2.4 per cent under ravines, which fall almost entirely in the northern and north-western districts, primarily in Bhind, Morena, Guna and Shajapur districts. Seeing land use over the last 20 years, there has been a very small increase in net sown area, from 46 per cent of total geographic area in 1977-78 to 49 per cent in 2005-06. In the same period, gross cropped area has increased from 52 per cent to 66 per cent, resulting from increase in area sown more than once.

TABLE 3.2

Land Use Classification in Madhya Pradesh

Category	*As % of Total Geographical Area*		
	1977-78	*1998-99*	*2005-06*
Forest	26.4	27.6	27.93
Not available for cultivation	11.5	10.4	11.02
Other uncultivable land excluding fallow land	6.8	5.6	4.42
Cultivable wasteland	5.1	3.8	3.77
Fallow land	4.1	3.4	3.85
Net area sown	46.1	49.2	49.01
Gross sown area	51.6	66.6	64.09

Source: Compendium of Agriculture Statistics 2006-07 MP, Government of Madhya Pradesh.

The forest area in the period from 1977-78 to 2005-2006 has increased marginally by 1.5 percentage points. Land not available for cultivation has shown a small decline of 0.5 percentage points. "Other cultivable land excluding fallow land" too has shown a decline of 2.4 percentage points. "Cultivable wasteland" and "Fallow land" have both shown a decrease of 1.3 and 0.2 percentage points respectively.

The land under wasteland with or without scrub and degraded forest land make up almost 16 per cent of the state's land area. Such a vast tract of land needs to be put under much more productive usage. The former wastelands can be developed and used

TABLE 3.3

Region-wise Land Use Classification in Madhya Pradesh, 2004-05

Agro-Climatic Region	*Geographical Area (in hectares)*	*Net Sown Area as % of Geographical Area*	*Gross Cropped Area as % of Geographical Area*	*Irrigated Area as % of Net Sown Area*	*Cropping Intensity*	*Cultivable Wasteland (in hectares)*
Chhattisgarh plains	924500	27.1	32.8	29.2	120.9	28080
Northern hills of Chhattisgarh	3782400	31.1	39.7	10.7	127.6	178500
Kymore plateau	2246500	48.8	64.6	29.4	132.4	90000
Central Narmada valley	2525900	49.4	73.1	58.4	147.9	111800
Vindhya plateau	5362800	55.7	74.2	40.2	133.3	161400
Gird region	3065400	44.9	55.4	51.9	123.3	172200
Bundelkhand region	2365800	46.6	60.2	56.1	129.1	162900
Satpura plateau	2192700	40.4	51.6	24.9	127.8	62600
Malwa plateau	5216200	67.0	100.8	38.1	150.5	129800
Nimar plateau	2466900	42.6	50.6	43.4	118.7	37400
Jhabua hills	675716	53.3	63.1	15.2	118.5	25502

Source: Commissioner of Land Records, Government of Madhya Pradesh, Gwalior.

either in cultivation or in common grazing land etc., and the latter should either be forested properly or given away to dwellers for agriculture uses or for social or commercial forestry. We have seen only a small increase in area under cultivation in the state over the last many years, and while we find that large tracts lie fallow or as wastelands, we have a large population without land (estimated to be around 28.7 per cent of the workforce).

Bringing in greater emphasis in wastelands development, dovetailing the process with the state's fairly successful watershed development, wherever possible, or with separate livelihood initiatives would be very helpful.

Regionally, Malwa stands out with the highest use of its land resources in agriculture. It also has a very high gross cropped area. Next to the Malwa belt come the districts in the central Narmada valley, with high land use, and very high levels of irrigation. In terms of cropping intensity, Vindhya plateau, Satpura plateau and the Nimar plateau require to substantially increase it. There are also regional land tracts of wastelands under cultivable wastelands, and this resource show tremendous potential along with increasing the double cropped area.

4. Operational Holdings in Madhya Pradesh

Percentages of marginal holdings have increased from 35.5 per cent in 1995-96 to 38.6 per cent in 2001 in Madhya Pradesh. However, percentages of small holdings and semi-medium holdings have remained more or less same in the above period. Small holdings have shown an increase of 4 percentage points over the same period because medium holdings become fragmented. The average landholding size has also decreased from 2.6 ha to 2.2 ha over this period. Thus, the majority of the farmers come in the category of marginal and small. They mostly practice subsistence farming and do not have adequate resources to invest in their land. It is evident from Figure 3.2 that nearly 65 per cent of the farmers are marginal and small. Much of these farmers are involved in subsistence farming and

FIGURE 3.2

Category-wise Number and Operational Holdings in Madhya Pradesh, 2001

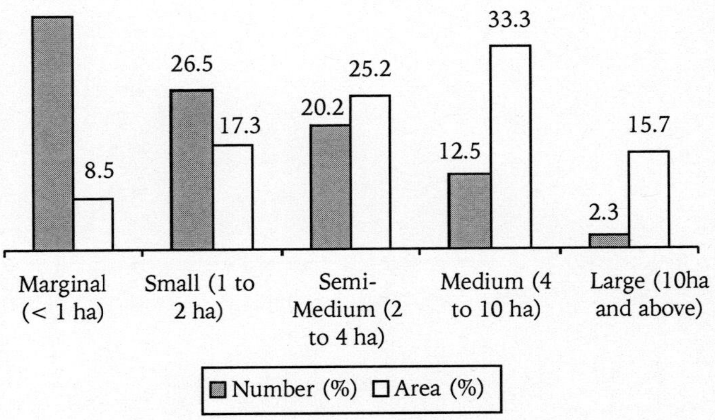

most of them are dependent upon a basket of livelihood activities for their survival. What is therefore needed is introduction of varieties of seeds and farming practices to improve the yields that are scale neutral so that the poorest of the farmer is able to adopt the proposed technology.

5. Agriculture Growth Rate in Madhya Pradesh

Growth of agriculture during the period from 1999-2000 to 2006-07 was very uneven without any specific trend. It was only in the years 2005-06 and 2006-07 that the growth rate was positive but reported miniscule growth rather shows decline in 2006-07 over 2005-06. The reason for fluctuating growth in agriculture is owing to severe droughts in the years 2000-01, 2002-03 and 2004-05. High growth in years 2001-02 and 2003-04 is mainly due to good rainfall.

From employment point of view, agriculture sector is one of the prime sectors in Madhya Pradesh. Although over a decade the employment share of agriculture has declined from 77.7 per cent in 1993-94 to 69.1 per cent in 2004-05, the decline is not substantial and it has always remained higher when compared to national average. Table 3.4 gives the employment share by different sectors for Madhya Pradesh and India.

Of the main workers recorded in census in 2001, 46.7 per cent were engaged as cultivators, with nearly a quarter of them either make a living as agriculture labour or working in sectors allied to agriculture. With the non-farm sector engaging just about a quarter of the workforce, agriculture is the livelihood source for the state, and trends in employment do not foretell any major shift in the coming decade.

The data from latest NSS round (61st) reveals the importance of agriculture sector in rural economy. From Table 3.5, it is clear that 82 per cent of the usually

TABLE 3.4

Employment Share by Sector

Sector	*1993-94*		*2004-05*	
	Madhya Pradesh	*All India*	*Madhya Pradesh*	*All India*
Agriculture	77.7	64.5	69.1	57.0
Manufacturing	5.5	10.5	7.5	12.4
Services	13.4	20.7	8.2	24.1

Source: Directorate of Economics and Statistics, GoMP and Economic Survey for MP and India.

TABLE 3.5

Distribution of Usually Working Persons in the Principal Status by Broad Industry Division (in %) for MP

Sectors	*Rural*			*Urban*		
	Male	*Female*	*Person*	*Male*	*Female*	*Person*
1. Agriculture & allied	79.0	87.6	82.0	8.8	16.7	10.2
2. Mining and quarrying	0.7	0.9	0.8	2.4	0.3	2.0
3. Manufacturing	4.5	5.7	4.9	17.9	28.7	19.9
4. Electricity, water etc.	0.2	0.0	0.1	0.8	0.2	0.7
5. Construction	4.6	2.4	3.8	8.5	3.2	7.5
6. Trade, hotel & restaurant	5.2	1.8	4.1	29.4	12.8	26.3
7. Transport etc.	1.2	0.0	0.8	8.7	0.7	7.2
8. Services						
8a. Finance, business act etc.	0.4	0.0	0.2	4.4	1.3	3.8
8b. Public administration etc.	4.3	1.6	3.3	19.2	36.2	22.3

Source: NSS 61st Round, Report no. 515, part I, "Employment and Unemployment Situation in India, 2004-05".

FIGURE 3.3

Growth Rate of Agriculture in MP

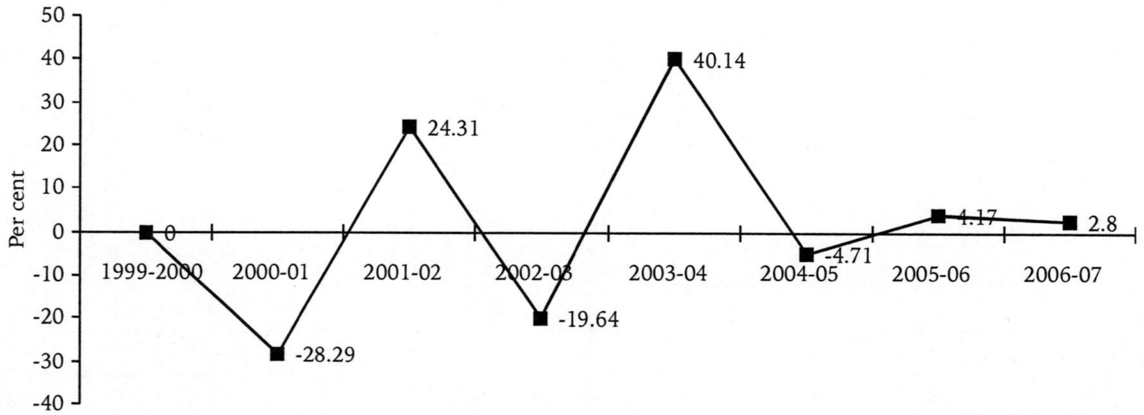

working persons are engaged in agriculture and allied activities in rural areas in 2004-05. While the further bifurcation by sex shows that 79 per cent male and 87.6 per cent female are dependent on agriculture and allied activities as the main source of livelihood.

This chapter analyses the data, both current and historical changes in production, area under cultivation, yields, agriculture inputs and infrastructure in the state of Madhya Pradesh and for the different agro-climatic zones of the state. The situation analysis of agriculture is accompanied by an analysis of the situation, the potential in the state and the problems, and some reflections on strategy that the government could consider for developing agriculture and its allied sectors in the state and the direction that the agriculture policy-making should take in the state. The significance of organic farming in the state is emphasised and the chapter includes the interesting and absorbing debate that organic farming has generated among the policy makers at the national and the state level.

6. Growth of Agriculture Production in Madhya Pradesh

Nationally, Madhya Pradesh plays a very important role in the agriculture sector. Currently (2006-07), Madhya Pradesh produces around 13.75 million tonnes of food grains and about 5.81 million tonnes of total oilseed (soyabean production is 4.785 million tonnes). The state produces 22.7 per cent pulses, wherein production of gram is highest at 40.4 per cent, and soyabean production at 55.0 per cent. Similarly, its oilseed production is 25 per cent in the country's total production. The diverse climatic and soil conditions make it possible to grow a broad range of agricultural products. The state has 11 agro-climatic zones and 5 crop zones (rice, though much reduced after division of the state, still covers the second largest agriculture area in *kharif* after soyabean, rice-wheat, wheat, wheat-*jowar* and cotton-*jowar*). But one has to be cautious as productivity of the major crops in Madhya Pradesh is low compared to national figures except the yield of

TABLE 3.6

Annual Growth Rate in Production of Crops in Madhya Pradesh, 1979-80 to 2006-07

(In '000 tonnes)

Crops	*1979-80*	*1989-90*	*1999-2000*	*2006-07*	*Annual Compound Rate of Change between 1980 and 1990*	*Annual Compound Rate of Change between 1990 and 2000*	*Annual Compound Rate of Change between 2000 and 2006-07*
Cereals	5928	12341	12637	10544	7.61	0.24	-1.79
Pulses	1517	2505	3427	3204	5.14	3.18	-0.67
Oilseeds	394	2353	5745	5813	19.57	9.34	0.12
Total	7839	17199	21809	19561	8.17	2.40	-1.08

Source: Compendium of Agriculture Statistics 2006-07 MP, Government of Madhya Pradesh.

TABLE 3.7

Annual Compound Growth Rate of Production in Madhya Pradesh

(In '000 tonnes)

Crops	*Long Term Growth Rate (1970-71 to 2006-07)*			*Short Term Growth Rate (1990-91 to 2006-07)*		
	1970-71	*2006-07*	*Growth Rate %*	*1990-91*	*2006-07 (FFC)*	*Growth Rate %*
Rice	950	1368	1.10	1435	1368	-0.29
Wheat	2536	7326	3.23	5742	7326	1.47
Jowar	1322	596	-2.36	1468	593	-5.29
Maize	505	840	1.54	1126	840	-1.74
Bajra	120	254	2.28	152	254	3.13
Gram	803	2413	3.36	1792	2413	1.80
Food grains	7380	13748	1.88	12896	13748	0.38
Groundnut	311	193	-1.42	218	193	-0.73
Soyabean	97	4785	12.41	2182	4785	4.82
Rape/Mustard	44	693	8.62	492	693	2.08
Cotton ('000 bales)	208	829	4.24	397	829	4.52

Source: Compendium of Agriculture Statistics 2006-07 MP, Government of Madhya Pradesh.

pulses, where it has maintained a record of high productivity over the decade and more.

The annual growth rates for production of major crops are given in Table 3.6. It shows that the growth rates of production in Madhya Pradesh in years prior to the 1990s than in the 90s themselves were higher. However, the situation changed drastically from bad to worse from the period 2000-2007. This has reiterated the fact that liberalisation, privatisation and globalisation has impacted negatively on agriculture growth. This has led to greater levels of food insecurity among the poor and developing countries as concluded from the analysis of Global Hunger Index.

One point to note is that between early 1980s and early 1990s, and during the overall period, the growth in yield was smaller than the growth in output because part of the increased output growth was provided by growth in gross cropped area. This growth, though small, was quite high compared to the rest of India. Growth rate for agriculture during nineties was merely 1.5 per cent per annum and subsequently for the period of 2006-07, it shows further decline.

What was behind this change in Madhya Pradesh's performance? Firstly, Madhya Pradesh's output growth pattern showed remarkable coincidence with the development of irrigation. Between 1979-80 and 1997-98, created irrigation potential increased by 73 per cent. In the last decade from 1993-94 to 2004-05, however, this potential created has remained almost stagnant, increasing from 23.2 per cent to 32.37 per cent in 2006-07 in terms of gross area irrigated to gross area sown. Gross area irrigated was 44.39 lakh hectares in 1993-94 that rose to 65.43 lakh hectares in 2006-07 showing an increase of 11.31 per cent over previous year. This indicates that we could bring about additionally only 21 lakh ha area under irrigation in the span of more than a decade. This comes out to be bringing hardly 1.6 lakh ha area under irrigation per annum.

The fund allocations to irrigation in the Sixth Plan (1980-1985), Seventh Plan (1985-1990) and the two Annual Plans (1990-1992) gives an indication of why there was such a large increase in irrigated area. Compared to the Fourth Plan (1969-1974), Fifth Plan (1974-1979) and the Annual Plan (1979-80) allocations of 21.80, 70.8 and 118 crore rupees per year, the Sixth Plan (1980-1985), Seventh Plan (1985-1990) and the two Annual Plans (1990-1992) had allocations of 196.8, 312.6 and 378 crore rupees per year respectively. Even accounting for inflation, these figures are much higher. During the Eighth Plan (1992-1997), the annual allocation was 371 crore rupees which is actually lower than the 1990-1992 allocation. In the Ninth Five Year Plan (1997-2002), out of the total plan outlay, 13.56 per cent i.e., 2722.02 crore rupees were allocated to the department of irrigation and flood control. Per cent distribution of outlay for irrigation in Tenth Five Year Plan has rose to 19.1 per cent out of total outlay. In the 11th FYP, Rs. 15102.61 crore (21.64 per cent) has been allocated to the irrigation and flood control department.

There have also been changes in the cropping pattern in the state between early 1980s to early 1990s. The major change was shifting to cultivating soyabean at the expense of coarse cereals. Oilseeds were grown in 9.9 per cent of gross cropped area in 1980-1983, and their share went up to 21.1 per cent by 1992-1995, and that of soyabean increased from 2.16 per cent to 13.27 per cent in the same period. The area under coarse cereals declined by 12 per cent from 1990-91 to 2006-07 in MP. However, area under pulses likes gram, peas, *masoor* and soyabean has shown substantial rise in MP. The area under soyabean has been more than doubled in the same period. This happened because of relatively higher profitability of oilseeds compared to coarse cereals. There were large increases in administered prices of oilseeds as well as significant increases in yields of major oilseeds. This contributed considerable value addition to the state's agricultural output.

After separation from Chhattisgarh, cropping pattern of the newly formed state of Madhya Pradesh is as follows. Share of cereals is 41 per cent, pulses 22 per cent and oilseeds 31 per cent, area under commercial crops like cotton and sugarcane is 3 per cent while fruits, vegetables, fodder and medicinal crops are cultivated on 6 per cent of the gross cropped area in 2006-07. Dominating crops in the above crop groups are wheat in cereals; gram in pulses; and soyabean in oilseed group, with their contribution of 21.5 per cent, 13 per cent and 25.6 per cent respectively.

7. Cropping Pattern

Madhya Pradesh with its large land area is endowed with 11 agro-climatic zones, 5 crop zones and 7 soil types. The Malwa, Vindhya and Nimar plateau and the Narmada valley in west and central Madhya Pradesh have black to deep black soils. Bundelkhand and part of Gird area in northern Madhya Pradesh have mixed black to red laterite soil. The type of soil in far north (Morena, Bhind and Gwalior) is alluvial while the plateaus and plains in the east and south have black and red soils. This makes it possible to grow a wide range of agricultural crops in Madhya Pradesh.

In terms of area under crops, 60 per cent of the total cropped area is under food grains, while the remaining 40 per cent is under oilseeds, fibre crops and other cash crops. The major crops of MP are wheat, rice, maize and *jowar* in cereals; gram and lentil in pulses and soyabean and mustard in oilseeds.

The undivided Madhya Pradesh also contained Chhattisgarh, often referred to as the rice bowl of India. But even with the bifurcation of the state, there is still a fairly large rice growing area of 1.68 million hectares left in divided Madhya Pradesh. Major agriculture produce is listed in the box below. Apart from the produce mentioned below, some areas also grow medicinal plants and narcotics, especially in Neemuch and Mandsaur districts.

Major Produce of Madhya Pradesh

Cereals:	Wheat, Rice, *Jowar*
Pulses:	Gram, *Tur*, *Urad*, *Moong*
Oilseeds:	Soyabean, Niger, Mustard, Groundnut
Vegetables:	Green Peas, Cauliflower, Okra, Tomato, Potato, Eggplant, Onion, Gourd
Fruits:	Mango, Guava, Orange, Melon, Papaya, Banana, Grapes
Spices:	Garlic, Coriander, Ginger, Turmeric, Chillies
Flowers:	Tube Rose, Roses, Marigold, Gladiolus

7.1 Food Grains and Oilseeds

Kharif crops are sown in 63 per cent whereas *rabi* crops are sown in 37 per cent out of the total cropped area in the state. About 38 per cent of cropped area is generally occupied by cereals, while pulses occupied 22 per cent area and oilseed occupied about 31 per cent area. In the remaining 9 per cent area, vegetables, fruits, fodder and other horticultural crops are grown.

7.2 Area under Different Crops and Crop Groups

In last two to three decades, the cropping pattern of Madhya Pradesh has changed considerably. The first significant point is that area under cereals has declined over time. While area under wheat and maize has gone up, area under *jowar* and other cereals has declined. The land taken out of cereal cultivation seems to have gone over primarily to oilseeds and to pulses. In pulses, area under gram has gone up by nearly 65 per cent, and Madhya Pradesh today is the largest producer of gram in the country. Cultivation of *arhar* and other pulses however, registered a decline in the last 20 to 30 years. Two factors have promoted the growth in the acreage under gram. First, gram needs much less water than wheat, and second, gram crop never fails completely, where as in case of wheat less irrigation decreases the crop yield.

The real story of agriculture in Madhya Pradesh has been in oilseeds. Area under oilseeds doubled between

TABLE 3.8

Growth of Various Crops Over the Years in MP

Crop Group/ Crop	*Area (in '000 Ha.)- 1978-79*	*Area (in '000 Ha.)- 1988-89*	*Area (in '000 Ha.)- 1998-99*	*Area (in '000 Ha.)- 2006-07*	*Area as Percentage of Gross Cropped Area- 2006-07*	*Percentage Change in Area under Crop from 1978 to 1988*	*Percentage Change in Area under Crop from 1988 to 1998*	*Percentage Change in Area under Crop from 1998-99 to 2006-07*	*Percentage Change in Area under Crop from 1978-79 to 2006-07*
Jowar	1841	1795	753	573	3.1	-3	-58	-24	-69
Maize	609	761	760	861	4.6	25	0	13	41
Wheat	3658	3567	4575	3993	21.5	-2	28	-13	9
Total cereals	9031	8720	8537	7669	41.3	-3	-2	-10	-15
Gram	1634	2038	2580	2463	13.3	25	27	-5	51
Tur	430	409	321	323	1.7	-5	-22	1	-25
Total pulses	3461	3723	4222	4109	22.1	8	13	-3	19
Total food grains	12493	12443	12759	11778	63.4	-0.4	3	-8	-6
Soyabean	199	1474	4541	4757	25.6	643	208	5	2290
Rapeseed/Mustard	180	419	592	694	3.7	133	41	17	286
Total oilseeds	1494	2970	5766	6088	32.8	99	94	6	307

Source: Various publications of Agriculture Statistics, Commissioner of Land Records, Government of Madhya Pradesh, Gwalior.

1978 and 1988 and then doubled again between 1988 and 1998. The most massive growth was observed in soyabean, where it was sown in 199000 hectares only in 1978, whereas in 2006-07 it is being grown over 4757000 hectares, with whopping rise by almost 23 times.

Regionally, western Madhya Pradesh dominates agriculture in the state. The northern belt of Bundelkhand, central Madhya Pradesh regions, east of Bhopal and the southern and south-eastern districts are relatively poorer in agriculture. The three divisions of Bhopal, Sagar and Ujjain account for 45 per cent of the total cropped area of wheat. Similarly, Ujjain and Bhopal divisions account for nearly 80 per cent of the area that is under cultivation of various pulses. Again, Ujjain and Bhopal divisions account for 54 per cent of the total cropped area under soyabean. Indore, Jabalpur and Ujjain account for two-thirds of the area under vegetable cultivation. Finally, 66 per cent of the spices growing areas are concentrated in Ujjain and Gwalior divisions.

8. State's Share in National Agriculture Production and Their Status

A look at Madhya Pradesh's share in production of different crop groups reveals that Madhya Pradesh is the eighth largest producer of cereals in the country, after Uttar Pradesh, West Bengal and Andhra Pradesh, accounting for 5.1 per cent of the country's produce. As far as pulses are concerned, Madhya Pradesh is the largest producer in the country accounting for 24.1 per cent of the country's total production. Madhya Pradesh is also the second largest producer of oilseeds in the country with 20.4 per cent of the country's production coming from here (Table 3.9).

Detailed crop-wise production shows that among cereals, Madhya Pradesh is the third largest producer of *jowar,* the fourth largest producer of maize and ranks fourth in wheat production in the country. Madhya Pradesh contributes 42.3 per cent of the gram produce of the country, giving it the first position among the states. It is also the sixth largest producer of *arhar,* contributing 8.76 per cent of the country's total production. Among oilseeds, Madhya Pradesh is the largest producer of soyabean accounting for 54.4 per cent of the country's total production and the third largest producer of rapeseed/mustard accounting for 10.46 per cent of the country's total production. However, a look at the yields of different crops presents a different picture.

Madhya Pradesh lags far behind the national average in the productivity of rice, wheat and maize, *arhar,*

TABLE 3.9

Share of Madhya Pradesh in National Production and its Ranking in Comparison with Other States in 2005-06

Crop Group/Crop	*First Position*		*Second Position*		*Third Position*		*Position of MP if Not in First Three*	
	State	*[%] Share*	*State*	*[%] Share*	*State*	*[%] Share*	*Position*	*[%] Share*
Total cereals	Uttar Pradesh	19.56	Andhra Pradesh	7.98	West Bengal	7.91	Eighth	5.11
Total pulses	Madhya Pradesh	24.1	Uttar Pradesh	16.7	Maharashtra	15.02		
Total food grains	Uttar Pradesh	19.37	Punjab	12.1	Andhra Pradesh	8.13	Sixth	6.33
Total oilseeds	Rajasthan	21.3	Madhya Pradesh	20.4	Gujarat	16.73		
Rice	West Bengal	15.81	Andhra Pradesh	12.8	Uttar Pradesh	12.13	Thirteenth	1.81
Jowar	Maharashtra	51.11	Karnataka	21.9	Madhya Pradesh	8.26		
Maize	Andhra Pradesh	21.01	Karnataka	18.6	Bihar	9.25	Fourth	8.5
Bajra	Rajasthan	35.94	Uttar Pradesh	16.3	Gujarat	13.93	Seventh	3.52
Wheat	Uttar Pradesh	34.71	Punjab	20.9	Haryana	12.78	Fourth	8.59
Arhar	Maharashtra	28.83	Karnataka	16.1	Uttar Pradesh	13.87	Sixth	8.76
Gram	Madhya Pradesh	42.3	Maharashtra	12.7	Uttar Pradesh	11.79		
Masoor	NA		NA		NA			
Groundnut	Gujarat	42.43	Andhra Pradesh	17.2	Tamil Nadu	13.77	Seventh	2.88
Soyabean	Madhya Pradesh	54.4	Maharashtra	30.6	Rajasthan	10.4		
Rapeseed/Mustard	Rajasthan	54.37	Uttar Pradesh	11.2	Madhya Pradesh	10.46		
Cotton	Gujarat	36.59	Maharashtra	17.1	Punjab	12.97	Seventh	4.05
Sugarcane	Uttar Pradesh	44.62	Maharashtra	13.8	Tamil Nadu	12.49	Eleventh	0.86

Source: Department of Agriculture, Government of Madhya Pradesh, Bhopal.

TABLE 3.10

Comparison of Productivity (kg/ha) of Crops in MP with Other States, 2005-06

Crop	*National Average*	*Madhya Pradesh*	*State with Highest Productivity*	*Yield*
Rice	2102	1045	Karnataka	3868
Jowar	880	1048	AP	1324
Maize	1938	1455	AP	4073
Bajra	802	1490	MP	1490
Wheat	2619	1710	Punjab	4179
Gram	808	937	AP	1591
Arhar	765	744	Bihar	1291
Groundnut	1187	1105	Tamil Nadu	1775
Soyabean	1073	1050	AP	1949
Rapeseed/Mustard	1117	1032	Gujarat	1349
Sugarcane	66928	43220	Tamil Nadu	104671

Source: Compendium of Agriculture Statistics, Madhya Pradesh, 2006-07.

soyabean, rapeseed/mustard and sugarcane. On the other hand, the state's productivity level is better for the crops like *jowar, bajra* and gram when compared to national average. Overall the yield of food grains, though slightly more than that of the neighbouring states of Maharashtra and Rajasthan, is significantly less than that of Gujarat, UP and the national average. Though Madhya Pradesh is one of the top soyabean producers in the country and is one of the major exporters, its productivity is very poor when compared to other states and national average and it is almost half of the international average.

It is a fact that productivity of major crops has shown tremendous improvement over the period of 29 years from 1978 to 2007. The yield of cereals has increased by almost 124 per cent, that of pulses by 60 per cent and oilseeds by a tremendous 156 per cent. But this rise in the yield is not at par many a times with national figures and also quite a low with the best producing state. The reasons behind low yields are many. Firstly, of the total cropped area in Madhya Pradesh, only 29.8 per cent is under irrigation, and just 37 per cent of net sown area in under irrigation. Going by districts, 25 of the 45 districts have less than 30 per cent gross irrigated area to gross cropped area. This is in contrast to the national average of 38 per cent gross irrigated area to gross cropped area, and the ratio of 93 per cent for the best state in India.

Low yields are also a result of traditional and old farming practices still in vogue in large parts of the state. Most farmers, especially small and marginal farmers numbering 47 lakh in the state constitute 65 per cent of all land owners of operational landholdings. These farmers operate small landholdings where using modern machines are difficult due to costs, and most of these families would be under-employed and fairly poor.

Looking at data on consumption of agriculture inputs reveals that consumption of fertiliser in the state per hectare is less than half of the national average and nearly one-fifth of the consumption in the best state in India. Similarly, number of tractors per lakh hectares in Madhya Pradesh is half of the national average and nearly one-tenth of the tractors per lakh hectares in the best Indian state. The consumption of pesticides again is half of the national average and less than one-seventh of the best state in India. Thirdly, the non-availability of quality seeds due to the supply side constraints has resulted in the seeds replacement rates in Madhya Pradesh being half to one-third of the replacement rates elsewhere in the country. Credit advance in agriculture in Madhya Pradesh is also another constraint. On the contrary, credit advanced to agriculture sector in Madhya Pradesh has shown tremendous rise from Rs. 819 in 1999-2000 to Rs. 3528 per hectare of gross cropped area in 2004-05, a growth of about 200 per cent.

TABLE 3.11

Productivity of Different Crop Groups in Madhya Pradesh

Crop Group/ Crop	*Yield in (kg/ha)- 1978-79*	*Yield in (kg/ha)- 1988-89*	*Yield in (kg/ha)- 1998-99*	*Yield in (kg/ha)- 2006-07*	*Percentage Change in Yield from 1978 to 1988*	*Percentage Change in Yield from 1988 to 1998*	*Percentage Change in Yield from 1998-99 to 2006-07*	*Percentage Change in Yield from 1978-79 to 2006-07*
Total cereals	749	1030	1398	1680	38	36	20	124
Total pulses	486	663	799	780	36	21	-2	60
Total food grains	676	933	1200	1167	38	29	-3	73
Total oilseeds	373	755	946	955	102	25	1	156

Source: Various publications of Agriculture Statistics, Commissioner of Land Records, Government of Madhya Pradesh, Gwalior.

TABLE 3.12

Area and Production in Fruits, Vegetables and Spices etc., in Madhya Pradesh

(Area in ha and production in metric tonnes)

Year	Fruits		Vegetables		Spices		Flowers		Medicinal & Aromatic		Grand Total	
	Area	Prod.	Area	Prod.	Area	Prod.	Area	Prod.	Area	Prod.	Area	Prod.
1999-2000	52796	945585	171044	1902192	293232	357209	3425	2000	20825	124000	541322	3330986
2004-05	47856	1032704	184950	2621258	265811	315210	1747	1048	15582	93492	515946	4063712
2005-06	46777	1172904	195977	2796580	207563	233336	3667	2200	15650	93900	469634	4298920
2006-07	48180	1208079	219488	3132086	228312	256658	NA	NA	NA	NA	495980	4596823

Source: Compendium of Agriculture Statistics 2006-07 MP, Government of Madhya Pradesh.

TABLE 3.13

Horticultural Produce in Madhya Pradesh

Crop Group/Crop	Area (in ha)	Production (in metric tonnes)	Yield (tonnes/ha)	Major Districts
2005-06				
Banana	7308	292320	40	Khandwa, Khargone, Dhar, Raigarh
Mango	6746	60714	9	Rewa, Jabalpur, Satna, Umaria, Shahdol, Katni
Mosambi	169	2704	16	Hoshangabad, Khargone, Dhar, Shajapur
Papaya	462	12474	27	Dhar, Khandwa, Ratlam, Khargone, Hoshangabad
Total Fruits	46777	1172904		
Potato	45999	689985	15	Indore, Dewas, Shajapur, Ujjain
Sweet potato	4191	25146	6	Chhatarpur, Hoshangabad, Tikamgarh
Onion	37699	603184	16	Khandwa, Shajapur, Ratlam, Sagar, Indore
Peas	18084	198924	11	Ujjain, Indore, Ratlam, Hoshangabad
Tomato	22388	335820	15	Bhopal, Datia, Indore, Chhatarpur, Sagar, Satna
Cauliflower	9716	155456	16	Chhindwara, Indore, Betul, Hoshangabad
Total vegetables	195977	2796580		
2005-06				
Chillies	46658	42459	0.91	Khargone, Dhar, Khandwa, Indore, Betul
Ginger	5757	7254	1.26	Tikamgarh, Chhindwara, Khargone, Dewas
Garlic	33717	125090	3.71	Mandsaur, Ratlam, Indore, Ujjain, Dewas
Coriander	101352	38514	0.38	Guna, Mandsaur, Shajapur, Rajgarh, Vidisha
Total spices	207563	233336		

Source: Directorate of Horticulture, Bhopal, Government of Madhya Pradesh.

9. Horticulture in Madhya Pradesh

State government is implementing National Horticulture Mission promoted by Ministry of Agriculture since 2005-06. It aimed at increasing productivity and doubling the production of horticulture crops in the 11th FYP period. The programme is being implemented in 30 districts. The major fruits produced in Madhya Pradesh are mango, guava, orange, melon, papaya, banana, and grapes; main vegetables are green peas, cauliflower, okra, tomato, potato, eggplant, onion, and gourd; and in spices, the state produces garlic, coriander, ginger, turmeric and chillies. From Table 3.13, we will be able to get an idea of the area and production in fruits, vegetables and spices in the state.

Madhya Pradesh has been a large producer of spices in India, although horticulture is not very well developed in the state. The state is the largest producer of garlic (37 per cent of the country's production) and the second largest producer of coriander.

In vegetables, although the production is not very high, there are certain strengths in the state. Among vegetables, it is gaining a reputation for the Malwa potato, which is ideal for potato chips processing.

Around 15 per cent of the pea production is also concentrated here. Potato is grown in around 47 thousand hectares in the state. The potential in the Malwa potato needs greater marketing and industrial linkage support, and has the potential of becoming very beneficial to farmers in concentrated pockets. Peas can also be picked up in larger numbers for storage and sale in as dehydrated products or even fresh peas under refrigeration.

The main fruits being grown are mangoes, guavas, banana and citrus fruits. Mangoes and guavas' production is high, and they have a large potential for tinned and pulp items. The state enjoys a potential in oranges. The largest area covered in fruits is under banana and mango, averaging around 13,000 hectares.

In terms of national share, MP produces 10 per cent of oranges, 8 per cent of guavas, and 7 per cent of banana production in the country. The productivity of most of these fruits, especially citrus fruits (orange, *mosambi* and lime) is very good, and they offer tremendous potential through an expansion in area, and through more focused fruit cultivation.

10. Medicinal Plants

In India, on the whole there are nearly 400 species of plants which are used for medicinal purposes in *Ayurvedic, Unani, Siddha* and Tibetan medicine but out of these, only 20 species are under commercial plantation. To develop and undertake commercial cultivation of these plants, and ensure that under commercial plantation they retain their values and properties as required for medicinal purpose, knowing traditional knowledge on them is crucial, along with ethno-botanical knowledge on them. It is equally important that communities traditionally holding this knowledge and involved in their production/collection continue to have these rights and do not get marginalised or reduced to labour in the growth of industrial interventions in the production and processing of these plants. The equity element of the primary collectors and repositories of knowledge must be recognised and guaranteed by state and commercial transactions, otherwise they will be reduced to the same state that most tribals have been reduced to *vis-à-vis* the forests.

Madhya Pradesh has a vast reserve of medicinal plants in its valuable forest cover. Tribal population of the state has engaged traditionally in collecting and using medicinal plants in health care practice with the help of local knowledge of herbs and medicinal plants. These make for ideal conditions to produce or collect medicinal plants for commercial use. Government of India through Technology Information, Forecasting and Assessment Council (TIFAC), an autonomous organisation under the aegis of the Department of Science and Technology, has shortlisted 45 medicinal plants out of which 7 have been identified with vast potential, and are proposed for development.

Biodiversity conservation and biodiversity-based activity has been taken up in a serious manner by the state government, through the setting up of a State Biodiversity Board. It has many national level persons as experts, with Dr. MS Swaminathan in Chair, and this Board has recommended that these seven medicinal plants be taken up for focused supportive action. The Government of Madhya Pradesh and the Biodiversity Board have collaborated with TIFAC and the Foundation for Revitalisation of Local Health Traditions; they have been working to pull in herbal product manufacturers from the private sector and link them for marketing by ascertaining their needs and building linkages, and to simultaneously develop a detailed information base on these seven identified plants.

In Madhya Pradesh, three medicinal plants that are grown and have a tremendous potential are *safed musli*, lemon grass and mentha arvensis. Already there are certain very successful enterprises in the state based on these. In the last one decade, MP has become one of the leading states in the country as far as on-farm cultivation of medicinal and aromatic plants (MAPs) are concerned with as many as 10,000 trained as well as untrained farmers having taken up its cultivation on approximately 15,650 hectares of land.

11. Incidence of Natural Calamity

Natural calamities like droughts, floods and hail-storms are common features of the state. Almost every year, one or other part of the state is generally hit by natural calamities. Droughts frequently occur in the state. The history of the last 16 years including the period after the separation of Chhattisgarh supports this fact. During the period of last 16 years, except for only 3 years (*viz.*, 1990-91, 1993-94 and 2003-04) every year one or the other part was hit by drought. Year-wise number of districts affected by natural calamity is given in Table 3.14.

TABLE 3.14

Incidence of Natural Calamities in Madhya Pradesh

Year	*No. of Affected Districts*	*Natural Calamity*
1991-92	23	Drought
1992-93	4	Drought
1994-95	4	Drought
1995-96	8	Drought
1996-97	5	Drought
1997-98	35	Affected by excess and heavy rains and hailstorm
1998-99	23	Hailstorm
1999-2000	4	Drought
	6	Flood
2000-01	32	Drought
2001-02	6	Drought
2002-03	33	Drought
2004-05	21	Drought
2005-06	12	Drought and cluster
2006-07	13	Drought and cluster

Source: *http://www.mp.nic.in/agriculture*

It should be noted that the weakness of Madhya Pradesh with respect to low use of fertilisers and pesticide may turn out to be a boon in disguise as the demand for organically grown crops is on the rise and right policies and initiatives may lead to the state being able to take advantage of the situation. Already, Madhya Pradesh is taking a leading role in adopting organic farming in India. The state has officially declared 1565 villages (five villages from each block) as having adopted organic farming. What is of still greater significance is that, farmers from as many as 3000 villages have adopted organic farming on there own initiative. District Dindori has a negligible fertiliser consumption of 2-3 kgs per hectare and has the potential of being declared as an organic farming district.

12. Organic Farming

Before we end the discussion on agriculture in Madhya Pradesh, let us discuss the issues involved in organic farming. From the late 1960s, the years of the Green Revolution, there have been massive changes in agriculture practices, and HYV seeds, chemical fertilisers, pesticides, mechanised agriculture, have all become the hallmarks of progressive agriculture.

There have been even then, and now, critics of the Green Revolution and other people who have constantly pointed out that organic farming cannot be disregarded and if properly undertaken, it can give same results as modern agriculture.

Some distinct advantages of eco-friendly sustainable agriculture are:

- Reduces land degradation,
- Reduces substantially pollution of water bodies,
- Requirement of water less than drip irrigation,
- Decreases the dependence on non-renewable energy sources,
- Decreases the use and need of costly inputs in agriculture such as fertilisers and pesticides,
- Saves farmers from debt-cycle as input costs drop substantially,
- Fruits/vegetables are tasty and far more nutritious due to presence of micro and macronutrients,
- Consumers including farming community from ingesting poisonous residues from non-organically grown food, and
- No deficiency of any micronutrients and at the same time assists in vigorous growth of earthworms and other organisms, helping nature to help farmers.

Similarly, totally mechanised agriculture has reduced the need for cattle in agriculture. Integrating cattle with agriculture also has certain uses such as:

- Draught animal power (DAP) for agricultural operations, transport, water lifting and village industries.
- Use of dung/urine for manure, biopesticides, hygienic and health care products.
- Use of dung/urine without recurring cost for decentralised source of electric power to light up homes, for which successful experiments have already been made.

We would like to end this section of the report with the success story of village Malegaon in Khandwa district where the farmers saved Rs. 23 lakh by way of organic farming. The entire village has biogas, Nadep and vermicomposting units. They do not use chemical fertilisers and pesticides and are growing bio-cotton. The farmers have not found themselves earning lower returns than when they were growing cotton conventionally.

13. High Yielding Varieties

Crops for which seeds of high yielding varieties are grown in Madhya Pradesh are wheat, paddy, maize,

BOX 3.1

Bitter Harvest of BT Cotton

by Mihir Shah and Debashis Banerji

In March 2002, three hybrid Bt cotton seeds supplied by the Mumbai-based company, Mahyco, were approved by the Genetic Engineering Approval Committee (GEAC) for cultivation of Bt cotton in central and south India. The US multinational Monsanto has a 27 per cent stake in Mahyco. Bt cotton seeds have been genetically engineered to produce a toxin that can kill the bollworm, a major headache for cotton farmers. They are ineffective against other pests and even according to their suppliers do not have any mechanism to raise yields. The idea is that they would raise the net incomes of farmers since they are expected to reduce spending on pesticides.

But a simple calculation shows that the economics does not quite work out. Seeds currently being used by farmers cost an average of Rs. 325 per hectare. The pesticide cost is around Rs. 400 per hectare. The Bt cotton seeds are about four times as expensive as existing seeds, i.e., Rs. 1,300 per hectare. Some pesticide has to be used even with Bt seeds, particularly because 20 per cent of Bt cotton fields need to be covered with non-Bt seeds (to ensure that pest resistance to Bt cotton does not rapidly develop). Even if Bt seeds are presumed to lead to a dramatic reduction in pesticide costs to say Rs.150 per hectare, the total cost of seeds and pesticides would still be double in the Bt case—Rs. 1,450 compared to Rs. 725 per hectare for seeds currently in use.

The mandatory requirement of growing non-Bt cotton in each Bt cotton plot is based on "resistance management plans" devised in the US, where farmers have huge landholdings. The idea is that the surviving resistant insects to the Bt crop will intermate with susceptible ones on the non-Bt crop. But Indian cotton farmers with much smaller landholdings have found it quite impossible to set aside land for these "refugia". Their inability to do so will only accelerate the development of pest resistance to Bt cotton. There are also a large number of technical specifications for refugia management with which Indian farmers have not even been made remotely familiar. This is obviously not a technology meant for the poor, dryland small farmers of India.

A study by the Nanjing Institute of Environmental Sciences under the Chinese State Environmental Protection Agency reveals that Bt cotton is harming natural parasitic enemies of the bollworm and seems to be encouraging other pests. The Chinese experience needs to be taken seriously since Bt cotton accounts for more than 1.5 million hectares (35 per cent of total cotton acreage) in that country. The study finds the diversity index of the insect community in Bt fields is much lower than in conventional cotton farms in China. It also finds that the populations of pests other than bollworm have increased in Bt cotton fields and some have even replaced it as the primary pest. It would be pertinent to remember that since Bt cotton was developed in the US to tackle only one main pest, the bollworm, its applicability to regions of the world with higher pest diversity was always suspect from the word go.

Source: The Hindu, August 24, 2002.

jowar and *bajra*. Over the years, coverage under high yielding varieties has grown from 4.6 million ha in 1993-94 to 6.2 million ha in 2006-07 which is 31 per cent of the gross cropped area. Ninety-three per cent of the cropped area under wheat, 85 per cent of the cropped area under *jowar* and 53 per cent of the cropped area under maize grow high yielding varieties. Seventy-eight per cent and 67 per cent of the cropped area under paddy and *bajra* are under high yielding varieties in 2006-07.

Moreover, a high proportion of the released varieties are not adopted by the farmers because they do not meet the farmers' requirements. This represents a considerable waste of resources. According to one study, in Gujarat, Madhya Pradesh and Rajasthan combined, more than 30 per cent and sometimes half of the released varieties of rice, wheat, maize, pearl millet, chickpea, groundnut and sorghum have never been grown by farmers.

14. Fertilisers

Crops respond dramatically to fertilisers on most soils. Chemical fertilisers have contributed a lot in meeting the population requirements for food and fibre. Total fertiliser consumption has increased from 9.4 kg per ha in 1978-79 to 62.7 kg per ha in 2006-07, showing the increase by 6.7 times. Major growth is seen in the use of nitrogenous and phosphorus fertilisers. The use of nitrogenous fertiliser has increased by nearly 7 times over in the above mentioned period.

There has also been a shift in the consumption of fertilisers over the years. Whereas in the late 70s the consumption of fertilisers in the *kharif* season was nearly one-fourth of the consumption in the *rabi* season, now the consumption of fertilisers is more in the *kharif* season. This is mainly due to shift in cropping pattern from food grains to oilseeds due to growth in irrigation facilities.

FIGURE 3.4

Fertiliser Consumption in Madhya Pradesh (kg/ha)

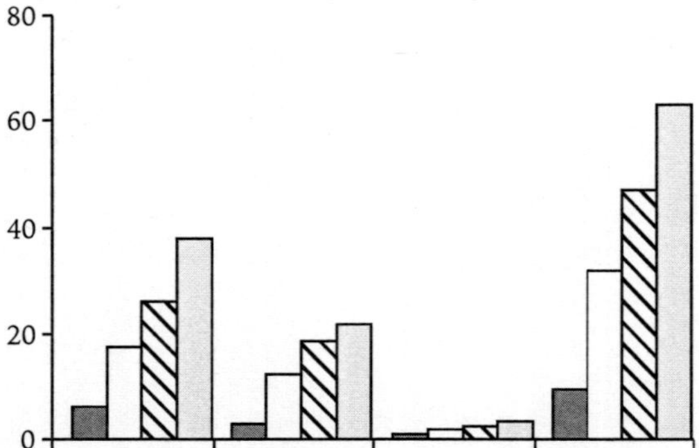

	N	P	K	Total
1978-79	5.79	2.91	0.7	9.4
1988-89	17.42	12.33	1.56	31.31
1998-99	25.88	18.27	2.17	46.33
2006-07	37.58	21.32	3.39	62.7

Source: Department of Agriculture, GoMP.

The emphasis placed on chemical fertilisers however, has had two major impact on agriculture. First is that there has been a decline in the use of organic fertilisers, that once swayed the land, and in fact organic fertilisers and organic modes of farming have been declining. Second, is that use of chemicals in agriculture is having its own debilitating effects on the environment, especially land and water in this case. While the use of fertilisers in Madhya Pradesh is much less than in other states of India and hence its negative effects are yet to appear in full force, we take evidence both from other states and from Madhya Pradesh to caution on the ever increasing use of chemical fertilisers, and emphasise that organic fertilisers and organic farming is a fairly viable and environmentally sound alternative. We will deal with this in more detail towards the end of this chapter.

15. Activities Allied with Agriculture

In the major activities allied with agriculture, we will take a quick review of animal husbandry and poultry in the state and then of fisheries. Animal husbandry (especially cattle, goats and sheep), poultry and piggery provide tremendous opportunities for landless and poor farmers in the state. Their contribution as supplementary incomes or providers of milk and meat, and a source of support as assets, is a tremendous source for the poor. The state has a very large cattle population, and is the third largest producer of milk in the country after Uttar Pradesh and Punjab.

15.1 Animal Husbandry

Livestock rearing has all along remained mainly a rural occupation practiced as a complementary to crop production. In the predominantly agriculture-based economy of Madhya Pradesh, livestock occupies a position second only to land. The contribution of cattle and buffalo to the national economy is vast. They are the main source of draught power in agricultural operation and rural transportation. They also provide essential food of animal origin like milk, meat and eggs etc. According to 2003 livestock census, the state has 3.56 crore of livestock and 117.05 lakh of poultry birds and ducks. Flesh production has doubled in the state from 10800 tonnes in 2001-02 to 21500 tonnes. Milk production has remained constant at around 53-54 lakh metric tonne from 2001-02 to 2004-05. It has increased to 63 lakh metric tonne in 2005-06 and 2006-07. Egg production has increased significantly from 7565 lakh in 2001-02 to 9518 lakh in 2006-07.

Nearly 70 per cent of animals are owned by small and marginal farmers and landless labour of the society who produces 62 per cent of milk production of the state. Improved animal husbandry practices have a major role in raising rural economy by providing employment to the tribals, scheduled castes, small and marginal farmers and landless labourers. Animal husbandry schemes are directly concerned with rural economy.

The state has two well known indigenous breeds of cattles namely Malvi and Nimari. Cattle is the most important economic asset in the rural agrarian sector of the state where 76 per cent people live in villages, out of which about 80 per cent are involved in livestock activity either as producer or as hired labourer. For upliftment of socio-economic status of the tribals, weaker section of the society, small and marginal farmers, animal husbandry has played a significant role. Most of the rural poor population are engaged in non-crop farming activities. Livestock rearing has helped the rural people through remunerative self-employment. The livestock rearing provides gainful employment through subsidiary occupations at the locality itself and makes better utilisation of essentially utilisable family labour comprising older people, women and children.

In the state, national project for cattle and buffalo breeding was launched with the objective to restructuring and reorienting cattle and buffalo breeding operations with a view to: (a) maximise returns on investments already made in livestock

BOX 3.2

Some Indigenous Breeds of Madhya Pradesh

Jamunapari (Goat)

Found in Bhind district of MP, white coloured with red spots on the body. It is the biggest breed of Indian goat. Dual-purpose breed combining meat and milk, well-developed Roman nose, pendulous and big ears. Short and flat horns, large udder, big teats. Milk yields 2.25 to 2.7 kg. per day.

Bhadawari (Buffalo)

Breed is found in the Gwalior and Bhind districts in MP. Animal of this breed are medium sized and of wedge shape. Small head, tail is long, thin and flexible with black and white or pure white marking reaching up to fetlock. Legs are short and stout. The body is usually light, copper coloured which is peculiar. The ears are scanty.

Malvi (Pride of Malwa)

Breed is found in the Malwa tract of MP—Shajapur, Rajgarh and Mandsaur districts. Animals are medium sized. Small head, horns are curved. Deep and compact body, tail is long. Strong and powerful legs. Colour is grey, black on neck and shoulders. Cows give 4-5 litre milk per day. Bullocks are very good for draught purpose.

Kadaknath (Pride of Madhya Pradesh) (Chicken)

Famous indigenous poultry breed of Jhabua and Dhar districts in Western part of MP. Characteristic feature of the bird is black beak, comb, legs, dark colour flesh that is very nutritious and tasty. Meat and eggs of this bird is rich in protein and haemoglobin. In tribal areas, this bird is used for medicinal purposes. Kadaknath is locally available in four sub-types *viz.*, black, golden, silver and pencil.

Nimari (Pride of Nimar)

Breed of Nimar region of MP—Khandwa and Khargone districts. Animals are of red colour with white patches on various part of body. Head is long bulging forehead. Horns are of medium size. Long body strong limbs. Well-developed udder. Cows give 4-5 litre milk per day. Bullocks are very good for draught purpose.

Source: Department of Animal Husbandry, GoMP.

breeding infrastructure, (b) to ensure sustainability of operations, and (c) quality in inputs and services. The project will, over a 10-years period, bring under organised breeding coverage, all the breedable female cattle and buffaloes in the state through a combination of: (i) vastly improved network delivering Artificial Insemination at the farmer's doorstep, (ii) strategically positioned bulls for natural services, and (iii) and training at all levels for skill upgradation both technical and managerial. Production of frozen semen is done in frozen semen station in Bhopal. Intensive castration of scrub bulls is also undertaken under this project.

15.2 Fisheries

The main potential in Madhya Pradesh is in fisheries. The inland fishery resources are approximately 3.98 lakh hectares in the form of irrigation reservoirs and ponds. The state has four major river systems *viz.*, Ganga, Narmada, Tapti and Mahi forming a network of 17088 kms. The state is also home to a large fishing community. In the year 2007-08, fish production in Madhya Pradesh was 61581.49 tonnes. The department earned nearly Rs. 189.28 lakh from fishery activities. Fishery as a livelihood option in the state can be divided into two broad categories. In certain cases, best exemplified by the tribal societies, it is a subsidiary source of livelihoods that primarily caters to the domestic needs. The largely subsistence household economy in such societies is supported by a diverse portfolio of options, (though often lacking market-driven specialisation), fishing in streams and ponds being one of them. Though a certain part of the produce may be sold in local *haats*, most of the produce in this case is sold domestically. The second case is of traditional fishing communities, like the Dhimars (in Tikamgarh and Chhatarpur), Barmaiyas (in Mandla, Dindori and other parts of eastern Madhya Pradesh) and the Bhois and Raikwars (in Raisen and Bhopal). In most cases, fishing continues to be the major livelihood option of these people and many of them are skilled fisher people.

In addition, a third category has also emerged in the last few decades. This is the case of people who have resorted to fishing as their major source of livelihood, after the construction of many large (and medium) sized reservoirs by the state during this period. Many of them are organised in the form of primary co-operatives, and have picked up fishing skills over years. These people belong to diverse social groups, though most of them hail from the backward communities.

The control of water bodies and the conditions governing fishing rights in reservoir and ponds is one of the crucial factors governing the exercise of this livelihood option. There is a diverse and rather intricate set of institutions and rules governing the control of water bodies in the state. For one, fishing in flowing water i.e., the streams and rivers is free and open. Stagnant water bodies below 2000 hectares in area have been brought under the control of three-tier Panchayati Raj bodies. From October 1996, the leasing out of these reservoirs is the responsibility of the Panchayati Raj bodies. While the *gram panchayat* had the responsibility for leasing out reservoirs up to a size (average size) of 10 hectares, the *janpad panchayat* and the *zila panchayat* were responsible for leasing out reservoirs between 10 and 100 hectares and between 100 and 2000 hectares respectively.[1] The royalties and lease amount for these different categories of tanks also go to the respective Panchayati Raj body.

The Panchayati Raj institutions are, however, bound to follow the rules and the norms prescribed by the state government for leasing as well as charging royalties. The state government has defined "fishermen" as a person who earns his livelihood exclusively either by pisciculture, or by fishing in water or through fish seed production. As per the government policy, water bodies below one hectare has to be leased out to an individual fisherman and above one hectare to 2000 ha average water area is to be leased out to primary fishermen co-operative societies/fishermen groups/ SHGs. Management of reservoirs above 2000 hectares average water area are under the control of the State Fisheries Federation for commercial fisheries. The MP State Fisheries Cooperative Federation Limited[2] controls and manages nine large and medium reservoirs occupying an area of 1.16 lakh hectares. Besides this, 44 reservoirs of 11000 ha water area has been retained with the department of fisheries, primarily to ensure availability of brood stock for fish seed production and for research and training purposes.

16. Institutions and Services Supporting Agriculture

16.1 Storage and Transport

Under institutional support to agriculture, let us take a look at the storage and marketing facilities available in Madhya Pradesh. There are around 240 market yards or *mandis* across Madhya Pradesh run by elected body of farmers and traders and equipped with infrastructure such as weighing machines and auction platforms, digital connectivity. The *mandi* network is a powerful and effective network in the state, with tremendous farmer participation in its politics and hence management. Madhya Pradesh does not boast of good and quality roads infrastructure, and its internal transport services also need a tremendous boost. As seen earlier, the tractor depth is low, and the state also lags much behind other states in trucks.

With poor transport and storage infrastructure, there is a very high level of cereal wastage due to rodent infestation, wastage of 20-30 per cent of fruits and vegetables due to poor packaging, multiple handling, transportation in open vans etc. There are 106 cold storage units owned by private sector and 18 units are in the hands of co-operative sector. The state government is putting up two food parks that allow pooling of various infrastructure and facilities proposed at Ratlam and Indore.

16.2 Agricultural Research

There are quite a few centres for research in agriculture in the state. The Jawaharlal Nehru Krishi Vishwavidyalaya, Jabalpur is the state agricultural university. It has colleges and centres at Rewa, Gwalior, Sehore, Indore, Khandwa and Mandsaur. Crop research centres are located at Dindori for minor millets and niger, Chhindwara for maize, Waraseoni for rice, Powarkheda for wheat, Khandwa, Badnawar and Ujjain for cotton, Khargone for pulses and groundnut, Mandsaur for poppy and maize, Jaora for sugarcane, and Morena for oilseeds. Rainfed wheat improvement is carried out at Sagar. There are also several farmer

1. The final ratification, however, has to be done by the collector in the case of tanks upto 100 hectares in size and by the commissioner for tanks bigger than 100 hectares but less than 2000 hectares.

2. In August 1999, the MP State Fisheries Development Corporation was merged with this federation of primary cooperative societies. Also known as the Matsya Mahasangh, the society owns three fish seed farms with hatcheries having a potential of 1600 lakh spawn and 300 lakh standard fry. The Mahasangh has taken up various welfare schemes for the fisherfolks of the state like interest free loans, Macchua Awas, Jalashaya Suraksha Samities, smart card yojana, training cum demonstration of different fish cultures, Janashree Beema Yojana, accident insurance, deferred wages scheme, awards (best fishermen and best society) and Macchua Charter Yojana.

training centres and *gram sewak* trainings centres in the state.

The other key institutes in the state:

- The MP State Agro Industries Development Corporation Ltd.– This has a mandate of promoting agro-industries.
- MP Agriculture Marketing Board (*mandi* board)- Oversees functioning of markets and provides supporting infrastructure.
- MP State Cooperative Marketing Federation (MARKFED)- Provides agriculture inputs and marketing facilities through member societies.
- MP Seed Certification Agency- Provides seed certification to ensure conformity.
- MP State Cooperative Dairy Federation Ltd.- Umbrella body of three-tier dairy cooperatives.
- MP Fisheries Federation- fairly active in developing water bodies, providing raw material etc.

17. Policy Initiatives by the State Government

State government is implementing various schemes under Agriculture Development Programme like distribution of chemical fertilisers, protection of seedlings and saplings, culture distribution, farm pond scheme, National Crop Insurance scheme, Annapurna and Surajdhara schemes, distribution of certified seeds, organic and sustainable farming.

17.1 Lowering Risks and Cost of Agriculture

- Crop credit interest brought down from 16 per cent to 7 per cent in 2006-07 and further to 5 per cent in 2007-08. This includes state subsidy of Rs. 100 crore.
- Nearly 2/3rd farmers i.e., 39.48 lakh farmers are covered under Kisan Credit Card scheme upto 31st August 2006.
- Bonus of Rs. 100 per quintal was declared in 2007-08.
- State level debt waiver scheme for loans upto Rs. 50,000 was announced in the latest state legislative elections.
- Madhya Pradesh will have a Farmers' Welfare Fund in order to impart modern training and ensure other facilities to the farmers. Two outstanding farmers including a female one would be awarded in every district and at state level.

17.2 Strengthening Extension

- MP is the first state to introduce PPP model in Extension Reforms (ATMA) Scheme for agriculture extension. The state government also started the novel schemes namely *kisan mitra* and *kisan didi* and selected one *kisan mitra* and one *kisan didi* from each revenue village for agriculture-related training so that yield of various crops could be increased through technical advice. Training was imparted by Indian Society of Agribusiness Professionals for *kharif* 2007 to 70 thousand *kisan mitras* and as many *kisan didis*.
- First state level call centre has been started to sort out the queries related to agriculture.
- Initiated community radio station, monthly newsletter, TV and radio programmes with rich content on agriculture.
- Over 1500 farm schools have been mobilised.

17.3 Moisture Conservation Efforts

- Thrust on ridge and furrow techniques.
- Balram Tal scheme for onfarm ponds.
- Tubewell scheme for cultivators.
- Top-up subsidy for drip and sprinkler systems.

17.4 Rural Finance Institutions

- Comprehensive amendments were done in Co-operative Act and it has been passed.
- MP was the first north Indian state to sign Vaidyanathan MoU in 2006 and received assistance of Rs. 1200 crore.
- Wide range of reforms are underway for reforming primary agriculture cooperative societies.
- Focus on savings and financing portfolio through microfinance.

17.5 Marketing

- Modernisation of 240 market yards that includes computerisation, electronic scales etc.
- Single licence system for bulk buyers to facilitate direct farmer processor linkage.
- Government has expanded warehousing, storage and collateral services.

18. Irrigation

As seen earlier, irrigation has played a major role in the growth and development of agriculture in the state. The areas that have benefited from irrigation projects, have shown growth in agriculture, by increasing yields, changing cropping pattern and increasing gross cropped area, moving from a mono crop regime to double cropping. The gap between the level of development of agriculture in the state and other parts of India is also explained by the gap between the levels of development of irrigation in Madhya Pradesh.

The major perennial rivers of MP are Mahi, Narmada, Tapti, Chambal, Betwa, Son, Wainganga, Ken and Pench. These rivers originate in Madhya Pradesh and then flow to the neighbouring states. The annual run-off from the above watershed has been estimated at 1,41,419 MCM. Out of this, it has been estimated that 56,857 MCM can be harnessed for irrigation purposes.

TABLE 3.15

Irrigation Statistics

S.N	Salient Features	Unit	Area
1	Geographical area	Lakh Ha.	308.0
2	Net sown area	Lakh Ha.	147.7
3	Total sown area	Lakh Ha.	179.7
4	Total Irrigated area	Lakh Ha.	112.9
5	Irrigation from surface water	Lakh Ha.	60.9
6	Irrigation from groundwater	Lakh Ha.	52.0
7	Total population (2001)	Thousand	60385.0
8	Rural population (2001)	Thousand	44282.0
9	Surface water (SW) available (75% dependable yield)	Lakh Ha. Metre	81.5
10	Utilisation of available SW in MP	Lakh Ha. Metre	56.8
11	Utilisation of available SW by neighbouring states	Lakh Ha. Metre	24.7
12	Groundwater availability in MP	Lakh Ha. Metre	34.5

Source: Compendium of Agriculture Statistics, GoMP 2006-07.

Together, the cumulative surface water irrigation potential and the groundwater irrigation potential created in Madhya Pradesh works out to 20 lakh hectares in the Ninth Five Year Plan period of 1997-2002 which had further increased to 24.48 lakh ha in 2006-07. But total utilisation has been 9.37 lakh hectares, which is just 38.28 per cent of the cumulative potential created. This leaves a very wide scope for increasing irrigation just by increasing the efficiency of the created potential of irrigation.

The development of irrigation potential created from government sources during different plan periods is as follows:

TABLE 3.16

Irrigation Potential Created and Utilised over the Years in Madhya Pradesh

Plan	Period	Cumulative Potential Created	(Lakh ha.) Utilisation	% Utilisation
To end of per plan	1950-51	4.69	3.54	75
First Plan	1951-1956	4.84	3.63	75
Second Plan	1956-1961	5.52	4.13	75
Third Plan	1961-1966	8.65	5.07	59
Three Annual Plans	1966-1969	11.51	7.44	65
Fourth Plan	1969-1974	12.35	8.63	70
Fifth Plan	1974-1979	17.7	12.22	69
Annual Plan	1979-80	19.14	12.07	63
Sixth Plan	1980-1985	24.52	15.27	62
Seventh Plan	1985-1990	28.11	18.22	65
Two Annual Plans	1990-1992	29.91	19.53	65
Eighth Plan	1996-97	32.68	19.74	60
Ninth Plan	1997-2002	20.59	9.24	46
Tenth Plan	2002-2007	24.48	9.37	38.28

Source: Department of Agriculture, Government of Madhya Pradesh and Economic Ssurvey, 2007-08.

It is proposed to create additional irrigation potential of 2 lakh hectares of major irrigation, 0.15 lakh hectares of medium irrigation and 1.25 lakh hectares of minor irrigation during the Tenth Five Year Plan. In order to increase the present utilisation, it is proposed to take up four new externally aided programmes and two modernisation schemes during the Tenth Plan. In addition, 0.40 lakh hectare of irrigation potential would be created under the schemes of Narmada Valley Development Authority (NVDA). Irrigation capacity developed and utilised is given in Table 3.17.

While the potential utilised in major government irrigation projects has remained around 46 per cent, it has been falling very drastically for medium irrigation projects from 68 per cent in 1999-2000 to as low as 43.2 per cent in 2006-07. This has fallen steadily in the case of minor projects as well. It is evident that special attention needs to be paid to these categories in order to increase the extent of utilisation.

18.1 Gross Irrigated Area

As can be observed from Figure 3.5, the proportion of gross irrigated area to gross area sown has always

TABLE 3.17

Developed Irrigation Capacity and Utilisation in Madhya Pradesh

Year	*Large Irrigation Project*			*Medium Irrigation Project*			*Small Irrigation Project*			*Total*		
	Capacity	*Utilisation*	*% Utilisation*	*Capacity*	*Utilisation*	*% Utilisation*	*Capacity*	*Utilisation*	*% Utilisation*	*Capacity*	*Utilisation*	*% Utilisation*
1999-2000	950	443	46.6	378	257	68.0	672	225	33.5	2000	925	46.3
2000-01	960	421	43.9	389	186	47.8	682	129	18.9	2031	736	36.2
2001-02	977	497	50.9	390	242	62.1	713	201	28.2	2080	940	45.2
2002-03	1019	408	40.0	390	184	47.2	731	176	24.1	2140	768	35.9
2003-04	1069	528	49.4	391	232	59.3	740	247	33.4	2200	1007	45.8
2004-05	1116	575	51.5	391	232	59.3	751	227	30.2	2258	1034	45.8
2005-06	1174	544	46.3	393	172	43.8	774	156	20.2	2341	872	37.2
2006-07	1243	574	46.2	403	174	43.2	802	189	23.6	2448	937	38.3

Source: Economic Survey of Madhya Pradesh, 2007-08.

lagged way behind the national average in Madhya Pradesh. Considering the fact that there are at least 10 perennial rivers that originate in Madhya Pradesh, the performance of the state in bringing areas under irrigation is not at par. If the rate of growth in the period under consideration is analysed then it is observed that the state of Madhya Pradesh has fared better than India but this is only due to the low magnitude of areas that were irrigated in the initial period in Madhya Pradesh.

FIGURE 3.5

Percentage of Gross Irrigated Area to Gross Area Sown

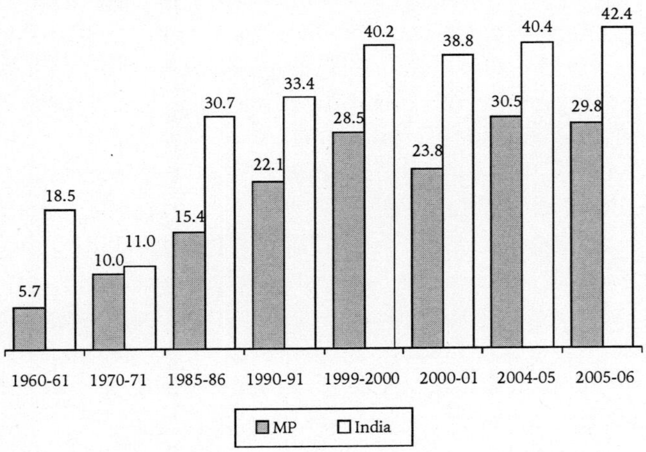

Wells and tube wells are the biggest and fastest growing source of irrigation in Madhya Pradesh accounting for 66 per cent of the net irrigation in the state, followed by canals with 18 per cent, other sources by 14 per cent and tanks by 2 per cent in 2005-2006. Area irrigated by well has jumped from 937500 hectares in 1978-79 to 2347000 hectares in 2005-06. The share of canals in irrigation has declined from 35 per cent in 1978 to 18 per cent in 2005-06, largely due to the growth in well irrigation and other sources.

Hoshangabad, Harda, Tikamgarh, Sheopur and Morena districts have the highest percentage of net sown areas under irrigation. Datia, Narsingpur, Sehore, Indore and Gwalior follow them, and Dindori, Mandla, Shahdol, Jhabua and Sidhi have very low level of development of irrigation facilities. Wheat is the major crop that avails the facility of irrigation in the state. This is particularly true of the northern and the western part of the state. Khandwa uses its irrigation facilities for cotton, Morena primarily for mustard and Mandsaur for opium and other cash crops.

The groundwater situation in MP can best be understood by analysing the data collected by the Central Ground Water Board through its 1300 monitoring station and also from the data collected by the State Ground Water Survey Department from 4000 wells. According to an Environmental Planning and Coordination Organisation report, the total replenishable groundwater resource for the state is 5.09 m ha m. Fifteen per cent of the total resources i.e., 0.76 m ha m may be apportioned for meeting the drinking water supply, industrial water supply, balance flow requirements catering to the needs for lift irrigation and maintenance of ecological balance. The remaining 85 per cent of the total groundwater resource may be considered as resource available for irrigation purposes that work out to 4.86 m ha m. If the utilisable groundwater resource for irrigation in net terms is assumed to be 90 per cent of the available resource, the utilisable groundwater resource works out to be 4.37 m ha m. The net groundwater draft for 2002-03 was estimated to be 0.63

TABLE 3.18

Irrigation Revenue Recovery for the Last Five Years

S.No.	Year	Opening Balance at the Beginning of the Financial Year	Current Demand	Total Target	Recovery against Total Target	Recovery (Rs. in Lakh)		
						From Arrears	From Current Demand	Total Recovery
1	1998-99	13536	4415	17593	10005	1431	2250	3681
2	1999-2000	14792	5109	19901	12500	2399	3621	6020
3	2000-01	7981	3202	11184	5401	921	1787	2708
4	2001-02	8431	2529	10960	6643	567	1110	1677
5	2002-03	9868.95	3406.99	13275.9	5730.0	3766.43	2085.58	5852.01
6	2003-04	11450.25	2747.36	14197.6	6717.0	877.8	3145.74	4023.54
7	2004-05	18970.41	3740.96	22711.4	9000.00	618.99	3675.20	4294.19
8	2005-06	30262.49	4401.90	34664.39	6900.00	926.14	2494.40	3420.54
9	2006-07	37120.80	5816.27	42937.07	8026.00	452.79	1428.82	1881.61

Source: Administrative report, Water Resource Department GoMP, 2006-07.

m ha m. Hence, the balance groundwater resource for future use works out to 4.23 m ha m. It may, however, be noted that the groundwater utilisation is maximum in the western part of the state which has witnessed many of its blocks being categorised as dark and grey areas (where digging of wells and installation of tube wells is not permitted). In fact, large-scale efforts have been made under National Watershed Development Mission Programme and the Rajiv Gandhi Mission for Watershed Management by the state government to arrest rainwater through people's participation and it is hoped that with a good monsoon, the problem of groundwater depletion may be mitigated to some extent.

For Madhya Pradesh, area covered by groundwater irrigation has grown tremendously in the period from 1986 to 2005. During this period, irrigation through groundwater increased by more than 200 per cent in Vidisha, Raisen, Sarguja and Seoni. In this period in the districts of Jhabua, Rajgarh, Guna, Datia, Hoshangabad, Narsingpur, Satna, Rewa, Sidhi and Shahdol, the groundwater irrigation has increased by over 100 per cent. In the remaining districts too, the growth in the period under consideration has been significant.

The following section of the report presents irrigation revenue recovery for the last five years in the state, some relevant irrigation statistics, a list of externally aided projects and finally some information related to some of the major, medium and minor irrigation projects.

18.2 Lift Irrigation Schemes

Efficient water distribution systems have enabled development of small individual irrigation schemes in which the farmer owns the system and taps post-monsoon collection of water in the riverbeds. The areas under lift irrigation are counted by the land record commissioner as other sources and as this depends on the surface water in riverbeds in the post-monsoon period, it does not have much further scope of being expanded except in a few districts like Narsingpur, Dhar and Khargone that lie in the bed of river Narmada and may have surface flowing water due to the Bargi reservoir. Most of the district has potential for development of groundwater irrigation. This is particularly so in the districts of Hoshangabad and Vidisha. In order to avoid over-exploitation of groundwater resources, it will be necessary for the government to provide a fillip to the growth of tank/ canal irrigation in the western and the northern part of the state on the pattern of system that has been practiced in Tikamgarh where both groundwater irrigation and canal/tank irrigation systems ensure that the groundwater table does not deplete despite high utilisation.

This will have to be increased in due course. But the terrain of the state is such that it does not lend itself to medium and large irrigation structures. Therefore, the route of developing micro and minor irrigation project is what should be adopted by the state. Also, there should be an honest attempt to conserve groundwater through the use of water

BOX 3.3

The Rajiv Gandhi Mission for Watershed Management in Madhya Pradesh: An Assessment

Environmental Impacts

- Increase reported in cropped area, especially compared to villages that do not have a watershed programme.
- Increase in non-crop biomass area, unlike other villages.
- Improvement in groundwater situation in many of the project villages as evidenced by reduction in dry period of wells, especially during March and April.
- An increase in irrigated area has also been reported in nearly two-thirds of all villages.

Livelihood-related Impacts

- Increases in *kharif* and *rabi* cropped area and crop-mix change.
- Increase in direct wage employment from project interventions are also reported. However, the increases in wage employment from agricultural sector do not seem to be significant enough to neutralise the accompanying growth in workforce.
- Landless households have benefited significantly from direct wage employment.
- Evidence to suggest increased crop yield, land values and livestock and other asset ownership in the project villages.

Socio-Political Impacts

- Increased appreciation of the agenda for sustainable natural resource management in select quarters, especially the village water committee (VWC) presidents and secretaries.
- Water has started emerging as a subject of mainstream public discourse.
- RGMWM has been effective in creating space for government official-people interaction and negotiation, and mainstreaming women's concerns.
- Major achievements of RGMWM has been the emergence of leadership and management skill pools at the village level.

Vulnerable Groups

- RGMWM has brought investments in areas that have witnessed limited public investment in the past.
- The direct wage employment opportunities provided through the RGMWM have provided immense relief to the landless and small and marginal farmers.

Women and Children

- A major direct impact on women has been in terms of equal wages for labour.
- Reservation of women representation in VWCs can have far reaching impacts on gender equity, although currently their participation in VWC activities is limited.
- Significant changes in sensitivities of government officials towards women and there are cases where women have started asserting their position.

Milli-Watershed Selection

Milli-watershed selection criteria envisaged are reported to be followed in most study districts. In some cases, however, additional criteria relating to people's demand as articulated by local representatives have been factored in. Even though this can indicate a shift towards a 'demand-driven' approach, there are dangers of the 'demand criteria' overwhelming other selection criteria and leading to politicisation of watershed selection.

Source: Study of RGMWM by TARU.

conserving, cost effective and locally adaptable technologies. Of the total capacities generated for irrigation, merely 50 per cent is under utilisation. Attempts should be made to utilise the unused capacities that are already in place.

18.3 Crop-wise Irrigation

In Table 3.19, the share of each crop to net irrigated area and gross irrigated area in the state is presented. Crop-wise irrigation is maximum in case of wheat, which accounts for nearly 50.3 per cent of the irrigated area. This is followed by pulses 24.58 per cent.

In terms of gross cropped area under irrigation, of the major crops wheat has a fairly good irrigation percentage of 78 per cent, while all other produce, pulses and oilseeds are very poor in terms of irrigated area to gross cropped area. There is a need for substantial increase in irrigation under these crops.

TABLE 3.19

Gross Irrigated Area under Major Crops in Madhya Pradesh, 2005-06

Crop	*% of Gross Irrigated Area under Major Crops*
Rice	3.95
Wheat	50.29
Pulses	24.58
Oilseeds	7.89
Sugarcane	1.48
Cotton	3.69
Spices	2.97
Fruits and vegetables	3.36

Source: Compendium of Agriculture Statistics, Madhya Pradesh, 2006-07.

19. Water Budgeting for Agriculture

The state is basically rich in water resources barring a few patches, which are water shortage zones. The state has an estimated surface flow of 8.15 million ha m (at 75 per cent dependability) of which 5.68 million ha m is usable by the state and remaining 2.47 million ha-m is left for use of neighbouring states. After considering the reservation of surface water for down-stream state under various interstate instruments and after considering the annually practicability, it is estimated that the state can utilise annually approximately 56.8 km^3 of water from the surface sources and about 34.5 km^3 from the groundwater sources. Thirty per cent of the surface water available in the state is stored in ponds and lakes and the remaining 70 per cent in the irrigation reservoirs. In terms of utilisation, the state is currently using only 49 per cent of the surface water.[3] Current annual utilisation in terms of withdrawal is around 14.0 km^3 from surface water and 10.0 km^3 from groundwater, while that in net (evapotranspiration) terms would be considerably lower. The groundwater development has taken place through about 9,16,108 open wells, 1,24,970 shallow tube wells/bore wells and 45 deep tube wells. Most structures, excluding the deep tube well are privately owned.

The gross cropped area of the state is 19.71 million hectare; out of that net cropped area is 15.07 million hectare. Total irrigation capacity of Madhya Pradesh state is 13.70 million hectare. The gross irrigated area is around 83 ha per thousand persons which is slightly larger than the all-India figure of 77 ha.

The irrigation potential created through government sources at the time of re-organisation of the state in 1956 was nearly 0.484 million ha. After bifurcation of state, the total irrigation potential created from government sources stands at 2.41 million hectare.

20. The Road Ahead

In order to give a boost to the agriculture sector, to make a direct and substantial dent in the poverty scenario and to make livelihoods of labourers, small and marginal farmers sustainable, certain suggestions have been listed here. These are divided into three sections, the first concerns agriculture, the second concerns issues in land, and the third with services related to agriculture.

20.1 Agriculture

The strategy for the state government should be to improve agriculture production and productivity through research, better dissemination of information and technology, and facilitating easy availability of agricultural inputs.

- In order to work on increasing productivity, a strengthened extension system needs to be evolved. While extension workers do not have to be increased, the *panchayat samitis* or the relevant *gram sabha* committees (wherever functioning) can now be used for such dissemination of practices. The primary objective of the extension infrastructure should be to provide effective and solution-oriented services to the maximum number of people possible. The mechanisms to provide services shall have to be strengthened and innovative ideas to reach the target group would have to be thought of and implemented.
- Crops must be picked up for focused promotion, and promotion must be crop-specific. This means that the strategy needed to promote say Durram wheat would be different from promoting Malwa potato. Examples of the produce that can be picked for focused promotion are wheat (including increased production of Durram wheat), productivity issues in soyabean, processing linked production in mangoes, peas, guavas etc.

3. WaterAid India (2005). *Water and Sanitation in Madhya Pradesh: A Profile of the State, Institutions and Policy Environment.*

- The state has low productivity in number of crops. The emphasis should be on increasing income of farmers by making the best use of the agro-climatic condition which give higher productivity in crops such as oilseeds pulses, vegetables, tubers, potatoes.
- The average size of holdings is small with very poor irrigation facility and poor cropping intensity. More than 60 per cent of the land-holdings are small and marginal. The following need to be addressed with a view to improving the cropping intensity:
  a) Irrigation works should be completed expeditiously.
  b) Watershed development programme should be taken up in potential areas.
  c) Joint Forest Management Committee should be formed in forest and other wastelands. Efforts should be to harness water and improve the chances of saving crops from inadequate rainfall by innovative farm ponds and other water conservation measures.
- Niche products like medicinal plants have a tremendous scope in the state. Work to identify, promote these has already started with the Bio-diversity Board. The Government of India is also offering financial assistance in developing bio-diversity, and this facility could also be used. However, the first steps are to map these and to develop strategies for their development, something already underway to some degree in Madhya Pradesh.
- Horticulture has considerable potential in the state due to its diverse agro-climatic conditions. For extensive promotion and quality, appropriate planting materials are required and the state horticulture units have to ensure that these are available in plenty. There are number of nurseries in the state from where planting material is available but both their numbers as well as the scale of their operations need upgradation.
- On-farm water management needs special attention. The existing experiments that have given good results in the state have to be identified and efforts made to ensure the adoption of these technologies in larger area and by small and marginal farmers.
- The yield of most crops is low by national averages as well as compared to best states of India. Not just this, there is also a wide gap between the yields in districts and the yields achieved in demonstration/research fields. This yield gap between farmer's yield and demonstration/research yield has to be filled as much as possible. The many factors that lead to this are in the agriculture practices, use of technology and quality and type of inputs. The state administration must ensure that this yield gap is closed as much as possible by first ensuring that basic needs such as water, soil related issues, seeds, machinery, pest harvest, processing etc., are taken care of. This will be the responsibility of not just the inputs but also of efficient and invigorated extension machinery. These also include balanced use of fertilisers, use of farm organic waste, Integrated Nutrient Management/Integrated Plant Nutrition System (INM/IPNS), soil testing and basic infrastructure development.
- In associated effort to both increase the yield and ensure that crops are not damaged or produce acceptable levels, major pest problems need to be kept in check, measures for promotion of integrated pest management (IPM), measures to ensure that quality pesticides are available to farmers and farmers use pesticides in optimal measures. There must also be a strengthening of the system to check pesticide residue testing/ monitoring in crop commodities and livestock produce. The members of *panchayats* at the *janpad* level could effectively be used for all such tasks.
- Administrative restrictions and controls on movements, marketing, credit, storage and export of agricultural products have been impending agriculture—by disabling farmers to look for better opportunities of markets and prices from markets across the nation, and by taking advantage of national and international opportunities and demands of agriculture products. While there have been some initiatives both by Government of India and the state government towards freeing trade and movement of agriculture produce, and in its control over storage, these issues need to be examined in greater detail and the sector freed from such controls, while ensuring that basic food security is not compromised.

- Efficient marketing of produce, especially perishable commodities ensures farmers get maximum returns as a percentage of the prices the goods fetch from consumers. To ensure this, reforms are required in this sector and there is an urgent need to do away with restrictions on the movement, storage, processing etc., of agricultural produce by the farmers. The existing laws and marketing arrangements along with credit availability should be carefully examined and suggestions given to ensure that the farmers get better price for his produce. Implementation of the recommendations of Guru Committee on Agriculture Marketing must also be undertaken.

20.1.1 Kisan Credit Card

Credit is the foremost requirement for ensuring adequate and timely availability of agriculture input to farmers, leading to enhanced agriculture productivity and better returns on agriculture produce for farmers. Therefore, kisan credit card should be issued to all remaining eligible farmers, within next two years. As we know that Madhya Pradesh has 72.30 lakh farmers with 65 per cent of them falling under small and marginal farmers, therefore, a special programme needs to be undertaken to issue kisan credit card to all remaining farmers with priority to 47 lakh small and marginal farmers. At present, only 2/3rd of farmers are covered under Kisan Credit Card scheme.

20.1.2 Vermicompost Units

Low cost vermincompost units should be promoted through demonstration on priority in horticulture crop area. This single unit should aim at meeting year round requirement of half acre area. This would have multiple benefits, in terms of reduced expenditure on fertilisers/ pesticides and irrigation, apart from enhanced yield of better quality crop produce. The state should target to bring at least 10 per cent of total cropped area under vermicompost application through providing 75 per cent cash subsidy on construction cost of low cost vermicompost unit during the next five years.

20.1.3 Dairy Promotion

Dairy can be a primary occupation for small and marginal farmers living in low rainfall area. Here, in the state of MP, comprehensive dairy cluster can be started in major *jowar* producing districts of Khandwa, Khargone, Badwani, Chhindwara, Shajapur, Guna and Betul.

Under this programme, initially, one block of this district should be taken for intensive dairy development. Under this dairy development programme, aspect of feeding, vaccination, housing and breed improvement should be covered and dairy should be made primary occupation of that block and subsequently, this programme should be scaled up to the entire district. Further, this dairy development programme should focus on indigenous cow, since scientific management of indigenous cow in terms of feeding and improved housing can ensure a monthly income of Rs. 700 or more from single cow. Further, these are low cost cows; therefore, funds for cow purchase can be successfully generated through women SHG formation and subsequently, their successful linkage with banks.

Further, state government should focus on creating infrastructure for marketing of milk and breed improvement of *desi* cows by producing exotic bulls in a manner that bull is available in every *gram panchayat* through demand-driven schemes for these clusters.

20.1.4 Backyard Poultry

Low cost backyard poultry is a very good income generation activity in water deficient area. In this activity, broiler should be promoted, which do not require light and market feed for rearing. For promotion of this activity, one division, with local market potential should be selected and initially, one block should be taken for intensive promotion among landless and marginal farmers. Government should enter into partnership with private agencies for ensuring chick supply on desired scale.

20.1.5 Percolation Tanks

To enhance assured irrigation across the state, construction of percolation tanks should be undertaken in every village. This would ensure, holding excessive rainfall and thus recharging groundwater table and hence, farmers would be encouraged to go for digging of new wells on their own. Further, it would also reduce problem of drinking water in villages. MP has 55393 villages and if each of these percolation tanks leads to indirect irrigation of 10 ha land, then the state would have additional irrigated area of 5.53 lakh ha every year. Let us presume that each of these percolation tanks would cost Rs. 2 lakh. Thus, the state would require an annual budget of Rs. 1108 crore. If this is done within five years, 27.65 lakh ha land can be brought under irrigation in these 55393 villages and probably, it would be a big step to avoid starvation in poor villages.

20.1.6 Irrigation

Irrigated area can be further increased in the state. Wells and tube wells are the major source here, and with a fairly good groundwater situation, this source can be built upon even more.

- The state has large number of water bodies and rivers and estimates state that they provide for a substantial irrigation potential, as yet untapped. Using small irrigation schemes and a massive increase in lift irrigation, this potential can be tapped further. The programme of watershed development and the Pani Roko Abhiyan, which apart from building water conservation structures also works to repair, clean or build existing water bodies, shall certainly help in this regard. A poor efficiency level of existing irrigation schemes needs urgent attention to increase the actual irrigation from the potential created by irrigation schemes/ projects. Towards increasing irrigation, a fairly substantial credit inflow would also be required for lift irrigation schemes and for tube wells. Current credit flows are poor, and both the co-operative credit network and NABARD related financial institutions would need to upscale efficiency and credit flows.
- To complement basic irrigation, the state must enhance natural resource management, degraded/ wasteland development and utilisation, rainwater harvesting and groundwater recharge.

20.2 Land

- Large tracts of land in the state are undulating, and large canal based irrigation projects are not very feasibly everywhere. In this situation, the efforts of the Rajiv Gandhi Mission for Watershed Management must be upscaled further, with lot more emphasis on water conserving, cost effective and sustainable technologies at the local level. There is a need for orienting farmers and watershed managers on groundwater conservation and recharging of tube wells.
- To develop the large tracts of cultivable wastelands, substantial resources would be needed, and in this, private sector partnership can be called in. The state had attempted to involve the private sector previously in developing wastelands. Further, wastelands can even be given over to good self-help groups for either their own use or for community benefits, under suitably designed programmes that help both self-help group members and add to community wealth, along with helping to regenerate the wastelands.
- In terms of land, the new initiative by the state government to distribute land to all landless households belonging to Dalit and tribal population is a crucial move. The government is already in the process of identifying such land, from wastelands, fallow land, common lands, lands violating land ceilings etc., and the work of distributing it amongst landless families has also started. Care will need to be taken that this process is far better managed than earlier land redistribution programmes. In many earlier cases, *pattas* have still not been given to the allottees; where *pattas* have been given, *kabza* is still not with the allottees, or the original owners/rural powerful has pushed out the allottees etc. In redistribution programme this time, it must be ensured that *pattas* and *kabza* are ensured, and enough administrative care is taken to see that land is actually used by the allottees.

20.3 Services related with Agriculture

- Improving rural roads connectivity, as well as quality of major feeder routes has to be affected urgently. Funds today are available under the Pradhan Mantri Gram Sadak Yojana, the state initiated Kisan Road Fund from *mandi* cess, and loans from the Asian Development Bank. Funds from PMGSY and ADB will help in new construction; funds from *mandi* cess would be used for rehabilitation and repair of existing rural roads. Work on rural roads appears to have taken off in the state in the last year itself and good results may be expected in a year's time. Similarly, the large trunk routes and feeder routes have been selected for public-private partnership under different contract systems.
- Legally, private investments are not allowed in *mandis* in the state. If appropriate changes could be brought in here, and private investments encouraged, either by private entrepreneurs or even associations of producers or industrial manufacturers, it could go a long way in easing the shortage.
- Madhya Pradesh is being talked off as a "logistics hub" for the nation. Its central position offers tremendous scope for this. This can be further extended to connecting the state horticulture

production areas with markets, through a chain or network of cold chains, especially for products like mangoes, guavas, *sitaphal* (custard apple), bananas etc. Further, appropriate infrastructure should be created at the *mandis* for fruits and vegetables such as grading, pack houses, sorting and cold storage.

- The potential offered by fisheries needs to be explored further. The entire process of granting *pattas* must be made open and ensure that true co-operatives of fishermen get these *pattas*. There is also a need to input technical assistance for fishermen, introducing fish seeds of high yielding varieties, producing fingerlings of relevant varieties, decentralising of water bodies through *panchayats* where pisciculture can be practiced, handing over the fisheries or reservoirs to the co-operatives, initiating *jhinga* culture in the fresh water areas, conserving the native species, providing the right to fisheries in all water bodies under any government department to the fisheries department, developing the aquarium sub-sector and encouraging angling facilities with an eye on the tourism industry.
- In order to get more credit into agriculture, there is a pressing need to encourage institutional credit into agriculture and to strengthen the co-operative movement. The Madhya Pradesh Swayatta Sahakari Adhiniyam (1999) provides opportunities for co-operatives to enter into a legal regime that will grant them greater autonomy.
- In order to promote quality seed research, the government is committed to develop a life sciences gateway at Bhopal. This would comprise a life sciences institute and a biotech park. It is envisaged that the gateway would be a centre for cutting-edge research in varieties of seeds that are suitable for the agro-climatic zones of MP.
- There has to be greater mechanisation in processes related with soil and water conservation, seeds, horticulture, crop residue management, post-harvest handling/processing.

Chapter 4

Finance

1. Introduction

State government is one of the important development agencies and its prime responsibility is to look after the development of the state and its citizens. A state's ability to undertake development functions more effectively is largely determined by its fiscal position. Hence, finances of the state government play a crucial role as far as less developed states like Madhya Pradesh is concerned. Under the Indian Constitution, there are some subjects that are included in the state list like health, education, agriculture, drinking water facility, roads, employment opportunities etc. Not only are these subjects directly related to day-to-day life of the state's citizens but also has a close relevance to the quality of life of the citizens. In order to provide the basic services to the people, state government formulates various policies and programmes on concerned subjects. Government's social and economic policy priorities are truly revealed in the budget document, mainly through the allocations made in different sectors and means through which the fund would be mobilised for the same. State government's budget affects the lives of the people both in direct and indirect ways. It is particularly the people belonging to the weaker sections of the society having low incomes and less political influence who get the most affected by budgetary decisions.

Finances of all the state governments witnessed deterioration in late nineties and Madhya Pradesh was no exception. It was mainly due to implementation of the Fifth Pay Commission. However, in the past few years, fiscal scenario of the divided Madhya Pradesh has shown significant improvement. It is the sound fiscal management that has brought under control the deteriorating fiscal position of the state government. There has been a qualitative change in the state of the state finances since 2004-05. Between 2001-02 and 2003-04, the state carried a revenue deficit. But since 2004-05, the state has turned around and has generated revenue surpluses.

BOX 4.1

Recommendations of the 12th Finance Commission for Restructuring Public Finance

- Centre and states to improve the combined tax-GDP ratio to 17.6 per cent by 2009-10.
- Fiscal deficit to GDP targets for the Centre and state to be fixed at 3 per cent.
- Revenue deficit of the Centre and state to be brought down to zero by 2008-09.
- Interest payment relative to revenue receipts to be brought down to 28 per cent and 15 per cent in the case of Centre and state respectively.
- States to follow recruitment policy in a manner so that the total salary bill, relative to revenue expenditure, net of interest payment, does not exceed 35 per cent.
- Each state to enact Fiscal Responsibility and Budget Management (FRBM) Act, providing for elimination of revenue deficit by 2008-09 and reducing fiscal deficit by 3 per cent of state domestic product.
- The system on lending to be brought at end over time. Long term goal should be to bring down debt-GDP ratio to 28 per cent each for the Centre and state.

Source: Report of the 12th Finance Commission, GoI.

1.1 12th Finance Commission (2005-2010)

The Commission submitted its report in November 2004, for the period 2005 to 2010. Recommendations of the Commission include a plan for restructuring of public finances of the Centre and state through improvement in revenue mobilisation and bringing down debt levels, and through enactment of FRBM Act by states, debt relief to states linked to fiscal reforms, doing away with the present system of central assistance to state plan in the form of loan and grant and transfer of central assistance to states on the same conditions as attached to such assistance by the external funding agencies.

This transition of Madhya Pradesh from being a revenue deficit state to a revenue surplus one has brought about a qualitative change through the way development in the state is being financed. For instance, during the era of revenue deficits, in FY 2003-04, the net public debt[1] had to be utilised first for financing the revenue deficit and the deficit on account of state government's "loans and advances", with only the balance being used for financing the developmental capital expenditure. This invariably resulted in developmental capital expenditure as a proportion of net public debt being small. But from financial year 2007-2008, the net public debt is entirely used to finance the developmental capital expenditure. Besides, the revenue surplus would not only be able to meet the deficit on account of state government's "loans and advances", but also augments further the developmental capital expenditure. Hence, the developmental capital expenditure as a proportion of net public debt has gone above 100 per cent. The next section here deals with time series analysis of receipts and expenditure of Madhya Pradesh government.

2. Receipts

Aggregate receipts of the state government consist of revenue receipts and capital receipts. Revenue receipts comprises tax revenue, non-tax revenue and grant-in-aid from the Central government. While components of capital receipts are recovery of loans and advances, net public debt and net receipts from public accounts. Table 4.1 below shows that total receipts of the state government has turned out to be more than double in the period from Rs. 17321.57 crore in 2001-02 to Rs. 40887.27 in 2008-09 (RE). Average share of revenue receipts and capital receipts in the total receipts is 79.53 per cent and 20.46 per cent respectively.

In the subsequent paragraphs, we will discuss in detail the components and trends in revenue and capital receipts of the state government mainly because they are the major components of the consolidated fund receipts.

2.1 Revenue Receipts

2.1.1 Composition of Revenue Receipts

Components of revenue receipts of the state government are tax revenue, non-tax revenue and

TABLE 4.1

Total Receipts for the Madhya Pradesh Government

(Figures in '000 Rs.)

S.No. Heads	*2001-02 AC*	*2002-03 AC*	*2003-04 AC*	*2004-05 AC*	*2005-06 AC*	*2006-07 AC*	*2007-08 AC*	*2008-09 RE*
1. Revenue receipts (2+3+4)	11200.98	13390.4	14288.96	19743.25	20596.8	25694.28	30688.73	34403.78
2. Tax revenue	8108.18	9893.29	11036	12849.65	15456.06	18561.67	22221.14	24745.04
(i) Own tax revenue	4668.88	6189.48	6805.1	7769.91	9113.83	10472.2	12017.63	14001.68
(ii) Share in central taxes	3439.3	3703.81	4230.9	5079.74	6342.23	8089.47	1023.51	10765.83
3. Non-tax revenue	1601.68	1635.48	1479.82	4461.86	2208.2	2658.46	2738.18	3145.31
4. Grants-in-aid from Central government	1491.12	1861.63	1773.14	2431.74	2932.54	4474.15	5729.41	7036.17
5. Capital receipts (6+7+8)	6120.59	3653.79	7574.95	6504.54	7451.75	2408.66	1932.64	6483.49
6. Recovery of loans & advances	1590.61	42.71	35.84	53.2	2851.98	38.42	118.10	49.83
7. Net public debt	2759.32	3455.68	7663.35	5457.62	4206.69	2871.44	1693.95	4754.26
8. Net receipts from public account	1770.66	155.4	-124.24	993.72	393.08	-501.2	120.59	1679.40
9. Total receipts (1+5)	17321.57	17044.19	21863.91	26247.79	28048.55	28102.94	32621.37	40887.27

Note: AC - Actuals; BE - Budget Estimate; RE - Revised Estimate.
Source: State Budget Books, GoMP, various years.

1. The difference in the receipts and expenditure under the heads "Internal debt of the state government" and "Loans and advances from the central government" taken together.

grants-in-aid from Central government. Tax revenue comprises state's own taxes and state's share in central taxes. Receipts from state's own taxes[2] are mobilised through levying of taxes by states. State's share in central taxes[3] is an entitlement of the state government that are transferred by the Central government from its divisible pool of taxes on the recommendations of the Central Finance Commission.

The non-tax revenue comprises: (i) fiscal services, (ii) interest receipts, dividends and profits and (iii) other non-tax revenue on account of general, social and economic services. The grants-in-aid from the Central government comprise non-Plan grants (provided either on the recommendations of the Central Finance Commission or central ministries) and Plan grants that are received by the state for financing state plan schemes, central plan schemes and centrally sponsored schemes. Plan grant allocations are made according to the recommendations of the Planning Commission of India.

FIGURE 4.1

Revenue Receipts of the State Government

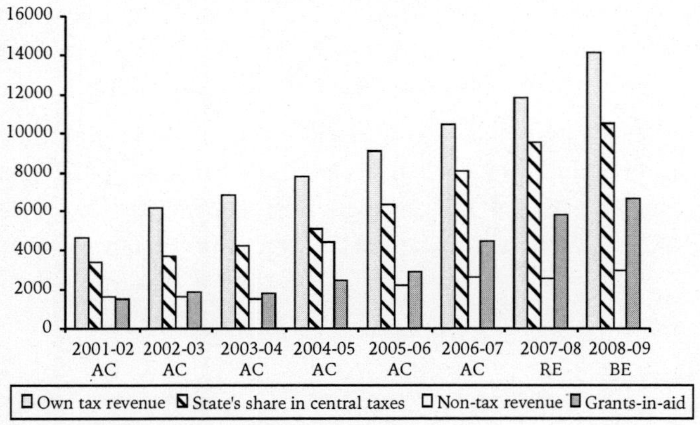

Source: State Budget Books, GoMP, various years.

Figure 4.1 describes the trends in revenue receipts of the state government.

- State's own tax receipt (SOTR) is the largest contributor to the state's revenue receipts. It consists of tax on goods and services (85 per cent), tax on property and capital transaction (14 per cent) and tax on income and expenditure (1 per cent).
- SOTR, state's share in central taxes and grants-in-aid from the Central government have steadily increased over the years.
- Receipts on account of non-tax revenue, which primarily comprises incomes from mining and forestry, however, has not been at par with other components.
- The primary reason for no increase in the non-tax receipts is that the payment of royalty for exploitation of natural resources of the state like forest and mines is made on the basis of volume rather than on the basis of monetary value of the resources.
- State's share in central taxes is a fixed proportion of the divisible pool of taxes collected by the Union government. The proportion is decided objectively and equitably by the Central Finance Commission for a period of five years. State's share in central taxes is an entitlement of the state. An increasing trend signifies good buoyancy in the central taxes rather than benevolence of the Union government towards the state.
- Grants-in-aid from the Central government flow to state in two forms, that is Plan and non-Plan grants. The non-Plan grants are again based on the recommendation of the Central Finance Commission and is based on objective criteria.
- Plan grants, however, are becoming increasingly conditional in nature, thereby, compromising the scope of the state government in designing their own schemes.

Table 4.2 attempts to give the picture of proportionate share of various components of revenue receipts over the years.

It is clear from the table that on an average, own taxes (40 per cent) and non-taxes (10 per cent) together constitute 50 per cent share in the revenue receipts. Remaining 50 per cent contribution comes from the Centre in the form of share in central taxes (30 per cent) and grants-in-aid (20 per cent) respectively.

The trends in these components reveal that own revenue effort of the state has increased from 42 per cent in 2001-02 to 44.2 per cent in 2005-06 but remained

2. Taxes on income and expenditure (this includes hotel receipts and other taxes on income and expenditure), taxes on property and capital transactions (this includes land revenue, stamp and registration and tax on immovable property other than agriculture land) and taxes on commodity and services (this includes state excise, sales tax, taxes on vehicle, taxes on goods and passengers, electricity duty and other taxes on commodities and services) together form state's own tax revenue.

3. State's share in central taxes mainly comes from corporation tax, tax on income other than corporation tax, tax on wealth, customs, central excise duties and service tax.

TABLE 4.2

Proportionate Share of Various Components of Revenue Receipts

Components	*2001-02*	*2002-03*	*2003-04*	*2004-05*	*2005-06*	*2006-07*	*2007-08*	*2008-09 (RE)*	*2009-10 (BE)*
Own tax revenue	42.0	46.2	47.6	39.4	44.2	40.9	39.2	40.1	40.2
State's share in central taxes	30.4	27.7	29.6	25.7	30.8	30.7	33.2	30.8	27.6
Non-tax revenue	14.3	12.2	10.4	22.6	10.7	9.4	8.9	9.0	9.9
Grants-in-aids	13.3	13.9	12.4	12.3	14.2	19.0	18.7	20.1	22.3

Source: State Budget Books, GoMP, various years.

stagnated at around 40 per cent from 2006-07 onwards. Non-tax revenue also shows steady decline over the years except in 2004-05 when MPSEB retuned a huge amount to state government after its restructuring. State's share in central taxes shows decline during the period from 2001-02 to 2004-05, but thereafter shows rise till 2007-2008. Grants-in-aid, however, shows rise in its support to the state receipts from 2005-06 except 2007-08.

2.1.2 Trends in Revenue Receipts

Table 4.3 describes trends in overall revenue receipts, its growth rate, and share of various components in total revenue receipts and proportion of revenue receipts to GSDP since 2001-02.

Revenue receipts of the state have shown steady increase from Rs. 11,201 in 2001-02 to Rs. 34,404 in 2008-09 at an average annual growth rate of 15.1 per cent. In the composition of revenue receipts, the respective share of tax revenue is 72.46 per cent, non-tax revenue 12.24 per cent and grants-in-aid contributed 15.30 per cent. In 2008-09, contribution of state's own resources, that is own tax revenue and non-tax revenue is 49.51 per cent. The balance amount has come from the state's share in central taxes and grants-in-aid from Central government.

Contribution of state's own tax revenue in the revenue receipts of the state has stagnated at around 42 per cent over the years and the state's share in central taxes too has stayed at around 30 per cent since 2001-2002 till date. While the state government is doing its bit to improve its share in central taxes,[4] the state government has introduced a regime of value added tax (VAT) since the beginning of the FY 2006-07 to help improve the mobilisation of own tax revenue.

The share of non-tax revenue has declined remarkably from 14.3 per cent in 2001-02 to 8.77 per cent in 2008-09 BE. In the budget estimates for 2008-2009, nearly three-fourth of non-tax revenue based

TABLE 4.3

Trends in Revenue Receipts

(Figs in Rs. Crore)

Indicators	*2001-02 AC*	*2002-03 AC*	*2003-04 AC*	*2004-05 AC*	*2005-06 AC*	*2006-07 AC*	*2007-08 RE*	*2008-09 BE*
Revenue receipts (RR)	11201	13390	14289	19743	20597	25694	29840	34404
Tax revenue	8108	9893	11036	12850	15456	18562	21459	24745
Non-tax revenue	1602	1635	1480	4462	2208	2658	2560	3018
Grants-in-aid	1491	1862	1773	2432	2933	4474	5821	6641
Proportion of tax revenue in RR	72.39	73.88	77.23	65.08	75.04	72.24	71.91	71.93
Proportion of non-tax revenue in RR	14.30	12.21	10.36	22.60	10.72	10.35	8.58	8.77
Proportion of grants-in-aid in RR	13.31	13.90	12.41	12.32	14.24	17.41	19.51	19.30
Growth rate of revenue receipts	(-) 12.68	19.55	6.71	38.17	4.32	24.75	16.13	15.29
Growth rate of own tax revenue	(-) 17.03	31.63	9.95	14.18	17.30	13.11	13.54	19.76
RR as % of GSDP	13.23	16.42	14.56	19.16	18.36	20.04	21.41	21.78
Own tax revenue as % of GSDP	5.6	7.6	6.9	7.5	8.1	8.0	8.4	8.9

Source: State Budget Books, GoMP, various years.

4. The state has tried to improve its share in central taxes by improving upon its tax effort and strengthening its fiscal discipline. The 12th Finance Commission has worked out the tax effort criterion by taking three-year average of the ratios of own tax revenue to comparable GSDP weighted by the square root of the inverse of the per capita GSDP. The index of fiscal discipline measures the improvement in the ratio of own revenue receipts of a state to its total revenue expenditure, related to a similar ratio for all states. Both the criteria of tax effort and fiscal discipline have been accorded a weightage of 7.5 per cent each.

income of the state is expected to come from the mining and forestry sectors. These sectors have always been the major contributors to the non-tax receipts of the state. However, the policies pertaining to these sectors are primarily formulated by the Union government, thereby considerably reducing the state's ability to augment its receipts by improving the mobilisation of non-tax revenue.

The grants-in-aid from the Central government in the last few years has been increasing in absolute terms as well as a proportion of total receipts. Contribution of grants-in-aid has shown considerable increase from 13.3 per cent to 19.3 per cent over the period. However, the 12th Finance Commission (FC) has indicated that non-FC grants[5] have shown a weekly positive correlation (of +0.16 as against a correlation of -0.87 for FC grants) between the quantum of non-FC grants and the per capita incomes of the states. In other words, the poorer the state, the lesser is the quantum of non-FC grants to them. Hence, the progressiveness of the non-FC grants stands questioned, as they are not furthering the cause of addressing regional disparities in the country. Another issue of importance is the rising trend in the quantum of non-FC grants that are conditional in nature, thereby severely limiting the latitude that the state governments should rightfully have in planning their expenditure.

The state's own tax revenue, as a proportion of GSDP is an important indicator that the Central Finance Commission has adopted as a standard measure for 'tax effort' by the state government. The more is the state's own tax revenue/GSDP ratio, the more would be the state's share in central taxes. As can be observed from Table 4.3, there was an exceptional rise in this ratio from 5.6 per cent in 2001-02 to 7.6 per cent in 2002-03. This happened because the receipts from taxes and duties from electricity swelled from Rs. 268.18 crore to Rs. 801.25 crore. However, in 2003-04, the ratio once again fell to 6.9 per cent but since the very next fiscal year, it has risen steadily to 8.9 per cent in 2008-09 (BE). This is one of the important achievements on the part of state government as it has crossed the 12th Finance Commission's target of OTR/GSDP ratio of 6.8 per cent in 2007-08.

The indicator assumes further importance in light of the fact that not only does its increase result in a higher balance on current revenue (BCR), thus affording a higher contribution from the state in funding its annual plan, but also enables the government to make higher allocations for the social services like health and education (the expenditure on them being mostly of a revenue in nature), without ending up with a revenue deficit. Further, the revenue surpluses generated have a salutary impact on the developmental capital expenditure.

2.2 State's Own Tax Revenue

In the context of the above analysis, it would be pertinent to look at the various components of state's own tax revenue as given in Table 4.4. State's own tax revenue comprises sales tax, state excise, stamps and registration, electricity duties, taxes on goods and

TABLE 4.4

Components of State's Own Tax Revenue (SOTR) as a Proportion of Total SOTR

Components of Own Tax Revenue	*2001-02 AC*	*2002-03 AC*	*2003-04 AC*	*2004-05 AC*	*2005-06 AC*	*2006-07 AC*	*2007-08 RE*	*2008-09 BE*
Hotel receipts tax	0.07	0.06	0.06	0.06	0.06	0.05	0.05	0.05
Other taxes on income and expenditure	3.80	3.12	2.77	1.93	1.68	1.56	1.51	1.38
Land revenue	1.03	0.65	0.64	0.60	0.85	1.26	1.03	0.90
Stamps and registration	9.46	8.64	9.03	10.15	11.08	11.95	12.96	12.95
Tax on immovable property other than agricultural land	0.00	0.00	0.00	0.00	0.00	0.00	0.00	0.00
State excise	14.99	14.38	15.96	15.35	15.04	14.77	14.73	14.60
Taxes on sale trade etc.	50.20	46.95	48.39	50.35	49.47	50.24	47.96	46.44
Taxes on vehicles	8.36	6.93	6.68	6.29	6.10	6.06	6.52	7.04
Taxes on goods and passengers	5.58	5.67	5.75	6.02	6.35	7.11	8.08	8.44
Taxes and duties on electricity	5.70	12.95	10.24	9.10	9.24	6.82	7.00	8.09
Other taxes and duties on commodities and services	0.80	0.63	0.47	0.15	0.15	0.18	0.16	0.13

Source: State Budget Books, GoMP, various years.

5. Non-FC grants comprise Plan grants provided to the states by the Union government on the recommendation of the Planning Commission of India and non-Plan grants provided by the central ministries to the state governments across the country.

passengers, taxes on vehicles, other taxes on income and expenditure, land revenue, other taxes and duties on commodities and services, hotel receipts and tax on immovable property other than agriculture land. Time trend of composition of state's own tax revenue is as follows:

- State's own tax revenue is growing at CAGR of 16.43 per cent from 2001-02 through 2008-09.
- Sales tax (50 per cent), state excise (15 per cent) and stamps and registration (12 per cent) together contribute more than three-fourth (76.82 per cent) to the receipts from state's own tax revenue. Over the years, CAGR of sales tax and state excise is growing at 16.49 per cent and 15.81 per cent respectively.
- CAGR of "taxes on goods and passengers" is 20.93 per cent and of "taxes on vehicles" is 12.37 per cent. This is in line with the CAGR of registered vehicles in MP. The CAGR for registered passenger and goods vehicles has increased from just 0.52 per cent and 1.83 per cent respectively between 2001 and 2003 to a whopping 9.55 per cent and 9.69 per cent respectively between 2003 and 2005. This has come about owing to improved road conditions in the state on the one hand and a stronger tax mobilisation effort on part of the state government on the other, in the last few years. Recent media reports have indicated that the government is trying to plug leakages in collection of vehicle taxes. For instance, in the state capital alone the government is losing vehicle taxes worth 0.47 crore annually, arising out of non-registration of vehicles whose registration period of 15 years has lapsed in 2007.
- Although the electricity duty is recording a growth rate of 19.93 per cent, its contribution had been more than doubled from 2001-02 (5.70 per cent) to 2002-03 (12.95 per cent), but then in the subsequent years it has declined, recording its lowest at 6.82 per cent in 2006-07.
- Stamps and registration is the third major contributor to state's own tax revenue and it is growing at CAGR of 19.42 per cent.
- Taxes such as other taxes on income and expenditure, land revenue, other taxes and duties on commodity and services, hotel receipts and tax on immovable property other than agriculture land are not contributing significantly as a percentage of total state's own tax revenue. Their combined share has shown a decline from 5.7 per cent to 3.32 per cent in 2008-09. However, among them, receipts from land revenue is growing the fastest at a CAGR of around 12.92 per cent.

Thus, it can be concluded that there is a strong need to evolve an efficient tax system and to undertake appropriate policy measures so as to cope with the changing pace of growing economy. One of such examples of measures undertaken by the state government in scoring its own taxes is of Anti-Evasion Bureau (AEB). Commercial tax department of the state government had constituted AEB, first of its kind in the state. The chief function of AEB is to curb growing tax theft by traders and transporters by showing proxy movement of goods through trucks from one state to another. AEB have six extension offices, one each at Bhopal, Jabalpur, Gwalior and Satna and two offices at Indore.

2.3 Increasing State's Non-Tax Revenue[6]

Generation of adequate revenues to finance expenditure responsibilities is one of the major challenges before the state government. But again, resource generation through non-debt sources is very crucial in order to avoid debt burden. Over the last three decades, MP has witnessed a steady decline in its own non-tax ratio. It was 4.1 during 1980-1990, declined to 3.4 during 1990-2000 and further declined to just 2.1 during the period 2000-2009. The national average however, for the same period has come down from 1.9, 1.7 and 1.4 respectively. Thus, the state government needs to take appropriate steps in improving cost recovery from various public services. Again, the recovery is heavily dependent on the quality of service delivery by the state. Restructuring of state PSUs for making them profitable and closing the sick units would be one of the measures.

2.3.1 Cost Recovery

The non-tax revenue of the state governments consists of a wide range of receipts ranging from interest receipts on the loans provided by the state governments, dividends and profits received by the state governments, revenue from general services such as state lotteries, revenue from user charges imposed on

6. *Source:* RBI (2008). *State Finances: Study of State Budgets 2008-09.*

different social and economic services provided by the state governments. During the recent years, the revenue from user charges contributed more than 50 per cent of the total own non-tax revenue of the state governments. However, it is well known that the user charges hardly finance the cost of providing these services (both social and economic) to the public. In the absence of firm data on cost recovery, the ratio of non-tax revenue to non-plan revenue expenditure is taken as a proxy for the cost recovery from these services. This ratio stands at 4.0 per cent for the social services and 32.3 per cent for economic services in 2007-08 (RE), indicating low cost recovery in respect of both these services. This brings out the urgent need for redesigning the system of user charges.

However, there are several issues that need to be considered while raising user charges on these services. The advocates of user charges argue that user charges will enable the state governments to pass on the cost of providing the services either fully or partially to the public. This can prevent the financing of these services from the tax revenue of the government, whose benefits accrue to specific individuals rather than the society as a whole. Illustratively, government water supply to the individual households can be charged based on a meter reading. Such a system once implemented may also prevent the wasteful usage of water by the households. The user charges are also useful in changing the mass consumer behaviour. For example, tolls on roads can be differentiated based on peak and off-peak hours. This will encourage the public to reduce the use of a particular road or bridge during the peak hours, thus, reducing congestion.

Other social services such as education and health provided by the government, fall into the category of merit goods, which all the citizens can consume irrespective of their economic background. Further, the private sector is also equally active in providing these services to the public. However, the market determined user charges as in the private hospitals and educational institutions may not be affordable to the poorer sections of population. Thus, providing quality education and health care to the poorer sections of population becomes a primary responsibility of the government. The same argument applies to water supply also, where the water connection to below poverty line households needs to be subsidised. Thus, in addition to identifying specific individual beneficiaries, the government may also have to differentiate between the beneficiaries based on their economic background.

In the case of economic services where the service such as power is used to generate profit, government should impose market-determined user charges. This can finance the expenditure for providing that particular service to the public. Further, if the government is providing pure private goods to the public, it should impose market-determined user charges to compete qualitatively with the private sector. Since the user charges are a *quid pro quo* receipt, the maximum amount collected through the user charges should not be more than the cost of providing services to the public. The entire money collected through user charges should be spent on that particular service and should not be diverted to finance other expenditure of the government. The user charges should also be linked to the quality of service provided to the public to make it more acceptable.

3. Capital Receipts

Capital receipts comprise recovery of loans and advances of the state government, net public debt (that comprises net internal debts of the state government and net debt from the Central government) and net receipts from public account. Before we dwell upon the trends in capital receipts, it would help the readers build their perspective, if we mention some of the trends in major components of gross capital receipts in consolidated fund.

Figure 4.2 should be read in light of the recommendation of the 12th Finance Commission that said that it should not be mandatory for the state governments to fund their annual plans though 70 per cent debt from the Central government. It is mainly because Central government is providing only 30 per cent of the Plan funds on a grant basis to the states. The recommendation was based on the fact that the loans provided by the Central government was one of the costliest[7] of all the options that were available to the state and that costlier loans were burning a sizeable hole in the states' pockets because of higher revenue expenditure owing to interest payments made by the state governments. The recommendation took effect from the beginning of the financial year 2005-06. The behaviour of the curves in the figure may be explained primarily through the implementation of the above recommendation. As may be observed from the figure,

7. For Madhya Pradesh, Central government loans are the second most costly source of credit at 9 per cent. National Small Savings Fund (NSSF) of the Central government is the costliest with an average interest rate of 9.5 per cent for FY 2006-07.

from 2001-02 to 2004-05, the loans from the Central government constituted 13-17 per cent of the gross capital receipts in the consolidated fund. But in 2005-2006, it dipped to 3.7 per cent. This was on account of a spike in the gross capital receipts through loans and advances of the state government owing to receipts made against loans advanced for electricity projects to 35.6 per cent from the sub-zero levels.

FIGURE 4.2

Major Components of Gross Capital Receipts in Consolidated Fund

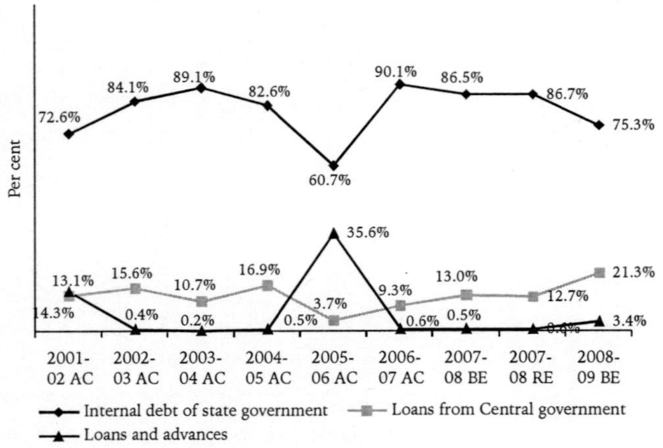

Source: State Budget Books, GoMP, various years.

In 2005-06, the loans from the Central government continued to be lower than in 2004-05 at 3.7 per cent. From the year 2006-07 onwards, however, once again loans from the Central government have pegged, reaching a maximum at 21.3 per cent, thus claiming the lower end of the level from 2001-02 to 2004-05. This increase is primarily owing to the fact that the Central government continues to provide loans for funding Plan expenditure of the state governments for externally aided projects. It would be pertinent to note that the state's borrowings to the tune of Rs. 2096 crore is budgeted to be sourced from NSSF—the costliest source of credit at 9.5 per cent. Can NSSF be avoided? Can the state avail itself of loans cheaper than 9 per cent—the rate at which Central government used to lend for funding state's plan? Is there anything done by the state to ensure access to cheaper funds? If yes, what are those steps?

Figure 4.3 illustrates the following findings:

- All the four components of the net capital receipts were substantial in the total net capital receipts in 2001-02, with the net capital receipts from the Central government constituting 17.6 per cent of the total net capital receipts.

FIGURE 4.3

Components of Capital Receipts as a Proportion of Total Capital Receipts

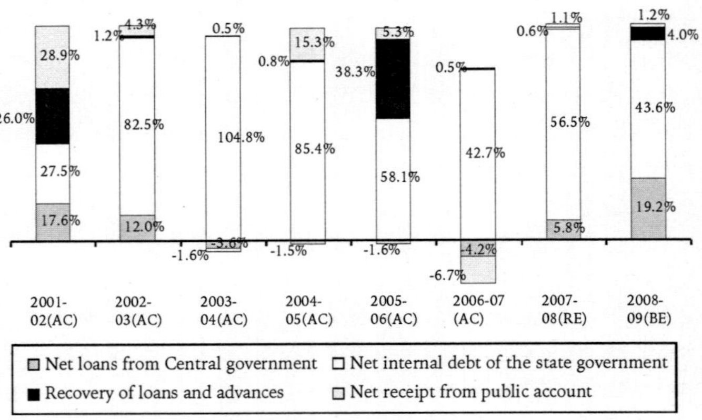

Source: State Budget Books, GoMP, various years.

- Since 2002-03, the situation has changed dramatically with the state's debt portfolio undergoing a significant change, with the net internal debt of the state government constituting the bulk of net capital receipts—more than 80 per cent has started falling down from 2005-06 onwards. Also recovery of loans and advances contributed as much as 38.3 per cent of the net capital receipts. The sudden rise in recovery of loans and advances in 2005-06 came about due to power sector reforms as the electricity companies returned their loans to the state government.
- In the period between 2003-04 to 2006-07, the net capital inflows from the Central government has been in the negative or sub-zero zone, indicating that during this period the state government borrowed just enough from the Centre to repay the principal amount of the loans taken by the state in the earlier years from them.
- The budgeted debt to be sourced from the Central government is 5.8 per cent in 2007-08 as the Central government continues to provide loans to the state governments for the externally aided projects. With nearly 2096 crore budgeted from the NSSF (one of the components of the internal debt of the state government) which is the costliest source of credit for the state government (carrying 10 per cent rate of interest for FY 2005-06), one would hardly have any quarrel with the idea of the state sourcing some of its debt requirements from the Central government if the latter are willing to provide it for externally aided projects.

4. Debt/GSDP Ratio

The debt-to-GDP ratio measures how important the debt is in proportion to the overall economy. Higher the ratio, less productive or developmental would be the economy. It also indicates greater proportion of the state's income being used to repay the huge burden of debt and its interest payment that would have been utilised for the most needed developmental cause. The Twelfth Finance Commission in its recommendations mentioned that the system of on-lending to be brought to an end over time. The long term goal should be to bring down debt-GDP ratio to 28 per cent each for the Centre and the states.

TABLE 4.5

Debt/GSDP Ratio

Year	*Total Outstanding Liability of the MP Govt. (in Rs. Crore)*	*Total Outstanding Liability as % of GSDP*
2001	22127	27.9
2002	26043	30.0
2003	29882	34.4
2004	37967	36.9
2005	44586	41.6
2006	49647	42.7
2007	53971	42.1
2008 (RE)	56280	39.5
2009 (BE)	61370	38.9

Source: State Budget Books, GoMP, various years.

It is amply clear from Table 4.5 that the debt-GSDP ratio for the state of MP has shown a steady rise over the years. It has grown from Rs. 22127 crore in 2001 to Rs. 61370 crore in 2009, registering an increase by 2.77 times from 2001. As a per cent of GSDP, it comes to 27.9 per cent in 2001 which has increased to 38.9 per cent by 2009, with an increase of nearly 40 per cent over nine years. Definitely, it is not a positive sign of the economy from the developmental point of view as public debt is highly considered as a non-developmental expenditure. It is expected that it should reduce over a period of time; unfortunately, the current debt/GSDP ratio for MP is on very high levels compared to the recommendations of 12th Finance Commission. It is only in the past two years that the proportion has come down to less than 40 per cent. But again its estimates for the last two years are revised/budgeted, the real position would only be clear with actual figures.

5. A Citizen's View of Public Debt

The per capita growth in GSDP, per capita expenditure and per capita debt in the state makes for interesting analysis. Here, it may be noted that GSDP for 2007-08 and 2008-09 have been assumed to be the same as provided by the GoMP in the FRBM Report 2008-09. Table 4.6 provides these indicators from the year 2001-02 through 2008-09.

TABLE 4.6

A Citizen's View of Public Debt

Year	*Per Capita GSDP*	*Per Capita Expenditure*	*Per Capita (Debt + Interest)*	*Per Capita (Debt + Interest) as a % of Per Capita Expenditure*
2001-02 (AC)	14208	2692	4281	159%
2002-03 (AC)	13935	2808	4811	171%
2003-04 (AC)	16190	3408	5963	175%
2004-05 (AC)	16576	4062	6903	170%
2005-06 (AC)	17649	4251	7377	174%
2006-07 (AC)	19108	4255	7788	183%
2007-08 (RE)	20814	5029	8368	166%
2008-09 (BE)	22673	5662	8944	158%
CAGR 2002-2008	6.91	11.20	11.10	159%

Note: Figures are calculated by author based on statistics from State Budget Books, GoMP, various years.

- The CAGR of per capita GSDP, expenditure and debt including interest at current prices are at 6.91 per cent, 11.20 per cent and 11.10 per cent respectively.
- For every Rs. 100 that the government spends on a citizen, it runs a debt of Rs. 158.

The silver lining, however, is that not only is the state now not financing its revenue deficit through public debt but also is using higher percentage of its public debt for financing developmental capital expenditure.

Among the sources of state's gross capital receipts of the state government, internal debt of the state government has always contributed the most in percentage terms.

5.1 Time Trend of Components of Internal Debt of the State Government

From the above analysis, it would be pertinent to look at the various components of the internal debt of the state government and their respective contribution over the years. Table 4.7 gives the time trend of composition of internal debt of the state government. Major components of the internal debt of the state government are market loans, special securities issued to NSS fund of Central government, ways and means advances from RBI and loans from NABARD. While the contribution of other elements like loans from other institutions (was highest at 6.7 per cent in the year 2004-05), loans from NCDC and loans from SBI and

TABLE 4.7

Components of Internal Debt of the State Government

Components of Internal Debt	*2001-02 AC*	*2002-03 AC*	*2003-04 AC*	*2004-05 AC*	*2005-06 AC*	*2006-07 AC*	*2007-08 RE*	*2008-09 BE*
Market loans	6.50%	10.00%	14.90%	15.50%	15.70%	17.70%	50.80%	36.50%
Loans from General Insurance Corporation of India	0.00%	0.00%	0.00%	0.00%	0.00%	0.00%	0.00%	0.00%
Loans from NABARD	2.70%	3.10%	2.60%	2.70%	5.40%	6.20%	8.70%	9.60%
Compensation and other bonds	0.00%	0.00%	16.50%	12.70%	0.00%	0.00%	0.00%	0.00%
Loans from SBI and others	0.00%	0.00%	0.00%	0.00%	1.50%	0.00%	0.00%	0.00%
Loans from National Co-operative Development Corporation	0.10%	0.10%	0.10%	0.10%	0.20%	0.10%	0.20%	0.00%
Loans from other institutions	0.00%	0.40%	0.10%	6.70%	0.00%	0.00%	1.70%	1.80%
Ways and means advances from RBI	56.10%	56.40%	39.80%	20.10%	0.00%	0.00%	6.20%	25.00%
Special securities issued to NSS fund of Central govt.	7.20%	14.10%	15.10%	24.80%	37.90%	26.50%	6.70%	10.00%
Loans from Central government	13.10%	15.60%	10.70%	16.90%	3.70%	9.50%	12.50%	21.90%
Loans and advances	14.30%	0.40%	0.20%	0.50%	35.60%	0.10%	0.20%	0.20%

Source: State Budget Books, GoMP, various years.

others is miniscule. Internal debt in the form of compensation and other bonds was exceptionally high in subsequent years 2003-04 and 2004-05 at 16.5 per cent and 12.70 per cent respectively.

In the year 2001-02, the composition of internal debt of the state government were as follows—the ways and means advances from RBI was one of the highest at 56.1 per cent, followed by loans and advances at 14.3 per cent and loans from Central government at 13.1 per cent. Borrowings from market were much lower at just 6.5 per cent. But one would see from Table 4.7 that the composition of internal debt of the state government has undergone considerable changes over the years.

- Ways and means advances from RBI which constituted more than half of the state's internal debt in 2001-02 has come down to 20 per cent in 2004-05. There were no ways and means advances from RBI in 2005-06 and 2006-07. But again, it surged to 6.2 and 25 per cent respectively in the subsequent two years.
- Share of market loans has shown a steady rise from 6.5 per cent in 2001-02 to its maximum at 50.8 per cent in 2007-08. Market loans would be a better source as it is one of the cheapest available source of loan to the state government.
- Over the years, loans taken by the state government from NABARD has risen to 9.6 per cent in 2008-09 from 2.7 per cent in 2001-02.
- Securities issued to NSS fund of the Central government has raised from 7.2 per cent in 2001-2002 to its peak at 37.96 per cent in 2005-06 but shows decline thereafter. This is definitely going to strain the state finances in future as it would either pull down the revenue surpluses (or increase the revenue deficit) owing to higher outflow on account of interest payment. Although it has dropped to 26.5 per cent and 6.7 per cent in 2006-07 (AC) and 2007-08 (RE) respectively, it has the highest interest rate among all the other available sources of loans to the state government (See Table 4.7).

5.2 Interest Rates and State Government Liabilities

Table 4.8 throws light on weighted average interest rates both for the outstanding amounts and loans raised during current fiscal years by the state government.

TABLE 4.8

Weighted Average Interest Rates on State Government Liabilities

Category	*Raised during the Fiscal Year*		*Outstanding Amount (as on 31st March)*	
	Previous Year 2005-06 (AC)	*Current Year 2006-07 (RE)*	*Previous Year 2005-06 (AC)*	*Current Year 2006-07 (RE)*
Market borrowings	7.59	8.31	8.06	7.58
Loans from Centre	9.00	9.00	7.68	7.92
Special securities issued to the NSSF	9.50	9.50	10.36	10.04
Borrowings from financial institutions/ banks	7.87	7.50	8.56	8.18
WMA/OD from RBI	7.50	7.50	0.00	0.00
Public account	8.00	8.00	8.66	8.00
Other deposits				
Overall average rate	8.66	8.60	8.77	8.60

Note: WMA - Ways and Means Advances; OD - Overdraft.
Source: FRBM Report 2007-08, Government of Madhya Pradesh.

6. Expenditure

6.1 Size of the State Budget

Total expenditure of the state government includes revenue expenditure, capital expenditure and loans and advances. Total expenditure or size of the budget of Madhya Pradesh has gone up from Rs. 16438 crore in 2001-02 to Rs. 39442 crore in 2008-09 (BE). It is being observed that the revised estimates are always more than the budget estimates owing to supplementary demands. Actual expenditure has always been on the lower side (except in 2004-05) than the revised estimates of expenditure indicating that the state government lack efficiency in utilising the amounts fully (Figure 4.4).

6.2 State Budget Size in Real Terms

- The total budget size of the state has grown since 2001-02 in real terms.
- But 2006-07 witnessed a slowing in expenditure of the state government in real terms over the preceding two years.

FIGURE 4.5

Total Expenditure at 1999-2000 Constant Prices (in crore)

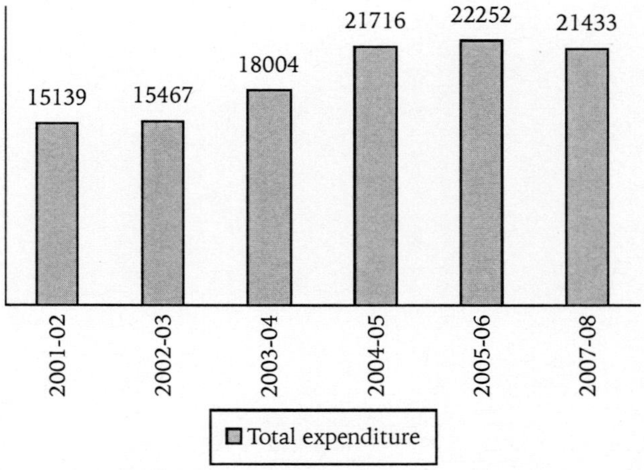

Source: State Budget Books, GoMP, various years.

6.3 Plan and Non-Plan Expenditure

Expenditure of the government is broadly classified into Plan and non-Plan category. Plan expenditure is defined as expenditure made to add new productive

FIGURE 4.4

Total Expenditure (in crore)

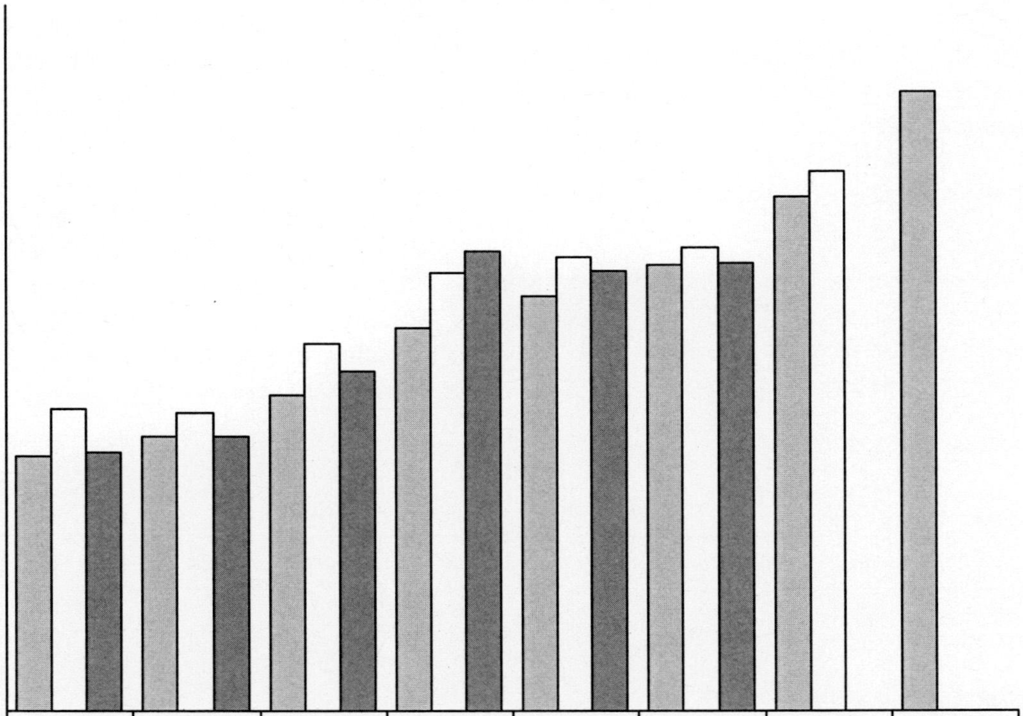

	2001-02	2002-03	2003-04	2004-05	2005-06	2006-07	2007-08	2008-09
BE	16280	17537	20065	24361	26341	28398	32694	39442
RE	19194	18984	23318	27818	28909	29451	34383	
Actuals	16438	17495	21648	29288	28021	28547		

Source: State Budget Books, GoMP, various years.

capacity in the economy. While non-Plan expenditure is defined as expenditure made to maintain the previously added productive capacity in the economy.

FIGURE 4.6

Plan and Non-Plan Expenditure

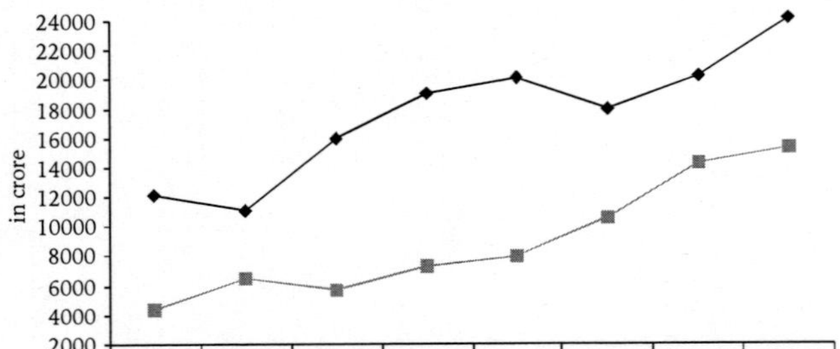

	2001-02 AC	2002-03 AC	2003-04 AC	2004-05 AC	2005-06 AC	2006-07 AC	2007-08 RE	2008-09 BE
Plan	4311	6433	5685	7269	7950	10572	14217	15352
Non-Plan	12127	11062	15963	19019	20071	17975	20166	24090

Source: State Budget Books, GoMP, various years.

- At the end of each five year plan, the state government takes a conscious decision and declares the expenditure incurred on schemes started in the previous five year plan as non-Plan. This is the reason why non-Plan expenditure of the state is always higher than the Plan expenditure.
- Increase in Plan expenditure indicates supply of more schemes for the people from the government. All non-Plan expenditure is not necessarily bad as also all Plan expenditure may not be necessarily good. This needs to be decided on a case to case basis.
- The steeper rise in Plan expenditure as against non-Plan expenditure from 2006-07 to 2007-08 is explained by the fact that the latter was the first year of the 11th Five Year Plan.
- The steeper rise in the non-Plan expenditure as against Plan expenditure in 2008-09 is explained by the fact that many schemes from the 10th Five Year Plan would have been declared non-Plan by the government.
- Proportion of non-Plan expenditure has come down from 73.8 per cent in 2001-02 to 61.1 per cent in 2008-09 while the Plan expenditure has increased from 26.2 per cent in 2001-02 to 38.9 per cent in 2008-09.

6.4 Revenue and Capital Expenditure

Revenue and capital expenditure are the major components of total expenditure. Revenue expenditure indicates expenditure incurred on day-to-day activities for running the government while capital expenditure is incurred for creating or building assets. Average proportion of revenue and capital expenditure in total is 78.53 and 21.73 per cent respectively.

It is evident from Table 4.9 that the total expenditure of the state has increased at 11.6 per cent per annum during the period 2001 to 2009. Annual growth rates of revenue and capital expenditure are 10.5 and 19.5 per cent respectively. In absolute terms as well, the total expenditure and revenue and capital expenditure got more than double during the period of eight years. This definitely indicates towards the growing economy of the state of MP with growth in capital expenditure preceeding over revenue expenditure.

The indicator of total expenditure as a proportion of GSDP is also called public expenditure ratio (PER).[8] PER of Madhya Pradesh has increased over the years from 19.41 per cent in 2001-02 to 24.97 per cent in 2008-09. If a government is to allow for sufficient spending in priority areas, a public expenditure of 20-25 per cent is desirable.[9] The average of public expenditure

TABLE 4.9

Revenue and Capital Expenditure

	2001-02 AC	*2002-03 AC*	*2003-04 AC*	*2004-05 AC*	*2005-06 AC*	*2006-07 AC*	*2007-08 RE*	*2008-09 BE*
Total expenditure	16438	17495.4	21647.72	26288.22	28021.2	28546.93	34382.61	39442.33
Revenue expenditure	14368.78	14559.8	18764.72	18026.38	20563.48	22362.6	26483.64	31564
Capital expenditure	1470.64	2454.9	2678.64	4950.98	6623.28	5169.94	6781.67	6099.93
Total expenditure as % of GSDP	19.41	21.46	22.06	25.51	24.98	22.27	24.67	24.97

Source: State Budget Books, GoMP, various years.

8. Public expenditure ratio is the proportion of state income that goes towards public expenditure. It is calculated as total budgetary expenditure as a proportion of GSDP.
9. Planning Commission/UNDP (2007). "Strengthening State Plans for Human Development", *Training of Trainers Workshop on Human Development* (Module 6: Financing Human Development), 15th-19th January.

to GDP is almost 23 per cent for MP. In consonance with the above-mentioned standard, the level of public expenditure of the state would be desirable.

6.5 Segregation of Total Expenditure into its Components

Total expenditure gets distributed among the components of general services, social services, economic services, and grants-in-aid and contribution to PRIs. On an average, out of total expenditure 30.1 per cent is being incurred on general services. Expenditure on social and economic services as a proportion of total expenditure is 29.7 per cent and 37.3 per cent respectively, while the share of grants-in-aid and contribution made to PRIs is 3.5 per cent of total expenditure. Figure 4.7 explains the segregated proportionate share of various services in total expenditure over the years. Over the years, there is slight decline in general services and economic services. Share of economic services remained stagnant but grants-in-aid from Central government has shown substantial rise over the years.

Performance of economic services has direct impact on performance of GSDP. It is mainly because elements of economic services such as agriculture and allied activities and mining constitute a substantial chunk of primary sector of GSDP. In case of Madhya Pradesh, the state's economy is largely agrarian; agriculture and allied activities together contributes more than one-third (34.4 per cent) of GSDP. In the light of the fact that state's GSDP is highly sensitive towards performance of agriculture and allied services, declining expenditure in economic services is definitely a cause of concern.

6.6 Expenditure on General Services

General services comprises expenditure on organs of the state, fiscal services, interest payment and servicing of debt, administrative services and pension. Table 4.10 gives the year-wise break-up of various components of general services and their respective shares in total expenditure over the years.

Among the other components of general services, interest payment and servicing of debt is a major player with an average of 13.33 per cent of total expenditure. Following interest payment, the maximum expenditure is incurred on administrative services and pension.

FIGURE 4.7

Proportionate Distribution of Total Expenditure into its Components

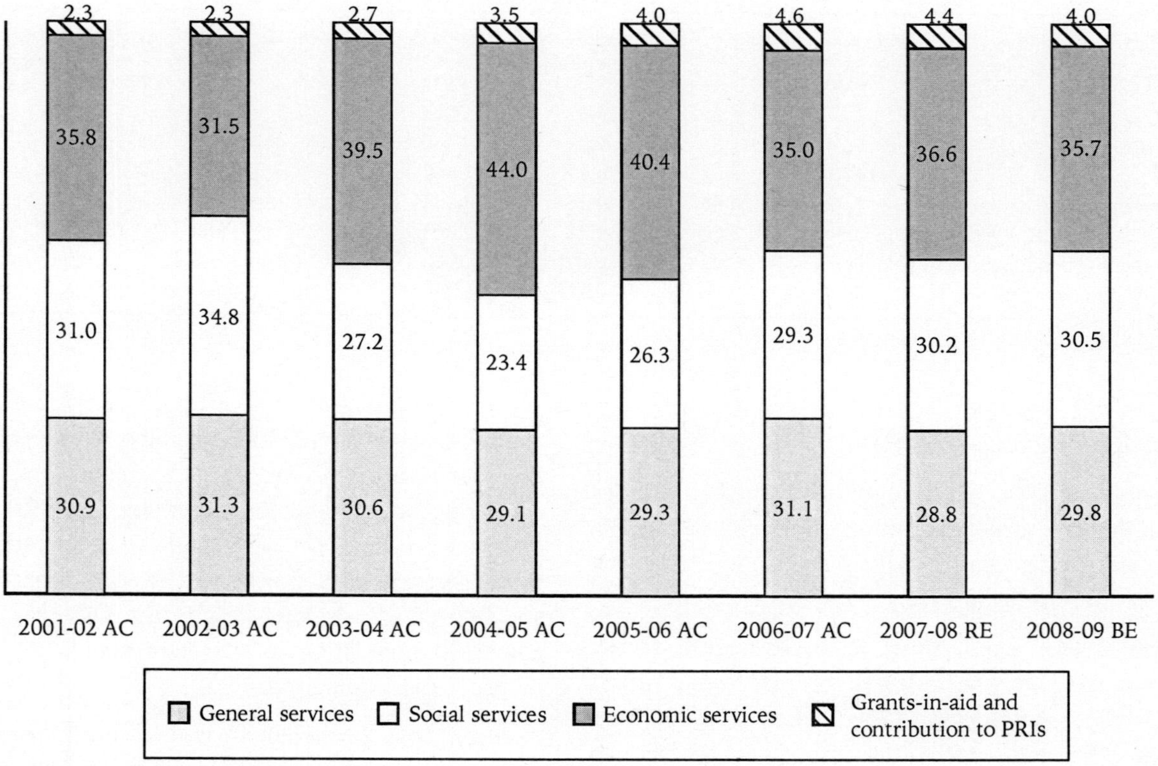

Source: State Budget Books, GoMP, various years.

TABLE 4.10

Expenditure on General Services

General Services	*2001-02 AC*	*2002-03 AC*	*2003-04 AC*	*2004-05 AC*	*2005-06 AC*	*2006-07 AC*	*2007-08 RE*	*2008-09 BE*
Organs of the state	0.73	0.85	0.82	0.77	0.63	0.74	0.75	0.83
Fiscal services	2.27	2.46	3.49	3.14	3.19	3.35	3.48	3.5
Interest payment and servicing of debt	13.71	14.3	14.81	13.93	12.21	14.14	12.22	11.38
Administrative services	7.84	7.3	5.7	5.49	5.13	5.43	5.32	7.16
Pension and miscellaneous services	6.16	6.2	5.55	5.08	5.94	6.54	6.11	5.84

Source: State Budget Books, GoMP, various years.

TABLE 4.11

Expenditure on Social Services

Social Services	*2001-02 AC*	*2002-03 AC*	*2003-04 AC*	*2004-05 AC*	*2005-06 AC*	*2006-07 AC*	*2007-08 RE*	*2008-09 BE*
Education, sports, art and culture	12.93	13.22	10.98	9.81	10.54	13.14	12.22	13.34
Health and family welfare	4.19	4.45	3.69	3.42	3.53	4.02	3.84	4.13
Water supply, sanitation, housing and urban development	5.79	6.06	3.91	2.95	3.62	4.56	5.82	4.98
Information and broadcasting	0.1	0.14	0.09	0.09	0.09	0.11	0.11	0.11
SC, ST and OBC welfare	4.58	5.35	4.52	4.25	4.61	3.13	3.55	3.51
Labour and labourer welfare	0.32	0.32	0.27	0.22	0.2	0.24	0.28	0.28
Social welfare and nutrition	3.05	5.21	3.67	2.66	3.64	4.06	4.29	4.11
Other social services	0.05	0.06	0.05	0.04	0.04	0.04	0.1	0.08

Source: State Budget Books, GoMP, various years.

TABLE 4.12

Expenditure on Various Economic Sectors

Economic Services	*2001-02 AC*	*2002-03 AC*	*2003-04 AC*	*2004-05 AC*	*2005-06 AC*	*2006-07 AC*	*2007-08 RE*	*2008-09 BE*
Agriculture and allied activities	6.97	7.31	5.70	4.97	4.83	5.96	6.37	6.76
Rural development	4.67	4.89	3.85	3.84	5.37	6.85	7.64	7.34
Irrigation and flood control	5.76	6.88	6.28	7.60	5.64	6.08	6.80	5.46
Energy	14.81	8.62	20.37	24.47	19.26	8.51	7.04	8.90
Industry and minerals	0.42	0.46	0.35	0.34	1.02	1.30	1.12	0.82
Transport	2.94	3.08	2.76	2.61	3.95	5.94	7.15	5.85
Science technology and environment	0.01	0.02	0.02	0.02	0.14	0.03	0.15	0.17
General economic services	0.24	0.26	0.21	0.15	0.22	0.32	0.37	0.36

Source: State Budget Books, GoMP, various years.

6.7 Expenditure on Social Services

Education, sports, art and culture, health, water supply, sanitation, urban administration, SC, ST, OBC welfare, social welfare and nutrition are some of the key elements of the social service.

In social sector expenditure-wise, education sector alongwith sports, art and culture occupies top position with an average spending of 12 per cent share in total expenditure. Expenditure in the important sector like health has remained stagnated at around 4 per cent over the years. A very disheartening feature of the above analysis is that the state's performance in expenditure earmarked for marginalised sections like SCs and STs is abysmally poor. Not only is it just investing less on these sections, but expenditure trends over the years is showing steady decline, despite the fact that SC and ST combined population in the state stands at 35 per cent of the total population.

There was observed an overall decline in the water supply and sanitation (WSS) and urban development but

TABLE 4.13

Developmental and Non-Developmental Expenditure

	Developmental Expenditure	*Non-Developmental Expenditure*
Revenue account	Expenditure on social services, economic services and grants-in-aid to local bodies	Expenditure on general services
Capital account	Capital account expenditure on social and economic services and loans and advances made by the government	Expenditure on repayment of principal amount of public debt

Source: Report on State Finances, Reserve Bank of India.

with the significant variations. On the other hand, expenditure on social welfare and nutrition has increased over the years. But the fact is that the increase is not in line with the high level of incidence of malnutrition in the state and deaths occurring out of that.

6.8 Expenditure on Economic Services

Economic services comprised of agriculture and allied activities, rural development, irrigation and flood control, energy, industry and minerals, transport and science and technology.

Expenditure on agriculture sector has declined over the years, despite the fact that the state's economy is basically an agrarian economy and needs greater attention in terms of investment in different aspects. However, rural development has shown substantial rise, in the light of heavy investment being done by the Central government in this sector. Again investments in irrigation and flood control remains stagnated over the years. Increased expenditure is seen in the transport sector. At the same time, expenditure in industry sector is not very satisfactory and remained as a neglected sector over the years.

6.9 Developmental and Non-Developmental Expenditure

The analysis of the expenditure data would be disaggregated further into developmental and non-developmental expenditure. All expenditure relating to revenue account, capital outlay and loans and advances are categorised into social services, economic services and general services. Broadly, the social and economic services constitute developmental expenditure, while expenditure on general services is treated as non-developmental expenditure.

FIGURE 4.8

Developmental and Non-Developmental Expenditure as a Percentage of Total Expenditure

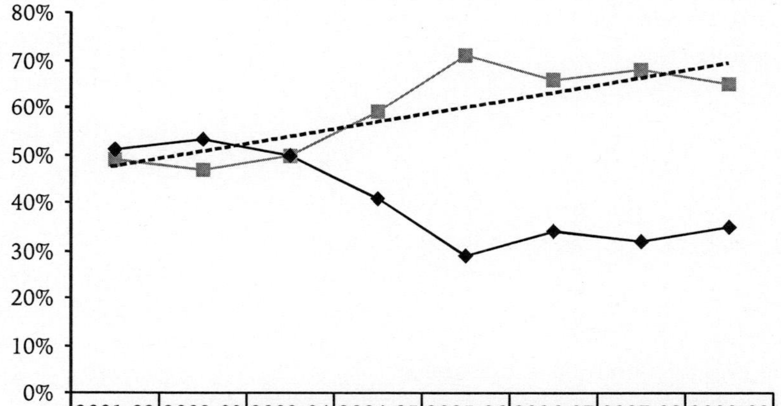

	2001-02 AC	2002-03 AC	2003-04 AC	2004-05 AC	2005-06 AC	2006-07 AC	2007-08 RE	2008-09 BE
Developmental expenditure	49%	47%	50%	59%	71%	66%	68%	65%
Non-developmental expenditure	51%	53%	50%	41%	29%	34%	32%	35%

Source: State Budget Books, GoMP, various years.

Thus, the developmental expenditure includes the development components of revenue expenditure, capital outlay and loans and advances by the state governments. The social sector expenditure includes expenditure on social services, rural development, and food storage and warehousing under revenue expenditure, capital outlay and loans and advances by the state governments. Capital outlay includes both developmental and non-developmental capital outlay. This has been summarised in Figure 4.8.

Analysis of the figure indicates that:

- FY 2003-04 onwards, the state's development expenditure has been increasing and has stayed above 65 per cent in the last three years. This augurs well for the state.
- From the year 2005-06 onwards, a decline in developmental expenditure is observed but this may not be taken seriously as this was an exceptional year due to return from MPSEB Rs. 1750 crore.
- Developmental capital expenditure comprises capital account expenditure on social and economic services and loans and advances provided by the state government.
- In 2006-07 and 2007-08, more than three quarters of the capital expenditure was developmental in nature. This augers well for the state.
- The budgeted developmental capital expenditure for 2008-09 has declined to two-thirds of the total capital expenditure. This is owing to expected greater outflow on account of repayment of principal amount of loans previously taken by the government.

7. Fiscal Priority

Table 4.14 reveals the changing fiscal priority of the state government over the years. As a proportion of GSDP both development expenditure as well as social sector expenditure shows rise, indicating good signs in terms of reaping the benefits of a growing economy and taking it to the people. However, one has to be cautious here in the sense that mere increasing ratios would remain rhetoric unless its reach to the poor people is not efficient.

TABLE 4.14

Fiscal Priority by MP State Government

Sr. No.	*Indicators*	*2004-2007 (Avg.)*	*2007-08*
1	Development expenditure as % of GSDP	15.8	16.3
2	Social sector expenditure as % of GSDP	7.7	9.4
3	Capital outlay as % of GSDP	4.8	4.8

Source: RBI (2008). *State Finances: Study of State Budgets 2008-09.*

8. Per Capita Expenditure

Per capita expenditure is one of the important measures of efficiency of the expenditure. There are at least eight states namely, Bihar, West Bengal, Uttar Pradesh, Orissa, Rajasthan, Kerala, Jharkhand and Maharashtra whose performance is below the national average on all the three per capita indicators mentioned in Table 4.15. Madhya Pradesh is no exception to this fact.

TABLE 4.15

Per Capita Expenditure, 2007-08 (in Rs.)

States	*Per Capita Development Expenditure*	*Per Capita Social Sector Expenditure*	*Per Capita Capital Outlay*
MP	3343	1923	979
India	4308	2492	1120

Source: RBI (2008). *State Finances: Study of State Budgets 2008-09.*

Low levels of spending in any sector in particular state may happen mainly due to two reasons: one, low fiscal priority attached by the state government and second, low fiscal capacity of the state government. In some states, both the factors work together resulting in a low level of spending.

9. The FRBM Act, 2005—Targets and Achievements on Fiscal Indicators for MP

The Fiscal Responsibility and Budget Management (FRBM) Act or the Madhya Pradesh Rajkoshiya Uttardayitva Evam Budget Prabandhan Adhiniyam, 2005 and the Rules under the Act or the Madhya Pradesh Rajkoshiya Uttardayitva Evam Budget Prabandhan Niyam, 2006 made under Section 12 of the Adhiniyam, have come into force on 1st January 2006 and 30th January 2006 respectively.

The Act is aimed to "provide for responsibility of the state government to ensure prudence in fiscal management and fiscal stability by progressive elimination of revenue deficit, reduction in fiscal deficit, prudent debt management consistent with fiscal sustainability, greater transparency in fiscal operations

TABLE 4.16

Targets and Achievements on Fiscal Indicators for MP

Fiscal Indicators	*2006-07 AC*	*2007-08 RE*	*2008-09 BE*	*Targets for 3 Years*		
				2009-10	*2010-11*	*2011-12*
Revenue surplus as a % of GSDP	2.60	2.36	1.80	2.06	2.21	2.38
Fiscal deficit as a % of GSDP	2.20	3.16	3.00	3.00	3.00	3.00
Total outstanding liabilities as a % of GSDP	46.57	44.49	43.65	42.20	41.16	40.22

Source: Memorandum of Finance Secretary, GoMP, various years and FRBM report, 2007-08.

of the Government and conduct of fiscal policy in a medium term framework".[10] The Act and the rules framed under it, require the state government to place before the state assembly, the macroeconomic framework statement, medium term fiscal policy statement, fiscal policy strategy statement and disclosure statements along with the state budget.[11]

The medium term fiscal policy statement (MTFPS) provides five-year rolling targets for some of the crucial fiscal indicators. Table 4.16 above provides information on fiscal indicators and rolling targets under FRBM Act.

Figure 4.9 describes the performance of various fiscal indicators as a proportion of GSDP over the years.

- Revenue deficit to progressively reduce (eliminated) by 2008-09: MP has already achieved the target. Since 2004-05, the state is a revenue surplus state. In 2008-09 BE, it stands at (+) 1.80. Revenue surplus of higher order help the state to finance its capital expenditure, thereby reducing reliance on borrowed funds.
- Fiscal deficit to reduce to 3 per cent of GSDP by 2008-09: This target is also well achieved two years ahead of the recommended time frame. It stands at (-) 2.20 for 2006-07 (AC); budgeted and projected at (-) 3.00 per cent for the years 2008-09 through 2011-12.
- Total outstanding liabilities to progressively reduce to 40 per cent of GSDP by FY 2015 end;

FIGURE 4.9

Fiscal and Revenue Deficit (-)/Surplus (+) as a Percentage of GSDP

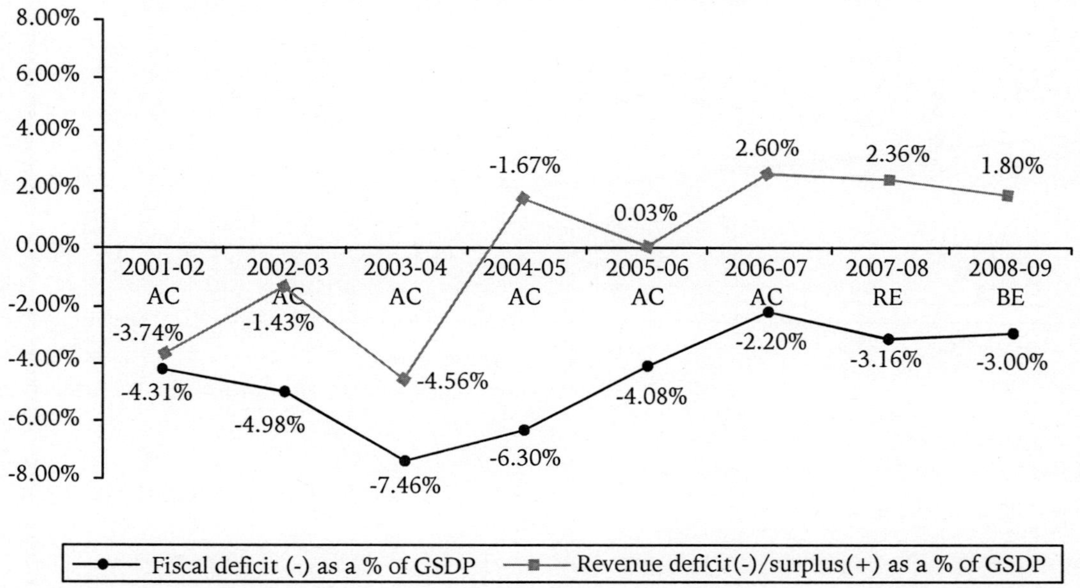

Source: State Budget Books, GoMP, various years.

10. Budget comprises the Annual Financial Statement and Demands for Grant.
11. FRBM Act, 2005.

43.65 per cent as per BE 2008-09; 40.22 per cent by FY 2011-12 as per rolling targets in FRBM report

- Total cumulative guarantees not to exceed 80 per cent of the revenue receipts of the previous financial year. It has been already achieved (69.4 per cent) for 2005-06.
- If fiscal prudence ordains that a fiscal deficit of 3.00 per cent is desirable, is it advisable for the state—the largest investor in one of the poorest state—to reduce its expenditure to the extent that the fiscal deficit goes as low as 2.20 per cent of the GSDP for 2006-07.

10. Quality of Expenditure

In the light of fiscal corrections, it is pertinent on the part of the state government that fiscal corrections should not be done at the cost of reducing expenditure on the most needed and crucial sectors. The 12th Finance Commission has also emphasised on the significance of improving outputs and outcomes by restructuring the expenditure. For example, it was observed in the analysis that in order to reduce revenue deficit, revenue expenditures were cut down.

FIGURE 4.10

Trend in Total Revenue Expenditure in Madhya Pradesh

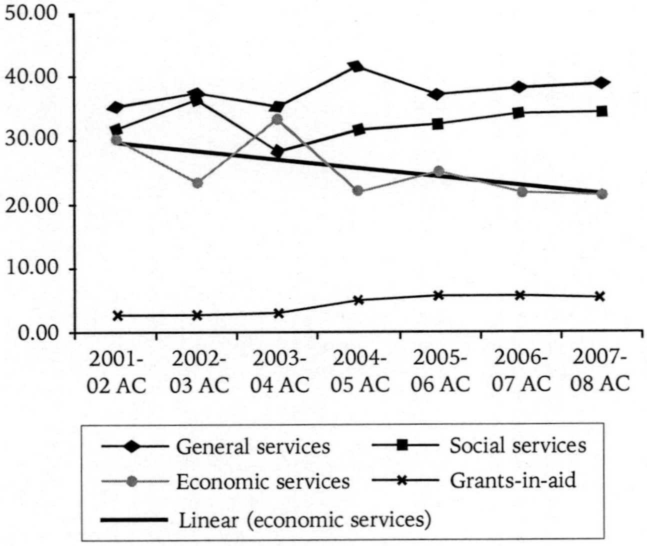

Source: State Budget Books, GoMP, various years.

Figure 4.10 puts forth the evidence that revenue surplus has been achieved at the cost of economic services out of other components in Madhya Pradesh. Expenditure on general services which in majority includes administrative expenses has remained more or less the same over the years. Social sector expenditure after witnessing the dip until 2003-04 has picked up as it is said that social sector expenditure are mostly of revenue in nature. On the other hand, economic services bears the brunt of reducing revenue expenditure to the greater possible extent as no way was left out to achieve the revenue surplus.

Further analysis points out that within the economic services, it is the agriculture and allied activities and irrigation sectors which are the victims of fiscal correction in the state. The counter argument in favour of economic services given is that it has the latitude of attracting the capital investment for its boost. Again, it is clear from the deeper analysis that the above arguments do not hold true in both cases of agriculture and irrigation. In the capital account expenditure, agriculture and allied services are attracting least investment that has come down from 1.59 per cent in 2001-02 to 0.85 per cent in 2007-08. Similarly, although the investment on irrigation and flood control is one of the highest, it is coming down very sharply from 46.6 per cent in 2001-02 to 30 per cent in 2007-08. Probably this would provide a very good example of neglecting one of the significant sectors of the economy that carries huge potential to reduce poverty of the state.

Another serious issue pertains to the utilisation of bulk of funds by majority of departments in the last quarter of every financial year, which has an adverse impact on the quality of work. In the financial year 2006-07, state government used about 52.25 per cent of resources in the first three quarters whereas remaining 47.75 per cent were utilised in the last quarter. In monetary terms, various departments used Rs. 4926 crore till December 2006 and spent Rs. 4503 crore in the last three months that is, January–March 2007. In these, agriculture, water resource, energy, school education, Narmada valley development authority, medical and public health, SC, ST and OBC welfare, rural development and industry and mining were the departments that failed to use their funds on time.

11. Principle of Accurate Budgeting

This is one of the principles of good budgeting. Principle of "accurate budgeting" ordains that the variance between the budgeted and actual receipts or expenditure should not exceed 10 per cent. Figure 4.11 plots the variance of the actual estimates and the budget estimates for both receipts and expenditure separately for

FIGURE 4.11

Variance of Actuals from Budgets

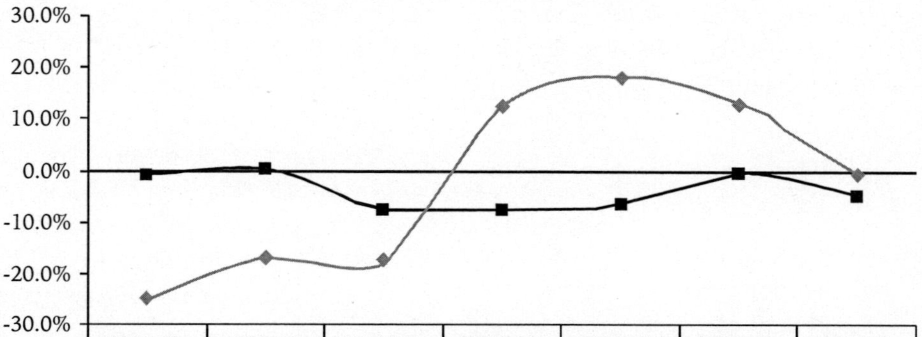

	2001-02 (AC)	2002-03 (AC)	2003-04 (AC)	2004-05 (AC)	2005-06 (AC)	2006-07 (AC)	2007-08 (RE)
Receipts	-25.0%	-16.7%	-17.2%	12.4%	18.0%	13.0%	-0.8%
Expenditure	-0.97%	0.24%	-7.89%	-7.91%	-6.38%	-0.53%	-5.16%

Source: State Budget Books, GoMP, various years.

various years. The figure should be interpreted with the "10 per cent criterion" mentioned above.

- Ideally, we would like the deviation of actual from the budget to be in the range of +/- 5 per cent for both the receipts as well as the expenditure.
- The state has maintained a good record with reference to variance in expenditure over the years.
- However, on the receipt side the deviation of accounts from the actual is not in acceptable range.
- It may, however, be noted that deviations for the entire budget hides huge deviations in various sectors.

RBI, in its report *State Finances: A Study of Budgets 2008-09* observed that the states generally overestimate grants-in-aid from the Centre while the amount of sharable taxes is underestimated in the state budgets. Loans from the Centre are also generally overestimated in the state budgets.

In order to minimise the variations, some steps need to be followed very stringently. There should be 2-3 budget reviews in each financial year. These reviews would help in keeping checks on anticipated revenue earnings and expenditure incurred on various heads more promptly. Appropriate forecasting methods and models should be used in for both income and expenditure side estimates. Majority of the state's income come from the taxes and hence, proper tax planning and its forecasting to generate adequate income is a very crucial task. The following guiding principles for good tax policy would help this task.[12]

a. *Simplicity:* The tax law should be simple so that tax payers understand the rules and can comply with them correctly and cost-efficiently.

b. *Fairness:* Similarly, situated tax payers should be taxed.

c. *Economic Growth and Efficiency:* The tax system should not impede or reduce the productive capacity of the economy.

d. *Neutrality:* The effect of the tax law on a tax payer's decisions on how to carry out a particular transaction or whether to engage in it at all should be kept to a minimum.

e. *Transparency:* Tax payers should know that a tax exists and how and when it is imposed on them and others.

f. *Minimising Non-Compliance:* A tax should be structured to minimise non-compliance.

g. *Cost-Effective Collection:* The cost of collecting a tax should be kept to a minimum, for the government and tax payers.

h. *Impact on Government Revenues:* The tax system should enable the government to determine how

12. *http://www.thehindubusinessline.com/bline/2005/12/08/stories/2005120800761000.htm*

much tax revenue is likely to be collected and when.

i. *Certainty:* The tax rules should clearly specify when and how the tax is to be paid, and how the amount is to be determined.

j. *Payment Convenience:* A tax should be due at a time or in a manner that is most likely to be convenient for the tax payer.

For curbing the expenditure side analysis, one has to keep vigil on the departmental spending, very particularly the departments that tops the list of supplementary budgets. More and more allocations through supplementary budgets itself indicate improper planning and budgeting exercise; thus, questioning the general functioning of the department.

Also, one has to give serious thoughts to the remarks in CAG reports. As a practice, it is been overlooked many a times; but provides rich content on the usual financial management at the overall departmental and on specific activities. It certainly highlights the irregularities in handling finances and if proper steps are taken on those issues, it would help the variations in due limit.

12. Implications of Sixth Central Pay Commission

The Sixth CPC, which was constituted by the Government on October 5, 2006, submitted its Report on March 24, 2008. Pay scales and revision of pension have been proposed to take effect retrospectively from January 1, 2006. Many of the state governments, by and large, follow the CPC award to improve the pay structure of their employees. However, some state governments constitute their own Pay Commissions. State governments have declared that the benefits of the Pay Commission's recommendations will be payable to state government employees with effect from January 1, 2006, and added, it would benefit around five lakh (500,000) state government employees, and around three lakh (300,000) pensioners. This decision on an average sees a hike of 30 per cent in the salary of the state government employees. State Pay Commission for MP has already been constituted. The commission has submitted its recommendation in 2008 but would submit its revised updates by June 2009. The decision of implementing 6th Pay Commission will put the financial burden of Rs. 2500 crore per annum on the state's exchequer. And if decided to implement from 1st January 2006, state government would need Rs. 7500 crore to pay arrears till August 2008.

13. Decentralisation

The last decade has experienced a remarkable shift in development strategies. This is remarkable in the sense that with the advent of 73rd and 74th Constitutional Amendment, rural local bodies came in to vogue. Decentralisation is now being considered as an instrument of poverty reduction and enhancing social welfare. Madhya Pradesh emerged as a leader in decentralised development in the mid-1990s. It was the first state in India to hold elections after the 73rd Amendment and to pass its own Decentralisation Act.

Fiscal decentralisation has been a topic of public finance literature for almost 40 years. The concept of fiscal decentralisation has got widest recognition during the last two decades. It has been considered as the most effective strategy from the point of view of welfare of the society. It is also believed that it has inherent merit of allocative efficiency that can respond more efficiently to community and regionally and nationally stated goals as well. Generally, allocative efficiency calls for assigning to lower levels of government those responsibilities where the costs and benefits are confined to a local jurisdiction and reflects the preferences of the local community. The Eleventh Schedule added to the Constitution by the 73rd Amendment lists 29 functions devolvable by states to Panchayati Raj Institutions (PRIs).

In line with the above, an attempt was made by Indira Rajaraman and Darshy Sinha in the paper entitled "Functional devolution to PRIs by states", where a quantitative measure of the extent to which functional transfers have been achieved through the budgetary transfer of funds, with respect to the fiscal year 2006-07, were studied for four states: Madhya Pradesh, Chhattisgarh, Rajasthan and Orissa. Major findings emerging out of the study are as follows:

- PRI share in total revenue expenditure for MP is 10.66 per cent.
- Per capita revenue transfer comes out to be Rs. 56.34 in MP.
- Devolved or total expenditure on 21 functions comes out to be 26.47 per cent.

14. State Finance Commission

The legislative acknowledgment to local governments was accorded with the 73rd Constitutional Amendment in 1992. With this, each of the state governments was required to appoint a State Finance Commission to assign taxes and fees to local governments, and recommend tax devolution and grants. The recommendations of the State Finance Commissions can be divided into three categories:

(i) Assignment of taxes, duties, levies and tolls to local bodies;

(ii) Sharing of revenue proceeds; and

(iii) Transfers on account of grants-in-aid and other financial assistance.

The Second Finance Commission for Madhya Pradesh was constituted under clauses (c) of Article 243-I (1) and (c) of Article 243-Y (1) of the Indian Constitution and Madhya Pradesh State Finance Commission Act, 1994. The Commission was constituted on 17th June 1999, the notifications on Terms of Reference were issued on 10th December 1999 and the Commission's report was submitted in July, August and December 2003. The recommendations were made for the period 2001-2006. While on one hand the report was inordinately delayed, on the other hand, the government too did not accept many of the Commission's recommendations while stating that it would take up some of the recommendations for further examination. This was evident from the Action Taken Report of the Finance Minister dated 14th March 2005. The report was presented in three parts. The first two pertained to fiscal packages for ULBs and PRIs. The third titled "Beyond Fiscal Package" related to restructuring local bodies' finances and administration, both rural and urban.

14.1 Action Taken Report on the Recommendations of the SFC as in March 2005

14.1.1 For Urban Local Bodies

- The government has accepted the SFC's recommendations on the share of ULBs in the state taxes, without any modifications.
- The SFC recommendations on general-purpose grants have been completely rejected by the government with likely support to the ULBs from the Central government based on 12th Finance Commission recommendations being cited as the reason for rejection.
- The SFC recommendation relating to inclusion of revenue from entertainment tax, presently being collected by state government, being assigned to the respective municipalities, from whose jurisdiction it is collected, has been rejected by the government. The reason cited for rejection is increase in receipts of the ULBs owing to increase in ULB's receipts under 'ULB's share in state taxes'.
- The SFC recommended continuation of previous provisions related to assigned tax revenue. The government accepted this recommendation without modifications.
- The recommendation related to non-transfer of funds, devolvable to ULBs, to urban administration department has been rejected by the state government for now. The government has indicated that their position may change once fiscal management of ULB improves.
- The recommendation on appointing a designated authority to redress a ULB's grievance of underestimation of its allocations has been accepted by the government.

14.1.2 For Rural Local Bodies

- The recommendations pertaining to share of PRIs in state's tax revenues were accepted by the government with the modification that the distribution among the *panchayats* with the already prevalent criteria of population, area and tax collection would be retained with their respective weights at 70 per cent, 25 per cent and 5 per cent, instead of the SFC recommended 100 per cent weight to the population of *panchayats*.
- The recommendations of SFC on grants were implemented with the government rejecting Rs. 50 crore worth of general purpose grant, accepting general-purpose grant of 14.65 crore for *janpads* and 2 crore to *zila panchayats*, accepting establishment-specific grant of Rs. of 28.4 crore but reducing the annual increase in the same from the recommended 10 per cent to 5 per cent and accepting specific grant recommendation of Rs. 5 crore to *zila panchayats* for capacity building of elected PRI representatives.
- The SFC recommendations on assigned tax revenue comprising net proceeds of land revenue, surcharge on stamp duty and cess on sales tax were the same as the pre-existing norm in the state and were accepted without any modifications.

Although the state government has now improved its fiscal position by eliminating its revenue deficit and begins to increase social spending, still its attempt to improve poverty reduction and impact of public expenditure has been met with limited success. The major cause behind this lies with lack of adequate capacity to prepare robust state level medium-term fiscal framework (MTFF) and absence of medium-term expenditure framework (MTEF) linking to goals and strategies and monitoring impacts of programmes and policies at the field level.

To remove these drawbacks, the state government has initiated activities like building Mudra Software and strengthening performance management in government.

15. Measures taken by Finance Department to keep Financial Discipline

- *Mudra Software:* Finance department of GoMP has developed a software called "Mudra" for enhancing computerised budget preparations. This not only enables the line departments to their budget estimates in a more detailed form but also helps the finance department to keep check on compilation, monitoring and evaluation of the budget estimates prepared by the administrative departments. The respective budget controlling officers are putting their efforts consciously owing to string fiscal discipline. Besides, with this software all the budget related information is now available in 'soft copy' form with the finance department. It also generates structured and desired output formats relieving it from tedious manual calculations.
- *Off-Budget Figures:* As a measure to improve transparency, the state government is presenting off-budget figures since last year (2007-08). Off-budget are the funds that are received directly from the Centre by various nodal implementing agencies and do not reflect in the state budget documents.
- *Strengthening PRIs:* In order to strengthen the PRIs, Madhya Pradesh plans to conduct independent audit for *panchayats* and also will constitute separate directorate for the purpose.
- *Strengthening Performance Management in Government:* A DFID (UK) assisted programme in the state of Madhya Pradesh is being implemented. The project will assist to strengthen management of public expenditure in the state as a part of the larger programme to strengthen performance management. Main purpose of this is to strengthen the links between policy, planning and budgeting to achieve more effective and efficient use of public resources so as to bring about poverty reduction and human development in the state. Here the focus would be on five outcomes.

  a. Improved Public Expenditure Management: To strengthen capacities of the state government to prepare robust MTFF for enabling better forecasting of long term revenue and expenditure, better management of liabilities like debt and pension, facilitate allocation of resources more objectively through departmental planning.

  b. Poverty Monitoring and Policy Support: Capacity building of Data Encryption Standard (DES) for better collection and analysis of poverty related data and share the specialised research within and outside the government for devising better policies and programmes.

  c. Strengthening Monitoring and Evaluation: This would involve monitoring and evaluation of projects and policies in State Planning Board and in few selected departments, where key performance indicators are designed, systems of collection of qualitative and quantitative data are formed and further analysis and dissemination of collected data would be undertaken. This would help the state government to report performance targets against MTEF, strengthen decision-making in prioritising resources and providing disaggregated data on key poverty and human development indices to help improved planning at the district level.

  d. Policy Framework for Better Management of PSEs: Here the performance and functioning of public sector enterprises would be reviewed. This would help the state government to channelise the resources for welfare spending either through closing of loss-making public sector enterprises or restructuring them to be functional.

  e. Strengthen System of Government Procurement: Under this, the state government's procurement systems, existing financial systems including internal audit would be reviewed and capacity of the finance department would be built so as to enable them to advice line departments in engaging with private sector for delivery of public services.

16. Way Forward

16.1 Fiscal Space[13]

Fiscal space is an evolving concept. It is defined as "a gap between the current level of expenditure and maximum level of expenditure a government can undertake without impairing its solvency".[14] It is also defined as "the availability of the budget room that allows a government to provide resources for a desired purpose without any prejudice to the sustainability of a government financial position.[15] Fiscal space is also characterised as "concrete policy actions for enhancing domestic resource mobilization and the reforms necessary to secure the enabling governance, institutional and economic environment for these policy actions to be effective".[16] The Eleventh Five Year Plan document has stated that for achieving the growth target of 9 per cent, it is important to overcome the infrastructure deficit in the country. Creating fiscal space would enable the undertaking of large investment in both social and physical infrastructure sectors of the country.

Fiscal space at the sub-national level can be created in number of ways like increasing tax rates, strengthening tax administration, cutting down low priority expenditure, implementing expenditure programmes efficiently, raising additional borrowings and acquiring higher transfers from the Central government. In India, raising the ratio of state's own tax and non-tax revenues to GSDP would be a possible way of creating fiscal space at the state levels. On the spending side, it would be created by structural reforms like:

1. Reducing inefficiency in public spending.
2. Eliminating programmes that have no strong reason to be in the public sector and can be shifted to private sector.
3. Cutting down non-merit subsidies.
4. Systematically enforcing the processes of budget preparation, execution, accounting, reporting and auditing.
5. Developing appropriate indicators for measuring effectiveness of programme implementation.
6. Facilitating an assessment of programme efficiencies through benchmarking of performances.

The Debt Swap Scheme (DSS) operated during 2002-2005 and Debt Consolidation and Relief Facility (DRCF) recommended by 12th Finance Commission have created fiscal space at the state levels in India, by reducing the expenditure on interest payments. Also, ruled-based FRBM enactment brought in considerable fiscal discipline at the state levels. Further, many state governments are using public-private partnership (PPP) as a way to create fiscal space for financing, mainly the infrastructure. Through PPP, state government can access the private funds in non-debt creating manner to finance the public projects.

16.2 Quality of Expenditure

Quality of expenditure involves three aspects, *viz.*, expenditure adequacy (i.e., adequate provisions for providing public services), effectiveness (i.e., assessment of performance/output indicators for select services) and efficiency of expenditure use.

State government is spending sizeable part of its expenditure (35 per cent in non-developmental expenditure) on interest payments, wages and salaries, pension obligation and administrative expenditure. This ultimately reduces the due share of productive and growth-oriented expenditure. Various schemes/ programmes run by the state government should be well-designed and implemented with utmost sincerity to reach the desirable outcomes. Improving public service delivery is the need of the hour and also in the wake of the fact that nearly 38 per cent of the population in the state is living below poverty line which is at high risk owing to their poor socio-economic status.

---

13. RBI (2008). *State Finances: A Study of Budgets 2008-09*.
14. IMF-World Bank (2006). *The Interim Report on Fiscal Policy for Growth and Development*.
15. Heller, P.S. (2005), "Understanding Fiscal Space," Policy *Discussion Paper*, IMF.
16. Roy, Ratin *et al.* (2007). "Fiscal Space for What? Analytical Issues from a Human Development Perspective", paper presented at G-20 workshop on *Fiscal Policy*, July 1-2, Istanbul.

Chapter 5

Governance

1. Introduction

The concept of governance is in practice with the evolution of human civilisation. In simple terms, governance means the process of decision-making and the process by which decisions are either implemented or not implemented. Government is one of the actors in governance. Other actors involved in governance vary depending on the level of government, for example influential landlords, associations of peasant farmers, co-operatives in rural areas, and NGOs, research institutes, religious leaders, finance institutions, political parties in urban areas. At the national level, in addition to the above actors, media, lobbyists, international donors, multinational corporations, etc., may play a role in decision-making or in influencing the decision-making process. All actors other than government and the military are grouped together as part of the "civil society".[1] Thus in short, 'governance' in general pertains to what 'government' does. It is an exercise of management power and policy.

The terms of governance and good governance are more often referred to, in the development sector, since past few years. The World Bank defines governance as "the exercise of political authority and the use of institutional resources to manage society's problems and affairs". According to UNDP's regional project on local governance for Latin America, governance has been defined as the rules of the political system to solve conflicts between actors and adopt decision (legality). It has also been used to describe the "proper functioning of institutions and their acceptance by the public" (legitimacy). And it has been used to invoke the efficacy of government and the achievement of consensus by democratic means (participation). Major donors and international financial institutions are increasingly basing their aid and loans on the condition that reforms that ensure good governance are undertaken and bad governance is being increasingly regarded as one of the root causes of all evil within our societies.

The demonstrated link among poor governance, poverty and nation state failure makes strengthening the quality of governance in the developing world an urgent task. In weak, troubled states, there is a strong likelihood that an excess of grievances will offer fertile ground for the nurturing of terrorism. Thus, improving the governance capabilities and effectiveness of developing countries is crucial not only to fostering their economic development, but also to reducing the potential for local and global conflict.[2]

2. Ranking of India on Governance Indicators[3]

While India may score high with the World Bank on growth, the story on governance is very different. A report on governance indicators released at the IMF-World Bank annual meeting in Singapore puts India at abysmally low levels. In the database of 213 countries that measures the political, economic and the institutional aspects of governance, the World Bank report ranks India at half or below half on most indicators.

---

1. Source: *http://www.unescap.org/pdd/prs/ProjectActivities/Ongoing/gg/governance.asp*
2. Rotberg, Robert I. (2004-05). "Strengthening governance: Ranking countries would help", *The Washington Quarterly* 28(1): 71–81.
3. Source: *http://www.indianexpress.com/news/world-bank-ranking-slams-india-on-governance/12748/*

The six facets of governance, each based on a number of underlying indicators itself, are: (i) voice and accountability, (ii) political stability, (iii) government effectiveness, (iv) regulatory quality, (v) rule or law, and (vi) control of corruption. A score is given for each indicator based on a number of sources, and then each country is placed in one of the six groups based on its percentile. The data reflect the views on governance of public sector, private sector and NGO experts, as well as thousands of citizen and firm survey respondents worldwide.

TABLE 5.1

Performance of India based on Governance Indicators

Sr. No.	*Indicators of Governance*	*Score*		*No. of Sources*	
		1996	*2008*	*1996*	*2008*
1	Voice and accountability	0.12	0.45	5	15
2	Political stability and absence of violence/ terrorism	-0.99	-0.99	6	11
3	Government effectiveness	-0.15	-0.03	7	13
4	Regulatory quality	-0.01	-0.21	7	12
5	Rule of law	0.34	0.12	8	17
6	Control of corruption	-0.38	-0.37	7	16

Source: World Bank (2009). *Governance Matters VIII: Aggregate and Individual Governance Indicators 1996-2008*, by Daniel Kaufmann, Aart Kraay and Massimo Mastruzzi, Brookings Institution, June.

3. Interstate Comparisons based on Quality of Life

It would be interesting to know the status of governance in various states within India over a period of time. NHFS has attempted to rank 20 Indian states based on quality of life offered in the big states. Big states are those that have land area over 35,000 sq. km. and population over one million. The eight parameters taken into consideration for ranking include: law and order, agriculture, primary education, primary health, infrastructure, environment, budgets and prosperity.

Geographically, Madhya Pradesh is the second largest state in India and is the ninth state in terms of GSDP. It has been ranked at 13th position with a score of 1.33, among 20 big states in the country in 2007 in terms of quality of life provided in the state. Compared to 2003 ranking, its position has improved in the next two years by one point but again rounded up to the same position in 2007. This definitely point out towards the scope for improvement in the quality of life offered in the state.

TABLE 5.2

Definitive Ranking of Quality of Life Across Indian States

Name of State	*Score in 2007*	*Rank*				
		2007	*2006*	*2005*	*2004*	*2003*
Punjab	2.72	1	1	1	1	1
Kerala	2.52	2	2	2	2	2
Himachal Pradesh	2.38	3	3	3	3	3
Tamil Nadu	2.36	4	4	4	4	4
Gujarat	2.11	5	7	7	7	6
Maharashtra	2.07	6	6	6	6	7
Karnataka	2.2	7	8	8	8	8
Haryana	1.89	8	5	5	5	5
Uttarakhand	1.84	9	9	9	9	N.A.
Andhra Pradesh	1.77	10	10	11	11	10
Jammu & Kashmir	1.66	11	11	10	10	9
Rajasthan	1.38	12	12	12	13	11
Madhya Pradesh	1.33	13	14	14	12	13
Assam	1.29	14	16	16	15	14
West Bengal	1.29	15	13	13	14	12
Chhattisgarh	1.17	16	15	15	16	N.A.
Uttar Pradesh	0.98	17	17	17	17	15
Orissa	0.98	18	18	18	18	16
Jharkhand	0.88	19	19	19	19	N.A.
Bihar	0.60	20	20	20	20	17

Source: NHFS, October 2007.

Even though National Housing and Facility Survey (NHFS) included key eight governance parameters for arriving at the definitive ranking of quality of life, it did not include some other vital characteristics of governance, like institutions, democracy, state of poverty, regulation and promotion, combating corruption, etc. So, let us first try to understand what one would call a good governance? The following exhibit attempts to answer the question.

4. About Good Governance

Good governance has eight major characteristics. It is participatory, consensus oriented, accountable, transparent, responsive, effective and efficient, equitable and inclusive, and follows the rule of law. It assures that corruption is minimised, the views of minorities are taken into account and that the voices of the most vulnerable in society are heard in decision-making. It is also responsive to the present and future needs of society.[4]

4. Source: *http://www.unescap.org/pdd/prs/ProjectActivities/Ongoing/gg/governance.asp*

FIGURE 5.1

Characteristics of Good Governance

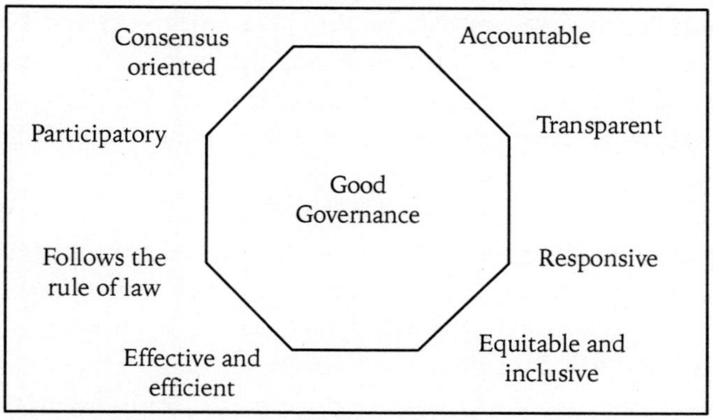

Source: *http://www.unescap.org/pdd/prs/ProjectActivities/ongoing/gg/governance*

Key characteristics of governance are described in the following paragraphs. Thus, it is clear that good governance is an ideal situation which is difficult to achieve in its totality. Very few countries and societies have come close to achieving good governance in its totality.

4.1 Participation

Participation by both men and women is a key cornerstone of good governance. Participation could be either direct or through legitimate intermediate institutions or representatives. It is important to point out that representative democracy does not necessarily mean that the concerns of the most vulnerable in society would be taken into consideration in decision-making. Participation needs to be informed and organised. This means freedom of association and expression on the one hand and an organised civil society on the other.

4.2 Rule of Law

Good governance requires fair legal frameworks that are enforced impartially. It also requires full protection of human rights, particularly those of minorities. Impartial enforcement of laws requires an independent judiciary and an impartial and incorruptible police force.

4.3 Transparency

Transparency means that decisions taken and their enforcement are done in a manner that follows rules and regulations. It also means that information is freely available and directly accessible to those who will be affected by such decisions and their enforcement. It also means that enough information is provided and that it is provided in easily understandable forms and media.

4.4 Responsiveness

Good governance requires that institutions and processes try to serve all stakeholders within a reasonable time frame.

4.5 Consensus Oriented

There are several actors and as many viewpoints in a given society. Good governance requires mediation of the different interests in society to reach a broad consensus in society on what is in the best interest of the whole community and how this can be achieved. It also requires a broad and long-term perspective on what is needed for sustainable human development and how to achieve the goals of such development. This can only result from an understanding of the historical, cultural and social contexts of a given society or community.

4.6 Equity and Inclusiveness

A society's well-being depends on ensuring that all its members feel that they have a stake in it and do not feel excluded from the mainstream society. This requires all groups, but particularly the most vulnerable have opportunities to improve or maintain their well-being.

4.7 Effectiveness and Efficiency

Good governance means that processes and institutions produce results that meet the needs of society while making the best use of resources at their disposal. The concept of efficiency in the context of good governance also covers the sustainable use of natural resources and the protection of the environment.

4.8 Accountability

Accountability is a key requirement of good governance. Not only governmental institutions but also the private sector and civil society organisations must be accountable to the public and to their institutional stakeholders. Who is accountable to whom varies depending on whether decisions or actions taken are internal or external to an organisation or institution. In general, an organisation or an institution is accountable to those who will be affected by its decisions or actions. Accountability cannot be enforced without transparency and the rule of law.

5. Governance Issues in MP

5.1 Human Development in MP

Over the last decade, the human development index (HDI) of Madhya Pradesh has improved by over 20 per cent, rising from 0.328 in 1991 to 0.394 in year 2001. The National Human Development Report prepared by the Planning Commission of India reveals that in the decade of 1990s, momentum for improving HDI was maintained in only three states in the country. Madhya Pradesh was among these selected states in the country. Madhya Pradesh, which stood at 13th place in 1991 in terms of HDI in the country, has now improved its position to the 12th place.

Madhya Pradesh has a historical edge over all other states of India, because it was the first state that published its first *Human Development Report* (HDR) in 1995. And after that, Madhya Pradesh followed it up with 1998-HDR, the 2002-HDR and recently the 2007-HDR. District-wise HDI, gender index, child mortality, IMR, longevity index, Gini coefficient and human development-wise ranking of each district of MP; besides giving special developmental thrust in each HDR report like to livelihood, to education, to *Panchayati Raj*, to social and public health and to infrastructure, etc., have underscored the state of community, its resources, role and responsibility of the state, emerging opportunities and interpretations, have helped policy makers, researchers and development practitioners to comprehend the complex situation of contemporary development in a more focused, systematic and concrete manner.

5.2 Poverty and Hunger in MP

The current poverty estimate from Planning Commission shows that even while poverty is reducing, it is getting more pronounced in states with a bad history and is becoming more chronic: the poorest are not able to move out of the poverty trap. India had 301.7 million 'poor' people in 2005, according to the new estimate. Of these, 72 per cent were in rural areas. More than 57 per cent were concentrated in five states: Maharashtra, Uttar Pradesh, Madhya Pradesh, Bihar and West Bengal.

The country's first *Social Development Report 2006* prepared by the autonomous body Council for Social Development (CDS) states that poverty and inequality in India are increasingly becoming polarised along regional and class lines. The report also speaks of a 'fourth world' of marginalised peoples that exists within the country of 1 billion-plus. Although India is aspiring to be an economic superpower, it is also a home to one in four of the world's undernourished. On the social development front, Bihar, Jharkhand, Uttar Pradesh, Madhya Pradesh and Orissa are at the bottom of the social indicators list in rural India. The social indicator list include demography, gender ratios, health care, education, unemployment, poverty and social deprivation. In urban India, Bihar, UP, Jharkhand, Chhattisgarh and Orissa are at the bottom. This clearly spelt out that the issues of poverty in Madhya Pradesh and Chhattisgarh are to be looked into more critically.

The latest entry into the realm of poverty indication has been made by the International Food Policy Research Institute (IFPRI). IFPRI has come up with a research document on the state of 'Hunger' in the world. It studied 88 countries of the globe and ranked them. As per the global hunger index (GHI), India has been ranked at 66th position among 88 countries that it studied. And the state of Madhya Pradesh with its alarming food situation has been ranked along with Ethiopia and Chad. IFPRI has further broken down the GHI into nation-wide indices, like Indian State Hunger Index (ISHI); Madhya Pradesh and other states of India will be scaled on ISHI. One of the implications of this study is that Madhya Pradesh government ought to proactively start making large investments in social security, protection, drought-proofing, health and nutrition programmes.

Various poverty alleviation programmes are being implemented in the state but the incidence of poverty has not been reduced substantially in MP. Poverty rate in MP is at 38.3 per cent, or 249.68 lakh persons are still living below poverty line. In the past two rounds of NSSO, rural poverty in MP has declined marginally from 37.06 per cent in 1999-2000 to 36.9 per cent in 2004-05. Urban poverty on the other hand has increased from 38.44 per cent in 1999-2000 to 42.1 per cent in 2004-05.

Understandably, the gap between the national and state income figures has widened during the last decades[5] although the state has maintained its ranking (or even gone up one place) among the states due to poorer performance of other backward states. The low

5. Gap in per capita income of MP and national average is Rs. 15,232 and per capita income of MP is higher only than UP and Bihar (Economic Survey, GoI, 2008).

economic growth in the state, particularly in agriculture, forestry and non-farm rural activities, is responsible for high poverty, both in urban and rural areas of the state, way above the national average.

5.3 Law and Order Situation and State of Vulnerable Communities

Madhya Pradesh is one of the few states that is a safe and relatively a crime-free state. A glimpse into the state of crimes brought to fore by the 2005-06 National Crimes Record Bureau, Government of India and MP-Lokayukt's 2005-06 report proves that Madhya Pradesh is relatively a safe, secure and peaceful state of India. MP, like any other normal state in the country does not invoke fear, anxiety or apprehensions about night-outs, shopping, wildlife safaris or for routine. MP does have its small quota of Maoists or Naxalites, but these elements unlike in Chhattisgarh are wary to strike at will, or cause wanton killings. Random and rare incidents related with Naxals' violence, only in a couple of thickly forested districts, take place, that too in few numbers, in the state. However, a snapshot of general crime statistics reveal the exact situation of law and order in the state.

There seemed to be a fairly reasonable and acceptable situation of law and order in the state. But Madhya Pradesh cannot afford to be very complacent about its extant state of crime. Table 5.3 clearly indicates that the law and order situation in MP has changed in the last few years. The first scenario that should attract the attention of the state government is that MP takes the lead position in terms of its share of the total IPC crimes in the country. Incidences of different types of crime particularly against the marginalised sections like women, children SCs and STs have shown rise, pointing towards loopholes in the overall governance in the state. There are at least four areas of concern that ought to be addressed with a long-term perspective to improve these considerably.

5.4 Corruption in MP

Indian political parties and their elected representatives are the most corrupt in the country. This was the perception which emerged in the global survey across 69 countries conducted by Transparency International. It says that for availing the basic services, people in the country have to pay bribe to the tune of Rs. 900 crore in a year. Thus, the most serious implication of corruption were observed on the poor people. Either many of the government schemes and programmes does not reach them properly or in case if it is reaching, they have to pay bribe. The report

TABLE 5.3

Categories of Different Crimes in Context to MP

Particular	*2006*	*2007*	*Remark*	*Context of MP*
IPC crime rate	167.7	175.1	Recorded growth of 4.4 per cent over previous year.	1. Madhya Pradesh has accounted for 10.2 per cent of total IPC crimes reported in the country, followed by Maharashtra 9.8 per cent. 2. Indore reported the highest crime rate (792.7) among the mega cities in the country, followed by Bhopal (760.8) and Jaipur (606.8).
Crime against women	14.7	16.3	The proportion of IPC crimes committed against women towards total IPC crimes has increased during last 5 years from 7.6 per cent in 2003 to 8.8 per cent during 2007.	Madhya Pradesh has reported the highest number of rape cases (3,010), 6772 of molestations against women and 742 dowry deaths (3rd position). Madhya Pradesh bags the 4th position in terms of total incidences of crimes against women and girls.
Crime against children	1.7	1.8	7.6 per cent increase was reported in incidence of crime against children in 2007 over 2006. Cases of child rape went up by 6.9 per cent during 2007 (5,045) over 2006 (4,721).	Madhya Pradesh reported 21.0 per cent (4,290 out of 20,410) of total crimes committed against children in the country.
Crime against SCs STs	 2.4 0.5	 2.5 0.5	The rate of crime against scheduled castes increased from 2.4 in 2006 to 2.6 in 2007 while rate of crime against scheduled tribes in 2007 remained 0.5, - the same as in 2006.	Madhya Pradesh reported 27.1 per cent of total (1,501 out of 5,532) crimes against scheduled tribes in the country.

Source: http://ncrb.nic.in/cii2007/cii-2007/Snapshots.pdf

released in June 2008 shows that the level of corruption in Madhya Pradesh is alarming. Madhya Pradesh is counted among the five most corrupt states in India, besides, Bihar, Assam, Jammu & Kashmir and Uttar Pradesh. The study, like the earlier ones, is based on perceptions about corruption in general, but specific in context of a service and more importantly, actual experience of paying bribe by BPL households in availing one or more of the 11 selected public services.

Depending on the frequency of interaction, the 11 services are divided broadly into "basic services" like PDS, hospital, school education (up to class XII), electricity and water supply services and "need based services" like land records/registration, housing, forest, NREGS, banking and police service (traffic and crime). In Himachal Pradesh, the level of corruption is "moderate" in all the 11 services studied whereas in the case of Madhya Pradesh and Assam, corruption level in all the 11 services was high or very high or alarming. The research was carried out in 5 districts (Shivpuri, Jhabua, Bhopal, Balaghat and Sidhi) of Madhya Pradesh.

6. Democratic Institutions

6.1 State-level Commissions and Statutory Bodies

These are also key democratic institutions that are either enacted by the legislature or are strategic tools in the hands of state cabinet and the executives. Box 5.1 gives a list of 16 commissions that were in operation in Madhya Pradesh in mid-2007. State-level commissions, in many ways define the policies and priorities of the government and in some ways these provide necessary shock-absorbing capability to the executive. Some of these commissions are very temporary and temporal, like Commission for Safai Karamchari and Commission for Economically Weak among the General Category and also the pay commissions (if and when instituted); but most of these institutions, like public service commission, human rights, minorities and women's commissions, SC, ST and backward castes' commissions, consumer disputes redressal commission and Gau Seva Ayog are such bodies that need full-time, tenured experts to run these. Whereas election commission remains dormant for a long time and then gets activated in spurts, as and when elections fall nearby.

6.2 Law and Order Institution

At least one statutory institution that came into inception in MP by 1982, consequent upon an enactment in 1981, was the institution of ombudsman (*Lokayukt*) and deputy ombudsman (*Uplokayukta*). This institution is critical to the governance because it is the legitimate body of check and balance in the state's governance at all levels and especially at the level of ministries and the state secretariat.

BOX 5.1

State-level Commissions in Madhya Pradesh

There are 15 state-level commissions in Madhya Pradesh. These are:

1) Madhya Pradesh State Finance Commission
2) Madhya Pradesh State Election Commission
3) Madhya Pradesh State Consumer Disputes Redressal Commission
4) Madhya Pradesh State Planning Commission
5) Madhya Pradesh Electricity Regulatory Commission
6) Madhya Pradesh Public Service Commission
7) Madhya Pradesh State Information Commission
8) Madhya Pradesh State Safai Karamchari Commission
9) Madhya Pradesh State Human Rights Commission
10) Madhya Pradesh State Commission for Economically Weak among the General Category
11) Madhya Pradesh State Scheduled Castes Commission
12) Madhya Pradesh State Scheduled Tribes Commission
13) Madhya Pradesh State Women's Commission
14) Madhya Pradesh State Minorities Commission
15) Madhya Pradesh State Backward Castes Commission
16) Madhya Pradesh Gau Seva Ayog

Source: General Administration Deptt., GoMP, Bhopal.

6.3 Ombudsman (Lokayukt)

The office of MP state ombudsman office works as an economic offence's wing of state government. It has exclusive jurisdiction to enquire into the complaints against chief minister, deputy chief minister, state ministers, leaders of opposition and all secretary level officers. *Uplokayukta* is empowered to look into the complaints against all those government, semi-government, quasi-government and autonomous institutions like the vice-chancellors and registrars of universities, officers that are not covered by the office of *lokayukt*. The *lokayukt* or the *Uplokayukta* cannot look into any complaint the subject matter of which is more than five years old. They cannot also enquire into any case which is the subject matter of an enquiry under the Public Servants Inquiries Act, 1850 or which has been referred for enquiry under the Commission of Inquiry Act, 1952. Meanwhile, the *lokayukt's* and

TABLE 5.4

Record of MP Ombudsman's/*Lokayukt's* Office Getting Complaints and their Disposal

Period	*No. of Pending Cases at the Beginning of Year*	*Complaints Received in the Current Year*	*Total Complaints*	*Complaints Filed Post-Prelim. Exam.*	*Complaints Sent to Depts. for Action*	*Registered Complaints for Inquiry*	*No. of Pending Cases at the Year End*
1999-2000	49	3438	3487	1992	179	1195	21
2000-01	21	3790	3811	2139	661	966	38
2001-02	38	3215	3253	1778	566	840	69
2002-03	69	3168	3237	1664	626	826	121
2003-04	121	2577	2698	1287	541	651	119
2004-05	119	2887	3006	1801	507	525	173
2005-06	173	3126	3299	2065	475	598	161

Source: Lokayukt office, GoMP.

Uploayukta's office in MP, with the help of Special Police Establishment, under its aegis, has taken action against 483 government employees (in five years between 2001 and 2006) and 376 of them were gazetted officers. Moreover, there were 905 special cases that were tried by special court between April 2002 and March 2008, of which 494 or 54 per cent of the 905 tried were convicted.

The rate of primary complaints' conversion into authorised complaints and thus being filed by the *lokayukt's* office, or dropping of complaints at the first level of screening subsequent to preliminary examination shows some improvement. Earlier, only 53 per cent of the initial complaints were getting recognised as bonafide complaints after the first level of screening. This figure rose to 62 per cent, in recent years. Further, success of the second level of screening such that finally the office of *lokayukt* sends recommendations to the concerned parent departments of the accused persons, to take appropriate action, is also being found improving, but it does not show any clear trend. Success rate at the second screening level for the year 1999-2000 improved from 8 per cent to 30 per cent and then dropped to 18 per cent and again rose to 23 per cent.

If the cumulative progress of the ombudsman's office is examined, one finds that the office received 22201 complaints over seven years including the pending cases, the total cases received by the *lokayukt's* office were 22791 or 3285 cases per annum, on an average. Fifty-five per cent of these complaints or 12726 cases were filed after preliminary screening and 3555 or 27 per cent of these filed cases were forwarded to the concerned departments of the accused officials for taking action against them. Further, 44 per cent of the filed complaints or 5601 cases were registered for inquiry. Actually, 45 per cent were screened out at the first inquiry and only 15 per cent of the initial lot of complaints (22791) made way to the parent departments of the accused officials and 24 per cent of the initial set of complaints got registered for further inquiry. In other words, about 39 per cent of the primary level complaints were destined to invite some kind of punitive action against the accused.

7. Decentralisation

The main aim of decentralising the powers at the district level is to reduce the delay in securing sanctions and to empower the people's representatives in the districts to take decision at the district level itself.

7.1 Panchayati Raj Institutions

Three-tiered Panchayati Raj bodies are the vital democratic institutions of rural India. The institution of Panchayati Raj was brought into modern independent India's political set-up exactly five decades ago. Panchayati Raj institutions were born with the Nagaur Convention of 1958, but these remained at their level of infancy before 1993. 73rd Amendment to the Indian Constitution that was passed in 1992 and subsequently which was applied with effect from 1993 planted actual teeth to these institutions. With passing of this bill, the *panchayats* which used to linger in Directive Principles of the Constitution and hence were not mandatory, suddenly became a very powerful tool when many grassroot development programmes got implemented through them. *Panchayats*, block level *panchayats* and district level *panchayats* became the harbingers of development schemes to the villages. This churning process of participatory village-level democracy at one level heralded the golden phase of power devolution that hastened the process of development and in many cases facilitated equity and at the other level, it divided each village into parties and camps and in some cases, it bred patronage sharing and clout mongering too.

As far as Madhya Pradesh is concerned, *panchayats* offered great opportunity to the state. Since 1993, MP has moved *panchayats* through many circles and bends; some of which were minor shifts in nuances or were such insinuations that strategically changed the implications, by a big way. This chapter accounts for these evolution phases of *panchayats* in Madhya Pradesh that helped turn *panchayats* into cornerstones of government policy and practice.

7.2 *The District Planning Committee (DPC)—Key Coordinating Institution*

In pursuance of the Article 243 ZD of the Constitution, the Madhya Pradesh government enacted the Madhya Pradesh Zila Yojana Samiti Adhiniyam, 1995 that received the assent of the Governor on 19th May 1995. The Zila Yojana Samiti Act provides for the constitution of the district planning committee (DPC) in all the districts of the state. As a part of revitalisation of Panchayat Raj institution and urban local bodies, the DPC is constituted in every district. Further, the districts were categorised as comprising of 15, 20 or 25 members in the committee. The membership to DPC has been provided to the elected members of the *panchayats*, municipalities, *zila panchayats* and the *prabhari* minister of the state government[6] and the district collector. The *prabhari* minister has been designated as the Chairperson of the committee. Apart from the Chairperson, other members of the DPC are elected from amongst members of *panchayats* and municipalities. The appointment of the minister-in-charge as Chairperson has, however, been controversial. As DPC, the committee has the powers of planning, raising resources for financing their plans, and to monitor and evaluate the programmes and schemes that are implemented under the system of decentralised planning, including the money to be allocated by the MP/MLA fund.

BOX 5.2

Guiding Principles of Devolution of Power to PRIs

Role of state government will be that of a policy regulating agency:

- *Panchayats* should be developed as institutions of self-governance and not merely as institutions of local governance.
- *Zila panchayat* should gradually evolve as district government and block *panchayat* should become its main administrative unit.
- The main responsibility of *panchayats* is to plan for economic development and social justice. To enable *panchayats* to fulfil this role, the staff and the budget should be transferred to the *panchayats*.
- At the district and sub-district level, the work should be distributed between the state and the *panchayat* sector. This division should avoid duplication of control and authority of state and *panchayat* sector.
- *Gram panchayat* be given functional control of those departments that need to be managed at the local level.
- Participation of *panchayats* to be ensured while preparing welfare and development programmes.
- State employees will work for the state government and the *panchayat* employees will work for the *panchayat*. There may be officials from the same department under the *panchayat* and the state sector—their roles and responsibilities and co-ordination should be well defined.
- Since the work of the departments has to be transferred to the *panchayats*, all the budget with the exception of establishment cost should be transferred to *panchayats*.
- The power of the departments should be given to an institution, and not to any particular official.
- The process of use of powers should be based on rules of procedure in the same manner as the state government. For this, working rules and procedures should be prepared for *panchayats* that will define the roles and responsibilities of the committees and the officials are empowered to take decisions.
- In no condition the *panchayats* will be given the ad hoc control of departments. Either there will be no control or there will be total control of *panchayats*.

Source: Madhya Pradesh Panchayat Raj & Gram Swaraj Adhiniyam, 2001.

The guiding principles were a major breakthrough for the state in transferring the work, the staff and the budgets to *panchayats*. In pursuance of the principles, works of 19 departments and the budget under demand number 15, 80 and 82 of these departments was placed at the discretion of *panchayats*. All the functions

6. The state government has a minister designated to specially look after the interests and development of each district. This minister of the state cabinet is called the *prabhari mantri*.

indicated in Schedule II have been transferred to *panchayats* and all concerned departments (nearly 23) have issued circulars and orders that effectively transferred their work, as well as issued orders that transferred the staff under the purview and control of *panchayats*.

The state government that is responsible to conduct elections for *panchayats* has also constituted the State Election Commission. In the past, the Election Commission has conducted two general elections and elections for seats and posts as and when they become vacant. Since 1994, there have been three rounds of elections for *panchayats* in the state—1994, 2000 and 2004. The *panchayat* elections was held in Madhya Pradesh in year 2004, in 48 *zila panchayats*, 313 *janpad panchayats* and 22051 village *panchayats*. Presently, there are 3,44,424 *panchayat* representatives in the state, which includes 22,387 members as leaders of their respective *panchayat* bodies. Among these, 61.4 per cent of the representatives belonged to the scheduled castes (15.6 per cent), scheduled tribes (27.6 per cent) and other backward class (18.1 per cent) categories. Of the total representatives, 33.8 per cent are women. If the women were not given the reservation, they would not have found the chance to contest and win the election and prove their calibre as administrative leaders. In one of its commendable steps, the state government has increased the women quota in *panchayat* reservation from 33 per cent to 50 per cent, thus motivating women's participation in local government.

In pursuance of the mandatory provisions of the 73rd Constitutional Amendment, the state government had also constituted the first and the second State Finance Commission to decide upon the principle of devolution of funds to the *panchayats*. Both the Finance Commissions have submitted their reports and in response to that State Government has prepared action taken report.

Section 129 of the Madhya Pradesh Panchayat Raj and Gram Swaraj Act, 1993 provides for the constitution of separate audit organisation for the conduct of audit of *panchayats* in order to strengthen the PRIs. State government has constituted separate directorate to undertake the work and it will soon be functioning in the state.

Madhya Pradesh has qualified for the Central government's award worth Rs. 1.50 crore by topping the list of states ranked for encouraging PRIs under Panchayat Empowerment and Accountability Incentive Scheme during 2008-09. States were evaluated and given scores based on the devolution index by National Council for Applied Economic Research, New Delhi for the task assigned by Ministry of Panchayati Raj.

TABLE 5.5

Ranking of States for Empowering PRIs and Making them Accountable

Rank	*States*	*Score of Functions*	*Score of Finances*	*Score of Functionaries*	*Overall Score*
1	Madhya Pradesh	4.52	4.08	4.71	4.44
2	West Bengal	5.00	3.68	4.43	4.37
3	Tamil Nadu	5.00	3.62	4.29	4.30
4	Kerala	5.00	2.82	4.29	4.04
5	Karnataka	5.00	3.29	3.64	3.98
6	Sikkim	5.00	3.20	3.29	3.83
7	Himachal Pradesh	3.83	2.97	4.14	3.65
8	Haryana	4.45	2.53	3.29	3.42
9	Chhattisgarh	4.31	2.89	2.86	3.35
10	Assam	4.60	2.47	2.64	3.24

Source: Study on an Index of Devolution for assessing environment for Panchayati Raj Institutions in the States Empirical Assessment, 2008 by NCAER.

Madhya Pradesh stood sixth in the ranking during 2007-08, it astoundingly came back and topped the list in 2008-09. Rest of the top five states are West Bengal, Tamil Nadu, Kerala and Karnataka.

7.3 Gram Nyayalaya

Madhya Pradesh had a unique concept of *gram nyayalaya*, where disputes regarding land encroachments were dealt with. The experience has been that the orders passed by *gram nyayalayas* are not implemented properly as no separate agency has been provided to them. The *gram nyayalayas* have to seek assistance of police and revenue officials for this purpose that leads to avoidable delay. The decision to restore the powers under Sections 248 and 250 of the Madhya Pradesh Land Revenue Code to *tahsildar* has been taken with a view to curb the tendency of encroaching upon government land and to ensure prompt removal of encroachments.

The state cabinet approved the draft Gram Nyayalaya Amendment Bill, 2005. The amendment bill seeks to withdraw the powers of hearing and disposing off the cases under Sections 248 and 250 of the Madhya Pradesh Land Revenue Code, 1959 from village courts (*gram nyayalayas*) and to place them under the exclusive jurisdiction of *tahsildar* again. The proposed amendment bill provides for restoring the powers to *tahsildar* for dispossessing such persons under Section 248 of the Madhya Pradesh Land Revenue Code who has encroached upon the land of somebody else or the land reserved for some special purpose or service or government land. Under Section 250, *tahsildar* would be authorised to restore the possession of land to the rightful owner who might have been dispossessed from it.

7.4 Gram Swarajya

The existing *panchayat* system was constantly being criticised for two major weaknesses or problems. One was the growing and almost over-bearing influence of *sarpanch* over the *panchayat*, and the second was the *gram sabha* not being able to establish its role, character and importance and there was dwindling interest in *gram sabhas* and therefore, declining attendance in its meetings. The *gram sabha* actually had considerable powers under the existing provisions of decisions and planning, but most of this had become redundant in practise.

Recognising both these problems, the idea of *gram swaraj* was evolved, inspired also by the ideals and thinking of Mahatma Gandhi. Empowering *gram sabhas* further and granting them a greater role, the idea is to tone down the unnecessary influence of the *sarpanch* and to give a comprehensive role to *gram sabha* so that people find it worthwhile to attend the meetings and thereby participate directly in their concerns—a change towards direct democracy.

The Madhya Pradesh government amended the Madhya Pradesh Panchayat Raj Act to give effect to *gram swaraj* in the state. The amendment has brought in substantive changes in the Act and in the nature of *panchayat* institutions, especially at the village level. The main features of the amendment are given in Box 5.3.

8. CSOs and NGOs

Madhya Pradesh has a strong network of more than 5000 civil society organisations including NGOs, voluntary organisations, donor agencies etc. These

BOX 5.3

Gram Sabha: New Role under the _Gram Swarajya_ Initiative

- The *gram sabha* of every revenue and forest villages in the state has been recognised as a legal entity. That is, the *gram sabha* can sue and be sued, and it will have its own seal and signature.
- The *gram sabha* itself will convene the meeting of *gram sabha*. One meeting of the *gram sabha* every month is mandatory.
- The condition for the fulfilment of the quorum has been made mandatory for the meeting of the *gram sabha*. The quorum for the *gram sabha* is 20 per cent of the membership of the *gram sabha*. Of the members present, one-third should be women.
- Decisions in the *gram sabha* will be unanimous. In case there is any dispute, attempts will be made to arrive at a general consensus, and if the matter is still not resolved, the majority opinion will prevail.
- There is provision for appeal on the decision taken by the *gram sabha*.
- Every *gram sabha* will constitute seven standing committees, namely, agriculture, education, health, infrastructure development, community resources, village protection, and social justice. The chairpersons of each of these committees along with the *sarpanch* and the *upsarpanch* of the *gram panchayat* will constitute the Village Development Committee.
- The amendment is flexible enough to provide space to the *gram sabha* to constitute ad hoc committees for specific work. These committees could be made and dismantled by the *gram sabha*.
- Every *gram sabha* will have a Village Fund, comprising of the cash (bank) fund; the grain fund; the labour fund; and the material fund. The purpose to which this fund will be put to use will be decided by the *gram sabha* operated by the Village Development Committee.
- *Gram sabha* has been entrusted with the responsibility of the village; of the work that is to be performed by the *gram panchayat* (e.g. express opinion on the budget of the *panchayat*, and its annual audit etc.); control over natural resources and control over institutions and their functionaries. With respect to responsibility of the village, the *gram sabha* will have lay down the principles for implementation of development schemes, identify families below poverty line, and controlling the implementation and monitoring of beneficiary-oriented schemes. The *gram sabha* also has the responsibility of ensuring equality of benefits in the implementation of various schemes and programmes.
- *Gram sabha* has three sources of income—donations, incomes from other sources, receipts from *panchayat nidhi*, funds under various schemes sponsored by the Central and the state government, and taxation. As a legal entity, the *gram sabha* has the option of imposing optional taxes and fees. At the same time, it has to levy and collect property tax, professional tax and tax on services provided to the village.
- Every *gram sabha* will ensure that there is an annual audit of its accounts.

Source: Madhya Pradesh Panchayat Raj & Gram Swaraj Adhiniyam, 2001.

organisations are active in the field of education, health, livelihood, poverty alleviation, environment and overall development sector. This group of organisations is working outside the government; at the same time, working towards welfare of different sections of society, taking the benefits of the government schemes and programmes to the beneficiaries and for improving governance. This section of organisations would be a potential player in improving new ideas and concepts of good governance, if their participation is ensured due to its mass-based work with footprints across all the districts, blocks and maximum number of villages. It would be exaggerating to expect to do all the work by these organisations which are a prime domain of state government. But yes, definitely one can use their services in increasing transparency and accountability of government's work through monitoring and evaluation.

9. Urbanisation

Urbanisation process in India had been slow, from the beginning of the 20th century, in 1901 to the new millennium census of 2001, i.e., in 100 years. Meanwhile, the total population of India trebled between 1947 and 2001 and population of urban areas have in the neighbourhood of 50 per cent of its total population by 2021. Various projections reveal that the urban areas will reach population worth 50 per cent of the total population in India. There are, however, some demographers who believe that actually the present urban population of India is near to 40 per cent and not 28 per cent. Madhya Pradesh contributed around 7.04 per cent to India's urban population in 2001. Only Maharashtra, UP, Tamil Nadu, AP and West Bengal were the five states that had more urban population than MP in 2001.

If we closely monitor the growth rates of 35 million plus towns, three of them fall in MP (Indore, Bhopal and Jabalpur. Gwalior and Ujjain are two towns that fall between 36th and 100th ranked towns of India). The growth rate of Bhopal and Indore towns is comparable to some of the fastest growing towns of India. Similarly, average annual exponential growth rate of Madhya Pradesh is better than that of India, confirming that the urban areas of MP are moving quite fast. See Table 5.6 for more details on growth rates and exponential growth rates of key 35 towns of India.

With rapid growth of urban areas, the problems, challenges and crises of towns are going to multiply in Madhya Pradesh and India. Great need of additional infrastructure that includes housing, roads, bridges, transport system, clean drinking water, sewage disposal, education, health, employment, electricity, parks, markets, malls, plazas etc., will be felt by these galloping towns. Investment and preparedness for addressing the paucity of these infrastructures through requisite investments, along with targeted programmes for the urban poor and slum dwellers shall be required.

TABLE 5.6

Growth of Population in Million Plus Cities as per 2001 Census 1981-2001

S. No.	City	Population in Million	Urban Agglomeration (Growth Rate %)		City Proper (Growth Rate %)	
			1981-1991	1991-2001	1981-1991	1991-2001
1	Greater Mumbai	16.43	33.7	29.9	20.4	20.0
2	Kolkata	13.20	19.90	19.9	6.6	4.10
3	Delhi	12.87	46.9	51.9	43.2	36.2
4	Chennai	6.56	26.4	18.5	28.9	9.70
5	Bangalore	5.70	41.3	37.8	7.4	61.3
6	Hyderabad	5.74	66.5	27.4	39.2	12.8
7	Ahmedabad	4.52	29.5	36.4	22.9	18.9
8	Pune	3.76	44.8	50.6	30.2	38.3
9	Surat	2.81	66.4*	85.1*	62.2*	62.3
10	Kanpur	2.71	23.8	32.5	25.8	35.00
11	Jaipur	2.32	49.6	53.1	49.2	59.4
12	Lucknow	2.24	65.7*	35.8	70.8*	36.3
13	Nagpur	2.12	36.4	27.6	33.2	26.2
14	Patna	1.69	19.7	55.3	18.1	33.4
15	Indore	1.51	33.7	47.8	31.6	46.3
16	Vadodara	1.49	44.0	32.4	40.4	26.6
17	Bhopal	1.45	58.4*	36.9	58.3*	34.9
18	Coimbatore	1.46	19.6	31.4	15.9	13.1
19	Ludhiana	1.39	71.8*	33.7	71.7*	33.7
20	Kochi	1.35	38.3	18.8	13.5	2.40
21	Visakhapatnam	1.34	75.1	25.7	33.00	28.9
22	Agra	1.33	26.9	39.4	28.5	29.2
23	Varanasi	1.20	29.3	17.5	29.6	18.4
24	Madurai	1.20	19.7	10.00	14.6	-1.9
25	Meerut	1.16	56.5*	37.4	67.9*	42.6
26	Nasik	1.15	63.7*	58.8	80.6*	63.9
27	Jabalpur	1.09	17.4	25.7	20.8	22.00
28	Jamshedpur	1.10	21.9	32.9	5.10	23.8
29	Asansol	1.06	52.00	42.7	42.9	85.4
30	Dhanbad	1.06	18.9	30.5	26.2	31.1
31	Faridabad	1.05	86.7*	70.8*	86.7*	70.8
32	Allahabad	1.04	29.9	24.3	28.7	24.9
33	Amritsar	1.00	19.9	42.6	19.2	27.3
34	Vijayawada	1.03	37.8	19.6	32.9	17.6
35	Rajkot	1.00	47.1	53.1	25.7	72.8

Note: * Cities that have >50 per cent decadal growth for at least two of the previous three decades.

Source: Census of India, 2001.

It is often argued that the states trapped in the vicious cycle of poverty report higher demographic growth. The logic is that the correlates of poverty that leads to high fertility and demographic growth like low levels of literacy, poor medical facilities and poor state of social and economic infrastructure is arguably as extant in Madhya Pradesh, as in any other poor state of India. Probably, the conundrum of much higher urban population growth rates that soar above the national average could be explained away with this logic. Importantly, however, migration factor has also played an important role in pushing up the urban demographic growth in MP.

10. Migration

This sub-section embarks upon unravelling the phenomenon of people's movement from their native households, either from rural to rural (RR), rural to urban (RU) or urban to urban (UU). These people in most cases emigrate either because of availability of better opportunities in their target new destinations or they respond to disasters like floods, earthquakes, famines, etc. Meanwhile, there are some very poor or chronic poor rural people who migrate for about six to eight months, every year. This movement of people may be either for only two months or eight months or for a couple of years, which certainly jeopardises their well-being. Owing to their departure from native environment, they face deprivation and misery related to livelihood, health, education, housing and transport, lack of communication with native habitations and absence of support groups in urban areas and so on. A detailed Census of India study, conducted every decade on interstate migration generates migration tables.

Table 5.7 gives the number of out-migrants for Madhya Pradesh; there were about 15 lakh of out-migrants during the year 2000-01. People from Madhya Pradesh mainly migrate to the three states of Maharashtra, UP and Rajasthan in large numbers, i.e., 5.4 lakh, 4.7 lakh and 2.7 lakh respectively. Whereas Gujarat received relatively low number of migrants from MP. These four states and Chhattisgarh share MP's boundaries. Besides, Orissa got 60,000 migrants from MP. Greater than 10,000 migrants from MP went to Bihar, Punjab, AP, West Bengal and Haryana, each. The three southern states of Kerala, Karnataka and Tamil Nadu received negligible number of migrants from MP, in 2001. As for the in-migration of people to MP from other states (and a few foreigners) are concerned, about 23 lakh people migrated to MP from various states in 2001.

TABLE 5.7

Migration from Madhya Pradesh to Other States, 2001

Maharashtra	5.40 lakh
Uttar Pradesh	4.70 lakh
Rajasthan	2.70 lakh
Gujarat	0.62 lakh
Orissa	0.60 lakh
Bihar	0.23 lakh
Punjab	0.20 lakh
Andhra Pradesh	0.19 lakh
Haryana	0.14 lakh
West Bengal	0.13 lakh
Tamil Nadu	0.08 lakh
Karnataka	0.04 lakh
Kerala	0.01 lakh
Total	15.04 lakh

Source: Census of India, 2001.

Madhya Pradesh shows the unique characteristic of low per capita income and economic growth, yet it gets more in-migrants than the out-migrants. This is partly because of the investment in heavy industries (Bhopal, Indore, Dewas, Jabalpur, Katni and Gwalior) in MP, during the post-Independence phase. Skill requirement for employment in the upcoming industries like steel, heavy electrical, heavy engineering was high and MP did not have adequate number of capable persons to get employed in these industries. Hence, a big rush of in-migration with industrialisation was observed in the state.

The low rate of out-migration for a backward state of Madhya Pradesh has important implications in the context of human development. It reflects that the poor in the state are not in a position to shift out to other states in search of livelihood despite serious socio-economic deprivations. This should be a matter of alarm. Unfortunately, while plight of migrants at the place of destination has received some attention of researchers and policy makers, the plight of people who are forced to stay back, due to socio-political factors, has not been given much concern. Increase in urban poverty indicates that the urban centres seem to have absorbed a segment of rural poor through the window of migration or emergence of new towns, relieving the pressure of poverty in rural areas.

11. Social Inequality

Around 35 per cent of the state's population comprised of marginalised sections of SCs (15.2 per cent) and STs (20.3 per cent). The state has 8 predominantly tribal districts. *Adivasi* or ST population in Madhya Pradesh are extremely vulnerable in the development process, primarily because of their poverty, illiteracy, assetlessness and location in environmentally sensitive areas. Similarly, *Dalit* community in the state is also lagging in reaping the benefits of development compared to the general population. Social discrimination against this marginalised community is a curse in MP. The process of their integration with the mainstream economy and socio-political system has been slow also due to their geographical isolation. In the post-Independence, period, they had to bear the brunt of the problems of displacement as their land were taken away or encroached upon for mining and industrial activities or construction of dams, roads or other infrastructural facilities, without proper rehabilitation measures. Despite the high profile negotiations, resettlement of the people in villages coming under submergence due to Narmada dam has not been resolved satisfactorily.

The state government has tried to address the problems of these marginalised sections of population through Tribal Sub-Plan (TSP) and Scheduled Caste Sub-Plans (SCSP). Despite the positive impact of this and several other targeted programmes of the Central and state government, one would note that the gaps in terms of various socio-economic indicators between ST and general population has not declined significantly over the past couple of decades.

12. Government Initiatives for Improving Governance

12.1 Maintaining Law and Order

Some of the steps which the state government has proposed to maintain law and order situation in the state are as follows:

- Constitution of a high-level committee headed by the chief minister for constant monitoring of law and order.
- New Police Act soon.
- All the police control rooms in the state to be strengthened.
- Automatic weapons, bullet proof jackets, helmets etc., will be made available at the control rooms of all the major cities in the state.
- Armed vehicles will be available in Bhopal, Indore, Gwalior and Jabalpur.
- Necessary equipment will be provided to make the police communication system effective.
- Security will be beefed up at places of historical, religious and archaeological importance.
- Separate investigating agencies will be constituted for incidents related to underworld and terrorism. Act will be promulgated for giving information about tenants, house servants and customers and employees of hotels and Internet cafes compulsory.
- Special measures will be undertaken for checking terrorism, and plan in this connection will be sent to the Union government.
- Every superintendent of police will maintain his daily routine. SPs will chalk out plans for curbing criminal tendency.
- Training programmes will be organised for police personnel at all the levels.
- Anti-Terror Squad (ATS) has been constituted in the state. Constitution of a parallel force can also be contemplated if need be.
- Efforts will be undertaken to increase the strength of police force every year. Necessary budgetary allocations will be made to provide better arms and facilities to the police force.
- Priority will be given to welfare programmes of the police force. Necessary instructions will be given by the state government in this connection.
- Public hearing would be organised in police stations and collectorate where common people can voice his/her complaints and inconvenience without any fear to the highest authority and seek for easy sorting out of cases and demand for justice.

12.2 Establishment of School of Good Governance and Policy Analysis (SGPA)

SGPA has been set up by the government of Madhya Pradesh to work as a think tank in the context of prevailing trends in global and local governance and also to analyse government policies and their effects. The school works as an autonomous organisation of GoMP. The chief minister of the state is the chairman of the governing body. The school is working towards providing a platform for various organisations and welfare groups to make administration people-oriented. It will also provide technical guidance and services to local bodies and organisations of national and international standard for research in their programme and administrative reforms.

12.2.1 Steps for Moving Towards Cherished Goals of Good Governance

- Creating space and motivation for innovations and their applications in governance by functionaries at different levels.
- Facilitating an environment of change for adoption/adaptation of best practices for their replication and upscaling.
- Measuring impact and monitoring quality of delivery systems for continuous improvement.
- Creating public value propositions that command legitimacy and support from a variety of stakeholders.
- Strategies for effective governance in rural, less developed and distant dwellings.
- Strategies for development of public-private partnerships (PPP).
- In-built systems for capacity building to deal with emerging challenges.
- Community empowerment and participation in governance.

12.3 e-Governance

IT policy of the state government has ushered the following objectives to take the state into 21st century.

- Improve the life of the common man by leveraging the strengths of e-Governance.
- Attracting investment in the sector so that the educated youth is able to contribute to the development of the state.
- Create a pool of highly skilled professionals who are at par with the best in the country.
- Transforming resource-based economy to knowledge-based economy.

12.3.1 e-Governance Initiatives of Madhya Pradesh Government

Madhya Pradesh in the last two to three years has implemented several e-Governance projects. The state's IT policy emphasises induction of IT in all walks of government functioning with the focus on masses and aims to leverage IT for transparency and better governance. The following are the major projects that have been undertaken:

1. *Commercial Tax Department:* The department is the largest revenue-earning department of the government of Madhya Pradesh. A comprehensive computerisation project which offers instant information access to the dealers and also offers major processes of the department 'online' has been implemented. The department's internal functions such as payroll, pension related activities, personal information processing has also been made online.

2. *Treasury and Accounts:* Integrated Treasuries Computerisation Project (ITCP) is a major e-Governance initiative by Government of Madhya Pradesh. Its coverage extends to the entire state (229 locations), through 53 district treasuries, 159 sub-treasuries, serving almost 8000 drawing and disbursing officers belonging to all departments of the state government. The project won the Golden Icon Award for exemplary horizontal transfer of ICT-based best practice for the year 2007.

3. *Land Records:* The state of Madhya Pradesh has prepared a database of land records in the country. In the state, the land records of all revenue villages have been computerised, i.e., the textual data of land records are 100 per cent converted into electronic form. Computerised land records are updated on regular basis with the facility of automatic weekly back-up. Thirty-five million *khasra* (plot/survey) comprising 11 million landowners have been computerised.

4. *Directorate of Technical Education:* Directorate of Technical Education, Madhya Pradesh acts as the co-ordinating agency between government, industry and institutions, and to advice and assist the government in the all round development of technical education. Letter entry system, pay bill system, admission system, gradation system, court system, management information system (MIS) and budget system work towards the e-Governance initiative.

5. *Transport Department:* This project aims to computerise transport department's activities by issuing smart cards for driving licences and vehicle registration. The project was implemented on BOO (Build Own Operate) basis by a service provider. MP is a pioneer state in usage of IT for better service delivery on PPP model. Presently, all activities of RTO offices are computerised. Information of vehicles registered in MP is available via SMS and Internet. A citizen-friendly site *www.mptransport.org* has been created for that matter.

6. *Mandi Board:* The project is modeled on PPP basis. The project empowers the farmers with the latest

information on the rates, arrivals etc., in the neighbouring state/national *mandis*. This not only improved the effectiveness of trading in the *mandis* but also brought transparency in the *mandi* operations. It has received several e-Governance awards (Golden Icon, CSI, Development Gateway etc.).

7. *Urban Administration and Development Department:* In Madhya Pradesh, the following cities have taken initiatives in e-Governance and has resulted in improved public service delivery: Indore, Bhopal, Gwalior, Jabalpur, Khandwa, Ujjain, Raisen, Dabra and Balaghat.

8. *Krishinet:* Krishinet project is developed for strengthening/promotion of ICT at the state, district, agricultural block and grassroot level and departments for faster information exchange/dissemination.

9. *e-Tendering in Madhya Pradesh:* As part of its e-Governance plan for the state and as an effort to standardise the procurement process, the state government decided to implement an electronic tendering solution for use by all its departments/PSUs and authorised Madhya Pradesh Agency for Information Technology (MAP_IT) to select a suitable service provider for the implementation.

10. *Department of Registration and Stamps:* This department is responsible for the stamps and registration of various types of documents, mostly related to property transfer in the state.

11. *MPOnline:* The Government of Madhya Pradesh has developed its online citizen services portal by the joint venture of Government of Madhya Pradesh and TATA Consultancy Services Limited. MPOnline on the lines of the vision of GoMP, provides citizen services in the areas of health, education, agriculture, government services and business to the majority of masses in rural Madhya Pradesh.

12. *State's ICT Initiatives in Education:* The state strongly believes that information and communication technology can yield significant outcomes in improving the quality of education.

13. *Headstart—A Computer-aided Learning Programme for Students and Teachers:* Under the District Primary Education Programme, the state in the year 2000, initiated a computer-enabled education programme called "Headstart". The programme uses computer as a teaching-learning tool at elementary education level.

14. *Edusat—Connecting the Isolated:* Edusat—the satellite launched by Indian Space Research Organisation, Ahmedabad, is full of communication technology potentials in terms of provision of video/data broadcast using the Digital Video Broadcasting-Return Channel via Satellite (DVB-RCS) technology. The state strongly believes that the potential of Edusat should be utilised at the optimum level in the school education sector. In collaboration with IGNOU and ISRO, Initiative for Edusat supported elementary education programme was started on December 17, 2005. As of date, 700 schools in Sidhi district and 30 schools in Jabalpur district have been provided Receive Only Terminal (ROT) facilities. Based on the research findings, the programme shall be reviewed and modified accordingly.

15. *Common Services Center (CSC) Project:* The Government of India has formulated the National e-Governance Plan with the vision of providing all government services in an integrated manner at the doorstep of the citizen, at an affordable cost. The NeGP envisions a three-pillar model for delivery of "web-enabled anytime, anywhere access" to information and services in rural India. These are: Common Services Centers (CSCs), State Wide Area Networks (SWANs), National Data Bank/State Data Centers (SDCs). The CSC Scheme, as approved by the Government of India operates as the front-end delivery point. Madhya Pradesh has about 55,000 villages. A total of 9232 CSCs is being set by January 2009, one for every six villages spread over the entire 48 districts of the state.

16. *State Wide Area Network (SWAN) Project:* The Department of IT, Government of India has approved the project for the establishment of SWAN up to block level in MP at a cost of Rs.174.21 crore. The establishment of SWAN will be extremely helpful in providing reliable connectivity for various e-Governance applications of different departments. The project envisages connecting all block headquarters to the state capital through districts and commissions. MP State Electronics Development Corporation Ltd. has been designated as the implementing agency of the project. The first instalment of the grant has been received by MPSEDC.

17. *Appointment of CIOs, Creation of Websites by Departments & Training:* With the efforts of the IT department, presently, around 30 departments/agencies have appointed their Chief Information Officers (CIOs). This initiative is expected to contribute in having a nodal officer for IT activities in the department, making an IT plan of the department, and allocation of resources for the department. IT department is co-

ordinating with various departments to have their websites/portals for better delivery of information and services to citizens. The department also conducts seminars, workshops and organises training programmes to create awareness among senior officers of the government about IT, its uses and how IT can improve governance.

18. *National e-Governance Plan (NeGP):* The capacity gaps are identified in the capacity building roadmap and the amount of money required for sustaining these activities are elaborated in the detailed project report. MAP_IT has been identified as the State e-Governance Mission Team [SeMT] which shall act as a catalyst for e-Governance projects. It is also expected to play the role of a friend, philosopher and guide.

19. *National Informatics Centre (NIC):* NIC, Madhya Pradesh has played a big role in providing e-Governance solutions to the state. It provides state-of-the art networking solutions for the establishment of Internet/Intranet/Extranet and providing specialised services over specialised technologies such as LAN/WAN/wireless/VSAT/leased line/dialup etc. NIC, Madhya Pradesh is connected over 2x4 Mbps leased line with the headquarter (HQ) and 44 district locations are connected over 2 Mbps leased line with the state HQ.

20. *Video Conferencing:* Video conferencing services are operational since September 2004. NIC has established video conferencing studios at 48 district locations, secretariat, CM residence and state HQ. On an average, 35 video conferencing sessions are held per month and Madhya Pradesh is at the highest among all states in the utilisation of VC services. The utilisation of video conferencing services has also been registered in the Limca Book of Records.

21. *Mail Messaging, Internet and Virtual Private Network (VPN) Services:* NIC has provided approximately 5000 e-mail and 300 Internet accounts for various government officials. NICNET/Internet services have also been extended to various bhawans like MP Vidhan Sabha, *Mantralaya*, Satpura Bhawan, Academy of Administrations and Narmada Valley Development Authority over wireless.

22. *e-PDMS (Public Distribution Monitoring System) for Directorate of Food, Civil Supplies & Consumer Protection, Bhopal:* In order to strengthen the public distribution system, under Government of India notification for PDS (control), NIC, state unit Bhopal, has developed a computer-based system for Directorate of Food, Civil Supplies and Consumer Protection, MP.

23. *e-CCENAIS (Crop Cutting Experiments for National Agricultural Insurance Scheme):* National Agricultural Insurance Scheme (NAIS) was introduced in the country from the 1999-2000 *rabi* seasons, replacing the Comprehensive Crop Insurance Scheme (CCIS) which was in operation in the country since 1985.

24. *e-PROOFS (Electronic Processing of Firms & Societies) for Registrar, Firms and Societies, Bhopal, MP:* The system (e-PROOFS) deals with the computerisation of the registration process and other activities of societies and firms at the Registrar's office, MP.

25. *Agricultural Marketing Information System Network (AGMARKNET):* AGMARKNET caters to the availability of prompt and reliable market information about arrivals and prices of commodities which considerably improves the decision-making capability of the farmers and strengthens their bargaining power.

26. *PANCHLEKHA:* A Panchayat Raj Institution Accounting System Software (PRIASoft), designed, developed and implemented in most of the districts of Madhya Pradesh since 2005. The system is aimed at efficient management and monitoring of funds at *janpad panchayat, zilla panchayat* and state headquarters, and is empowering the administrators to monitor the fund receipt, availability and expenditure at all four-tier administrative set-up of PRIs.

27. *Result Processing System for Rajya Shiksha Kendra, Bhopal:* Designed and developed to computerise basic students' information, processing of results (for 5th and 8th class board examination), followed by subsequent dissemination of information on Internet and generation of analytical reports. It has been successfully implemented in 38 districts of Madhya Pradesh since September 2006.

28. *e-Gram Suvidha:* Implemented in collectorates/*zilla panchayats* of five districts (Chhatarpur, Bhopal, Mandla, Dhar and Damoh). e-Gram Suvidha is a geomatics-based decision support system towards creation and management of facilities at village level in rural areas. It covers about 20 facilities organised under 10 major sectors like education, health, communication and roads etc.

29. *Departmental Monitoring System in Mantralaya, MP:* It is the Intranet-based system which allows all the departments at *mantralaya*, MP to access the information pertaining to CM letters, CS references, cabinet decisions, CM announcements and other related information and update its status over the net. The information is retrieved by all the concerned for the monitoring purposes

such as G2G system, information retrieval, updation of the status and speedy disposal of matters.

30. *Computerisation of the Office of Chief Minister:* Implemented in office of chief minister, Government of MP. Lot of computerisation is done in the office of the chief minister. This includes development of softwares for keeping track of mail received from public and its representatives, monitoring of CM announcements and implementation of manifesto, maintenance of CM relief fund and petitions received during Jan Darshan Programme.

31. *Computerisation of the Office of Chief Secretary:* The office of the chief secretary (CS) being the office of head of administration deals with various important issues. The various softwares developed and implemented for the purpose of monitoring includes mail monitoring system, cabinet decision monitoring system and file monitoring system.

32. *PARAKH (Basic Services/Amenities Management System):* Government of Madhya Pradesh, recognising the fact that access to minimum level of social infrastructure facilities must be an integral part of a strategy for improving the quality of life of the people and for eradicating poverty, has introduced the Basic Services/Amenities Management System called PARAKH for improving the delivery of the basic services/ amenities in rural areas of the state. For this purpose, a computerised system for maintaining the basic services/ amenities is put into place.

33. *Web-based RuralSoft Monitoring System:* RuralSoft is a computerised web-based monitoring system for monthly progress of various developmental schemes of department of rural development, Government of Madhya Pradesh.

34. *WaterSoft (PHEMIS):* WaterSoft (PHEMIS) is a web-based solution for effective management of water resources, schemes/programmes (rural/urban water supply schemes), equipment information, water quality, contractor information, material and stores, total sanitation campaign, finance and works accounting.

12.4 Some of the Major Outcomes of Adopting e-Governance

- The citizens benefit because there is transparency, efficiency and integrity in their dealings with the government; furthermore, there is an easy access to information. There is a convergence of services and delivery mechanism for deserving beneficiaries and vulnerable groups and an extending outreach.
- The government benefits because it reduces redundancy and duplication. The processes of data collection, analysis and audit are made much easier. Decision-making gets expedited and there can be tremendous improvements in specialised areas such as criminal justice, transport etc.
- The business community benefits because e-Governance can become a catalyst and a channel for e-Business. Furthermore, a web-based government will enable tax paying online, reduce corruption and bending of laws.

12.5 Right to Information Act

The RTI Act was notified on June 15, 2005, and implemented in Madhya Pradesh from October 12, 2005. Samarthan, a Poorest Areas Civil Society (PACS) Programme partner, has prepared a status report on the RTI Act in Madhya Pradesh. The report highlights several implementation problems. Public information officers (PIOs), appointed in all departments to handle RTI queries, are often unaware of rules and guidelines such as the application of fees and what information is excluded from the Act.

Citizens complained that they were kept waiting for hours before their applications were accepted, did not get the information within the stipulated time-frame, and were provided irrelevant information.

Taking note of these lapses, the general administration department (GAD) of the Madhya Pradesh government issued detailed instructions regarding implementation of the Act. This resulted in some positive changes, although the status report claims that there are still areas that need to be addressed:

- GAD has mandated that updated manuals on self-disclosure be prepared and uploaded on departmental websites. However, the manuals have not been updated; in some cases, even the names of district-level PIOs and APIOs have not been put up.
- The list of district-level applications received and addressed was to be uploaded, but this has not happened.
- Although BPL applicants do not have to pay photocopying charges, they continue to do so.
- Applicants living at a distance from government offices should be able to pay fees through post offices.

The State Information Commission (SIC) has been quite active in Madhya Pradesh. In all, the SIC received 347 complaints and 155 appeals till March 2006.

Most of the complaints/appeals were from urban areas; only 91 of the total 502 complaints/appeals were from rural areas. Those who are relatively better-off economically, go in for second appeals. Most complaints/appeals were received by the revenue department (59 complaints and 29 appeals), followed by the education department (39 complaints and 17 appeals), and urban administration (27 complaints and 14 appeals).

12.5.1 Challenges in Promoting RTI Applications

There are several challenges in promoting the filing of applications under RTI in both rural and urban areas.

- There is a significantly low level of awareness amongst people about their rights under the RTI Act, particularly in rural areas.
- Vested interests or politically connected individuals often misuse the Act to settle personal scores or blackmail officials. What is needed is a strong mechanism to track application disposal rates and the use of RTI-obtained information in order to minimise misuse of the Act.
- The legal aid support system for the poor needs to be linked with RTI so that many of those opting for legal action can get free legal support. Information centres at the district or block level, with assistance from CSOs, could help citizens draft applications and withstand the pressure of *panchayats*, etc.
- PIOs at the district/block level have fixed timings or days for receiving applications. People who approach PIOs at other occasions waste time, money and energy.
- Even designated PIOs avoid giving receipts for applications.
- The cost of seeking information sometimes deters genuine poor citizens from exercising their right.

Hong Kong-based Political and Economic Risk Consultancy said in its report that Singapore's civil servants are the most efficient among their Asian peers while India stands on the other end with 'worst bureaucrats'. According to the business survey on 12 economies, India's bureaucracy was ranked the least efficient. The survey said, working with the civil servants was a "slow and most painful" process. They are a power centre in their own right at both national and state levels and are extremely resistant to reforms that affects them or the way they are going about their duties.

BOX 5.4

Good Governance in the Clutches of Red Tapism

We have seen one of the characteristics of good governance is responsiveness. It entails that the institutions and processes try to serve all stakeholders within a reasonable time-frame. Here is an example of apathy of the implementing agency on part of delivering social schemes to its citizens.

State government is running a scheme: Janashree Bima Yojana under which breadwinner of the BPL family would be able to avail free life insurance. The scheme is being run by the social justice department. Bhopal Municipal Corporation's programme cell is co-coordinating in urban wards.

- Number of centres established for Bhopal district - 17.
- Expected number of benficiaries - 1.70 lakh BPL card holders.
- Number of forms distributed – 34,000.
- Due date for the form submission would be revised and new date would be declared depending upon the availability of the forms.
- No idea when the new forms would release.

The above facts throw light on the prevalent red tapism in the government. Reasons for low form distribution were given as shortage of staff at the centres and less number of forms were distributed by the original department itself.

Source: *Nav Duniya*, 26/02/2009.

12.6 Road Map

1. In order to improve governance in the state, the government has to finish its work within the stipulated time limit and should attempt to work on pending as well as regular matter papers with minimum time lag. This should be applicable to all the officers irrespective of their ranks and positions.
2. Functioning of various state government departments needs a face lift in order to improve service delivery mechanism, particularly those departments that are implementing beneficiary-oriented schemes/programmes.
3. Many of the schemes are being run that have overlapping objectives. Such schemes/programmes should be clearly identified and should be

reworked as they are causing greater misuse of public money.

4. It was also observed that many more departments are involved in delivering to a particular sector despite their capabilities to do so, ultimately creating a huge mess. For example, in delivering to the education sector, there involves as many as 14 departments. Such anomalies should be removed in order to establish proper co-ordination and fixing specific responsibilities among them.

5. On paper, government schemes appear to be picture perfect, but when it gets actually implemented in the field, major impediments are observed like delays, corruption, ineffective co-ordination, apathy, improper monitoring and supervision and lack of proper planning. These inefficiencies should be overcome to serve the people in better ways.

6. On one hand, lack of resources is given as the most usual excuse for not serving the public facilities, but on the other hand, persistent quality of departments of non-spending is definitely an indication of inefficient system. As rightly pointed out by CAG in its reports, majority of the public serving departments have the habit of saving 30-40 per cent of the allotted amount annually and by virtue, it gets lapsed at the end of the year. This is definitely a cause of serious concern that has to be checked.

7. In order to improve the law and order situation in the state, old and outdated abiding laws should be reworked.

8. Regular monitoring and supervision along with frequent reviews would help to keep check on the situation.

9. e-Governance is one of the milestones the state government has achieved but it was observed that many a times, official websites of the different departments are not providing updated information. Thus, they lack both transparency in functioning and accountability of the system.

Chapter 6

Education in Madhya Pradesh

A Story of Success and Future Challenges

1. Introduction

Education is one of the important elements of social sector. Under the Constitution of India, the Directive Principle contained in Article 45 stipulated that the state shall endeavour to provide within a period of 10 years from the commencement of the Constitution, for free and compulsory education to the children until they complete the age of 14 years. Accordingly, the first national policy on education was formed in the year 1968 and education was primarily a state subject. In 1976, an amendment was done under Article 42 and education was transferred from state list to Central government list. As a result of which education became a concurrent subject. Thus, financial and administrative responsibilities are shared between state and Central government. However, the task of providing basic education for all, with concrete plans of actions, gained greater momentum only after the National Policy of Education (NPE), 1986 (revised in 1992). Although education is on the concurrent list of the Constitution, state government continues to play very important role particularly in the field of elementary education. At the same time, the greater responsibility of enforcing national education policy, monitoring educational requirement in regard to manpower development lies with the Union government. In the last 10 years, this state has impressive achievements in education to its credit. Strengthening its existing school system and innovating for reaching the unreached, increasing enrolment and ensuring widespread adult literacy in the state have led the effort. In view of the above, we present the scenario on development in education sector of Madhya Pradesh from the aspects of access, retention, dropouts, achievements and quality for different levels of education, namely, elementary education, secondary and higher education and technical education. The scenario provides the level of progress in education as revealed by measures of improvement in enrolment, reduction in dropout and improvement in pass percentage.

2. Status of Elementary Education

As the critical beginning of education starts from literacy, the only universally acceptable and appropriate measure is, therefore level of literacy, although that itself does not really tell us about the depth and quality of education levels of people. Nevertheless, it is an indicator that shows the current spread and reaches of basic ability in education and perhaps also shows the expanding and deepening of education in people. The 1991 Census revealed that in Madhya Pradesh, 56 per cent of the population was illiterate and 70 per cent women were not literate. Literacy rates were lowest for the scheduled castes and scheduled tribes i.e., 35.1 per cent and 21.5 per cent respectively. Access to schools was a problem, which had both physical and social implications. Other academic problems like no systematic plan for regular in-service teacher training, no effective system of academic supervision, higher student teacher ratio and no feedback and discussion existed at the school level. Education of the community had no lateral accountability to the local community. This was perhaps reflected in the dysfunctioning of the schools, teacher absenteeism and low quality of teaching.

It is significant that whereas the National Policy on Education of 1987 (revised 1993) stipulated universal elementary education (UEE), the state documents of policy and programme do not talk about UEE till about 1994. Prior to 1994, the state's action for education is evinced in discreet, dispersed, small incremental accretions of schools. The year 1994 marks the first ever efforts to address the goal of UEE, beginning with an increasingly growing concern of the state for universal primary education and by 2000, moving up to a concern for universal elementary education. It is significant that this concern sparks off with the emergence in the state of the elected *panchayats* dotting almost each village with a Panchayati Raj Institution (PRI).

3. Growth in Literacy Rate

The last 7 to 8 years have witnessed sustained action towards educating people in the state—making children and adults literate, bringing children to school and ensuring that they remain there, and that they receive quality and useful education. The progress in literacy has been very satisfactory. According to Census of India 2001, Madhya Pradesh has recorded an unprecedented jump of 20 per cent in literacy in the period of the nineties, from 45 per cent to 64 per cent.

3.1 Gender Differences in the Level of Literacy

- In the period 1991-2001, male literacy in Madhya Pradesh increased from 58.54 per cent in 1991 to 76.80 in 2001, indicating an increase of 18.26 per cent.

FIGURE 6.1

Growth in Male Literacy in MP

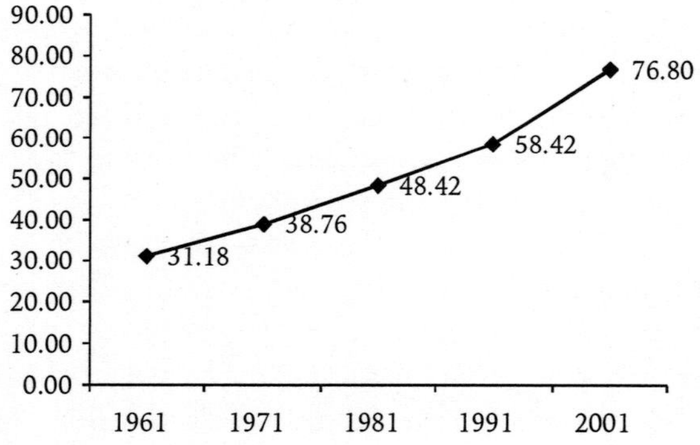

Source: Census, 2001.

FIGURE 6.2

Growth in Female Literacy in MP

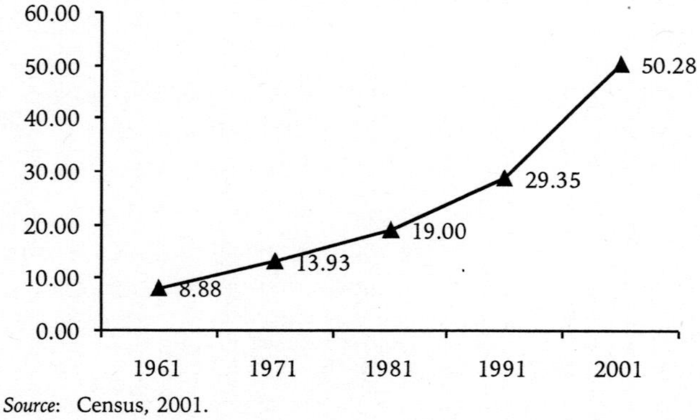

Source: Census, 2001.

- Madhya Pradesh has moved ahead of the national average of 75.85 in male literacy and is ahead of the two southern states of Andhra Pradesh (70.85 per cent) and Karnataka (76.29 per cent, marginally lower) in male literacy.
- In female literacy, Madhya Pradesh has condensed the growth of three decades into one decade. Taken as a combined state, the growth in female literacy has been 22.49 per cent in the decade of the nineties and reached to 50.28 per cent in 2001.
- Female literacy growth rate exceeds not only the male literacy growth rate but also the national average. At the national level, female literacy went up from 39.3 per cent in 1991 to 54.2 per cent in 2001, registering a 14.9 growth whereas in Madhya Pradesh the growth has been 22.5 (combined) and 20.93 (after division).
- For the first time, the gender gap between male literacy and female literacy started to decline in the decade of the nineties.

Following is the status of literacy pertaining to different categories in the state in 2001.

TABLE 6.1

Literacy Rates for Different Categories in MP

Category	*MP*	*National*
SC Female	43.28	41.90
SC Male	72.33	66.64
Total SC	58.57	54.69
ST Female	28.44	34.76
ST Male	53.55	59.17
Total ST	41.16	47.1

Source: Census of India, 2001.

It is evident from Table 6.1 that the literacy rates in SCs in MP for both male and female are far ahead of the national average but at the same time, the state is lagging behind the national figures for the literacy among the STs. Improvement in this section is necessitated in the light of fact that tribals constitute 20.3 per cent of the total population in the state.

4. Enrolment in Primary Schools

Mere literacy displayed by the figures of literate population does not show the education deficit if we are looking for at least eight years of schooling. However, the general enrolment numbers show that at the primary level, almost all children are now enrolled across the state and this is as true for girls as for boys.

TABLE 6.2

Gender-specific Gross Enrolment Rate

GER as per LSA 1996			GER as per LSA 2000-01			GER as per RSK 2007-08		
Boys	*Girls*	*Total*	*Boys*	*Girls*	*Total*	*Boys*	*Girls*	*Total*
81.5	70.7	76.5	97.9	94.3	96.2	102.27	102.39	102.33

Note: LSA - Lok Sampark Abhiyan.
Source: Rajya Shiksha Kendra, 2007-08.

TABLE 6.3

Age-wise Population, Enrolment and GER at Primary and Upper Primary Levels, 2007-08

Age Group	*Population (in lakhs)*			*Enrolment (in lakhs)*			*GER (in %)*		
	Boys	*Girls*	*Total*	*Boys*	*Girls*	*Total*	*Boys*	*Girls*	*Total*
5+ to 11 year	60.25	55.22	115.47	62.79	57.66	120.46	104.23	104.41	104.32
11 to 14 year	25.95	22.03	47.98	25.36	21.44	46.80	97.73	97.32	97.54
5+ to 14 year	86.20	77.25	163.45	88.15	79.10	167.25	102.27	102.39	102.33

Source: www.ssa.mp.gov.in

There has also been improvement in the gross enrolment ratio (GER). It has risen from 76.5 per cent in 1996 to 102.33 per cent in 2007-08. It means that most of the eligible children are enrolled in some school or the other. The GER of girls has risen from 70.7 per cent in 1996 to 102.39 per cent in 2007-08. The gap in GER of boys and girls has also narrowed from 25 in 1992 to 10.8 in 1996 to 3.6 in 2000-01, indicative of the fact that girls' enrolment has increased in the past eight years. In the year 2007-08, the gap in GER of boys and girls is miniscule.

In the state, presently 1.63 crore children are enrolled at the elementary level. Out of these 77.25 are girls, which is 46 per cent of the total enrolment. The increase in enrolment is a result of a series of mobilisation activities along with opening of Education Guarantee Scheme (EGS) schools in areas of deprived of education facility.

4.1 Status of Education based on Various Indicators

Table 6.4 describes the education status of elementary education in Madhya Pradesh based on selected indicators. Average attendance of the students in primary and upper primary levels is around 72 per cent which is quite good. Regularity of attendance is some thing which cannot be said with surety; however, field experience bears out that in the last three to four years, attendance in school has improved and the reasons for this are accessible schools within the habitation, an effective midday meal scheme, timely distribution of incentives such as textbooks, school uniforms to girls and increased number of local teachers.

TABLE 6.4

Status of Attendance, Retention Rate and Completion Rate (At Primary and Upper Primary Level, 2007-08)

Indicators	*Primary*			*Upper Primary*		
	Boys	*Girls*	*Total*	*Boys*	*Girls*	*Total*
Average attendance	73.4	71.6	72.6	73.7	71.7	72.8
Dropout rate	14.1	17.0	15.6	12.9	17.0	14.7
Retention rate	85.9	83.0	84.4	87.1	83.0	85.3
Overall repetition rate	16.5	16.8	16.7	16.9	16.9	16.9
Completion rate	66.2	62.3	64.3	62.7	60.4	61.5

Source: SSA, Madhya Pradesh, Bhopal.

Retention rate has shown improvement over the years if one goes by the statistics available. But the retention of girl students to upper classes is still found challenging, particularly in the rural areas.

But then the state is still struggling to cope with the slow change in dropout rate. At around 15 per cent in both primary and upper primary levels, it is definitely a cause of concern. Majority of out of school children belong to SC (17 per cent) and ST (43.5 per cent) categories. A survey undertaken in 2006 by SSA also indicates the growing number of children in urban poor areas who are out of school. As per latest statistics, still around 2 lakh (1.81 lakh) children in the state are out of school. Out of school children comprises the never enrolled and dropout children. Of the total out of school children, the never enrolled children are 66 per cent. To bring these children in to school is, of course, the immediate challenge for education sector.

TABLE 6.5

Out of School Children by Reason

Working in Fields, Agricultural Labour or Other Labour Work	*Sibling Care*	*Cattle Grazing*	*Weak Financial Condition*	*Lack of Educational Facilities (Middle School)*	*Social Belief due to which Parents are Reluctant to Educate Children*	*Handicapped or Prolonged Illness*	*School Environment not Conducive*	*Migration*
25.1	18.5	14.9	11.2	6.0	5.9	3.0	2.8	12.6

Source: Rajiv Gandhi Shiksha Mission, Madhya Pradesh, 2004-05.

Broad reasons for children being out of school, either as never enrolled or dropout are as follows:

- About 80 per cent girls remain out of school due to the following five reasons i.e., sibling care (24.6 per cent), engaged in economic activities (18.5 per cent), cattle grazing (13.6 per cent), weak financial condition (13.6 per cent) and migration (9.3 per cent).
- About 86 per cent boys remain out of school due to the following five reasons i.e., engaged in economic activities (21.6 per cent), cattle grazing (22.4 per cent), sibling care (15.6 per cent), migration (11.5 per cent) and weak financial condition (14.4 per cent).
- Other factors responsible for children being out of school are social belief and parental reluctance to send children to school, especially girls, lack of upper primary educational facilities (8.0 per cent), prolonged illness or handicap (2.4 per cent) and school environment being not conducive (1.6 per cent).
- Social belief and parental attitude is responsible for a higher girls' out of school (8.24 per cent) in comparison to boys (3.1 per cent). Similarly, migration affects the boys more (11.5 per cent) in comparison to girls (9.3 per cent).
- To work as child labour (25.1 per cent), along with weak financial condition (11.2 per cent) of the family are the major reasons for keeping the children away from schooling.
- Sibling care (18.5 per cent), cattle grazing (14.9 per cent), migration (12.6 per cent) are the other reasons why children are out of school.
- Besides, other factors like lack of educational facilities i.e., middle school (6.0 per cent), social belief of the parents to educate children (5.9 per cent), prolonged illness or handicapped (3.0 per cent) and non-conducive school environment (2.8 per cent) are responsible for children being out of school.

But once again, comparatively lower completion rate questions the quality of education being provided in the government schools. Although the transition rate from primary to upper primary level is 97 per cent, only 64 per cent of them complete the upper primary level. One has to be cautious here because state level average figures many a times hide the disparity among the districts. Given the performance of district on the basis of education development index (EDI), it indicates that the state has miles to go specifically taking the education in SC and ST dominating districts at par. With 10 predominantly tribal districts, the state has the additional challenge of multi-lingualism and appropriate materials for schools in these districts.

Pass percentage in board examinations presented in Table 6.6 provide scope for further improvement.

Annual Status of Education Report (ASER), 2007 indicates a significant progress in learning levels; however, at class III level the proportion of children who read level two texts is 18.7 per cent and 40 per cent children cannot write a simple dictated sentence. Although there is improvement from 2005-06 to 2006-2007, the same pace has not been maintained in 2007-2008. This clearly spelt out the need for consistent efforts that should be undertaken to improve upon student's learning achievements.

TABLE 6.6

Pass Percentage of Children in Class V and VIII Board Examination, 2006-07

Board Examination	*Boys*	*Girls*	*Total*	*"A" Grade Achievers*
V	81.8	81.2	81.5	22.5
VIII	71.2	71.9	71.5	17.3

Source: Rajiv Gandhi Shiksha Mission, Madhya Pradesh, 2004-05.

5. Education Incentives

To increase women/girls' literacy and retention in tribal areas of MP, the following schemes are being

TABLE 6.7

Enrolment in High and Higher Secondary School, 2006-07

Level	*Enrolment Total (in thousand)*					
	Total		*SC*		*ST*	
	Boys	*Girls*	*Boys*	*Girls*	*Boys*	*Girls*
High school (class 9 to 10)	1009	597	205	110	119	67
Higher secondary school (class 11 to 12)	579	344	85	47	64	31
Total (class 9 to 12)	1588	941	290	157	183	98

Source: Administrative Report, School Education Department, GoMP, 2007-08.

TABLE 6.8

Dropout Rates, 2006-07

Level	*Total*			*SC*			*ST*		
	Boys	*Girls*	*Total*	*Boys*	*Girls*	*Total*	*Boys*	*Girls*	*Total*
Class 9-12	31.98	27.96	30.55	41.27	35.61	39.37	39.16	37.80	38.72
Class 1-10	56.38	65.48	58.69	59.46	71.14	55.49	70.29	79.96	74.77
Class 1-12	70.93	78.54	74.91	81.28	84.71	82.49	83.04	89.69	84.04

Source: Administrative Report, School Education Department, GoMP, 2007-08.

implemented through the Department of School Education of the state.

- Free textbooks and uniform are provided at the primary school to SC, ST and OBC students.
- Free textbooks are also being distributed to the SC and ST students for middle and secondary level education.
- The girls studying in primary schools and belonging to the SC, ST and the OBC communities are being provided with free school uniform.
- Free textbooks are being distributed to girl students of general class studying in class I to class III.
- Free textbooks are being distributed to boy students of below poverty line studying in class I to class III.
- Throughout Madhya Pradesh, schooling facilities have been provided within one km for the primary level and within three kms for middle level education. For this, sufficiently large numbers of primary schools and schools under the Education Guarantee Scheme have been started. Also district primary education programmes (DPEP) are being implemented in 34 districts of the state.
- Midday meal scheme is being implemented in the primary schools in the state to improve the retention of the poor children.
- Various other schemes are in implementation under SSA, like opening of new schools, school complexes for girls, provision for boys and girls hostels and provision for special coaching classes throughout the state.

6. High and Higher Secondary School

Gender-specific enrolment by social groups separately for high school and higher secondary levels has been presented for the year 2006-07 in Table 6.7. It is an abysmally poor situation for Madhya Pradesh that out of its 163 lakh children enrolled in elementary education, hardly 15.33 per cent (25.29 lakh) are getting enrolled in high school and higher secondary schools. Further, in this group the proportionate share of SCs and STs is too low. This implies that the secondary education sector in the state needs fundamental reviving to retain the children in the schools. One of the major reasons for this is low access to secondary education in the state. It indicates that the students completing their elementary education do not have enough secondary education facilities to educate themselves further.

Dropout rate for secondary education is presented in Table 6.8 for the year 2006-07. Again on this front, the state is fairing very poorly as it is evident from the statistics given in the table. The table also reveals that the situation among both the deprived groups is poor but worse in case of scheduled tribes.

7. Basic Infrastructure

Eleventh Five Year Plan document of Madhya Pradesh states that the state is still lagging behind in terms of basic infrastructure and quality of education provided in the elementary and secondary government schools. This includes school building[1], drinking water facility, separate toilet facility to girl students[2], inadequate secondary education facility[3] and large gender and social equity gap in secondary education. The state is still struggling with the problems of higher pupil teacher ratio than recommended[4], proportionately less number of trained teachers[5], inadequate teaching and learning material, lower levels of learning achievement, low retention of girl students, considerable number of out of school children[6] and lower literacy rates in weaker sections, particularly SCs and STs.

8. School Facilities

The state has 52086 inhabited villages and 111780 habitations and it has a primary school within a distance of 1 km for every village and habitation. Distribution of school education facilities in the state is given in Table 6.9.

TABLE 6.9

Number of Schools in MP

Schools	*Numbers*
Primary schools	
a. Govt. schools	81550
b. Private unaided	15862
c. Private aided	933
Total primary schools	98345
Middle schools	
a. Govt. schools	24765
b. Private unaided	11936
c. Private aided	394
Total middle schools	37095
High schools	4688
Higher secondary schools	4456

Source: Administrative Report, School Education Department, GoMP, 2007-08.

As discussed previously, number-wise, the reach of primary schools is adequate today but the efforts should be made to increase the numbers of middle and secondary schools in the state. The average students per primary and middle school in MP in 2007-08 were 122 and 126 whereas the national figures were 180 and 185. This average in MP is even lower in tribal dominated districts such as Jhabua, Betul, Mandla, Dindori etc. Similarly, average students per high school and higher secondary schools is little higher. The state is confronted with the challenge of a large number of relatively small schools.

As evident from Table 6.11, nearly 15,000 primary and 2000 middle schools are single teacher schools in the state. The shortage of teachers in the school definitely has an adverse impact on the student's learning as the teacher is not being able to give adequate attention to the students.

TABLE 6.10

School in Madhya Pradesh, 2006-07

Type of School	*Schools*	*Average Students Per School*	*Pupil-Teacher Ratio*
Primary school	98345	122	44.2
Middle school	37095	126	31.3
High school	4688	342	41
Higher secondary school	4456	207	13

Source: Administrative Report, School Education Department, GoMP, 2007-08.

TABLE 6.11

Status of Single Teacher School

Level	*No. of Single Teacher School*
Primary	14593 (17.9%)
Upper primary	1996 (7.7%)

Source: SSA, Madhya Pradesh, Bhopal.

1. 2.3 per cent of primary schools and 48 per cent of the middle schools do not have their own school building (RGM, 2005-06).
2. Nearly 21 per cent of primary and 40 per cent of middle schools do not have drinking water facility and 45 per cent do not have toilet facility (RGM, 2005-06).
3. Out of 4688 high schools and 4456 higher secondary schools in the state, almost 50 per cent are in the hands of private players (Annual Administrative Report, Department of School Education, 2007-08).
4. According to 2005-06 statistics, primary pupil-teacher ratio is 48:1, as against the recommended ratio of 40:1 by Sarva Shiksha Abhiyan.
5. Thirty per cent teachers of primary and middle level are without any proper training. This comes to more than one lakh teachers in numbers (MPHDR, 2007).
6. According to RGM in 2006-07, approximately 3 lakh (2,96,979) remained out of school.

Table 6.12 gives a fair idea of the infrastructure available in the schools. Nearly 92 per cent schools avail the facility of drinking water, but still more than one-fourth of the schools in the state lack toilet facility. Similarly, less than half of the schools are having separate girls' toilet. Unavailability of separate toilet for girls in the schools is one of the major hindrances for girl children to continue with schooling. These gaps in basic amenities in schools need to be plugged first. The state has gone for financing of school buildings in a major way by taking loan from NABARD and converged with Total Sanitation Campaign, Rashtriya Sam Vikas Yojana and other rural development programmes to bridge the infrastructure gap.

TABLE 6.12

Infrastructure in Schools in 2007-08

	% Schools having Drinking Water Facility	*% Schools having Common Toilet*	*% Schools having Girls' Toilet*	*% Schools having Boundary Wall*
All schools (primary and middle)	91.95	71.62	46.98	46.23

Source: DISE report 2007-08.

In addition to the formal schools, primary education facilities have been started to ensure that the children who are out of the ambit of formal education, also get an opportunity to education that will ultimately lead to their mainstreaming in the formal education sector. The details and status of these alternative facilities are given in Table 6.13.

TABLE 6.13

Alternative School Facilities in MP, 2005-06

S. No.	*School Facilities*	*Numbers*	*Number of Beneficiaries*
1	Non-residential bridge courses	1244	25158
2	Residential bridge courses	337	24865
3	Madarsas under 'Modernisation of Madarsa' scheme	2603	167488
4	Sanskrit schools	595	10609
5	Human development centres for urban deprived children	5841	12,011
6	Transitional education centres (TEC) under INDUS project	200	10000

Source: Rajya Shiksha Kendra, Bhopal.

9. Higher Education

There are 9 universities, 18 national level institutions, 78 engineering colleges (including 5 university institutions, 4 government declared autonomous colleges, 1 self financing institution and 64 private institutions), 12 medical colleges, 6 dental colleges and 47 polytechnics. Renowned educational institutes and other apex institutions like Indian Institute of Management (IIM), Indore; Maulana Azad National Institute of Technology (MANIT), Bhopal; ABV Indian Institute of Information Technology and Management, Gwalior; Indian Institute of Forest Management, Bhopal; Indian Institute of Hotel Management, Bhopal; National Judicial Academy, Bhopal; National Law Institute, Bhopal; Central Institute of Agricultural Engineering, Bhopal; Indian Institute of Soil Science, Bhopal; National Technical Teacher's Training Institute (NTTTI), Bhopal; Central Farm Machinery Training and Testing Institute, Budni; Water and Land Management Institute (WALMI), Bhopal; PSS Central Institute of Vocational Education (PSSCIVE), Bhopal; Disaster Management Institute, Bhopal; Agriculture University, Jabalpur; Academy of Administration and Management, Bhopal; Central Institute of Plastic Engineering and Technology (CIPET), Bhopal; Centre for Advanced Technology (CAT), Indore are already functional in various parts of Madhya Pradesh.

UGC has identified educationally backward districts (EBDs), based on the GER (higher education)[7] which is below the national average of 12.4. Based on this indicator, 374 out of 593 districts in India are educationally backward. GER (higher education) for Madhya Pradesh is 8.92, indicating only 9 in 100 students in the age group 18-23 are enrolled in higher education. In Madhya Pradesh, around 87 per cent of the districts turned out to be educationally backward, that is 39 districts out of 45 districts (as per Census 2001). To categorise this further, 16 districts fall in Category B (GER 3.1-6.0), 18 districts fall in Category C (GER 6.1-9.0) and 5 districts fall in Category D (9.1-12.4). Educationally backward districts in MP includes 15 ST dominated districts (25 per cent and above) and 10 SC dominated districts (20 per cent and above). Thus, the overall performance of the state in higher education in general and among weaker sections particularly, is far below the national levels.

7. GER (higher education), is calculated as a proportion of all enrolled in post-higher secondary classes to total population in 18-23 age group.

TABLE 6.14

Details of Technical Education Institutions and Admission Capacity

Year	Progress of Govt./Aided/Private Engineering College		Progress of Govt./Aided/ Polytechnic College		Total Number of Courses Accreted by NBA		No. of Reserved Category Students Benefited Through Computer Training in Polytechnic College	Campus Selection in Govt./Aided/ Private Engineering College
	No.	Seat Capacity	No.	Seat Capacity	Engineering College	Polytechnic College		
2001-02	37	9636	43	6005	Nil	Nil	172	312
2002-03	49	12801	44	6035	6	Nil	577	474
2003-04	56	15350	44	6165	28	15	453	1548
2004-05	63	19810	44	6245	37	Nil	552	1945
2005-06	69	23794	44	8479	37	25	1086	1456

Source: Department of Technical Education and Training, GoMP, 2007-08.

TABLE 6.15

Recent Growth in Number of Technical Education Institutions and Admission Capacity in Different Courses

Sl. No.	Course	2006-07		2007-08		Growth Compared to Last Year			
		Institutions (number)	Admission Capacity (number)	Institutions (number)	Admission Capacity (number)	Institutions		Admission Capacity	
						No.	Per cent	No.	Per cent
1	2	3	4	5	6	7	8	9	10
1	Engineering and architecture	86	29433	124	38085	38	44.18	8652	29.39
2	Pharmacy (degree and diploma)	95	5409	107	6420	12	12.63	1011	18.69
3	MCA	67	3790	77	4720	10	14.92	930	24.54
4	MBA	63	4900	66	5060	3	4.76	180	3.67
5	Diploma (engineering syllabus)	44	9034	44	9785	0	0	691	7.65

Source: Department of Technical Education and Training, GoMP, 2007-08.

10. Technical Education

There has been a high increase in number of technical education institutions and admission capacity over years as may be seen from Table 6.14.

The scenario of technical education in regard to growth in recent number of technical education institutions and admission capacity during 2006-07 and 2007-08 is shown in Table 6.15.

In addition to these 5 courses, 2 more courses namely hotel management degree and hotel management diploma are also awarded. The number of institutions for the courses are 3 with admission capacity 180 and 1 with admission capacity 60 respectively. For extension of technical education, Dr. Ambedkar polytechnic institutions and Eklavya polytechnic institutions have been started for SC and ST students with full facilities.

11. Quality of Education

11.1 Learner Achievement

NCERT carried out learning achievement tests throughout the country in the year 2004-05. The tests were carried out in classes III, V, VII and VIIII. MP has not been included for class VII but results are available for rest of the three classes. In class III, the state's performance has been the worst among all states. The mean scores in this class were 36.94 per cent in maths and 45.21 per cent in languages compared to all-India figures of 58.25 and 63.12, respectively. In class V, mean scores in EVS, maths and language were 54.09, 49.03 and 58.25, respectively. Again these scores were worse than all-India average except the last category where it has been marginally better. In class VIII, the situation was no better. The mean scores in language, maths, science and social sciences were 50.63, 36.14, 41.71 and 43.50, respectively. Again except for science, the mean scores have been worse than all-India average. The more disturbing fact is that the sampled districts in this survey were all non-tribal districts whereas the state has a sizeable tribal population where reach of government services is even worse.

However, the ASER, 2006 mentions that the quality of education in MP has improved significantly within one year from 2005-06, after the implementation of "Learning to Read Programme" that was conducted in classes III-V in 45 districts of MP from October 2005 to January 2006. Simultaneously, the teachers of all the schools in classes VI to VIII undertook similar efforts. Subsequently, Pratham, an NGO organised a volunteer based camping from April to June 2006 that was aimed at classes II and I. While in 2005, the proportion of children studying in classes I and II, who could read letters, words or more was 57.31 per cent; it increased to 89.17 per cent in 2006. Similarly, while in 2005, the proportion of children studying in classes I and II, who could recognise numbers or more, was 48.59 per cent, it increased to 84.32 per cent in 2006. While in 2005 the proportion of children studying in classes III to V, who could read level I or more was 57.74 per cent, it increased to 78.91 per cent in 2006. Similarly, while in 2005, the proportion of children studying in classes III to V who could do subtraction or more, was 56.09 per cent, it increased to 81.56 per cent in 2006.

Thus, it is clear from the above statistics that MP has shown a big jump between 2005 and 2006 in change in the ability to read standard textbook of classes 1-8. But it shows little increase in 2007, indicating lack of energetic follow-up to further improve the situation.

Factors responsible for unsatisfactory academic achievements can be identified as being both academic and non-academic. Among the non-academic factors, the commonest is the absence of the teacher from the classroom mainly due to non-teaching tasks, which affects the time on transaction and completion of the course. It has also emerged that a large number of children do not have textbooks. Although the state has a commitment to provide free textbooks, the resources required to support this do not match the need. Among the academic factors, attention needs to be given to deploying qualified teachers for appropriate tasks, professional development of teachers, improving classroom processes and learner evaluation systems, and academic supervision.

11.2 Equity

The issue of equity is central to education both because the delivery of education should target the disadvantaged group traditionally deprived of the opportunities of education, and because education is understood as a process of empowerment. This involves a distributive aspect and a qualitative one. The distributive aspects, in terms of the spread of resources, have been measured through indicators of access and participation. Primary schools have been established within one kilometre of each habitation, with more than 50 per cent of the EGS schools coming up in tribal areas. This universal spread of primary education gives every child the opportunity to access basic education. In addition, there has been an improvement in the share of girls' participation in schools and the gender gap in children in and out of school has reduced. Lower enrolment and higher dropout rate in secondary schooling is observed particularly among the deprived sections of *dalits* and *adivasis*. As discussed in earlier sections, overall improvement in the education status of these groups is a real challenge before the state government as these groups together constitute nearly 35 per cent of the population.

While the state has made progress in terms of providing access and enrolment of children, however, concentrated efforts are required to improve the status of retention and learner achievement in the state. While the education goals are expected to be achieved under the broader framework of Sarva Shiksha Abhiyan (SSA), need specific programmes are also being implemented. These are for addressing the issue of equity through National Programme for Education of Girls at Elementary Level (NPEGEL), Kasturba Gandhi Balika Vidyalaya Yojana (KGBV) and Midday Meal (MDM) Programme.

11.3 Access for Children with Special Problems

While the problem of basic access has been addressed and many provisions and efforts have ensured that children do get access to schools we still have two basic problems, one dealing with children with disabilities and the other dealing with children with special abilities or those who require a different care pattern in education. There are some institutions in Madhya Pradesh who look after children with special needs, but overall the state primary education system does not have the wherewithal to make provisions for proper learning of all students with disabilities and special needs.

11.4 Access to Urban Deprived Children

In MP, 26 per cent population resides in urban areas. The concentration of urban deprived children is more in the 4 major cities—Bhopal, Indore, Gwalior and

Jabalpur. The urban deprived children are generally found in slum pockets and unauthorised areas. Capturing the out of school children is also a major problem as the habitation pattern undergoes changes and mere survey cannot capture the real reasons for the children being out of school. Thus, the survey needs to be accompanied by an in-depth study to identify the urban deprived children and the hurdles that come in the way of education of such children. Access is a problem for slum areas and unauthorised areas; private schools with low base of minimum facilities keep mushrooming. Also, the survey of slum pockets and unauthorised area is difficult and hampers identification of out of school children.

Detailed survey and study of the areas with slum concentration would help in planning area-specific interventions for such children. It is proposed that on the basis of the above assessment, provision for education and other factors will be made through human development centre. The concept of human development centre involves providing a place for such children where their educational and health related needs are given due attention. The human development centre will also provide guidance and counselling for the children, as most of these children do not have a conducive atmosphere in their homes, where they can talk about their hopes, aspirations and their future. The centre will also provide a platform for interaction between the children, their parents/guardian, counselors and community so that issues concerning these children can be discussed and addressed to.

12. Provisioning of Teachers

A suitable pupil teacher ratio is necessary for ensuring quality of learning. The system of multi-grade teaching affects the efficiency of teaching/learning, reduces time for transaction and specially for process of continuous evaluation alternative for diagnostic and remedial action. Comparison of data of enrolment and teachers of different years shows a rising trend in pupil-teacher ratio (PTR) because of increase in enrolment. At the primary level, the higher PTR shows that the recommended norm of SSA for PTR as 1:40 is not followed.

The state government has taken a number of decisions about teachers. First, the cadre of teachers appointed on a permanent basis on a government pay scale has been brought to an end. In its place, teachers are appointed on a contract basis. Teachers are employed by *panchayats* on a fixed contract, which has been pitched at a lower level than the old scale. This has been the corollary to the *panchayat*-based decentralisation. The eligibility criteria, in terms of minimum educational qualifications have been the same as for the earlier lot of teachers. There are three main types of teachers i.e., the traditional assistant teachers; teachers appointed by local bodies comprising of the *shiksha karmi* and *samvida shikshak* who are the contract teachers and the *gurujis* of EGS schools. The latter two types are appointed against schools and are not transferable. EGS *gurujis* are chosen by the local community and are local residents. The same minimum educational qualification is applicable to all but the recruitment procedure differs which affect their perception of themselves as teachers. The *shiksha karmis* and *samvida shikshaks* are accountable to block and district level *panchayat* bodies, while *gurujis* are accountable to the local community.

Fixing teacher remuneration at a lower level and devolving teacher recruitment to block *panchayats* led to a rapid provisioning of teachers. Sample data reveals that the new policy towards teachers has encouraged a greater number of women and persons from SC and ST and OBC groups to enlist as teachers. This can be attributed to three reasons; first, local recruitment, therefore, greater dissemination of information and awareness; second, recruitment against school and therefore non-transferability of service; and third, broader-based character of *panchayats* as recruitment agencies, therefore, greater sensitivity to issues of caste and gender.

12.1 Status of Professionally Trained Teachers

Another major blockade observed in imparting quality education is about low strength of professionally trained teachers. Resultantly, it impacts to a greater extent on the quality of output from untrained staff. As it is found many of the times that such para-teachers or guest teachers are trained enough to impart quality education to the children which has a direct impact not only on the learner's achievement but also influence the decision of parents to enrol their children in private schools rather than continuing in the government schools.

The variety of challenges posed in training are as follows:

- Differences of training requirement get aggravated, and that too, on a very large scale.
- The state government has not had a policy of pre-service training as a mandatory prerequisite for

TABLE 6.16

Per cent of Untrained Teachers

	Numbers & % of Untrained Teachers
Primary	82903 (48%)
Upper primary	27995 (38%)
Total	110898 (45%)

Source: Rajya Shiksha Kendra, Bhopal.

teacher recruitment. Therefore, quite a large number of teachers and specially *shiksha karmis*, contract teachers and *gurujis* do not have pre-service training. This creates a need for careful perspective planning for developing their capabilities.

- In addition, there are pedagogical challenges created by first generation learners and heterogeneous multi age-multi ability groups.

The strategy for training, therefore, has been sensitive to these complexities. Besides compulsory in-service trainings, the state government has also initiated the mode of distance learning to supplement teacher training. In the year 2006-07, nearly 45 per cent teachers at elementary level were untrained according to Rajya Shiksha Kendra, Bhopal. This constitutes around 48 per cent teachers at primary level and 38 per cent teachers at upper primary level who are professionally trained (Table 6.16).

Teacher training till recently tended to be highly centralised. Training modules were developed at the state level and run uniformly throughout all districts. Over the recent years, because of continuous decentralisation of programme management and focus on learner evaluation especially in terms of learning outcomes, the need for decentralised and contextualised responses to teacher training requirements was acknowledged. The state teacher training policy now has decentralised basic induction and in-service training at the district level. This policy has been put into effect in full scale for the year 2001-02. For the professional development of existing teachers, new contract teachers and *gurujis*, a decision has been taken by the state government to reserve the seats of D.Ed. and B.Ed. courses in government institutes for them. Along with this, an important development has been the safeguards built against the use of school teachers for any and every purpose by the state government in the Jan Shiksha Adhiniyam. This Act does not permit easy and anytime use of teachers for purposes of surveys, and other uses that state government often put teachers to, thereby affecting teaching and teacher attendance in schools. But the desired outcomes would be reached only if the Act is being implemented very stringently.

13. Curriculum

The curriculum of primary level was reviewed in 1994 to introduce elements of competency-based, activity-based and child-friendly pedagogy. Based on the new curriculum, the state has now introduced new teaching learning materials at the primary stage. Textbooks are self-contained and each textbook is divided into a number of lessons covering several teaching sessions, each of which comprises signposting to the specific competencies addressed, student material and teacher guidance in the form of footnotes. The textbooks have a shelf life of five years, after which they are revised in the light of experience, evaluation and changing ideas about teaching and learning. Review of the curriculum and materials for the upper primary is in process. The need for a rich pool of useful teaching learning materials as alternative learning sources beside the textbooks has been recognised.

The potential of information technology has been recognised to enrich educational processes. A programme for computer-enabled education has been introduced at the elementary school level to provide computer–enabled education to rural school children. Positioned in rural schools, "Headstart" aims at bridging the digital divide. A syllabus for Headstart has been developed. Educational softwares on Language (Hindi and English), Mathematics and Environment Sciences has been developed to help the teachers reinforce textual materials and encourage children through interactive learning. These multimedia rich lessons aim at strengthening learning competencies and expand the knowledge base of students and teachers and develop computer literacy along with it.

14. Learner's Evaluation

The state government followed the policy of non-detention till the upper primary level with only the district board examinations at the end of the Vth and VIIIth classes. This policy was changed in the academic year 2000-01 wherein an annual examination had to be cleared for promotion to the higher grade. The new policy of learner evaluation stipulates quarterly tests conducted internally with cumulative credits classifying achievements under grades. Diagnoses of assessment outcomes are expected to be followed up by remedial

BOX 6.1

Headstart: Improving Quality of Learning through Computer-enabled Education

Headstart is a programme for computer-enabled education introduced in selected government elementary schools in rural areas. Headstart aims at improving the quality of education by providing CD-based multimedia rich lessons (MMRL) for the use of children and teachers based on an analysis of their knowledge base and learning needs. These MMRLs aim at strengthening learning competencies and expand the knowledge base of students and teachers and develop computer literacy along with it.

The educational software is developed in-house by the Rajiv Gandhi Shiksha Mission based on research into curriculum, materials, teaching learning processes and knowledge levels leading to the identification of concepts that pose difficulties in transaction as well as areas for knowledge enrichment. The challenge is to use technology shift for a paradigm shift in pedagogy, by making it interactive, interrogative, self-learning and discovery through error, enquiry and reasoning. Since Headstart aims at quality improvement, it is not seen as a standalone intervention, but an integral part of a total teaching learning process within built online-offline activities to be evaluated for assessing the quality of learning outcomes. A syllabus for Headstart has been formulated to guide material development. Educational software on Language, Mathematics and Science has been produced and provided to schools. The distinctive features of Headstart are customised culturally. Educational softwares in Hindi, Mathematics, Science and English emphasise on learning through computers whereby computer literacy is an inevitable spin-off and integration with a total teaching learning process. Currently, Headstart is located in 648 elementary level government schools that also act as a school cluster resource centres (*Jan Shiksha Kendras*) where teachers meet once a month for academic sharing. It is poised to expand to 70 *Jan Shiksha Kendras* by 2003 and during the year 2005-06 it was again expanded in 494 JSKs of the state. As of date, 3212 JSKs have been developed as Headstart centres. Interactive Multi Media Rich Lessons (IMMRLs) and video films for students and teachers have been developed by *Rajya Shiksha Kendra* to support teaching-learning process in classrooms. The programme, appreciated by MHRD, has received national acclaim and is perhaps the largest computer-enabled education programme in India. During the year 2006-07, the programme will be expanded under the innovations head. Provision has been made for equipments, furniture, electrification and renovation of existing room for new Headstart. For the Headstart already functional, provision has been made for recurring expenditures like insurance, annual maintenance contract and contingency. The Headstart JSKs will be reallocated, so that problems associated with power supplies can be addressed to.

Some 4000 teachers have been trained on the technical and academic aspects of Headstart. A Headstart unit includes 3 computers, 1 printer, 3 UPS and ancillaries and costs about Rs. 0.14 million.

Source: Rajya Shiksha Kendra, GoMP, Bhopal.

action. This is to be done at all levels starting from school to *jan shiksha kendras* (JSKs), block, district and state level to evolve clear methods to provide academic support to the school. Difficulties captured through this learner evaluation analysis are expected to enable the teachers to focus on problem areas so that remedial action can be taken at the school level. Periodic external evaluation is planned in order to create a more detailed understanding of the factors that promote quality of learning. This is expected to enable the teacher to undertake remedial action for low achievements.

Table 6.6 earlier revealed that in the academic year 2006-07, pass percentage of children in the Vth board and VIIIth board examination is 81.5 and 71.5 respectively. However, proportion of "A" grade achiever is considerably low, 22.5 per cent in Vth board examination and just 17.3 per cent in VIIIth board examination.

15. Decentralisation of Academic Support

To strengthen the academic support system, there are 236 block resource centres (*Janpad Shiksha Kendra*) at the block level and 4325 cluster resource centres (*Jan Shiksha Kendra*) located within primary or middle schools and serving groups of 10-15 schools. The JSK has an academic coordinator, *jan shikshak,* who is a senior teacher. The *jan shikshak* is expected to visit the schools for purpose of academic monitoring and facilitates teacher discussions at monthly JSK meetings. The JSKs have the potential to grow as peer support hubs at levels closer to the school context.

15.1 Restructuring of Academic Support Institutions

Restructuring of academic support institutions has been acknowledged as a key area of concern and the state has initiated review of the academic requirements of key institutions. The state government has recently undertaken professional reorganisation of academic support institutions (State Council of Educational Research and Training and District Institutes of Education and Training) seeking to restructure these institutions on the following premises to create the necessary pre-conditions of quality support.

- Clear delineation of academic criteria comprising knowledge specialisation, academic qualifications, school experience and evidence of professional development for the purpose of staffing.

- Rotational placement between academic support institutions and school to ensure mutual enrichment of theory and practice.
- Emphasis on subject faculty structure to ensure that core curricular inputs are designed and implemented by competent professionals.

While technical and financial support from the state to the district level (DIETs) will continue, district level academic support institutions are to be made laterally accountable to districts for management purposes. DIETs will be responsible for the academic planning of their districts, ensuring its implementation and quality assessment.

15.2 School Management

School management has been decentralised to the district and sub-district levels. Recognising the need to strengthen the school as a unit, the Parents Teacher Association (PTA) and the Village Education Committee (VEC) have been given powers to decide on issues that impinge on the daily functioning of the school, such as school timing, local holidays, monitoring the regular functioning of the school. Teachers are now expected to be accountable to the local PTA and the VEC. This is expected to make the school management responsive to the needs of the children.

Emphasis has been given to each school to develop its own development plan with participation of parents. This would then be the basis of the village education planned upward to get integrated into a district education plan. Teachers are expected to help in developing village education registers to record and track each child's movement through school.

Decentralisation of school management and the policy to make it accountable to the local structures such as PTA, VEC and *panchayats* is expected to help in enabling school management to orient itself to the educational needs of the children. However, the process of institutionalising these lateral relationships is new and needs to be firmly grounded and strengthened for it to yield expected results that can become effective indicators of the transition of school managed as end–links of a bureaucratic machinery to becoming community schools locally managed with sufficient autonomy, such as is evident in relatively greater measure in the state's education guarantee scheme (EGS) schools. In the EGS schools, the local community chooses the teacher, gets a grant from the state government to run its school and forms a PTA that manages the school completely, also academic support coming in from the *jan shiksha kendra*.

BOX 6.2

Jan Shiksha Adhiniyam : An Act for Creating Public Accountability for Quality

MP Jan Shiksha Adhiniyam, 2002 is shaped by the vision of education as a collaborative process of the teachers, learners and the local community and the role of the government as facilitating this process towards the twin goals of equity and quality. The Act recognises the right of every child to basic education and seeks to remove impediments to access and participation in schools both by improving delivery as well as by creating social pressure. Parental responsibility for compulsory education upto age 14 is enforceable by *gram sabha*. Strengthening decentralisation, the Act lays down clearly the roles and responsibilities of key agencies: parents, teachers, local bodies and government. A crucial role is assigned to the PTA to be set up for every school.

The aim is to foster processes that help school emerge as a strong unit accountable to the local community of parents, with all other structures performing the role of school support institutions. Perceiving academic and administrative functions as constitutive of educational management, structural convergence has been effected at all levels of support institution for enabling holistic planning for qualitative learning outcomes.

Human resource support has been enlisted at school-level through voluntary teachers (retired) or *shiksha bandhu*. Incentive framework for teachers and students has been stipulated. Teachers are not to be normally deployed for non-teaching tasks. Private sector has been encouraged. No prior permission required to open schools up to middle level.

To make planning responsive to the local educational needs, a Jan Shiksha Yojana emanating from the PTA level is envisaged. Educational funds at the school, district and state level designated as *shala, zilla* and *rajya shiksha kosh* are to be set up for enabling mobilisation of additional resources. Public education report (*Jan Shiksha Prativedan*) will be presented on the status of education, specially learning outcomes, every quarter to the PTA and to the district government and annually to the legislative assembly, constituency-wise. These reports are expected to feed back into the Jan Shiksha Yojana for incremental improvement; thereby creating an organic relationship between planning and evaluation, placing their outcomes in public space for reinforcing people's right and the state's responsibility for better quality education.

Source: Jan Shiksha Adhiniyam, GoMP, 2003.

15.3 Institutional Restructuring

Institutional restructuring, which is the most critical premise of educational reform, is being affected through internal rationalisation of resources and does not require any additional financial support. In fact, it has led to a better utilisation of existing resources.

16. Budget

As government policies and programmes get fully reflected in the budget, we present an overview of quantum of fund being invested in education sector by the state and the Central government based on time series analysis of both outcome indicators of education and budgetary performance. It enables us to estimate the magnitude of concrete efforts to be put in so as to achieve the set targets committed on various national and international platforms and in the Five Year Plans of the state. Going by state government classification, state expenditure on education sector is around 11-12 per cent of the total expenditure. Large chunk of this gets spent on salaries. But besides the budget flowing through the state budgets, there is also an amount which is bypassing the state budget and does not appear in the state budget like funds of SSA and the UGC funds to colleges. In the next section, we attempted to give a comprehensive picture of investment in education from all sources possibly. The investment in education comprises three kinds, namely, state components, Central component that gets rooted through state budget and Central component of Centrally sponsored schemes which is bypassing the state budget that does not appear in the state budget.

16.1 State Expenditure, State and Centre Combined Expenditure on Education as Percentage of GSDP

In 1960, Kothari Commission recommended 6 per cent of GDP for spending on education, but even after more than 40 years the norm has not been achieved, taking together the state and Central government expenditure. Under the common minimum programme (CMP) of UPA government, Wada Na Todo Abhiyan was initiated in 2006 which emphasised on 9 per cent of GDP to be spent on education (6 per cent) and health (3 per cent) through the children's campaign "Nine is Mine". However, state and Centre are together spending 3.77 per cent of GSDP on education.

Table 6.17 reveals that state expenditure on education as percentage of GSDP is showing an increase from 2.93 per cent in 2001-02 to 3.55 per cent in 2007-08, except in the year 2003-04 where there was a dip to 2.78 per cent, the lowest in eight years. Also, it is clear that addition of Central funding bypassing the state budget does not yield much difference in percentage share to GSDP in 2007-08 RE except in years 2005-06 and 2006-07. Thus, there is a room for the government to increase its allocation to education sector.

TABLE 6.17

Expenditure on Education through State Budget and by Both State and Centre as a % of GSDP

Year	*State's Share in GSDP (%)*	*State & Centre Combined Share in GSDP (%)*
2001-02	2.93	2.93
2002-03	3.51	3.63
2003-04	2.78	3.07
2004-05	3.30	3.79
2005-06	3.45	4.17
2006-07	3.40	4.37
2007-08 RE	3.55	3.77

Source: Education Sector Analysis using Budget as a tool, Sanket Development Group, 2008.

16.2 State Expenditure on Education as Percentage of Social Services

In the total state budget, expenditure on social sector share is comprised of 30 per cent. Within the social sector, education is one of the important sub-sectors attracting more than 50 per cent of the social sector funding compared to its other counterparts.

TABLE 6.18

Share of Expenditure on Education Sub-sector to Expenditure on Social Sector

Year	*% Share in Social Sector*
2001-02	49.8
2002-03	50.4
2003-04	49.4
2004-05	58.2
2005-06	55.1
2006-07	52.3
2007-08 RE	49.9
2008-09 BE	51.3

Source: State Budget Books, GoMP, various years.

16.3 Total Investment by Government in Education Sector, MP (Through and Bypassing the State Budget)

There is direct funding from Central government in the account of a nodal agency for centrally sponsored schemes such as SSA, NPEGEL, KGBV etc. In MP, Rajiv Gandhi Mission (RGM) is the nodal agency in education sector. Table 6.19 indicates the total investment being done in education sector which includes expenditure incurred by both the state and the Central government taken together but excludes the UGC grant that goes directly to the colleges for higher education, bypassing the state budget.

TABLE 6.19

Total Investment by Both State and Centre in Education, MP

(Figs. in Rs. Crore)

Year	*BE*	*RE*	*AC*
2001-02	2869	3331	2543
2002-03	3625	3431	3154
2003-04	4356	3709	3155
2004-05	4347	4194	4071
2005-06	5027	4860	4854
2006-07	5724	5439	5598
2007-08 RE	6240	5363	

Source: State Budget Books, GoMP, various years.

The table reveals that:

1. Investment in education sector has been steadily rising in budget estimates, revised estimates and accounts. Increasing investment in education sector is a positive sign as it is one of the important social sectors.
2. Budget estimates for education has gone up by 2.15 times from Rs. 2869 crore in 2001-02 to Rs. 6240 crore in 2007-08.
3. Revised estimates too has gone up by 1.61 times from Rs. 3331 crore in 2001-02 to Rs. 5363 crore in 2007-08.
4. Although actual expenditure has more than doubled since 2001-02 to 2006-07 to Rs. 5598 crore, but the actual expenditure has always been less than what was budgeted for. This shows the tendency of under-spending in the initial years from 2001-02 to 2003-04. But thereafter, the situation has improved. Year 2003-04 was particularly worst where around Rs. 10 crore were less spent.

16.4 Proportionate Share of State and Centre Expenditure on Education

Inter-temporal changes in the share of expenditure on education for state and Centre component presented in Table 6.20 reveals that central funding has grown up steadily from 6.8 per cent in 2001-02 to the highest of 29.4 per cent in 2006-07. There is a need to look at how best these investments are getting translated into outcomes.

TABLE 6.20

Per cent Share of State Component and Centre Component on Education

Year	*State Component*	*Centre Component*
2001-02	93.2	6.8
2002-03	89.1	10.9
2003-04	83.1	16.9
2004-05	80.2	19.8
2005-06	77.6	22.4
2006-07	70.6	29.4

Source: Education Sector Analysis using Budget as a tool, Sanket Development Group, 2008.

16.5 Investment in Education by State Government and Central Governments—Through and Bypassing the State Budget

Table 6.19 on investment in education by state and Central government—through and bypassing the state budget reveals that over the years, the actual total investment in the education has been doubled and in 2006-07 is to the tune of Rs. 5598 crore and the quantum of Central component which is bypassing the state budget has increased over the years. In 2006-07, the amount bypassing the state was to the tune of 22.13 per cent of the total expenditure on education.

16.6 Intra-sectoral Investment in Education

Inter-sectoral changes in different levels of education as percentage of total expenditure presented in Table 6.21 reveal that:

1. Elementary education attracts maximum investment ranging from 52 to 64 per cent from 2001-02 through 2008-09. Maximum expenditure was in the year 2006-07 because of large chunk of SSA amounting to Rs. 1140 crore.
2. Expenditure on secondary education has increased from 9 per cent to 19 per cent but needs attention compared to elementary education.
3. Over the years, expenditure on university and higher education has been reduced and expenditure on technical education is a very small component of education sector owing greater participation from private players.

TABLE 6.21

Intra-sectoral Investments in Education

Year	Elementary Education	Secondary Education	University and Higher Education	Technical Education	Others
2001-02	52	9	14	3	22
2002-03	53	12	13	3	19
2003-04	59	9	11	3	18
2004-05	56	10	11	3	21
2005-06	60	9	9	3	19
2006-07	64	13	9	2	12
2007-08 RE	54	17	11	3	15
2008-09 BE	54	19	11	3	12

Source: Education Sector Analysis using Budget as a tool, Sanket Development Group, 2008.

Reducing administrative expenditure is long pending since decentralisation really does allow a thinning down of top-level structures because their powers and functions have been devolved. This is needed not just for cutting out redundant financial expenditure, but most urgently for liberating the new empowered decentralised arrangements. This would also imply administrative efficiency. But in reality, state government is saving Rs. 455 crore per year by curbing the expenditure on fresh recruitment of regular cadre teachers and instead shifting to contract teachers.[8] There is a need to closely scrutinise and understand choices on the basis of a cost-benefit analysis, to adjudge cost-effective inputs.

16.7 Partners in Education

Besides the state government, many agencies and NGOs are working in the field of education. To meet the challenges of UEE, it is important that there should be convergence of resources flowing to the education sector. The experiences of NGOs are also being elicited by involving them as active partners in various fields of education. The details of partnership with the NGOs are discussed below:

1. Room to Read

Room to Read (children's libraries) started its operations in India in 2003. It partners with local communities throughout the developing world to establish schools, libraries and other educational infrastructure, and working towards strengthening the Government's efforts to meet its goal of universalising quality elementary education. It runs four programmes, including establishing libraries and computer labs, publishing children's books in Hindi and a girls' scholarship programme. Room to Read has been partnering with five state governments namely, Delhi, Himachal Pradesh, Madhya Pradesh, Rajasthan and Uttarakhand. Room to Read visualises library as an active learning centre and facilitates the learning of children through different activities based on books and focused capacity building of the school teachers and the library facilitators. It provides print-rich environment through books, posters and materials developed by children. Room to Read has partnered with Rajya Shiksha Kendra, Madhya Pradesh Government to establish school libraries covering all 70 Kasturba Gandhi Balika Vidyalayas (KGBVs) across 27 districts.

2. MV Foundation

In Madhya Pradesh, bridge course has been started for the out of school children with the objective of mainstreaming them in the formal education system. The design of the bridge course and training had been planned and finalised in co-ordination with MV Foundation. A group of 60 persons from the state was sent to Hyderabad to learn from the experience of MV Foundation. These persons are the resource persons for training of bridge course volunteers. The resource persons from MV Foundation are working in the state conducting motivation camps, helping to enrol girls in the Residential Bridge Course (RBC), monitoring the functioning of RBC and mainstreaming the girls in regular schools.

3. Pratham

Pratham has started 25 learning centres in the slums of Bhopal and worked in 10 government schools for improving the reading abilities of children. This was followed by Learning to Read campaign in 40 districts. The resource persons of Pratham are involved in training of teachers on accelerated learning approach and monitor the "Learning to Read" programme. Follow-up activities will be taken up.

4. Naandi Foundation

In Madhya Pradesh, Naandi would help to implement the Midday Meal programme through MP Kitchen in Bhopal and Jabalpur city. Besides, the Foundation is also working on early childhood education and quality improvement of education and girl's education. The organisation is providing reading, writing support to children, support library in schools,

8. Sen, Tapas K., H.K. Amarnath, Mita Choudhury and Amit Mukherjee (2007). *Tackling Poverty Constraint on Human Development: Financing Strategies in Madhya Pradesh.* New Delhi: NIPFP, August.

fairs, competitions, exposure visits. It also engages the community through forming dynamic youth force (Bal Mitra), open black board, regular village meeting and *sandesh vahini* and forming *mahila jagrati manch*.

5. Azim Premji Foundation (APF)

The mission of the Foundation is to catalyse a national movement for UEE in India. The Foundation believes that the only way to sustained universalisation of elementary education is to improve the quality of learning in schools. All efforts are therefore, directed at interventions, partnerships and communication towards guaranteeing learning in the schools. The Learning Guarantee Programme, conceptualised by APF and tested in Karnataka is being implemented in two districts of MP—Vidisha and Datia as a coordinated activity of GoMP and APF. Efforts are being made to bring all the schools of these districts in this programme voluntarily.

6. Education Development Centre (EDC)

EDC is an international non-profit organisation that has been a pioneer in building bridges between research, policy and practice for the last four decades. The EDC has been chosen to execute the dot-EDU Technology Tools for Teaching and Training (T4) project in India, in cooperation with the Government of India and the various state governments. The goal of dot-EDU is to strengthen quality, expand access and enhance equity, especially for girls and the rural poor, through carefully planned applications of digital and broadcasting technologies. Dot-EDU strengthens education and learning systems through customised ICT interventions and content for educators, students and professionals. Its activities revolve around implementation of the T4 initiative. The T4 initiative works in close co-ordination with SSA (Sarva Shiksha Abhiyan) of the Government of India and the state governments. Dot-EDU activities, especially learning English through interactive radio instruction, was implemented on a pilot basis in three blocks, each in three states of Karnataka, Chhattisgarh and Jharkhand. This was run on pilot basis in two tribal dominant districts of MP, namely Jhabua and Mandla and was then implemented in the whole state. Next year also, it will be continued. It is also proposed to use Interactive Radio Instruction (IRI) technique for subjects like Hindi, Maths and EVS.

7. Parwarish—Project DISHA

Parwarish was established as a registered trust which provides comprehensive care to all children in the age group of 0 to 18 years with an emphasis on infant stimulation and early childhood care. The basic objective of the project is to study school readiness in pre-school education, manner of teaching, identify gaps in early childhood education. It worked with RSK and UNICEF, Bhopal under the project DISHA (school readiness programme) under SSA-NPEGEL.

8. Samavesh

Samavesh Society for development and governance is running a project titled 'Community Based Participatory Programme', for strengthening elementary education in two blocks of two districts Dewas and Harda of Madhya Pradesh. The specific objectives of the programme is to evolve a support programme covering around 50 villages to provide good and effective education. On a more extensive basis, to strengthen the overall education system i.e., strengthening the Block Resource Co-ordinators (BRCs) of two blocks and training and monitoring of Cluster Resource Co-ordinators (CRCs). It involves and motivates community to achieve 100 per cent enrolment and retention of children in schools. It also helps and trains the PTAs to support the schools.

9. Microsoft—Project Shiksha

Government of Madhya Pradesh School Education Department in collaboration with Microsoft is working in the area of computer training. This programme is known as Project Shiksha. To ensure effective implementation of the programme, an MoU has been signed between GoMP School Education department and Microsoft.

The main objectives of the project are:

- Empower teachers and student to make optimum use of the potential of ICT by providing greater access to latest technologies.
- Develop high quality ICT literacy and development skills in teachers to enable them to use ICT in education.

10. UNICEF

UNICEF is the main UN agency which is partnering the state in improving quality of education under SSA.

With UNICEF's support, the state is implementing quality package in four districts *viz.*, Guna, Shivpuri, Bhind and Jhabua. A state-wide enrolment drive with special focus on tribal children and girls was also carried out. UNICEF also facilitated the development of the communication materials for this drive. For the first time, the chief minister sent out letters to PTAs and community to request them to ensure that all children enrol and attend schools regularly. UNICEF is supporting development and implementation of quality package to help address issues in the area of teacher effectiveness, school-community linkages and school environment with the main focus on reducing gender disparities.

17. New Opportunities

The main emphasis in Madhya Pradesh, since 1994 has been on universalising primary education and since 1999, this concern has enlarged to encompass universalisation of elementary education. The strategic framework for this was created by new opportunities in the state.

17.1 Decentralisation of Governance

The key objective for educational planning was decentralisation of educational management. It should be remembered here that decentralisation of educational management and the attempt to give greater space to direct community participation has been an end in itself because it expresses the belief that strengthening processes of democracy is itself a larger understanding of education. The effort of the government has been to move increasingly towards user groups at the grassroot level, and so establishing structures that enable their direct participation in the management of schools. From 26th January 2001, management, control and maintenance of schools have been transferred to *gram sabhas*. With the introduction of Panchayati Raj in the state, *panchayats* and urban bodies are entrusted with functions like management and running of school education guarantee centres, construction, repair and expansion of school buildings, providing equipments, recruitment of *shiksha karmees* and implementation of incentive schemes.

The education sector saw a very substantive delegation of powers to the local *panchayat* bodies and VECs. Recruitment and transfer of teachers, construction of school buildings and procurement of school equipment have become the responsibility of the *panchayats*. The VEC have been reconstituted under the recent amendment in the Gram Swaraj Act, further decentralising powers to the village government which acquired a statutory existence and has been entrusted with powers to supervise the local schools. A PTA has been envisaged for each school with substantive powers in school management. The PTAs are in the process of being set up.

17.2 Road Ahead

1. In elementary education, involvement of 6-7 departments is seriously affecting the delivery system owing to lack of proper co-ordination, which needs to be resurrected for effective implementation.
2. State must rejuvenate its dying cadre of teachers and should go for appointment of full time teachers rather than depending upon varying category of para-teachers if it is really sincere in its efforts to improve quality of education provided in the government schools of the state.
3. The functioning of school education needs strong reforms in terms of training and capacity building of present teachers, their involvement in non-academic tasks, effectiveness of training institutes in terms of delivery, demand based planning from bottom level, efficiency in spending the allotted budgets etc.
4. Higher education is totally in the hands of private sector which has resulted in taking away the opportunities of higher education owing to escalating costs.
5. Quality of education provided in these private institutes is also debatable. Besides, various discrepancies are observed in its regular functioning.
6. More focus should be put on the market-oriented skills and further linked up with business groups to know the demands that have higher job opportunities like wise the strategy adopted by the ITI institutes in Rajasthan state.

Chapter 7

Forests in Madhya Pradesh

1. Background

Forest is of paramount importance not only from the economic point of view but also from the ecological point of view. It has a multifarious role in maintaining the ecological balance and moderation of environment besides providing livelihood opportunities to people depending on forests. From ancient times, forest and people have symbiotic relationship due to the peculiar characteristics of forest as an economic resource, as a legacy and a part of future. Fossil evidence reveals that the first plant appeared 450 million years ago. Rich coal deposits confirm that there were rich forests 300 million years ago. Pale botanical evidences indicate that India was covered by rich forests more than 135 million years ago. After the advent of kingship in India until the pre-British days, forests happened to be the property of the king with no ownership rights for commoners. However, people were free to utilise for economic gain or domestic needs, in this supply-dominated era. During the British rule, the main objective was to exploit the colonial forest resources in order to supply timber for expansion of the railways and the ship-building industry in England.

After Independence, the princely states were either carved into states of India or merged into adjoining states. Some of these states had organised forest departments whereas others had engaged trained foresters from the neighbouring provinces of British India and brought their forest under reasonable state of management. This left a further category which had no scientifically managed forests like the small states, *zamindaris* and private holdings. With the abolition of the *zamindari* system and the application of land ceiling laws, large private forest areas were taken over by the government. A major task of the forest service in the early 1950s was to control heavy felling by erstwhile owners, notify and bring such forests under scientific management. In 1950-51, recorded forest area was 40.48 million ha in India. It increased to 66.80 million ha in 1976-77 and further 76.52 million ha in 1996. However, the intervening period witnessed large scale felling to get maximum returns, thus reducing the forest cover to 67.71 million ha which is 20.60 per cent of the total geographic area of the country in 2005. The growing human population[1], and consequent large scale urbanisation, industrial development and political consolidation have put heavy demand on forest for fuel, fodder, food, medicine and small timber causing degradation of forests.

An assessment by Forest Survey of India (FSI) in 2005 shows that 5.46 million ha (1.66 per cent of GA) of forests are having over 70 per cent crown density, 33.26 million ha (10.12 per cent of GA) are having 40 to 70 per cent density, 28.99 million ha (8.82 per cent of GA) are having 10 to 40 crown cover. Around 3.85 million ha (1.17 per cent of GA) of forest is scrub area. Thus only 11.78 per cent of the land area has reasonably good forest cover over 40 per cent crown density against 33 per cent stipulated in the National Forest Policy of 1952 and 1988.

The National Forest Policy, 1952 appreciated the multiple benefits of forests and the policy of 1988 emphasised to ensure environmental stability, maintain ecological balance and secure forest products for meeting the requirements of rural and tribal people. The policy further stated participatory forest

1. 361.1 million in 1951, 846.3 million in 1991 and 1129.7 million in 2008.

management with involvement of people in management, protection and conservation of forests. Madhya Pradesh is the first state to implement participatory approach through formulation of village level Joint Forest Management Committees (JFMCs) in 1991. The new State Forest Policy, 2005 of Madhya Pradesh lays special emphasis on checking forest encroachments as well as efforts to curb forest-related crimes.

2. State of Forests in Madhya Pradesh

2.1 Forest Area

Madhya Pradesh is the second largest state in the country with an area of 30.82 million ha constituting 9.38 per cent of the geographical area of the country. Also, the state has the largest forest area in the country with the recorded forest area 94,689.38 sq km constituting 30.72 per cent of the geographical area of the state (3,08,245 sq km).

Total forest cover in MP can be classified as reserved forest 65.36 per cent (61886.49 sq km), protected forest 32.84 per cent (31098.04 sq km) and unclassified forest 1.7 per cent (1704.85 sq km) of the total forest area. The per capita forest area is 0.16 ha against the national average of 0.07 ha (MPFS, 2004) which indicates positive trend towards maintaining own forest resource.

2.2 Forest Cover

As compared to the forest cover of other states/UTs, Madhya Pradesh with 76,013 km^2 has the largest area under forest cover, followed by Arunachal Pradesh (67,777 km^2), Chhattisgarh (55,863 km^2), Orissa (48,374 km^2) and Maharashtra (47,476 km^2). Further, the state's forest cover is 24.66 per cent of the state's geographic area. This is an increase of 1653 square kilometre over the previous survey of 1997.

TABLE 7.1

Forest Cover in Different Assessments

(Area in sq km)

Year	*1997*	*1999*	*2001*	*2003*	*2005*
MP	74,760	75,137	77,265	76,429	76013
India	633,397	637,293	675,538	6,78,333	677088

Source: Forest Survey of India, 2005.

If we look at the tree cover in Madhya Pradesh, it is 2.03 per cent of the total geographical area of Madhya Pradesh (Table 7.2).

TABLE 7.2

Tree Cover in Madhya Pradesh *vis-à-vis* India

	Geog. Area (km^2)	*Tree per ha*	*Tree Cover*	
			Area (km^2)	*% of Geog. Area*
MP	308,245	9.68	6267	2.03
India	3,287,263	12.14	91663	2.79

Source: Forest Survey of India, 2005.

The total tree and forest cover together in Madhya Pradesh is 82,280 sq km, more than 10 per cent of the country's tree and forest cover (Table 7.3).

TABLE 7.3

Total Forest and Tree Cover

Total forest & tree cover	82,280 km^2
Of state's geographic area	26.69 %
Of country's forest & tree cover	10.70 %
Per capita forest & tree cover	0.16 ha*

Source: * MP Forest Department website & Forest Survey of India, 2005.

Distribution of total forest in the state is as follows: 4,239 km^2 (5.58 per cent) is very dense forest, 36,843 km^2 (47.12 per cent) is moderately dense forest and 34931 km^2 (45.95 per cent) is open forest. Thus, out of total forest cover, 54.05 per cent has reasonably good forest cover with over 40 per cent crown density (Table 7.4). As shown in the table, Madhya Pradesh is relatively better in terms of forest resources. Following districts have relatively large forest cover in the state namely, Balaghat, Betul, Chhindwara, Damoh, Dindori, Khandwa, Sidhi, Mandla, Panna, Raisen, Seoni, Sheopur, Shivpuri, Umaria and Harda.

As shown in Table 7.5, the loss of forest cover in Madhya Pradesh is mainly due to submergence of area for construction of dam, in the districts of East Nimar, Harda and Dewas (Indira Sagar and Omkareshwar dams), and Shivpuri district (Madikheda dam). The gain in forest cover is due to plantation raised outside forest and rehabilitation of degraded forests.

2.3 Notified Forest Area versus Actual Area under Cover

The districts like Balaghat, Betul, Raisen, Chhindwara, Sidhi, Panna, Shivpuri, Mandla and Sheopur have larger share in the total forest area cover (Table 7.4). Whereas districts *viz.*, Khandwa, Jabalpur, Shahdol, Barwani, Chhindwara, Dindori, Narsimhapur, Shajapur, Bhind, and Gwalior have good forest cover as compared to the forest area (Tables 7.4 and 7.5). The

TABLE 7.4

Extent of Forest Cover in Different Districts of Madhya Pradesh in 2005

(Area in sq km)

Sr. No.	District	Geographical Area	Forest Cover Very Dense	Moderate Dense	Open Forest	Total
1	Balaghat	9229	1022	2368	1467	4857
2	Betul	10043	94	1825	1604	3523
3	Bhopal	2772	0	116	208	324
4	Sehore	6578	0	756	686	1442
5	Raisen	8466	39	1612	1061	2712
	Rajgarh	6153	0	26	155	181
7	Vidisha	7371	14	503	365	882
8	Chhindwara	11815	115	2335	1946	4396
9	Bhind	4459	0	37	79	116
10	Indore	3898	0	319	268	587
11	Dhar	8153	0	176	419	595
12	Dewas	7020	17	986	754	1757
13	Jhabua	6778	0	295	541	836
14	Khandwa (East Nimar)	10776	22	2000	1420	3442
15	Rewa	6314	46	251	394	691
16	Satna	7502	18	972	712	1702
17	Sidhi	10526	524	2032	1403	3959
18	Sagar	10252	1	1707	1207	2915
19	Damoh	7306	3	867	1803	2673
20	Chhatarpur	8687	18	845	834	1697
21	Tikamgarh	5048	0	96	208	304
22	Panna	7135	29	1586	1122	2737
23	Narsimhapur	5133	43	550	766	1359
24	Seoni	8758	169	1312	1527	3008
25	Shivpuri	10277	36	1090	1316	2442
26	Guna	11064	10	713	1348	2071
27	Ujjain	6091	0	0	21	21
28	Ratlam	4861	0	27	156	183
29	Shajapur	6195	0	1	120	121
30	Gwalior	4560	3	538	772	1313
31	Datia	2691	0	81	77	158
32	Mandsaur	5535	0	83	177	260
33	Neemuch	4256	0	199	685	884
34	Jabalpur	5211	40	407	630	1077
35	Katni	4950	94	435	641	1170
36	Mandla	5800	746	965	1060	2771
37	Dindori	7470	605	1450	642	2697
38	Morena	4989	0	238	541	779
39	Sheopur	6606	7	1904	1723	3634
40	Hoshangabad	6707	198	1328	868	2394
41	Harda	3330	0	592	434	1026
42	Khargone (West Nimar)	8030	0	418	670	1088
43	Barwani	5422	0	362	530	892
44	Shahdol	9952	86	1330	1047	2463
45	Umaria	4076	240	1110	524	1874
Total		308,245	4,239	36,843	34,931	76,013

Source: Forest Survey of India, 2005.

TABLE 7.5

Change in Forest Cover during 2003 and 2005 Assessment Extent of Change in Forest Cover in Different Districts of Madhya Pradesh

(Area in sq.km)

Sr. No.	District	Geographical Area	Total Forest Cover in-2003	Total Forest Cover in-2005	Change in Forest Cover
1	Balaghat	9229	4859	4857	-2
2	Betul	10043	3537	3523	-14
3	Bhopal	2772	312	324	12
4	Sehore	6578	1464	1442	-22
5	Raisen	8466	2732	2712	-20
6	Rajgarh	6153	179	181	2
7	Vidisha	7371	902	882	-20
8	Chhindwara	11815	4409	4396	-13
9	Bhind	4459	121	116	-5
10	Indore	3898	554	587	33
11	Dhar	8153	585	595	10
12	Dewas	7020	1803	1757	-46
13	Jhabua	6778	842	836	-6
14	Khandwa (East Nimar)	10776	3580	3442	-138
15	Rewa	6314	708	691	-17
16	Satna	7502	1678	1702	24
17	Sidhi	10526	4013	3959	-54
18	Sagar	10252	2922	2915	-7
19	Damoh	7306	2678	2673	-5
20	Chhatarpur	8687	1706	1697	-9
21	Tikamgarh	5048	325	304	-21
22	Panna	7135	2728	2737	9
23	Narsimhapur	5133	1374	1359	-15
24	Seoni	8758	3038	3008	-30
25	Shivpuri	10277	2479	2442	-37
26	Guna	11064	2092	2071	-21
27	Ujjain	6091	13	21	8
28	Ratlam	4861	182	183	1
29	Shajapur	6195	123	121	-2
30	Gwalior	4560	1323	1313	-10
31	Datia	2691	164	158	-6
32	Mandsaur	5535	264	260	-4
33	Neemuch	4256	895	884	-11
34	Jabalpur	5211	1078	1077	-1
35	Katni	4950	1191	1170	-21
36	Mandla	5800	2732	2771	39
37	Dindori	7470	2643	2697	54
38	Morena	4989	777	779	2
39	Sheopur	6606	3632	3634	2
40	Hoshangabad	6707	2402	2394	-8
41	Harda	3330	1045	1026	-19
42	Khargone (West Nimar)	8030	1089	1088	-1
43	Barwani	5422	901	892	-9
44	Shahdol	9952	2483	2463	-20
45	Umaria	4076	1872	1874	2
Total		308,245	76,429	76,013	-416

Source: Forest Survey of India, 2003 and 2005.

south, south-east and eastern part of the state is composed of maximum forest area and forest cover. The districts Khandwa, Hoshangabad, Chhindwara and Narsimhapur form the compact block in south. The districts Seoni, Balaghat, Mandla and Damoh form the compact block in the south-eastern part of the state. In the east, Shahdol, Umaria, Sidhi and Panna form the compact block. In the north, Sheopur and Shivpuri districts comprise of maximum forest and tree cover. Forest area under these 14 districts forms 49.03 per cent of the total forest area and bear 55.27 per cent of total forest cover. In the other parts of the state, the forest and tree cover is sporadic and sparse.

2.4 Change in Forest Cover between 2003 and 2005

It was observed from the forest cover assessment that the forest cover has increased in the districts Bhopal, Indore, Satna, Mandla and Dindori from 2003 to 2005 by more than 10 sq km. However, forest cover in other districts shows a declining trend.

2.5 Dense Forest Cover as Percentage of Total Geographical Area

The dense forest comprise 41082 sq km, which forms 54 per cent of the total forest cover. When compared with total forest cover, the area under very dense forest cover is 8 per cent and moderately dense forest cover is 48 per cent of the total forest cover. The very dense forest cover is around 10 per cent (4239 sq km) and moderately dense forest cover is 90 per cent (36843 sq km) of the total dense forest cover.

The districts Umaria and Balaghat have 37 and 33 per cent of their total geographical area under dense forest cover respectively. The districts Mandla, Sheopur, Sidhi, Dindori and Sheopur have more than 25 per cent of their total geographical area under dense forest cover. However, the districts Balaghat, Betul, Sehore, Raisen, Chhindwara, Sidhi, Damoh, Panna, Seoni, Mandla, Dindori, Sheopur, Hoshangabad, Umaria have more than 33 per cent of their total geographical area under forest cover. Whereas in other districts, the forest cover is very low and hence to bring 33 per cent of the total geographical area under good forest cover, scrub forest area and other barren areas need to be undertaken for raising the plantations of desired species.

3. Forest Types and Resources

There are four major forest types found in the state of Madhya Pradesh (FSI, 2005).

- Dry thorn;
- Dry and moist deciduous;
- Subtropical semi-evergreen; and
- Tropical moist evergreen.

The common wood species found in these forests are *Tectona grandis* (teak), *Shorea robusta* (*sal*) and other miscellaneous species. The *Dendrocalamus strictus* sp. (bamboo) found distributed across the state. The non-wood forest products (NWFPs) yielding species are *Diospyros melanoxylon* (*tendu* leaves), *Shorea robusta* (*sal*), *Terminalia chebula* (*harra*), gum of *Sterculia urens* (*kullu*), *Anogeissus latifolia* (*dhaora*) and *Acacia nilotica* (*babool*), *Emblica officinalis* (*aonla*), *Terminalia bellirica* (*behada*), *Buchanania lanzan* (*chironji*), flowers and seeds of *Madhuca indica* (*mahua*) etc. With a view to reduce pressure on the natural forests, plantations have been undertaken in forest and non-forest areas to supplement the availability of fuel wood, small timber, fodder etc.

4. Growing Stock and Productivity

The total growing stock (volume of timber/wood) is 500 lakh cu. m whose valued worth is Rs. 2.5 lakh crore (*www.forest.mp.gov.in*). The average growing stock per ha of recorded forest is estimated to be about 40 cu. m, which is 29 per cent of the total growing stock of India. While the growing stock figure is better than the all-India average figure of 26 cu.m, however, it compares poorly to the world average of 110 cu. m. Similarly, the mean annual increment in the stock is about 1.00 cu. m/ha/year which is double the all-India average of 0.5 cu. m/ha/year., whereas it is half the world average of 2.0 cu. m/ha/year. The growing stock per ha of actual forest cover in the state works out to be about 47 cu. m, while the average for the country works out to 65 cu. m and for the world 110 cu. m. These figures clearly show that our forests do not enjoy good health compared to world figure but is generally better than the all-India figure. The average annual production in the state is 4.24 million cu. m against the all-India average annual production of 27.5 million cu. m for the country.

5. Long-term Bio-conservation—Regulatory Status of Protection Categories

5.1 Biosphere Reserves

The Government of India has recently proposed that examples of the country's richest and most distinctive biomes should be given the extra attention as biosphere reserves. Though this proposal aims at attaining top conservation status, it does not bear direct legal status.

Following the concepts developed by UNESCO under its Man and the Biosphere (MAB) Programme, such reserve should ideally be large planning areas which are integrated ecosystems containing legally protected core-zones (e.g., parks and sanctuaries), within a framework of human settlement and resource exploitation areas. The essence of these reserves is that all land use and resource exploitation should be co-ordinated by a high level planning committee. The core units do not lose their legal status or management requirements as parks or sanctuaries. There is thus, no conflict in objective or management strategy between biosphere reserves and older conservation categories. The programme is a pioneering effort at pursuing the increasingly difficult yet urgent task of conserving ecological diversity under mounting pressures. The emphasis of the programme is on conservation of landscapes, ecosystems, species and genetic variations; promote economic development which is culturally, socially and ecologically sustainable and to provide support for research, monitoring, education and information exchange related to local, national and global issues. The Government of India, Ministry of Environment and Forests has notified 16 biosphere reserves (BR) in the country (Table 7.6).

The Pachmarhi biosphere reserves (notified on 3.3.1999), covers an area of about 5000 sq km. It includes Bori Sanctuary, Satpura National Park and Pachmarhi Sanctuary. It is the 11th biosphere reserve of the country and the first of Madhya Pradesh. These 16 BRs not only aim to protect representative ecosystems but also serve as laboratories for evolving alternation models of development. Ministry of Environment and Forests, Govt. of India provides funds to the respective state governments for conservation and management of these reserves, besides supporting individual research and development project on BR directly to R&D organisations.

5.2 National Parks (NP)

According to guidelines for declaration of National Parks, mere notification of park status alone is not enough. Unless the full provisions of the PA (protected area) are implemented, such status is of no significance. It also says that no consumptive utilisation of land or resources is permitted except what is necessary for the achievement of conservation objectives. Villages have to be shifted and resettled and land use rights and privileges in NP areas have to be revised. This category is, in theory, the ultimate level of protection that can be given to an area. In practice, the level is dependent on the magnitude of problems and the ability and commitment of the management agency. Park status is, however, necessary for the total long-term protection of species and community values. Such total protection is a key component of the national conservation policy, which says that representative portions of each biological unit should be maintained inviolate. Madhya Pradesh is a home for some of the

TABLE 7.6

Biosphere Reserves (BRs) in the Country

S.No.	*Biosphere Reserve*	*Date of Notification*	*Location (State)*
1	Nilgiri	01-08-1986	Part of Wynad, Nagarhole, Bandipur and Mudumalai, Nilambur, Silent Valley and Siruvani Hills (Tamil Nadu, Kerala & Karnataka)
2	Nanda Devi	18-01-1988	Parts of Chamoli, Pithoragarh and Almora districts (Uttarakhand)
3	Nokrek	01-09-1988	Part of Garo Hills (Meghalaya)
4	Manas	14-03-1989	Part of Kokrajhar, Bongaigaon, Barpeta, Nalbari, Kampup and Darang districts (Assam)
5	Sunderbans	29-03-1989	Part of delta of Ganges and Brahmaputra river system (West Bengal)
6	Gulf of Mannar	18-02-1989	Indian part of Gulf of Mannar between India and Sri Lanka (Tamil Nadu)
7	Great Nicobar	06-01-1989	Southern most islands of Andaman and Nicobar (A&N) Islands.
8	Simlipal	21-06-1994	Part of Mayurbhanj district (Orissa)
9	Dibru-Saikhowa	28-07-1997	Part of Dibrugarh and Tinsukia districts (Assam)
10	Dehang Debang	02-09-1998	Part of Siang and Debang valley (Arunachal Pradesh)
11	Pachmarhi	03-03-1999	Parts of Hoshangabad, Chhindwara and Betul districts (Madhya Pradesh)
12	Khanchendzonga	07-02-2000	East Himalayan region of Sikkim.
13	Achankamar-Amarkantak	30-03-2005	Parts of Anuppur and Dindori districts of MP and Bilaspur district of Chhattisgarh.
14	Agasthyamalai	12-11-2001	Parts of Tirunelveli and Kanyakumari districts of Tamil Nadu, Thiruvananthapuram, Kollam and Pathanamthitta in Kerala.
15	katchchh	2008	Parts of Kuchh, Rajkot and Surendranagar districts of Gujarat.
16.	Cold Desert		Jammu Kashmir & Himachal Pradesh.

Source: Ministry of Environment and Forest, Government of India.

finest national parks in the country. Most of them are famous for tiger and elephant safari.

5.3 Wildlife Sanctuary (WLS)

The intention behind this is that the conservation of biological values (species or communities) holds priority over other forms of resource utilisation; such resources may only be exploited if such activity does not detract from conservation objectives. Timber fuel wood and minor produce, harvesting and livestock grazing are other possible forms of resource utilisation. The level of actual conservation achieved is thus, dictated by the strength of the political support and the administrative and conservation effort at any one time. The better sanctuaries have core areas free from utilisation and which do permit long-term conservation, but the poorer sanctuaries are rapidly losing value in the face of intense resource exploitation.

In Madhya Pradesh, there are 9 national parks and 25 wildlife sanctuaries spread over an area of 1.1 million ha constituting 11.40 per cent of the total forest area and 3.52 per cent of the geographical area of the state. There are five tiger reserves in the state namely, Kanha, Panna, Bandhavgarh, Pench and Satpura (FSI, 2005).

6. Role and Importance of the Forestry Sector in State's Economy

Madhya Pradesh is famous for its rich forest reserves like timber, fuel wood and bamboo besides wildlife and biodiversity. They are also a key source of minor forest products such as *tendu, harra, sal* seed and gum etc. These products not only generate revenue but also generate employment through trade/business. However, over the years, due attention has not been given to the efforts and the cost the state has paid for maintaining its huge natural resource and environmental stability in the country. However, there is no return on such investment on the state's part.

The judgment of Supreme Court regarding compensation to states having forest cover above national average is a significant step towards maintaining ecological balance and the costs thereof. It suggests that an equitable arrangement would be to calculate the cost of forest assets by capitalising the stock, attributing it a value and making incremental return available to the states as a rate of return. On this basis, Madhya Pradesh has an excess forest cover of 33036 ha. Net present value of the same would be Rs. 165172 crore at Rs. 5.80 lakh per ha of capital stock. This capital stock would yield an annual return of Rs. 8285 crore at the minimum interest rate of 5 per cent. The Hon'ble President of India has also mooted the idea of "forest credit" which needs rigorous follow-up. Although GoI has used this argument at all the international forums in the national interest, but little has happened in practice. Presently, 13th Finance Commission has flagged this issue and is working on it.

Original allocation for forestry sector was Rs. 352.75 crore in the 10th FYP that was revised to double the amount of Rs. 756.61 crore. Similarly, plan outlays for forestry sector in the 11th FYP have increased to Rs. 1210 crore, an increase by 59 per cent. This increased allocation definitely indicates the raised recognition towards the sector.

7. Forest Produce in the State

The key forest products are listed in Table 7.7.

TABLE 7.7

Key Forest Products

Wood Products	*Nationalised Minor Forest Products*	*Non-Nationalised Minor Forest Products*
Timber, small timber, fuel wood and bamboo	*Tendu* leaf, sal seed, *kullu* (gum)	*Harra*, all other gums, *satawar, kalmegh, giloe, achar*, arjun bark, *aonla, gudnar, chiratia, nagarmocha, baheda, bael, bhilwa, mahua, van, tulsi* (more than 155)

Source: Forest Department, GoMP.

7.1 Production of Wood and Bamboo

Table 7.8 shows production of wood and bamboo.

TABLE 7.8

Production of Timber, Fuel Wood and Bamboo

Year	*Timber (in lakh cu.m)*	*Fuel Wood (in lakh cu.m)*	*Bamboo (in lakh notion tonne)*
2001-02	4.63	3.47	0.89
2002-03	3.92	3.34	1.32
2003-04	4.15	4.11	1.33
2004-05	2.65	2.71	1.08
2005-06	2.68	2.96	1.04
2006-07	2.08	2.19	2.65
2007-08	2.45	3.02	1.17

Source: Administrative Reports, Forest Department, GoMP, various years.

Disposal of forest products like timber, poles, fuel wood, bamboo etc., is done through auction in commercial depots and through sale on notified rates in the *nistar* depots. The revenue earned is shown in Table 7.9.

TABLE 7.9

Revenue from Sale of Timber, Poles, Fuel Wood, Bamboo and *Nistar* Supply

Year	*Total (Rs. in crores)*
2002-03	509.96
2003-04	496.4
2004-05	558.06
2005-06	490.4
2006-07	523.11
2007-08	608.01
2008-09	311.16*

Note: * figure upto September 2008.
Source: *www.forest.mp.gov.in*

7.2 Nistar Supply

Madhya Pradesh, as a state has accepted the responsibility of providing *nistar*, i.e., requirements of villagers of forest produce, to all agriculturists, village artisans and agricultural labourers living within 5 km of forest fringes. Further, supply of bamboo, fuel wood, poles and small timber is available at concessional rates for bona fide domestic needs of people. The supply is given from the notified *nistar* depots at specified rates. There are 1,896 *nistar* depots and 309 central/consumer depots. Thus, a total of 2205 depots are supplying *nistar* material in the state. On an average, the forest department provides a concession of Rs. 9.93 crore. Table 7.10 shows the *nistar* supplied in terms of quantity and concessional value by Madhya Pradesh forest department.

TABLE 7.10

***Nistar* Supplied in Terms of Quantity of Forest Products and Concessional Value by Madhya Pradesh Forest Department**

Year	*Bamboo (no. in lakhs)*	*Pole (no. in lakhs)*	*Fuel Stack (no. in lakhs)*	*Nistar Value (Rs. in crores)*	*Market Value (Rs. in crores)*	*Concession* (Rs. crore)*
2004	94.38	3.57	0.55	6.54	15.67	9.13
2005	94.41	3.29	0.55	7.09	17.1	10.01
2006	86.35	3.92	0.69	7.60	17.64	10.04
2007	71.62	2.71	0.70	8.65	19.19	10.54
Average	94.395	3.43	0.55	6.815	16.385	9.93

Note: * market value - *nistar* value.
Source: *www.forest.mp.gov.in*

With the formation of the state of Madhya Pradesh, the reserve forests were exclusively for the use of the state, except for certain rights given to forest villagers. The villagers had the rights of *nistar* and grazing in the protected forest but the requirements were not satisfactorily available. *Nistar* depots are the centres from where villagers were given forest produce for their use. The process had begun in early 1955 in Mahakoshal region and in Madhya Bharat regions but it was unacceptable, particularly to those villagers who were not living near the forest and were denied the right of *nistar*. Therefore, in 1958 the state government brought the resolution wherein it was said that the *nistar* requirements of cultivators to be fulfilled by nearby forests and that there should be no distinction whatsoever. The forest Nistar Policy of Madhya Pradesh also stated that material extracted from *nistar* forests would be supplied at concessional rates. Every villager was entitled 250 bamboos and 30 poles per year at fairly cheaper rates.

But the conflict between people and foresters still exists where the latter blames the former exercising *nistar* rights that have reduced the forests, especially the partially regenerated areas that are completely destroyed. The picture of *nistar*, which emerges from the point of view of villagers, is that the supply of timber, bamboo, fuel and fodder is crucial for his/her ordinary livelihood. Next to agriculture, *nistar* becomes the most important element in village life.

The real problem of *nistar*, therefore, is not necessarily the enormous gap between demand and supply, but the failure to provide those critical items, especially fuel, which is leading to an increasing biotic pressure on forests through unregulated extraction of material. To avoid this, the government would have to evolve short and long-term strategies which would increase satisfaction rate in the matter of *nistar*. (Extracted from *The Forests of Madhya Pradesh* by M.N. Buch, 1991.)

7.2.1 Nistar Policy of GoMP

In order to create better conditions to encourage the villagers to raise trees on their marginal lands and achieve self-reliance in forest produce requirement, and meanwhile help reduce pressures on natural forests, the Government of Madhya Pradesh declared a new Nistar Policy in 1994. According to this new policy, the prevailing *nistar* facility shall be restricted to those villages that are located within the 5 km of forest boundary. This policy provides for supply of *nistar* forest produce at concessional rate to the residents of villages, located beyond 5 km radius of forest boundary. The supply of such materials in villages beyond 5 km from forest boundary is to be organised through village *panchayats* who shall buy necessary *nistar*-material from scheduled depots of the forest department. To dissuade villagers from resorting to illicit felling to satisfy their *nistar* requirements, it was felt necessary to arrange supply of such material through *panchayats*, at market rates. The control and domain of state government exercised through the Department of Forests, over forests and even on reserved lands, is fragmented and has been constrained by external factors. Given the case of access to forests to people for legitimate as well as illegitimate uses, and the socio-political environment that often prevents strict control, it has not been very easy for the state to enforce its property rights.

The trade of forest products other than timber, fuel and bamboo is done by Madhya Pradesh Minor Forest Produce (Trading & Development) Federation. It deals with products like *tendu* leaf, *sal* seed, *chebulic myrobalan* (*harra*) etc.

8. Production of Non-Timber Forest Produce (NTFP) or Minor Forest Produce (MFP)

The minor forest produce (MFP) of Madhya Pradesh can be categorised as nationalised and non-nationalised products based upon the state control on the trade of these products. The major nationalised products are *tendu* leaves, *sal* seed and gums. The major forest products that come under the non-nationalised category are *chironji*, mahua flower, *bahera*, *bel* etc.

8.1 Tendu Leaf

Prior to 1964, *tendu* leaves growing on government lands were sold unplucked to contractors and those that grew on private lands were disposed off by the owners of the land in the manner they saw fit. This provided a space for market intermediaries. Also, there was high volume of theft of *tendu* leaves from government lands. In order to control this and check the exploitation by middlemen, the state took over the trade of *tendu* leaves by enacting the Madhya Pradesh Tendu Patta (Vyapar Viniyaman) Adhiniyam, 1964.

Under this Act, agents were made responsible for the collection of *tendu* leaf. The price paid by the purchaser depended upon the number of standard bags delivered to him. However, the agents who were usually private individuals or private companies heavily exploited the primary collectors in this system. To improve the condition of the collectors, the Madhya Pradesh State Minor Forest Produce (Trade and Development) Co-operative Federation was formed in 1984, whose mandate was to free the primary collectors from the exploitation of the middlemen. Between 1984 and 1988, the Federation carried out experiments in collecting *tendu* leaves under the auspices of institutions such as MARKFED, LAMPS and PACS.

The state government in 1988 decided to eliminate the middleman totally, following which a three tier co-operative institution was designed. At the first tier, the body consists of primary forest produce co-operative societies whose members were the *tendu* leaf collectors. The primary society appoints a *phad munshi* for procuring the leaves and paying the wages to the pluckers. The secondary level consists of the district primary forest produce co-operative unions headed by the district collector. At the apex level of this institution is the Madhya Pradesh State Minor Forest Produce (Trade and Development) Co-operative Federation. Each tier is allotted commission rates on societies. The premium is borne by the Government of India and Madhya Pradesh State Minor Forest Produce Co-operative Federation.

Madhya Pradesh is the biggest *tendu* leaves producing state of India. The average annual production of *tendu* leaves in Madhya Pradesh is around 25 lakh standard bags, which is nearly 25 per cent of the total *tendu* leaves production of the country. One standard bag of *tendu* leaves in Madhya Pradesh means 1000 bundles of 50 *tendu* leaves each.

Tendu leaf is the most suitable wrapper and is used mainly for *bidi* rolling in India. *Bidi* rolling is the primary job which is very simple and can be done at any place at any time. The procedure for collection and processing of *tendu* leaves has almost been standardised and almost the same procedure is used everywhere. The *tendu* plants are pruned in the months of February and March and the mature leaves are collected after about 45 days. The leaves are collected in bundles of 50 leaves, which are dried in sunlight for about a week. The dried leaves are sprinkled with water to soften them and then filled tightly in jute bags and exposed to direct sunlight for 2 days. The bags, thus packed and cured can be stored till their use in *bidi* manufacture. Great care is needed while plucking, curing and storage of *tendu* leaves. It is a sensitive product and with the slightest mistakes or oversight during any of these processes their quality deteriorates rendering them unfit for making *bidis*. Table 7.11 shows quantity collected, revenue received and expenditure incurred on *tendu* leaves. The maximum revenue was obtained in the years 1989, 1998, 1999 and 2007.

TABLE 7.11

Data of *Tendu* Leaves Trade

Year	Collection	Collection Rate per S.B.	Collection Wages	Quantity Stored	Quantity Disposed Off	Revenue	Expenditure	Net Receipt
1989	43.61	150	65.42	43.58	43.58	405.15	114.7	290.45
1990	61.15	250	152.88	60.57	60.57	248.47	209.12	39.35
1991	46.16	250	115.4	45.79	45.79	298.07	180	118.07
1992	45.06	250	112.65	44.64	44.64	285.99	201.47	84.52
1993	41.31	300	123.93	40.98	40.98	252.77	198.29	54.48
1994	42.38	300	127.14	42.08	42.08	299.4	210.95	88.45
1995	39.56	300	118.68	39.36	39.36	289.39	197.8	91.59
1996	44.6	350	156.1	44.43	44.43	338.85	269.38	69.47
1997	40.14	350	140.49	39.95	39.95	338.69	244.05	94.64
1998	45.47	400	181.84	45.23	45.23	407.66	309.55	98.11
1999	49.37	400	194.2	49.12	49.12	402.2	283.87	118.33
2000	29.59	400	114.78	29.49	29.49	176.31	160.08	16.23
2001	21.28	400	83.09	21.22	21.22	111.05	136.07	-
2002	22.74	400	89.04	22.65	22.65	165.77	143.83	21.94
2003	22.25	400	87.56	22.21	22.21	152.95	140.71	12.24
2004	25.77	400	101.61	25.72	25.72	167.71	145.86	21.85
2005	16.83	400	66.37	16.82	16.82	131.41	106.9	24.51
2006	17.97	400	71.88	17.97	17.97	151.33	97.78	53.55
2007*	24.21	450	108.95	24.21	24.21	373.62	138.52	235.1
2008*	18.02	550	99.11	-	15.52	182.24	124.33	57.91

Note: Quantity: In lakh standard bags (1 standard bag=50,000 leaves); Amount: In Rs. crores.
* Figures for 2007 & 2008 seasons are to be finalised.
Source: *http://www.mfpfederation.com*

8.1.1 Group Insurance Scheme

A group insurance scheme for the *tendu* leaves pluckers was launched in 1991. It is the biggest insurance scheme of its kind in the whole of Asia. All *tendu* leaves pluckers between 18 and 60 years of age (about 28 lakh) are insured free of cost under this scheme. The scheme is run by the Life Insurance Corporation of India. Following insurance amounts are paid under this scheme. In case of disability due to accident, the plucker is paid an amount of Rs. 12500. In case of death or permanent disability caused due to accident, the amount of insurance is Rs. 25000. The nominees of the pluckers are provided all help and guidance in the submission of claims. The settlement of claims is also monitored regularly. Till now, 177274 claims have been settled and an amount of Rs. 68 crore paid to the nominees of the deceased pluckers. Year-wise break-up of the settled claims is given in Table 7.12.

TABLE 7.12

Details of Settlement of Claims

Year	No. of Claims Settled	Amount of Insurance Paid (in Rs. crores)
1991-92	1194	0.36
1992-93	3235	0.99
1993-94	8238	2.48
1994-95	10699	3.37
1995-96	10361	3.54
1996-97	16522	5.75
1997-98	13249	4.69
1998-99	10215	3.76
1999-2000	15026	5.26
2000-01	18242	7.11
2001-02	16271	6.69
2002-03	10750	4.75
2003-04	11040	4.6
2004-05	10564	4.63
2005-06	4130	2.04
2006-07	13737	6.47
2007-08	3801	1.79
Total	177274	68.28

Source: *http://www.mfpfederation.com*

8.1.2 Incentive Wages to *Tendu* Leaves Pluckers

Looking at the huge profit margin of 1989 season, the state government decided to distribute Rs. 150 crore as incentive wages to the *tendu* leaves pluckers out of the profit of 1989 season. This amount was paid in 4 instalments through accounts of pluckers opened in local branches of cooperative banks or credit societies. This payment was discontinued from 1990 season and was again started from 1995 season. For 1995 to 1997 seasons, nearly 20 per cent of net income was paid as incentive wages.

As a consequence of the 73rd Amendment to the Constitution, the state government decided to pass on all the net income from the trade of NWFP to the societies and the societies, in turn, distributed 50 per cent of this net income to the *tendu* leaves pluckers as incentive wages from 1998 season. From 2004 season, the proportion of incentive wages has been enhanced to 60 per cent of the net income. The amount of incentive wages paid in various years is shown in Table 7.13 (*http://www.mfpfederation.com*).

TABLE 7.13

The Amount of Incentive Wages Paid in Various Years

Collection Season	*No. of Pluckers (in lakhs)*	*Amount of Incentive Wages Paid (in Rs. crores)*
1989	21.31	150
1995	15.76	10.76
1996	18.02	12.29
1997	22.41	15.3
1998	18.84	57.27
1999	15.5	48.22
2000	4.5	7.3
2002	5.23	8.22
2003	4.64	5.51
2004	7.95	11.8
2005	9.41	13.23
2006	10.62	27.41

Source: http://www.mfpfederation.com

8.2 Harra

Chebulic myrobalan or *harra* was a specified forest produce under the MP Van Upaj (Vyapar Viniyaman) Act, 1969 and only the state government or an agent appointed by the state government could collect it. Its collection till 2002-03 was done by the MP State Minor Forest Produce Co-op. Federation Ltd. through primary societies in 17 *harra* producing districts of the state. The disposal of *harra* collected in this manner was done through tenders/auctions. *Harra* has been taken out of the list of specified produce in June 2003. The data pertaining to collection and sale of *harra* during the last nine years is shown in Table 7.14.

8.3 Sal Seed

Sal (*Shorea robusta*) is a large evergreen tree belonging to the family *Dipterocarpaceae*. *Sal* forests occupy about 16.5 per cent of the total forest area of the state and are confined to the eastern part of the state. The data of *sal* seed collection and disposal during the last 11 years is given in Table 7.15. MP State Minor Forest Produce Co-op. Federation Ltd. collects *sal* seed, a nationalised forest produce, through primary forest produce co-operative societies in 12 districts of the state which are *sal* forest areas. Valuable edible oil is extracted from these seeds. The seed contains 19-20 per cent of oil. The oil is used as a substitute of butter and also in confectionaries and eatables. The oil cakes remaining after oil extraction contains 10-12 per cent protein and is used as feed for

TABLE 7.14

Data of *Harra* Collection and Disposal

Year	*Collection Rate (Rs. per Qntl.)*	*Quantity Collected*	*Collection Wages*	*Quantity Sold*	*Total Expenditure*	*Sale Price*	*Average Sale Rate (Rs. Per Qntl.)*
1994-95	110	55065	60.56	53972	106.81	152.69	282.90
1995-96	130	107150	139.30	105916	230.37	366.17	345.72
1997-98	200	25753	51.51	25692	77.26	250.93	976.98
1998-99	300	55430	166.29	52083	188.46	369.56	709.56
1999-2000	550	47993	263.96	47076	287.96	321.70	683.36
2000-01	300	42230	126.69	42130	148.00	162.56	683.36
2001-02	250	29682	74.20	29679	82.57	77.56	261.33
2002-03	200	10948	21.9	10948	38.32	25.63	234.11

Note: Quantity: in quintals, amount in Rs. lakhs.
Source: http://www.mfpfederation.com

chicken. All the *sal* seed collected in the state is being sold by open tenders/auctions.

TABLE 7.15

Data of *Sal* Seed Collection and Disposal

Year	*Collection Rate (Rs. per Qntl)*	*Quantity Collected*	*Collection Wages*	*Quantity Disposed Off*
1995	160	361687	578.7	355557
1996	160	795111	1272.17	779369
1997	200	223412	446.82	217149
1998	300	44179	132.54	41637
1999	300	77635	232.91	75439
2000	320	347645	1112.46	336384
2001	330	12060	39.79	12060
2002	330	6273	20.7	6273
2003	330	709	2.34	709
2004	330	570	1.88	570
2005	330	3834	12.65	3834
2006	450	3319	14.94	3319
2007		Collection Banned		
2008	1000	40000*	-	-

Note: Quantity: in quintals, amount in Rs. lakhs, figures from 2001 season are for the new state of MP, * collection estimate for 2008 season.

Source: *http://www.mfpfederation.com*

8.4 Gum

Gum is an important minor forest produce. Gums are exuded by plants in response to injuries so as to seal the wound. Gums have both commercial and medicinal uses. Many trees in the forest produce gum like *dhaora, khair, babool, kullu, palas, salai* etc. *Kullu, dhaora, khair, babool, salai* gums were notified in Madhya Pradesh state as "specified forest produce" under the MP Van Upaj (Vyapar Viniyaman) Act, 1969 and only the state government or an agent appointed by the state government could collect these gums.

Gums extracted from *kullu* (*Sterculia urens*) and *salai* (*Boswellia serrata*) trees are valuable forest produce. In addition, gum from axlewood tree or *dhaora* (*Anogeissus latifolia*), cutch tree or *khair* (*acacia catechu*) and Indian gum Arabic tree or *babool* (*Acacia nilotica*) are also extracted and are economically important. These gums came under the category of nationalised minor forest produce. Extraction of these gums was carried out through primary forest produce cooperative societies and the district unions. The collected quantity is sold through open tenders/auctions either in advance or after godowning. However, all gums except *kullu* gum have been taken out of the list of specified produce in 2003.

8.4.1 Kullu Gum

Kullu (*Sterculia urens*) is a beautiful tree with white skin. It is found in dry forests in rocky areas. Extraction of gum is done during summer season. It has great medicinal value and is a highly valued gum in the international market. It is also used in confectionaries and chewing gums. In Madhya Pradesh, these trees were being destroyed due to deep tapping. Therefore, the state government had banned extraction of gums in early 80s. This ban was lifted in 1995 and controlled extraction was permitted in Sheopurkalan, Khandwa and Bastar districts. Extraction of *kullu* gum (*gum karaya*) is done through primary forest produce cooperative societies and the district unions. The data of last 11 years in respect of gum *karaya* is given in the Table 7.16 (*http://www.mfpfederation.com*).

TABLE 7.16

Data of *Kullu* Gum Collection and Disposal During the Last 11 Years

Collection Year	*Quantity Collected*	*Quantity Disposed Off*	*Sale Price*
1996-97	184.45	184.45	3.91
1997-98	28.18	28.18	1.72
1998-99	74.25	74.25	4.23
1999-2000	304.05	304.05	19.23
2000-01	352.2	352.2	15.67
2001-02	328.91	328.91	16.01
2002-03	529.4	529.4	25.72
2003-04	215.93	215.93	11.21
2004-05	422	422	26.22
2005-06	333.9	330.9	23.09
2006-07	567.25	567.25	50.31
2007-08	224.55	-*	-

Note: Quantity: in quintals, amount: in Rs. lakhs, * Figures of sale for 2007-08 season are being compiled. The extraction rate of gum *karaya* for the year 2007-08 was Rs. 7500/quintal.

Source: *http://www.mfpfederation.com*

8.4.2 Salai Gum

Boswellia serrata is a medium sized deciduous tree with ash coloured papery bark. It yields a valuable gum of high medicinal value—astringent, antipyretic, antidysentric, expectorant, diuretic and stomachic. Its collection was banned by the state government due to over-exploitation in the past. *Salai* gum was notified in Madhya Pradesh state as "specified forest produce" under the MP Van Upaj (Vyapar Viniyaman) Act, 1969 and only the state government or an agent appointed by the state government could collect these gums. It has been taken out of the list of specified produce in June 2003.

In 1997, the state government lifted the ban on extraction of *salai* gum in Gwalior, Shivpuri, Ujjain and Khandwa forest circles. It was also permitted in Narmada Sarovar submergence areas of Badwani and Jhabua forest divisions. The data for *Boswellia* gum collection during the last seven seasons are given in Table 7.17.

TABLE 7.17

Data for *Salai* Gum Collection During the Last 7 Seasons

Collection Year	*Collection Rate (Rs. per quintals)*	*Quantity Collected*	*Quantity Disposed Off*	*Sale Price*
1996-97	1550	4577	4577	118.14
1997-98	1800	5919	5919	165.46
1998-99	2000	4877	4877	129.02
1999-2000	3000	5432	5432	210.3
2000-01	3000	7036	7036	185.79
2001-02	3000	5947	5947	165.62
2002-03	2500-3000	5072	5072	138.47

Note: Quantity in quintals, amount in lakh rupees.
Source: *http://www.mfpfederation.com*

8.4.3 Class-II Gums

Dhaora, babool and *khair* gums are grouped together as Class-II gums to distinguish them from *kullu* and *salai* gums. These gums have been taken out of the list of specified produce in June 2003. MP State MFP Cooperative Federation had carried out trade of the specified gums as an agent of the state government, through primary forest produce co-operative societies till 2002-03.

Details of the Class-II gums (*dhaora, khair* and *babool*) collection during the last five collection seasons are given in Table 7.18.

TABLE 7.18

Details of Collection of Class-II Gums

Collection Year	*Collection Rate per Qntl.*	*Quantity Collected*	*Quantity Disposed Off*	*Sale Price*
1998-99	2200 - 3000	721.39	721.39	20.27
1999-2000	2200 - 4500	2338.61	1992.61	52.6
2000-01	2200 - 4500	447.99	443.51	20.8
2001-02	2200 - 6000	391.68	391.68	15.18
2002-03	2000 - 3000	210.37	210.37	7.42

Note: Quality in quintals, amount in lakh rupees, variable collection rates for wet and dry seasons.
Source: *http://www.mfpfederation.com*

8.5 Non-Nationalised Forest Products

The state government has deregulated non-nationalised forest produce trade from 1984 onwards, and any individual is free to collect any non-nationalised minor forest product in any quantity for domestic or commercial consumption.

Very important and valuable non-nationalised non-wood forest products like *mahua, aonla, chirota, neem, mahul patta, chironji,* honey, tamarind etc., are found in abundance in the forests of Madhya Pradesh. The villagers are free to collect and sell these produce. Generally, after meeting their own requirements, the villagers sell the balance quantity to small local traders or middlemen at very low rates. These middlemen, in turn, earn huge profits from these produce.

Therefore, with a view to save these villagers from the exploitation by the middlemen, the collection of these non-wood forest products was started through primary forest produce co-operative societies from 1995-1996. Primary societies purchase these produce from the villagers and later on, sell the collected produce in bigger markets. All the decisions regarding the quantity and rate of purchase and sale are taken by the elected officials of the primary co-operative societies and district unions. The forest officials give all necessary help and guidance to them. The Federation gathers information regarding the market price and supply conditions and transfers this information to the district unions so that the produce collected by the societies can be conveniently sold at remunerative prices.

In the year 1998-99, about 12,188.60 quintals of non-nationalised NWFP was collected through the primary societies. The details of item-wise quantity collected are given in Table 7.19.

The importance of minor forest produce of NTFP lies not only in the gainful employment provided through activities related to collection and utilisation of MFPs in conjunction with the usual agricultural activities, or in the annual revenues provided to the state government to the tune of around Rs. 75 crore. The importance lies in the role these produce play in the livelihoods of tribal communities and forest dwellers providing them with diverse products for consumption for their houses, for their requirements of energy etc.

8.6 Collection and Sale of MFP in the State

The collection and sale of MFP are done through three tier co-operative structure:

TABLE 7.19

Forest Product-wise Quantity Collected

S. No.	Name of the NWFP			Quantity (in qntls)
	Local	English	Botanical	
1	*Achar-guthli*	Chironji tree	*Buchanania lanzan*	466.00
2	*Aonla*	Indian gooseberry	*Phyllanthus emblica*	5692.00
3	*Aonla* (Dry)	Indian gooseberry	*Phyllanthus emblica*	15.00
4	*Baheda*	Belleriee myrobalan	*Terminalia bellirica*	264.00
5	Chirota Seed	Ringworm plant	Cassia tora	404.00
6	*Shahad*	Honey		6.00
7	*Imli*	Tamarind	*Tamarindus indica*	166
8	*Mahua*		*Madhuca indica*	1555.00
8a	*Mahua gulli*		*Madhuca indica*	20.00
8b	*Mahua patta*			1004
9	*Safed musli*	Indian spider plant	*Chlorophytum borivilianum*	4.00
10	*Nagarmotha*	Nut grass	*Cyperus rotundus*	51.00
11	*Shatwar*	Asparagus	*Asparagus racemosus*	12
12	Others			858.00
	Total			10517.00

Source: *http://www.mfpfederation.com*

- An apex federation at the State level;
- The district union at the forest district level
- The primary forest co-operative societies at the village level.

After the 76th Amendment to the Constitution and enactment of Panchayats (Extension to the Scheduled Areas) Act, 1996 (PSEA, 1996), the Government of Madhya Pradesh defined the term MFP as follows: "MFP is the first produce which can be harvested on a non-destructive basis." The Government of Madhya Pradesh has also decided that the entire net profit coming out of the business of MFPs will be given to co-operative societies. Out of the total profit to the societies, 20 per cent would be spent on forest regeneration, 50 per cent would be distributed among *tendu patta* collectors and remaining amount would be spent for village development.

8.7 Collection of Non-Nationalised MFP

The Madhya Pradesh State Minor Forest Produce (Trade and Development) Co-operative Federation was given the job of collection of non-nationalised MFP in the year 1995-96 through its primary co-operative societies. The process adopted for collection is that a shortlisting of species has been done by the apex federation in which 100 species of commercial importance have been identified. The primary co-operative societies and the district unions have been asked to survey the possibilities of collection and marketing of these produce. The apex federation acts as a facilitator in marketing of the produce collected by the primary co-operative societies.

The role of the forestry sector in the state's economy is significant. The average contribution of forests to the state's total revenue receipt is around 1.74 per cent and its range is between 2.06 per cent to 1.49 per cent (Table 7.20).

TABLE 7.20

Showing the Contribution of Forests to the State's Total Revenue Receipt

(Figs. in Rs. '000)

Year	*State's Total Revenue*	*Total Revenue from Forestry and Wildlife**	*Percentage Contribution of Forests*
2001-02 (AC)	222870137	3317863	1.49
2002-03 (AC)	248295243	5125691	2.06
2003-04 (AC)	304102304	5227178	1.72
2004-05 (AC)	308801977	5742385	1.86
2005-06 (AC)	286094208	5061085	1.77
2006-07 (AC)	303356735	5696322	1.88
2007-08 (RE)	367115034	5949286	1.62
2008-09 (BE)	432130474	6556196	1.52
Average	309095764	5334500.75	1.74

Note: AC-actual, RE-revised estimate, BE-budget estimate;
* includes revenue from the sale of forest products and capital receipts.

Source: Volume 2 of state budget book, GoMP.

Table 7.21 shows revenue received through the sale of wood and non-wood forest products. The average revenue for the year 2001-02 to 2008-09 is Rs. 503.69 crore.

Figure 7.1 shows that the revenue from the sale of forest products is increasing. The average contribution of timber to the total revenue is 72 per cent. Apart from its significant contribution to the state exchequer, the forest sector plays an important role in the socio-economic upliftment of the people, especially the rural population who lives in and around the forest areas. It provides around 100 million person-days of employment to the rural poor every year. About 43,000 persons are regularly employed in the various establishments of the forest department. The tribals forming a quarter of the total population of the state are almost entirely dependent on forest for their livelihood. It is estimated

TABLE 7.21

Revenue Earned under Various Heads by MP Forest Department

(Figs. in Rs. '000)

Head	*Year*							
	*2001-02AC**	*2002-03AC*	*2003-04AC*	*2004-05AC*	*2005-06AC*	*2006-07AC*	*2007-08RE**	*2008-09BE**
Timber and other forest products	366997	444996	403697	604256	374332	584174	584000	720000
Social and farm forestry	242	17	25	321	0	11	130000	131500
Environment forestry	0	26	1750	0	0	0	80	90
Tendu leaf	151541	102064	0	1996	1974	4888	1865	401399
Minor forest products	216	7417	0	414	175	1	545	606
Timber	2042925	3346765	3798378	4013143	3787659	3880805	3951689	4110210
Bamboo	225976	225354	283107	335971	218275	265394	357935	107100
Khair	15880	5995	15427	18852	11641	8123	7140	1020
Others	260724	840394	465094	616118	509904	621642	396746	528075
Total	3064501	4973028	4967478	5591071	4903960	5365038	5430000	6000000

Note: *AC-actual, RE-revised estimate, BE-budget estimate.
Source: Volume 2 of state budget book, GoMP.

that the sector generates employment opportunities to the tribals to the tune of around 70 million person-days (*Source:* MP Forest Department). However, these benefits are not been recorded in the conventional system of Forest Resource Accounting (FRA).

FIGURE 7.1

Revenue from the Sale from Forest Products

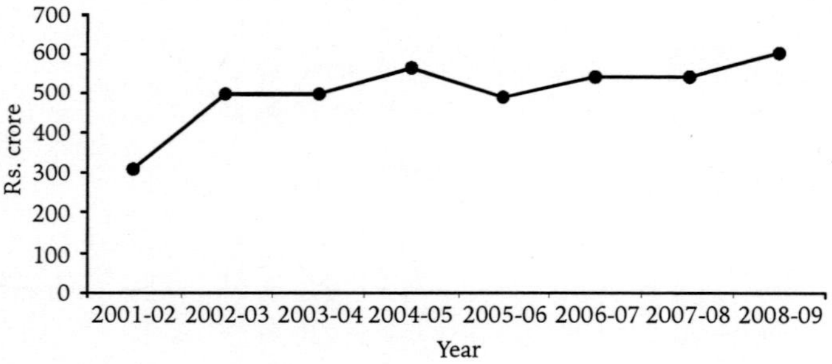

Source: State Budget Books, GoMP, various years.

8.8 Contribution of Forest Sector to GSDP

In the conventional system of FRA of India, the income from forest resources is aggregated at the national and state level under the head "Income from Agriculture, Forestry and Fisheries" and the sub-head of "Forestry and Logging". This includes the income from the following sources: (i) industrial wood, (ii) fire wood, and (iii) minor forest produce respectively (CSO, 2002). Gross domestic product (GDP) and net domestic product (NDP) from the forestry sector are computed as follows:

GDP = [Value of Output – Repairs, Maintenance and other Operational Costs]

NDP = [GDP – Consumption of Fixed Capital*]

* Consumption of Fixed Capital = Depreciation of Fixed Assets

In the state of Madhya Pradesh, the average (2000-2001 to 2005-2006) contribution of forest sector to gross state domestic product (GSDP) at current price was estimated at Rs. 11472.3 million. As shown in Figure 7.2, the forest sector contributed in the range between 2.01 to 2.78 per cent. The contribution shows the slightly declining trend over the years.

FIGURE 7.2

Percentage Contribution of Forest Sector to Gross State Domestic Product (at Current Prices)

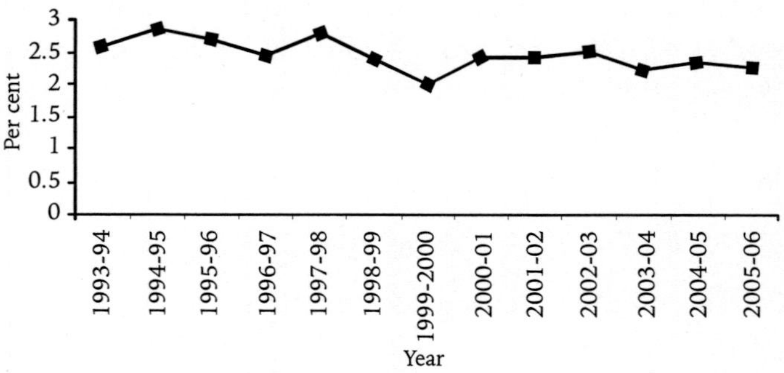

Source: Economic Survey, GoMP, 2006-07.

8.9 Expenditure on Forest

The total expenditure (non-Plan and Plan) required for the protection, conservation and management of

TABLE 7.22

Expenditure State of Forest Sector

(Figures in Rs. '000)

Particulars	*Year*							
	2001-02 AC	*2002-03 AC*	*2003-04 AC*	*2004-05 AC*	*2005-06 AC*	*2006-07 AC*	*2007-08 RE*	*2008-09 BE*
Total expenditure for forest department (1)	4615369	4835356	4586830	5645235	6509868	6295407	8203929	8408990
Public relations (Non-Plan) (a)	9836	14750	18270	17164	17498	15052	16000	16000
Relief expenditure for the areas affected by natutal calamities and drought-prone areas—revenue department (Plan and non-Plan) (b)	5681	1946	4757	3315	4152	4373	0	0
Financial assistance to three-tier PRIs-rural development (Plan) (c)	903	738	0	0	0	0	0	0
Total expenditure on forest sector by other departments (2=a+b+c)	16420	17434	23027	20479	21650	19425	16000	16000
Total expenditure for forest sector (3=1+2)	4631789	4852790	4609857	5665714	6531518	6314832	8219929	8424990
Proportion of forest sector expenditure to total state expenditure	2	1.91	1.53	1.78	2.25	2.09	2.25	1.95

Note: (1) includes non-Plan: police, housing, social security and welfare, loans for crop husbandry and roads and bridges; Plan: capital expenditure on forestry and wildlife; Non-Plan and Plan: soil and water conservation and forestry and wildlife.

AC-actual, RE-revised estimate, BE-budget estimate.

Source: Volume 3 of state budget book, GoMP.

forest resources of Madhya Pradesh is shown in Table 7.22. The average non-Plan expenditure accounts for 71 per cent of the total expenditure. The average proportion of forest sector expenditure to total state expenditure is 1.97.

As shown in Figure 7.3, the expenditure incurred on forestry and wildlife is higher than the revenue generated. However, if the values of unrecorded forest benefits are taken into consideration, the deficit in revenue would be wiped off.

FIGURE 7.3

Showing the Total Revenue and Expenditure Statement

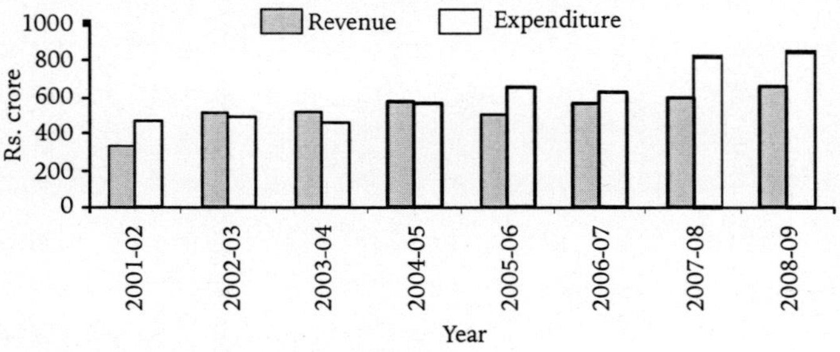

Source: State Budget Books, GoMP, various years.

8.10 Demand and Supply

A wide gap in demand and supply (Table 7.23) has put excessive pressure on the forests. In addition to home consumption, wood is also extracted for sale. As per the estimates, the ratio of firewood to food grain price doubled in 1975-1985, which made cutting wood for sale an attractive economic proposition. There has been a rapid increase in the incidence of head loading, which in itself was attributable to declining opportunities to the landless in rural areas to earn a livelihood.

TABLE 7.23

Estimated Demand and Supply of Timber, Fuel Wood and Fodder (undivided MP)

Forest Produce	*Total Domestic Demand*	*Present Production from Forests*	*Surplus/ Deficit*
Timber	2.00 m tonnes	00.50 m tonnes	-01.50 m tonnes
Fuel wood	24.30 m tonnes	00.60 m tonnes	-23.70 m tonnes
Fodder	83.20 m tonnes	41.90 m tonnes	-41.30 m tonnes

Source: Madhya Pradesh Forest Department.

Thus, there is a need to differentiate between urban and rural demand patterns and their effect on wood fuel supplies, as well as inter-fuel substitution. Urban wood fuels are usually traded with a much wider effect where reasonably-sized trees are cut, with a more degrading effect on forests, than with village supplies which comes from lopping, pruning or pollarding trees.

In the past, deforestation had often been associated with sudden policy change or period of uncertainty, like take-over of private forests and abolition of landlordism. Once large trees are felled, the old harmony between people's demands and supplies through twigs and branches gets disrupted, and government's efforts towards replanting come to naught. As these examples indicate, local patterns of deforestation vary and it is 'never a simple matter of numbers outstripping environment' (Westoby, 1985). It occurs as a result of not just local pressure on resources, but also any momentary disruption of the institutional framework responsible for resource protection and management.

8.11 Social Forestry Phase

The degradation of village lands and protected forests led to increased pressure from the people on the reserved forests. In order to reduce this pressure, the National Commission of Agriculture recommended growing trees on land accessible to village people. To quote from its report of 1976, "Free supply of forest produce to the rural population and their rights and privileges has brought destruction to the forest. Having over-exploited the resources, they cannot in all fairness expect that somebody else will take the trouble of providing them with forest produce free of charge. One of the principal objectives of social forestry is to make it possible to meet these needs in full from readily accessible areas ... Such needs should be met by farm forestry, extension forestry and by rehabilitating scrub forests and degraded forests."

By the mind-seventies, the realisation became clear that if peoples' demands were not met, it would be impossible to save forests. This was to be achieved through social forestry on village and private lands. As such, a Five-Year Social Forestry Project was launched in Madhya Pradesh in 1981-82 and continued up to 1985-86, in 21 districts. Plantations were raised over 41,875 ha of village common lands and 2,328 ha of such land was brought under pasture development. In all, nearly 31 million seedlings were distributed, mainly to the agriculturists.

Social forestry was not tried on forest lands, as such lands were sought to be used for producing timber and pulpwood and people's participation on such lands was not encouraged. Thus, social forestry was seen as a programme which would release industrial forestry from social pressures. But in order to keep people out, it was necessary to make them produce what they consumed free of charge using community and private lands to draw off the pressure on forest lands.

8.12 Evaluation of Social Forestry

It is now acknowledged that social forestry was an initiative that just did not take off, and did little to address the negative policy impacts referred to above. Evaluations have brought out the factors responsible for this lack of success.

According to the government, revenue and community wastelands were not made available to the forest department on time and this was one of the major reasons for the lack of success. The role of the village community was not in conformity to the needs of the programme. The *panchayats* did not come forward to take charge and control of the community plantations in the manner expected. The grazing of village cattle being a crucial issue, the co-operation of villagers was inadequate. Since non-forest public lands in villages are devoid of administrative control, and there are large-scale encroachments on them, it was impossible to locate compact areas even to the extent of 5 ha. There was an almost total lack of organisational ability at the village level, and women's participation was poor in most districts, especially in the north. To compound these weaknesses, there was no continuity or linkage in the wastelands so developed and they were scattered.

The villagers felt that they or the *gram panchayat* had little say in the programme. The villagers whose common lands were developed insisted on benefits being made available to them only, whereas *gram panchayats* wanted to have control over the forest products and services arising out of the developed wastelands. *Gram panchayat* could not become a viable organisational or administrative unit at the grassroot level for development and management of the public wastelands. The mid-term review of Madhya Pradesh social forestry project (USAID, 1985) commented that the principal aim of social forestry to build up institutional capacity of *panchayats* had fallen by the wayside because of the existing political economy of the *panchayats*. It concluded that short-term political motivation of the leaders and cattle pressure would not allow community managed plantations to last very long.

In the community forestry programme of a few villages in Madhya Pradesh, it was observed in a study by an independent agency, Centre for Development and Instructional Technology (CENDIT) in 1985, that there was factionalism in the villages, and the poor were hardly consulted about social forestry. Government officers were mainly interested in fulfilling targets, and often adopted the line of least resistance. The *panchayats* were not keen to take over plantations. Often community land was handed over to the forest department to avoid encroachment by the poor. The practice of the *panchayat* auctioning grass from such plantations reduced the availability of fodder for the poor.

Social forestry on village lands failed to take off in Madhya Pradesh because the local people were not involved. Village councils are multi-village bodies which do not inspire confidence in every constituent village; and there is no tradition of management (meaning protection, fresh planting and punishment to offenders) of common lands. The area available as village lands was also far less than anticipated at the project stage. Besides these structural constraints, there were shortcomings in the programme which was conceptualised and implemented, leading to a marked divergence between the stated objectives of social forestry and the actual outcomes.

First, market-oriented trees were planted which did little to improve consumption within the village. Fodder trees were generally ignored. Close spacing to accommodate more trees affected grass production. Second, as projects did little to meet the demand of the poor for fuel wood and fodder, pressure on forest land continued.

Third, as deforestation was perceived to be due to fuel wood and fodder demands of the people, it was assumed by the policy makers that given government help, people would willingly invest their labour and capital in raising fuel wood and fodder trees. However, as fuel and fodder were often collected for free, farmers preferred income generating trees, and continued to collect branches, twigs, leaves and grasses from forests as before. Thus, the assumption in social forestry about how village farmers would react to a given crisis was untenable. Producers were interested in increasing their incomes, and not in the national objective of providing fuel wood and fodder to the poor.

Fourth, as state funds got locked to meet the matching contribution required for external assistance for social forestry project, forest lands got starved of funds, with several adverse effects. The neglect of forest lands hurt forest dwellers and tribals. It reduced timber supplies to the markets, resulting in price escalation, which further increased smuggling from forest lands.

Fifth, species selection and spacing were considered technical questions, and hence were not examined carefully at the project stage. Benefits which could flow to the poor from species-yielding intermediate products were not properly appreciated. The value of the tree was linked in the minds of foresters with the final product obtained through felling. Thus, production of grasses, legumes, fodder, fruit and non-timber forest produces (NTFP) was neglected. Spacing has often been reduced to avoid intermediate management operations to reduce plantation cost, and to cut down on staff supervision time. As a consequence, spacing, thinning and pruning, which could have produced intermediate yields of grass and tree products for the people, have not been made use of. Technology with which the foresters were familiar for large-scale plantations for markets within forest areas was applied to small-scale village woodlots, where the need was more for fodder and subsistence than for timber.

8.13 Future Directions in Social Forestry

The policy and management issues which would be valuable for the continuation of the expansion of the MP farm forestry programme include the following:

- Formalisation of a state-wide farm forestry strategy incorporating collaboration with other land management agencies, and revision of planning rules and legislation to encourage farm forestry including harvesting and marketing mechanisms.

- The major trust for the advancement of farm forestry would be with respect to farm forestry demonstrations; many demonstrations often contain only one regime, and normally as a plantation design, when most farmers do not have the land available for such plantings. The following aspects should be borne while designing the demonstration plots: Tree species—while there is considerable concentration on eucalypts and a very successful programme for commercial production of clonal eucalyptus hybrids, which generally show the best performance, other species comparisons would be instructive. Tree spacing—many designs had trees planted at one metre intervals, which from basic silvicultural principles, will result in many tall slender trees which will take some time to reach merchantable size. Fewer trees planted, say at three metre intervals, would result in a shorter rotation period and quicker return. Also any impact on adjoining agricultural crops would be reduced. Planting designs—most demonstrations were in the form of plantations; of more relevance would be plantings on bunds, wastelands, water conservation areas, village surrounds and in intercropping arrangements. Coppicing many plantings assume a second crop being from the stump of the harvested trees. The resultant coppice will consist of many stems which will need to be reduced to one or two per stump in the first year after harvesting. Such demonstrations have not been established and developed as yet which would show treated and non-treated coppice. Mulching/fertilising—there were many instances where crop and tree litter was being burned resulting in a loss of organic matter and nutrients from the site. Demonstrations of mulching and litter retention *versus* removal would be valuable. Irrigated/non-irrigated—most research and extension (R&E) demonstrations were regularly irrigated on regimes not possible when combined with normal agricultural practice. Demonstrations on actual working farms would be more appropriate. Self tolerance—while not always obvious, salinity occurs in a number of regions of MP as a result of applying saline irrigation water. Demonstrations and research is needed to determine the salt tolerance of the preferred eucalyptus clones and other species advocated for farm forestry. Strategic plans—each R&E centre should be encouraged to review their objectives and their audience's needs to assist and identify the most relevant demonstrations of farm forestry. There are numerous farmers with suitable plantings who indicated to us that they were prepared to co-operate with the R&E centres and convert existing plantings or be prepared to establish new plantings on their land to serve as demonstrations.

- Underlying the need for on-farm demonstrations is the acceptance that a failed demonstration too is a success in itself since considerable knowledge can be gained explaining why the demonstrations failed. In general, we observed a reluctance to demonstrate improper techniques, inappropriate species selection or silviculture. The existing demonstrations provide the opportunity to compare and contrast.

9. Forest Policy, 1988

The new Forest Policy announced in 1988 gives higher priority to environmental stability than to earning revenue. It discourages monocultures and prefers mixed forests. Relevant paragraphs from the policy are: "The life of tribals and other poor living within and near forest revolves around forests. The rights and concessions enjoyed by them should be fully protected. Their domestic requirements of fuel wood, fodder minor forest produce, and cost ruction timer should be the first charge on forest produce."......... "As far as possible, forest based industry should raise the raw material needed for meeting its own requirements, preferably by establishment of a direct relationship between the factory and the individuals who can grow the raw material...."

The Ministry of Environment and Forests, GoI, in an official paper in March 1991, stated, "This (National Forest Policy, 1988) reverses the recommendations of the NCA, which favoured commercial plantations on forest lands, and tree planting for meeting the subsistence needs on private lands of the rural people. It is visualised that industrial raw-material supply from the forest areas would eventually be phased out so that the industry meets its requirements largely from trees raised on private degraded lands." The reasons attributed for this change in approach for formulating policy, since the late eighties can broadly be summarised as follows:

- The definition of "development" and the strategy for achieving it has changed world over, and it is no longer equated with economic development or industrialisation.
- In all sectors, generally the government looks after the infrastructure or welfare needs of people, whereas market needs are met from the private sector. In forestry, this distribution of responsibility was not being followed and the reverse was being attempted so far.
- Several fruit trees demanded by farmers and which would also have produced wood, were not encouraged in the social forestry projects. In Madhya Pradesh, large farmers wanted to grow teak, but the social forestry programmes could not satisfy this, as teak is not classified as fuel wood or fodder tree.
- It appears that interests of the local population were often directly pitted against department considerations. Forests were sought to be protected not for the people, but against them. Although it was being realised at the Government of India level that other usufruct based species were required, as planting of teak only transfers biotic pressure from one region to another, yet large scale propagation techniques are important.

Minor forest produce (MFP) like tamarind, *neem* and *mahua* are still to be developed for specific sites. On the other hand, teak, the major planted species in forest lands, is not preferred by tribals.

- Another issue at stake in the planting of teak and other such timber-only species is of sustainability. Planting teak encourages smugglers or undisciplined behaviour. When priorities are to be fixed, livelihood products like NTFPs, on which the local population might be depending, should rank high. In the prevailing environment of smuggling of timber, it was ironic that tribals, who for centuries lived in harmony with forests, were tempted to eke out a living by felling timber trees, although there is some evidence to suggest that the poor do not cut trees which provide usufructs, but only such trees where the value is in stem only.

10. Joint Forest Management (JFM)

There are over 22,000 villages in the state which are situated on the forest fringes. These villages constitute almost 42 per cent of the total villages in the state. The tribal population of the state is nearly 20 per cent, out of which substantial population is living on the forest fringes. These villages are greatly dependent on forests for their livelihood and have an intimate and reciprocatory relationship with forests. It is generally understood that the biotic pressure from villagers seeking fuel wood, fodder and timber, both for their needs and for generating cash, is the main cause of degradation of the forests. Any effort of the government could not check the increasing damage to the forests.

After experiencing from the past that government alone cannot effectively protect and manage the forest resources, the state government decided to take the co-operation of people living adjoining to the forest area and finally introduced the concept of participatory management in forestry sector. With a view to involving local people in forest management, not only to check further degradation of forest for their basic needs, but also to introduce the concept of sustainable forest development together with village development, the Government of India issued a circular on 01/06/90 supporting joint planning and management of degraded forests in all parts of India. The state of Madhya Pradesh took a lead in JFM.

The concept of JFM may be defined as, "the sharing of products, responsibilities control and decision making authority over forest lands between forest department and local user group. It involves a contract specifying the distribution of authority responsibilities and benefits."

JFM is the best way to protect, regenerate and manage forests. The basic object behind it is to create awareness in local people that they are the owners of the forests collectively and the forest department is only a manager. It is important for people to realise the fact that they have stake in the protection of forests and that their social and economic life becomes enriched by tangible and intangible benefits flowing from well protected and managed forests tract near their habitation, and all this is possible if they actively participate in forest management.

In accordance with the guidelines of Government of India, the state government passed a resolution in December 1991 for community participation in forest management for preventing illicit felling in sensitive forest areas and rehabilitation of degraded forests. Two types of village committees were prescribed.

Village forest committees to be formed for rehabilitation of degraded forests (density upto 40 per cent) and forest protection committees to be formed to protect well-wooded forests (density more than 40 per cent). The state government resolution of 1991 proved to be a milestone in the taking-off of JFM activities. JFM activities in Harda division set the wheel of JFM in motion and it was followed in many more forest areas of the state.

In order to reduce the dependence of the villagers on forests, village resource development programmes/eco-development programmes have been taken up as one of the important activities of the JFM. Eco-development is based on the belief that if foresters support village development—resources, cattle, veterinary inputs, schools, health, water, roads, etc.—then the people will appreciate the role of forests and help in its protection.

Eco-development is different from social forestry in one respect, that is, it is implemented in fringe areas, whereas social forestry was generally in areas remote from forest lands. However, the two share a common assumption—if resources outside forest lands become more productive, people will give up gathering from forests. There are some success stories, but these are mostly pilot experiments, and their large-scale replication is still to be tried.

By itself, poverty alleviation does not reduce dependence on open resources. However, it may facilitate it if combined with measures like JFM. JFM should not mean just giving a share from forest produce to the people. Only when people are given greater security of access to the forest products that they depend on and a sense of partnership in forest management, will they have a greater motivation to ensure that the forest resource is not degraded. They themselves will then assist or undertake the protection of the resource though regular patrolling and regulation of use. This will require fulfilling of several conditions, which seem to be lacking at present in Madhya Pradesh.

To make the provision of 1991 resolution more effective, in 1995, a revised resolution was issued by the state government which included elaborate arrangements to ensure participatory micro planning for the protection and management of forests and a clear approach for integrated village resource development programme (VRDP). VRDP is viewed as a complementary activity to forest protection. Women's participation was ensured by offering them 50 per cent membership in committees. Further amendments were made through the JFM resolutions in the year 2000 and 2001.

There have been many instances of petty conflicts amongst people in JFM areas, but they do not relate to usufruct distribution among themselves. Whereas conflicts do take place sometimes when the members of the committees apprehend forest offenders, but these conflicts are resolved internally. According to the new Nistar Policy, concessions are available to the people regarding forest produce within 5 km periphery of forests. People living in such forest areas are eligible for the forest produce at concessional rates.

10.1 Some Important Components of JFM Strategy

- *Introduction of village resource development programme:* It is based on the strategy of involving communities in the management and sustainable utilisation of forests and creating alternative sources of income and employment to reduce pressure on the forest. The creation of village assets have gained the confidence of the villagers and hence, consolidating the JFM approach.
- *Micro planning:* In this approach, people are being involved in planning and it helps in proposing the management of the forests and development of village resources the way people want.
- *Participation of non-governmental organisations:* NGOs are being encouraged to work as an intermediary between government and the villagers in various JFM activities.
- *Training:* The training programmes are tailored to inculcate attitudinal changes of the staff so that they are able to communicate with the local people living especially in the vicinity of the forest areas in preparing micro plans of that area. This also sensitises them towards working together.

10.2 Gender Focus of Forest Management

Gender has become an inseparable issue of forestry development recently. With the role of community in management of forest resources through participatory management being widely accepted now, true participation cannot be achieved without involving women. Fuel wood and fodder for domestic needs are generally collected by women. Therefore, they are being actively involved in efforts to generate alternate sources for fuel wood and fodder on field bunds by the state government. An even more critical move has been involving women in formulating micro plans in areas allotted to VFCs. Women leaders in villages and women *panchayat* representatives are entrusted with the task of motivating and organising women to play an effective role in these activities. Existing women's groups such as the *mahila mandals* are also being involved in participatory management of forests.

Most of the head-loaders in the state are women, whose livelihood is curtailed by the new forest management arrangements. They have very few alternative sources of income, so they need to be compensated. The formation of self-help groups (SHGs) of women is one of the most significant strategies being adopted to involve women and compensate them. The initiation of thrift and credit activities under SHGs enables women to realise their productive potential and they could be seen as and helped to become economic actors. Making women effective income-earners helps reducing their dependency on forests.

The functioning of SHGs follow almost similar pattern, *viz.*, homogeneous groups of 10-20 women form a SHG. The group carries out compulsory thrift on weekly basis ranging from Rs. 5-10 per person. Some of the SHGs are also linked with the Development of Women and Children in Rural Areas (DWCRA) programme.

A study conducted in 24 villages of district Harda found that 40 per cent of the villages having JFM committees has a positive impact on agriculture. The advancement was in the form of strengthening of the irrigation infrastructure, increased farm mechanisation and increase in availability of agriculture credit. In 60 per cent villages, no significant improvements were noted as result of JFM in the village.

In 20 of the 21 non-control villages, the JFM impacted negatively on livestock rearing as a source of livelihood. The main reason was that many compartments were closed for grazing and the remaining available compartments could not be managed efficiently. Secondly, the area faced severe problem of weed infestation. The weeds like lantana, *van-tulsi* and *chirita* posed problems for the villagers by suppressing the growth of fodder species. The JFM programme contributed significantly in increasing opportunities for wage labour in three out of four forest villages. But in other villages, the contribution was only marginal and insufficient. Manish Shankar (2005).

11. Forest Development Authority

Four centrally sponsored schemes were merged to form National Afforestation Programme for promoting forest cover on degraded forests and adjoining lands including national parks and sanctuaries. This programme is implemented through the Forest Development Authority established as a confederation of selected JFM committees. The FDAs are working on the participatory project management approach with an aim to holistic development of the ecosystem which includes the forests and inhabitations under the forest committees. The operational parts of FDA include components like awareness, micro planning, entry point activities, soil and water conservation, plantations, monitoring and evaluation, and social fencing, ensuring active participation in the forest committees. Madhya Pradesh has constituted 49 FDAs with 15188 JFM committees and an amount of Rs. 72.30 crore has been released by the GoI so far. Further, proposals to constitute FDA in more territorial divisions are in the process.

12. Greening of Non-forest Lands: *Lok Vaniki*

In the state of MP, there are large number of small patches of private tree-clad areas and forests. They have not been yielding any income to the owners. Such private landholdings of the thousands of farmers are small, generally ranging from 0.5 ha to 15 ha.

The owners of such private forests are tempted to somehow get rid of the standing tree crop and convert the land into agricultural fields or they become indifferent to their forests. In order to achieve the overall goal of conservation and sustainable development, a scheme based on private forestry, called *Lok Vaniki* was launched by the Government of MP in April 1999 on a pilot basis. The scheme envisages that felling of trees in private forests of willing owners, will take place as per a duly approved management plan. Such management plans would prescribe multi-tier scientific management of privately held forest. The management plan is to be prepared for each private holding to ensure continuity of management and improvement of the area.

The *bhumi swami* or the *lok vaniki* beneficiary has to sell the timber growing on his or her land to the forest department only, and the price of the timber so sold is paid to the *bhumi swami* as per the rates fixed by the state government. Vide the government of MP's forest department circular no. F-4267/289/05/10-3 dated 5 November 2005, a provision has been made for the benefit of the *bhumi swami* (land owner) and the *lok vaniki* beneficiaries that they can have a separate lot of the timber grown on their land at the time of sale through the forest department. The *bhumi swami/lok vaniki* beneficiary may opt for fixing of the upset price of the lot of his/her timber and the final disposal of the lot to be done as per departmental procedures. He/she may reduce the price so fixed if the need arises in future auctions (*www.forest.mp.gov.in*).

12.1 The MP Lok Vaniki Act, 2001

The state of Madhya Pradesh has recently enacted the MP Lok Vaniki Act, 2001 (MP Act No. 10 of 2001) to give a boost to scientific management of privately owned 'forests' and other 'tree-clad areas' in the state. The Act provides an opportunity to the willing landholders to take up management of their tree-clad holdings for optimising economic returns to themselves and simultaneously ensuring environmental benefits to the society. The Act is voluntary as its application as provided in the Section 1 clause(3). Section 3 of the Act deals with the preparation of management plan by chartered foresters. Sections 4, 5 and 6 of the Act deal with the approval, implementation and monitoring of the implementation of such approved management plans respectively. Section 7 of the Act provides for the enrolment of chartered foresters. The provisions regarding punishment for contravention and appeal against such punishments are contained in Sections 8 and 9 respectively. The remaining four sections, i.e., Sections 10, 11, 12 and 13 contain provisions.

12.1.1 Objectives

- *Lok vaniki* aims at arresting degradation in private forests and improving their productivity by linking scientific management of these areas with the livelihood system and economic returns.
- *Lok vaniki* aspires to bridge the increasing gap between the demand and the supply of forest produce by improving the productivity of private forests, tree-clad areas and wastelands. This would help in greening large barren stretches, improve the environment and substantially assist in the eradication of rural poverty.
- The major thrust of the scheme is on 'handing back' to the people, the management of their own forests for economic and environmental benefits by 'unlocking' the neglected and degraded forests on private holdings.
- It also aims at considerably spreading green cover on areas unsuitable for 'good' and profitable agriculture, by facilitating development of a culture of cultivation of trees, medicinal herbs, shrubs and climbers as a regular source of earning for land owners.
- The Lok Vaniki programme intends to facilitate the production of improved and certified planting stock by improvement in technologies of production of planting material through use of microbiology, biotechnology and tissue culture.

12.1.2 Progress

The scheme is being implemented in 10 districts of the state, namely Dewas, Damoh, Sidhi, Hoshangabad, Narsimghapur, Seoni, Dindori, Mandla, Katni and Jabalpur. More than 100 management plans have so far been prepared in three districts and many more are under preparation. Cultivation of aromatic grasses and medicinal plants is covered by regular and attractive income to the farmer. Training programme for such activities is supported under the scheme. One distillation plant for aromatic grasses has been set up by the farmers themselves in Pokhar village of Dewas. This distillation unit has started production of *Rosha* oil which is being sold at attractive prices. Efforts for entrepreneurship development have begun with the help of private individuals and government agencies. The MP Lok Vaniki Act, 2001 has been enacted and rules are in the process of finalisation.

13. Forest Department Initiatives under State Plan Development Funds

13.1 PPA or the People's Protected Areas

This new initiative undertaken by the MP State Minor Forest Produce Co-operative Federation is based on sustainable livelihood approach with biodiversity conservation (SLAB) and involves conservation and development along with non-destructive and sustainable harvesting of non-wood forest products (NWFP). The activities planned in this initiative include *in-situ* and *ex-situ* conservation, training, processing, value addition and green marketing. In the first phase, PPA programme was being undertaken in eight districts of the state. As on date, PPA programme is being undertaken in 17 districts of the state.

13.2 Hi-tech Plantations

The productivity of important species like teak, bamboo, *aonla* and *gamhar* are raised with high technology inputs of irrigation and fertilisation. These plantations are raised on a small scale with 2-10 ha of area in plantation working circles under the working plan. The planting stock for the plantation is obtained from known progeny with established productive potential. The theme is two-pronged for raising such plantations. One, to establish the good stock progeny in forests and two, to demonstrate that the best growth requires best inputs (like agriculture) for sustaining high productivity. During the last five years, 1600 ha of high-tech plantations have been raised throughout the state.

13.3 Privatisation of Forest Lands

The present policies regarding government forests have not been adequately successful in either improving productivity, or improving welfare of the people. Several alternatives have been suggested, including leasing of forests land to user-industries.

The estimated demand for wood and bamboo has been assessed to be 6.4 million tonnes by the industry in 1991 as against the current utilisation of 3.2 million tonnes, rising up to 20.2 million tonnes by the year 2015. Assuming a low productivity of 3 tonnes per ha per annum, the requirement can be met from 2 million ha. There is 141 m ha of cultivated land in the country, 60 per cent of which is owned by rich and affluent farmers, who are market-oriented and can be trusted to fulfil the requirements of the industry. Industries required fast growing species *viz.*, eucalyptus or bamboos, which can be easily produced in 5-8 years time, and are eminently suitable for farm forestry. Leasing out lands to industries is thus not necessarily the only solution to meet this demand.

It may be relevant here to mention the recent upsurge in the number of companies offering private teak plantations to the urban rich. Commercial sector in forestry, if desirous of acquiring large chunks of degraded land to take the advantage of economy of scale, can follow this example and learn from the experience of such private sector initiatives. Leasing of forest lands on a large scale even to the poor is not desirable. First, a great deal of private land, often with the poor, is uncultivated, but may be suitable for trees. More than 5 to 6 million hectare lands have been leased to the poor in the last two decades. In addition, in semi-arid regions a great deal of private land is either uncultivated or yields very low output. The total area of such land is estimated at 45 million hectares, which is comparable with the area of degraded forest lands. Hence, there is no case for further privatisation, unless suitable technological and institutional arrangements have been worked out to bring this huge chunk of land under trees of agro-forestry. Second, privatisation would encourage farmers or the poor to plant short-term exotics, or use land for agriculture. Both forms of land use for degraded lands are environmentally not desirable. The limited market demand is another constraint. What is required is to put degraded public lands under shrubs, bushes, or slow growing multi-purpose trees (MPT), which are environmentally more sustainable. This option, however, does not bring immediate returns; hence, the poor are unlikely to do so on leased lands.

Third, the number of the poor families is very large, and privatising in favour of some, while ignoring others, is likely to produce social tensions. Fourth, villagers have the right of collection on most of degraded forest lands, and privatisation would perhaps be against the existing settlement laws, and will be opposed by other villages, having usufructory rights in the concerned forest land. Fifth, the experience of some of the NGOs like Sewa Mandir in Rajasthan shows that they were more successful when they undertook afforestation of public lands, rather than of private lands. This is because the constraints in semi-arid monocropped areas are such that individual approach is less likely to succeed than working with groups. And lastly, most of the forest lands are in tribal areas, where market penetration is weak. The population per village is not high, and hence working with groups does not raise the kind of problems encountered in non-forest public lands, where penetration of markets and large size of villages have eroded the cohesive nature of village society. On the whole, there is no escape from continuing the present system of government management on forest lands.

13.4 Other State Level Initiatives

13.4.1 Encouraging Tree Planting and Private Investment and Private Investment on Non-Forest Wastelands

In view of the above concern, the state government has taken many important decisions to encourage and assist the farmers and other private growers for raising of plantations on private and public wastelands. Efforts have also been made to overcome the factors that discourage the farmers to go for plantations thinking that the farmers can play an important role to abridge the big gap between the demand and supply of the forest produce. In 1997, the state government amended MP Land Revenue Code, 1959, where the following changes have been introduced. Some of the efforts made by the state government are enumerated below:

- Powers to permit felling of dead/dying trees of mango, jamun, tamarind, *mahua*, sandalwood, *harra* on private lands have been delegated to *panchayats*.
- No permission for felling and transit for timber in the holding of any private owner will be required when such trees are planted, including commercial plantations.
- The state government declared a policy in 1997 about leasing non-forest (revenue) wasteland to private companies to produce tree-based raw material for their industries. This will definitely go a long way in reducing pressures on natural forests, and stabilise tree-based industries.
- Lands under tree plantations have been exempted from the provisions of Land Ceiling Act.
- Transit permit rules have been liberalised to promote tree plantation on private lands.
- Contractual supplies to industries beyond 31.12.1998 have been terminated to create better market condition for private growers.

These efforts made by the government have encouraged farmers to take up more forestry activities on private degraded/wastelands.

Market information—There is generally little awareness amongst farmers about the kind of price that they could reasonably expect to get for their trees. To overcome this problem, forest department has established an Industrial Liaison Unit, which would co-ordinate between the tree grower and consumer and will provide all necessary market information.

Research is needed to identify other short-rotation, high-value species besides eucalyptus. Farmers should have a range of trees on their land, which meet their various needs, and spread the risk of the collapse of any one market. Such activities have already been initiated in 14 R&E divisions and State Forest Research Institute, Jabalpur.

There is urgent need of huge quantities of improved high-yielding and disease-resistant planting materials. Assurance of purity of the material is more vital in fruit and forest seedlings than in seasonal crops since the taste of the fruits and trees can be had only after 3 to 5 years. Secondly, not much research data has been generated on the rainfed horticultural crops.

The primary stated objective of every forestry project includes that it wishes to help people. However, in many cases it has been seen that direct support in people's lives does not extend beyond wages. It is advisable that programmes attempt to both aim for as well as assess the non-monetary benefits to people, so that programmes in future can be evolved and designed with increased direct and tangible benefits for communities.

The state government has taken a number of measures to modernise the forest protection mechanism. However, the shortage of financial resources is a limiting factor here also.

The states with rich and large forest area need to be provided with increased allocation from Government of India under Integrated Forest Protection Scheme.

The state government's efforts for saving forest are not adequate enough as emphasised through the following facts and figures. Here is the reality check.

1. At many places in the forest, illegal mining is carried out. Measures taken to stop the activity are not strong and adequate enough.
2. In the absence of alternative energy sources, there is uncontrolled cutting of trees that are providing firewood.
3. On the account of heavy encroachment on forests in the districts like Khargone, Barwani and Burhanpur, forest is on the diminishing way.
4. Incidences of illegal forest cutting and poaching are continuing in the state owing to growing poverty and unemployment.
5. The forest manual prepared in 1949 is greatly outdated, no updated version has come out in the past 30 years.
6. Out of 95 thousand sq km forest in the state, more than 40 per cent falls in the category of deteriorated forest.
7. Compared to 1978-79, production of bamboo has fallen down nearly four times. In 1967-68, production of wood was 62.49 lakh cubic metres, that has declined to its lowest at just 3.60 lakh cubic metres in 2008-09.
8. Number of production divisions in the state has reduced from 37 to 14.

13.4.2 People and Forest Management

With livelihood forestry, subsistence and consumption would be met more from forest land, and market demand would be met more from private land. Using private lands for short rotation products will permit the large area of forest lands to be used for long gestation trees, which enrich the environment and provide a range of products to the poor. Choice of species and management practices should be radically changed to suit the new policy. In Madhya Pradesh, the changes at policy level has allowed government to harness the tremendous attachment of the tribals for forests. The schemes have been conceived to demonstrate that the development of forests also bestowed benefits on the tribals, and this has initiated a new era of partnership between the tribals and the government.

Technical—If the site is bare, degraded to the point that it cannot support trees, then grasses, legumes, local shrubs and agave may be the only alternative. Attempting to plant trees on bare soil would result in low survival or poor growth. Besides, grass cover can reduce run-off of rain and soil loss. Protection of bare area has given excellent growth of grasses in Jhabua and it has become a good source of income generation for the members of village forest committee.

Environmental—The maintenance of life support system is a function performed mainly by the crown biomass of trees. It is this component of trees that can contribute positively towards the maintenance of the hydrological and nutrient cycles. Trees, which provide a lot of leaves, twigs and branches, enrich the soil much better than those which provide poles and timber alone. One of the main outputs from forests should be water, which is possible only when forests are considered more in the context of local rather than national needs.

Political—If trees for timber are grown primarily on forest lands, no matter what instructions are issued by the government for giving a particular share to the poor (such as in Hitgrahi scheme in Madhya Pradesh), they are difficult to implement as supply is not equal to demand. Besides this, the chances of intermediaries and trader-smugglers benefiting from this arrangement increases. If low value (low in market value terms, but high in biomass) output is planned, the government may try to restrict the entry of people in the forests but the poor will still manage to access the forest lands and to fulfil their needs. If species suitable for individual gathering by households are planted, the poor would directly appropriate the benefits. Unlike commercial timber species, relatively low value non-rotational trees for intermediate products would not attract the attention of rich farmers and contractors.

Economic—Since the demand for marketed wood in India is limited, by duplicating the same species like eucalyptus on forest lands as on farm lands, we are ultimately cutting into the profits of the farmers, and thus undermining the farm forestry programme itself. It would be ironic if production of eucalyptus on farm lands, which is far cheaper, is discouraged because of production of more expensive eucalyptus on government lands. Although there is as yet no glut of eucalyptus in Madhya Pradesh, looking at the experience of several parts of the country, the possibility of market saturation cannot be ruled out, if common species are planted on both forest and private lands.

Demand and supply position shows that the demand for commercial wood, although at present unsatisfied, is only a small fraction of the demand for fuel wood. The gap between supply and demand of timber and pulpwood can be met by afforestation of private and revenue wasteland. Unlike timber, which is bought from markets, fuel wood is generally gathered by rural people and even by the urban poor, and only the lower middle class (the middle class use kerosene and the rich use gas) in urban areas and the very rich in rural areas buy fuel wood. Moreover, in some parts of the country, cow dung and husk are used as fuel. The source of supply is thus varied; farmer's produce has to compete with supplies from head-loaders, bullock carts and merchants who buy wood from forest auctions.

The fact is that fuel wood markets supply hardly 10-15 per cent of the total fuel wood consumed. It has two implications. First, the gatherers can always beat the producers over the pricing of fuel wood; the producers would be price-takers, rather than price-makers. Second, the market price of fuel wood would always be lower than its social cost for replacement of growing stock through investments in plantations. These make production of wood for fuel wood markets a non-viable proposition. It may also be mentioned here that although the real price of fuel wood in urban markets increased steadily between 1975 and 1985, it started declining after 1985, causing further loss to the producers (Singh, 1985; Chambers, 1989; Saxena, 1990). These considerations prove beyond any doubt that the fuel wood gaps can be met only through such trees on public lands that produce a lot of twigs and branches.

There are several implications of this. First, in cases when degraded lands are to be used for wood production, there must be reservation for this sector as far as pole, pulpwood and timber (to the extent possible) are concerned, and these species should not be raised on forest lands. Second, research needs to identify other short rotation, high value species, which suit farmers' requirements of planting on marginal lands and bunds. Third, such species should be promoted in forest lands where the main product is different from wood, like MFP.

Managerial—A further advantage of planting "trees of the poor" (which are essentially employment augmenting trees, as they require labour for gathering and collection, as opposed to trees which are clear-felled) on forest lands is the likelihood of improved co-operation. People are reluctant to protect trees, which will be auctioned or felled, to the benefit of government, contractor and forest staff. They are much more likely to collaborate in protection of trees from which they are, much more than others, in a position to benefit.

Forest lands have a comparative advantage in growing long gestation trees which may be less attractive to farmers. Fortunately, these are also the source of several MFPs. Instead of raising plantation crops, these lands should be used for non-rotational trees and natural forests, the produce of which is gathered. Bamboo, *aonla*, fruit and oil bearing trees like *mahua* and *karanj*, which provide income to poor and raw material for artisans, should get a high priority. These should be supplemented with shrubs, grasses and bushes to yield fibre, fuel wood and fodder in the shortest possible time, and some trees, which can go well with teak and can provide fuel wood in the short time. Thus, the policy should be to encourage usufruct-based trees in place of trees that require felling.

The suggestions given here require 'productivity' and 'economic value' to be redefined in terms of multipurpose utilisation and satisfying basic human needs. Rather than maximise the timber value, the objective of scientific forestry should be to maximise biomass, by allowing a tree to expand horizontally rather than to grow in the vertical direction only. In place of stem-based forestry, crown-based forestry will be environmentally superior, besides satisfying people's needs and thus being more sustainable to conventional forestry. This requires a new outlook and a new silviculture, in which the interests of all poor people to secure rights of gathering would be paramount.

The lessons of experience are clear. Addressing upfront the livelihood security needs of the poor has to be the essential touchstone of any vision that seeks to ensure the long-term sustainability of forest resources.

14. Road Ahead

The constraints such as lack of natural regenerations and low productivity, grazing pressure beyond the carrying capacity of forests, over-exploitation of forest produce, forest fire affecting regeneration and causing damage to forests, inadequate institutional capabilities, lack of people's participation and less effective investment affects the enhancement of forest resources (NFAP, 1999). Besides, the investment in the forestry sector has been very low ranging between 1.53 to 2.25 per cent of the total outlay of the state plan, which is the main constraint in the development of forests.

- The well-stocked forest area should be brought under protected area network.
- Assisted natural regeneration should be undertaken for rehabilitation of degraded forest and open forests with people's participation.
- The livestock improvement programme should be encouraged and fodder production programme in the non-forest area should be taken up to reduce the pressure of grazing on forest.
- The gap between demand and supply will be minimised by rehabilitation of degraded forest and undertaking large-scale plantations of fuel and fodder species on the degraded forest and outside the forest areas.
- The summer season in Madhya Pradesh is very favourable for wild fire. The wild fire is responsible for loss of valuable forest resource. With a view to avoid the negative effects of fire, it is necessary to develop efficient fire protection and management mechanism with well-development network of wireless system and adoption of geographic information system (GIS) technology.
- The time-to-time capacity building programmes on forest protection, management and conservation should be undertaken.
- People's participation for sustainable forestry development should be ensured with encouraging the income generating activities.
- The unrecorded forest benefits should be incorporated in the existing system of forest resource accounting to reflect the real contribution of forest sector. This in turn helps in formulating appropriate policy and planning for the forest conservation and management.
- NGOs working on forestry development, uplifting poverty, increasing literacy, improving health and generating employment opportunities should be involved in motivating the forest dwelling people for their overall socio-economic development.

Chapter 8

Status of Women and Children in Madhya Pradesh

1. Introduction

This chapter is an attempt at understanding the status of women and children in the state of Madhya Pradesh. In building this understanding, we have taken the help of available and reliable statistical data. These data on social indicators enable us in arriving at conclusions over their situation. With the help of these social indicators, an attempt has been made to examine the gender disparity that exists in the state. Further, an attempt has been made to bring in the cultural, social, political, environmental and developmental context of the region along with the temporal and spatial behaviour of social indicators to draw a comprehensive picture of the situation of women and children in MP. Very often, inferences that may point towards the possibility of a particular social phenomenon have been drawn and often the need for further analysis of the phenomenon has been suggested.

A precise definition of the term 'status' is a difficult proposition as it is still an evolving term and encompasses a variety of indicators to assess the position of a particular group in a social system or sub-system. In studying the status of women, different authors have perceived and interpreted status in different ways in their studies. Each of their study has brought in a range of qualitative and quantitative indicators and contributed a great deal to the understanding of the position of women in society. These include the extent of women's access to social and material resources within the family, community and society (Dixon, 1978), her authority or power within the family/community and the prestige commanded from those other members (Mukherjee, 1975), or her position in the social system distinguishable from, yet related to, other positions (Committee on the Status of Women in India, 1974). Each of these attempts has been to understand the gender-related disparities, and thus finding ways and means of minimising them.

As such, women and children are identified as the key components of marginalised sections of the society although women constitute half of the societal population, while children in 0-18 age group (including both the gender groups) constitute 40 per cent share in total population. Hence, the overall status of these groups assumes greater social importance first and then the economic development of the society. In the current study of the status of women and children in Madhya Pradesh, indicators related to health, demography, education and employment have been studied.

2. Key Survival Indicators

A look at the key survival indicators reveals extremely high levels of mortality. Comparing the transition over the last decade, one does notice an improvement, although very marginal. Prevalence of high mortality rates does call for immediate and earnest attention from all quarters.

Deaths due to pregnancy and childbirth are common among women in the reproductive age groups. Reduction of mortality of women has thus been an area of concern, and governments across the globe have set time-bound targets to achieve it. The International Conference on Population and Development in 1994 had recommended reduction in maternal mortality by at least 50 per cent of the 1990 levels by the year 2000 and further one-half by the year 2015. The Millennium Development Goals (MDGs) has set the target of achieving 200 maternal deaths per lakh of live births by 2007 and 109 per lakh of live births by 2015. Let us see the progress made by Madhya Pradesh on these key survival indicators in Table 8.1.

TABLE 8.1

Key Survival Indicators for Madhya Pradesh

Indicator	*Year*	*Value*	*Source*
Life expectancy at birth (in years)	2002-2006	Total- 58.0 Male- 58.1 Female- 57.9	Economic Survey of India, 2008-09
Total fertility rate	2005-06	Total- 3.12 Rural- 2.58 Urban- 3.34	NFHS-III
Maternal mortality rate (per lakh)	2004-2006	335	SRS
Infant mortality rate (per thousand)	2005-06	70	NFHS-III
Child mortality under 5 (per thousand)	2005-06	94.2	NFHS-III
Malnutrition under 5 (%)	2005-06	60	NFHS-III

Note: SRS - Sample Registration Survey.

Madhya Pradesh has the highest infant mortality rate (IMR) among Indian states. The state ranked second in child mortality and anaemia in children under 5. On similar lines, it ranked third in infant mortality and maternal mortality in the country. Surprisingly, life expectancy at birth for females in Madhya Pradesh is lower than the males; in other states, the scenario is just the opposite. Also on various socio-economic indicators, MP is performing below the national average. The above facts are good enough to explain the status of women and children in Madhya Pradesh. It was also observed in the analysis that these indicators show little change from its position in the early nineties. Therefore, it is definitely a cause of serious concern on one hand and reflects poor programmatic interventions and implementation on the part of the state government on the other.

2.1 Trends in CBR, CDR and TFR in the Last Three Decades

As seen in Figure 8.1, crude birth rate (CBR) (SRS estimates) has been declining consistently from 1991 to 2005, but only marginally with close to 10 per cent rural-urban differential. The state's crude death rate (CDR) also declines steadily from 1991 onwards till 2005 and is at 7.6 (Figure 8.2). It can be observed that the state has performed poorly as compared to the nation from 1971 through 2005. The rate of decline, however, has kept pace with the national rate of decline. In the context of the state, higher birth rate is a result of higher mortality among the children, greater perceived economic value generated due to their labour once they are seven years of age, inaccessibility to the modern methods of birth control and sometimes social and

FIGURE 8.1

Birth Rates: MP and India (SRS)

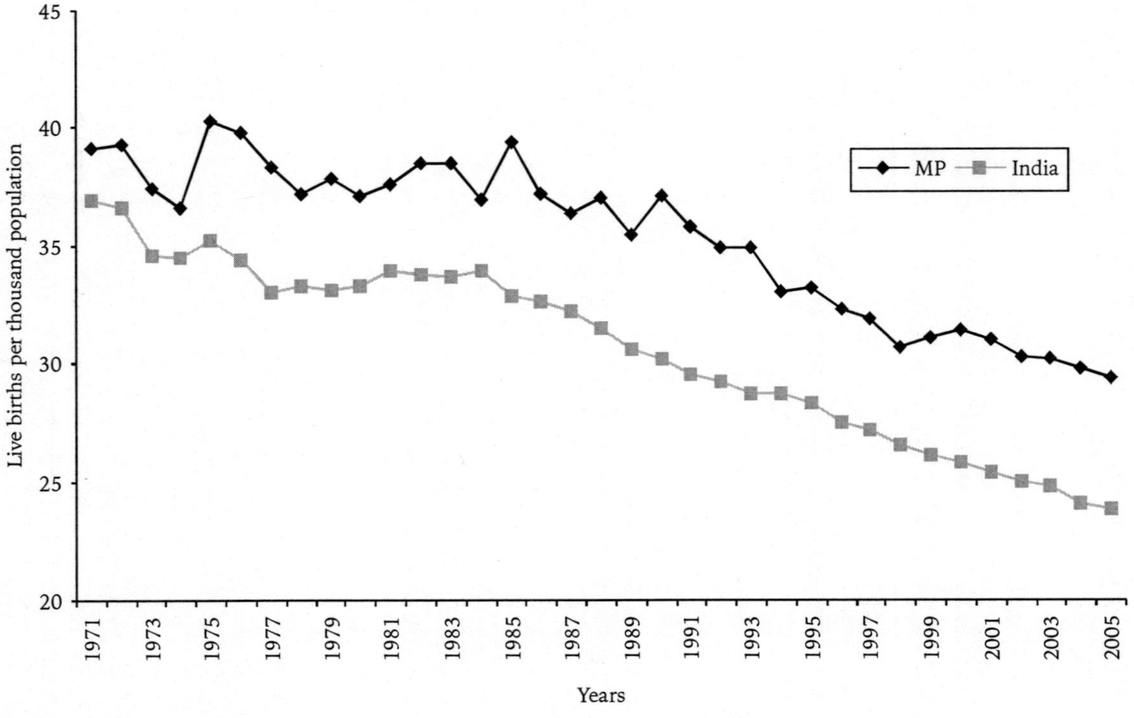

Source: Sample Registration Survey Bulletins, various years.

FIGURE 8.2

Death Rates: MP and India (SRS)

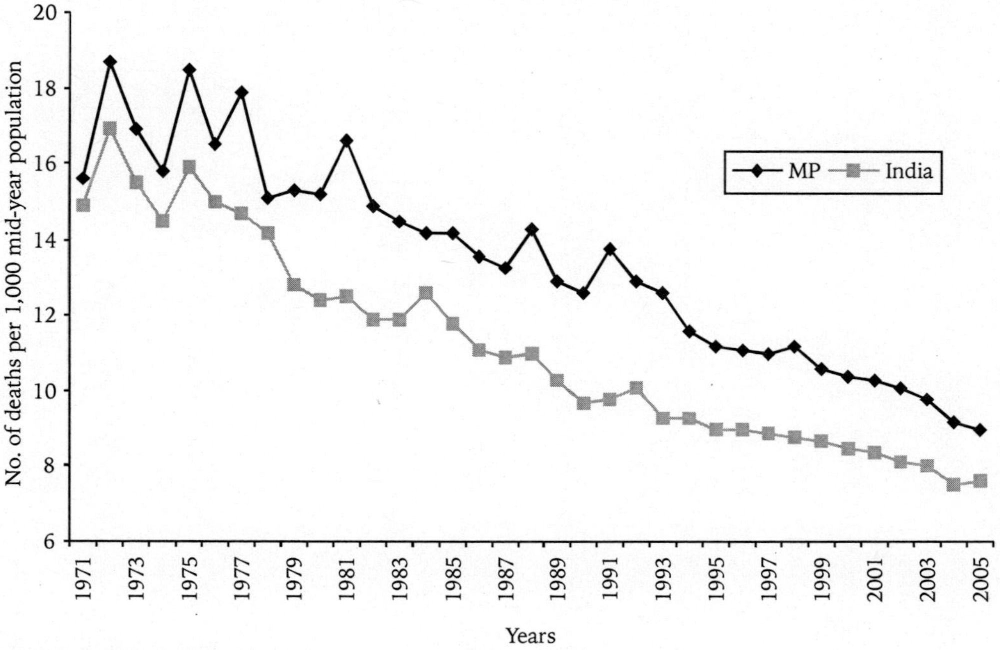

Source: Sample Registration Survey Bulletins, various years.

religious practices that take birth control beyond the pale of general behaviour.

Figure 8.2 shows that the death rates in both the state and India have declined but is much higher in the former than in the latter. In late nineties, the rate of decline in death rate caught up with the rate of decline at the national level. Another observation is that since mid-nineties, the rate of decline in the death rate has become low to the extent of being labelled as stagnant. The gender differential in the age-specific mortality rates has been analysed in another section of the chapter.

High death rates in Madhya Pradesh is another indicator of pervasive poverty and the very poor performance standards of the health delivery system. The bodies of the poor from their very childhood become prone to common diseases and succumb far more easily to disease due to malnourished and weak bodies.[1] Also, large sections of the population are unable to access quality care in health. Primary health care facilities in the state are pretty abysmal, and health centres are poorly equipped with both doctors and medical necessities. Access in a state with undulating terrain, large forested belts and sparsely populated areas adds further to the problems of health.

Figure 8.3 shows that the total fertility rate has declined at a rate much lower than that of the rate of decline for the nation in the initial years but in the last decade, Madhya Pradesh has tried to catch up with the national average and in 2005, TFR (MP) is 3.12 and TFR (India) is 3 (NFHS-III), only marginally less than that of Madhya Pradesh. It is estimated that the state of MP would attain the replacement level TFR of 2.1 in about 3-4 decades at the present annualised rate of decline in the TFR. If the extent of undernourishment of children under 5 is taken as an indicator of the quality of life for the future population, Madhya Pradesh draws a dismal picture as it has the highest percentage (51 per cent) of children chronically undernourished.

3. Child Mortality

Factors responsible for child mortality are attributed to maternal factors, nutrient deficiency, environmental contamination, injury and personal illness control, which include both the availability of health services and the capacity to use them.[2] Malnutrition is a critical risk factor, increasing the probability of succumbing to major childhood infections, particularly diarrhoea and

1. The large number of persons succumbing to malaria in the districts of Betul and Chhindwara have been largely due to malnourished and weak bodies.
2. Ibid.

FIGURE 8.3

Total Fertility Rate: MP and India (NFHS-II and NFHS-III)

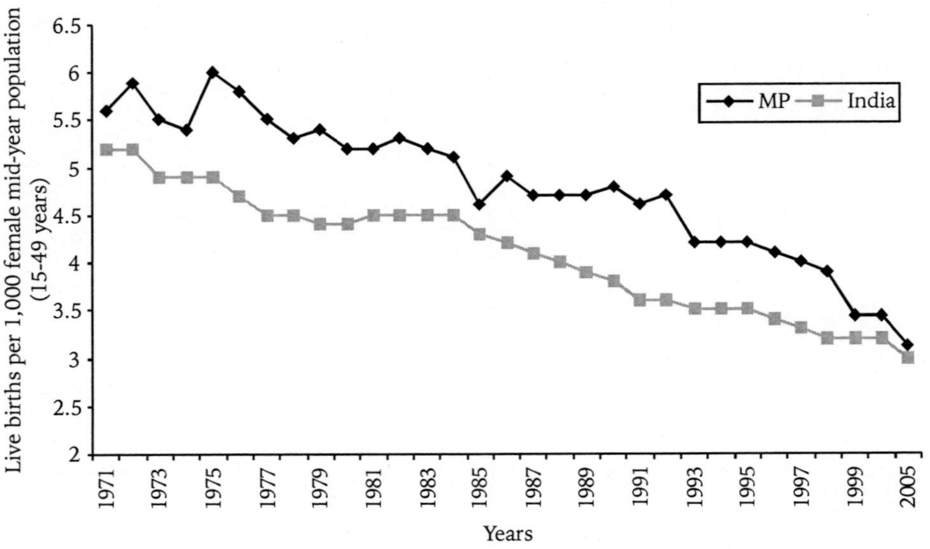

Source: NFHS II and NFHS III.

acute respiratory infections. It is also identified as the main factor retarding improvements in human development and hindering further reductions in infant mortality. Low birth weight is a key factor leading to malnourished children and an important determinant of child mortality. As per NFHS-III, more than half (60 per cent) the children under age 3 are underweight and little less than half (40 per cent) are stunted. Thirty-three per cent children are wasted (weight-for-height).

Further, acute respiratory infection (ARI), diarrhoea, asthma, tuberculosis, jaundice and malaria are all the prevailing morbidity affecting children's health and thereby endangering their lives. In addition to these, the identified six major child health preventive diseases are tuberculosis, diphtheria, pertussis, tetanus, poliomyelitis and measles. As per the Universal Immunization Programme (UIP) that aims to cover 85 per cent of all infants against the six vaccine-preventable diseases, only 40.3 per cent of children between 12-23 months are fully vaccinated. One of the major reasons for stagnation in infant mortality rates is "declining or levelling off of coverage rates of preventive and curative child health services". Coverage of as low as 40 per cent full immunisation in the state does reflect a poor delivery system.

The IMR is favourable to girls than to boys, but there is a substantial loss of girl children against male children in the 1-5 age group (16.9) reflecting gross medical, nutritional and general neglect of girl child resulting in higher mortality. Further, neonatal mortality (NN) of boys is higher than girls, but post neonatal (PNN) i.e., between the age of one month and one year, survival of girls becomes adverse as compared to the boys, once again reflecting gross medical and nutritional neglect of girl child. Sex ratio at birth (SRB) for male children is high for biological reasons, perhaps nature's way of balancing the fact that the male of the species is more likely to die in the initial period after birth than the female of the species. Perhaps one of the reasons for lower infant morality rate for girls could be because of higher NN rate for boys. The discrimination against girl children is best revealed in the PNN stage that ultimately reflects under 5 mortality rates.

4. Maternal Mortality and the Status of Nutrition among Women in MP

Maternal mortality rate (MMR) as per SRS was 498 in 1997. The latest figure for MMR for Madhya Pradesh is 335 for the year 2004-2006, again provided by SRS. Of the total registered deaths in MP as per records of the Department of Health, the share of registered female deaths is 44.4 per cent (1,89,389) that accounts for 2466 (1.3 per cent) maternal deaths. The proportion of maternal deaths owing to haemorrhage and fever during pregnancy accounts the maximum per cent of 26.2. Toxaemia of pregnancy (19.0 per cent) and abortion and related complications (14.3 per cent) are other major causes of maternal mortality deaths.

TABLE 8.2

Maternal Health Indicators for Madhya Pradesh

Indicators	*NFHS-II (1999-2000)*	*NFHS-III (2004-05)*
Mothers who had at least 3 antenatal care visits for their last birth (%)	27.1	40.2
Mothers who consumed IFA for 90 days or more when they were pregnant with their last child (%)	na	11.8
Births assisted by doctor/nurse/LHV/ ANM/other health personnel (%)	28.9	37.1
Institutional births (%)	22.0	29.7
Mothers who received postnatal care from a doctor/nurse/LHV/ANM/ other health personnel within 2 days of delivery for their last birth (%)	na	27.9

Source: National Family Health Survey.

The following eye-opening facts given by NFHS-III highlight the true causes and poor status of maternal health in the state of Madhya Pradesh. Although proportion of institutional deliveries is dismal in the state, it has shown a little improvement over the previous NFHS survey. Miniscule proportion (11.8 per cent) of pregnant women is consuming iron and folic acid tablets for 90 days or more, one of the crucial caring factor during pregnancy. Hardly 37 per cent women are receiving the help of trained birth attendants during their deliveries.

Further, we know from SRS data that the mortality rates for rural women is much higher than that of their urban counterparts in the age groups 0-4 years, 5-9 years, 10-14 years, 20-24 years, 30-34 years, 40-44 years, 55-59 years and 65-69 years. The same is the case in the "all ages" category. This is obviously due to poorer access that the rural women have to the medical services as compared to their urban counterparts.

Maternal mortality is high amongst anaemic women. Anaemia results in increased risk of premature delivery and low birth weight, thus leading to high infant mortality. Over 57 per cent married women and pregnant women in 15-49 age group are anaemic (NFHS-III). Scheduled tribe women are found to be the most anaemic (70.3 per cent). With this, it is not surprising that women in MP are at high risk of mortality.

As long as girls are married at an early age and the birth of the child is followed in quick succession, maternal mortality rates will continue to remain high. Women of poor health give birth to children with poor health. Girl children with poor health, who further receive inadequate attention during their growing years, fare poorly in their pregnancies and deliveries experiencing high maternal morbidity and mortality. By increasing the spacing between two deliveries, family planning can at best partly ensure that female new-borns are not underweight or unhealthy. But family planning definitely cannot address the problems that arise out of the neglect of the girl children in our society or the problems that arise due to early marriage of girls.

NFHS-III states that 40.1 per cent women in the age group of 15-49 are those whose body mass index (BMI) is below normal indicating that they are nutritionally at risk. It also observes that short stature is directly related to poverty. Thus, women with low standard of living, subsequently illiterate, belonging to scheduled castes or tribes tend to fall within this category of 'nutritionally at risk'.

5. Overall Gender Ratio

The gender ratio of the new state of MP has improved in 2001 (920) since the last decade (912) for the second time since 1901 but it is well below the national average of 933. Although there has been an improvement in the overall gender ratio in 2001, 14 out of 45 districts in the state record sex ratio less than 900 with Morena recording the lowest at 822 in 2001.

A clear spatial pattern emerges with respect to the overall sex ratio in the state. The northern and the central region, including the capital Bhopal, record a sex ratio less than 900. In fact, the overall sex ratios in these areas are quite low as compared to the western, eastern and southern parts of the new MP. Betul, East Nimar, Narsimhapur and Damoh worsened between 1991 and 2001. The other 41 districts show some improvement in overall sex ratio with 11 districts having a sex ratio between 950 and 1000. Mandla and Balaghat have a sex ratio of over 1000 and it is explained by the fact that large proportion of the population in these districts happens to be from the scheduled tribe category.

6. Child Sex Ratio

For the first time, the 1991 Census tabulated sex ratio for the age group 0-6 and 7 and above separately. Besides the fact that information of a crucial age group is available, the 0-6 is also a convenient age group to study the impact of the integrated child development services (ICDS) programme, one of the major programmes in the country to address malnutrition amongst women and children. This information has come in as a rude shock and put the entire nation in a state of alert, calling for immediate intervention. Although the overall sex ratio has shown an improvement, the child sex ratio (CSR) of 0-6 age group shows a shocking decline in the decade from 1991-2001. All the major states like Rajasthan, Punjab, Haryana, Chandigarh, Himachal Pradesh in the northern belt, Tamil Nadu, Andhra Pradesh, Karnataka in the southern belt and even West Bengal and Maharashtra have recorded dismal decline in CSR.

Madhya Pradesh too shows a similar trend of declining child sex ratio. CSR in Madhya Pradesh records a decline from 941 to 929 between 1991 and 2001. This raises critical questions on the deteriorating living conditions of girl child over the past decade and also on the possibility of practice of female infanticide/ foeticide in recent years.[3] Table 8.3 gives district-wise details of CSR in the state.

The table very clearly demarcates the northern region with alarmingly low child sex ratio. Mandla and Dindori districts stand out prominently with high CSR; these districts also have very high overall sex ratio of more than 1000.

A favourable overall sex ratio indicates that the all-pervading neglect of women in certain districts is gradually diminishing. The better overall sex ratios and better 7+ sex ratios are a matter of some satisfaction. What is happening which is leading to it? An easy explanation forwarded could be the impact of migration, but we do not have sufficient evidence to rely fully on this alone, and migration cannot impact on such large numbers across the districts. There are some other factors also that would certainly have contributed towards such an increase. One is the increase in economic value of women as they increase their numbers in the workforce, often working in visibly productive economic activities, with many of them taking to full-time jobs and remunerative professions. Also we cannot totally ignore the impact of government programmes which may have had made a dent in the general appreciation towards women and girls, and better access of health for women.

TABLE 8.3

District-wise Child Sex Ratio in MP

District Name	*Juvenile Sex Ratio*
Bhind	832
Morena	837
Gwalior	853
Datia	874
Shivpuri	906
Indore	908
Tikamgarh	916
Chhatarpur	917
Narsimhapur	917
Bhopal	925
Harda	925
Rewa	926
Sehore	927
Hoshangabad	927
Sheopur	929
Dewas	930
Guna	931
Sagar	931
Satna	931
Neemuch	931
Jabalpur	931
Panna	932
Damoh	935
Shajapur	936
Raisen	936
Ujjain	938
Rajgarh	938
East Nimar	941
Dhar	943
Vidisha	943
Mandsaur	946
Katni	952
Sidhi	954
Ratlam	957
Chhindwara	958
Umaria	959
West Nimar	962
Balaghat	968
Betul	969
Barwani	970
Shahdol	972
Jhabua	974
Seoni	977
Mandla	981
Dindori	990
Madhya Pradesh	934

Source: Census 2001.

3. Premi, M.K. (2001). "The Missing Girl Child", *EPW* XXXV1(2), May 26-June 1.

But a declining CSR portends gross neglect of girl children who are not only undernourished but also suffer owing to the inability of their parents to protect them against illnesses—both communicable and non-communicable. Also, a study in district Bhind has shown strong evidence of the prevalence of female infanticide[4] among the non-Rana Rajputs, Gujjars and Jats. This too might be contributing, even though to a lesser extent, to a declining child sex ratio. Since the data of sex ratio at birth (SRB) is not yet available for the districts, the magnitude of the problem of foeticide in various districts cannot be quantified or authoritatively commented upon. However, what we at least know is that the practice of female foeticide is rampant among certain castes in the state.

Looking at the data for juvenile sex ratio for the different districts of Madhya Pradesh, we find that the districts Bhind, Morena, Gwalior and Datia are the worst performers with JSR below 900 level. The top performers are Dindori, Mandla and Seoni, predominantly tribal districts. The average for Madhya Pradesh is 934.

7. Age at Marriage

The UNICEF's "State of the World's Children Report 2007" states that the average age for marriage of girls has been increasing during the last 20 years, but 46 per cent girls are still married off before they reach 18 years. The reason for early marriage of girls is not only financial. People also feel that by getting their daughters married off early the girls could be saved from sexual harassment and getting pregnant prior to marriage. It also points out that the girls marrying before 15 years have five times more chances of dying while giving birth.

Child marriage, although illegal, still persists in India. It is most common and deeply rooted among the populous northern states namely, Rajasthan, Madhya Pradesh, Uttar Pradesh and Bihar. The Child Marriage Restraint Act of 1978 has set the minimum age for marriage for girls at 18 years. The social practices prevalent in the state have however made the implementation of the Act rather weak. According to 2001 census, 6.4 million Indians under the age of 18 were married, with Rajasthan and Madhya Pradesh accounting for a large chunk of such marriages. Many researches across the country on this topic have pointed out the overall negative implications associated with child marriages. It aggravates some social problems like soaring birth rates, grinding poverty and malnutrition, high illiteracy and infant mortality, and low life expectancy, especially among rural women.

The NFHS-III (2005-06) says that 53 per cent of the women of age group 20-24 were married by the age of 18 years. It further states that 13.6 per cent of the women of age group 15-19 years were already pregnant or mothers at the time of survey. The median age at first birth for women aged 25-49 is 19.4 years. According to non-government sources, nearly 20,000 children were married off last year (2008) on the auspicious day of *Akshaya Tritiya,* in Madhya Pradesh alone. Madhya Pradesh comes second to Rajasthan as far as marriage of minor girls is concerned. While the average age of marriage for an Indian girl is 20 years, it is 17 in Madhya Pradesh.

The situation in Madhya Pradesh can be judged from one of the incidents that in 2005, a man chopped off a woman official's hands with a sword in Madhya Pradesh for trying to stop child marriages in Dhar district. Realising that such malpractices cannot be curbed through government efforts alone, there is a need to generate awareness in the society. The state government has directed to organise awareness camps at every block headquarters, where influential people should be invited to brainstorm against such malpractices.

8. Educational Profile

Census 2001 records a major leap in the literacy rate in the state—from 44.67 in 1991 to 64.11 per cent in 2001. The trend in the last 50 years has seen more than double the increase in male literacy rates and 10 times an increase in female literacy rates. In fact, female literacy has progressed far better (by 20.93 per cent) than male literacy (by 18.26 per cent) since the last decade.

TABLE 8.4

Literacy Rates in Madhya Pradesh—1951 to 2001

	1951	*1961*	*1971*	*1981*	*1991*	*2001*
Total %	13.6	21.4	27.2	38.6	44.6	64.1
Male %	20.2	32.9	39.4	49.3	58.5	76.5
Female %	4.9	8.9	13.9	26.9	29.4	50.6

Source: Census of India, 1951; 1961; 1971; 1981; 1991 and 2001.

4. A study in district Bhind, "Born to Die: Female Infanticide in MP" (1994) by Mahendra K. Premi and Saraswati Raju talks of the practice of female infanticide.

In the state, all the 45 districts have recorded an increase in the literacy rate. As far as female literacy is concerned, the three districts of Sheopur, Jhabua and Barwani have fared the worst. The extreme eastern parts and the northern parts of the state (barring Morena, Bhind and Gwalior) have performed somewhat poorly as compared to the rest of the state. Datia, though in the northern part of the state, has outperformed all its neighbours in the northern part of the state in female literacy. This clearly exhibits that simple declaration of feudal control and regional cultures cannot describe everything.

9. Economic Profile of Women in MP

Women's contribution to the economy of the nation continues to be under-reported largely because of underestimation of the role of women in various sectors. International Labour Organization (ILO) studies attribute this to four principal factors:

1. The persistent differences in men's and women's pay.
2. Unequal access to stable employment.
3. The perpetuation and sometimes the accentuation of job segregation.
4. The growth of "ghost work" (i.e., invisible work, unpaid but economically necessary, in the domestic, agricultural and informal sectors).[5]

According to the Registrar General of India, the work participation rate for women has been 25.68 in 2001. This rate witnessed an improvement during the earlier two decades from 19.67 per cent in 1981 to 22.73 per cent in 1991. The notable aspect of the women's work participation is that women from rural areas are more in workforce than their counterparts in urban areas. In 2001, work participation rate for women in rural areas was 30.98 per cent as compared to 11.55 per cent in the urban areas. In rural areas, women are mainly involved as cultivators and agricultural labourers, where they undertake as many as activities right from sowing, weeding, harvesting, maintenance of the harvest and marketing as well. In the urban areas, almost 80 per cent of the women workers are working in the unorganised sectors like household industry, petty trades and services, building and construction.

As evident from Table 8.5, women's participation in every sphere of economic activities has increased in a decadal period in Madhya Pradesh. It is observed that

TABLE 8.5

Women Participation in Economic Activities in MP (in %)

Economic Activity	*1991*	*2001*
Share of women main workers	26.33	26.19
Share of women cultivators	24.74	37.29
Share of women agriculture labourers	44.42	52.77
Share of women in household industries	37.04	50.36
Share of women in other works	10.44	16.29

Source: Census of India.

the percentage of women agriculture labourers in the northern parts of the state (barring Shivpuri) and in the central part of the state is comparatively lower than in the other parts of the state. These incidentally are also the areas that have a lower overall sex ratio in the state. The participation of women in the agriculture labour force is the highest in the districts of Mandla, Dindori, Shahdol, Betul, Chhindwara, Neemuch, Ratlam and Jhabua. Most of these districts are predominantly tribal. There is also a positive 0.87 correlation between sex ratio and women workers, and positive 0.86 correlations between sex ratio and female WPR. We also see in extreme examples that Balaghat and Mandla have over 40 per cent women cultivators, and Bhind has the lowest FWPR (2.01 per cent) along with very low sex ratio. A clear relationship between economic value/ participation of women and their status emerges.

The Census defines work as "participation in any economically productive activity", which includes subsistence agriculture in rural areas. This leaves out the contribution of hard labour by girls and women. These may even include the demanding physical and mental work of running the household and looking after young children that involves long hours each day and can be very intense, requiring considerable skill. Women may not do 'heavy' work with the plough (studies actually have shown that women do work with ploughs, but due to cultural taboos often do not report) but may be seen carrying heavy head loads like fuel and water over great distances as a part of their services in the household. Thus, most work that produces goods or services used within the household falls outside the Census definition unless the worker is paid. Such work involves long hours to fulfil the needs of the family, and women and girls are not at leisure or unemployed. Thus, women's 'non-work' (defined as unemployed and available for work) is often mistakenly seen as unused national resource, yet essential to the

5. ILO (1996). *Remuneration for Women's Work: A Curious Paradox.*

survival and advancement of the people of India. There would thus be recorded a large share of women as 'non-workers' which in effect means a large per cent of women engaging in unpaid household work. In comparison with men, women tend to lose out in acquiring steady jobs. More women are employed in the informal and unorganised sector, which is not only underpaid but also hazardous with no legal protection.

More often than not, girls and women lose opportunities to read and write in the demand to fulfil the household needs, thereby bearing the related disadvantages. Ignoring this reality if opportunities of paid work are created for women, without a support system in place by planners, it often ends either in increasing burden for the woman or additional workload on the girl child with further loss of opportunity or both.

10. Child Labour

Child labour represents a fundamental abuse of child right and a violation of various laws. Many working children are engaged in occupations that negatively affect their physical, mental and emotional well-being and are below their minimum age for employment. According to a UNICEF report, "State of the World's Children 2006", India has the largest number of working children and 17 per cent of them are under the age of 15. Girls aged 12-13 are the preferred choice of 90 per cent households. ILO estimates that 218 million children were involved in child labour in 2004, of which 126 million were engaged in hazardous work. Estimates from a 2000 study suggest that 5.7 million were in forced or bonded labour, 1.8 million in prostitution and pornography and 1.2 million were victims of trafficking. In India, 1104 lakh children are working as labourers. NSS 55th Round survey in 1999/ 2000 estimated that around 17 per cent children in the age group 10-14 years were employed as workers in Madhya Pradesh, as against the national average of 11 per cent.

Child labour is still a major problem in India. The Hindi belt, including Bihar, Madhya Pradesh, Rajasthan and Uttar Pradesh, account for 1.27 crore working children in the country, engaged in both hazardous and non-hazardous occupations and processes. Over 19 lakh child labourers in the 5-14 age group are in Uttar Pradesh. Rajasthan accounts for over 12.6 lakh workers followed by Bihar with over 11 lakh and Madhya Pradesh with 10.6 lakh. However, according to the 2001 Census, in state-wise distribution of working children in the 5-14 age group, Andhra Pradesh with 13.6 lakh child labour stands second in the national list after UP.

Prevalence of child labour is amongst communities and groups that are at the lower rungs of the traditional, caste-based social hierarchy. This includes the SCs, STs, OBCs and minorities, especially Muslims. They also constitute a bulk of the small and marginal farming community, landless, agricultural labourers and artisans. Poverty builds pressures on already resource-strapped families, especially on the women to increase family income. This ultimately results in children either stepping into the adult role of taking care of household chores including siblings, as in the case of girl children, or else step out to add to the meagre family income or both. Our own data shows that there has been a substantial increase in the female worker participation rate, perhaps owing to poverty pressures. An unskilled, illiterate and vulnerable person, that too a woman, ends finding her source of income in the informal sector. With pressures on children to take care of the home or add to the family expenses, the dropout rate in school tends to increase. Employment of children appears to be mostly in districts where the construction industry has shown growth. These include districts such as Panna, Mandsaur, Ratlam, Jhabua, Dhar, Khargone, Khandwa, Rajgarh, Betul, Mandla, Chhindwara and Seoni.

FIGURE 8.4

Children (5-14 Years) Working as Main and Marginal Worker in MP

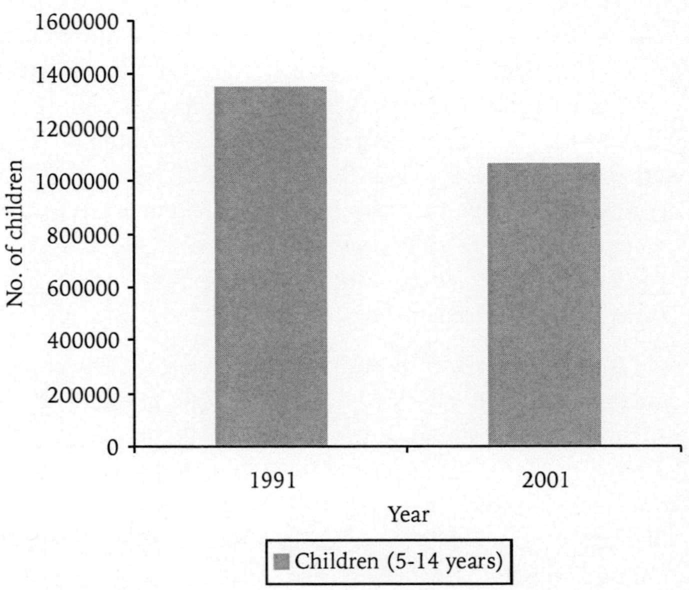

Source: Census, 2001.

If we look at the 2001 Census data, 10,65,259 children between ages 5-14 in Madhya Pradesh work as main and marginal worker. It stands at 6.7 per cent of the total main and marginal workers of Madhya Pradesh. Jhabua still has 23.1 per cent children of the district as part of the workforce. Dindori has 14 per cent children working as main and marginal workers. The number has come down but still more than a million children between 5-14 age group in Madhya Pradesh are working to earn their bread and butter. In 2006, the state went for total ban on child labour (below age 14 years) but it is yet to give positive effect.

11. Political Voice—As Elected Representatives

Women in the state are yet to find their political voice in any significant way. Although amendments in the Panchayat Acts to reserve 33 per cent seats exclusively for women were accepted without much of a debate in the parliament, the men in the political parties resist a similar resolution. In any case, amendments in the Panchayati Raj Acts in 1992 to ensure political space for women has been a path-breaking opportunity for women to actually hold and utilise the cudgels of power. While there is still a long way to go before women representatives in the *panchayats* mature politically as women, the journey itself has been very empowering.

Madhya Pradesh has been one of the first states to make amendments in the Madhya Pradesh Panchayati Raj Act, 1993 in accordance with the 73rd and 74th Constitutional Amendment. It has provided reservations for women on 33 per cent of the total number of seats at each of the three tiers of the Panchayati Raj system. The 1994 figures from the State Election Commissioner show that the number of women elected in *panchayats* were marginally more than what was reserved for them (10620 elected against 10156 reserved), and similarly for urban bodies (2352 elected against 2300 reserved). The figures also show that the number of women elected in district *panchayats* (DP), *janpad panchayats* (JP) and *gram panchayats* (GP) were slightly more than what was statutorily required.

The figures portend well for an emerging leadership amongst women as elected representatives. Many have suggested that active and genuine participation by the elected women representatives would depend more on their social status than on their level of education. It is hoped that women would gain acceptance in the political apparatus gradually and would become effective in due course owing to the enabling local governance structures that have been put in place as a result of the 73rd and 74th Amendments to the Indian Constitution.

TABLE 8.6

Number of *Panchayats* and Elected Women Representatives in the Three Tiers of PRIs (as on 30/6/2009)

States/UT	*No. of States' Panchayats of All Three Tiers*	*Total Representatives (in numbers)*	*Women Representatives*	
			Number	*%*
Andhra Pradesh	22945	224003	74019	33.0
Arunachal Pradesh	9356	9471	3889	41.1
Assam	2431	25436	9903	38.9
Bihar	9040	130091	70400	54.1
Chhattisgarh	9982	160548	54159	33.7
Goa	191	1559	534	34.3
Gujarat	14068	114187	38068	33.3
Haryana	6293	67277	25854	38.4
Himachal Pradesh	3330	24581	9552	38.9
Jharkhand	3979	0	0	0
Karnataka	5833	96090	41210	42.9
Kerala	1165	18482	6518	35.3
Madhya Pradesh	23412	396516	136196	34.3
Maharashtra	28283	229740	77997	34.0
Manipur	169	1736	758	43.7
Orissa	6578	92454	33630	36.4
Punjab	12604	90963	31809	35.0
Rajasthan	9457	120247	42543	35.4
Sikkim	258	986	394	40.0
Tamil Nadu	13031	116488	39364	33.8
Tripura	540	5733	1986	34.6
Uttar Pradesh	52890	771661	299025	38.8
Uttarakhand	7335	61021	33610	55.1
West Bengal	3705	51499	19812	38.5
A&N Islands	75	856	296	34.6
Chandigarh	19	187	62	33.2
D&N Haveli	12	125	47	37.6
Daman and Diu	15	97	37	38.1
Lakshadweep	11	110	41	37.3
Pondicherry	108	1021	406	39.8
Total	247115	2813165	1052119	37.4

Source: A Study on Elected Women Representatives (EWRs) in *Gram Panchayats*, 2007-08, Ministry of Panchayati Raj.

12. Crime against Women and Children in Madhya Pradesh

Violence against women is one of the most sensitive indicator of well-being and status of women in the society. Violence against women includes a whole range of forms of violence committed against women. Right from inside the womb, where her very survival is at threat, she encounters assaults (both physical and mental) till her last breath. Crime against women is not clinical but social. In India, crime perpetrated against women is largely patriarchal violence.[6] The problem of under reportage of crime against women has resulted in the inability of the government to respond adequately through legislation and the media to highlight the problem in a way that enhances sensitivity of society towards problems faced by women. The low sex ratio in the state itself is a reflection of one of the forms of violence.[7]

According to statistics of National Crime Record Bureau, Madhya Pradesh and Maharashtra have earned the dubious distinction of topping the list of states reporting the most number of crime cases in the country, which registered over 19.89 lakh cases. Madhya Pradesh has accounted for 10.2 per cent of total IPC crimes reported in the country followed by Maharashtra at 9.8 per cent. Madhya Pradesh has reported the highest number of rape cases (3,010) and 6772 of molestations against women and 742 dowry deaths (3rd position). Madhya Pradesh bags the 4th position in terms of total incidences of crimes against women and girls. Madhya Pradesh reported 21.0 per cent (4,290 out of 20,410) of total crimes committed against children in the country. This data draws the attention towards increasing crime against women and children in the state that needs sincere and immediate attention.

The categories of crime against women include murder, rape and suicide, dowry act, dowry murder, kidnapping, outraging and assaulting modesty of women, dowry harassment, selling or buying of women for prostitution and others. In addition, cases of custodial violence against women go largely unreported and unrecorded. Often women are vulnerable from both ends. If they do find courage to share details of atrocity with the family and find support from them, there is pressure from the family to quietly suffer it from fear of inviting the wrath of those in authority upon the entire family or community.

Domestic violence is most prevalent in India. NFHS-III survey, which included questions related to prevalence of domestic violence, found that 47 per cent of women in MP experienced violence since age 15. It was also found that literate/educated women, working women and those living in non-nuclear families were less prone to experiencing violence. Some of the reasons quoted for abuse within marital relation are suspicion by the husband, wife not bringing enough money or other material from her natal family, wife disrespects in-laws, wife goes away without informing her husband, wife neglects house and children and does not cook properly.

TABLE 8.7

Comparative Statement of Crime against Women

S. No.	*Head*	*2002*	*2003*	*% Change from 2002-03*	*2004*	*% Change from 2003-04*
1	Murder	437	402	-8.01	425	5.72
2	Attempt to murder	229	204	-10.92	285	39.71
3	Hurt	3305	3515	6.35	3367	-4.21
4	Grevious hurt	681	692	1.62	710	2.6
5	Molestation	6615	6610	-0.08	6680	1.06
6	Kidnapping	548	250	-54.38	511	104.4
7	Rape	2618	2452	-6.34	2582	5.3
8	Suicide	569	505	-11.25	583	15.45
9	Dowry deaths	597	565	-5.36	652	15.4
10	Torture	2739	2612	-4.64	3195	22.32
11	Criminal intimidation	5053	6097	20.66	6347	4.1
12	Robbery	157	211	34.39	229	8.53
13	Sell-purchase, Prostitution	3	4	33.33	7	75
14	Dowry act	35	30	-14.29	77	156.67
15	Arson	50	55	10	52	-5.45
	Total	23636	24204	2.4	25702	6.19

Source: Home department, GoMP.

In Madhya Pradesh, crime against women for period January to November 2002, 2003, 2004 are 23636, 24204, and 25702 respectively. The crime rate has increased by 2.40 per cent if compared between year 2002 and 2003 and has increased by 6.19 per cent for the period between 2003 and 2004. Since 1996, the dowry deaths in MP have increased from 432 to 652 in 2004, an increase of over 50 per cent. In 2004, attempt to murder and kidnapping saw a steep increase from previous year levels.

Cases of sexual abuse, especially of children rarely get reported, especially if the abuse is within the

6. Sonpar, Shobna, Ravi Kapur (2001). "Non-Conventional Indicators: Gender Disparities under Structural Reforms", *EPW*, January 6.

7. The state government has responded with the Prenatal Diagnostic Techniques (Regulation and Prevention of Misuse) Act that it amended in 2001. The government has also made it mandatory for all ultrasonography machines to prevent their misuse by invoking the Medical Termination of Pregnancies Act, 1971.

private sphere. Further, many cases of domestic violence such as marital rape, child marriages, physical and mental abuse by members of family, never get reported.

13. Gender Budgeting

With the consistent lobbying by the gender economists and women's groups, the Ministry of Finance, for the first time, gave a mandate to all ministries to establish a Gender Budgeting Cell by January 2005, and 18 ministries and departments were asked to submit annual reports and performance budgets highlighting budgetary allocations for women.

The Government of Madhya Pradesh has presented the gender budget for the first time in 2007-08. The effort has covered only 13 of the 51 odd departments in its gender budget. The Department of Finance is the nodal agency and a Gender Budgeting Cell is being set up under a budget director to monitor the flow of funds to women-specific schemes and pro-women schemes in these 13 departments. A separate booklet on gender responsive budgeting in the above stated departments has been published for the year 2007-08.

However, gender budgeting and gender budget analysis should not remain as a mechanical or academic analysis, instead it would matter the most when it reaches and impacts the lives of women of the state in reality. Therefore, there is strong need to pursue the realistic gender budgeting and gender budget analysis. According to the commitments of Ministry of Finance in the Union Budget 2005-06, a review of public expenditure profile must be undertaken. It should be then followed by conducting beneficiary incidence analysis and then recommending specific changes in the operational guidelines of the schemes with gender perspective which would enable gender budgeting in a holistic manner.

14. Women Empowerment

The study on gender development in Indian states particularly with respect to education and health shows that the gender development is substantially high in Kerala, Haryana, Punjab, Maharashtra, Gujarat and Tamil Nadu. But it is significantly low in Orissa, Madhya Pradesh, Rajasthan, Assam and Bihar. Literacy has been taken as an indicator to education while life expectancy and infant survival rate (ISR) are considered the indicators to health. It also finds that the performance of poor states remains poor and rich states remains rich over the years. But no state is extremely good or bad in all the basic dimensions of gender development except Kerala. It finally suggests that there is need to stress on all dimensions of gender development simultaneously in order to maintain a high gender development in the economy. For this, the government (both Central as well as respective state governments) has to play a significant role.[8]

The Tenth Five Year Plan documents define women's empowerment in the following ways:

- *Social Empowerment:* To create an enabling environment through various affirmative developmental policies and programmes for development of women besides providing them easy and equal access to all the basic minimum services so as to enable them to realise their full potentials like health, education, water and sanitation etc.
- *Economic Empowerment:* To ensure provision of training, employment and income-generation activities with both 'forward' and 'backward' linkages with the ultimate objective of making all potential women economically independent and self-reliant through economic identity, employment opportunities, assets, credit, skills etc.
- *Gender Justice:* To eliminate all forms of gender discrimination and thus, allow women to enjoy not only the *de jure* but also the *de facto* rights and fundamental freedom at par with men in all spheres, *viz.*, political, economic, social, civil, cultural, etc., through political participation, gender equality in inheritance, marital laws, security etc.

15. State Women's Policy

The state government of Madhya Pradesh has declared the new 'Women Policy-2008-12' for the state in August 2008. The policy tries to address various critical issues related to women in the state. It aims at ensuring total and dignified participation of women in the development process and integrating them with the mainstream development. Specific objectives of the policy include providing protection to women in every field, their empowerment and ensuring result-oriented implementation of the various policies, programmes and schemes for their all-round development and welfare.

8. Pradhan, Rudra Prakash (2007). "Gender Development in Education and Health: A Study of Indian States", *Journal of Health Management* 9(1): 1-14.

Declining juvenile sex ratio in the state is the area of prime concern. The policy seeks to prevent female foeticide through enforcing relevant laws and creating social awareness to maintain gender balance. It proposes that proper mechanism needs to be undertaken to curb violence and crime against women in a more effective manner in order to secure women's safety. The new policy envisages augmenting employment opportunities for women and to enhance their capacities to earn better income. Special efforts would be made for development of adolescent girls with particular emphasis on their health, education, nutrition and prevention of their sexual abuse and exploitation and enhance their participation in decision-making. The women's policy also seeks to ensure public spending on women through gender budgeting exercise.

The Madhya Pradesh government has also prepared an action plan to provide benefit of the policy to women. The action plan has incorporated the different points as per the provisions of the policy. It specifies as to what would be the institutional arrangement, what activities would be carried out and which departments would be responsible for them.

It is true that the state government is doing its bit to harness congenial condition for the women in the state, but the policy on paper would turn out to be effective in its true spirit only when it is implemented with utmost sincerity and great care.

16. State Government's Efforts Through Schemes/Programmes

16.1 Supplementary Nutrition under Integrated Child Development Services (ICDS)

Persistence malnutrition is a critical problem in the state. Supplementary nutrition under ICDS aims to cater nutritional requirements to children in 0-6 age group, pregnant and lactating mothers and adolescent girls. However, the reality of ICDS implementation is abysmally poor in terms of its beneficiary coverage. Though the orders of the Supreme Court states that the universalisation of the ICDS and providing all the 7 services to all its beneficiaries is mandatory, the latest report from DWCD shows that still 60 per cent children and more than 73 per cent eligible women beneficiaries are out of the focus. According to the government statistics, no adolescent girls in the age group 11-17 years were covered under the nutrition programme although they are one of the eligible beneficiaries under universalisation of ICDS.

16.2 Project Shaktiman

The state government is implementing this programme in order to reduce incidences of malnutrition among the pockets of malnutrition in tribal areas of 19 districts of the state. The government through its own resources is spending Rs. 4 besides the Rs. 2 allocations per head under ICDS on the nutrition of malnourished children in tribal areas.

16.3 Ladli Laxmi

It is the state government's one of the most ambitious schemes being implemented to bring in change in the society's attitude towards girl child and improving the sex ratio. The scheme is in implementation from January 1, 2006, for the benefit of the girl child belonging to below poverty line families. Under it, Rs. 6,500 would be deposited by the state government in the name of a girl child on the day she is born, which would accumulate to Rs. 1 lakh after 18 years. This money will be then handed over to the girl. Keeping up the popularity of Ladli Laxmi Yojana, the state government has decided to give its benefit to the first girl child from 2008, but the condition of family planning after second delivery has been continued as before so that the objective of the scheme can be fulfilled. Now twin girls and girls whose mother or father has died are also being extended benefit of the Ladli Laxmi Yojana.

16.4 Usha Kiran

Domestic Violence Act, 2006 is implemented in the state through Usha Kiran Scheme. However, once again the field implementation of the scheme is not only effective as the provisions under scheme are not adequate enough to tackle the problems faced by the women suffering from domestic violence.

16.5 Swayam Siddha

Under this scheme, self-help groups of the women are formed and are trained to become financially capable.

16.6 Swadhar Scheme

The scheme is implemented with the view to provide shelter, nutrition and other necessary facilities to rehabilitate those women, who are living in difficult situation.

16.7 Tejaswini Rural Empowerment Programme

The programme is implemented by the Mahila Vitta Evam Vikas Nigam with the help from International Fund for Agriculture Development, Rome in six districts namely, Balaghat, Panna, Mandla, Tikamgarh, Chhatarpur and Dindori. The project is aimed at empowering 12000 women SHG groups in these districts.

Chapter 9

Tourism in Madhya Pradesh

A Thriving Sector

1. Introduction

The process of "globalisation" has led to greater travel, and India although not anywhere near to being a travel destination of any great preference, does appear to be emerging and developing to enable itself to become a decent-sized tourism player internationally. Globally, the research shows that travel and tourism currently employs nearly 240 million people and creates 10 per cent of the world GDP. Research on the world's strongest travel and tourism performers by World Travel and Tourism Council (WTTC), defined countries set to grow the fastest in 2007 and over the coming decade. The result show that China, Montenegro and India are at the top of the list with the demand in the respective countries growing at each year at the rate of 9.1 per cent, 8.6 per cent and 7.9 per cent respectively. These countries have consistently ranked in the top three positions over the past four years, consolidating their growth year on year.

1.1 Tourism in India

Within India, the tourism sector has witnessed impressive growth. According to the WTTC,[1] travel and tourism contributes about 5.6 per cent to India's GDP. In addition, the contribution of the travel and tourism economy to employment is expected to rise from 31 million jobs in 2009 that comes to 6.4 per cent of total employment, or 1 in every 15.6 jobs. This would further grow to 40 million jobs with 7.2 per cent of total employment or 1 in every 13.8 jobs by 2019.

Real GDP growth for the travel and tourism economy is expected to be 0.2 per cent in 2009 and to average 7.7 per cent per annum over the coming 10 years.

1. World Travel and Tourism Council, 2009.

BOX 9.1

Tourism in the World Economy

Tourism is emerging as a major economic activity. It is highly employment-oriented and has a huge foreign exchange earning potential. It had a 10 per cent share in the world GDP which is more than the world military budget put together. In global terms, the investment in tourism industry and travel trade accounts for 7 per cent of the total capital investment. Tourism accounts for 8 per cent of total world exports, more than 31 per cent of international trade in services, and more than 100 million jobs worldwide. It employs more people than any single industrial sector and its infrastructure (lodging, transportation and restaurants) investment is conservatively estimated to exceed $3 trillion. In future, this industry is likely to see unprecedented growth.

Source: WTTC Report.

The growth of tourism in India has made it one of the largest foreign exchange earners. Arrivals are rising at a steady pace, and tourists have a longer length of stay than other international destinations. In 2005, there were over 3.9 million foreign tourist arrivals, which increased to more than 4.4 million foreign tourists during 2006. In 2009, India ranked 14th in the world in terms of absolute size and 144th relatively in terms of contribution to national economy.

1.2 National Tourism Policy

The National Tourism Policy, 2002 seeks to enhance employment potential within the tourism sector as well as to foster economic integration through developing linkages with other sectors. Broadly, the policy paper attempts to:

a. Position tourism as a major engine of economic growth;

b. Harness the direct and multiplier effects for employment generation, economic development and providing impetus to rural tourism;

c. Focus on domestic tourism as major driver of tourism growth;

d. Position India as global brand to take advantage of the burgeoning global travel trade and the vast untapped potential of India as a destination;

e. Acknowledge the critical role of private sector with government working as a proactive facilitator and catalyst;

f. Create and develop integrated tourism circuits based on India's unique civilisation, heritage and culture in partnership with the state, private sector and other agencies;

g. Ensure that the tourists to India gets physically invigorated, mentally rejuvenated, culturally enriched, spiritually elevated and "feel India from within".

The policy document takes into consideration seven key areas that will provide thrust to tourism development. These are: *Swagat* (Welcome), *Soochana* (Information), *Suvidha* (Facilitation), *Suraksha* (Safety), *Sahyog* (Co-operation), *Samrachana* (Infrastructure Development) and *Safai* (Cleanliness).

TABLE 9.1

Foreign Tourist Arrivals in India

Foreign Tourist Arrivals			Percentage Change	
2005	*2006*	*2007**	*2006/05*	*2007/06*
3918610	4447167	4977193	13.5	11.9

Note: * Provisional estimates.
Source: WTTC.

Table 9.1 suggests that there has been an increasing trend not only in tourists' arrival in India but also in share of tourists' arrivals in India as against the world tourists' arrival. Table 9.2 indicates that the preference towards India as a tourist destination has increased.

The share of India in international tourist arrivals has progressively increased from 0.37 per cent in 2001 to 0.54 per cent in 2007. Foreign tourist arrivals (FTAs) rose from 3.46 million in 2004 to 5.0 million in 2007. Tourism makes a significant contribution to foreign exchange earnings, which grew from Rs. 27944 crore (US$ 6.17 billion) in 2004 to an estimated Rs. 49413 crore (US$ 11.96 billion) in 2007. The share of India in world earnings from tourism registered an increase from 0.98 per cent in 2004 to 1.21 per cent in 2006. Domestic tourism too has grown phenomenally over this period. The number of domestic tourists in India has risen from 366.23 million in 2004 to an estimated 462 million in 2006 (Ministry of Tourism, *Annual Report 2007-08*).

TABLE 9.2

Share of India in World Tourist Arrivals

(Figs. in millions)

Year	*World Tourist Arrivals*	*Tourist Arrivals in India*	*Share of India in World Tourism*
2001	683.8	2.54	0.37
2002	702.8	2.38	0.34
2003	690.9	2.73	0.39
2004	766.0	3.46	0.45
2005	808.0	3.92	0.49
2006	847.0	4.4	0.52
2007	903.0	4.9	0.54

Source: WTTC.

TABLE 9.3

Estimated Foreign Exchange Earnings Per Tourist

Country	*Average Per Tourist Estimated Foreign Exchange Earnings (In US $), 2005*	*Average Per Tourist Estimated Foreign Exchange Earnings (In US $), 2008*
World	844	948
France	556	662
Spain	862	976
USA	1653	1727
Italy	970	977
China	626	766
India's Neighbourhood		
Sri Lanka	984	N.A.
Hong Kong	685	802
Malaysia	520	670
Thailand	763	1077
Singapore	892	1089
Indonesia	863	971
India	1462	2156

Source: World Tourism Organization.

Table 9.3 indicates that average per tourist estimated foreign exchange earning is the second highest in

India, next only to USA in 2005 but it is far more than USA by 2008. Rather by 2008, India stands at first position in terms of average per tourist foreign exchange earnings.

TABLE 9.4

Foreign Exchange Earnings from Tourism in India

(In crore Rs.)

Foreign Exchange Earnings			Percentage Change	
2005*	2006*	2007 #	2006/05	2007/06
33123	40375	49413	21.9%	22. %

Note: * Revised estimates; # Advance estimates.
Source: Ministry of Tourism.

1.3 Employment Generation

Table 9.4 presents the status of estimated employment generated in India through tourism.

TABLE 9.5

Employment Generated by the Tourism Industry

Year	Employment Generated (In million)
2002-03	38.6
2003-04	41.8
2004-05	44.7
2005-06	47.8
2006-07	51.1

Source: Ministry of Tourism.

2. Why Tourism

a. High growth, high potential sector – The travel and tourism industry plays an important role in generating wealth throughout the economy. This sector is expected to grow at the rate of 8.4 per cent per annum in India. It currently accounts for 5.6 per cent of the GDP. This contribution is expected to increase to 6.6 per cent of the GDP by 2010. It, therefore, offers a huge opportunity.

b. Employment-intensive industry – Tourism generates employment opportunities at various levels especially for the unskilled and semi-skilled people. It contributes to direct employment through the activities like tourist guide, employees in hotels, restaurants, transport etc., as well as indirect employment through construction, telecommunications and agriculture activities. By 2010, it is expected to account for at least 1 in every 15 jobs in India.[2]

c. A large multiplier effect – A major benefit of tourism is the multiplier effect as tourist expenditures are recycled through the local economy. A traveller's spending flows through the entire economy and increases the purchasing power and circulation of money in the state.

d. Poverty alleviation – Tourism can be used as an instrument for poverty alleviation. It offers employment opportunities at various levels especially for the unskilled and the semi-skilled workers and therefore, helps in increasing the per capita income of the state. It also has a huge multiplier effect that helps in creating employment in other sectors.

e. It catalyses the growth of other sectors – Tourism acts as a catalyst for the development of other sectors. It stimulates the provision for better infrastructure, impacts industry, especially the small scale and rural industry and also creates a pull for agricultural produce.

f. It is a *relatively non-pollutant industry*, which if properly managed, can contribute to the conservation and promotion of natural and cultural heritage.

g. Tourism is also an important vehicle for *promoting cultural exchange*, which enhances international understanding and goodwill among people.

Tourism thus has a large role to play in the economic development of any state. Madhya Pradesh has the advantage of large number of diverse tourist destinations. In view of the huge economic benefits, the potential growth rates, as well as the potential for broad-based balanced regional growth that can be achieved, the Government of Madhya Pradesh has identified tourism as one of its growth engines.

3. Tourism in Madhya Pradesh

3.1 Tourist Destinations

Madhya Pradesh is located at the centre of the nation with considerable connectivity channels with other states. There is considerable diversity in terms of the tourism attractions within the state, and these extend not just to destinations but also to heritage, cuisine, festivals and art and craft. Some of the important tourist destinations of Madhya Pradesh are given in Table 9.6.

2. World Travel and Tourism Council.

Madhya Pradesh, located in the central region of the country, has three principal forms of tourism—the traditional holiday locations; the local tourism for fairs, religious events and the work related and cross-border travelling. The first is attracted to the state as a tourism destination, the second group already has their travel destinations, and the third moves across or into the state and utilises its various services. Presently 382 tourist centres in the state are attracting tourists from all over the world. Out of this, about 20 centres are renowned at national and international levels.

The state has a number of hill ranges, and is the source of some of India's important rivers. The few developed destinations on the hill ranges provide an incredible experience for the tourists, but it must be remembered that most of the hill destinations are also environmentally fragile areas. The rivers and their banks provide innumerable spots and flavours as potential tourist destinations.

The state is also a treasure trove of Indian art, home to the earliest paintings of India. The caves of Bhimbetka, with paintings that date back to 10,000 BC, are remarkably well-reserved, and provide a fascinating insight into pre-historic life; the Udaygiri paintings are equally attractive.

A seemingly endless number of palaces, temples and forts dot the state. The oldest and most renowned Buddhist stupa—the Sanchi Stupa originally constructed by Emperor Ashoka in the 3rd century BC can be found here. A number of pillars in the Greco-Buddhist tradition are also found here, including the Ashoka Pillar, the national emblem of India. In almost every district, be it in the Bundelkhand belt in north, or in Mandla district, there are forts, often existing side by side with forests and other places of natural beauty. The magnificent fort at Gwalior dates back over a thousand years, which speaks of its glorious past. The

FIGURE 9.1

Tourist Map of Madhya Pradesh

TABLE 9.6

Important Tourist Destinations in Madhya Pradesh

	Places of Importance	*Facilities*
Cultural Tourism	Gwalior, Orchha, Khajuraho, Sanchi, Mandu.	Heritage hotels, Museums, Craft villages.
Wildlife & Adventure Tourism	Pachmarhi, Kanha, Bandhavgarh, Panna, Satpura, Pench Valley National Parks, Tigra Lake (Gwalior), Upper Lake (Bhopal), Gandhi Sagar (Mandsaur).	Log huts, Camping Grounds,Trekking, Water sports, Aero-sports, Angling, Cruises, Caravans, Tents etc.
Leisure & Business Tourism	Pachmarhi, Khajuraho, Bhopal, Gwalior, Indore, Mainpat, Tamia, Raipur, Jabalpur etc. Golf Courses,Country	Convention centres, Exhibition grounds, Shopping, Evening entertainment, clubs, Weekend getaways etc.
Pilgrim Tourism	Ujjain, Maheshwar, Omkareshwar, Chitrakoot, Amarkantak, Rajim, Sanchi, Bhopal, Orchha etc.	Budget accommodation, Day shelters, Cafeterias etc.

Source: Madhya Pradesh Tourism Development Corporation (MPTDC).

temples of Khajuraho, bedecked with exquisite carvings, are one of mankind's finest dedications to God, and draws pilgrims and art lovers by the thousands.

One-third of the state is forested, offering a unique and exciting panorama of wildlife in the national parks of Kanha, Bandhavgarh and Shivpuri, and smaller but exciting and adventurous forest zones and national parks in places like Bori provide a treasure house for the adventure traveller.

Customs and beliefs in each area have added colour to the fairs and festivals. Shivratri in Khajuraho, Bhojpur, Pachmarhi and Ujjain; Ramnavami in Chitrakoot and Orchha; Bhagoriya in Jhabua and the annual festival of dances at Khajuraho, are events for the tourists to remember. There are a large number of local events that have a potential for attracting the tourist. These are the pilgrimages related with walks on the banks of the Narmada. These walks are a mix of religion and trekking.

Apart from these destinations and potential that would call the attention and interest of the tourist on a holiday, the tourism of the business traveller, those travelling for religious purpose and those using the roads of the state to go across are equally crucial. These travellers also use facilities and services associated with tourism such as restaurants and hotels, transport, etc.

TABLE 9.7

Important Tourist Destination and their Connectivity

S. No.	*Destination*	*Facilities to Reach*
1	Amarkantak	**By Air:** Nearest airports are Jabalpur (228 km) and Raipur (230 km). **Rail:** The nearest railhead is Pendra Road (42 km) on the Katni-Bilaspur section of the South-Eastern Railway. **Road:** Amarkantak is connected by regular bus service with Shahdol, Umaria, Jabalpur, Rewa, Bilaspur, Anuppur and Pendra Road.
2	Bandhavgarh	**By Air:** Nearest airport is at Jabalpur (164 km). The most convenient route to Bandhavgarh is to fly from Delhi to Khajuraho from where it is a five and a half hour drive (237 km). **Rail:** The nearest railway stations are Jabalpur (164 km), Katni (102 km) and Satna 120 km) on the Central Railway and Umaria (35 km) on the South-Eastern Railway. **Road:** State/private transport buses ply between Katni and Umaria and from Satna and Rewa to Tala (Bandhavgarh). Taxis are available at Satna, Jabalpur, Katni, Umaria, Bilaspur (300 km) and Khajuraho.
3	Bhedaghat	**By Air:** Jabalpur (23 km) is the nearest airport connected to Bhopal and Delhi with regular flights. **Rail:** Jabalpur, on the Mumbai-Howrah (via Allahabad) main line, is the main railhead. All mail, express and passenger trains halt here. **Road:** Frequent buses, tempos and taxis are available from Jabalpur.
4	Bhimbetka	**By Air:** Bhopal (46 km from Bhimbetka) is the nearest airport. It is connected with Mumbai, Delhi, Jabalpur, Indore and Gwalior. **Rail:** Bhopal, on the Delhi-Chennai and Delhi-Mumbai mainline is the most convenient railhead. **Road:** Bhimbetka is connected by bus with Bhopal.
5	Bhojpur	**By Air:** Bhopal (28 km from Bhojpur) is the nearest airport. It is connected with Mumbai, Delhi, Jabalpur, Indore and Gwalior. **Rail:** Bhopal, on the Delhi-Chennai and Delhi-Mumbai mainline is the most convenient railhead. **Road:** Bhojpur is connected by bus with Bhopal.
6	Bhopal	**By Air:** Regular flights connect Bhopal with Delhi, Gwalior, Jabalpur, Indore and Mumbai. **Rail:** Bhopal is on the Delhi-Chennai main line. Major trains going from Mumbai to Delhi via Itarsi and Jhansi also go through Bhopal. **Road:** Regular bus services connect Bhopal with Indore (186 km), Mandu (285 km), Ujjain (188 km), Khajuraho (383 km), Pachmarhi (195 km), Gwalior (423 km), Sanchi (46 km), Jabalpur (295 km) and Shivpuri (311 km).
7	Chanderi	**By Air:** The nearest airports are at Bhopal (258 km) and Gwalior (259 km). **Rail:** Lalitpur (36 km) and Jhansi (124 km) on the Delhi-Chennai and Delhi-Mumbai main line, are the convenient railheads. Ashok Nagar (46 km) and Mungaoli (38 km) also serve Chanderi. **Road:** Chanderi is connected by bus with Gwalior, Indore, Guna, Shivpuri, Ashok Nagar, Jhansi, Lalitpur, Tikamgarh, Vidisha, Sanchi and Bhopal.
8	Chitrakoot	**By Air:** The nearest airport is at Khajuraho (175 km), connected with Delhi and Agra. **Rail:** The nearest railhead is at Chitrakoot Dham (Karwi) (11 km) on the Jhansi-Manikpur main line. **Road:** Regular bus services connect Chitrakoot with Jhansi, Mahoba, Chitrakoot Dham, Harpalpur, Satna and Chhatarpur.

Contd...

...contd...

S. No.	Destination	Facilities to Reach
9	Gwalior	**By Air:** Gwalior is connected with regular flights from Delhi and Bhopal. **Rail:** Gwalior is on the Central Railway's main Delhi-Mumbai and Delhi-Chennai lines. Among other major trains, the Shatabdi and the Taj Express connect Gwalior with Delhi and Agra daily. **Road:** Gwalior is connected by regular bus service with Agra, Mathura, Jaipur, Delhi, Chandigarh, Lucknow, Bhopal, Chanderi, Indore, Jhansi, Khajuraho, Rewa, Jabalpur, Ujjain and Shivpuri.
10	Indore	**By Air:** Indore is connected with Bhopal, Delhi and Mumbai. **Rail:** Indore is on the Western Railway and is connected with major Indian cities. **Road:** Indore is connected by bus with Mumbai, Ahmedabad, Aurangabad, Bhopal, Gwalior, Mandu, Maheshwar, Omkareshwar, Ujjain, Sanchi and Vidisha.
11	Jabalpur	**By Air:** Jabalpur is connected with regular flights from Delhi and Bhopal. **Rail:** Jabalpur is on the Mumbai-Howrah (via Allahabad) main line. All mail, express and passenger trains halt here. **Road:** Jabalpur is connected by regular bus services with Bhopal, Indore, Satna, Raipur and Nagpur among other places.
12	Kanha	**By Air:** Nearest airport is at Jabalpur (156 km), connected with regular flights from Delhi and Bhopal. **Rail:** Most convenient railheads are at Jabalpur and Bilaspur. **Road:** Daily bus service available for Kisli and Mukki from Jabalpur and back. Taxis are available for hire from Jabalpur, Bilaspur and Raipur. Vehicles are not permitted within the park after dark.
13	Khajuraho	**By Air:** Khajuraho is connected to Delhi and Agra with regular flights. **Rail:** The nearest railheads are Mahoba (64 km) and Harpalpur (94 km). Jhansi (175 km) and Satna (117 km) are convenient railheads for visitors from Delhi, Mumbai, Calcutta, Chennai, Agra and Varanasi. **Road:** Khajuraho is connected by regular bus services with Mahoba, Harpalpur, Satna, Jhansi, Gwalior, Agra, Jabalpur and Bhopal.
14	Maheshwar	**By Air:** Nearest airport is at Indore (91 km), connected with Mumbai, Delhi and Bhopal. **Rail:** Nearest railheads are Barwaha (39 km), Indore (91 km), Khandwa (110 km), and Mhow on the Western Railway. **Road:** Regular buses are available from Barwah, Khandwa, Dhar and Dhamnod.
15	Mandu	**By Air:** Nearest airport is at Indore (99 km), connected with Mumbai, Delhi and Bhopal. **Rail:** Convenient railheads are Ratlam (124 km) on the Mumbai-Delhi main line and Indore (99 km). **Road:** Regular bus services connect Mandu with Indore, Dhar, Mhow, Ratlam, Ujjain and Bhopal.
16	Omkareshwar	**By Air:** Nearest airport is at Indore (77 km), connected with Mumbai, Delhi and Bhopal. **Rail:** Nearest railhead is Omkareshwar Road (12 km) on the Ratlam-Khandwa section of the Western Railway. **Road:** Omkareshwar is connected to Indore, Ujjain, Khandwa and Omkareshwar Road by regular bus services.

Contd...

...contd...

S. No.	Destination	Facilities to Reach
17	Orchha	**By Air:** Nearest airport is at Gwalior (119 km), which is connected with regular flights from Delhi and Bhopal. **Rail:** Nearest railhead is Jhansi (16 km), on the Delhi-Mumbai and Delhi-Chennai main lines. All major mail and express trains stop at Jhansi. **Road:** Orchha lies on a diversion from the Jhansi-Khajuraho road. Regular bus services connect Orchha with Jhansi. Tempos and taxis are also available.
18	Pachmarhi	**By Air:** Nearest airport is at Bhopal (195 km) connected by regular flights with Delhi, Gwalior, Jabalpur, Indore and Mumbai. **Rail:** Pipariya (47 km), on the Mumbai-Howrah mainline via Allahabad, is the most convenient railhead. **Road:** Pachmarhi is connected by regular bus services with Bhopal, Hoshangabad, Nagpur, Pipariya and Chhindwara. MP Tourism also operates regular coach services between Bhopal and Pachmarhi. Taxis are available at Pipariya.
19	Panna	**By Air:** The nearest airport is Khajuraho (25 km), connected with Delhi and Agra. **Rail:** Jhansi (180 km) for those travelling from Mumbai, Delhi and Chennai. Satna (90 km) for those travelling from Delhi, Kolkata and Varanasi. Katni (150 km) for those travelling from Mumbai, Chennai and Nagpur. **Road:** Reserve does not have any transport facility for the visitors. Four wheel drive petrol vehicles are best for wildlife watching and going around the reserve. Rough terrain, unmedalled roads, steep inclines are difficult for other vehicles. Private vehicles can be hired at Khajuraho/Panna.
20	Pench	**By Air:** Nagpur (92 km); 80 km along National Highway 7 to Khawasa and then 12 km to Turia gate. **Rail:** Jabalpur (195 km); 165 km along National Highway 7 to Sukhtara village via Seoni and then 30 km to Karmajhiri. **Road:** Jabalpur (195 km), Nagpur (92 km), Chhindwara (120 km), Seoni (60 km).
21	Sanchi	**By Air:** Nearest airport is at Bhopal (46 km via Diwanganj and 78 km via Raisen) which is connected with Delhi, Mumbai, Jabalpur, Gwalior and Indore. **Rail:** Sanchi lies on the Jhansi-Itarsi section of the Central Railways. However, the most convenient railheads are Vidisha (10 km) and Bhopal (46 km). **Road:** Good, motorable roads connect Sanchi with Bhopal, Indore Sagar, Gwalior, Vidisha and Raisen, besides other places.
22	Shivpuri	**By Air:** Nearest airport is at Gwalior (112 km), which is connected with regular flights from Delhi and Bhopal. **Rail:** Nearest railheads are at Jhansi (101 km) and Gwalior which are on the Delhi-Chennai main lines. **Road:** Shivpuri is connected by regular bus services with Gwalior, Indore, Bhopal, Jhansi and Ujjain.
23	Ujjain	**By Air:** Nearest airport is at Indore (55 km) which is connected by flights with Delhi, Bhopal and Mumbai. **Rail:** Ujjain is connected with Mumbai, Delhi, Bangalore, Ahmedabad, Allahabad, Kolkata, Chennai and Cochin. **Road:** Regular bus services connect Ujjain with Indore, Bhopal, Ratlam, Gwalior, Mandu, Dhar and Omkareshwar.

Source: Department of Tourism, GoMP.

4. Hospitality

The state has more than 50 graded hotels. Apart from this, there are several hotels/lodges/ accommodation facilities run and maintained by MP Tourism Development Corporation. Since the state houses various heritage buildings and bungalows, several of these have been converted into heritage hotels. The government has acknowledged the need of more 5, 4 and 3 star hotels and is inviting private players to invest in the state. Further, there are various heritage properties which the government is keen on converting into heritage hotels with the association of private parties.

TABLE 9.8

Hospitality Ratings

S.No.	*Hotel Ratings*	*No.*
1	Heritage	5
2	5 star deluxe	1
3	5 star	3
4	4 star	1
5	3 star	23
6	2 star	13
7	1 star	4
8	Classification awaited	1

Source: Department of Tourism.

5. Tourist Arrival in Madhya Pradesh

5.1 Tourism Traffic Data

Table 9.9 presents the tourist arrival in Madhya Pradesh. It indicate towards primarily domestic tourists at places of pilgrimage with marginal foreign tourists. The foreign tourist arrival at pilgrim centres is much less compared to domestic tourist arrivals. This ratio reduces to almost one–ten–thousandth by the year 2008. The same ratio for major centres is about one-tenth. Major destinations in the state are once again flooding with domestic tourists. Overall, the period between 2004 and 2005 shows a decreasing trend in tourist arrivals especially in case of the domestic tourists. Beyond 2005, the tourist arrival in Madhya Pradesh has grown at the rate of 20 per cent per annum. The overall tourist arrival has gone up by three times from 2004 to 2008.

The earnings from the domestic tourists far exceed the earnings from the foreign tourists due to the number of domestic tourists (more than a thousand times of the foreign tourists). The above data indicates the need for development in terms of facilities and target marketing of these destinations given the two categories of tourists.

Table 9.10 indicates the trends in foreign and domestic tourists' visit to the key tourist destinations in Madhya Pradesh. Amarkantak, Chitrakoot and Omkareshwar has the maximum tourist visits with Chitrakoot accounting for almost half the tourist visits as compared to the total tourist visits across the state.

For the foreign tourists, Gwalior, Orchcha, Khajuraho and Sanchi seem to be the choice locations. Here, it can be stated that out of the four places mentioned, Khajuraho and Sanchi are the key tourist destinations. Gwalior and Orchcha fall on the route to Khajuraho while travelling from Delhi by road/rail. With old palaces and forts, a stop-over by these tourists have got these centres limelight. This example can be used as a strategy while developing tourist centres.

TABLE 9.9

Tourist Arrivals in MP

Year	*Pilgrim Centres*			*Major Centres*			*All Tourists*		
	Domestic	*Foreign*	*Total*	*Domestic*	*Foreign*	*Total*	*Domestic*	*Foreign*	*Total*
2004	7457518	7224	7464742	1161908	138151	1300059	8619426	145375	8764801
2005	6128953	7192	6136145	1121999	156231	1278230	7250952	163423	7414375
2006	9535760	9330	9545090	1504430	180307	1684737	11040190	189637	11229827
2007	11917333	6074	11923407	1977167	228130	2205297	13894500	234204	14128704
2008	20074113	8006	20082119	2014814	243727	2258541	22088927	251733	22340660

Source: MPTDC data.

TABLE 9.10

Tourist Arrival during Calendar Years 2005 to 2008

Tourist/Pilgrim	*2005*			*2006*			*2007*			*2008*		
Centres	*Domestic*	*Foreigner*	*Total*	*Domestic*	*Foreigner*	*Total*	*Domestic*	*Foreigner*	*Total*	*Domestic*	*Foreigner*	*Total*
Amarkantak	1172000	41	1172041	1131006	29	1131035	1260000	24	1260024	1995000	48	1995048
Bandhavgarh	23244	4068	27312	18877	3421	22298	38614	6812	45426	69641	24781	94422
Bhedghat	462085	2423	464508	392013	2341	394354	548853	3044	551897	559320	1382	560702
Bhimbetka	0	0	0	0	0	0	24632	390	25022	36782	1492	38274
Bhuranpur	39130	39	39169	38845	96	38941	42925	107	43032	54594	150	54744
Chitrakoot	2673847	460	2674307	3242200	198	3242398	6096835	499	6097334	9142009	664	9142673
Gwalior	112382	12261	124643	108445	9811	118256	140766	11953	152719	197220	17841	215061
Kanha	68424	4200	72624	66932	3325	70257	80223	6411	86634	96707	18169	114876
Khajuraho	145987	70726	216713	140466	62109	202575	164406	73843	238249	201443	89169	290612
Maheshwar	89891	1058	90949	79635	1044	80679	130072	2508	132580	173884	2250	176134
Mandu	269341	6789	276130	270149	7085	277234	308933	6488	315421	514892	7247	522139
Omkareshwar	1731130	3210	1734340	2612664	3612	2616276	1500000	3255	1503255	2364000	1447	2365447
Orchha	65006	42691	107697	58267	37602	95869	75832	46881	122713	78958	53373	132331
Pachmarhi	316363	101	316464	373436	241	373677	480068	97	480165	497270	138	497408
Panna	0	0	0	0	0	0	33346	7679	41025	56325	14419	70744
Pench	0	0	0	0	0	0	24174	572	24746	54641	4530	59171
Sanchi	70511	15278	85789	71977	14346	86323	78021	18929	96950	139603	12333	151936
Shivpuri	11611	78	11689	14514	115	14629	12490	145	12635	16738	85	16823
Ujjain	0	0	0	0	0	0	0	0	0	5839900	2215	5842115

Source: MPTDC.

TABLE 9.11

Growth Rate of Tourism in Madhya Pradesh

Year	*Domestic*	*Foreign*	*Total*
2001-02	1.3	-25.4	0.8
2002-03	-9.2	-9.3	-9.2
2003-04	34.85	47.19	35.05
2004-05	40.81	46.98	40.91
2006	52.3	16.0	51.5
2007	25.9	23.5	25.8

Source: MPTDC.

In Table 9.11, growth rate of tourist arrivals between 2001 and 2007 is given. Foreign tourists have been around 2 per cent of the tourist traffic, and tourists to centres of pilgrimage constitute about 70 to 80 per cent of the tourist traffic.

The years 2003-04, 2004-05 and 2006 showed a high growth rate in the tourist arrivals in Madhya Pradesh. The domestic tourist inflow increased by 35.05 per cent, 40.91 and 52.3 per cent respectively. Further, the foreign tourist inflow increased at the rate of 47.19 per cent, 46.98 per cent and 16 per cent, respectively. The need of the time is to take proactive steps to maintain this growth and try to further increase it.

Despite MP's strengths as a tourist destination and the government's initiatives, MP has still a lot to realise in terms of its potential. The recent developments in tourism sector in building tourism infrastructure, focusing on marketing initiatives and development of newer tourism products have shown results and the way forward for tourism development in the state. With current focus on private investments into the sector through public-private partnership, the state is poised to harness optimum results in tourism development in the state.

6. Tourism Policies in Madhya Pradesh

6.1 State Tourism Policy, 1995

In order to ensure growth and development of tourism in MP, the state government announced a Tourism Policy in January 1995. This policy envisaged the creation of an environment conducive to attracting private investment. The focus of this policy was mainly on the improvement and creation of adequate basic infrastructure including water, electricity; upgradation and augmentation of accommodation; catering and recreational facilities; augmentation of transport facilities; and on marketing the state.

BOX 9.2

Tourism Policy of Madhya Pradesh

With the view to speed up development of tourism in Madhya Pradesh, the state government announced a New Tourism Policy in January 1995. The new tourism policy envisages creation of an environment conducive to attracting increased private investment in the tourism sector, and a more meaningful role for the government.

Strategy for Development

The focus shall be on the following areas:

- Improvement and creation of adequate basic infrastructure—land, roads, water, electricity etc.
- Upgradation and augmentation of accommodation, catering and recreational facilities.
- Augmentation of transport facilities.
- Marketing of destinations to ensure optimal use of infrastructure.
- Evolving suitable policies for increasing foreign exchange earnings.
- Promotion of the arts and crafts of Madhya Pradesh.

Role of State Government

The state government will confine its efforts to infrastructure development ensuring uninterrupted electricity, water supply and provision of basic medical facilities. It will also be responsible for dissemination of information, organisation of festivals and inter-departmental co-ordination to create conditions for attracting private sector investment for the tourism sector. For this, it will provide fiscal incentives, assist in providing suitable sites and remove bottlenecks, especially those connected with infrastructure development.

Incentives

A special package of incentives for the tourism industry has been prepared. These incentives will also be available for private entrepreneurs for any of the following activities:

- Hotels, motels and restaurants.
- Heritage hotels, health farms, recreation centres, ropeways, golf courses, museums, amusement parks, craft villages, convention centres, and all other bona fide tourism-related activities recognised by the government.
- A/C luxury coaches, A/C mini buses and imported limousines purchased by registered tour operators for tourist transport.
- Activities connected with adventure tourism, such as hang gliding, parasailing, river rafting, boating, trekking, rock climbing etc.

The specific incentives are:

Land

1) Government land will be offered with the approval of the Empowered Committee as equity participation on behalf of the government at current market value for setting up joint ventures;
2) The companies thus formed who are given any kind of government land will be expected to complete the project within a period of three years from the date of transfer of land, failing which the land will revert to the government. The company will not be allowed to transfer the land to anybody else, or use it for any purpose other than that for which it is allotted;
3) For construction of approved category hotels, etc., in the urban areas, exemption under Section 20 of the Urban Land Ceiling Act will be made available on a case-to-case basis as decided by the Empowered Committee.

Luxury Tax

New projects shall be exempt from luxury tax for five years from the date of commencement of commercial operations.

Sales Tax

New projects shall be exempt from sales tax for five years from the date of commencement of commercial operations.

Entertainment Tax

Entertainment centres will be exempt from entertainment tax for five years from the date of commencement of commercial operations.

Source: MPTDC.

The private sector was to be involved in achieving the above. A special package of incentives was prepared which included land as equity participation on behalf of the government and exemption under Section 20 of the Urban Land Ceiling Act for construction of approved category hotels. Exemption on sales and luxury tax on new projects for 5 years from the date of commencement of commercial operations was also given. Entertainment centres were also exempted from entertainment tax for 10 years from the date of commencement of commercial operations.

BOX 9.3

Ecotourism

It is that form of tourism in which the tourist is able to enjoy nature and see wildlife in its natural habitat in quiet and serene surroundings.

Adventure Tourism

It provides the tourist with special thrill and feeling of adventure whilst participating in sporting activities in river, water bodies, hills and mountains. Madhya Pradesh with its richly endowed natural environment has immense potential for such sports.

Source: Madhya Pradesh Tourism Development Corporation.

6.2 Eco and Adventure Tourism Policy, 2001

The tourism policy of Madhya Pradesh, 1995 had as one of its major objectives, the promotion of eco and adventure tourism. This was keeping in view the demand for such tourism and the potential for the same in the state.

Instead of depending upon its limited resources, the state government has decided to open up this sector for private participation for optimum utilisation of these resources.

While on one hand, with these efforts, the government hopes to attract tourists in large numbers, on the other hand, it is expected that it would help in generating a greater demand for local products and in creating new employment avenues for the local communities.

BOX 9.4

Heritage Hotel

As per the definition of the Department of Tourism, Government of India, all those buildings, forts, *havelis, kothis* and castles that have been constructed prior to 1950 and are being run as hotels shall fall within the category of heritage hotels. A heritage hotel can be of any size or dimension.

Source: Madhya Pradesh Tourism Development Council.

6.3 Heritage Tourism Policy, 2002

One of the objectives of the tourism policy of Madhya Pradesh, 1995 was to convert the heritage wealth of the state i.e., forts, palaces, *havelis* and *kothis* into heritage hotels. The efforts made in this direction in Rajasthan and Gujarat have been highly successful both in conservation of heritage wealth and generating economic benefits.

The state is committed to promote and support private investment and community effort for the conversion of these historic buildings into heritage hotels and development of heritage buildings.

7. Institutional Mechanism

7.1 Madhya Pradesh Tourism Development Corporation (MPTDC)

MPTDC in the recent years has taken a multi-pronged strategy towards improving tourism in Madhya Pradesh. On one hand, the corporation has focused upon building tourism infrastructure in the state and increasing tourism products; on the other hand, it has put a lot of effort into marketing the state to provide the much required visibility, both nationally and internationally, as a potential tourist destination.

Over the last couple of years, however, the corporation has undertaken a number of initiatives to promote tourism, which includes production and showing of national and international films of tourist locations in the state. These films have been credited as being of particularly good quality and showcase the state's attractions well. The corporation is also in the process of attracting private investments under the public-private partnership model. The corporation has earned the revenue of Rs. 35.11 crore in 2006-07 which is 51.93 per cent higher than the previous year.

While MPTDC is directly responsible for promotion of tourism in the state, there are in fact some other agencies, which have played and have the capacity to play a significant role in tourism promotion in the state. We briefly mention them and their roles here.

7.2 Special Area Development Authority (SADA)

SADA was created to look after special areas and it administered full control, initially even overriding local self-governments in their designated areas. But now *nagarpalikas* and *nagar panchayats* have been put in-charge of the operations. Some of the major tourism sites in the state are under the administrative control

BOX 9.5

Madhya Pradesh Tourism Development Corporation: Formation and Functions

Madhya Pradesh Tourism Corporation (MPTDC) was incorporated in 1978. MPTDC has seven regional offices and five satellite offices functioning outside the state. The MPTDC has a body of 768 employees who looks after the running of the management units, housing units and transportation units of the corporation. The MPTDC has made 42 residential units, seven non-residential units and 39 vehicles available for the tourists.

The corporation was incorporated with a corpus of Rs. 1 crore. The corpus has since increased to Rs. 25 crore. MPTDC strives to attract the tourists to various tourist sites in the state through appropriate advertisements. The corporation helps the tourist coming from outside the state by offering tour packages. The corporation also organises festivals/fetes with a view to encourage the folk art and culture of the state.

Functions of MPTDC:

1) Managing the residential and non-residential units at the tourist sites.
2) Providing information and literature to the tourists related to their tours.
3) Publication of tourism literature about the tourist destinations from time to time.
4) Making transportation available at the tourist sites.
5) To collect data related to the domestic and foreign arrivals at the 18 tourist destinations of MP through the directors of national parks and the Archaeological Survey of India.
6) Expedite reservation of accommodation in the residential units managed by the corporation.
7) To implement the decisions taken by the Advisory Committee, division level committees and the government.
8) To prepare proposals for the state and Central plans and the annual budget.

Source: MPTDC.

of SADA—Mandu and Khajuraho. SADA has been able to prevent to a large extent illegal construction and encroachments, and keep these sites relatively safe and secure from urban growth and environmental damages.

7.3 Adivasi Lok Kala Parishad

The state's Adivasi Lok Kala Parishad has been an active agency managing, planning and implementing a large number of tribal folk performances, including national and international level festivals across Madhya Pradesh. Further, this agency has also been promoting local events. Its role in initiating events of tourist interest in major tourism locations and in building a momentum around tribal and folk culture is a strength for the state to explore further.

7.4 Madhya Pradesh Ecotourism Development Board (MPEDB)

The state government through its forest department constituted the MPEDB in July 2005 to act as the nodal agency for development and promotion of ecotourism in the state. It shall be the board's mandate to ensure the attainment of the objectives and adherence to the guiding principles set forth in the policy for ecotourism development. For this, the board shall develop the necessary systems, standards and institutions. The board shall be equipped with required technical and financial resources to implement this policy. It shall liaise with local, national and international stakeholders for planning, developing and implementing projects compatible with this policy.

The board shall also be empowered to oversee and approve specific ecotourism projects, activities and site management plans that are in conformance with this policy and other statutory requirements.

8. Eleventh Five Year Plan[3]

The following goals have been clearly defined with these objectives, during the 11th Five Year Plan:

- Increase employment generation.
- Promote and market destination with and outside India.
- Develop basic infrastructure at lesser known tourist locations.

3. *Source:* State Planning Board, Government of MP.

- Develop eco-friendly and sustainable tourism facilities.
- Develop and promote eco and adventure tourism, and
- Convert old palaces into heritage hotels under the public-private partnership scheme.

An outlay of Rs. 147.60 crore has been proposed for the 11th Five Year Plan. The figure is more than double when compared with the 10th FYP of Rs. 53.60 crore.

Plan allocation under some important schemes is as given below:

(i) An amount of Rs. 10.00 lakh has been allocated to give training to guides at important tourist centres.

(ii) During 11th Five Year Plan, for the year 2007-2008, an amount of Rs. 1,000.00 lakh has been provided for upgradation of units of MPTDC.

(iii) During the 11th Five Year Plan, for the year 2007-08, an amount of Rs. 1,675.00 lakh has been provided under the 12th Finance Commission to fulfil the special needs of the tourists in the state.

(iv) An amount of Rs.10.00 lakh has been provided to give interest subsidy for heritage hotels during 2007-08.

(v) For Annual Plan 2007-08, an amount of Rs. 100.00 lakh has been provided for development of tourist centres at every district.

The activities of the tourism department like publicity and promotion, fair and festivals, development of tourist circuits of MPTDC units in the state will be performed during the 11th Five Year Plan period 2007-2012.

9. Achievements in the Tourism Sector

9.1 Awards (2007-08)

- Government of India, National Award by the Ministry of Tourism.
- National Tourism Award—Best Performing State.
- National Tourism Award—Best Maintained Tourist Friendly National Park—Pench National Park.
- National Tourism Award—Best Maintained Tourist Friendly Monument—Sanchi.
- National Tourism Award—Most Innovative Product—Shaan-e-Bhopal Rail Coach Restaurant.

9.2 ISO Certificates

The MPTDC has received ISO 9001:2000 certificate for their following units:

i. Paryatan Bhawan,

ii. Shaan-e-Bhopal,

iii. Boat club,

iv. Resident Office, New Delhi, and

v. Highway Treat, Dodi.

The organisation is now in the process of getting ISO certificates for the following units:

i. Delawari Jungle Camp (ISO 14000),

ii. Bargi-Maikal Resort (ISO 14000),

iii. White Tiger Forest Lodge, Bandhavgarh (ISO 14000),

iv. Hotel Lake View Ashoka (ISO 22000), and

v. Hotel Palash Residency (ISO 22000).

10. A Tourism Strategy for Madhya Pradesh

10.1 Reorientation of Institutions

MPTDC as the apex agency for promoting tourism in the state has been showing marked improvement in the recent past in terms of its outcomes right from increased tourists to national awards in tourism. To support this growth in the sector, given the limited funds available, the role of private investors through the PPP model needs to be promoted. The institution needs to be reoriented towards leveraging greater private investments.

10.2 Role of MPTDC

The MPTDC needs to come out of its role as a manager of tourism facilities. If it moves towards a greater promotional role, the current budgetary allocations to it and to the tourism sector need to be substantially increased. There is already a proposal for creation of a Tourism Development Fund. This fund should be flexibly managed but have definite work streams that would help MPTDC promote activities like festivals, events, advertising budget, liaison offices, touch screen information booths for tourists etc. Further, the state would require a master plan for promoting tourism, which will have cross linkages with other units of the state such as those involved in infrastructure, revenue and culture.

Preparing a tourism master plan for the state—The development of a policy does not complete the picture needed for strategic action. A tourism master plan will be required that puts elements into place apart from incentives for tourism players and putting together required infrastructure, facilities etc.

Marketing and promoting tourism in Madhya Pradesh—The economic development policy of MP has outlined this strategy very effectively and it is led by three actions:

i. A positioning platform for the state,

ii. Increased promotional activities, and

iii. Developing joint circuits with other states.

In the new envisaged role of MPTDC, it will have to bridge the gap between the needs in tourism and the desire and capacity of private sector and its role in services and infrastructure required. This role as a facilitator and as a promoter would require the corporation to undergo a system change wherein, both its nature, its personnel capacity and its culture and knowledge base will have to be upgraded substantially. This cannot be done without a reorganisation and institutional reforms process within tourism.

10.3 Improved Connectivity

The biggest bottleneck in the development of tourism in MP is the lack of physical connectivity to the destinations. Most of the tourist towns do not have air and rail connectivity. The road linkages across tourist towns are in bad condition. The absence of good quality intra-state connectivity leads to tourists restricting their visits to one or two destinations only. Even before the state can start promoting tourism, it has to ensure access to the destinations.

The government will have to work for promoting air linkages between major cities and major tourism destinations such as Khajuraho, Indore, Bhopal, Jabalpur etc. These must then get linked to good rail or road transport to tourism destinations which are being aggressively promoted.

A fair amount of work has already started in the state to better connect with roads some of the important tourist destinations like Orchha, Pachmarhi, Khajuraho, Mandu, Bandhavgarh, Chitrakoot, Sanchi, Kanha, Omkareshwar, Maheshwar, Satna, Maihar etc. These linkages must be ensured to be of high quality and covering many of the other destinations. There must also be good linkages to destinations of natural beauty such as Shivpuri, Jabalpur, etc.

10.4 Promoting Rural Tourism

Religious tourism abounds in the state, and all rural areas, especially around the Narmada and other rivers have major fairs, pilgrimages and other events all round the year. Very little has as yet actually been done to promote rural tourism and most of this is restricted to the adjoining wildlife sanctuaries or tourism centres such as Khajuraho or Mandu.

By itself, identifying and promoting locations in rural areas has to be launched and a system of promoting these by profiling them, then identifying and building an infrastructure that would attract the tourist towards them has to be undertaken. Each location must also be identified for the type of tourist they may attract, since every tourist is not attracted to every location. Government must be conscious that it does not land up putting up restaurants or kiosks or other facilities themselves, but attempts to bring in private players along with promotional role of popularising these areas.

10.5 Marketing

The marketing of the state being done by MPTDC, has seen a major turnaround in the recent years. The marketing has now taken a multi-dimensional focus with aggressive campaigning through TV and print media, organising festivals and road shows across the state and country, increased participation of MPTDC officials in national and international tourism conventions and greater focus on the tourism promotion offices in and outside the state.

In addition, the corporation needs to and is also working towards:

- Building tourism packages, both to carry tourists to and within the area.
- Develop proper literature and other requirements of information.
- Ensure through government, proper infrastructure and provision for reaching the places of travel therein.
- Encourage and ensure private participation in designing tourism products and in putting in place infrastructure and utilities such as vehicles, accommodation, etc.

- Put into place an effective selling proposition for the state and the different tourist places. Unlike successful cases such as Kerala, MP does not have just one type of option for the tourists and hence, the different types of tourism that the state offers would need a more comprehensive and well thought out strategy to encourage tourists.
- Such strategies apart from getting tourists must also plan to put in place provisions that shall facilitate more nights spent per tourist in MP.

A critical factor that is affecting the foreign tourists visiting India is the perception of threat due to terrorist activities. Though the issue requires a more comprehensive strategy at a national level, Madhya Pradesh needs to do its bit in promoting Madhya Pradesh as a peaceful and a tourist-friendly state.

10.6 Adding New Tourism Products

The tourism promotional agencies must try and identify a unique selling proposition for the state and should then arrive at a positioning plank. The marketing and the promotion plan should be developed around this. Themes for each destination should then be woven around this positioning plank. Further, rather than spread out thin, a few selected tourist circuits could be selected for promotion. The best option could be to focus on the major heritage sites and the eco-adventure tourist circuits. Already, the state government is envisaging a MP Heritage Development Trust. Some of the new developments in the new tourism potential products are mentioned below.

10.6.1 Ecotourism

Madhya Pradesh is endowed with a very rich spectrum of scenic and relatively undisturbed landscapes, forests, wildlife and cultural diversity. The state has the largest forest area (94,669 sq km) in the country of which more than 10,000 sq km is under protected areas and the largest tiger population housed in five world famous tiger reserves. It is also home to several endangered species including the Gangetic dolphin, the *ghariyal*, the great Indian bustard and the *kharmor* amongst others. More than 80 per cent of tourism in Madhya Pradesh is centred on nature and wildlife. The state has long been a premier wildlife destination especially for 'tiger viewing'. Excessive and exclusive focus on tigers and tiger reserves, however, has the potential to lead to problems including resource degradation, neglect of other areas, erosion of the local culture and other management problems associated with excessive centralisation. Besides, a majority of tourists are deprived of experiencing other lesser known but equally rich facets of the state's natural heritage, which could also lead to stagnation in the growth of tourist inflow to the state.

It is in this context that "ecotourism" has gained its relevance. Ecotourism or ecologically sustainable tourism has been defined as "responsible tourism to natural areas that conserves the environment and improves the well being of local communities". It has been recognised as an important conservation tool as it encourages local communities, government as well as private agencies to protect natural resources that attract visitors resulting in economic benefits and at the same time caters to the growing worldwide popular demand for opportunities to savour natural wilderness. Ecotourism also has potential to play an important role in creating environmental as well as cultural awareness amongst all the stakeholders—local communities, tourists, government and the private sector.

With this background, the Government of Madhya Pradesh has resolved to make the promotion of ecotourism in the state a priority area. The focus shall be on conservation of natural resources through awareness building, diversification of tourism activities and destinations, and local community participation. This policy is aimed at informing and sensitising the general public and related government departments towards ecotourism and laying down the framework for its growth in the state in an environmentally, socially and economically sustainable manner.

Following are the activities and facilities that may be undertaken for promoting an area as an ecotourism destination within the state.

a. Nature Camps

Camping sites may be identified and provided with basic facilities to enable the tourists to stay in natural surroundings, either solely to experience the wilderness or additionally for participating in other activities requiring overnight stay in forests.

b. Eco-friendly Accommodation

Adequate facilities for boarding and lodging of tourists may be developed. The infrastructure must be eco-friendly and strictly in accordance with guidelines laid down in this regard. Suitable existing buildings, located in picturesque locations, may also be developed for tourist accommodation; where feasible, local community members may also be encouraged to provide lodging and boarding facilities to the tourists, subject to prescribed quality standards.

c. Trekking and Nature Walks

Trekking routes of varying distances and guided nature trails through designated paths may be identified and developed in scenic landscapes rich in biodiversity, causing minimum disturbance to the natural vegetation and soil. Staff and local persons, especially youth may be appropriately trained to act as nature guides and naturalists so as to assist visitors during wildlife viewing and trekking.

d. Wildlife Viewing and River Cruise

Wildlife viewing in eco-friendly vehicles or on elephant backs may be promoted at appropriate sites for observing wildlife. Sites having suitable water bodies may be developed for providing river cruise facilities in non-polluting boats.

e. Adventure Sports

Facilities for adventure sports such as rock climbing, rappelling and parasailing along with water sports such as river rafting, boating and canoeing may be developed in consultation and co-operation with experts and the concerned department or agency having control over the water bodies.

f. Angling

Angling facilities for Mahseer and other suitable fish species, strictly on a catch and release basis, may be developed on suitable rivers/water bodies flowing through or along the forest areas in consultation with the concerned department. Angling guidelines to be formulated by the Madhya Pradesh Ecotourism Development Board (MPEDB) shall be strictly followed in this regard. If necessary, water bodies may be artificially stocked by rearing and releasing fish seed into the rivers that have been depleted of the target species over time.

10.6.2 Herbal Ecotourism

Herbal ecotourism may be made the thrust area at suitable locations having a rich herbal heritage. Traditional medicinal practices of such locations may be explored and based on these; authentic herbal inputs having appropriate certifications and recognition may be made available to the tourists. These activities may be promoted in collaboration with Madhya Pradesh Minor Forest Produce Co-operative Federation.

10.6.3 Urban Ecotourism through Eco-Parks

In order to promote urban ecotourism, eco-parks may be developed in various urban centres. Such eco-parks may contain provisions for various ecotourism activities including interpretation centres, trekking, nature walks, biking, bird watching, camping, angling, herbal centre, adventure sports etc., on a small scale depending upon the area being developed. For this purpose, existing public parks in urban localities may also be utilised.

10.6.4 Visitor Interpretation Centres

Existing interpretation facilities may be strengthened to make them more comprehensive to accommodate the requirements of various classes of visitors envisaged. Each destination must incorporate ways to enhance and enrich the visitor experience.

10.6.5 Conservation Education

Conservation education must be promoted in and around each destination for creating awareness amongst school and college students, local communities, government staff and visitors in order to maintain and enhance support for ecotourism and environmental conservation. Various means that may be adopted include media campaigns, formation of eco-clubs at schools and colleges, exposure visits to destinations, displays and hoardings, community centres etc. New and innovative methods shall also be encouraged.

10.6.6 Other Facilities

Facilities for any other eco-friendly activities may also be provided based on specific requirements of a site, provided the activity is compatible with the overall objectives of this policy and in conformance with the various standards and guidelines laid down in this regard.

10.6.7 Proposed Ecotourism Destinations of Madhya Pradesh

- Orchha Nature Reserve
- Ratapani Wildlife Sanctuary
- Ralamandal Wildlife Sanctuary
- Amarkantak and Dindori Forests
- Chambal River
- Dumna Ecotourism Centre, Jabalpur
- Kathotia Adventure Point
- Jhinna Forest Camp

10.6.8 The World Heritage Centres in Madhya Pradesh

The Archaeological Survey of India, except the monuments of Orchha, which are with the State Department of Archaeology, protects most of the major heritage monuments. Out of these, UNESCO has declared Khajuraho, Bhimbetka and Sanchi as world heritage sites. The ASI and the State Department of Archaeology have their expert engineering cells to undertake annual conservation programmes. At Khajuraho and Sanchi, the UNESCO also participates with expertise and financial backing. Sanchi, being an important place of pilgrimage for the Buddhists from Japan and South-East Asia, has received financial aid and expertise for complete renovation and environmental development of the adjoining stupa of Satdhara. The Madhya Pradesh government should focus on development of basic infrastructure at these places. The availability of infrastructure will result in the full tourism potential realisation of these world heritage sites.

11. Road Ahead

a. The tourist destinations that Madhya Pradesh has to offer will get greater leverage if the accessibility to these centres is increased. There has been significant infrastructure development in the state in terms of national highways, state highways and connecting roads to important tourist destinations. The effort has been and should also be to expedite linking of the key tourist destinations from major cities of the state with a view that the travel time for domestic and foreign tourists is minimised. The rail network also needs to be reviewed.

b. In terms of foreign tourists, the current scenario is that foreigners land in India at international airports where they get packaged tours to the known locations in India. In fact, a lot many tourist sectors have been delineated to cater to foreign tourists. With international airport now coming to Madhya Pradesh, thematic sectors can be mapped out for the target groups including domestic and international tourists.

c. Madhya Pradesh has been marketed as a tourist destination through advertisements like "India ka dil dekho". This has been a very nice campaign and projects Madhya Pradesh as a holistic tourist destination. In addition to this, site-specific campaigns also need to be promoted like religious tourism—Ujjain, wildlife tourism—Kanha, Bandhavgarh, historical tourism—Sanchi, Khajuraho etc.

d. In addition to the above, thematic marketing of tourist destinations like ecotourism, cultural tourism, wildlife tourism, wild sports tourisms etc., also needs to be given impetus. This should be supplemented with better targeting of the niche customers.

e. The institutional reform process, especially to do with the present role of MPTDC and to attract private capital in tourism, being undertaken by the state government needs to be expedited.

Chapter 10

Infrastructure in Madhya Pradesh

1. Introduction

The definition of infrastructure, as described in Edna Carew's book *The Language of Money*, is "the stock of basic facilities and capital equipment needed for the functioning of a country or a region". She further explains that it is the basis or framework on which something is built. The term is popularly used to describe the services—roads, electricity supply, sewerage, phone lines, bus routes, water pipes, railways and so on—which enable a business, industry or economy to function. As per American Heritage Dictionary, the term 'infrastructure' has been used since 1927 to refer collectively to the roads, bridges, rail lines and similar public works that are required for an industrial economy, or a portion of it, to function. Ben Fine and Kwame Sundaram Jomo write in their book entitled *The New Development Economics* that infrastructure means, "social capital put to work in development practice". They however caution that infrastructure, in the context of political power and social relationships may not always lead to equitable development. The Congressional Budget Office of the US stated in 1983 that infrastructure included those facilities that have the common characteristics of capital intensiveness, long economic life and high public investment at all levels of government. They are, moreover, directly critical to any activity in the nation's and state's economy. Developing infrastructural sectors of roads, railways, airports, telecom and power involve very tangible and concrete structures, with well-defined capital outlays, capacity installations and their measurable performance.

India initiated an ambitious reform programme of commercialising the infrastructure about a decade and a half ago, ascertaining a shift from a controlled to an open market economy. However, the market showed very few signs of private or foreign direct investment getting into the infrastructure. Reason being, so far, the bulk of infrastructure in India was in the public sector which meant that this sector operated in a protected set up and hence, had been largely subsidised by the government. Since the launching of reform, the government is trying to reduce its borrowing which means that further subsidisation will not be possible. Because of the long gestation period and many social implications, the infrastructure sector compares unfavourably with manufacturing and many other sectors that flourish with the private and foreign capital. For reversing this trend, specific policies in this area were needed to make infrastructure attractive. There is a wide gap between the potential demand for infrastructure for high growth and the available supply; which required bridging. And this was the challenge that was placed before Madhya Pradesh state and the whole of India.

Madhya Pradesh state was formed on 1st November, 1956. Exactly after 44 years, on 1st November 2000, a significant area of MP state was carved out to make the Chhattisgarh state. With this partition, the state of MP lost some roads, airports, railway lines and other key infrastructure elements, like power plants to Chhattisgarh state. However, in the last eight years, Madhya Pradesh has been able to not only substantively compensate the infrastructure lost but has gained a lot more also. In recent years, since the year 2003, the rate of growth of infrastructure in India has always been above 5 per cent. Easing the monopoly of public sector in telecom; introducing provision of income tax exemptions or benefits under section 80-IA (12) of Income Tax Act to private enterprises for undertaking infrastructure projects; Electricity Act, 2003; Electricity Regulatory Commission Act, 1998; turnaround of railways; Madhya Pradesh's decision to scrap the loss-making state roadways transport corporation and introduction of public-private partnership scheme, have been some of the new developments that have hastened the growth of infrastructure in Madhya Pradesh.

This chapter provides key information for six core infrastructure sectors in Madhya Pradesh. These are: 1) Roads, 2) Railways, 3) Telecom, 4) Airports, 5) Electricity and 6) Water Supply and Sanitation.

2. Roads

Roads and bridges are one of the very fundamental instruments of connectivity. Good roads are essential for the development of the country; not only economic but also equally necessary for social development and reducing regional disparity by providing access to the remotest part of the country. Roads are important as they connect people and places through the means of travel and trade and keep the economy running.

This section of the chapter provides a general overview of the road sector in the state. It begins with comparing the state of MP with national figures based on some of the crucial indicators and a comment on the priority accorded to the state in terms of provisioning of national highways including the Golden Quadrilateral project. This is followed by information on different types of roads (like rural roads, major district roads and state highways) and classes of roads by their surface types for the people of the state. The next part of the section focuses on functioning and major roles of different institutions involved in delivering various categories of roads like national highway, state highway, major district roads, rural roads etc. Names of these institutions are NHAI, MPRDC, PWD and MPRRDA. The next section deals with financial and physical performance of roads and bridges in the state. The section concludes with achievement of the various institutions over the years.

2.1 Roads in MP: A General Overview

On 31st March 1999, Madhya Pradesh state had total roads worth 67284.2 km. However, the state lost about 45 per cent of its total road length to Chhattisgarh state in November 2000. Gradually, MP recouped the loss and went up to attain a total road length of 73314 km by March-end 2008. It constitutes only 2.2 per cent of the total road length of 3.3 million km in India.

The road network of the state as compared to other states is very poor. The national average for road network is 74.9 km/100 sq km whereas in MP, it is only 45.1 km/100 sq kms. The national average for Class-I roads per 100 sq km is 35.55 km whereas in MP, it is only 18.71 km. Similarly, the national average for tarred roads is 21.4 km/100 sq km whereas it is only 8.4 km/100 sq km for MP. This is not only an indicator of the backwardness of the state but also the cause of its backwardness.

2.2 Road Length in Madhya Pradesh

The state of Madhya Pradesh had 73314 km of roads by March 2008. Nearly 6 per cent of these roads were national highways, 16 per cent were major district roads, 12 per cent were state highways and the remaining 66.5 per cent were village roads and other district roads.

TABLE 10.1

Length of Roads in Madhya Pradesh: 2007-08

S. No.	*Particulars*	*Length of Roads (in Km)*	*Percentage*
1	National highways	4280	5.8
2	State highways	8729	11.9
3	Major district roads	11572	15.8
4	Rural roads	48733	66.5
5	Total	73314	100.00

Source: Annual Administrative Report, PWD, GoMP, 2007-08.

Nearly 8499 km or 11.59 per cent of the total road length in the state is classified as *kutcha* roads whereas the remaining 88 per cent of roads are classified as *pucca* roads.

TABLE 10.2

Classification of Road Length in MP

Type of Road	*Road in MP during 2007-08*			
	Pucca Road		*Kutcha Road*	*Total (in Km)*
	BT	*WBM*		
National highway	4280	—	—	4280
State highway	8729	-	—	8729
Major district roads	10286	1286	—	11572
Village road	16715	23519	8499	48733
Total	40010	24805	8499	73314

Note: BT - Black Top; WBM - Water Bound Macadam.
Source: Administrative Report, PWD, GoMP, 2007-08.

The Golden Quadrilateral (GQ) comprehensively misses Madhya Pradesh with just 621 km of North South-East West corridors passing through the state. Again, it may be noted that the East West corridor has only a fleeting presence in the northern fringe of the state while much of the 621 kms of road comes under the North South corridor. Of the total length of GQ, only 4.68 per cent passes through the state. Though the state covers 10 per cent of the nation's area, it has only 8 per cent of the national highways passing through them. As per the proposed National Highways Vision 2121, out of total national highway network, only 6.25 per cent of the total would pass through Madhya Pradesh.

Madhya Pradesh has 18 national highways, with total length of 4280 km. These highways are: NH-3, NH-7, NH-12, NH-12A, NH-25, NH-26, NH-27, NH-59, NH-59A, NH-69, NH-75, NH-75Ext., NH-76, NH-78, NH-79, NH-86, NH-86Ext, NH-92.

Because of the central location of the state and surrounded by five states, traffic from all the neighbouring states passes through the state's road/rail network. The scanty railway network and the low density of population scattered across small and distant villages and hamlets, demands more roads on the one hand while on other hand, makes the business of construction of roads less cost-effective than in states with dense rural population.

2.3 Distribution of Institutional Responsibilities

A brief description of the division of responsibilities between the different agencies related to roads are given below.

2.3.1 NHAI

The National Highways Authority of India (NHAI) was constituted by the Indian Parliament in 1988. It is the authority responsible for the development, maintenance and management of national highways entrusted to it. The Authority was made operational in February 1995 and is currently undertaking the developmental activities under National Highways Development Project (NHDP) in phases.

2.3.2 PWD

The Public Works Department (PWD) in Madhya Pradesh has traditionally played the role of governing the maintenance and construction of roads. But in the last few years, this role has been perceived as much more significant and strategic and thus, has witnessed significant change in the way the roads are being governed in MP now.

2.3.3 MPRDC

However, for strengthening the state highways, to develop projects in the state on the basis of public-private partnership and to act as the State Highway authority, the state of Madhya Pradesh has incorporated Madhya Pradesh Road Development Corporation (MPRDC) as an independent company on 14.07.2004. MPRDC has also been entrusted with the responsibility of constructing state highways that comprise nearly 12 per cent of the total road length in the state. Of the total outlay for 2005-06 for PWD, nearly 61 per cent had been spent through MPRDC. Yet PWD continued to work on state highways using the funds from Central Road Fund (CRF), economic and interstate importance (E&I) and under Fast Track Schemes that were designated for developing roads that were not covered under any other scheme.

2.3.4 MPRRDA

The Madhya Pradesh Rural Road Development Authority (MPRRDA) is the implementing agency (IA) for central flagship programme Pradhan Mantri Gram Sadak Yojana (PMGSY). The MPRRDA is a registered society under the Societies Registration Act of 1860. It was registered on the 25th of December 2000. The Authority has a general body that is headed by the chief minister, an executive council headed by the rural development minister and an empowered committee that is headed by the chief secretary.

A senior IAS officer heads MPRRDA as its CEO. The empowered committee is responsible for monitoring the progress of the project. It also makes the financial and administrative decisions. The project proposals are scrutinised and sanctioned by this committee. It also accords final sanction to the master plan/core network of the state. Thirty-eight project implementation units (PIUs) for 48 districts have been constituted to co-ordinate the works executed by the contractors and supervised by the consultants. The general body lays down the policy guidelines and monitors the programme. MPRRDA has the mandate to organise public consultation meetings with *sarpanches* (village heads) and inform the stakeholders/villagers about the road improvement scheme, and the positive and possible negative impacts of it.

2.4 Outlays for Roads and Bridges in Five Year Plans

Out of the total outlays of 10th FYP, roads and bridges account for 5.15 per cent; in monetary terms it comes to Rs. 1325 crore. During the Plan period, 71 major bridges, 530 medium bridges, 13,174 culverts, 8 railway overbridges, and a road length of 6448 kms were expected to be constructed by March 2007, providing connectivity to 1,308 villages.

In the 11th FYP, the outlays for roads and bridges have been increased by near about six times to the tune of Rs. 7770 crore. The target set to achieve during the 11th FYP is construction of 101 major bridges, 79 medium bridges, 5 railway overbridges, 66,535 culverts and a road length of 21,587 kms.

TABLE 10.3

Time Series Analysis of Outlays and Expenditure for Roads and Bridges through PWD

Year	*Outlays*	*Actual Expenditure*	*% of Utilisation*
2002-03	265.00	203.49	76.8
2003-04	390.77	331.31	84.8
2004-05	789.02	563.91	71.5
2005-06	857.99	778.6	90.7
2006-07	1215.28	1024.93	84.3
2007-08 (Upto Dec. 2007)	1995.74	949.55	47.6

Source: *Annual Administrative Report*, PWD, GoMP, 2007-08.

Table 10.3 above shows the gap in the approved outlay and actual expenditure over the years. It is clear from the table that the department was able to spend nearly three quarters of its approved outlay in 2002-03. This increased to 85 per cent in 2003-04. In 2004-05, it declined once again to 71.5 per cent. Year 2005-06 is observed as one of the most efficient year in terms of 90 per cent of the utilisation of the approved outlays. The pace was almost tried to retain in following year 2006-07. But once again it shows decline in utilisation, nearly upto 50 per cent by the end of third quarter of the financial year 2007-08. It would be pertinent to share that the above-mentioned approved outlays and expenditures include the outlay and expenditure for MPRDC as well.

2.5 *Physical Performance*

If one were to look at the trends in terms of the length of roads constructed by PWD, it would be found that the gap between the target and the achievement has persisted despite commendable efforts on the part of the government to speed up the process through institutional and other changes that were brought about in the last few years.

In 2002-03, PWD achieved nearly 66 per cent of its targeted construction for the length of 929 km. In 2003-04, it declined to 63 per cent and the declining trend continued in 2004-05 too, when it posted an achievement of 60 per cent of its target. It was in 2005-2006 that for the first time, the pace was speeded up and target was nearly achieved with 97 per cent. But again in the consecutive years, the set targets fell short in its achievement.

FIGURE 10.1

Targets and Achievements in Road Construction

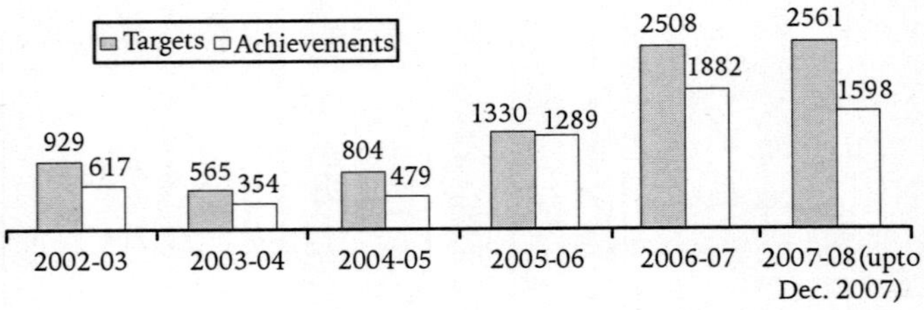

Source: Annual Administrative Report, Public Works Department, GoMP, various years.

TABLE 10.4

Targets and Achievements for the Construction of Big and Medium Bridges

Year	*Targets*	*Achievements*
2002-03	20	19
2003-04	97	81
2004-05	64	57
2005-06	43	39
2006-07	61	45
2007-08 (upto Dec. 2007)	55	13

Source: Annual Administrative Report, PWD, GoMP, 2007-08.

Similarly, Table 10.4 explains the targets and achievements for the construction of big and medium bridges.

It seems the performance is positive in achieving the targets for constructing big and medium bridges in the state. In 2002-03, the set targets were nearly accomplished. Years 2003-04 and 2004-05 shows little dip in the achievement which is then speeded up in 2005-06. But again, the next two years were not promising compared to 2005-06.

Keeping aside the performance of MPRDC, PWD also worked on different types of roads under various schemes over the years. Some of these schemes are:

1. Fast Track.
2. Farmer's Road Fund (FRF): In order to undertake road development, a surcharge has been imposed at the agriculture *mandi* level. It may be pertinent to note that the funds under FRF comes in MPRRDA's kitty from where a part of it is transferred to PWD who work under the conditions set by the general body of MPRRDA.

3. Central Road Fund (CRF): The scheme is in implementation since 2000-01, wherein, certain proportion of tax collected by imposing a cess of Re. 1.00 on each litre of petrol and diesel is distributed among state governments for improving the state highways and major district roads in the state. Out of CRF, MP is getting Rs. 93.29 crore annually on 100 per cent funding basis. During the Eleventh Five Year Plan, the state is likely to get Rs. 525 crore for construction of 1700 km of roads under this scheme.
4. NABARD (RIDF): NABARD under its Rural Infrastructure Development Fund gives loans to the state government for development of rural roads.
5. Special Central Assistance (SCA): SCA is provided by the Centre in Tribal Sub-Plan (TSP) to cater for basic infrastructure development like road construction.
6. Roads of Economic and Interstate Importance (E&I): Roads and bridges of economic and interstate importance are being constructed under this scheme. It is sponsored by the Central government with 50 to 100 per cent central finance being given to the state government for construction purpose.
7. 12th Finance Commission: The state government has started the development of road infrastructure in the state on the recommendations of the 12th Finance Commission. Under this, state government will get Rs. 52.00 crore per annum for development of road infrastructure from 2006-07 to 2009-10 which will be a total of Rs. 208.00 crore. The state government will complete 550 kms of road construction out of this fund.

The state government has developed some roads in past few years by issuing of bonds and taking loan from Housing and Urban Development Corporation Limited (HUDCO). The state government is currently developing many roads by taking loan from Asian Development Bank (ADB). Also it is negotiating a loan of from ADB for upgradation of 1768.16 km roads. The approach roads to villages are being undertaken by the state government under National Bank for Agriculture and Rural Development (NABARD). Currently, rural connectivity is being provided under the PMGSY in a big way. Besides the road construction being undertaken through the state plan, significant quanta of roads and bridges/culverts are being constructed under PMGSY. Rs. 2,959.00 crore is expected to be spent under the scheme constructing 13,500 km of road providing single connectivity to 3,372 villages during the 10th FYP.

2.6 State Highways

2.6.1 Institutional Changes: Advent of MPRDC, its Objectives and Work Culture

MPRDC was incorporated as its fully owned company by the government with the following objectives:

- To upgrade, construct and strengthen the total length of state highways;
- To develop projects in the state on the basis of public-private partnership;
- To act as a planning consultant to PWD in the state;
- To act as the State Highway Authority under Section 4 of the State Highway Act;
- To upgrade the entire 8729 kms of state highways in the next three years (by 2008-09).

For improving the work culture within the organisation, the company relied on outsourcing of expertise needed for building good quality roads in the state.

- Consultants are appointed for the preparation of detailed project report, for affecting financial closure and for supervising the construction work.
- Experts like legal advisors, company secretaries, environmental and management information system (MIS) experts are engaged on a contract basis with their continuation based on their performance.
- Every officer within the organisation is required to attend at least two training programmes in a year.
- Contractor is treated as a partner in development.
- Bills are cleared in 4-5 working days.

MPRDC as the sole State Highways Development Authority is committed to develop the high standard and quality road development/building in the state. The standard maintained by MPRDC is at par with the Indian Roadways Congress (IRC) Standards. As per Table 10.5, MPRDC is able to complete successfully the construction for 3543 km or 43 per cent worth of state highways, as on March 2008, against the assigned work of 8133 km of state highways worth Rs. 1897.82 crore.

TABLE 10.5

Road Length Completed by MPRDC

Type of Project	*Numbers of Project Completed*	*Length in Kms*	*Expenditure (Rs. Crore)*
Built, Operate and Transfer (BOT)	11	1532.66	760.97
Regular contract	7	559.71	235.85
ADB-Phase I	4	332.59	250.31
ADB-Phase II	10	1118.24	650.69
Total	32	3543.20	1897.82

Source: MPRDC, GoMP.

TABLE 10.6

Ongoing Road Projects by MPRDC

Type of Project	*Numbers of On-going Project*	*Length in Kms*	*Expenditure (Rs. Crore)*
Built, Operate and Transfer (BOT)	6	656.26	1836.53
Regular Contract	9	667.28	506.29
ADB-Phase II	1	153	83.87
ADB-MPSRSP II	17	1670.11	1348.27
Total	33	3146.65	3774.96

Note: MP State Road Sector Project.
Source: MPRDC, GoMP.

Besides, still 38 per cent of the assigned projects to MPRDC are in progress. These projects are worth Rs. 3774.96 crore and expected to build 3146.65 km roads in the state in the coming years.

2.7 Public-Private Partnership in Roads Sector

MPRDC is executing the projects both through contract scheme and by providing grant/subsidy to the concessionaire on competitive bidding basis. While the former route is being adopted in projects that are funded through loans (from ADB and HUDCO), the latter route leads to public-private partnership (PPP) that results in roads being built on built-operate-transfer (BOT) basis. The story of PPP in MP is a successful one as it is attracting private partners for building the state highways in MP. This has been achieved by the state through creating an enabling environment that has been nurturing PPP since its inception.

- Eleven roads covering a length of 1,664 kms, have already been undertaken under PPP of which two are already under construction.
- Six road projects covering a length of 652.64 kms costing Rs. 1,519.12 crore were recently bid out and will be developed with GoI assistance under Viability Gap Funding.
- The intermediate link roads are in a bad shape and unless these roads are upgraded, the development of the rural roads would be of no avail. It is expected to upgrade about 3,290 kms of roads at a cost of Rs. 1,167 crore during the Eleventh Plan period. At the same time, there are certain missing links between roads which, if developed would provide good connectivity to the rural population. It is estimated that about 1,866 km of such roads need to be developed which will require Rs. 675.36 crore.
- It is estimated that for upgradation of those major district roads whose performance guarantee period is over, Rs. 1,774.35 crore will be required to upgrade about 3,800 kms of road. Provision has accordingly been proposed.
- All the villages having more than 50 per cent SC/ST population are proposed to be provided road connectivity on priority. It is proposed to construct 200 kms of such roads.

The enabling environment being provided by the state comprises the following elements:

- Minimising project-related risks.
- Making the projects bankable.
- Keeping the user charges at a level that not only the public is willing to pay but also is less than their opportunity cost.
- Scrupulously avoiding discretion (avoiding any kind of patronage).
- Treating concessionaire/developer as an entrepreneur.
- Containing red tape, and
- Government acting as a facilitator rather than a controller.

The last five years of running PPP in MP prove that it has many obvious advantages. Seven such advantages have been enumerated here. First, the cost of building roads gets shared between the government and the private developer, thereby reducing the burden of government. Second, the government neither have to answer nor deploy manpower for maintaining roads. Third, the government does not have to divert any part of its budget on the maintenance of roads. Fourth, more than 95 per cent of the budgeted expenditure accrues to the project development head because the administrative cost under this system is less than 5 per cent of the total project outlay. Fifth, the quality standards maintained are much higher than the roads built sans the participation of private entrepreneurs. Sixth, there are many other aspects attributed to efficient management that flourish owing to the private sector participation. Finally, the users get good quality roads that are built fast, without any time and cost overruns, providing satisfaction to road users and enhancing the image of the state government. Thus far, the experience that the public has had of the roads built by MPRDC has been good. This is primarily on account of two factors. First, the BOT system, by itself, creates a charge in favour of the concessionaire, delivering good quality roads, as it is the concessionaire who would have to maintain and operate it for the upcoming 15 years. Second, for the non-BOT roads undertaken by contractors, the developers are made to furnish performance guarantees. Besides, MPRDC supervises the work directly as well as through independent supervision consultants appointed by them.

2.8 Rural Road Connectivity in MP

The broad objective of MPRRDA is to provide rural road connectivity to human habitations in the state under PMGSY. It aims at providing connectivity to all unconnected habitations with 500 and above general population and population of 250 in tribal areas with all weather roads and construction and upgradation of connecting rural roads. Currently, MPRRDA has been entrusted with the task of constructing 36636.46 kms of village roads in MP, expected to benefit 9571 villages worth Rs. 7751.69 crore in different phases. This is nearly 66 per cent of the total rural roads of Madhya Pradesh. This works out to nearly 49 per cent of the total road length in the state and makes it one of the most important road-constructing agencies in the state.

Since its inception in 2001-02, MPRRDA has become synonymous with village road connectivity in MP. Since the beginning of its operations, MPRRDA has been able to connect, mostly through good quality village roads, nearly 44 per cent of the habitations having a population of 1000 and 500 and more. MPRRDA has been funded by the funds allocated under PMGSY by the Central government and by an ADB loan. The MPRRDA's effort, though commendable, still leaves MP with nearly 56.6 per cent of its habitations unconnected.

TABLE 10.7

Physical and Financial Performance under PMGSY in MP (November 2007)

Sr. No.	*Particulars*	
1	No. of sanctioned road projects	8093
2	No. of road projected constructed	3462
3	Road length (km)	15892.21
4	Expenditure (in Rs. crore)	3672.89
5	No. of villages benefited (1000 and 500+ population)	4286

Source: Economic Survey, GoMP, 2007-08.

2.9 The Challenge of Providing Village Road Connectivity

The task of providing rural connectivity remains one of the most daunting challenges that the state faces today. MPRRDA's efforts in this direction are most appreciating but at the same time, its operations needs to be upscaled if it were to achieve the set targets within the stipulated timeframe. Since the Authority is banking upon Bharat Nirman for providing the funds for its future operations, it would be apposite to understand the targets set for the authority under Bharat Nirman. It can be seen in Figure 10.2 that the year-wise targets under Bharat Nirman far exceed what the Authority can deliver even if it utilises the present infrastructure to its full capacity by augmenting both its headquarter and field formations set-up. The maximum length that the MPRRDA was able to deliver in any one year since its inception was 4000 kms approximately. Hence, it is quite evident that the Authority would need to upscale its operations substantially if it were to meet its noble target of connecting nearly 5285 habitations by constructing the road lengths shown in the figure. In light of the limitations faced by the Authority in meeting the daunting challenge of achieving the targets set under Bharat Nirman, it is planning to not only upscale its operations but also to compensate for the exhausted capacity of MP-based contractors by roping in construction PSUs[1] and major private national and multi-national construction companies. Here the

1. EIL, NHPC, NHDC, NPCC, PEC, TCIL and IRCON International Limited.

Authority is aiming to take a leaf out of Bihar's experience under PMGSY where PSUs have been allotted 2-3 districts to effect timely completion of work. It is mooting the idea of having large size packages worth Rs. 50-100 crore to attract national and multinational construction companies.

FIGURE 10.2

Targets under Bharat Nirman for MPRRDA

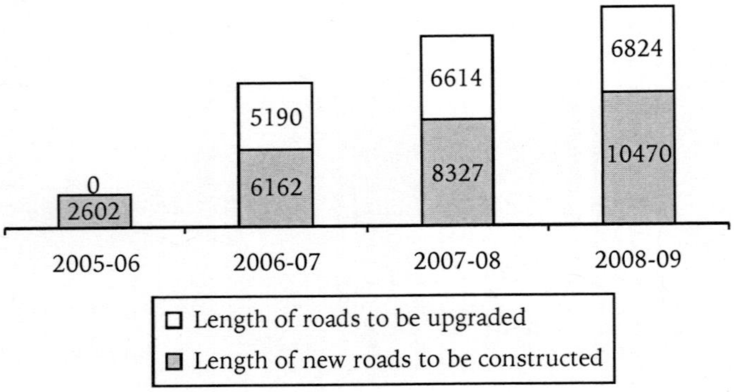

Source: Madhya Pradesh Rural Road Development Authority.

2.10 *MPRRDA: The Road Ahead*

The Authority has proposed a five-pronged approach to enable it to face the challenges posed by the targets set under Bharat Nirman.

First, it proposes to augment administrative set-up at its headquarters. The team at MPRRDA's headquarters is proposed to be made multi-disciplinary where apart from the officers with engineering and accounting backgrounds, officers from forest department, mining department and revenue department may also be deputed. Presence of a DFO/CF ranked officer at the headquarters would help resolve the forest disputes and obtain timely clearance of forest cases. A mining officer at the headquarters would help resolve the mining related problems that are a major stumbling block in progress of work. Huge quantities of construction material like moorum, metals, etc., are required and their availability is often hampered by mining related problems. As most of the village roads are being constructed on existing cart tracks, improving their geometrics and widening them necessitates acquisition of land, both government and private. Though normally the farmers voluntarily donate their land, occasionally compensatory land needs to be allotted in lieu of private land. Presence of deputy/additional collector in the team would help resolve revenue/land acquisition cases speedily.

Second, the Authority has proposed to strengthen its administrative structure at the field level. The number of project implementation units (PIUs) needs to be increased from 38 to more than 45. Every district may have one PIU, with districts having more unconnected habitations than others having two of them. The personnel appointed in PIUs may be made to undergo regular technical and contract management trainings. Since the inception of the scheme, the Authority has engaged consultants to assist the departmental staff in preparing project reports, providing supervision and affecting quality control. The expenditure on consultants will now be met by the Central government unlike in the past when the state government was meeting these expenses. The Authority is contemplating to affect two significant changes with respect to the functioning of consultants. It not only plans to switch over from state controlled development to a more liberalised regime by diluting the control of the government officials on the consultants but also to expand the role of consultants by broadening their current scope of work that comprises supervision and quality control. It proposes to add functions like preparing district project reports (DPRs) and bill of quantity, drafting tender documents and assisting in drafting of NITs, managing information systems, identifying capable contractors, taking measurements and preparing the bills and ensuring progress and timely completion of work to the current scope of work of the consultants. The Authority wants the recommendations of the consultants to be accepted normally both by the state and the Central government, unless rejected for reasons recorded in writing. It further wants to limit the role of departmental officers to overall management of the project, 10 per cent measurement of the works executed by the contractors and exercising quality control by taking random samples.

Third, the Authority is considering a different strategy for award of contracts. The following issues need to be flagged:

- Larger packages: The current approach of sanctioning 50-75 kms of roads scattered all over the district and costing Rs. 3-6 crore needs to be shelved in favour of larger packages worth Rs. 50-75 crore within a defined geographical area. This will address the twin problems of exhausted execution capacity of MP-based contractors (who have enough work for the next two years) and non-participation by the larger contractors owing to small sizes of the contracts currently offered by the Authority.

- Longer construction period: The prevailing regime of allowing 12 month construction period including the rainy season should give way to an arrangement where the construction period may be 2-3 years long in view of the fact that contracts worth Rs. 50 crore for roads scattered all over a district cannot be otherwise successfully executed.
- Provision of escalation: Since longer contract period is being mooted, an escalation clause, which is currently absent in the PMGSY tender document owing to the fact that the construction period allowed is only 12 months, should be included keeping in view the rising labour and material costs.
- Schedule of rates: SOR needs to be revised in view of the rising prices of diesel and bitumen and increase in royalties for construction material and labour charges. Despite a recent revision of the same by the Authority in July 2005, there may be cases where tender rates may exceed SOR.
- Tender premiums to be borne by the Government of India: Currently, only sanctioned amount is allowed by the Government of India with tender premium being paid by the state government. In view of the ambitious targets and huge amount of investments, the GoI should meet the entire cost of construction.
- Limiting re-tendering: In order to keep the construction cost within the sanctioned amount, re-tendering is resorted to repeatedly, resulting in a lot of time being lost. Therefore, the Authority is mooting the idea of sanctioning the contract after the second call if the rates are reasonable.
- Ensuring timely availability of building material: The mining rules need to be relaxed if the contractors are to ensure timely availability of construction materials like muroom, sand and metals so that the projects are not delayed. Currently, the contractors are not able to mine the material even after they have deposited the royalty for want of permission from the mining department. Alternatively, department officials may be given the responsibility to recover the royalty as per the prescribed rates and deposit it in the treasury.

Fourth, for the construction of 12,000 kms of road in a year, the volume of sanctions should be around two and a half times of this road length. To achieve the target fixed up to the end of FY 2009, at least 50 per cent of the targeted road length needs to be sanctioned by June 2006 and the remaining by October 2006 so that the agency for execution of all works could be fixed by March 2007. The Authority hopes that the Government of India would give clearance for the proposed road lengths to be constructed in the next three years so that work for preparation of DPR may be taken up urgently.

Fifth, the Government of India has indicated that it would henceforth bear the expenditure on supervision and quality control consultants also. If the targets set under Bharat Nirman were to be achieved, then appointment of project implementation consultants (PICs) is necessary by the end of FY 2006. The proposal is under active consideration of the Central government for the last six months.

2.11 Conclusions

The following conclusions can be arrived at based on the above analysis:

- If everything goes as per the plans set for the state under Bharat Nirman, then the lengths of roads that MPRRDA is planning to work on (by way of upgradation as well as construction), would bring the entire rural roads (village roads plus other district roads) under the sole control of MPRRDA. PWD then would be left with the construction and maintenance of major district roads alone. The larger packages that MPRRDA is mooting would most probably include most of the other district roads. As per the administrative report 2007-08, the PWD is planning to declare nearly 15910.73 kms of other district roads to major district roads, in order to avoid any further encroachment on their turf by MPRRDA. This is reminiscent of the past and if this happens then the turf war may result in unnecessary delays in providing rural road connectivity to the state population. The government may either lower the targets under Bharat Nirman and let PWD handle the ODRs or ask PWD to keep completely off ODRs and concentrate solely on MDRs. Alternatively, the government may ask MPRRDA to bite only as much as it can chew and have only a part of the ODRs to work on instead of all of them. It is pertinent to note that the government while deciding would have to consider the fact that the establishment cost of MPRRDA is much lower than that of PWD and therefore, the former can deliver more roads in the same cost than the latter.

- As the State Highway Authority, MPRDC would do well to concentrate on developing the state highways. Though it is actively engaged in nearly 64 per cent of the state highways currently, it still has a long way to go before it completes the upgradation of the entire network of 8729 kms of state highways. Attempts to get involved with four laning of national highways and major district roads would result in unnecessary infringement in PWD's domain. If they are to meet their targets of upgrading the entire state highway network to conform to IRC norms, then a focused attempt at achieving it is more likely to lead it to success.
- The time series analysis of PWD's performance (that includes the work done by MPRDC as well) shows that it was not as good as its standalone performance sans MPRDC's work under various schemes. While the achievement as a percentage of targets for the former is in sixties, it is in seventies for the latter. It is common knowledge that the technical competence of PWD is very high and curtailing its role in the development of a road network in the state can prove to be costly in the long run. The government would help its cause if it puts to rest any speculation on the respective areas in which the road agencies discussed above have to operate. Also, unwarranted comparisons of PWD as has been referred to earlier in this report with MPRRDA or with MPRDC are not in order and each agency should be free from the fear of diminishing domain with their objectives clearly defined and adhered to in letter and spirit.
- If the MPRRDA is to reach any where near the targets set for the state under Bharat Nirman, then it would have to up scale its operations substantially. The conditions under which the funding would come from the Central government shall have to be suitably amended with many steps to be taken by the Central government in quick time. Lobbying intensively to secure the state's interests with the Central government would be in order.
- The government has done well to increase the period of toll collection for 5 roads from 15 to 30 years so that the subsidy provided may be brought down to not more than 40 per cent of the project cost. This would enable the state to attract 20 per cent of the subsidy from the Central government and increase the state's capacity to go for more roads on BOT basis.
- Although the PPP effort in the state has been christened "Bond BOT" but it may be noted that the government is yet to raise any resources through bonds for the roads. All BOT roads have been done on the basis of subsidies made available on the basis of competitive bidding. Since the government plans to take up the remaining lengths of 16 per cent of the state highways at the beginning of 2008-09, and since no other source of funding than the state budgets appear to be available and since one is acutely aware of the fact that much of the state budgets in roads sector would be tied up with prior commitments, the government would do well to explore the possibility of floating road bonds that may finance RDC's operations beyond 2008-09 on the remaining 16 per cent of the roads.
- Some of the major district roads in the state has good volume of traffic and PWD may be entrusted to carry out these projects under BOT scheme.

3. Aviation Sector in MP

As a mean of transport, aviation is faster, comfortable and provides quality travel to people on one hand but is expensive and out of reach for most people on the other. It is an essential service for the growth of industry and business as it provides opportunities to people, finances and knowledge.

With a growth rate of 18 per cent per annum, the Indian aviation industry is one of the fastest growing aviation industries in the world. The government's open sky policy has led to many overseas players entering the market and the industry has been growing both in terms of players and number of aircrafts. Today, private airlines account for around 75 per cent share of the domestic aviation market. India has jumped to 9th position in the world's aviation market from 12th in 2006. The scheduled domestic air services are now available from 82 airports as against 75 in 2006.

Madhya Pradesh is generously endowed with places of historical and cultural importance and has vast natural heritage. There is the industrial town of Indore, one of India's leading manufacturing centres, the capital at Bhopal and the tourist attraction at Khajuraho would rank amongst the world's best known places of tourist interest. Yet the state of air infrastructure and air services is very poor. There are two aspects to air transport infrastructure—one is the airports themselves, their capacity to take aircrafts of different types at different frequencies, night parking capacity etc; the second being basic air services, number of flights into and out of various airports of the state, the cities connected to it, size of aircrafts, and so on.

Madhya Pradesh government constituted the Department of Aviation on 1.6.1982 that undertakes the following activities:

1) To upgrade and extend existing airstrips under the control of state government and construct new airstrips.
2) To arrange for the maintenance of the state government aircraft and to make available government aircraft for VIP flights.
3) To promote facilities of aviation and training in the state.

3.1 Airports in MP

The main airports in Madhya Pradesh are Indore, Bhopal and Khajuraho, along with some flights into and out of Gwalior and Jabalpur. All these have only domestic terminals, and cannot take larger aircrafts (larger than Boeing 737s). Khajuraho takes only tourism passengers, and Indore, Bhopal, Gwalior and Jabalpur are the airports that bring in people with business, both public and private. Earlier, the stations that were connected by Vayudoot (small aircraft airline) were Bhopal, Khajuraho, Satna, Rewa, Guna, Indore and

TABLE 10.8

Airstrips/Airports in Madhya Pradesh

S. No.	*Name of Airstrip*	*Other Details*
1	Neemuch Airstrip	Can be used in all weathers, operated by Garrison Engineer, Mahu
2	Ratlam Airstrip	Can be used in all weathers, operated by PWD
3	Indore Airport	Can be used in all weathers, operated by Airports Authority of India (AAI)[2]
4	Khargone Airstrip	Can be used during clear weather, operated by PWD
5	Khandwa	Can be used in all weathers, operated by AAI
6	Gwalior Airport	Can be used in all weathers, operated by Indian Air Force and AAI
7	Shivpuri Airstrip	Can be used in all weathers, operated by PWD
8	Bhopal Airport	Can be used in all weathers, operated by AAI
9	Guna Airstrip	Can be used in all weathers, operated by PWD
10	Tekanpur Airstrip, Gwalior	Can be used during clear weather, operated by BSF
11	Sagar Airstrip (Dhana)	Can be used in all weathers, operated by PWD
12	Pachmarhi Airstrip	Can be used during clear weather, operated by PWD
13	Khajuraho Airport	Can be used in all weathers, operated by AAI
14	Damoh Airstrip	Can be used during clear weather, operated by Diamond Cements
15	Jabalpur Airport	Can be used in all weathers, operated by AAI
16	Satna Airstrip	Can be used in all weathers, operated by AAI
17	Sidhi Airstrip	Can be used in all weathers, operated by PWD
18	Rewa Airstrip	Can be used in all weathers, operated by PWD
19	Shahdol Airstrip (Lalpur)	Can be used in all weathers, operated by Orient Paper Mill
20	Kanha Airstrip (Mandla)	Can be used during clear weather, operated by Forest Department (May not be suitable for wildlife tourists)
21	Birwa Airstrip, Baihar, Balaghat	Can be used during clear weather, operated by PWD (Suitable for wildlife tourists to Kanha National Park)
22	Chhindwara Airstrip	Can be used in all weathers, operated by PWD
23	Sarani Airstrip (Betul)	Can be used in all weathers, operated by MP State Electricity Board (Not being used recently)
24	Nagda Airstrip (Dhar)	Can be used in all weathers, operated by Grasim Industries
25	Datana Airstrip (Near Ujjain)	Can be used in all weathers, operated by PWD
26	Jhabua Airstrip	Can be used in all weathers, operated by PWD (Not being used recently)
27	Panna Airstrip (Sakria)	Not functional. Renovation and reconstruction of the airstrip underway
28	Umaria Airstrip	Under construction

Source: http://mpaviation.nic.in/deptrespon.htm

2. Airports Authority of India manages 120 airports in India.

Jabalpur. All major flight connections are still restricted to Delhi and Mumbai only and all other stations are connected to cities of Madhya Pradesh via these two cities. Major air carriers, i.e., Indian Airlines, Jet Airways and Kingfisher Airlines operate their flights through these two cities. Though there are more than two dozen airports located within the state, Gwalior, Khajuraho and Jabalpur are the key airports, besides the aforesaid two airports in Bhopal and Indore. Many public and private airlines operate flights to these five airports. Government of MP intends to set up an aviation city near Dabra Sugar Mills, near Gwalior, with investment worth $ 5 billion. Around 7000 acres of land have been identified for setting up this project. This project is bound to have facilities for repair and maintenance of aeroplanes. The state has 28 airstrips/ airports, details of which are given in Table 10.8.

3.1.1 Raja Bhoj International Airport (Bhopal)

Raja Bhoj Airport is located about 12 km away from the old city of Bhopal. Domestic airlines like Indigo, SpiceJet, GoAir, Indian Airlines, Jet Airways, Sahara Airlines, Kingfisher Airlines, Alliance Air, Paramount Airways and Air Deccan, connect the terminus to the places in and around the state. International flights of Indian Airlines and Air India also operate from here, to places like Dubai, Singapore, Sharjah and Bangkok. Keeping in mind the convenience of the travellers, the airport is well equipped with facilities like comfortable lounge, facilities for refreshments, clean washrooms and car hire.

3.1.2 Gwalior Airport (Gwalior)

Gwalior Airport is situated 8 km to the northeast of the city and is one of the important domestic airports of the state. There is one domestic terminal in the airport. Key domestic airlines connect Gwalior to the rest of India. Some of the places from where one can avail flights to Gwalior Airport are Bhopal, Mumbai, Delhi and Indore. Flights of Indian Airlines are available thrice a week. At present, there are no provisions for international travel from the airport. The runway length of the airport is 9000 feet and its height is 617 feet. There are facilities for trolley, wheelchairs and telephone.

3.1.3 Devi Ahilyabai Holkar International Airport (Indore)

Named after the legendary Holkar Queen, Devi Ahilyabai, Indore airport is located 8 km to the southeast of the city centre and caters to the air traffic needs of people travelling to/from Indore. Domestic airlines (like Jet Airways and Indian Airlines) and private airlines (like Sahara Airlines, Kingfisher, SpiceJet and Indigo) shuttle regular flights to different parts of India. SilkAir, Air Arabia, Indian Airlines and Air-India Express are international airlines that fly from this airport. Facilities include parking, restaurant, coffee shop, luggage keeping, information desk, medical facilities, pre-paid taxi booth, baggage wrapping and gift shop.

3.1.4 Civil Airport (Khajuraho)

Located 3 km to the south of the Khajuraho town, Civil Airport is one of the most important air terminals of Madhya Pradesh and furnishes air travel facilities to the state. Though small, the airport provides air linkage to different cities of India. Flights of major airlines like Jet Airways (to Varanasi, Delhi and Mumbai), Air Sahara (to Bhopal, Indore and Delhi), Indian Airlines (to Varanasi, Delhi and Agra) and Kingfisher Airlines (to Bhopal, Allahabad, Indore, Mumbai and Delhi) operate from Khajuraho. There are also flights that connect Khajuraho to the neighbouring country of Nepal.

3.1.5 Dumna Airport (Jabalpur)

Jabalpur Airport, also called 'Dumna', is situated 20 km from the city centre. Both chartered and regular flight services operate from Jabalpur to other important air destinations in India. Some of the key airlines that operate from the Jabalpur Airport are Kingfisher Airlines, Indian Airlines and Air Deccan. Air Deccan provides regular services on the Delhi-Bhopal-Jabalpur route. Kingfisher Airlines operates daily services from Jabalpur to Indore and Mumbai and also connects Hyderabad and Nagpur, via Indore. Indian Airlines flies four days a week on Delhi-Gwalior-Jabalpur route. Vayudoot flights also enable tourists to travel to Jabalpur by air.

3.2 Air Traffic in MP

Details of some of the key flights is given in Table 10.9.

The data on traffic from the airports is displayed in Table 10.10. Madhya Pradesh handles an abysmal share of our national air flights and passenger traffic, just about 1.6 per cent of flights and just about one per cent of passengers only. This is way below the total area under Madhya Pradesh, or the share of population in all of India's.

TABLE 10.9

Details of Key Flights

Name of Carrier	*Flight No.*	*From*	*To*	*Departure Time*	*Schedule*
Indian Airlines	IC-133	Bhopal	Delhi	08.45	Daily
Indian Airlines	IC-134	Bhopal	Delhi	18.30	Daily
Indian Airlines	IC-133	Mumbai	Bhopal	05.40	Daily
Indian Airlines	IC-134	Delhi	Indore	18.30	Daily
Indian Airlines	IC-817	Delhi	Jabalpur	07.30	4 days a week
Indian Airlines	IC-817	Delhi	Gwalior	07.30	4 days a week
Indian Airlines	IC-818	Jabalpur	Delhi	10.30	4 days a week
Indian Airlines	IC-406	Delhi	Khajuraho	10.05	3 days a week
Indian Airlines	IC-405	Khajuraho	Delhi	14.00	3 days a week
Jet Airways	9W724	Khajuraho	Delhi	13.25	Daily
Jet Airways	9W723	Delhi	Khajuraho	10.40	Daily
Jet Airways	9W731	Delhi	Bhopal (via Indore)	07.40	Daily
Jet Airways	9W731	Bhopal	Delhi (via Indore)	11.00	Daily
Jet Airways	9W737	Bhopal	Delhi (via Indore)	21.20	Daily
Jet Airways	9W737	Delhi	Bhopal (via Indore)	18.10	Daily
Jet Airways	9W3106	Bhopal	Mumbai	20.00	Daily
Jet Airways	9W3418	Bhopal	Ahmedabad (via Indore)	18.45	Daily
Jet Airways	9W3417	Bhopal	Hyderabad (via Indore, Raipur)	09.35	5 days a week
Jet Airways	9W382	Indore	Mumbai	08.00	4 days a week
Kingfisher Airlines	IT2553	Ahmedabad	Indore	06.30	Daily
Kingfisher Airlines	IT4397	Delhi	Indore	18.30	Daily
Kingfisher Airlines	IT4375	Delhi	Jabalpur	07.10	Daily
Kingfisher Airlines	IT0331	Delhi	Khajuraho (via Varanasi)	09.20	Wednesday & Sunday
Kingfisher Airlines	IT2801	Hyderabad	Indore (via Nagpur)	06.25	Daily, except Tuesday

Source: Department of Civil Aviation, GoMP.

TABLE 10.10

Airport Traffic

Destination	*Average Number of Flights Handled per Day*			*Average Number of Passengers Handled per Day*			*Average Cargo handled per day (In Tonnes)*		
	All	*Int.*	*Domestic*	*All*	*Int.*	*Domestic*	*All*	*Int.*	*Domestic*
				2003-04					
Bhopal	9	0	9	300	0	300	1	0	1
Indore	12	0	12	622	0	622	6	0	6
Khajuraho	3	0	3	43	0	43	0	0	0
Gwalior	1	0	1	2	0	2	0	0	0
Jabalpur	0	0	0	1	0	1	0	0	0
All MP	25	0	25	968	0	968	7	0	7
All India	1919	359	1560	137922	45679	92243	3071	1918	1153
MP's share	1.30%	0.00%	1.60%	0.70%	0.00%	1.05%	0.23%	0.00%	0.61%
				2002-03					
Bhopal	8	0	8	289	0	289	1	0	1
Indore	12	0	12	599	0	599	4	0	4
Khajuraho	2	0	2	85	0	85	0	0	0
Gwalior	1	0	1	2	0	2	0	0	0
Jabalpur	1	0	1	4	0	4	0	0	0
All MP	24	0	24	979	0	979	5	0	5
All India	1551	314	1237	121284	40605	80679	2818	1802	1016
MP's share	1.55%	0.00%	1.94%	0.81%	0.00%	1.21%	0.18%	0.00%	0.49%

Source: Department of Civil Aviation, Government of India.

In air transport, with private airlines and public air carrier also looking at commercially profitable destinations, the state government must look at promoting Madhya Pradesh as a tourist destination.

Thus, it is clear from the above analysis that air connectivity in the state needs greater boost up in order to open up more and more opportunities for investment and tourism from the larger perspective of drivers of the economy. The Government of India is taking up airport modernisation (including upgradation and expansion of airports) in a big way. The airports of Bhopal, Khajuraho and Indore must be picked up in Phase II of this expansion plan, and there must be facilities developed to take larger aircrafts, especially in Khajuraho where direct international chartered tourist flights can be encouraged, the way Goa has successfully done. Further, Mumbai, Hyderabad and Delhi airports are heavily congested and hence, private airlines are looking for airports for parking at night which are not very far from these cities; Bhopal and Gwalior are ideally located. Proactive work must be undertaken to grasp this opportunity.

4. Railways

Railways are a unique provider of transport, a connector and a lifeline for this nation. The railways perhaps is the most pro-poor of all mass transport systems—they offer relatively cheap, affordable and safe travel for all economic levels, and transport basic goods, food grains, minerals, manufactured goods, even essential commodities such as medicines and perishable commodities such as fruits, fish and milk from one place to another—offering better markets to farmers and providing essential commodities to commodity scarce areas. Access to railways opens up a world of opportunities to labourers, especially during times of distress or to prospective and current migrants. Railways enable long distance migration as well as a lifeline linking back home.

As a centrally located state, the major north-south rail lines and some east to west rail lines pass through the state. Main junctions in the state are Bhopal, Bina, Gwalior, Indore, Itarsi, Jabalpur, Katni, Ratlam and Ujjain. The divisional railways headquarters are at Bhopal, Ratlam and Jabalpur.

4.1 Rail Density in MP

Madhya Pradesh has rail density of 15.9 km rail lines per 1000 sq km, which is much lower than the national average of 20 km per 100 sq km of area. The average length of railway lines per 10 lakh population in MP is 75.8 km. The state fares poorly in comparison to some of its peers like Bihar, UP, Maharashtra, Rajasthan and Gujarat. Rail connectivity in terms of railway lines in km/1000 sq km for all the major states is given in Table 10.11.

TABLE 10.11

Rail Connectivity Across the Country

Sr. No.	*States*	*Railway Line in Km/1000 sq km*
1	Delhi	138.2
2	West Bengal	43.4
3	Punjab	41.6
4	Haryana	36.1
5	Bihar	35.9
6	Uttar Pradesh	35.8
7	Tamil Nadu	32.1
8	Assam	31.9
9	Kerala	27
10	Gujarat	26.9
11	Jharkhand	24.3
12	Andhra Pradesh	18.9
13	Goa	18.6
14	Maharashtra	17.9
15	Rajasthan	17
16	Madhya Pradesh	15.9
17	Karnataka	15.5
18	Orissa	14.6
19	Chhattisgarh	8.6
20	Uttarakhand	6.4
21	Himachal Pradesh	5.1

Source: http://www.kbkrail.orisaalinks.com/documents/Documents-slides.ppt

India has about 63000 route km worth of railway network (18000 route km is electrified) that is criss-crossed by 8000 trains, everyday. Whereas the total length of the railway network in Madhya Pradesh is 5992 route km, which makes about 9 per cent share of the total network and the number of trains that pass through MP every day is 475. Of 5992 km, almost 1,880 km is electrified track. Currently, railway upgradation projects in the state that includes adding 1,151 km of railway lines, have been in progress. In November 2000, Madhya Pradesh lost about 1150 route km to Chhattisgarh; unfortunately MP could barely recompense the route length that it lost to Chhattisgarh over the last eight years.

There are interregional disparities among the various regions of the state in terms of railway connectivity. Till today, large parts of the state do not have the benefit of any rail line. For instance, the central region is most poorly connected by rail as there are only 27.6

km of railway lines serving every 10 lakh population in the region. Compare this with the state average of 75.8 km or with south-western, north and south-central regions, each of which have nearly 100 km of railway lines serving per 10 lakh population. The second most poorly connected region by railways is Vindhya region that has just 56.5 km of railway lines serving every 10 lakh of its population. The Malwa region (at 73.0 km of railway lines per 10 lakh population) fares better than the Vindhya region, but only marginally worse than the state average. Out of the 48 districts of MP, there are 4 districts that do not have any railway lines connecting them. These districts are Barwani, Dhar, Dindori and Sheopur.[3]

A large part of railway network in Madhya Pradesh is covered by the West Central Zone of Indian Railway, headquartered in Jabalpur. West Central Zone has three divisions, *viz.*, Jabalpur Division, Bhopal Division and Kota Division. However, four other divisions also cover a large part of Madhya Pradesh. These are:

1) Bhusawal Division of Central Railway: Khandwa, Burhanpur, etc.
2) Jhansi Division of North Central Railway: Gwalior, Bhind, Bina, etc.
3) Ratlam Division of Western Railway: Ratlam, Nagda, etc.
4) Nagpur Division of South East Central Railway: Balaghat, Nainpur, etc.

On an average, 140 trains cross Itarsi station, 175 trains pass Bhopal station and about 75 trains pass through Jabalpur station daily. Bhopal is going to be one of the 19 railway stations that are scheduled to become a world-class station in near future.

4.2 Importance of Rail Connectivity in the State's Economy

In the emerging plans of new rail lines and gauge conversions, Madhya Pradesh does not seem to be getting its due share and attention. With the advantages of the state in agro produce, mineral ores, fisheries, forest based produce, and its potential as a national central warehouse due to its strategic location, increased rail routes in the state would become critical. The inadequate availability of rail infrastructure gets compounded when one considers the fact that the state produces nearly 81,000 MTs of mined materials every year and nearly 15 per cent of its NSDP at current prices comes from mining activities.

The plan for a dedicated freight corridor proposed recently also does not address the concerns of Madhya Pradesh. MP would receive its meagre share in the railway golden quadrilateral only when the railways set out to begin work on the Delhi-Chennai corridor which is not being taken up with any degree of urgency by the ministry of railways. The state needs to join forces with Tamil Nadu to mobilise government support for the Chennai–Delhi corridor.

Every year, Indian Railway plies about 5500 goods trains that carry about 750 million tonnes per annum. Some part of dedicated (railway) freight corridor or DFC that is scheduled to connect Delhi and Mumbai by the year 2015 will pass through Madhya Pradesh.

MP being a landlocked state, the potential to develop it through port infrastructure is limited. Railways play a major role through the inland container depots (ICD), also called dry port. These ICDs are operated by Container Corporation of India Ltd. The state had two dry ports in Pithampur (near Indore) and Malanpur (near Gwalior) while the third one in Mandideep (near Bhopal) has commenced operations in February 2006. The talks are going on to have a fourth dry port at Ratlam on Delhi-Bombay track. The cargo handled by the two ICDs Pithampur and Malanpur in the last three years is given in Table 10.12.

TABLE 10.12

Cargo Handled by ICD

Name of ICD	*2003-04*	*2004-05*	*2005-06*
		ICD Pithampur	
Export	9525	10540	12515
Import	9113	10297	13053
Total	18638	20837	25568
		ICD Malanpur	
Export	2850	3870	4172
Import	3270	4267	3539
Total	6120	8137	7711

Source: Container Corporation of India, data in Twenty-Foot Equivalent Units (TEUs).

While not much in terms of data on rail traffic—both passenger and goods—is available, it can be said with some certainty based on rail line density, number of stations, both normal and junctions and movement

3. *Source: Madhya Pradesh Human Development Report*, 2007.

of fright wagons, that Madhya Pradesh is still under-serviced and under-equipped in terms of rail infrastructure.

5. Telecom

Of all the key infrastructure sectors, telecom emerged as the most recognised and popular sector in India. By 1995, the telecom sector has been a success story of India. Telecom Regulatory Authority of India (TRAI) played a crucial role in promoting competition among multiple telecom providers and rapid improvement in telecom technology.[4] A revolutionary change has occurred in past few years in terms of increased market share by telecom service providers. India has emerged as the third largest telecommunication network in the world after China and the US with the total telephone (mobile+fixed line) subscriber base touching 257 million at end-October 2007. With this, the overall teledensity has reached 22.5 per cent as against 16.9 per cent in December 2006.[5] In October 2008, the two public sector companies, namely BSNL and MTNL had a market share of 15.42 per cent for mobile telephones in India compared to private telecom companies. In basic telephones, MP was the first state to have private sector investment.

5.1 Telephones in MP

Cellular connections in MP have grown at a whooping rate of 242.91 per cent during the period from December 2006 to March 2009. During this period, mobile connections have increased from 43.52 lakh to 1.49 crore, indicating awesome expansion of the sector in the state. Position of Madhya Pradesh comparing other states is mentioned in Table 10.13.

TABLE 10.13

No. of Mobile Connection in MP (March 2009)

Sr. No.	*States*	*No. of Mobile Connections (in Crore)*	*% Share in India*
1	UP	3.348	11.6
2	Maharashtra	2.177	7.5
3	Gujarat	1.843	6.4
4	Rajasthan	1.604	5.6
5	MP	1.492	5.2
6	Bihar	1.598	5.5
7	India	28.836	100.0

Source: Cellular Operators Association of India.

As evident from the table, MP is lagging behind states like UP, Maharashtra and Gujarat in terms of number of mobile connections, but is in lines with Rajasthan and Bihar. Its share in all-India mobile connections is at 5.2 per cent.

Similarly, fixed line connections have shown a growth of 89.5 per cent during the period from March 2006 to May 2009. During this period, number of fixed line connections increased from 22 lakh to 2.1 crore.

5.2 Teledensity

The Indian telecom industry has witnessed impressive growth in the recent past. Between 31 March 2002 and 31 March 2007, the number of phones increased from 44.9 million to 205.9 million. The teledensity of 1.30 per cent as of 31 March 1996 rose to 18.2 per cent by 31 March 2007.[6] Teledensity is measured as the availability of phones per 100 persons.

TABLE 10.14

State-wise Rural-Urban Teledensity: July 2007

(Per cent)

No	*State*	*Rural*	*Urban*
1	Himachal Pradesh	23.3	98.3
2	Kerala	20.7	80
3	Punjab	17.5	73.8
4	North East I	4.8	66.8
5	Bihar	2	63.5
6	Assam	2.4	60.1
7	Karnataka	8.3	60.1
8	Andhra Pradesh	7.4	57.7
9	Haryana	12.7	52.6
10	Jammu and Kashmir	5.8	49.9
11	Gujarat	11.5	48.8
12	Rajasthan	8	47.3
13	Maharashtra (including Mumbai)	8.7	43.8
14	Tamil Nadu (including Chennai)	10.9	43
15	Uttar Pradesh	3.5	42.5
16	Orissa	4.8	42.4
17	Madhya Pradesh	3.5	42.1
18	West Bengal (including Kolkata)	5	40.3
19	North East II	3.1	23.9
20	Uttarakhand	4.4	23.1
21	Andaman and Nicobar Islands	14	23
22	Chhattisgarh	1	11.5
23	Jharkhand	1.1	11
	All-India	6.5	52.3

Note: North East I - Meghalaya, Mizoram, Tripura.
North East II - Arunachal Pradesh, Manipur, Nagaland.

Source: www.trai.gov.in

4. Mukherji, Rahul (2007). "Promoting Competition in India's Telecom Sector", in Vikram K. Chand (ed.), *Reinventing Public Service Delivery in India*. India: Sage Publication.
5. *India Infrastructure Report*, 2008.
6. *Source: www.trai.gov.in*

Urban teledensity as on 31 March 2007 was 49.5 per cent, whereas rural teledensity (RTD) was 2.0 per cent. Low RTD leads to lack of quality access to markets, non-optimal production decisions, and lack of supply to rural demands in a timely manner. One of the main reasons for the low teledensity is that the cost involved in setting up infrastructure in the rural areas is high, and recoveries could be lower as there are not many users.

The overall teledensity across all the states has been rising consistently, though the disparity between rural and urban teledensity has disturbingly widened. Table 10.14 depicts the acute nature of interstate disparities in telecom development in India. As on July 31, 2007, India's overall urban and rural teledensity stood at 52.3 and 6.5 per cent, respectively. The state of Himachal Pradesh ranks first in the country with the highest urban and rural teledensity of 98.3 per cent and 23.3 per cent, respectively. Kerala state ranks second, registering urban and rural teledensity of 80 and 20.7 per cent, respectively. The rural and urban teledensity in the state of Madhya Pradesh is quite low despite being a more populous and better-off state than Bihar and UP. The urban and rural teledensity in MP stood at 42.1 per cent and 3.5 per cent, respectively. MP's share in population is 60.35 million or 5.9 per cent of the country.

It is believed that popularisation of mobiles in the rural areas will facilitate the attainment of millennium development goals. Pradip Baijal and Rekha Jain argue in the rural telecom chapter of *Indian Infrastructure Report*, 2007 (of 3i-Network) that communication technologies help in poverty reduction in three ways: (i) increasing the efficiency of the individual and thereby, of the entire economy, (ii) ensuring better delivery of public services, such as health and education and (iii) creating new sources of employment, income and training particularly for the poor population. Low cost mobile solutions are now available for rural areas at affordable prices. Business innovations such as pre-pay options for mobiles have reduced the entry price at the lower end of the market and enabled easy access for multiple services in areas where fixed telephone infrastructure is poor. Only 22 per cent of total mobile users in December 2007 lived in rural areas. But the penetration of mobiles in rural areas was barely 1 per cent. Hence, major mobile operating companies started focusing on increasing their rural clientele.[7]

However, there are some key problems en route to higher market penetration by the mobile in rural Madhya Pradesh or rural India. The low population density in rural areas shall necessitate more towers of higher altitudes raising the costs further. Language is another problem; there are many dialects that have no alphabets in rural India. To meet these challenges, operators must come up with solutions like simplifying product access, offering customer centric solutions (like songs, music, hello tunes that are popular), and infrastructure sharing. The DoT, GoI, is also interested in research in telecommunication and has decided to fund innovations in communication technologies developed by small companies, entrepreneurs, universities or NGOs. The Universal Service Obligation Fund (USOF), where currently over Rs. 10,000 crore lie unutilised, will be used for this purpose.

5.3 Initiatives of Private Players for Improving Rural Teledensity

It is a fact that universal service objectives are affected by multiple policies and one needs to analyse in detail before embarking on the plan to increase rural teledensity. Airtel, a major private mobile company has set up a joint venture with IFFCO, called IFFCO Kisan Sanchar Ltd. (IKSL). IFFCO will have the majority 50 per cent stake while Airtel and Star Global will have 25 per cent equity each. The target of IKSL is the 55 million strong members of IFFCO (*The Hindu*, May 2, 2008). The Finnish mobile phone maker Nokia is already selling handsets adapted for rural India with longer battery life, dust-resistant covers and local language interface in 10 Indian languages. Moreover, Nokia is running a pilot project to gauge consumer response to initiatives such as the use of microfinance to fund the purchase of mobile phones by rural consumers.[8]

6. Power

Electricity is one of the many forms of energy and is widely used as a source of energy as it is available at the doorstep of the people, can be conveniently transferred from one place to another and has divergent uses. It does significantly affect our day to day life whether on official, home or business fronts equally and in gender neutral manner. Availability of electricity of appropriate quality and quantity can reduce energy costs for people and therefore, can be a commercially

7. *India Infrastructure Report* (2008) by 3iNetwork, Indo-Asian New Service and *The Times of India*, June 17.

8. *www.livemint.com*, 20/10/2008.

viable proposition even for the poor in the long run. Data from household survey in India suggests that, while both education and electricity can lead to higher non-farm income, delivering these services together amplifies the effect by as much as 2.3 times of annual household income.[9] Therefore, these investments should be planned and implemented together to realise the full and intended impact.

India is the fifth top power producing country of the world. Only USA, China, Japan and Russia produce and consume more power than India. Per capita power consumption in the country is about 650 units per annum. K.K. Chakarvarti, Manager, Power Plant Component, Indo-German Energy Programme states that India has an installed power generating capacity of 1,43,061 million units (MUs) as on March 31, 2008 of which, the thermal power stations share is 91,906 MUs (64 per cent). It is noted that the plant load factor of thermal stations have improved progressively over the years. It improved from 52.4 per cent in 1985-86 to 78.6 per cent in 2007-08, registering a remarkable improvement of 50 per cent during the period.

In mid-1990s, power sector witnessed innovative reforms with the introduction of incentive-based schemes funded by the Central government and the sector was opened up for private participation. Different states are at dissimilar stages of development. In the policy statements of early 1990s, it was projected that the foremost ailment affecting the power sector is power shortage. The slogan was "power at any cost is preferable to no power". The experience of the privatisation of Delhi power distribution suggests that there is no shortcut to improve efficiency of the distribution system. There are now many private power generation companies and under the Electricity Act, 2003, there will be many others in the foreseeable future.

6.1 Provisions in the Electricity Act, 2003

The Electricity Act, 2003 which governs the development of the electricity sector, has number of provisions for facilitating rapid expansion and improvement in quality and reliability of supply for consumers. It provides for:

i. National policy on standalone systems for rural areas and non-conventional energy systems.

ii. National policy on electrification and local distribution in rural areas.

iii. Obligation to supply electricity to all areas including villages and hamlets on the government.

iv. Exemption from the need to obtain licence for supply by *panchayat* institutions, users' associations, co-operative societies, NGOs and franchisees.

v. Multiple licensees and the incumbent service provider do not have the exclusive right.

vi. Open access in distribution and transmission for facilitating competition in generation and retail supply.

vii. Duty to supply on request by the owner or occupier of any premises by incumbent service provider.

viii. Standards of performance to be specified for the distribution licensee and non-achievement of these standards may result in imposition of penalty. These standards may be different for different licensees.

ix. Tariffs to be based on efficient cost and principles of competition. The tariffs may, however, be differentiated according to geographical location.

x. Provisions for consumer forum and ombudsman for resolving consumer disputes.

6.2 National Electricity Policy

The National Electricity Policy notified by the Central government in compliance with Section 3 of the Electricity Act, 2003 reinforces the intent of the Act to facilitate human development. The policy aims at achieving the following objectives:

i. Providing access to all households in next five years.

ii. Availability of power demand to be fully met by 2012. Energy shortages to be overcome and adequate spinning reserve to be available.

iii. Supply of reliable and quality power of specified standards in an efficient manner and at reasonable rates.

iv. Per capita availability of electricity to be increased to over 1000 units by 2012.

v. Minimum lifeline consumption of 1 unit/household/day as a merit good by year 2012.

vi. Protection of consumers' interests.

9. Barnes, Fitzgerald and Peskin.

6.3 Current Trends in Electricity Generation, Demand, Sale and Use for Different Purposes

In the fiscal year 2000-01, the same year when Madhya Pradesh was partitioned to carve out the state of Chhattisgarh from it, MP had total installed capacity to generate 4368.21 MW power. Of which, thermal power was worth 3437.5 MW and hydel power was worth 949.91 MW. In the year 2000, about 1360.2 MW of installed power capacity was transferred to Chhattisgarh and MP state was left with 2768.01 MW worth installed capacity.

For effective management of electricity sector, some institutional reforms were brought in through larger reconstitution of MP Electricity Board. Under the Company Act, 1956 five companies were reconstituted in July 2002 for electricity production, transmission and distribution in the state. From 1st July 2005, these companies act as autonomous bodies. Although they were entrusted with different responsibilities, they were accountable to Madhya Pradesh State Electricity Board (MPSEB).

Madhya Pradesh has a total installed electricity generation capacity of 6,449 MW. Thermal energy is the prime source of electricity in the state. About 95.66 per cent of electricity generation capacity in the state is based on thermal energy. The remaining source comes from hydel sources. On a per capita basis, electricity consumption in Madhya Pradesh stands at 352 kWh per annum, which is much closer to the national average of 355 kWh per annum. Madhya Pradesh Power Generating Co. Ltd. (MPPGCL) is a wholly owned company of MP government engaged in generation of electricity in the state of Madhya Pradesh. Total electricity generation capacity of Madhya Pradesh was 9458 MW (along with its Central share) as on 31st October 2007. Table 10.15 describes electricity generation capacity in the state from different sources.

Electricity generation capacity has increased by 1253.23 MW over previous year's 7934.85 MW in October 2006. Out of the total electricity generation capacity, nearly 63 per cent was the state's share and 21 per cent was the Central share which is 5 per cent of the country's electricity generation capacity. Electricity production in the state from various sources has estimated to rise from 26438 million units in 2001-02 to 39630 million units in 2007-08.

Normal power demand in the state remains at 4800 to 5000 MW nearly. In addition to this, the state receives approximately 2050 MW share from Central sector. High demand of about 2000 MW is observed in the state during the *rabi* season i.e., from November to March, which creates a gap between availability and demand and the state is forced to purchase the extra requirement.

TABLE 10.15

Electricity Generation Capacity through Different Sources

Sr. No.	*Source*	*Electricity Generation Capacity (in MW)*
1	State thermal power station	2647.5
2	State hydropower station	922.95
3	Joint venture water programme (Narmada project)	2356.5
4	Share received from Central electricity generation area	2050.13
5	Captive generation capacity	1481.00
	Total	9458.08

Source: Economic Survey, GoMP, 2007-08.

Figure 10.3 explains the electricity sold year by year.

FIGURE 10.3

Electricity Sold in Million Units

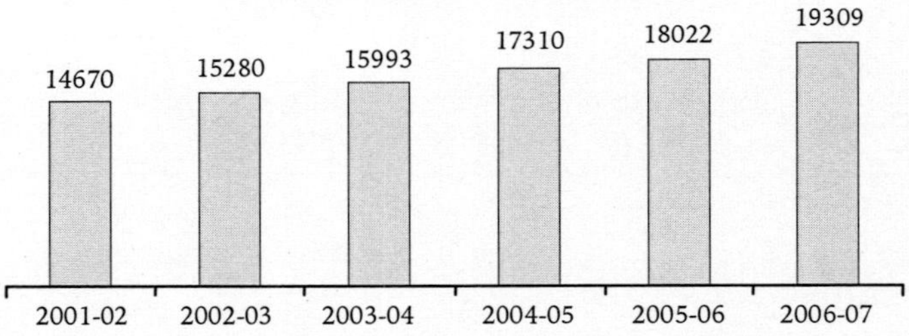

Source: Compendium of Power Statistics, GoMP, various years.

Figure 10.4 gives category-wise use of electricity in Madhya Pradesh.

FIGURE 10.4

Category-wise Use of Electricity in MP in 2006-07

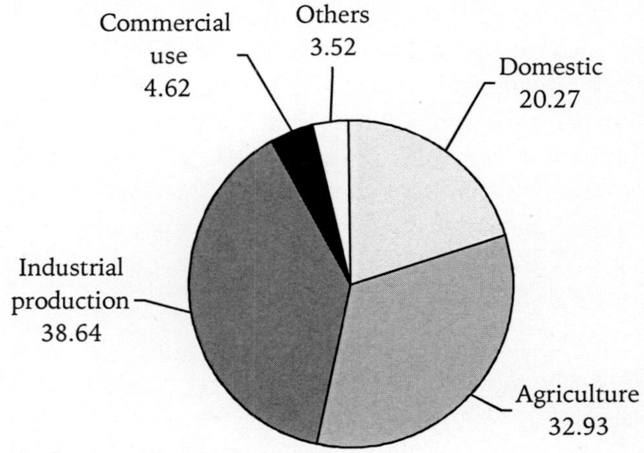

Source: Economic Survey, 2006-07.

High tension-based power for industrial production accounted for the highest proportion (39 per cent) of the consumed electricity, followed by agriculture and domestic consumption and commercial use respectively. Others include use of electricity by coal mines, traction etc.

A news item of 20th August 2008 from *Financial Express* carries Central Electricity Authority's (CEA) assessment that during the fiscal year 2008-09, there will be power shortage in India to the tune of 8.8 per cent and the peak shortage will be worth 18.1 per cent. Moreover, owing to the capacity addition of 10,178 MW in 2008-09, the shortfall in power availability will be lower than what was experienced in 2007-08. CEA recalled that during 2007-08, the total ex-bus energy availability in the country was 6,66,007 MU against a requirement of 7,39,343 MU leading to a shortage of 73,336 MU or 9.9 per cent. The total peak availability for the country was 90,793 MU against a peak demand of 108,866 mw, resulting in a peak power shortage of 18,073 MU or 16.6 per cent.

TABLE 10.16

Power Supply Position of Madhya Pradesh and its Four Neighbouring States

State	January – 2007 (Figures in Million Units)			
	Requirement (MU)	Availability (MU)	Surplus (MU)	Deficit (%)
Madhya Pradesh	6,919	5,753	-1,166	-16.9
Chhattisgarh	2,257	1,783	-474	-21.0
Rajasthan	5,794	4,823	-971	-16.8
Uttar Pradesh	8,248	7,071	-1,177	-14.3
Gujarat	10,203	7,670	-2,533	-24.8
All-India	1,00,411	85,088	-15,323	-15.3

Source: Central Electricity Authority.

Madhya Pradesh experienced power shortage of 13.9 per cent and peak shortage of 16.9 per cent. In terms of peak power shortage, MP state fared better than Chhattisgarh and Gujarat but marginally worse than Rajasthan and UP. Based on the capacity addition programme, peak availability for the state has been assessed. Peak requirement and peak availability from 2006-07 to 2011-12 have been worked out as indicated in Table 10.17.

For the year 2006-07, the peak availability has been assessed as 5,651 MW against the estimated peak demand of 6,881 MW resulting in peak shortage of about 1,230 MW (17.63 per cent). For the year 2007-2008, peak availability has been assessed as 6,939 MW against the peak demand of 7,547 MW resulting in peak shortage of 608 MW (6.95 per cent). The peak availability at the end of the 11th Plan (2011-12) has been assessed as 10,521 MW against the peak demand of 10,491 MW. It may, therefore, be seen that the power supply position of the state will improve by the end of 11th Plan.

TABLE 10.17

Peak Requirement and Peak Availability of Electricity in MP

Year	Peak Requirement in MW	Peak Availability in MW	Shortage/ Surplus	Shortage/ Surplus in %
2006-07	6881	5651	(-) 1230	(-) 17.88
2007-08	7547	6939	(-) 608	(-) 6.95
2008-09	8144	7623	(-) 521	(-) 6.40
2009-10	8938	8295	(-) 643	(-) 7.19
2010-11	9753	9254	(-) 499	(-) 5.12
2011-12	10491	10521	(+) 30	(+) 0.29

Source: *http://www.mp.gov.in/spb/fiveyearplan/VolumeIsep07/chapter-9%20Power%20final.pdf*

6.4 Transmission and Distribution

Due to paucity of funds, the development of transmission and distribution system suffered badly during the 9th Plan. This has been compensated during the 10th Plan.

FIGURE 10.5

Transmission and Distribution Loss in MP

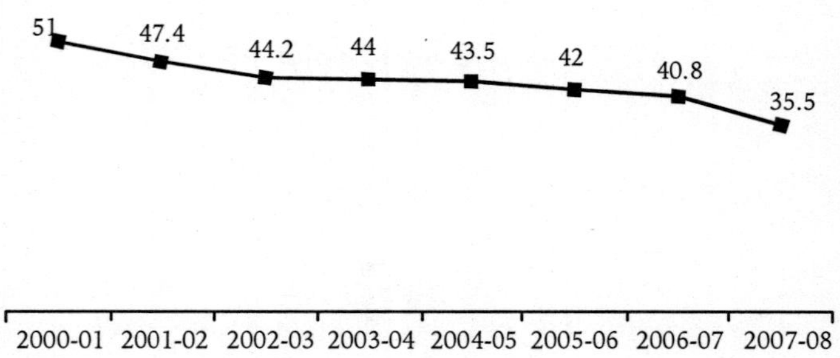

Source: Economic Survey, GoMP, 2007-08.

The state government is taking strong efforts to curb transmission and distribution losses. In the past 4-5 years, more than 37 lakh electronic meters have been installed. Level of meterisation in the state is now around 80 per cent. 106 special courts have been set in order to sort out cases of electricity stealing. The state has geared up the process of identifying areas with more electricity losses through intensive vigilance. In these areas, low tension open lines have been replaced with armed cables and High Voltage Distribution System (HDVS) systems. In addition, energy audits have also been undertaken in such areas through 100 per cent meterisation of extra high voltage (EHV) 33KV and 11KV feeders. As a result of strengthening and upgradation, the transmission and distribution system got an impetus and the state has been able to reduce the transmission and distribution loss from 51 per cent in 2000-01 to 35.5 per cent in 2007-08.

6.5 Access to Electricity

The basic issue of household access to electricity has seen some impressive progress in the state. While in 1991, 43.3 per cent households were estimated (Census 1991) to be electrified, this figure has gone up substantially to 70 per cent for all households and 62.3 per cent for rural households (Census 2001). However, there are two disturbing factors—one is that if we see the number of households with domestic connections, as registered in the MPSEB, it is just 43 per cent overall, and 29 per cent in rural Madhya Pradesh—signifying that either many households do not have a valid connection, or that actually only 29 per cent rural households have proper connections that deliver power as supplied. The high loss levels till 2005 indicate that the probability of the former is higher.

The second disturbing factor is the low per capita energy consumption. If we compare it with some of the other 'more developed' states such as Maharashtra and Gujarat, the difference becomes very clear. The inter-district variations within MP place some regions in a very poor power scenario. While the average per capita domestic consumption is the highest in Bhopal, Indore, Gwalior, Jabalpur and Ujjain, it is the lowest (below 500 kWh per year per person) in Mandla, Seoni, Jhabua, Damoh and Dindori which are sparsely populated areas. However, this low per capita consumption does not present the right picture because the losses on account of illegal connections are actually consumption and hence, actual data for per capita consumption may be higher than indicated.

The National Electricity Policy envisages that the per capita availability of electricity will be increased to over 1000 units by 2012. Based on the information released, even in 2012, per capita availability of power in India would be woefully short going by the current pace of per capita consumption. Also, the state-wise consumption data reveals large disparities between states.

TABLE 10.18

Per Capita Electricity Consumption and Status of Rural Electrification

State	*Per Capita Electricity Consumption (in kWh) 2005-06*	*Number of Unelecrified Rural Households (2007)*	*% of Unelectrified Households*
Haryana	1090.39	527649	21.5
Himachal Pradesh	765.86	60551	5.51
Jammu & Kashmir	711.01	293016	25.23
Punjab	1436.79	292537	10.54
Rajasthan	572.20	4006147	55.98
Uttar Pradesh	311.82	16505786	80.2
Uttarakhand	654.84	593902	49.7
Chandigarh	1553.96	552	2.6
Delhi	1766.94	24580	14.5
Gujarat	1283.77	1641203	27.88
Madhya Pradesh	580.34	3061371	37.68
Chhattisgarh	685.81	1810152	53.89
Maharashtra	934.43	3829566	34.83
Goa	1970.08	10650	7.6
Daman & Diu	8300.12	562	2.5
Dadra & Nagar Haveli	11567.67	5695	17.4
Andhra Pradesh	723.10	5114485	40.35
Karnataka	720.43	1858260	27.84
Kerala	424.13	1703651	36.47
Tamil Nadu	976.81	2384419	28.8
Lakshadweep	368.29	14	0.3
Pondicherry	2509.25	13713	19
Bihar	85.86	12010504	94.87
Jharkhand	548.74	3422425	90.01
Orissa	633.93	5470135	80.65
West Bengal	380.61	8899353	79.7
Andaman & Nicobar	407.77	15846	31.9
Sikkim	429.81	22915	25
Assam	170.65	3522331	83.46
Manipur	215.21	140675	47.47
Meghalaya	517.54	229916	69.74
Nagaland	179.34	114405	43.12
Tripura	190.62	368323	68.2
Arunachal Pradesh	297.66	91251	55.47
Mizoram	250.15	44334	55.86
All-India	631.41	78090874	56.5

Source: http://www.mperc.org/Rural-electrification-households.html

National per capita electricity consumption is 631.41kWh and more than half of the rural households are deprived of electricity facility. Per capita electricity consumption of Madhya Pradesh at 584.30 kWh is below the national figure. But it is faring better in terms of the proportion of unelectrified households with respect to the all-India figure. Performance of Madhya Pradesh is downturning compared to Gujarat and Maharashtra on both the indicators of per capita consumption and per cent of household unelectrified. However, it augurs well for the state when compared with other neighbouring states like Bihar, Rajasthan, UP and Chhattisgarh.

Some of the challenges in rural electrification in the state are as follows:

- High investment cost due to increased network expansion costs as compared to urban areas.
- High supply cost owing to widely dispersed load to be spread on low volumes of energy consumption, low uncertain demand and high supervision cost in problematic areas.
- Weak institutions and sector governance due to presence of several national and state agencies with overlapping mandates.
- Low recovery rates from agriculture connections.

6.6 Non-Conventional Energy Sources

MP Urja Vikas Nigam (MPUVN) was constituted by the Government of Madhya Pradesh in August 1982. The main activities of the Urja Vikas Nigam are as under:

1. Establishment of various power projects based on the non-conventional energy sources in private sector.
2. Implementation of various non-conventional energy based projects in the state.
3. Promotion and popularisation of use of non-conventional energy sources.
4. Promotion of research and development activities in the field of non-conventional energy sources.
5. With a view to encourage energy conservation, arranging energy audits in selected industrial units and other institutions, offices etc.
6. Co-ordination among the Central, state government and investors for setting up power plants based on non-conventional energy sources.
7. Electrification of unelectrified villages through non-conventional energy sources under Integrated Rural Energy Programme (IREP).

Various efforts undertaken under these include, IREP, biogas, solar energy, energy conservation and management, rural electrification, biomass and solar photovoltaic, biofuel and energy parks.

6.7 Outlays in Five Year Plans

The outlay approved for 10th Plan is Rs. 2420 lakh. The expenditure incurred during the four years 2002-2006 is Rs. 350.99 lakh, Rs. 282.89 lakh, Rs. 309.80 lakh and Rs. 244.22 lakh respectively.

Outlay for the 11th FYP is Rs. 5,652 lakh. MPUVN has proposed to take mainly rural village electrification programmes during the 11th Plan period and proposed to electrify 943 villages through the projects based on non-conventional energy sources out of which 200 villages will be electrified in 2007-08. A target for installation of 10,000 biogas plants during the 11th Plan period is also proposed by the Nigam under biogas programme. Fifteen energy parks will be developed for display of all projects based on non-conventional energy sources and installation of 25 MW power plant is proposed based on wind energy.

TABLE 10.19

Targets and Achievements under Non-Convention Energy Sources during 10th FYP

S. No.	Item	Unit	Target	Actual/Anti. Achievement
1.	Biogas domestic	Nos.	21,000	6,815
2.	Solar photovalastic			
	a) Street light	Nos.	460	784
	b) Domestic light	Nos.	1,600	3,008
	c) Drinking water system	No. of villages	18	5
3.	Biomass power plant	MW	35	9.26
4.	Wind energy monitoring	No. of sites	38	2
5.	Wind energy power plant	MW		19.25
6.	Energy conservation energy audits	Units	300	505

Source: *http://www.mp.gov.in/spb/fiveyearplan/Volumelsep07/chapter-9%20Power%20final.pdf*

6.8 Post-Reform Scenario in MP

- MPSEB is heavily dependent on subsidy support from the state government. The amount of subsidy was around Rs. 794 crore in 2004-05 (about 15 per cent of the revenue earned by the DISCOMs from sale of power).
- The failure rate of DTs has increased by 4.75 per cent (from about 18.13 per cent in 2001-02 to 22.88 per cent in 2004-05).

- The percentage of metered domestic consumers has come down from 84 per cent in 2000-01 to 81 per cent in 2004-05, which is a disturbing trend.
- The collection efficiency in respect of agricultural and domestic consumer categories has suffered after the restructuring. In the case of agricultural consumers, the collection efficiency has deteriorated progressively from 88 per cent in 2000-01 to as low as 21 per cent in 2004-05. It is equally poor for the domestic consumers and have come down from as high as 95 per cent in 2000-2001 to 79 per cent in 2004-05.
- For prevention of theft of electricity, the state government enacted law in 2001. Several administrative measures have been undertaken by the companies to check power theft. However, enforcement measures for elimination of theft of electricity have slowed down in the state. The number of FIRs lodged has come down to 1,607 FIRs in 2003-04 to 522 FIRs in 2004-05 and the recovery towards the cases involved in theft declined from 78 to 75.8 per cent of the demand raised.
- Metered sale has come down from 50.59 per cent in 1996-97 to 38.23 per cent in 2004-05.
- MPPGCL has been able to improve the plant load factor (PLF) from 46 to 66 per cent and availability has increased from the level of 75 per cent in 1995-96 to 87 per cent during 2004-05.
- After reorganisation of the state, installed generating capacity left in the state was about 2,940 MW. There was only a marginal increase of about 50 MW hydro capacity. However, with regard to the thermal capacity, there has been no further addition since 2002-03.
- The state has been facing acute peak demand as well as energy shortages. The peak power deficit and energy shortages have been as high as 28 and 23 per cent respectively in April 2006.
- GENCO had spent a very little amount on repair and maintenance (R&M) activities as compared to the amount approved by the Commission under this head. The Commission, in its tariff order dated 10 December 2004, had allowed Rs. 140.31 crore under R&M of generating stations, but the GENCO failed to utilise the approved amount.
- For 2005-06, the Commission had approved Rs. 131.91 crore under this head. But the repeated failure to utilise the funds approved for the much-needed R&M activities is baffling when it is urgently needed to increase generation and improve the PLF.

6.9 Financial Sustainability

Major causes for the sector being financially unsustainable are tariffs not reflecting full cost, high cross subsidies, adverse consumer mix, collection inefficiencies, high distribution losses and other high distribution inefficiencies. The returns on investments consequently have been negative in the last few years.

TABLE 10.20

Profit and Loss of MPSEB

Profit and Loss Without Subsidy (Rs. crore)		*Subsidy Paid by the State Government (Rs. crore)*	
Pre-restructuring	*After restructuring*	*Pre-restructuring*	*After restructuring*
1996-97	2005-06	1996-97	2005-06
-464	-952	300.4	270

Source: *www.hpsldc.org/Presentations/Power%20Sector%20Reforms.ppt*

As seen from Table 10.20, the MPSEB even after restructuring is not able to come up with any profits, rather its loss has more than doubled over a pre-restructuring period at Rs. 952 crore in 2005-06. It is also evident that the state government has been providing significant amount of subsidies to the Board after restructuring has taken place. MP state government took over liabilities of MPSEB to the tune of Rs. 4,431 crore.

One of the major assumptions for restructuring was that it will enable cheap power by reducing T&D losses. However in reality, after restructuring, the reduction in the T&D loss levels has been slow and losses dropped by just 12 per cent over a period of 7 years from 2001-02 to 2007-08. Tariff comparisons over the years for various consumer categories are given in Table 10.21.

TABLE 10.21

Tariff Comparisons (Rs./unit)

Year	*Domestic*	*Commercial*	*Industrial*
1999-2000	1.30	4.30	4.36
2005-06	3.43	5.45	4.47

Source: *www.hpsldc.org/Presentations/Power%20Sector%20Reforms.ppt*

The first and the foremost thing that gets revealed from the table is that electricity has got costlier. Thus, the assumption of providing cheaper electricity after restructuring is proved to be a false promise. Although the tariff has increased in the entire consumer categories, it is very miserable on the part of domestic consumers, because the tariff rise is maximum in this category as high as 164.7 per cent. The tariffs in the state should be rationalised as average tariff of low tension (LT) consumers has risen while that of the high tension (HT) consumers has declined in real terms. It would be desirable to carry out a survey in Madhya Pradesh to determine the affordability and willingness of consumers to pay that are presently paying tariffs below cost of supply so that tariffs can be accordingly fixed.

7. Water Supply and Sanitation

Impact of global warming in terms of climate change, melting of glaciers, devastating cyclones and drying of large river basins have been observed and felt by majority of population all over the world. The provision of safe drinking water supply and sanitation facilities is a basic necessity of life. One of the MDGs identified as "Halve, by 2015, the proportion of people without sustainable access to safe drinking water and basic sanitation". Comprehensive data was available in 2002, hence it is considered as halfway mark towards achieving the 2015 MDG deadline. The UNDP's *Human Development Report* for 2006, focuses on access to water and sanitation; it states that today, some 1.1 billion people in developing countries have inadequate access to water and 2.6 billion lacks basic sanitation. India's rank on HDI stands at 126 out of 177 countries.

Although a large percentage of households have access to safe public water supply and sanitation in India, mortality and morbidity associated with water-borne diseases remains high in the country. In India, water and sanitation related infections account for 70-80 per cent of the burden of disease (Tenth Five Year Plan, 2002-2007).

As evident from Table 10.22, Madhya Pradesh is at par with the national figure in providing access to safe drinking water in both rural and urban areas. At the same time, its performance in providing sanitation facility generally and to rural areas particularly is the area of concern. The country has little hope of reaching the MDG for access to safe drinking water and sanitation if it continues at this pace. It is because these access figures are indicating miles to go. However, it does not speak about the access to minimum water requirement norms of 20-40 litres per capita per day for both drinking water and sanitation purpose as given by World Bank and WHO. Also, among the households that do not have access to safe drinking water, more than half belongs to BPL families whose per day income is less than $1.25. The above norms include the most basic recommended needs that are as follows: (a) Five litres of drinking water per capita per day, (b) Twenty litres for sanitation and hygiene, (c) Fifteen litres for bathing, and (d) Ten litres for cooking.

TABLE 10.22

Access to Safe Drinking Water and Sanitation

	Drinking Water Supply (%)			*Toilet Facility (%)*		
	Total	*Rural*	*Urban*	*Total*	*Rural*	*Urban*
MP	68.4	61.5	88.6	24.0	8.9	67.7
India	68.2	62.3	92.4	36.41	21.92	73.72

Source: Census of India, 2001.

It is true that most of the developing countries in Asia, Africa and Latin America use less than 50 litres per day.[10]

If we have a look on the sources of water supply in Madhya Pradesh, we find that about 86.4 per cent is dependent on groundwater in which hand pumps and tube wells are constituting 50.8 per cent and wells are contributing 35.6 per cent. Tap, river/canal, tank and others are contributing only 13.6 per cent of the total water supply.[11]

Water is a state subject. Providing drinking water facilities and sanitation becomes the primary responsibility of the state government. Supply of clean drinking water in the rural areas has always been one of the highest priorities of the government. Rural water supply is one of the six components of Bharat Nirman to be implemented during 2005-2009 to build the rural infrastructure. During the Bharat Nirman period, 55,067 uncovered and about 3.31 lakh slipped-back habitations are to be covered and 2.17 lakh quality-affected habitations are also to be covered. In terms of physical coverage in rural water supply, considerable success has been achieved.

10. Swain, Ashok (2004). *Managing Water Conflict: Asia, Africa and the Middle East.* Routledge.
11. Das, Keshab (2003-04). "Drinking Water and Sanitation in Rural Madhya Pradesh: A Review of Policy Initiatives". Ahmedabad: Gujarat Institute of Development Research.

In April 2005, 96.13 per cent of rural habitations in MP have been fully covered (FC) with drinking water facilities, 3.55 per cent are partially covered (PC) and 0.32 per cent is not covered (NC) with drinking water facilities.[12] These numbers are only giving physical coverage but not indicating towards the sustainabilty of sources and quality of water. Rural water supply schemes in India are facing well-known deficiencies: dependence on groundwater sources and hence lack of source sustainability; poor quality of electricity, which hampers water pumping; wastage from overflowing cisterns; bad quality of construction work; lack of institutional responsibility, especially for management of water; lack of a legal framework, etc.

At the national level, department of drinking water supply (DDWS) is dealing with the water supply and sanitation sector. This department works under the Ministry of Rural Development. At the state level, MP public health engineering department (MPPHED) is a nodal department for implementing water supply and sanitation programmes. From April 2008, centrally sponsored schemes like Swajaldhara and Total Sanitation Campaign (TSC) has been transferred to the department of rural development; that is why in Madhya Pradesh two departments are involved in water supply and sanitation. The supply-led schemes, like Accelerated Rural Water Supply Programme (ARWSP) is handled by Public Heath Engineering Department (PHED) and the demand-driven Swajaldhara is working under department of rural development.

7.1 Investment through Budgets

7.1.1 Proportionate Spending on Water Supply and Sanitation (WSS)

The total expenditure in WSS was Rs. 267 crore in 2001-02 that has been increased to Rs. 927 crore in 2008-09. The WSS spending has been increased by four times during this period; however, no consistency in the expenditure trend was observed. WSS expenditure shows rising trend with a growth rate of 16.24 per cent during 2001-02 to 2006-07. Share of WSS in total state budget has increased from 1.4 per cent in 2001-02 to 2.4 per cent in 2008-09. Although no consistency is seen in the expenditure pattern over the years, but the trend line is showing an upward growth. On an average, during 2001-02 to 2008-09, government spent about 2 per cent of its total state spending to WSS. Government is increasing the share of WSS in the state budget by spending by 0.10 per cent per annum. It was also found that there is high correlation between state budget expenditure and WSS expenditure (0.89).

In the period 2001-02 to 2004-05, estimated budgets were always higher than the actual expenditure, indicating lack of efficiency on government's part to spend whatsoever was budgeted for. However, after 2004-2005 the trend got reversed and government's actual expenditure became higher than the budget and the excess expenditure was met out through supplementary budgets. In the WSS sector as a whole, average share of

FIGURE 10.6

Percentage of WSS to State Budget

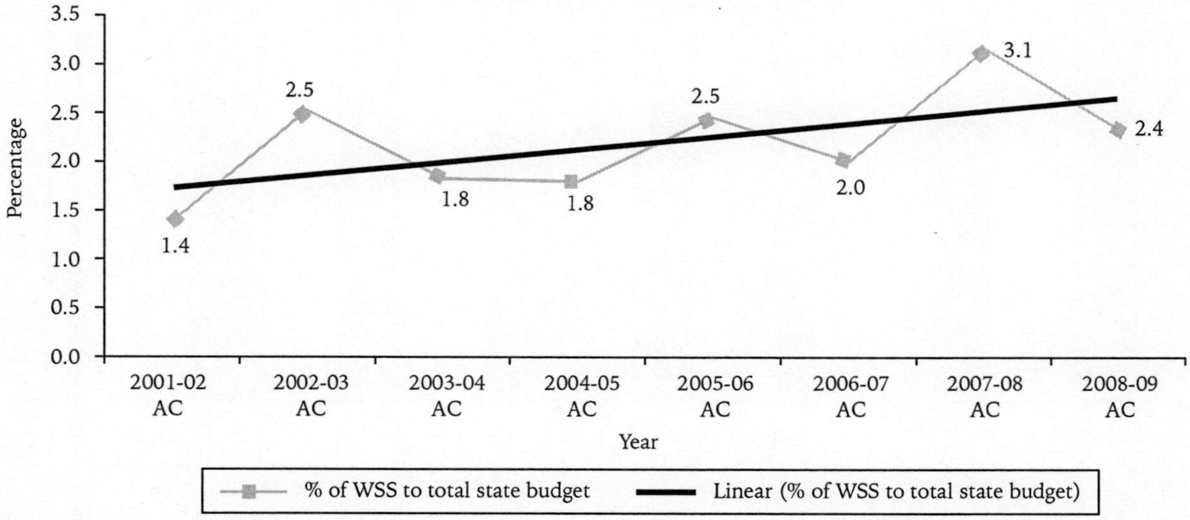

Source: State Budget Books, GoMP, various years.

12. National Portal of India: "Sectors—Rural Development, Rural Water Supply Programme", *India.gov.in*, *http://india.gov.in/sectors/rural/rural_water.php*

water supply and sanitation is 95 per cent and 5 per cent respectively. However, proportion of water supply is coming down from 97 per cent in 2001-02 to 93 per cent in 2008-09, indicating increasing stake of sanitation in the sector over the years. This too goes well with the figures of access to safe drinking water and sanitation for the national and state level figures as well.

7.2 WSS in Social Sector

Water supply and sanitation combined with housing and urban development is one of the important elements of social sector as it constitutes the basic amenities for human beings. WSS, housing and urban development together accounts for 16 per cent of total social sector spending and it ranks at second position among other social sectors after education. WSS, housing and urban development sector shows greater investments in 2007-08 and 2008-09 over past 4 years from 2003-04 to 2006-07; it is owing to heavy investment being done through schemes like Jawaharlal Nehru National Urban Renewal Mission (JNNURM).

In the broader sector of WSS, housing and urban development, share-wise position of its components is as follows. Water supply and sanitation is at top with average contribution of about 52 per cent, followed by urban development with a share of 39 per cent and housing with least 9 per cent share. As shown in the chart, WSS share has increased from 2002-03 till 2005-2006, and the share of urban development is coming down but after this, WSS is coming down and urban development is increasing. The trend is showing that whenever government increases the expenditure of urban development, it happens on the cost of decreasing share of WSS.

While the rural population in MP constitutes about 74 per cent of the total population, the rural water supply is getting only 57 per cent (average of 2001-02 to 2008-09) of total water supply budget. Also, the per head expenditure for water supply is always higher than the rural water supply. Similar to the case of WSS sector, it was observed that during the period of 2001-02 to 2004-05, estimated budget was always higher than actual spending, indicating inability of the state government to spend in the line with budgetary allocations. After 2004-05, government has been spending more than the allocated figures indicating increase in the budgets through supplementary demands. From 2005-06 to 2007-08, on an average around 42 per cent of the amounts was spent more than the estimated one.

FIGURE 10.7

Expenditure on Water Supply and Sanitation, Housing and Urban Development as a % of Social Sector Spending

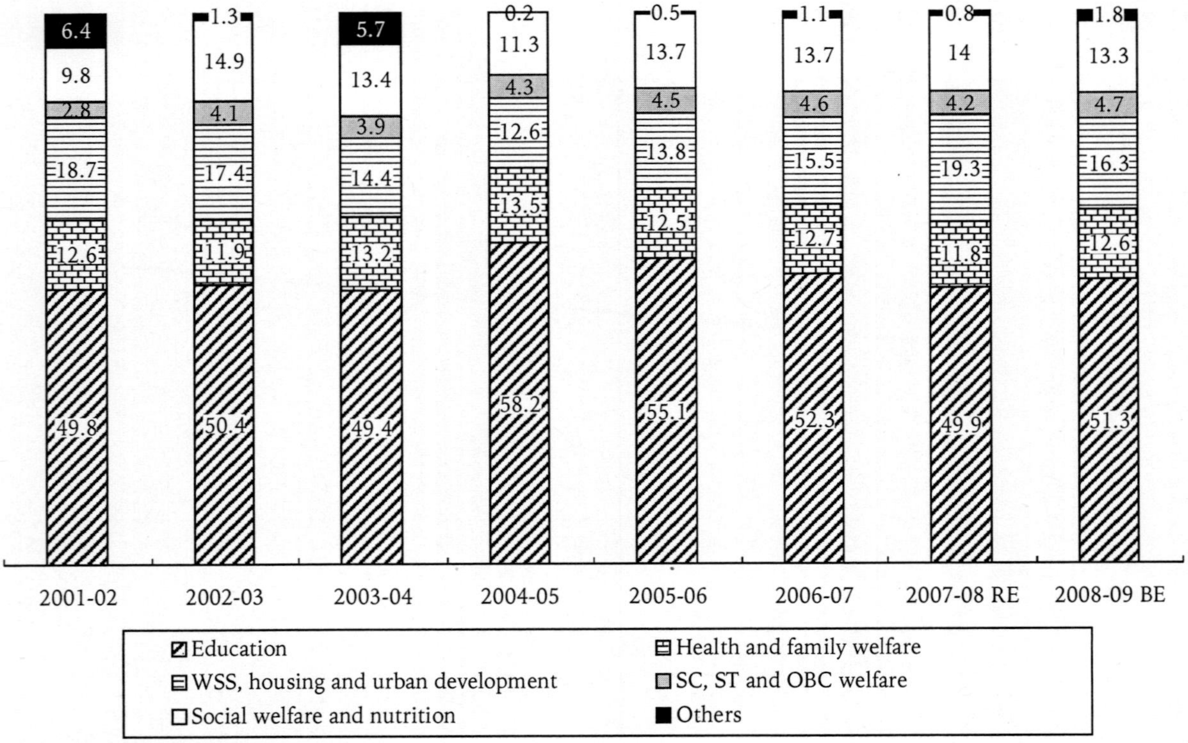

Source: State Budget Books, GoMP, various years.

7.3 Expenditure on Marginalised Section

Scheduled Caste (15.2 per cent) and Scheduled Tribe (20.3 per cent) together constitute 35 per cent of the state population. Adhering to the principles of Tribal Sub-Plan (TSP) and Scheduled Caste Sub-Plan (SCSP), sectoral spending should be proportionate to the population proportion.

TABLE 10.23

Expenditure on SCs and STs as a Percentage of Total Water Supply and Sanitation

Year	*SC*	*ST*	*Total SC/ST*
2001-02	12.47	6.58	19.05
2002-03	11.05	6.72	17.77
2003-04	10.51	5.87	16.38
2004-05	9.45	10.56	20.01
2005-06	12.80	11.29	24.09
2006-07	20.76	14.10	34.86
2007-08 RE	20.67	18.64	39.31
2008-09 BE	17.89	16.85	34.73

Source: State Budget Books, GoMP, various years.

Analysis shows that SCs and STs would have been able to attract on an average only 9 and 13 per cent respectively of the total WSS over the years. This is not only disproportionate to their population share but far below the proposed norms of TSP and SCSP.

7.4 Key Highlights

1) The state government should commit a definite proportion of the total budget/social sector budget/WSS budget to rural water supply (RWS) sector in order to achieve targets set by the Planning Commission of India and the state planning board.

2) Budgetary outlay for sanitation should form at least 1-2 per cent of government's annual budget (at different levels).[13] But the total budget for WSS forms only 2 per cent, and in this 2 per cent, sanitation is managed barely 5 per cent.

3) In the WSS, WS and RWS deviation of actuals from the budgeted figures are not in the acceptable range; this has to be corrected.

4) Allocation for SCs and STs should be in their population proportion in total WSS and WS budgets.

5) Considering the share of SCs and STs in the rural population, there should be 41 per cent of total RWS budget for them.

The major factor responsible for low economic growth in the state and high regional disparity is deficiency in infrastructure. Lack of connectivity, both physical and communication are the major bottlenecks in attracting industrial investment from within or outside the country. The other major infrastructural deficiency is in terms of irrigation, storage of food grains and marketing facilities. Due to low rates of investment through central sector projects and incapacity of the state to allocate substantial funds, very few assets have been created over the years. The state has failed to protect the small farmers and entrepreneurs against their national and global competitors through appropriate institutional support system. The decline in public investment, under the compulsions of globalisation, created serious problems of livelihood for the poor as community based organisations were extremely weak in the state and could not come forward to take up even a part of the responsibility. It is, therefore, not very surprising that in terms of employment growth, poverty reduction or human development, the southern and central regions having more serious deficiencies in infrastructure, performed much below the national average.

In case of percentage of households having access to safe drinking water, the gap has narrowed down but the more serious problem in the state is that of provision of sanitation facilities. Besides, there is no equity in spending on disadvantaged sections of the state, thus leaving them deprived of basic minimum facilities.

One area where the achievement of Madhya Pradesh seems to be satisfactory is in the field of primary education and amelioration of illiteracy. The state has allocated significant resources to education sector and directed its major programmes to rural areas. This has resulted in high growth in number of educational institutions, school-going children and literacy rate. It has almost caught up with the national literacy figure of 64 per cent in 2001, despite the state being 8 percentage points behind the national figure of 52 per cent in 1991.

13. "Suggested Action Points: Financing", Third South Asian Conference on Sanitation (SACOSAN-III), November 16-21, 2008, Vigyan Bhawan, New Delhi, India.

Chapter 11

Handlooms in Madhya Pradesh

1. Introduction

Handloom textiles constitute a timeless facet of the rich cultural heritage of India. As an economic activity, the handloom sector occupies a place second only to agriculture in providing livelihood to the people. It is estimated that the handloom industry provides employment to 65 lakh workforce directly and indirectly and there are about 35 lakh looms spread all over India. The handloom sector constitutes nearly 19 per cent and the power loom sector constitutes 60 per cent of the total cloth production of the country and both contribute substantially to the earning from exports. The contribution of power loom sector is increasing in order. On one hand, Indian textile industry is the second largest in the world, second only to China; on the other hand, handlooms as an important constituent of the textile industry is facing crisis nationally. The state of Madhya Pradesh follows the national trend. While weaving on handlooms is predominantly on cotton, the future yarn consumption pattern is expected to be equitably shared between cotton and other fibres. With technological developments, the handloom products are being increasingly replicated on power looms at a much lower cost. While the government's endeavour is to create conditions for the harmonious growth of the entire textile industry, at the same time it would also like to ensure that there is well-defined and delineated areas for handlooms which is not unduly encroached by the power looms and mills.

2. Handlooms in Madhya Pradesh

Madhya Pradesh has been an old centre for handlooms. The weaving traditions of *Chanderi* and *Maheshwar* go back several centuries. The weaves range from fine cottons and silks (both mulberry and *tussar*) to coarse and basic weaves including hand block printed cotton material. Data from the MP Hast Shilp Vikas Nigam (MPHSVN) or the MP Handicraft and Handloom Development Corporation shows that textiles have become the main product in their sales operations, mainly the silk saris, dress material (usually printed) and other textile items.

2.1 Status of Handlooms and Production

The estimates with respect to the units and numbers involved in handlooms in the state are given in Table 11.1 below. The number of handlooms declined over the period and has stabilised to around 21000 working handlooms in the state. As compared to the established handlooms, only about 63 per cent are in working conditions. There has been an increase in the number of persons employed in these handlooms since 2002-03 which indicates towards the promotional activities taken up in the state.

TABLE 11.1

Status of Handlooms and Numbers Employed

Year	*Handloom*		
	Established	*Working*	*Employed*
2000-01	35700	22200	70500
2001-02	39000	22500	71400 (including 14 SHGs and 445 weavers)
2002-03	33500	19200	54441
2003-04	37100	19700	59379
2004-05	34479	20837	62511
2005-06	34690	21568	64704
2006-07	34690	21910	65730

Source: Economic Survey 2001-02, 2003-04, 2004-05, 2005-06 and 2006-07 as per Directorate of Handloom and Handicraft Department Report.

TABLE 11.2

Status of Textile Sector in Madhya Pradesh

Particulars	*2000-01*	*2001-02*	*2002-03*	*2003-04*	*2004-05*	*2005-06*	*2006-07*
Total looms	35723	35723	33007	34260	34330	34690	34690
Working looms	20248	20229	19146	20101	20312	21568	21910
Est. looms in co-operative sector	20506	20652	30087	19676	20652	19884	18496
Working looms in co-operative sector	9628	9053	8843	8867	9053	8933	8389
Total weaving societies	654	689	647	674	627	670	635
Working societies	300	282	277	280	262	277	223
Training	558	197	506	497	560	1530	2036
Loom & equipment provides	559	75	124	223	255	315	624
Employment generation (in '000s)	61	58	54	59	61	65	66
Production (in million m.)	81.13	100.48	77.52	43.90	105.48	169.24	222.49

Source: Department of Rural Industries, GoMP.

2.2 Status of Textile Sector

The number of looms in the co-operative sector are about 57 per cent of all the looms in the state, though in terms of working looms, only 44-45 per cent fall under co-operatives, indicating that the weavers outside the co-operative sector are either more efficient or have found more ways and means to continue to remain working in handlooms than those under co-operative linkages. The progress on account of cloth and yarn production is unsatisfactory and the ground seems to be shaky especially in case of yarn production.

2.3 Provision for Handlooms by Rural Industries Department, Madhya Pradesh

If we look at the budget of rural industries department, Government of Madhya Pradesh, we find that for handlooms sector, a sum of less than 8 crore is assigned out of the total 34 crore budget for sericulture, handlooms, handicrafts, *khadi* and village industries. The sum is roughly equal to 25 per cent money allocated for all the sectors.

TABLE 11.3

Budget of Rural Industries Department in Madhya Pradesh

Sector	*Allotment (in Lakh Rs.)*	
	FY: 2006-07	*FY: 2007-08*
Handlooms	466.60	467.25

Source: Department of Rural Industries, 2006.

2.4 Handlooms Today

Handloom weaving is found in certain important clusters in the state, the most important of which are concentrated in Chanderi, Maheswar, Burhanpur and Jabalpur. A variety of traditional textile printing and dyeing craft clusters are in different parts of Malwa region.

In year 2001, 71,400 persons were working in 22,500 handlooms out of the established 39,000 handlooms in the state. Out of the total 20,506 handlooms established in the co-operative sector, only 9,053 looms are operating. There are only 282 out of 689 weaving societies working in the handloom sector.[1] Madhya Pradesh accounts for 3.53 per cent of mill-made fabrics and 5.62 per cent of the total spun yarn in the country in 2001-02.[2]

In 2005, only 30100 handlooms were established in the state and out of that 16100 are working. Some 17700 handlooms are under 650-plus co-operative societies. These societies employed 26600 people and the production of cloth was worth Rs. 23.68 crore.

Table 11.5 presents the performance of the handlooms in Madhya Pradesh during financial years 2004-05 to 2006-07. The increase in production in terms of length has been more than 20 per cent over the said period. All the other indicators also present an increasing trend, highlighting a growing handloom sector in the state.

1. *Source: Annual Report, 2001-02,* Department of Rural Industries, GoMP, till November 2001.
2. "Monthly Review of the MP Economy" (April 01-February 02), Centre for Monitoring Indian Economy.

TABLE 11.4

Status of Handlooms in Madhya Pradesh at the End of Financial Years 2005-06 and 2006-07

Handlooms in Madhya Pradesh	*2005-06*	*2006-07*
Total operational loomage	21568	21910
In the co-operative sector (Operational)	8933	8389
Production (Lakh mts.)	169.24	222.49
Employment	64704	65730

Source: Madhya Pradesh Handicraft and Handloom Development Corporation, 2006 and 2007.

TABLE 11.5

Performance Highlights of Handlooms

	Achievements		
Particulars	*2004-05*	*2005-06*	*2006-07*
Loom	725	798	993
Production	140.00 lac mts.	169.24 lac mts.	222.49 lac mts.
SHG formation	61 SHG, 700 beneficiaries	196 SHG, 2240 beneficiaries	272 SHG, 2800 beneficiaries
Credit cards	1882 submitted in banks, 267 sanctioned	4632 submitted in banks, 746 sanctioned	2700 submitted in banks, 890 sanctioned
Employment	62511	64704	64730
Manpower trained	1388	1530	2036
Trained women	589	933	1020
Operational loomage	20532	21568	21910
Women oper. loomage	10601	10804	11264
Total man-days generated	46,47,370	64,70,400	66,51,750
Govt. supply (man-days)	456300	819900	974020

Source: Madhya Pradesh Handicraft and Handloom Development Corporation, 2007.

2.5 Main Handloom-based Textile Production Clusters

The status of the main handloom-based textile production clusters as on 31st March 2008 is presented in Table 11.6. The table indicates that Chanderi, Maheshwar, Padhana (Sarangpur) and Gwalior clusters are the bigger clusters in terms of the total number of looms. The ratio of women weavers is almost half to one-third of the total weavers in the listed clusters.

2.5.1 Handloom Clusters

The major handloom clusters in Madhya Pradesh are discussed in detail below:

TABLE 11.6

Status of Main Handloom-based Textile Production Clusters as on 31st March 2008

Main Handloom Clusters	*Total Looms*	*Working Looms*	*Total Weavers Working*	*Women Weavers*
Chanderi	3729	3377	10131	4052
Maheswar	1658	1533	4599	1840
Sausar	700	464	1392	460
Waraseoni	618	383	1149	492
Padhana and Sarangpur	2044	744	2232	893
Ashta	1564	525	1575	630
Mandsaur	885	595	1785	714
Neemuch	764	118	354	142
Gwalior	2061	1383	4149	1660
Sidhi	1408	935	2805	1122
Total	15431	10057	30171	12005

Source: Directorate of Handloom and Handicraft M.P. Rural Industries, Bhopal.

i. Waraseoni Cluster: The Waraseoni cluster is situated in Balaghat district of Madhya Pradesh. It is one of the famous handloom clusters in Balaghat, like other clusters Maheshwar in Khargone and Chanderi in Guna district of MP. It is famous for its own quality and brand all over the country.

ii. Padhana-Sarangpur Cluster: It is one of the oldest clusters situated in Rajgarh district of MP. Muslims have been and are still the main weavers here since Mughal rule in India. At that time, they were weaving *rupmati, safa and pagari.* In 1954-55, they started cotton sari weaving and after some time (about 1970-1980), they were weaving *Janta* saris. At present, about 250 weavers in Padhana and 500 weavers in Sarangpur are working and are involved in weaving of *tericot* suiting, bed sheet for govt. supply, sprung cloth. The raw material (sized, long yarn) supply for the cluster comes from Indore and Ahmedabad. The Padhana cluster was famous for its expertise in bed sheet designing; its market demand was also high. After some time, due to lack of new design input, the market went down. Between the period of 1975-1980, most of the weavers connected with the traders of Kota, Rajasthan and were involved in *Kota jari* sari weaving.

iii. Khilchipur-Mandsaur Cluster: It is also one of the old clusters and currently 3-4 hundred weavers are involved in weaving of blankets, medical bed sheets and other cotton bed sheets.

iv. Gwalior Cluster: The weavers in and around Gwalior are not locals; they come from Mauranipur, UP. The cluster has not much importance.

v. Maheshwar Cluster: Maheshwar on the banks of Narmada, is an important centre. The *Maheshwari* sari, mostly in cotton and silk, is characterised by its simplicity. The body is either chequered, plain or has stripes, combined with complementary colours. The reversible border of the saree which can be worn either side, is a speciality. It has a variety of leaves and flowers on the border, in *karnphool* pattern, which is quite popular. The palla of *Maheshwari* sari is also distinctive with five stripes, three coloured and two white alternating. Nowadays, these saris are made in natural and artificial silk as well. The cluster size is increasing in order and currently, thousands of weavers are involved in weaving numbers of product like *Maheswari* sari, tissue sari (*zari* + cotton), and other dress materials. They are using good quality raw material as compared to other clusters.

vi. Chanderi Cluster: It is one of the biggest and oldest clusters in MP and currently, 3000 weavers are involved in weaving number of products like *Chanderi* sari and other dress materials. They have good market linkage.

2.5.2 Types of Prints

Apart from handlooms, connected with cloth-based handicrafts, there are certain other products of the state which need to be mentioned here to complete the picture of handicraft-based textiles.

i. Hand Block Printing: Hand block printing is among the important crafts of Madhya Pradesh. The popular colours used in this process are vegetable and natural dyes like indigo, turmeric roots, pomegranate skin, lac, iron, and other substances that create an effect that is rich yet subtle. The Malwa and Nimar regions are renowned for their hand block printed cotton textiles. Bherongarh near Ujjain, has large printer communities who specialise in *lugda, jajams, oudhnis* and quilts. Today in Bherongarh, a range of hand block-printed products like saris, *dupattas*, dress material, bed sheets, pillow covers, table cloths are available. Jawad specialises in *Nandana* prints which consist of traditional motifs in fast colours. In Tarapur and Umedpur, indigo is still used in printing.

The printed textiles of Bagh located in the Dhar district of Madhya Pradesh, are the *piéce de résistance* of hand block printing. The printers of Bagh as well as Kukshi and Manawar use vegetable and natural dyes, specially extracted from roots of *aal* or madder. These prints have a tonal and a three-dimensional effect which is impossible to replicate in the screen printing or machine printing process. Bagh printing—a connoisseur's choice, has become a national and international favourite. The other important printing centres in the state are Indore and Tarapur and Jawad in Neemuch.

ii. Tie & Dye: The art of tying and dyeing fabric is known as *Bandhani* or *Bandhej* in Madhya Pradesh. This delicate technique represents the earliest forms of resist patterning. In this process, parts of the fabric are tied with thread or twined into minute knots and then dipped in dye. Mandsaur produces excellent *bandhanis*. In Indore and Ujjain also, craftspersons produce exquisite samples of tie and dye.

iii. Batik: Batik is a resist process in which the fabric is painted with molten wax and then dyed in cold dyes. *Batik* is done on a large scale in Indore and Bherongarh. Multi-coloured and variously designed *Batik* saris are popular and attractive for their contrast colour schemes. Apart from saris, dress material, bed sheets, *lungis, dupattas* etc., are also made here.

3. Promoting Handloom Sector

Design and material used in different Handloom products have undergone change over a period of time but has not lost its charm of traditional value and does have a strong demand in domestic as well as international market. Textile weaving in Madhya Pradesh is as refined as the hand printing craft. Thousands of craftsmen practice hand printing, generally with vegetable dyes at a string of hand printing centres- Jawad, Bhairongarh, Mandsaur, Umedpura, Burhanpur, Bhopal, Indore, Gotampura, Sohawal and Tarapur. Handloom products like Sari, dress material, garments, bedspreads, tablecloths and curtain material quilt covers, *lungis, oudhnis, jajams* (floor coverings), carpets and *zari*-embroidery are the famous and popular ones.

The raw material (sized, long yarn) is sourced from mills of Indore, Ahmedabad and Coimbatore. Unlike earlier times, local dyeing at the cluster/village level has stopped. The traditional handloom clusters of Maheshwar and Chanderi have grown and are thriving. There are around 3,000-5,000 weavers in business in each cluster, and the traditional skills and craftsmanship have survived and developed over time. Products like saris and dress material are now made out of a variety of material like cotton, tissue (*zari* + cotton), silk, synthetic-blends, etc. They are using good quality of raw material compared to other clusters. Yarn is sourced from Maharashtra and Tamil Nadu.

Silk yarn produced from mulberry cocoon within the state is being used in different silk weaving clusters. *tussar* silk produced in MP, is also known by its Sanskrit name '*kosa*'. Tasar production being promoted in Balaghat, Mandla, Shahdol, Seoni, Dindori, Hoshangasbad, Betul, Chhindawara, Jabalpur, Jhabua etc., and mulberry cultivation in Hoshangabad, Harda, Betul, Narsinghpur, Vidisha, Rajgarh, Balaghat, Mandla etc., districts of Madhya Pradesh.

Larger, well-off weavers have good private market tie-ups, but the smaller weavers have marketing problems, particularly in the off-season. At least 75 per cent of the produce is bought/sold in the open market involving businessmen who are into wholesale and/or retail trade. Some traders provide yarn on credit to the weavers, who in turn sell back the produce to them. In such cases, the weavers get their piece-rates or wages. At most around 25 per cent of the produce is procured by the state government agencies. A third, very small channel is that of weavers selling directly to buyers at trade fairs (melas) held in larger cities and metros. In most cases, these promotional exhibition-cum-sales are organised by the state government agencies of national and state level. In the other 4-5 smaller, poorer clusters, the government is a big procurer of items such as bed sheets, gauze bandages, etc., for government supply, hospital supply etc. Handloom products are also marketed through showrooms owned by various state government undertakings located at various places in the country as well as through organising/participating in exhibitions. In order to provide marketing support to the handloom weavers, State Government is running 20 emporiums, out of which 10 are located outside the Madhya Pradesh. These emporiums organise more than 40 exhibitions-cum-sales every year and the handloom products of the state. Municipal corporations in Gwalior and Bhopal have established permanent urban haats, where the artisans and weavers can sell their produce on rotation basis directly to the consumers.

Government is also promoting sericulture development activities in the state with special focus on Mandla, Balaghat, Jabalpur, Katni, Shahdol and Narsinghpur, where Saja/Arjun cultivation for *tussar* silk and mulberry cultivation for mulberry silk is promoted.

In 2007-08, 231.52 lakh metre handloom was produced. In 2007-08, HSVN supplied handloom clothes worth Rs. 469.98 lakh to various government departments and provided employment to 4074 weavers.

TABLE 11.7

Budgetary Provision: Madhya Pradesh Khadi & Village Industries Board

			Financial Year 2006-07		
1	(a)	**State Government-**			
		1. Plan	Rs. 660.61 lakh		
		2. Non-Plan	Rs. 178.14 lakh		
		3. State Share-Vindhya Valley Project	Rs. 63.75 lakh		
		Total	Rs. 902.50 lakh		
	(b)	Central govt. assisted schemes-Margin Money	Rs. 716.36 lakh		
	(c)	Central govt. assisted schemes-Vindhya Valley	Rs. 191.25 lakh		
		Grand total	Rs. 1810.11 lakh		
2		**Production**			
	(a)	*Khadi*	Rs. 300.00 lakh		
	(b)	Village industries	Rs. 200.00 lakh		
		Total	**Rs. 500.00 lakh**		
3		**Marketing**			
	(a)	*Khadi*	Rs. 330.00 lakh		
	(b)	Village industries	Rs. 220.00 lakh		
		Total	Rs. 550.00 lakh		
4		**Training**			
	(a)	Financial	Rs. 31.01 lakh		
	(b)	Physical	1400 beneficiaries		
5		**Employment**	**Total**	**Female**	**Male**
	(a)	Production centre	1200	900	300
	(b)	Margin Money	7600	3800	3800
	(c)	Household-centric	7000	3500	3500
	(e)	Vindhya Valley	600	300	300
		Total	16400	8500	7900
6		**Special Projects**			
	(e)	Vindhya Project	480.00 lakh (Total sales target) & 40 new self-help groups		

Source: Madhya Pradesh Khadi and Village Industries Board.

The budget shows a provision of Rs. 300 lakh for supporting the production of *khadi* in Madhya Pradesh and a provision of Rs. 330 lakh to support marketing of the *khadi* produced in Madhya Pradesh.

The production of mulberry and tasar cocoon beneficiaries benefited as well as budgetary allocation for sericulture during 9th and 10th five year plan period is shown in the table below.

Traditional textile printing and dyeing clusters are located in different parts of Malwa and Nimar regions of MP. The hand-block printed textiles of Bagh are famous for the use of vegetable and natural dyes with colours derived from indigo, turmeric roots, pomegranate skin, lac, iron, etc. These natural colours do not fade easily, permeate the fabric and lend it an attractive look. Bherongarh near Ujjain has large printer communities who specialise in *lugda, jajams, oudhnis* and quilts whereas Jawad (Neemuch) specialises in Nandana prints. Mandsaur produces excellent *bandhanis*. In Indore and Ujjain craftspersons produce tie-and-dyed fabrics. *Batik* is done on a large scale in Indore and Bherongarh. Bhopal has a cluster famous for *zardozi* work on textiles. Intricate and traditional beadwork of the tribal women in Jhabua is now being taken up on textiles too.

TABLE 11.8

Production of Mulberry and *Tussar* Cocoon and its Beneficiaries

Sr. No.	*Plan Period*	*Expenditure (Rs. in lakh)*	*Production of Cocoon*		*Beneficiaries*
			Mulberry (in MT)	*Tussar (lakh kahan)*	
1	IXth Plan	1995.31	255.80	16629	20849
2	Xth Plan	2899.09	718.80	58762	58596

Source: Directorate of Sericulture, GoMP.

The performance of MP State Sericulture Development and Trading Co-operative Federation Ltd since 2001 is shown in the table below:

TABLE 11.9

Performance of MP State Sericulture Development

(In Rs. lakh)

Year	*Purchase*	*Sale*	*Net Profit*
2001-02	68.86	95.28	2.05
2002-03	72.78	73.71	5.21
2003-04	86.42	108.89	3.70
2004-05	125.44	123.94	2.83
2005-06	164.19	261.32	2.52
2006-07	200.32	194.32	2.70
2007-08	278.05	221.54	4.82

Source: Economic Survey, GoMP, various years.

In order to generate more demand for the products of handloom sector Department of Rural Industries is playing major role in collaboration with NABARD, Ministry of Micro, Small and Medium Enterprises. The strategy for development of handloom sector comprises of expansion of handloom industry, training of weavers and non-weavers for skill up gradation, improving quality and design of handloom cloth, providing modernized handlooms and developing entrepreneurship qualities among weaver community. State Government has also initiated some of the welfare schemes in order to increase the productivity of the weavers through congenial working environment and infrastructure facilities. In order to support handloom industry handloom cloth is being used in the Government departments.

4. Market Profile in Madhya Pradesh

Shopping for handicrafts and handlooms in Madhya Pradesh is a classic experience. Almost everywhere in the state there is a dual choice between old *bazaars* where shops 'specialise' in offering certain items, and modern streamlined shopping centres which tend to stock a 'cosmopolitan' range of goods. The older shopping centres in Madhya Pradesh have retained the lingering ambience of a bygone age. There is a hustle and bustle in the teeming *bazaars* and narrow bylanes but once inside a shop, the trader or shopkeeper displays an abundance of courtesy without a mite of impatience as one goes through the wares haggling and bargaining.

4.1 Bhopal

The *chowk*, which forms the heart of the old city, is a fascinating shopping centre. Old mosques and *havelis* around the area are reminders of a splendid past while the shops in the narrow alleyways are the storehouses of traditional crafts that entice the shoppers. One can also get delicately embroidered cushions and velvet purses, exquisite silver jewellery and exotic *zari* borders out here.

And if one has time for a quick shopping spree, s/he should head towards the modern, streamlined shopping centres. The Madhya Pradesh State Emporium with its range of handicrafts at fixed prices is situated here.

4.2 Indore

The city of Indore is a shopper's delight. Its oldest market, the Maharaja Tukoganj cloth market, popularly known as MT market, has a range of fabrics that could warm the heart of a princess. The famous *Maheshwari* saris with their distinctive borders and the prized *Chanderi* saris can be found here. Brocades and *zari* work in a host of designs charm the senses. Jail Road and the Topkhana rank as the second oldest markets in Indore. Smocking done at nearby Mhow can be found here, along with an assortment of handicrafts that range from the odd tribal mementos to utilitarian papier-mâché articles, terracotta pieces and wood-carved objects.

The old market at Rajwara has a predominance of traditional fabrics, while the Bara Sarafa and the Chotta Sarafa offer an impressive array of jewellery. A branch of the Madhya Pradesh State Emporium is also located in Indore.

4.3 Ujjain

In the holy city of Ujjain, beautifully carved objects such as penholders, glasses, plates, images of gods and goddesses are carved in stone with delicate hues ranging from pale green to rich, creamy brown. These can be bought along with papier-mâché articles, lacquerware and beadwork from the numerous stalls and shops outside the Mahakal Temple and in the small *bazaar* at Ujjain.

4.4 Gwalior

Perhaps the oldest *bazaars* in Madhya Pradesh are in Gwalior. In the lanes near the *chowk* at Bara, shopkeepers claim a lineage that dates back several centuries. *Chanderi* saris can be found here, along with choice fabrics with a traditional weave. The shops near Rajwara and Laskar, particularly at Patankar Bazaar, offer a mix of arts and crafts that are native to Gwalior. These include dolls, lacquerware, hand-woven carpets, wall hangings in the Gwalior style of painting, jewellery and crafts from other centres in Madhya Pradesh. The State Emporium is located at Sarafa Bazar, Gwalior.

5. Related and Supporting Industries

Handlooms are affected by a large range of promotional efforts by both national and state government. The support is through protective and promotional policies and schemes, through promoting other organisations, as well as running their own organisations. The state government's promotional activities are mainly through:

MP Hast Shilp Vikas Nigam (HSVN): Imparts basic and advanced training to unemployed/underemployed and traditional crafts persons, provides advanced tools at subsidised rates, technical and design guidance through 31 development centres. Marketing support is through its network of 20 emporia under the brand name Mrignayanee, as well as through exhibitions. Among the different state government agencies of all sectors, HSVN today accounts for the largest share of exports. More than 60 per cent is handlooms/textiles and 40 per cent is handicrafts. HSVN has its units in handicraft/handloom clusters. It is attempting wider collaborations with quasi-government, NGO and private agencies, such as with the National Institute of Fashion Technology (NIFT), Handloom Export Promotion Council and Export Promotion Council for Handicraft (HEPC and EPCH).

MP Powerloom Weavers Co-operative Federation Ltd.: It supplies raw material to poor powerloom weaver through the society and procure their products. The Federation has nine sale depots in various cities in MP. It also supplies cloth to state agencies and consumer federations all over India.

Roopmati Handlooms: During the 1970s-1980s, many handloom weaver societies were formed at the primary level and federated at the state level under Roopmati Handlooms. At one time, Roopmati Apex Handloom Weaver Society used to actively procure and sell from hundreds of weavers in many clusters but this has fizzled out. It has showrooms in large cities of MP.

MP Sericulture Development and Trading Co-operative Federation Ltd.: It is promoting sericulture (both mulberry and non-mulberry silk) through a gamut of activities. This includes marketing of produce on co-operative basis, organising cocoon production, collection, processing, yarn/cloth production, research and development. With an assistance of Rs. 749 crore from Overseas Economic Co-operation Fund (OECF), a comprehensive sericulture modernisation plan to benefit 50,000 families is being implemented by the federation.

Khadi and Village Industries Board (KVIB): Special efforts are being made by the state government and KVIB to promote *khadi* production and sale. Weaver societies are being encouraged to take to *khadi* weaving.

Some NGOs are also involved in research and development in the handloom sector. Some examples are: Rehwa Society, Maheshwar, Khargone district, they have been effectively involved in design and market development of Maheshwar weavers and promotion of the cluster for many years. Lupin is involved in the Technology Resource Centre at Sarangpur (Rajgarh) handloom cluster. Development Alternatives (DA) is engaged in research and development on silk weaving and improving the TARA loom in traditional weaving clusters of MP. DA is also working on *ahimsa* silk.

6. Some of the Key Initiatives by the State Government in 2007-08

- Promoting artisan participation in international festivals; tapping market access for direct artisans.

- To provide infrastructural facilities to Chanderi cluster, a DPR of Rs. 19.50 crore under Industrial Infrastructure Upgradation Scheme (IIUS) has been prepared and submitted to Govt. of India, Ministry of Commerce & Industries. Govt. of India has sanctioned a project of Rs. 27.45 crore and released the first instalment of Rs. 578.74 lakh.
- Under the Govt. of India's scheme, documentation of handlooms/handicrafts as living heritage in Sarangpur, Maheshwar and Saunsar.
- Support to weavers by procuring orders for supply of cloth required by different government departments. Orders worth Rs. 1323.00 lakh were received from health, medical education, forest, police, revenue, labour, home guards, tribal welfare, school/higher education and other departments. Thus, 10.00 lakh man-days were created.
- Organised two state-level fairs at Delhi and Mumbai.
- Organised 10 district-level and state-level fairs and exhibitions for marketing of handloom and handicraft products.
- 272 SHGs (2800 beneficiaries) were formed. Organisation of weavers/artisans at the cluster level into cluster clubs to enable them to access and share collective resources.
- Professional development of managers: 58 officers were trained on different subjects organised by the State Academy of Administration.
- Special project being implemented through Project Design and Product Development Project through NIFT for Saunsar and Sarangpur handloom cluster.

7. Handloom Development Scheme

Under the 11th Five Year Plan, modified Handloom Development Scheme has been introduced in place of State Project Package Scheme. Under this scheme, assistance has been provided to primary weavers co-operative societies/SHGs/entrepreneurs and individual handloom weavers. The following financial assistance is included:

1. Basic training;
2. Skill upgradation scheme (weaving/dying/designing);
3. Pre-loom and post-loom facilities (for new looms Jacquard-Dobby, dyeing and processing equipment);
4. Marketing assistance (to organise district/divisional level events, participation in state and national metros, participation expenses for two persons in state or outside state exhibitions and export exhibitions for sample display);
5. Organising health and education awareness camps;
6. Working capital to enhance borrowing capacity from the bankers. Under the aforesaid scheme, assistance can be obtained through district handloom officers/district rural development officer.

In order to strengthen the institutional support to the weavers, the state government has charted out the following action plan.

a) Structural Support to Weavers

- Organise weavers into collective entities for better access to resources, stronger production base and Negotiating space. Set up weavers' cluster clubs.
- Develop weavers' cluster resource centres for establishing and managing common resources and activities. Also to synergies production and training on-site.
- To establish basic requirements and infrastructure for pre- and post-loom facilities.

b) Capacity Building

- Project-based entrepreneurship development programmes for generic managerial skills in weavers through a mutual learning system that is participatory and on-site.
- Participatory action research for concurrent critical analysis of the project inputs and outcomes to improve quality consciousness.

c) Promotion and Documentation Support

- Facilitate global-local exhibitions for awareness generation, mutual learning and appreciation.
- Develop and promote handlooms and handicrafts as living heritage. A fundamental shift in the paradigm by adoption of cluster approach.
- Multi-media resources to document key initiatives as case studies for further learning and improvement.

- Develop a design studio and virtual design gallery.

d) Improve the Physical Environment of Worksites

- Physical infrastructure development on a need basis to be taken up largely through co-ordination of resources with other development agencies.

e) Convergence and Co-ordination

- Improve access to social services like functional literacy and basic health.
- With technical resource support agencies: Weavers service centre (WSC) for training.
- With market promotion agencies: The Handicrafts and Handloom Exports Corporation (HHEC), Central Cottage Industries Emporium, NIFT.
- With social services: Health, education with development programmes, tourism, rural development.
- With heritage conservation: Culture, archaeology.
- With horticulture/agri-business for incremental income through Gramodyog Plus.

f) Operational Plan

- Implementing a 'Weavers Package' in focus clusters on a pilot basis.
- Select a few clusters as focus clusters for weavers package.
- Twinning of clusters (global-local, local-local) for mutual support and value addition.
- Eleven handloom clusters—Chanderi, Maheshwar, Saunsar, Waraseoni, Padhana, Sidhi, Sarangpur, Ashta, Mandsaur, Neemuch and Gwalior selected on basis of potential resources for integrated production to market inputs. Two clusters in tribal areas.
- Three value addition clusters: Bagh and Jawad for vegetable dyeing. Hoshangabad, Bhopal for hand embroidery.
- Weavers 'cluster club' (A self-help group of about 10-20 member-weavers) in each cluster to be the main implementing agency. Selection of weavers on criteria of 'skill and need', i.e., weavers who have skills but for want of resources do not have sufficient work, and have not been able to keep pace with technology, market demand with adverse effect on their livelihood opportunities. Emphasis on women's participation.
- Set up weaver cluster resource centres to be managed by weaver cluster clubs for receiving, developing, demanding and managing common resources—funds, professional services, technical inputs.
- Federate weaver cluster clubs at the state level into a cluster development agency (CDA) to ensure structural support for effective, sustainable initiatives. WCDA will be part of the handloom directorate and help in additional resource mobilisation, canalising resource support and resource convergence, networking, facilitating public-private partnerships.
- Identify professional resource support agencies as per needs: production, training and entrepreneurship development, costs and marketing. Enter into partnership with professional bodies to help designing and marketing.
- Allocate and transfer funds to implementing/ supportive agencies.
- Conceptualisation of design and product diversification.
- Initiate technical improvement in production equipment and processes. Procurement of raw materials.
- Training and orientation.
- Prototype development; initiate promotional activities.
- Documentation.
- Test market of sample products, expose weavers to global markets.
- The above steps to form a continuous cycle of 'production to market to production' process with built-in follow-up and corrective measures.
- Handloom directorate to nodalise, co-ordinate review and evaluate (funds, professional services, technical inputs, production support, market intelligence and participation, capacity development, partnerships).
- Income from the sales proceeds will be transferred to the weavers cluster clubs so as to form a corpus of funds for rotation.
- The effort would be to encourage direct interface between weavers and market agencies so that over a period of time, the weavers develop as entrepreneurs and can access institutional credit

with increasing strength. This will enable the SHGs to evolve into micro-credit groups and then SMEs with decreasing dependence on subsidies.

- For other clusters, extend support through ongoing schemes like Integrated Handloom Training Programme, Handloom Development Scheme etc.

8. Strategy for Madhya Pradesh

a. Thriving clusters like Chanderi and Maheshwar need to be taken to a higher order of development. For this, the first step should be to change the promotional strategy followed hitherto, focusing on individual weavers and subsidies and using public sector institutions. Instead of looking at traders and entrepreneurial weavers as "exploiters", they should be seen as vectors of growth and means of adaptation of the produce to a constantly changing market. The new strategy should be built around the private sector.

b. To promote the sector, a concerted attempt should be made to establish industry associations. For this, selected organisations, such as marketing and technical consultancy organisations, entrepreneurship development agencies and NGOs that have a commercial orientation and track record, need to be invited to work in the clusters. Agencies with special competence and appropriate programmes, especially UNIDO, SBI and UPTECH should be brought in and SIDBI's experience in cluster development should be harnessed.

c. Market development and promoting products in newer market segments through new designs and wider end-use of the fabric should be an ongoing process required for all clusters, in order to diversify and develop new markets. For example, embellishing fabrics with *zardozi* and beadwork is in vogue. Within MP itself, Bhopal (*zardozi*) and Jhabua (beadwork) offer crafts resource-base of a high quality. Fabrics can be designed and put to more end-uses and types of garments apart from the usual saris and dress material. Examples are using for furnishings, modern garments, handicrafts etc. Promotional agencies should promote textile and garment designing with beadwork, *zardozi*, block printing, traditional painting styles, etc., through designers within and outside MP. For the above to happen, designers from institutes like NIFT/NID should be invited to work collaboratively in these clusters. However, instead of their being hired by government agencies, the funding to hire designers should be provided to the nascent industry associations.

d. Regarding marketing facilities for artisans, the MPHSVN is unable to handle all the volumes that artisans can produce. A more effective marketing linkage is required and in this the role of market-savvy NGOs such as Saarthi, Wal-Mart, Dastakaar Haat etc., can be utilised. These agencies can be persuaded to open local linked agencies or offices and assist through their existing networks and knowledge of handloom marketing.

e. An important contribution to weaver's direct welfare can be provision of micro finance for them. Towards this, using the existing promotional structure of state government and NGOs wherever they have linkages with weavers for organising weavers into self-help groups will be very effective. These can be done with institutional arrangements with NABARD, SIDBI and local banks.

f. Among the declining clusters such as Waraseoni, the ones with most potential should be taken up one-by-one for focused, sustained and concerted investment of resources and promotion activity. Once again, the revival based on tradition should be seen as a second step and instead, the first step should be to link the surviving weavers to markets for products, which are in demand. Once the cluster revives and re-establishes market links, some of the traditional products may also find a market.

g. To help weavers overcome their dependence on traders for input supply and buy-back, arranging for micro finance would improve their returns. Thus, established micro credit organisations can be invited to work in the weaving clusters.

9. Road Ahead

a. The handloom sector contributes substantially to the total cloth production in the country. In addition, it provides employment to about 66,000 persons in the state as per 2006-07 data. Madhya Pradesh has established and thriving handloom clusters. There is a need to further strengthen these clusters and develop other clusters in the state.

b. Handlooms can be an effective source of livelihood for women. Women weavers should be promoted in the profession. The skill trainings should target more and more number of women weavers.

c. The handloom products are much in demand and have been well marketed by various government initiatives like Mrignayanee etc. To increase the market for handloom products, there is a need to further diversify the product range with support from design institutions, marketing agencies etc. The current links and future collaborations should explore the scope and arenas where handloom products can be better placed. Product diversification would support in developing new markets and catering to newer market segments.

d. Madhya Pradesh has many thriving clusters in the handloom sector. There is a need to identify more clusters and select organisations with proven track record to develop these clusters like UNIDO, SIDBI, different NGOs etc.

e. The weaving community is often limited by the financial constraints. The existing promotional structure of state government and NGOs wherever they have linkages with weavers for organising them into self-help groups will be very effective. Micro finance support through NGOs, micro finance institutions can also play an effective role.

Chapter 12

Health in Madhya Pradesh—A Major Development Challenge

1. Introduction

Being physically healthy is of prime importance in life. Being ill or not feeling well can drastically affect one's work. Obviously, if one feels physically and mentally healthy, s/he can be more productive. That is the reason why public health has been assumed to be one of the important social sectors. It ultimately reflects in terms that healthy society will lead to a healthy nation.

According to the population census of India 2001, total population of Madhya Pradesh, after carving out the state of Chhattisgarh is around six crore. Urban population in the newly formed state was 26.7 per cent. Scheduled tribe and scheduled caste population in the state constitute 20.3 per cent (25.8 per cent rural, 4.9 per cent urban) and 15.2 per cent (15.6 per cent rural, 14.0 per cent urban) respectively. With low density of population (196 persons per square kilometres) compared to density of population at national level (324 persons per square kilometres), the state for the first time has shown a declining trend in the growth of population (2.2 per cent per annum) as may be seen from Table 12.1.

TABLE 12.1

Population (Actual and Projected) and Growth Rate—Madhya Pradesh

Population	*1991*	*2001*	*2005*	*2010*	*2015*	*2020*
Population, actual and projected	4.86	6.04	6.90	7.84	8.87	9.99
Growth rate per annum projected for next five years		2.70%	2.60%	2.50%	2.40%	2.53%

Source: Census of India, 2001.

The geographical vastness of the state and its social, cultural and economic diversity demand substantial inputs for healthy level of living including health. The state has large forest area and concentration of tribal population in around 1800 forest villages within or in the periphery of forests.

The health centres planned and established on population norms are spatially difficult to access due to sparsely located population. Infrastructure for health care delivery in the state, therefore, is not adequate enough to meet out the health needs of the people in an efficient and cost-effective manner. Thus, the most daunting challenge before Madhya Pradesh is the delivery of effective public health services.

Several national level evaluations have shown that Madhya Pradesh along with Orissa are two among the major states of India that have very poor record on different indicators of health and health needs. However, the cumulative outcome of multiple initiatives that have happened in the state in the area of women empowerment, female literacy, girl's education and political decentralisation has started resulting in improvement to some extent in the health indicators.

2. Indicators on State of Health

Life expectancy at birth, that is, the number of years a newborn is expected to live at the time of his or her birth, is the most comprehensive indicator of health from the point of longevity. It is different for different ages, and also changes over time, with improvement in medical and health systems. A better health status can be safely assumed to give a better life expectancy to people. However, the health situation in Madhya Pradesh is very poor. The latest estimate for life expectancy at birth in Madhya Pradesh is 58 years for the period 2002-2006 and this was the lowest amongst all major states in India and a good five years lower than the national average, as may be seen in Table 12.2.

TABLE 12.2

Life Expectancy at Birth, 1993-1997 and 2002-2006

States	*Life Expectancy at Birth 1993-1997*			*Life Expectancy at Birth 2002-2006*		
	Male	*Female*	*Total*	*Male*	*Female*	*Total*
Andhra Pradesh	61.2	63.5	62.4	62.9	65.5	64.4
Assam	56.6	57.1	56.7	58.6	59.3	58.9
Bihar	60.4	58.4	59.6	62.2	60.4	61.6
Gujarat	60.9	62.9	61.9	62.9	65.2	64.1
Haryana	63.7	64.6	64.1	65.9	66.3	66.2
Karnataka	61.8	64.9	63.3	63.6	67.1	65.3
Kerala	70.4	75.9	73.3	71.4	76.3	74.0
Madhya Pradesh	55.6	55.2	55.5	58.1	57.9	58.0
Maharashtra	64.1	66.6	65.5	66.0	68.4	67.2
Orissa	57.1	57.0	57.2	59.5	59.6	59.6
Punjab	66.7	68.8	67.7	68.4	70.4	69.4
Rajasthan	59.1	60.1	60.0	61.5	62.3	62
Tamil Nadu	63.2	65.1	64.1	65.0	67.4	66.2
Uttar Pradesh	58.1	56.9	57.6	60.3	59.5	60.0
West Bengal	62.2	63.6	62.8	64.1	65.8	64.9
All-India	60.4	61.8	61.1	62.6	64.2	63.5

Source: Economic Survey of India, 2008-09.

Over the years, life expectancy of both males and females has increased in Madhya Pradesh and India. Within the state, there are geographical differences in life expectancy, with rural life expectancy substantially less than urban life expectancy. Further, while naturally female life expectancy should be more than male life expectancy, it is the opposite case in Madhya Pradesh, pointing towards discriminatory practices against the girl child and women, leading to higher mortality than nature would otherwise determine. Therefore, equality in life expectancy of males and females in effect show that females in comparison to men do not enjoy an equal health status. It is evident from Table 12.2 that perhaps Madhya Pradesh, Bihar and Uttar Pradesh are the only states where female life expectancy is still on the lower side than its male counterpart in 2002-2006.

3. Death Rate

Over the last two decades, there has been sharp decline in death rate (number of deaths per thousand population). The death rates in rural and urban areas of Madhya Pradesh were 10.1 and 6.4 respectively in 2004 and have come down to 9.4 and 6.2 respectively in 2007. Present death rate in MP is 8.7 (per 1000) which is also higher than the national average of 7.4. MP would be the second highest following Orissa with death rate of 9.2 among the 15 major states in the country. Sex-specific death rate presented in Table 12.3 reveals that in both Madhya Pradesh as well as at all-India level, female death rate is less compared to male death rate.

TABLE 12.3

Sex-specific Death Rate

Sector		*Death Rate*					
		Male		*Female*		*Person*	
		2004	*2007*	*2004*	*2007*	*2004*	*2007*
Rural	MP	10.2	9.9	9.9	8.8	10.1	9.4
	All-India	8.7	8.5	7.6	7.4	8.2	8.8
Urban	MP	6.4	6.7	6.3	5.6	6.4	6.2
	All-India	6.1	6.5	5.4	5.4	5.8	6.0
Combined	MP	9.3	9.2	9.1	8.1	9.2	8.7
	All-India	8	8.0	7	6.9	7.5	7.4

Source: SRS, Bulletins, 2004, 2007.

4. Maternal Health

Maternal mortality rate is another area of high concern for the state of MP. The two issues, IMR and MMR are interrelated; their solutions also supplement each other. The MMR for the states per NFHS-II was 498 per lakh births. The latest data of MMR released by Registrar General of India (RGI) pertains to year 2003 that show MMR of MP as 379 per lakh births, a significant improvement from 498 but much worse than the national average of 301.

Despite improvements in the coverage of antenatal care for pregnant mothers, only 4 in 10 women in Madhya Pradesh received at least three antenatal care visits for their last birth in the past five years according to NFHS-III data. Among women who gave birth in the five years preceding the survey, almost three quarters (74 per cent) received antenatal care for their last birth from a health professional (33 per cent from a doctor and 41 per cent from other health personnel). One in five women (20 per cent) received no antenatal care. More than 9 in 10 urban women (92 per cent) received antenatal care from a health professional for their last birth, compared with 68 per cent of rural women.

Even when women receive antenatal care, they do not receive most of the services needed to monitor their pregnancy. About two in five women who received ANC had their blood pressure taken (41 per cent) or their urine tested (37 per cent). Forty-four per cent of women had their blood tested. Fifty-four per cent had their weight taken and 68 per cent had their abdomen examined.

Almost three out of every four births in Madhya Pradesh take place at home; only one in four births (26 per cent) take place in a health facility. However, the percentage of births in a health facility during the three years preceding the survey increased from 22 per cent in NFHS-II to 30 per cent in NFHS-III.

5. Infant and Child Mortality

The status of infant (children up to the age of one year) and child mortality (upto age group of 5 years) is considered to be indicators for the assessment of the state of basic health care, quality and reach of health delivery, general environment for health and facilities of crucial health determinants such as nutrition, sanitation, safe drinking water etc. It also helps as good determinants of the performance of development initiatives that focus on poverty, backwardness, gender equity and empowerment.

Infants and children up to age of five years die prematurely due to diseases such as measles, diphtheria, tetanus, diarrhoea, pneumonia etc.; due to combination of factors including poor nutrition for their mother while pregnant, lack of haemoglobin in their bodies, poor sanitation and health care conditions at birth, poor care during delivery, overall unhygienic conditions, poor level of awareness, unclean environment, poor health delivery system; and environment from which respiratory and water-borne diseases could be contacted etc. These are preventable through simple vaccination, nutritious diet and health care provisions and measures.

TABLE 12.4

Infant Mortality Rate in Madhya Pradesh and All-India

States	*Infant Mortality Rate (per 1000 live births, 2007)*		
	Male	*Female*	*Total*
Andhra Pradesh	54	55	54
Assam	64	67	66
Bihar	57	58	58
Gujarat	50	54	52
Haryana	55	56	55
Karnataka	46	47	47
Kerala	12	13	13
Madhya Pradesh	72	72	72
Maharashtra	33	36	34
Orissa	70	72	71
Punjab	42	45	43
Rajasthan	63	67	65
Tamil Nadu	34	36	35
Uttar Pradesh	67	70	69
West Bengal	36	37	37
All-India	55	56	55

Source: Economic Survey of India, 2008-09.

Madhya Pradesh ranks at the top with highest IMR 72 in 2007 among all the states. Kerala's IMR is the lowest at 13 while the national figure is 55. The high level of infant mortality rate indicates the general level of poverty and an ill-performing health system. Between 2004 and 2007, while the national IMR reduced from 58 to 55, the IMR in MP dropped from 79 to 72. Sex-specific difference separately for the rural and urban areas of MP and all-India presented in Table 12.5 reveals that in 2004, female IMR in MP was less compared to male IMR but in 2007, there is no such difference. However, in urban areas, female IMR is higher compared to male IMR which is probably resulting out of spread of illegal sex determination centres in the urban areas.

There appeared to be gradual decline up to 2004 in IMR in the state but a faster decline has been noticed in the year 2007. Compared to decline of 4 points and 3 points in rural and urban areas for males at the national level, the corresponding decline in Madhya Pradesh was 11 points and 8 points respectively. For females, compared to decline of 2 and 1 point at all-India level, the decline in MP was 3 points and 2 points respectively.

TABLE 12.5

Sex-specific Infant Mortality Rate

Sector		*Death Rate*					
		Male		*Female*		*Person*	
		2004	*2007*	*2004*	*2007*	*2004*	*2007*
Rural	MP	88	77	80	77	84	77
	All-India	64	60	63	61	64	60
Urban	MP	58	50	53	51	56	50
	All-India	39	36	40	39	40	37
Combined	MP	82	72	75	72	79	72
	All-India	58	55	58	56	58	55

Source: SRS, Bulletins, 2004, 2007.

The girl child being biologically healthier should normally survive better than the boy child which was not the case in MP as revealed by sex-specific IMR. However, the situation has changed. It has come out of a dangerous situation of male-female gap in IMR pointing against discrimination for the girl child.

Infant mortality rate categorised into early neonatal (infant deaths within first week of birth) and post neonatal (infant deaths within first month of birth) are presented in Table 12.6. As an indicator of quality and magnitude of risk faced shows that post-natal mortality rate in MP declined from 56.9 in 1980 to 30.4 in 1999.

The decline in perinatal mortality was much less, from 64 in 1980 to 56 in 1999 which means a reduction of 12.5 per cent. The situation in case of neonatal mortality compared to post-neonatal mortality as presented in Table 12.6 shows a matter of concern as any reduction in them have significant impact on survival of children.

TABLE 12.6

Mortality Rates for Different Age Groups in MP

Categories	*NFHS*	
	Phase-II	*Phase-III*
Neonatal	53.2	54.9
Post-neonatal	32	31.2
Infant	85.2	86.1

Source: NFHS II and III.

6. Immunisation

An attack on high infant and child mortality in particular has been led by programmes for universal immunisation, promoting and ensuring hygienic and safe delivery practices, promoting better natal and child care etc. However, a pathetic situation gets revealed out of the fact is that merely 40 per cent of the children in the state are recipient of full vaccination, while the national figures is 43.5 per cent. This highlights the poor health facility not only in the state but also nationwide.

BOX 12.1

Immunisation Schedule for Children

At birth	BCG
1½ months	DPT – I, Polio – I
2½ months	DPT – II, Polio – II
3½ months	DPT – III, Polio – III
9 months	Measles
18 months	DPT Booster, Polio Booster
5 years	DT

Source: Department of Public Health & Family Welfare, GoMP.

Among all the 29 states, Madhya Pradesh has the 9th lowest level of full immunisation coverage for children aged 12-23 months.

7. The Disease Burden

Exact rates of morbidity or affliction of diseases are difficult to estimate. Information on morbidity rates for diseases handled through vertical programmes of Government of India is available through their management information systems (MISs). Some of these diseases are malaria, tuberculosis, leprosy and blindness.

TABLE 12.7

Rural Persons Reporting Illness, NSS 52nd Round

	Percentage of persons reporting any ailment during the last 15 days by sex for all types of ailments		
	Male	*Female*	*Person*
India	5.4	5.7	5.5
MP	4.0	4.3	4.1

Source: "Morbidity and Treatment of Ailments", NSS 52nd Round.

Some indirect measures are available from the NFHS survey and NSS 52nd Round. NSS gives three estimates from its survey. Accordingly, nearly 1 out of every 25 persons in rural Madhya Pradesh was ill the period of 15 days preceding the survey. Applying this percentage to population size, we find that the number of ill persons at any point of time would be approximately 18 lakh in rural Madhya Pradesh. The data from NSS, however, does show that the persons reporting ailments are amongst the lowest compared to the other major states in India.

TABLE 12.8

Percentage of Spells of Ailments Treated (non-institutional) during 15 Days and Percentage Distribution of Treated Spells of Ailments by Source of Treatment in Major States

State/India	*Rural*			*Urban*		
	% of Spells of Ailment Treated	*Source of Treatment in (%)*		*% of Spells of Ailment Treated*	*Source of Treatment in (%)*	
		Government	*Private*		*Government*	*Private*
Bihar	81	5	95	88	11	89
Chhattisgarh	89	15	85	90	20	80
Kerala	87	37	63	90	22	78
Madhya Pradesh	87	23	77	95	23	77
Rajasthan	90	44	56	90	53	47
Uttar Pradesh	77	10	90	88	13	87
India	82	22	78	89	19	81

Source: NSS 60th Round, Report No. 507: *Morbidity, Health Care and the Condition of the Aged*, Jan.-June, 2004.

8. Factors Affecting Basic Health

8.1 Determinants of Health

Health is determined by many factors—personal, economic and social. It is convincingly argued that the most crucial determinant of health is poverty. We shall not dwell into poverty directly here but discuss more direct determinants of health, which are also directly associated with poverty, nutrition, sanitation, drinking water etc.

8.2 Nutrition

The nutritional status of any population is a complex and composite entity, being a reflection of the overall socio-economic status and stratification, livelihood and food security, intra-household food distribution patterns, food related practices and dietary habits. In addition, the effectiveness of various nutritional supplementation programmes, including those for micronutrient supplementation, affects the nutritional status of a community.

8.2.1 Child Nutrition

Table 12.9 throws light on the comparative nutritional status of children in MP using data for the few indicators as given by the NFHS rounds.

TABLE 12.9

Comparative Nutritional Status of Children in MP

Sector	*NFHS-II*	*NFHS-III*
Stunted (too short for age)	49	40
Wasted (too thin for height)	20	33
Underweight (too thin for age)	54	60

Source: NFHS II and III.

It is amply clear from the above table that children in MP are faring well only in one indicator. The proportion of stunted children has reduced from 49 per cent to 40 per cent between the two rounds of NFHS. Stunted growth is the reduced growth rate in human development. It is the primary manifestation of malnutrition in early childhood, including malnutrition during foetal development brought on by the malnourished mother. Children who fall below the fifth percentile of the reference population in height for age are defined as stunted, regardless of the reasons.

On the other hand, the data emerges as a contrasting scenario where the proportion of wasted (measured in terms of weight for height) and underweight (measured in terms of weight for age) children has rather increased over the previous NFHS figures. At present, 33 per cent children are wasted and around 60 per cent children are underweight in MP according to NFHS-III. Adding to the worst, the proportion of children who are anaemic in the age group 6-35 months has risen from 71.3 per cent in NFHS-II to the level of 82.6 per cent in NFHS-III. The empirical evidences unambiguously spelt out the deteriorating condition of child nutrition in MP despite the state government's make-believe estimates about malnutrition in the state.

8.2.2 Adult Nutrition

Adults in Madhya Pradesh suffer from a dual burden of malnutrition; two in five adult women and men (42 per cent) are too thin, and 8 per cent of women and 4 per cent of men are overweight or obese. Only 51 per cent of women and 54 per cent of men are at a healthy weight for their height. Undernutrition is much higher in rural areas than in urban areas. Undernutrition is especially serious among the young (particularly those in the age group 15-19), those in the lower wealth quintiles, and those belonging to scheduled tribes and scheduled castes.

On the count of global hunger index (GHI), hunger is a major threat in 33 countries says a report developed by US-based International Food Policy Research Institute (IFPRI) in 2008. The situation in these countries is either alarming or extremely alarming; world progress in hunger reduction since 1990 has been slow. The index uses a multi-dimensional approach that gives a very comprehensive picture of hunger in developing and transitional countries. GHI measures hunger on the basis of three indicators, namely child malnutrition, rates of child mortality and the number of people who are calorie-deficient. The problem of hunger is measured in five categories like low, moderate, serious, alarming or extremely alarming.

BOX 12.2

Hunger in MP

All 17 states of India have India State Hunger Index (ISHI) scores that are significantly worse than the "low" and "moderate" hunger categories. Twelve of the 17 states fall into the "alarming" category, and one—Madhya Pradesh—falls into the "extremely alarming" category. Madhya Pradesh's nutrition problems, it says, are comparable to the African countries of Ethiopia and Chad.

Source: IFPRI, 2008.

India's GHI 2008 score is 23.7 with the ranking at 66th position out of 88 countries. It is slightly better over the previous year's score of 25.03 and 94th rank out of 118 countries. These scores indicate towards little efforts made in curbing hunger and poverty in India.

Neighbouring countries like Pakistan, Sri Lanka and Nepal have faired better than India in the GHI list. The India State Hunger Index (ISHI) 2008 was constructed in a similar fashion as the GHI 2008 to allow for comparisons of states within India and for comparisons of Indian states to GHI 2008 scores and ranks for other countries. The ISHI 2008 score was estimated for 17 major states in India, covering more than 95 per cent of the population of India. ISHI 2008 scores for Indian states range from 13.6 for Punjab to 30.9 for Madhya Pradesh, indicating substantial variability among states in India. Punjab is ranked 34th when compared with the GHI 2008 country rankings, and Madhya Pradesh is ranked 82nd.

9. Household Food Expenditure

The disposable income available to a household and the related expenditure is one of the most important determinants of the quantity and quality of the household's food intake. What emerges from an all-India comparison is that Madhya Pradesh has the lowest per capita expenditure on food amongst all the Indian states. This is primarily a manifestation of widespread poverty and lack of livelihood security, and is arguably the most important factor responsible for determining the poor nutritional status of people in the state. Distribution of consumption expenditure between food and non-food items also reflects the economic well-being of the population. In general, poor households are expected to spend substantially more on food items as against the non-food items.

TABLE 12.10

Average Expenditure (Rs.) Per Person Per 30 Days on Groups of Items of Consumption

States/India	*Food Expenditure*		*Non-Food Expenditure*		*Total Consumer Expenditure*	
	Rural	*Urban*	*Rural*	*Urban*	*Rural*	*Urban*
Madhya Pradesh	234.43	336.04	202.91	457.33	437.34	793.36
Orissa	241.98	415.53	172.11	456.56	414.08	872.09
Bihar	260.59	375.49	181.9	408.53	442.49	784.02
Uttar Pradesh	280.23	364.29	257.95	462.67	538.18	826.96
Rajasthan	315.92	431.13	264.55	563.68	580.47	994.81
Gujarat	334.05	476.63	279.17	615.37	613.21	1092
Punjab	431.76	417.6	515.1	641.23	946.86	1058.82
All-India	304.6	441.48	260.1	618.68	564.7	1060.16

Source: NSS 60th Round, Report No. 505: *Household Consumer Expenditure in India, 2004.*

Despite the emergence of a number of health insurance programmes and health schemes, only 5 per cent of households in Madhya Pradesh report that they have any kind of health insurance that covers at least one member of the household (14 per cent of households in urban areas and 1 per cent of households in rural areas).

10. Availability of Food

Per capita consumption of food grains is one key indicator linked to food security. In this context, the latest NSSO report released by the Government of India on consumption patterns in India (which includes consumption on food and other essentials for life) shows a decline in levels of food consumption. Various analyses have shown that these findings actually reveal the true face of poverty elimination programmes and the result of development without protecting agriculture.

Overall, the level of food consumption in rural areas of our country is declining. In 2005-06, an average of 11.92 kg of food grain was consumed per month by a member of the family and to acquire this, the family had to spend Rs. 106.30 per month. But in 2006-07, the average food consumption came down to 11.69 kg per person (1.97 per cent decline) in the family, and the cost to acquire it had risen to Rs. 114.80 at this consumption level.

The changing consumption pattern in Madhya Pradesh in itself points towards a deep crisis of food security in the state. On an average, a person in rural Madhya Pradesh was consuming 11.48 kg food or grain per month in 2005-06 and was spending Rs. 86.46 to acquire this amount of food, but per person food consumption has declined to the level of 9.718 kg per month and shows negative change of 15.34 per cent while the expenditure level is almost the same i.e., Rs. 87.27. It clearly shows the impact of inflation on changing food consumption levels. Interestingly, Kerala people spend Rs. 83.69 on egg, fish and meat, while Madhya Pradesh's individual spends only Rs. 7.44 per month on these items. Punjab definitely spends less on food grain (Rs. 91.86) but the total expenditure on food group is Rs. 511.25 per person per month and they consume milk and milk products worth Rs. 167.24 (32.71 per cent of total food expenditure), while an individual from Madhya Pradesh spends only Rs. 44.75 per month on these items. Since Madhya Pradesh does not have such high purchasing capacity required for consumption of non-cereal food items, people have to depend mainly upon cereals. It is also serious to note that food grain production in Madhya Pradesh has declined rapidly in the last one decade. With this backdrop, low food grain consumption in Madhya Pradesh is a serious matter.

(Source: http://www.merinews.com/catFull.jsp?articleID=15772805)

11. Food Intake among Vulnerable Groups

Given this background of household food expenditure, we may briefly examine the situation of food intake by various vulnerable groups, particularly women and the tribal population, especially tribal children. The tribal or *adivasi* population of the state is especially vulnerable regarding food security and food intake, for a variety of reasons. One major factor is the process of alienation from traditional natural resources, which many such communities have undergone in the previous decades, due to various reasons such as deforestation, land degradation etc. Additional stresses due to drought may then contribute to tipping the balance critically towards severe food insecurity (see Box 12.3).

Among all the vulnerable population groups, inadequacy of protein/calorie intake is quite striking. Looking at the groups most at risk, namely the pre-school children and children below 10 years of age, we find that only about one-third of these tribal children receive a diet adequate in calories and protein. Similarly, among elder children (10-12 years) and pregnant and lactating women, only around half of the tribal population in these groups have adequate caloric and protein intake. It may be noted that an intake of less than 70 per cent of the recommended daily allowance constitutes a serious dietary deficiency. However, about one-fourth of tribal children do not receive even this bare minimum cereal intake, exposing them to the risk of severe malnutrition.

The NNMB survey shows that almost three-fourths of tribal children in Madhya Pradesh are underweight (74.1 per cent) and stunted (73.4 per cent). (This is somewhat higher than the NFHS proportions, perhaps because of sampling variation.) What is more worrisome is the very high proportion of severely underweight tribal children, at about 42 per cent, this being a group which is most vulnerable in situations of fluctuation of food supply or infectious illnesses. Similarly, a very high proportion has severe stunting (53.6 per cent).

BOX 12.3

Audit Body Criticises Madhya Pradesh for Low Nutrition Levels

Criticised by the Comptroller and Auditor General (CAG) of India for laxity in improving the nutrition levels of women and children, Madhya Pradesh has now increased its budgetary allocation to reduce malnutrition in the state. "The CAG had said that over 55 per cent of children in the state suffered from malnourishment in the year 2004-05. 'The impact of the implementation of Integrated Child Development Services was marginal on health and nutritional status of children, as more than 55 per cent of the children were malnourished in the state," stated the CAG report. The report further said: "Due to inadequate budget provision for nutrition and delay in release of funds to district offices, 52-62 per cent children and 46-59 per cent expectant and nursing mothers in the state were deprived of the nutritional support."

The state's budget for the overall development of women and children this year has gone up to Rs.5.9 billion. "This would not only help improve the socio-economic condition of women in the state but boost the physical, mental and intellectual development of children who suffer from malnutrition," the official added. Meanwhile, the CAG has also noticed instances of procurement of sub-standard nutritional food and non-observance of prescribed procedures in procurement. Besides, the implementation and monitoring of the scheme has been largely effected due to a number of posts in the department remaining vacant and improper manpower planning, said the report.

Source: *www.indiaenews.com/business*, July 28, 2006.

12. Health Infrastructure in Madhya Pradesh

The state government is the single largest health provider in Madhya Pradesh, especially when it comes to preventive care and public health issues. However, the direct role of government service providers is on a decline and a majority of people resort to private health providers, especially in rural areas for medical treatment.

Madhya Pradesh Economic Survey for 2007-08 states that there is a huge gap in the need and availability of health institutions in the state. It mentions that Government of India is still following the 1991 census indicators and because of that, the state is facing the lack of 1384 sub-health centres and 572 primary health centres. Though the state has adopted an innovative approach of mobile health dispensaries through public-private partnership and other health schemes, its impact on primary health has not been evaluated so far.

TABLE 12.11

Total Number of Health Institutions in MP

State	*No. of Blocks*	*District Hosp.*	*Civil Hosp.*	*CHC*	*PHC*	*SHC*	*Urban FW Centre*	*Urban Health Post*	*Civil Disp.*
Madhya Pradesh	313	50	56	333	1155	8860	96	80	92

Source: Administrative Report, 2008-09, Dept. of Health and Family Welfare, GoMP.

As per the norms, there should be one PHC per 20,000 people in tribal areas and 30,000 people in other areas. Similarly, there should be one SHC per 3,000 populations in tribal areas and 5,000 populations in other areas. The ground level situation of the state shows that the system is operating far below the norms. There is great shortfall of health facilities in rural areas. As per the population of MP, there is a great need to increase the facilities while the government is involved in privatisation of existing facilities which will further devoid general public from utilising them due to its cost implications.

Even if we look at the basic requirement of the health centres in terms of manpower, we will find that the health institutions in the state are under significant shortfall.

Looking at the condition, the MP government should focus on establishing more centres, allocate more budgets and employ more doctors and other staff rather than going for privatising the basic health facilities.

13. Accessibility to Health System

Accessibility and availability of health care is important for ensuring a community's general health status and reflects the coverage of health facilities. NFHS-III shows a decline in the number of people availing health facilities from public sector. In Madhya Pradesh, 62.6 per cent population generally does not use government health facilities, whereas for all-India level, the proportion is 65.6 per cent. Highest reasons for not using public health care facilities are as follows: poor quality of health care (62.9 per cent), no nearby facility (50.8 per cent), too long waiting time (26.4 per cent), non-convenient facility timings (10.0 per cent), health personnel often absent (7.7 per cent) and other reason (1.6 per cent).

14. Health Expenditure

14.1 Outlays on Health in State's Five Year Plans

Figure 12.1 portrays the share of the resource allocations to the health and family welfare in different five year plans. Trends in financial allocations to the health sector are subjected to greater degree of high fluctuations over the years. But very specifically, the allocations has come down in Xth and XIth Five Year Plans compared to IXth FYP, which is a major hindrance in providing health services to poor people and in remote areas.

TABLE 12.12

Resource Gaps in Health Facilities in the State

Particulars	*Required*	*In Position*	*Shortfall*
Health Infrastucture			
Sub Health Centre (SHC)	10402	8834	1568
Primary Health Centre (PHC)	1670	1149	521
Community Health Centre (CHC)	417	270	147
Human Resources			
Multipurpose worker (Female) ANMs at Sub centres and PHCs	9983	8718	1265
Health worker (Male) MPW (M) at sub centres	8834	4030	4804
Health assistant (Female)/LHV at PHCs	1149	741	408
Health assistant (Male) at PHCs	1149	495	654
Doctors at PHCs	1149	1042	107
Obstetricians & Gynaecologists at CHCs	270	53	217
Physicians at CHHs	270	51	219
Pediatricians at CHCs	270	66	204
Total specialists at CHCs	1080	220	860
Radiographers	270	162	108
Pharmacists	1419	603	816
Laboratory Technicians	1419	491	928
Nurse/Midwife	3039	901	2138

Source: RHS Bulletin, March 2008, MOHFW, GoI.

FIGURE 12.1

Outlays on Health in State's Five Year Plans

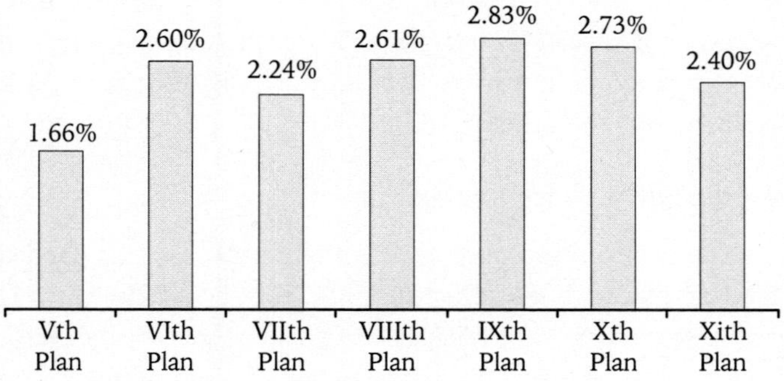

Source: State Five Year Plans, GoMP, various years.

14.2 State's Expenditure on Health

Table 12.13 gives information about the expenditure incurred by the state government on health. It is clear from the table that state government's expenditure on health as a proportion to total expenditure has declined sharply from 5.1 per cent in 2000-01 to 3.9 per cent in 2008-09. In Madhya Pradesh, public expenditure on health is just 25 per cent while out-of-pocket expenditure is one of the highest at 75 per cent.[1] Under the pressure of bilateral agencies like the World Bank and World Trade Organization (WTO), Indian government is shying away from its responsibility and exerting more pressure on people to spend on basic facilities like health. As a proportion of GSDP, the expenditure on health is not exceeding one per cent (0.93%).

TABLE 12.13

Health Budget of Madhya Pradesh Government

S. No.	*Financial Year*	*State's Expenditure on Health as a Proportion of Total Expenditure*
1	2000-01	5.1
2	2001-02	4.1
3	2002-03	4.1
4	2003-04	3.3
5	2004-05	3.1
6	2005-06	3.4
7	2006-07	3.8
8	2007-08 (RE)	3.7
9	2008-09 (BE)	3.9

Source: State budget books, GoMP for various years.

14.3 Per Capita Health Expenditure

Table 12.14 explains the per capita expenditure incurred by different states on health by diffent categories like public and out-of-pocket expenditure.

TABLE 12.14

State-wise Per Capita Expenditure on Health

State	*Per Capita Expenditure (Rs.)*	*Per cent Spent by*		
		Household	*Public*	*Other*
Andhra Pradesh	1118	73.4	19.4	7.2
Arunachal Pradesh	4365	86.5	13.5	0.0
Assam	1347	80.8	17.8	1.4
Bihar	1497	90.2	8.3	1.5
Delhi	1177	56.4	40.5	3.1
Goa	4564	79.2	17.5	3.3
Gujarat	1187	77.5	15.8	6.7
Haryana	1786	85.0	10.6	4.4
Himachal Pradesh	3927	86.0	12.4	1.6
Jammu & Kashmir	2082	77.3	20.7	2.0
Karnataka	997	70.4	23.2	6.4
Kerala	2952	86.3	10.8	2.9
Madhya Pradesh	1200	83.4	13.6	3.0
Maharashtra	1576	73.3	22.1	4.6
Manipur	2068	81.2	17.2	1.6
Meghalaya	664	36.5	58.4	5.2
Mizoram	1027	39.4	60.6	0.0
Nagaland	5338	91.7	7.6	0.7
Orissa	995	79.1	18.0	2.9
Punjab	1813	76.1	18.0	5.9
Rajasthan	808	70.0	24.5	5.5
Sikkim	2240	56.9	43.1	0.0
Tamil Nadu	933	60.7	26.6	12.7
Tripura	1101	69.0	27.4	3.6
Uttar Pradesh	1152	84.3	13.0	2.7
West Bengal	1188	78.4	17.3	4.3
Union territories	598	85.1	8.8	6.1
All-India	1377	73.5	22.0	4.5

Source: Report of National Commission on Macroeconomics and Health, Government of India, 2005.

Per capita heath expenditure in MP is Rs. 1200, out of which 83.4 per cent is incurred at the household level. When compared with the national figure at 73.5 per cent, it is very high indicating more burden on family resources and lower utility of public health facilities.

15. Rogi Kalyan Samiti

Rogi Kalyan Samitis (RKSs) are the registered societies constituted in the hospitals as an innovative mechanism to involve the people's representatives in the management of the hospital with a view to improve its functioning through levying user charges.

1. State Health Policy Draft for MP (*http://www.health.mp.gov.in*).

The state has initiated a scheme for citizen involvement in the management of state hospitals and health centres, following the successful experiment with a RKS in cleaning and refurbishing the Maharishi Yashwantrao Hospital at Indore. This scheme brings in citizen's participation in health centre management, introduces levying user charges, citizen bodies controlling user charge funds, and maintaining the health centres.

TABLE 12.15

Funds Collection by Rogi Kalyan Samitis

Year	*Income*	*Expenditure*
2000-01	3.70	2.78
2003-04	18.44	5.56
2004-05	11.59	11.36
2005-06	11.50	9.18
2006-07	12.02	10.06
2007-08	20.38	19.89

Source: Department of Health Services, Government of MP, Bhopal.

Presently, RKS has been constituted in every district/civil hospital, CHC and PHC. There are 830 RKSs functioning across the state. Income for RKS is generated through user charges or raised by citizens as donations for their hospitals and health centres. Details of income and expenditure are given in Table 12.15.

Many problems have also been identified with the RKS, but what has happened is that it has opened up the health system to the participation of people in their management, brought a sense of ownership amongst citizens; with user charges it has broken the bogey that people will not pay for good services, and has provided a system with the potential to be used to improve services of health units. It clearly shows that people's participation can definitely improve the status of public health delivery system.

16. The Institutional Response

The performance of the public health delivery system in MP faces several constraints: vacancies of staff and infrastructure gaps, particularly in the poorest 10 districts and tribal areas; lack of drugs and other essential supplies at local levels; weak implementation and monitoring systems; poor accountability of staff and low staff motivation and management capacity. The poor quality and low funding of the public health system has resulted in the growth of an unregulated and poor quality private sector. For poor households, use of the private sector has led to high out-of pocket expenditures (often pushing people further into poverty). The GoMP has taken a number of steps in the recent past to improve the functioning of the health system and facilities.

16.1 State Policies and Initiatives

The policy framework for health in MP state is guided by the national level health policies, and some specific policies and new initiatives that the state has evolved, which have a direct and indirect bearing on health. To overcome some of these constraints, the state government has undertaken some initiatives in health in the last eight years.

MP has set the example by promoting decentralised planning under Ministry of Family Health and Welfare (MoHFW)'s flagship programme, the National Rural Health Mission (NRHM). It has already signed a memorandum of understanding (MoU) with GoI, committing itself to: increasing public expenditure on health, increased decentralisation and community participation, providing funding for community level health workers and granting functional autonomy to local health facilities. GoMP is committed to improving health service delivery through improved and equitable access to quality health care especially targeted at the poor. Some of the core health strategies under the mission are as follows:

- Capacity building of Panchayati Raj Institutions (PRIs) to recognise their stakes in the public health system.
- Promote access to improved health care at household level through the accredited social health activist (ASHA).
- Promote formulation of village health plans for each village through village health and sanitation committees of the *gram sabhas*.
- Strengthening the sub-centres through better human resource development, clear quality standards, better community support and an untied fund to enable local planning and action and more ANMs.
- Strengthening existing PHCs through better staffing and human resource development policy, clear quality standards, better community support and an untied fund to enable the local management committee to achieve these standards.

- Provision of 30-50 bedded CHC per lakh population for improved curative care to a normative standard (Indian Public Health Standards (IPHS) defining personnel, equipment and management standards, its decentralised administration by a hospital management committee and the provision of adequate funds and powers to enable these committees to reach the desired levels).
- Preparation and implementation of an inter-sector district health plan prepared by the district health mission, including drinking water, sanitation, hygiene and nutrition.
- Integrating the management of vertical health and family welfare programmes at district level.
- Provisioning of technical support to state and district health missions for improved public health management.
- Strengthening capacities for data collection, assessment and review for evidence-based planning, monitoring and supervision.
- Formulation of transparent policies for deployment and career development of human resource for health.
- Developing capacities for preventive health care at all levels for promoting healthy lifestyle, reduction in consumption of tobacco and alcohol, etc.
- Promoting involvement of private and corporate non-profit sector, particularly in under-served areas.

Supplemenatry strategies would include regulation for private sector including the informal rural medical practitioners, promotion of public-private partnerships (PPP) for achieving public health.

Goals mainstreaming AYUSH (Department of Ayurveda, Yoga and Naturopathy, Unani, Siddha and Homeopathy): Revitalising local health traditions, reorienting medical education to support rural health issues, effective and visible risk pooling and social health insurance to provide health security to the poor. Besides, the state government has identified 10 districts performing poorly on the selected heath indicators which would receive special attention. These districts are Dindori, Damoh, Sidhi, Barwani, Anuppur, Chhindwara, Rewa, Betul, Raisen, Seoni, Chhatarpur, Morena and Sheopur.

The state government is implementing various innovative schemes and programme interventions to provide health facilities to the masses. The list of such schemes or programmes under various categories is as follows:

1. Maternal Health

- Vijaya Raje Janani Kalyan Beema Yojana
- Janani Express Yojana
- Janani Sahyogi Yojana
- Dhanwantari Block Development Scheme
- Prasav Hetu Parivahan Evam Upachar Yojana

2. Child Health

- Alternate Vaccine Delivery System
- Defaulter Tracking System
- Bal Shakti Yojana

3. Schemes for BPL Families

- Deendayal Mobile Hospital Scheme
- Deendayal Antyoday Upachar Yojana
- State Illnesses Fund - District Illnesses Fund

The state government is also working on improving the health status of women and children in the state through RCH-II programme with improved access and quality and special attention to vulnerable sections of the society. Some of the outcomes and goals decided under RCH-II are as follows:

TABLE 12.16

Outcomes and Goals under RCH II for MP

Outcomes	*Current Status*	*Goals for MP*	
		2007	*2010*
MMR	379	350	220
IMR	72	75	60
TFR	3.1	3.2	2.1

Source: RCH II & SRS Bulletin.

16.2 Local Helping Hand for Providing Health Care

There is another class of health providers, persons who have received some training or experience in health care, either under a government scheme, or with a field agency like Jan Swasthya Rakshak, a trained *anganwadi* worker, ASHA. They provide basic health care; look after symptoms in patients such as fever, cold, aches, injuries etc., at initial level. In case of further medical help, the patients are referred to district or state hospitals. There is no data or information available on the scale of such people or their impact on health. But in a way, it also offers an opportunity to utilise such semi-trained or oriented persons in developing a cadre of well-trained and oriented health watchers and basic service providers.

16.3 Private Health Services

Private health services dominate the health sector as far as share of patients is concerned. These are characterised by private doctor clinics and nursing home facilities in cities and towns, and small doctor clinics at town and municipal market centres and roving doctors, registered medical practitioners and footloose health service providers. Very little information is currently available about the non-government health care delivery system in the state. There has, however, been a very substantial expansion of the non-government health care delivery system in the state in recent years, especially in large urban areas. A major part of private health services providers, who are neither properly trained nor formally registered to provide health care services to the community, form a large part of the non-government health care delivery system, especially in small towns and rural areas. This quackery continues to flourish in the state because of a weak government health care delivery infrastructure and the absence of an effective mechanism to regulate. These health services providers do more harm than good to the people in terms of meeting their health needs.

There is no effective mechanism to regulate private health providers by the state or by medical associations as a self-regulatory exercise. There are very few norms existing if any, and the question of charges is normally market-based, rather than any price regime for a public utility service. The state government has a hospital regulation act that may help in regulating the non-government health sector but this act is still to be enforced because of a stay petition in the court. Very little is really known about the private health sector, apart from individual experiences and sporadic assessments.

16.4 Non-Government Organisations and Community Participation in Health Sector

The state of Madhya Pradesh has been rich in social and people's movements, which have created their own people's organisations and some very good non-government organisations across the state. There is very little organised knowledge of voluntary effort in health in the state. The state does have a long history of hospitals, dispensaries and community health care projects in the voluntary sector, which is growing over the years. Work on NGOs like Sambhavana Trust Clinic is well known in terms of their help and support to the victims of Bhopal gas tragedy. This has a large potential, which is still left relatively unexplored and could become a major partner in the people-oriented health policies of the state which seeks to empower the local elected bodies in health work. The social movements and elected local bodies are not mutually exclusive; in fact, the best agents for strengthening and sustaining local bodies are grassroot-level civil society organisations and NGOs who can act as resource/support agencies in health sector.

Community participation is one of the area negligible, if any, in the health system. The main role of community participation in Madhya Pradesh has been through the medium of the Panchayati Raj institutions. At the district level, *zila parishad* are entrusted with some responsibility of managing local health set-up and recruiting Jan Swasthya Rakshak. However, in practise, till now there has been very little interface between the health structure and people's representatives. It is only at the village level that multi-sector mandate combining health, safe drinking water, sanitation and nutrition has been entrusted to *gram panchayat*.

17. Log Frame for Medium-Term Health Sector Strategy (2006 to 2011)

The Department of Public Health and Family Welfare, Government of Madhya Pradesh has taken a decision to develop a medium-term health strategy, intended to serve the state for next five years. The situation analysis of the state has seen change in the last three years; and the state has considered all the new initiatives taken by the Government of India and the Government of Madhya Pradesh in planning the next five years' plan. This strategy would enable the government to better respond to the health needs of the population, in particular the poorest in the state.

The purpose of this medium-term health sector strategy is to set a manageable range of strategic themes related to core issues for the state department of health and family welfare over the next five years; to ensure that the department is able to deliver on its priorities; to focus its initiatives for poor and marginalised citizens in greater health need; to ensure inter-sectoral convergence that result in making government services becoming more people-oriented, effective and efficient; and to enable partners in better targeting of development assistance, increasing its synergy with government policy and making it more effective.

18. Road Ahead

"All people living in the state of Madhya Pradesh will have the knowledge and skills required to keep themselves healthy and have equity in access to effective and affordable health care, as close to the family as possible, that enhances their quality of life, and enables them to lead a healthy productive life"—State's vision on health.

TABLE 12.17

Health Care Service Delivery

Strategy	*Activity*	*Objectively Verifiable Indicators*	*Means of Verification*
Improved quality of services through appropriate staffing, infrastructure & capacity building.	• Ensuring 90% of the staff available across all cadres. • Upgrading the institutions as per population norms and package of services to be offered.	• Status of manpower. • No. of institutions established and upgraded against requirement.	• Department reports.
Promoting access to improved health care at household and community level through involvementof ASHA, PRIs, CBOs, etc.	• ASHA selected, trained and functional. • Village health plans prepared with involvement of PRI and CBOs.	• No. of ASHA functional. • Village health plans prepared.	• Department reports.
Capacity building to upgrade knowledge and skills of staff.	• Capacity building of staff across all cadres at regular intervals *viz.*, refresher, skill upgradation, etc.	• No. of capacity building sessions and staff trained.	• Training reports.
Strengthening supportive supervision, monitoring and reporting mechanism to ensure accountability and optimise outputs.	• Establishment of monitoring and evaluation cell. • Preparation of HMIS. • Establishing universal filing system (UFS). • Feedback and reporting mechanism at state & district level.	• Monitoring and evaluation cell functional. • Data collected & compiled as per HMIS. • UFS in place. • Sample checking of received reports.	• Monitoring reports. • Evaluation reports.
Introducing audits like referral audit, maternal and child death audit, medical audit, resource utilisation audit, etc., on sample basis to validate the authenticity of services.	• Formation of quality assurance team (QAT). • Establishment of audit system.	• Quality assurance team functional. • No. of audits conducted at regular intervals.	• Audit report.
Develop a drug policy to increase efficiency of procurement, streamline distribution mechanism and ensure timely supply of quality drugs in the public health system.	• Drug policy enforced. • Formation of drug corporation.	• Drug policy in place. • Drug corporation functional.	• Policy document. • GO issued. • Procurement & supply through the drug corporation.
New initiatives like introducing public health course and placement of hospital management professionals at government health facilities.	• PH course introduced. • Training of doctors in hospital administration. • Hiring of HM professional.	• No. of batches completed. • No. of doctors trained and placed. • No. of HM professionals in place.	• No. of pass outs. • Reports.
Implementation of medical insurance scheme.	• Formulation of medical insurance scheme. • Implementation of medical insurance scheme.	• No. of person benefited under medical insurance scheme.	• Government and insurance companies report.

Source: Log Frame for Medium Term Health Sector Strategy (2006-2011), Department of Public Health & Family Welfare, GoMP.

TABLE 12.18

Strengthening of Health Institutions

Strategy	*Activity*	*Objectively Verifiable Indicators*	*Means of Verification*
Equipping health institutions/ facilities through appropriate provision of manpower (for e.g. regular & contractual staffing), fiscal (for e.g. regular and untied funds) and physical resources (e.g. repair/ renovation, extension, equipments).	• Resource mapping and facility survey • Ensuring 90 per cent of the staff available across all cadres. • Upgrading the institutions as per population norms and package of services to be offered. • Supply of equipments based on facility survey and services provided by health institutions. • Upgrading community health centre to IPHS standards.	• Survey report status of sanctioned *vs.* filled positions. • No. of institutions established and upgraded against requirement. • List of equipment supplies as per norms. • No. of community health centre upgraded.	• Department reports. • Audit reports.
Introduce a logistics management system to enhance functionality of health institutions.	• Design logistic management system. • Establish LMS cell at state and district level.	• LMS operationalised at state & district level.	• Report from LMS cell.
Administrative & human resources reforms in the department, e.g., appraisal system, incentives, promotions, transfers, etc.	• HR policy revision.	• Policy document in place.	• Review/appraisal report.

Source: Log Frame for Medium Term Health Sector Strategy (2006-2011), Department of Public Health & Family Welfare, GoMP.

TABLE 12.19

Improving Maternal and Child Health Care

Strategy	*Activity*	*Objectively Verifiable Indicators*	*Means of Verification*
Improving maternal health through enhancing quality of ANC & PNC and increasing institutional deliveries.	• Skill upgradation of ANM to provide quality services at community level with involvement of ASHA and at SHC level. • Special schemes for referral transportation and cash incentives for all categories with pro-poor focus. • Availability of emergency obstetric care at health institutions within reach.	• No. of skill trainings organised. • Per cent increase in institutional deliveries. • No. of health institutions providing emergency obstetric care.	• Training reports. • Departmental report.
Improving child health to reduce mortality, morbidity and malnutrition.	• Improving quality of child health care as per New Born Care (NBC), Integrated Management of Neonatal and Childhood Illnesses (IMNCI) and Infant and Young Child Feeding (IYCF) norms. • Skill enhancement of service providers specially ANM and ASHA. • Availability of neonatal care at health institutions within reach. • Establish a functional referral system for malnourished and sick children.	• Guidelines for incorporating requisite norms. • Training calendar prepared and training started as per IMNCI norms. • Skill training of service providers organised. • No. of health institutions providing neonatal care. • Per cent increase in cases referred.	• Published & circulated. • Training reports. • Reports from health institutions.
Public-private partnership to enhance accessibility and availability of MCH services.	• Scaling up the mobile clinic scheme in remote inaccessible areas. • Accredition of private health clinics.	• No. of district with mobile clinic scheme. • No of private health clinics accredited.	• Report from partners.

Source: Log Frame for Medium Term Health Sector Strategy (2006-2011), Department of Public Health & Family Welfare, GoMP.

TABLE 12.20

Population Stabilisation

Strategy	*Activity*	*Objectively Verifiable Indicators*	*Means of Verification*
Enhancing the awareness, choice, acceptance and quality of family planning services.	• BCC activities (IEC & IPC) for socio-economic issues and utilisation of family welfare services. • Skill training of ANMs for IUD insertion and medical officers & staff nurse for injectable contraceptives on pilot basis. • Social marketing of contraceptives. • Establishing beneficiaries-oriented sterilisation ward cum counselling centres at health institutions.	• BCC activity framework. • No. of skill training of health functionaries. • No. of social marketing franchise established. • No. of wards/centres established.	• District plans. • District reports.
Strengthening the adolescent reproductive and sexual health (ARSH) services.	• Incorporating the health components/ recommendations as per National Youth Policy 2003 on pilot basis. • BCC activities for issues such as child marriage, age at marriage, RTI/STI, etc. • Establishing multipurpose youth friendly centres (YFC) at district level health institutions. • Incorporating ARSH component in school through involvement of teachers, parents and students.	• No. of pilot projects initiated. • BCC activities framework. • No. of YFC established. • No. of districts introducing ARSH education in schools.	• Reports and survey.

Source: Log Frame for Medium Term Health Sector Strategy (2006-2011), Department of Public Health & Family Welfare, GoMP.

In order to convert the vision into reality, the state government has to follow the strict action plan. Some of the relevant points in this direction would be as follows:

1. Measures should be taken to expand the health services to maximum beneficiaries and at affordable cost and improved quality.
2. Budgets to health sector should be increased substantially in order to provide satisfactory health services.
3. Need to work on various causes for low accessibility of public health services as mentioned in NFHS-III survey.
4. Shortfall of manpower has to be overcome by recruiting health professional and providing them with the incentives to work in rural areas specifically.
5. Pockets with SC and ST dominating communities as well as urban slums must be given the extra-ordinary attention.
6. There should be the better co-ordination with other departments in delivering health related services. For example, with Women and Child Development Department for implementing health related services in ICDS, with public health and engineering for water supply and sanitation related matters etc.

TABLE 12.21

Major Disease Control Programmes

Strategy	*Activity*	*Objectively Verifiable Indicators*	*Means of Verification*
Increase the involvement of community in awareness of IDSP.	• Establish and operate a central-level disease surveillance unit. • Strengthen disease surveillance at the state, district & sub-district levels. • Improve laboratory support. • Training for disease surveillance.	• Central-level disease surveillance unit is functional. • Epidemic response protocol established. • No. of blood slide collected. • No. of training conducted.	• Reports.
Increase the management capacity of NGOs involved with HIV/AIDS and blindness control programme.	• Effective implementation of the awareness programme in identified high risk areas. • Strengthening counselling centres in district hospitals. • Monitoring of NGOs activities.	• No. of cases identified. • No. of counselling cases identified. • Random sampling.	• Reports.
The malaria control programme needs to be reassessed in terms of its priorities, the data collection process and effectiveness.	• Identification of hotspot areas. • Specific plans as local needs. • Effective sample collection, testing and treatment. • Social marketing of mosquito nets. • Strengthening of data collection.	• No. of hotspots areas identified. • Plan developed. • No. of cases identified and cured. • Random cross verification of data collected.	• Reports.
The TB control programme to be strengthened and effective implementation at community level through DOTS.	• Effective IEC of DOTS for: 1. Community involvement. 2. Early detection and timely treatment.	• No. of DOTS providers. • No. of case identified and cured.	• Reports.
Improve the data collection strategy to enable accurate assessment of coverage of immunisations.	• Development of immunisation monitoring system. • Assessment of coverage of immunisation. • Regular supply of vaccine. • IEC for community mobilisation.	• MIS system in place. • Random sampling. • Vaccine is available. • No. of fully immunised children.	• MIS reports. • Field visit reports. • Reports.

Source: Log Frame for Medium Term Health Sector Strategy (2006-2011), Department of Public Health & Family Welfare, GoMP.

TABLE 12.22

Reducing Out-of-Pocket Expenditure

Strategy	*Activity*	*Objectively Verifiable Indicators*	*Means of Verification*
A public expenditure review to capture expenditure against various heads classified as fixed, semi-variable, variable; by target group (Poor/SC/ST) and by urban and rural. Health institutions to be opened according to the census population norms in the state.	• Identification and reallocation of funds available under different head. • Identification of areas for opening new centres with geographic information systems (GIS).	• Reallocation done. • GIS in place and list prepared.	• State budget. • Report and finalisation list.
Organising regular health *melas* in outreach areas.	• Calendar prepared and activity started.	• No. of health *melas* conducted.	• Monthly report.
Extending the existing pro-poor scheme like the Dindayal Antyoday Upachar Yojana (DDAUY), Janani Suraksha Yojana(JSY), Prasav Hetu Parvahn Avam Upachar (PHPAU).	• Effective implementation of pro-poor schemes. • Monitoring & feedback mechanism to be strengthened.	• No. of beneficiaries. • Random sample of reported cases.	• Reports.
New schemes for health check up, maternal & child health, adolescent reproductive and sexual health and family welfare programmes for poor, urban slums and other areas.	• Existing schemes to be reviewed and improved. • Develop new schemes as per need.	• Revised schemes in place. • No. of new schemes developed.	• GO. • State budget allocated.
Mobile units to be established between rural areas and referral centres.	• Strengthen present system. • Outreach areas identification. • PPP for effective implementation of mobile units.	• No. of fully functional mobile units. • No. of outreach areas covered. • No. of NGO involved.	• Reports. • Sample test & report.

Source: Log Frame for Medium Term Health Sector Strategy (2006-2011), Department of Public Health & Family Welfare, GoMP.

TABLE 12.23

Intersect Oral Convergence for Determinants of Health and Related Issues

Strategy	*Activity*	*Objectively Verifiable Indicators*	*Means of Verification*
Enhanced intersect oral convergence with department of W&CD (for nutrition, gender & equity issues, adolescent health etc.); Department of PHE (for environment health), DP&SW (for involvement of PRIs) and DISM (for integrating AYUSH) etc.	• Joint planning and review meeting at state level. • Specific schemes/activities designed with related departments. • Incorporating priority issues in integrated health plan. • Implementation at grassroot level through involvement of functionaries from respective departments. • Joint training of PRIs, ANM, AWW and ASHA.	• No. of review meeting organised. • No. of schemes/activities designed and implemented e.g. Bal Shakti Yojana. • Specific activities like IEC and schemes being implemented related to nutrition, determinants of health, water sanitation and ISM.	• GO issued and reports received.
NGO partnerships for community mobilisation.	• BCC (IEC/IPC) at community level on environment health, nutrition and AYUSH issues.	• No. of districts with NGO partnerships.	• NGO reports.

Source: Log Frame for Medium Term Health Sector Strategy (2006-2011), Department of Public Health & Family Welfare, GoMP.

Chapter 13

Industry in Madhya Pradesh

1. Introduction

The new state of Madhya Pradesh formed after reorganisation is the third largest Indian state covering 9.5 per cent of the country's area. The state is endowed with rich natural resources, a good climate, fertile agro-climatic conditions, good average rainfall, good central location and fairly upcoming industrial base. Located in central India, Madhya Pradesh has a unique advantage, bordered by the states of Uttar Pradesh, Rajasthan, Maharashtra, Gujarat and Chhattisgarh to increase its trade with neighbouring states.

TABLE 13.1

Comparative Structure of the MP's Economy with Other BIMARU States

(Figures in percentage)

Sector/Year	*Agriculture*		*Industry*		*Services*	
	1993-94	*2003-04*	*1993-94*	*2003-04*	*1993-04*	*2003-04*
MP	43.19	33.96	21.15	26.17	35.66	39.34
UP	39.80	35.11	21.45	20.97	38.75	43.91
Bihar	48.78	36.35	9.93	9.28	71.29	54.37
Orissa	44.95	38.85	19.78	19.17	35.27	40.98
Rajasthan	36.27	30.5	24.96	25.06	38.77	44.44

Source: FRBM Report 2006-07, Madhya Pradesh.

Comparison of the composition of economies of BIMARU states reflects some of the startling features. Over a decade, contribution of agriculture sector has deteriorated due to sheer negligence towards the sector. Service sector has grown significantly in all the states except Bihar. It is mainly due to poor law and order situation in the state. Industry sector however, has slightly declined, except in Rajasthan that shows slight increase. But very distinctly, it is the state of Madhya Pradesh that has shown a promising trend in industrial growth over a decade. It is a silver lining for the economy of state that Madhya Pradesh's industry sector has the highest share in GSDP when compared with other BIMARU states. At the same time, one also has to be cautious about the performance of service sector which is not at par with its counterparts.

Primary sector is contributing around 28 per cent in the state's GSDP. The economy of the state was largely agrarian, employing 77 per cent of the total workforce. However, in the past few years a significant change has been observed in the composition of sectoral contribution to the state's economy. Contribution of primary sector has come down over the years on one hand while secondary and tertiary sectors are showing stagnated growth. Dip in the primary sector from 2001 to 2003 is owing to severe drought conditions which

TABLE 13.2

Share of Different Sectors in State's Economy

(At current prices)

Sectors	*1999-2000*	*2000-01*	*2001-02*	*2002-03*	*2003-04*	*2004-05*	*2005-06*	*2006-07*
Primary	29.7	24.7	27.6	24.5	30.1	27.0	27.4	28.1
Secondary	24.2	25.8	24.6	24.8	23.8	25.9	25.6	25.1
Tertiary	46.0	49.5	47.8	50.6	46.1	47.1	47.0	46.8

Source: Economic Survey 2007-08, GoMP.

prevailed in the state. This stagnant growth of the secondary sector and tertiary sector is turning out to be one of the key impediments to take out the state from the clutches of BIMARU title. During the last 5 years, FDI inflow of Rs. 140 crore has been reported to the RBI office at Bhopal against a total inflow of Rs. 75,000 crore in the country, which is less than 0.2 per cent of the national pie. Surely, these figures do not do justice to the potential of the state.

Hence, efforts should be made in the direction of nurturing industrialisation in the state and promoting service sector equally to pave the way towards rising economy of the state through increased income and employment opportunities. Services sector does have the potential to grow impressively but cannot show continuous and sustained growth without the demand-related pull from both the primary and the secondary sectors. It is necessary that the positive features and competitive advantages of the state are shared with investors in general and foreign investors in particular.

2. Industry in State's Economy

The industrial sector contributes 8 per cent to employment of the state workforce and 25 per cent to state GDP. The rate of annual industrial growth in the recent past has varied from 4 per cent to 6 per cent. Further detailed analysis of secondary sector, particularly the industry in the state would throw light on the real picture of the sector growth. Since the last six years, the share of registered manufacturing to the state's GSDP has reduced from 11 per cent in 2000-01 to around 9 per cent in 2005-06 at constant prices, whereas that of unregistered manufacturing has come down from 6.95 per cent in 2000-01 to 4.31 per cent in 2005-06. The annual rate of growth of registered manufacturing has been unstable during this period. It was at its peak in 2000-01 and dropped to its lowest growth of just 0.23 per cent in 2003-04, that got momentum in two subsequent years. Annual growth of unregistered manufacturing unit is also quite fluctuating and registering a declining trend of growth over the years.

While the manufacturing sector has been growing at faster rates than the GSDP, these rates are not adequate enough to give a push to the state's economy. If we assume that the state's economy should grow at 5 to 6 per cent per annum or more, then manufacturing, especially registered manufacturing needs to give a boost to greater extent.

3. Key Industries in MP

The state's industrial base is quite diverse and vibrant. Industry is largely resource-driven, leveraging the state's natural wealth in the form of limestone, coal, iron ore, silica, bauxite, soya, cotton, etc. Therefore, the state has a strong industry base in sectors like cement, steel, textile and soya processing. Important and well-known companies having their manufacturing bases include ACC (cement), Bajaj Tempo (automobile—utility and LCVs), Cadbury India (confectionary), Coca Cola (beverages), Eicher Motors (automobiles—commercial vehicles), Grasim Industries, (cement, textile, fibric, viscos staple fibre), HLL (synthetics detergent) IPCA laboratories (pharmaceuticals), Kinetic Motor Company (automobiles—two wheelers), Nicholas Piramal (pharmaceuticals) Proctor and Gamble (detergents), Ranbaxy Laboratories (pharmaceuticals) , Ruchi Soya Industries, JP Associate, Bridgestone, Lupin (pharmaceuticals), Vardhaman Textiles and National Fertiliser Limited. In Madhya Pradesh, there is a strong

TABLE 13.3

Gross State Domestic Product of Madhya Pradesh, At Constant (1993-94) Prices

Year	*Manufacturing Registered*			*Manufacturing Unregistered*			*Combined (Registered+Unregistered)*		
	Number	*Share*	*Annual Growth*	*Number*	*Share*	*Annual Growth*	*Number*	*Share*	*Annual Growth*
2000-01	540330	10.96%	12.01	342532	6.95%	6.12	882862	17.91	9.72
2001-02	517621	9.66%	-4.39	348562	6.50%	1.73	866183	16.16	-1.93
2002-03	457936	9.12%	-13.03	240758	4.80%	-44.78	698694	13.91	-23.97
2003-04	458999	7.87%	0.23	251977	4.32%	4.45	710976	12.19	1.73
2004-05	483554	8.02%	5.08	255113	4.23%	1.23	738667	12.24	3.75
2005-06	527498	8.58%	8.33	265076	4.31%	3.76	792574	12.89	6.8

Source: Directorate of Economics and Statistics, Government of Madhya Pradesh.

auto, auto ancillary and pharmaceutical sector. Three major central government undertakings—Bharat Heavy Electricals Limited (BHEL), Nepa Mills and a Central Bank note press at Dewas are located in the state.

Various central ministerial undertaking in the state are as follows:

1. Security Paper Mill, Hoshangabad,
2. Ordinance Factory, Itarsi,
3. Ordinance Factory, Katni,
4. Ordinance Factory, Khamariya, Jabalpur,
5. Defence Vehicle Factory,
6. Gun Carriage Factory, Jabalpur,
7. Telecom Factory, Jabalpur,
8. Rail Coach Repair Workshop, Bhopal,
9. Bharat Heavy Electricals Limited, Bhopal.

Tables 13.4 and 13.5 give details of important industrial areas and centres as well as prominent manufacturing companies in Madhya Pradesh.[1]

TABLE 13.4

Important Industrial Areas and Centres in MP

S. No.	Industrial Areas	Location
1.	Special economic zones	Indore
2.	Growth centres	Gwalior, Jabalpur, Bhopal, Indore, Rewa
3.	Food parks	Bhopal, Nagpur, Indore, Gwalior, Jabalpur
4.	Crystal IT park	Indore
5.	Major industrial areas (Approx. 150 units under these areas)	Bhopal, Sehore, Raisen, Harda, Mandideep, Dewas, Pithampur, Khandwa, Jhabua, Dhar, Ujjain, Mandsaur

Source: Madhya Pradesh Audyogic Vikas Nigam (MPAVN).

TABLE 13.5

Prominent Companies in Madhya Pradesh

SRF Limited	Jaypee Group	Kirloskar
Airtel	Hindustan Lever	Pratibha Syntex Ltd.
Lupin	Cadburys	Avtec
JK Tyre	Tata	Bharat Petroleum
BHEL	Hindustan Motors	Ruchi Soya Industries
Ranbaxy	Aditya Birla Group	Godrej
Eicher	Dainik Bhaskar	Reliance
Bajaj	Indorama	TAFE
Bridgestone		

Source: Madhya Pradesh Audyogic Vikas Nigam (MPAVN).

4. Industrialisation of Madhya Pradesh

4.1 Establishment of Large and Medium Industries

Year-wise establishments in respect of large and medium size industry, employment generation and capital investment in the state of Madhya Pradesh is given in Table 13.6.

TABLE 13.6

Large and Medium Size Industry in Different Years, MP

Year	Units	Employment	Capital Investment (Rs. crore)
2002-03	2	54	13.46
2003-04	5	1105	156.09
2004-05	18	2949	666.64
2005-06	17	1370	482.69
2006-07	10	1819	545.27

Source: Economic Survey, 2007-08, GoMP.

Number of medium and large industrial units established in the state has increased steadily over the years, however the noted growth has been observed only after 2004-05. This growth has resulted out of the efforts of the state government for promoting industrialisation in the state following the adoption of 'New Industrial Policy-2004'. However, employment offered by these units and capital investment done in these units shows abrupt trends in past three years. Compared to 2004-05, in the year 2005-06, there was only one unit short, but the drop in employment was by 53 per cent, and capital investment also declined by Rs. 183.95 crore. On the other hand, 2006-07 turned out to be a better year despite the number of units being reduced to just 10; it has offered employment to the tune of 1819 and shows 13 per cent growth in capital investment.

4.2 Micro and Small Scale Industries

Small scale sector plays a significant role in the state's economy and is largely dependent on the type of raw materials locally available, local entrepreneurial capabilities, traditional skills and craftsmanship, the base of local infrastructure, support facilities in the form of credit, marketing and finally, the political will to implement the policy measures initiated at various levels from time to time. Table 13.7 describes trends in small scale industry in terms of establishment, capital invested and number of persons employed in the state of Madhya Pradesh.

1. *Source:* "India in Business", ITP division, Ministry of External Affairs, GoI.

TABLE 13.7

Number of Units, Investment (per lakh), Employment (no.), Employment (per unit)

Year	*Number of Units*	*Investment (per lakh)*	*Employment (No.)*	*Employment (per unit)*
2001-02	6338	10697	17371	2.74
2002-03	4297	5718	12110	2.82
2003-04	15358	9453	33000	2.15
2004-05	15873	13359	47732	3.01
2005-06	14949	12861	32372	2.17
2006-07	16733	17823	38958	2.33

Source: Economic Survey, 2007-08, GoMP.

The state has a large presence of small scale industries (SSIs). Industry Development Act, 2006 for micro, small and medium industries has been enforced in the state. The table reveals overall increase in number of units and investment but proportionately the employment offer is not at par, particularly the year 2005-06 was very bad on the count of all the three indicators. However, owing to lack of demand from mother units, fierce global competition, general economic slowdown and a paucity of finances, number of these units have become sick and in many cases non-viable. In keeping with the changing industrial environment, SSIs need to address themselves to global markets and demand conditions through institutional capacity building, organising themselves into clusters, expanding themselves towards a small medium enterprise (SME) position.

In the above background, it will be of interest to have a look on spatial and inter-temporal performance of factory sector in the state of Madhya Pradesh.

5. Comparative Performance of MP in Factory Sector

The spatial and inter-temporal data on registered factory sector in respect to 25-27 structural parameters for different states including the newly formed states and union territories of India are available from annual surveys of industries conducted by National Sample Survey Organisation, Ministry of Statistics and Programme Implementation, Government of India on their website. The latest published data is for the year 2005-06. Comparative performance of MP from 1999-2000 is given in Annexure 13.A. Key findings for MP are as follows:

5.1 Number of Factories

During 2000-01 and 2003-04, there was decline in the number of factories in the state of Madhya Pradesh and then it increased in 2004-05. At the national level, the decline was sharper compared to Madhya Pradesh. Relative position of MP among 19 states during 1999-2000 to 2004-05 has remained stagnant at 12th position. MP's share in number of factories in India was 2.22 per cent in 2004-05.

5.2 Fixed Capital

Fixed capital in MP has risen from 2001-02 to 2005-2006. There was a slight decline in all-India share and ranking too.

5.3 Productive Capital

Productive capital of MP has declined between the period from 2001-02 to 2003-04, whereas it was on rise at the all-India level during the same period. MP shares just 3.56 per cent of India's productive capital. Its ranking has declined from 10th in 2001-02 to 9th in 2005-06.

5.4 Working Capital

Working capital showed increasing trend from 2002-2003 in the state of MP. It ranked at 9th position in the country among 19 states in 2004-05.

5.5 Invested Capital

It has shown a steady rise from 2001-02 for MP. The ranking has declined from 11th to 9th in 2004-05 and shares 3.22 per cent of the country's invested capital.

5.6 Outstanding Loan

Trend in outstanding loan has gone up from 2002-2003 to 2004-05 in case of MP as well as its neighbouring states except Rajasthan in 2003-04 and at all-India level. Relative position of MP among the 19 states has improved from 11th in 2003-04 to 8th in 2004-05.

5.7 Number of Workers

There was an increase in the absolute number of workers in MP in 2003-04 and 2004-05. But MP's share in all-India has declined from 3.12 per cent in 1999-2000 to 2.48 per cent in 2004-05. Relative position remained stagnant at 12th position.

5.8 *Total Employees*

Trend pattern was similar to that of number of workers. The relative position of MP among 19 states deteriorated from 10th position in 1998-99 to 12th position in 2004-05.

5.9 *Value of Output*

Increasing trend was observed in terms of value of output, except a slight fall in 2002-03. MP shares 2.81 per cent of the country's value of output with relative position at 10th rank.

5.10 *Net Value Added*

MP does not show any perceptible trend compared to all-India pattern. The state contributed 2.14 per cent to the net value added from the factory sector at the national level in 2004-05. Among the 19 states, relative position of MP deteriorated from 7th position in 2000-01 to 14th position in 2004-05.

5.11 *Net Income*

Net income has increased only from 2002-03 in MP. Per cent share of MP in all-India has come down from 4.72 per cent in 2000-01 to 1.99 per cent in 2004-05. Relative position of MP among 19 states deteriorated from 12th position in 1998-99 to 14th position in 2004-2005.

5.12 *Net Fixed Capital Formation*

This is the only indicator where MP has shown promise. Among other states, MP was at the bottom most position in 2001-02 but improved to 7th position in 2004-05.

5.13 *Gross Fixed Capital Formation*

There was observed a steady rise in gross capital formation in MP from 2001-02 to 2004-05 with MP's share as 3.5 per cent. The relative position of MP improved from 15th position in 2001-02 to 9th position in 2004-05.

5.14 *Gross Capital Formation*

A similar trend has been observed to that of gross fixed capital formation. Share of MP in all-India increased from 2001-02 but fell in 2004-05. Relative position of MP deteriorated from 9th position in 1998-99 to 11th position in 2004-05.

5.15 *Profit*

Improvement was seen in only 2004-05 compared to previous years in MP. Relative position deteriorated from 5th in 2000-01 to 14th in 2004-05.

6. Structural Ratios

Based on Annexure 13.A, partial measures of productivity, identification for justification of investment in fixed capital, importance of expenditure on raw materials used in the product employing structural and technical ratios along with the rankings of the neighbouring states have been provided in Annexure 13.B.

7. Industrial Clusters

Madhya Pradesh has four geographic regions, namely Malwa and Vindhya, Satpura and Bundelkhand. With a view to promote balanced regional development, we recommend that the state should develop four focus clusters in four natural regions for fast paced industrial growth as under:

TABLE 13.8

Regional Foci for Industrial Development

Sl. No.	*Natural Region*	*Foci of Cluster Development*
1	Malwa	Indore - Pithampur - Dewas - Dhar
2	Vindhya	Bhopal - Mandideep - Satlapur- Pilukhedi
3	Satpura	Jabalpur - Katni - Rewa
4	Bundelkhand	Gwalior - Malanpur - Banmore - Ghirongi - Bina

Source: Madhya Pradesh Audyogic Vikas Nigam (MPAVN).

The following sectors have been identified as focus sectors based on the above factors: life sciences, agro/food, mineral, textiles and auto and auto ancillary. The corridor's excellent connectivity—lies on the NH-3 between Agra and Mumbai and near the main rail trunk line between Mumbai and Delhi—will be utilised for a dual market focus, national and exports.

7.1 *Vindhya and Malwa*

These plateaus with flat and rolling topography and black cotton soil are ideally suited for agriculture, particularly cotton. This has led to the development of a major textile industry in the region. Proximity to western coast, particularly Mumbai has helped in developing a significant industrial base in auto, chemical, pharma and textile. Indore has emerged as the commercial capital of MP with a developed urban infrastructure.

7.2 *Narmada*

The Narmada basin has relatively flat land with potential for agriculture. The region has developed a significant urban agglomeration based on services. Industrial activity in the region is limited to the following growth centres promoted by MP State Industrial Development Corporation (MPSIDC). Cluster analysis has shown that Bhopal-Mandideep-Satlapur belt could be positioned as a 'life sciences gateway' with development of pharma and biotechnology industry. The presence of a sizeable pharma industry and educational infrastructure makes it suitable for this positioning.

TABLE 13.9

Industrial Investment Scenario—Narmada Region

Growth Centre	*Total Area in ha.*	*Units under Production*	*Investment in Rs. Lakhs*	*Employment*
Mandideep	778	339	5779	13712
Pilukhedi	228	5	4453	2244
Satlapur	282	-	-	-

Source: MPSIDC.

7.3 *Satpura*

Madhya Pradesh accounts for nearly 20 per cent of the mineral production in the country by value producing 23 major minerals. Most of this comes from the Satpura region. Mining is a major economic activity in the region. The region is however characterised by low industrial activity. This is reflected in the statistics of growth centres promoted by MPSIDC.

TABLE 13.10

Industrial Investment Scenario—Satpura Region

Growth Centre	*Total Area*	*Units under Production*	*Investment*	*Employment*
Maneri	571	43	1776	1537
Boregaon	272	24	26944	4261
Purnea	106	37	2532	992
Rewa	134	49	15042	1840
Waidhan	34	16	548	126

Source: MPSIDC.

Much of the minerals mined in this region is exported as ores. Negligible value addition or processing is done before the ore/stone is exported. In order to maximise the gains to MP, the Jabalpur–Katni-Rewa belt will be developed as a mineral industry hub.

7.4 *Bundelkhand*

This northern outcrop of MP has seen the development of small and large-scale industry in textiles, cement, light engineering and fast moving consumer goods (FMCG). It has developed a strong industrial base and urban social infrastructure.

TABLE 13.11

Industrial Investment Scenario—Bundelkhand Region

Growth Centre	*Total Area in Ha.*	*Units under Production*	*Investment in Rs. Lakhs*	*Employment*
Malanpur	611	84	66285	8516
Ghirongi	716	40	82507	7171
Banmore	289	94	44625	5685
Pratappura	94	26	1772	609
Sidagawah	225	39	696	390
Chainpura	149	-	-	-

Source: MPSIDC.

Cluster analysis has reflected that Gwalior-Malanpur-Banmore-Ghirongi belt could be positioned as a FMCG and IT cluster. Its proximity to Delhi and strong linkages to the large, fast growing North Indian markets make it suitable for these activities.

8. Industrial Promotion Policy 2004: New Ray of Hope

It is perceived that the institutional framework for industry in Madhya Pradesh needs to be restructured and reorganised in line with the changing industrial paradigm. The new policy envisages on creating an industry-friendly administration, maximising employment opportunities, tackling industrial sickness, to rationalising rates of commercial taxes and bolstering private sector participation. The main thrust of the policy is:

- Establishment of a Madhya Pradesh Trade and Investment Facilitation Corporation.
- Enacting an Industrial Facilitation Act and to change rules of business with a view to make single window system decisive and result oriented.

- Developing infrastructure for enhancing identified industrial clusters.
- Reviving closed down/sick industrial units by granting special packages.

Industrial Promotion Policy, 2004 document envisages the creation of an "industry friendly administration, maximising employment opportunities, tackling industrial sickness, rationalising rates of commercial taxes and bolstering private sector participation". For shaping these goals, necessary institutional arrangement calls for:

i) Constitution of an industry advisory board;

ii) Creation of Madhya Pradesh Trade and Investment Facilitation Corporation (MPTIFC) for implementation of single window system;

iii) Formation of empowered committees at three levels for single window clearances;

iv) Creation of an Industrial Infrastructure Development Fund;

v) Abolition of dual taxation in the industrial areas;

vi) Development and promotion of industrial clusters in identified locations;

vii) Development of industrial parks;

viii) Special packages for sick industrial units for rehabilitation; and

ix) Implementation of various employment oriented schemes for UN employed youth.

Thus, the new policy is aimed to provide industrial investment promotional assistance, concessions in allotment of land, concessions for project of special importance, land on confessional rates, for warehousing, exemptions on stamp duty and registration charges, exemptions on electricity duty on captive power generation, exemption from entry tax, exemptions from *mandi* tax, subsidy on interest of term loans, subsidy to industry under thrust sector, subsidy on capital investment, and special packages for scheduled caste and scheduled tribe entrepreneurs and special packages for revival of sick units at small, medium and large scales.

In a bid to build a competitive environment, industries and their ancillaries would be promoted in clusters while keeping in mind the availability of raw materials, skilled labour and market potential. The following clusters and industrial parks have been identified by the state government to promote industrialisation in the state (Tables 13.12 and 13.13).

TABLE 13.12

Identified Clusters for Promoting Industrialisation

Indore	Pharmaceutical, textile, food processing, information technology, auto-components.
Bhopal	Engineering, fabrication, biotechnology, herbal products, information technology, food processing.
Jabalpur	Garment, mineral, forest and herbal based industries, food processing.
Gwalior	Electronics, information technology, fast moving consumer goods and commodities, light engineering, food processing.
Rewa	Refractories, lime stone and forest based industries.
Sagar	Major and minor minerals processing.

Source: MPSIDC.

TABLE 13.13

Identified Industrial Parks

Indore-Pithampur	Apparel park, gem and jewellery park, software technology park and herbal park
Bhopal	Life sciences institute
Jabalpur-Katni	Apparel park and stone park
Rewa-Satna	Herbal park
Tikamgarh-Sagar-Chhatarpur	Granite park

Source: MPSIDC.

9. Special Economic Zone in MP: Salient Features

A new Special Economic Zone (SEZ) Scheme has been introduced in the Export and Import Policy with a view to provide an internationally competitive and hassle-free environment for export production. Salient features of the policy are as given:

- A designated duty-free enclave to be treated as a foreign territory for trade operations and duties and tariffs.
- No licence required for import.
- Exemption from customs duty on import of capital goods, raw materials, consumables, spares, etc.
- Exemption from central excise duty on procurement of capital goods, raw materials and consumable spares, etc., from the domestic market.
- Supplies from DTA to SEZ units treated as exports.
- Purchases reimbursement of duty paid on furnace oil, procured from domestic oil companies to SEZ

units as per the rates of drawback notified by the directorate general of foreign trade.

- SEZ units may be for manufacturing, trading or service activity.
- SEZ unit to be positive net foreign exchange earner within three years.
- Performance of the units to be monitored by a committee headed by development commissioner and consisting of customs.
- Hundred per cent foreign direct investment in manufacturing sector allowed through automatic route except few sectors.
- Profits allowed to be repatriated freely without any dividend balancing requirement.
- Domestic sales on full duty subject to import policy in force.
- No fixed wastage norms.
- Full freedom for sub-contracting.
- Sub-contracting facility available to jewellers units.
- Duty-free goods to be utilised in five years.
- Job work on behalf of domestic exporters for direct expose allowed.
- No routine examination by customs of exports and import cargo.
- No separate documentation required for customs and exam policy.
- In-house customs clearance.

10. Advantage Madhya Pradesh

The state of Madhya Pradesh certainly carries some advantages over other BIMARU states. The promising growth in the industrial sector of the state may be attributed to the advantages which need to be explored in strategic ways to put the state on developing path. Some of the advantages for MP are as following:[2]

- Strategic geographic location.
- Excellent interstate connectivity (national and state highway, train and air links).
- Rich, fertile land and natural resources.
- Rich mineral wealth (copper ore, magnesium ore, limestone, diamonds, coal and coal-bed methane).
- Availability of land at a reasonable cost.
- Cheap labour.
- Unexploited species of rare, valuable medicinal, herbal plants.
- Industrially peaceful and stable with a vibrant industrial base.
- Peaceful political scenario (law and order).
- Rich cultural heritage.
- Major auto manufacturing base. Largest producer of radial tyres in India.
- Largest soya processing hub in India.
- Hub for FMCG, consumer electronics, pharmaceuticals, herbal products, textiles and apparel.
- Growing gems and jewellery centre.
- Largest producer of oil seeds and pulses in the country. Largest exporter of DOC (de-oiled cake) in India. Twenty-five per cent of pulses and 40 per cent of grams grown.
- Largest producer of garlic and coriander.
- Grower of commercially favoured varieties of wheat and potatoes. Largest producer of garlic and coriander.

11. Investment Opportunities for Promoting Industrialisation

Over a period of time, leveraging its agriculture and mineral resources, some key industries has gained a strong foothold in the state. However, there have been a few exceptions to the resource-driven industrialisation rule, as a result of the state's aggressive incentive policies and strong solicitation.

11.1. Agriculture and Agro Processing

Madhya Pradesh is the fourth largest producer of agriculture produce in India with lowest consumption of fertiliser per hectare. Agriculture contributes almost one-third of the GSDP and is the main source of employment for over 70 per cent population and constitutes about 60 to 75 per cent rural income. The state is major producer of pulses and oilseeds in the country. Important crops grown in the state are paddy, wheat, maize and *jowar* among *cereals*; gram, *tur*, *urad*

2. *Source:* "India in Business", ITP division, Ministry of External Affairs, GoI.

and *moong* among pulses, while soyabean, groundnut and mustard among oilseeds. Also commercial crops like cotton and sugarcane are grown in considerable area in few districts. Horticulture crops like potato, onion, garlic, along with fruits like papaya, banana, orange, mango and grapes are also grown in the state. Some area has also been brought under medicinal and narcotic crops. The investment opportunities in this sector are wheat processing, potato processing, spices, edible oil and processing of pulses. Also three agriculture export zone have been sanctioned for the state for: 1. potato/onion/garlic, 2. seed spices and 3. wheat.

11.2 Herbal Business

Madhya Pradesh is known for a wide range of herbs. It caters to about 40 per cent of Indian herbal industry's requirement across spread across the country. The main herbal centres are Shivpuri, Betul, Katni, Neemuch and Lalitpur. The natural occurrence of most of the herbs coupled with mass scale cultivation has made the state the herbal hub of the country. Madhya Pradesh is the raw material bowl of the herbal industry and is all set to become the main processing centre for several herbal products. Investment opportunities exist in this sector in the following industries:

- Aloe vera gel extraction and spray dried powder manufacturing units.
- Units to produce extracts of various herbs.
- Fractional distillation units for value addition in essential oils.
- Various *ayurvedic* drug formulation units.
- Promotion of food and vegetable colour dyes.
- Production of concentrates from flowers.
- Primary processing of raw herbs.
- *Isabgol* de-husking units.
- Herbal cosmetics.
- Units to make perfumery compounds.
- Production of bio-diesel.

11.3 Cement

The state is the third largest producer of cement in the country catering to 13 per cent of the national demand. Madhya Pradesh's key strength in cement industry is the presence of large limestone reserves, estimated to be over 2 billion tonnes. Considering the present scenario and the availability of raw material, there is a scope of further investment of $2.5 billion in this sector. Currently present several major groups are expanding their production capacities. Prominent cement companies present in the state include ACC, Grasim Industries, Jaiprakash Associates, Cement Corporation of India Ltd, Century Textiles and Mysore Cements. The districts of Balaghat, Damoh, Dhar, Hoshangabad, Jhabua, Katni, Khargone, Mandsaur, Morena, Narsinghpur, Panna, Rewa, Sagar, Satna and Sidhi are rich with limestone reserves.

11.4 Textiles and Apparels

Madhya Pradesh is known for its rich heritage of textiles in India for its distinctive style and individuality. Hand block printing is among the important crafts of Madhya Pradesh. The popular colours used in this process are vegetable and natural dyes like indigo, turmeric roots, pomegranate skin, lac, iron, and other substances that create an effect that is rich yet subtle. Tying and dyeing and *batik* prints are again well known arts in textiles sectors of MP.

TABLE 13.14

Textile Infrastructure in MP

Composite mills	20
Exclusive weaving units	8
Export-oriented spinning units	12
Handlooms	47,000
Looms	6,500
Power looms	43,290
Power loom units	17,524
Rotors	14,348
Spindles	14,14,000
Spinning units	40

Source: "Public-Private Partnership in India", Ministry of Finance, GoI.

Madhya Pradesh is famous for its delicate weaves in *Chanderi* and *Maheshwari* saris. Madhya Pradesh encompasses nearly 51 textile units. The textile export from MP is around $250 million approximately. There are vast opportunities for spun yarn, fabric, textile/ fashion designing, readymade garments. Some of the key industry players in the state are Bhaskar, Bhilwaras, Indo-Rama, Maikal Oswals, Parasrampuria and S. Kumar's.

11.5 Pharmaceuticals

The pharmaceutical sector in Madhya Pradesh envisages a potential of $1 billion investment in the next five years. There is tremendous scope for bulk drugs/formulations, herbal products, contract research, research centres/laboratories.

11.6 Chemicals

The chemical sector in Madhya Pradesh envisages an investment opportunity of over $75 billion, with a potential growth of 5 billion in the next 10 years.

11.7 Auto and Auto Components

This sector offers tremendous potential with reference to HCV/LCV/MCV/PC/2-3 wheeler, auto components—tyres, engines and gears. About 60 per cent of the auto industry in MP is dominated by auto component players. The size of the auto component industry in Madhya Pradesh is around $306 million. The Union Government of India has sanctioned an auto cluster in the Pithampur industrial area. The Government of India will grant an amount of $11 million.

11.8 Minerals/Stone

Madhya Pradesh is endowed with significant mineral resources. With 604,000 carats of proven diamond reserves, it accounts for 99 per cent of India's total reserves. It is the sole producer of diamonds in the country. It also leads the country in the production of copper ore, slate, pyrophillite, diaspore, and is second in production of rock phosphate, clay and laterite. The state has the country's largest open cast copper mine at Balaghat and the thickest coal seam of Asia at Singrauli coalfield in Sidhi district. The opportunities in this sector include stone cutting and polishing, marble, granite, sandstone, mineral/gas exploration, mineral excavation and power generation plant.

BOX 13.1

Reality Bites

In the past two years, the state government has organised investor's meets to attract various business houses from across the country and world. 309 MoUs worth Rs. 3.72 lakh crore were signed in 2007-08. Out of which the recent review of 155 MoUs in industry, IT and food processing sectors revealed that, actual production has began in only two, construction work has began in 59, preliminary survey has been carried out in 45 cases and 9 MoUs have been cancelled due to no interest shown by the investors in setting up units in the state. There was no mention about the 29 MoUs signed in the power sector. Several problems were identified in the review meeting about slow progress of MoU implementation. Some of them are, one, timely allocation of land to the investors and second, red tapism at the district level.

Source: Hindustan Times, 18/1/2009.

11.9 IT/IT Related Services

Four software technology parks (STP units) to be set up in Bhopal, Indore and Gwalior. There are 38 IT engineering colleges in the state providing education to future IT professionals. Large IT players, such as HCL and Genpact have shown interest in setting up the facilities in the state. Investment opportunities exist in the area of business process outsourcing and software/hardware segments. Madhya Pradesh is targeting 5-10 per cent of the Indian share of global IT/ITES market.

12. Multi-prong Strategies for Promoting Industry Sector in MP

12.1 Initiatives Required for the Textile Cluster

- Improvement of factory conditions: The government should take the following initiatives to enhance the competitiveness of textile industries in the corridor:
  - Develop a wholesale trade centre.
  - Facilitate the development of a technology centre.
  - Promote the development of an apparel park.
- Positive interventions influencing demand conditions to enhance competitive advantage of the textile cluster are:
  - Conducting regular market studies to focus private sector initiative.
  - Participating in international trade meets.
- To develop support industries and services, the government should set up an integrated school of textiles, which would offer courses at the graduate and postgraduate levels. In addition, the institute shall also offer training courses for workers and short-term vocational courses.
  - Invite an established institute of fashion design to set up a fashion design centre within the school of textiles.
  - Promote testing and certification facilities for the SSIs with private participation.

The government would offer special incentives in the form of tax concessions and credit facilities for new units set up in the cluster.

12.2 Initiatives Required for the Agro Food Industry Cluster

- Enhancement of factor conditions: In order to enhance factor conditions for the industry, the government should:
  - Develop a food park.
  - Assist the industry in setting up a research and development centre to enhance value addition, processing, packaging and instant quick-freezing (IQF).
  - Provide a framework for the creation of infrastructure relating to collection, sorting, grading, transportation and warehousing of products.
  - Promote with private initiative cold-chain infrastructure and vapour heat treatment facility catering to the industry.
  - Develop a testing and quality control facility for processed foods and raw materials with private participation.
- The government would influence demand conditions by:
  - Setting up a centre for monitoring markets and quality control.
- For the development of support industry and services, the government would:
  - Revamp dissemination mechanism for information about markets, agri-inputs and best farm practices to farmers.
  - Provide connectivity to farms and promote facilities of storage and transportation of agri-produce for processing.

In order to increase efficiency in the agro/food industry, the government should actively encourage disintermediation by promotion of direct selling, establishing a framework for contract farming and setting up co-operatives.

12.3 Initiatives Required for the Life Sciences Cluster

- The government would positively influence the factor conditions for the cluster by:
  - Facilitating the setting up of State Science Technology Institute.
  - Tying up with an academic institution of international repute for establishing a centre for life sciences research.
  - Facilitate the establishment of a cold-chain infrastructure and air logistics for life science industry by private sector participation.
- Demand conditions would be influenced by government's procurement policy. The government of MP would:
  - Procure for hospitals/state farms/seed corporation.
  - Allow free-testing in hospitals, states, farms/ seed corporation.
  - Set up a database for buyer and patent information.
- The government would take the following steps in influencing the industry structure:
  - Establishing incubation laboratories for life sciences start–ups.
  - Announcing an innovation policy for rewarding innovation.
  - Developing a framework for enabling contract research.

12.4 Initiatives Required for the Mineral Cluster

- The government would influence the factor conditions for the development of mineral-based industry by:
  - Facilitating the setting up of a stone park.
  - Stone village for demonstration/product display and to provide export outlet for stone crafts. The village would also serve as a training centre for artisans.
  - Export products display centre for catalogues, products, machinery etc.
  - Logistics infrastructure for handling stones.
- Demand conditions would be influenced by governments procurement policy. The government of MP would set up a mineral technology and trade information centre.
  - Mineral industry data bank.
  - Facilitating information on pricing, taxation and regulations.
  - Sector statistics relating to exports, imports, production, etc., country reports/profiles.
  - Library.

- Support services for the industry will be augmented by setting up a stone testing and technical consultancy (R&D centre) with the following facilities:
  - Testing of stones as per ASTM and other international standards.
  - Quality control, inspection and certification facility.
  - Technological upgradation for quarrying, processing, stone-craft, finishing, laying and cladding, packing.
  - Promote mechanised quarrying.
  - Undertaking market studies and analysis.
  - Geological investigations, quarry development and processing.
  - Promote development of stone craft through technological upgradation.
- The government would influence the industry structure by:
  - Inviting FDI for technology upgradation in the industry.
  - Announcing a mineral exploration policy.
  - Preferential allotment of mining rights for captive utilisation by industries to promote value addition in the state.
  - Influencing the development of a framework for enabling private mining.

12.5 Initiatives Required for the FMCG Industry Cluster

For the emergence of this cluster, as a first step a few large fast moving consumer goods (FMCG) manufacturers need to be attracted. The development of related and supporting industries and infrastructure as suppliers of machinery, equipment and packaging materials, industrial chemicals and containers will be triggered subsequently.

Some specific measures that should be taken are:

- Development of logistics infrastructure.
- Centre for testing and certification.

12.6 Initiatives Required for the IT Cluster

Among the sectors with potential for high growth, information technology has immense opportunities for entrepreneurship. Madhya Pradesh has few IT and related industries. Gwalior with its proximity to Delhi and excellent connectivity with other parts of the country is ideally suited to emerge as the state's focus for IT enterprises. We recommend the following initiatives for the purpose:

- The government should initiate changes in the labour laws to make them favourable to IT enabled services.
  - Allow 24×7 working days.
  - Allow the use of contract employees.
  - Allow women to work in night shifts.
- For the enhancement of factor conditions, it is imperative that telecom connectivity be enhanced. The government should invite Software Technology Park of India (STPI) to set up a centre at Gwalior focused on Information Technology Enabled Service (ITES).
- Government should contribute land for the setting up of an incubation facility for start-ups.
- An entrepreneurship development centre should be set up to disseminate information about opportunities in IT.
- The government should catalyse the setting up of an industry association that will promote co-operative marketing and business development effort, information sharing, benchmarking and best practices, etc.
- IT software industry should be exempted from the purview of the Pollution Control Act, except in respect of power generation sets.
- The government should totally exempt computer software from the payment of sales tax.
- For IT infrastructure companies establishing facilities on private lands outside the limits of the municipal corporations, relaxation of Floor Area Regulation (FAR) to the extent of 50 per cent of the prevailing norm should be available.

12.7 Promoting Small Scale Industries

The impending de-reservation of SSI sectors post-2005 with the coming of force of the WTO regime, will require mechanisms for the SSI sector that build on their strengths and remove constraints. International experience has borne out that SSIs can be made competitive when they are organised in collaborative framework. This framework institutes these smaller units with confidence, agility, flexibility and motivation to exceed expected norms of performance.

Despite such achievements, the majority of the Indian SSl clusters share significant constraints like technological obsolescence, relatively poor product quality, information deficiencies, poor market linkages and inadequate management systems. Moreover, with the Indian economy on the path of liberalisation, all SSI clusters (even the best performing ones) are increasingly feeling the competitive pressures coming from the international markets. Surprisingly, the state of Madhya Pradesh that has the maximum number of small-scale enterprises (12.7 per cent) as per the IInd All India Survey of SSI, but has very few clusters (1.4 per cent).

TABLE 13.15

List of Industrial Clusters in Madhya Pradesh

Name of Industrial Estate (I.E.) or Industrial Area (I.A.)	*Total Area in hectare*
Bhopal	382
Sehore	58
Raisen	325
Harda	46
Mandideep	151
Dewas	507
Khandwa	28
Jhabua	224
Dhar	326
Ujjain	280
Mandsaur	1379

Source: MPSIDC.

12.8 Initiatives Required for Cluster Development

As a part of the cluster development strategy, the government should take initiatives for the general development of SMEs and also initiatives focused on specific clusters. These initiatives will be facilitative in nature. The following interventions are required for developing the SME sector in general:

- Building up basic infrastructure on a local level, consisting of industrial areas, roads, water, electricity, telecommunications.
- Providing vocational training and promoting entrepreneurship from a cultural point of view, and educating existing or potential entrepreneurs in basic managerial techniques.
- Providing services to micro enterprises of the informal sector, in order to induce them to enter the formal sector, and reducing bureaucratic costs and complexity of bureaucratic procedures for enterprises.
- Providing information about incentives for the creation of new enterprises and for investment and providing micro credits to design mutual guarantee schemes.

The interventions for development of specific clusters should include:

- Promoting local products on foreign markets, such as export consortia.
- Supplying specific strategic human resource training for production and business processes, through technical schools and training programmes.
- Favouring networks of SMEs and setting up collective service activities, through sector-specific service centres.
- Providing temporary management guidance and mentoring for local SMEs.
- Offering adequate medium-long term financial support, in order to facilitate enterprises to buy new technical equipment, use consultancies, etc.
- Increasing the specialisation and quality of infrastructure.
- Creating international linkages for local enterprises, and possibly, joint ventures through international co-operation programmes.
- Attracting foreign investment in innovative and complementary activities.
- Connecting local enterprises to universities and research centres and transferring the results of scientific and experimental research through technological industrial parks.
- Reinforcing local identity and stimulating the circulation of information, through industrial museums and business associations.
- Stimulating international co-operation between institutions and creating institutional networks at the international level.

12.9 Improving Governance Practices for Industrial Development

There is a requirement for refocusing government interventions. Facilitation more than regulation will be the cornerstone for government initiatives in industrial development. A redefinition of organisational roles within the government is essential as some of the roles relevant to the licensing regime are redundant and need to be re-oriented in line with the new industrial paradigm.

In the existing industrial areas within the state, different agencies are at present responsible for providing civic amenities and other social infrastructure. There is a lack of proper co-ordination between such agencies and certain essential services are still to be provided keeping in view the needs of industry on one hand and local residents on the other. The multiplicity of administration, as a result of the overlapping functions and powers (exercised by local bodies like the municipality, *panchayat,* AKVN, OTIC etc.) lead to inordinate delays, turf issues and inconvenience for the industrial area occupants. There is thus, a need for a co-ordinated single authority that manages the estates and facilities in industrial estates/ clusters. Private contracting should be adopted as a model for the operations and maintenance of industrial areas as a precursor to the comprehensive privatisation of O&M in industrial areas.

12.10 Financial Incentives

The industrial promotion and development system has undergone substantial change since the period of liberalisation. Not only has there been a gradual reduction of such subsidies and financial incentives, there is also a coming closer of policies and incentive structures in different states. No longer do states differ from each other substantially in the kind and scale of incentives and subsidies they are offering. The opening up of the Indian economy and the approaching 2005 deadline where the WTO regime will come into play has also led to the realisation that markets are best positioned to connect demand with supply of goods and services. With the diminishing of trade barriers and unlimited access to markets, global competitiveness is the only source of sustainable industrial development. Given the scenario, subsidies and incentives are ineffective.

Current status of subsidies in Madhya Pradesh: Exemption and deferment from sales tax/commercial tax in line with the agreement reached between state chief ministers; Capital subsidy is available for SSIs only, Table 13.16 shows the basis for determination of capital subsidy for SSIs; Interest rate subsidy is available for SSIs only and is limited to 2 per cent (maximum 25,000 per year for three years) for general category and 6 per cent to SC/ST entrepreneurs (without any capital); Other subsidies are—subsidy for ISO 9000 certification, 50 per cent of fee paid, and exemption from payment of entry tax on purchase of raw materials, incidental goods and packaging materials.

TABLE 13.16

Capital Subsidy Classification

	% Age of Fixed Capital Investment	*Ceiling (Rs. lakh)*
Advanced districts	5% (only for thrust sector)	1.00
Backward districts		
Category A	7.5%	1.50 - 2.00
Category B	10%	2.00 - 2.50
Category C	10%	2.50 - 3.00
Growth centres	15%	5.0

Source: MPSIDC.

The state investment subsidy scheme offered for SSI along with projects in co-operative sector (minimum plant and machinery investment of Rs. 1 crore and membership of 100 persons) should be continued. However, the state government should re-examine the higher level of subsidies for location in growth centres and possibly confine the subsidy to a set of labour-intensive thrust industries or proposed clusters. The interest subsidy to SSI's needs to be re-examined. However, project report cost reimbursement, assistance for obtaining ISO 9000 certification scheme should continue.

A great benefit would come if 50 per cent exemption from stamp duty, registration fee and transfer duty of lands meant for industrial use is allowed. In order to exclude small businesses from incidence of tax and also reduce administrative burden, a threshold limit of turnover is prescribed. Businesses whose annual turnover does not exceed the prescribed limit are not liable to tax. Table 13.17 presents a comparison of the minimum levels for registration in select states.

TABLE 13.17

Minimum Turnover Level for Registration

(in Rs. Million)

State	*Delhi*	*Haryana*	*MP*	*Maha.*	*Punjab*	*Rajas.*	*UP*
Importer	Nil	Nil	0.05	0.10	Nil	0.05	Nil
Manufacturer	0.20	0.10	0.05	0.10	0.10	0.05	0.10
Other dealer	0.40	0.50	0.10	0.25	0.50	0.10	0.15

Source: Incentives for Industrial Development by Central and state govts.

In Madhya Pradesh, the turnover limits were fixed in 1984 and have not been revised since. The GoMP should revise the turnover limits in line with other states to suitably enhance the threshold.

12.11 Industrial Investment Promotion Assistance

The new policy would provide following concessions and facilities to industries commencing production on or after 1st April 2004. An industrial investment promotion assistance, equivalent to 50 per cent amount of commercial tax and central sales tax (excluding Commercial Tax on the purchase of raw material) deposited by the unit in the preceding year would be given to the industry; having fixed capital investment between Rs. 1.00 crore to Rs. 10 crore. Provision for this purpose would be made in the departmental budget. This would be available for 3 years in advanced districts and for 5 years in the backward districts. Assistance will not be more than fixed capital investment.

1. An industrial investment promotion assistance equivalent to 75 per cent amount of commercial tax and central sales tax (excluding commercial tax on the purchase of raw material) deposited by the unit in the preceding year would be given to the industry having fixed capital investment more than Rs. 10.00 crore. Provision for this purpose would be made in the departmental budget. The assistance would be available in the line of following criteria.

TABLE 13.18

An Industrial Investment Promotion

S.No.	Category of District	Minimum Eligible Fixed Capital Investment	Duration of Assistance
1.	Advanced district	Rs. 25 crore	3 years
2.	Backward district A	Rs. 20 crore	5 years
3.	Backward district B	Rs. 15 crore	7 years
4.	Backward district C	Rs. 10 crore	10 years

Source: MPSIDC.

Amount of assistance will not be more than fixed capital investment. For information technology industries, the above assistance would be available only in the IT parks.

2. Concessions to mega projects in allotment of land: Industrial units having fixed capital investment of Rs. 25 crore and above (excluding working capital) would be treated as mega projects. Five to twenty acres land at a concessional rate of 25 per cent of the stipulated premium rate would be made available to such projects, depending upon the size of investment.

3. Concessional package for mega projects and projects of special importance: Mega projects of special importance with infusion of modern technology management could be given special economic or other package, sanctioned by the Apex Level Investment Promotion Empowered Committee headed by the chief minister, on a case by case basis, keeping in view the requirements of such projects and resources of the state government. Industrial units in food and agro processing, milk products, herbal and forest based products would be treated as mega projects for this purpose, if their fixed capital investment is over Rs. 10 crore.

4. Exemption in stamp duty and registration charges:

   a. Industries that obtain loan for new units, expansion, diversification or modernisation would be eligible for exemption in stamp duty and registration charges in the legal documents as per the following table:

TABLE 13.19

Exemption in Stamp Duty and Registration

Category of Districts	*Stamp Duty*		*Registration Fee*	
	Small Industry	*Large and Medium Scale Industry*	*Small Scale Industry*	*Large and Medium Scale Industry*
Backward B	100% exemption	50% exemption	Re. 1 per thousand	50% of general rate
Backward C	100% exemption	100% exemption	Re. 1 per thousand	Re. 1 per thousand
N.I.B.	100% exemption	100% exemption	Re. 1 per thousand	Re. 1 per thousand

Source: MPSIDC.

   b. Stamp duty and registration charges would be levied on the premium amount as charged by the industry department for lease deeds of land and shed in industrial areas and industrial growth centres.

   c. Stamp duty and registration charges would be levied only on the transfer fee; charged by the industry department in cases of land transfer. Blood relations (husband/wife/mother/father/son/daughter/brother/sister/granddaughter/grandson) would not be included in the transfer category for ownership or partnership units. In such cases, no transfer fee would be charged. Appropriate amendments in the lease deed would be made for which Rs. 1000 as stamp duty and Rs. 100 as registration fee would be charged.

d. Stamp duty and registration charges would be fully exempted for the industrial units, which have been closed down and acquired by the financial institutions and banks or sick and closed units referred to Board for Industrial and Financial Reconstruction (BIFR) or liquidator for disposal.

e. Full exemption in stamp duty and registration charges for sale/transfer of sick units; as defined by RBI and closed down industrial units would be given.

f. If existing managements of an industrial unit did not succeed in running the unit at more than 50 per cent of its installed capacity, for 3 years and for better utilisation of capacity, he sells the unit as "ongoing concern" to another entrepreneur or the said unit. Merges/ amalgamates with another company, then in such cases the stamp duty and registration charges would be limited to a maximum of Rs. 10 lakh.

5. Exemption from electricity duty on captive power generation for a period of 5 years.

6. Entry tax: Exemption would be given to new industry for a period of 5 years from the date of the first purchase of raw material.

7. Interest subsidy on term loan: This subsidy will be available to the new units at a interest rate of 3 per cent to 5 per cent for a period of 5 years to 7 years for a total amount of Rs. 10 lakh to Rs. 20 lakh; depending upon the category of districts in which unit has been set up. This subsidy would also be available in "No Industrial Block" even though it falls in advance district.

8. Subsidy to industry under thrust sector: Industry under textile, information technology, bio-technology, automobiles, pharmaceuticals and herbal, food processing, agriculture and urban waste processing, sectors have been categorised as thrust sector. In order to encourage the establishment of industry in the thrust sector, a special subsidy will be given at the rate of 25 per cent of the fixed investment to a maximum of Rs. 10 lakh to 25 lakh as per the category of the district. These industries would not be eligible for other capital investment subsidy.

9. Capital investment subsidy: On fixed investment, the following particulars would be given to small scale industries (Table 13.20).

TABLE 13.20

Investment Subsidy for Districts

District Category	*Percentage of Fixed Investment as Subsidy*	*Maximum Amount*
Backward A	15%	Rs. 5.0 lakh
Backward B	15%	Rs. 10.0 lakh
Backward C	15%	Rs. 15.0 lakh

Source: MPSIDC.

10. Special provisions for entrepreneurs belonging to scheduled caste and scheduled tribes and women entrepreneurs:

- Interest subsidy on the term loan at a rate of 5 per cent for a period of 5 years without any ceiling would be provided to the industrial units owned by women, scheduled caste and scheduled tribe entrepreneurs.
- Investment subsidy at the rate of 15 per cent of the capital investment with a ceiling of Rs. 5 lakh would be given to said category of entrepreneurs in advanced districts.
- Upper limit for investment subsidy in the backward districts of A, B and C category would be Rs. 6 lakh, Rs. 12 lakh and Rs. 17.5 lakh respectively.

11. Concessions to the existing units: Existing units undergoing expansion/diversification/ technological upgradation will be treated as a new unit for the purpose of concessions and facilitate as a new unit subject to the condition that additional fixed investment is more than 50 per cent of the existing unit and with a minimum amount of Rs. 5.00 crore.

12. Exemption from *mandi* tax: *Mandi* tax would not be levied on the agricultural produce brought from outside the state as raw material by a food processing industry.

    Agricultural produce used as raw material in the industries set up in the food parks would be exempted from *mandi* tax.

13. Concessions to food processing industry: Commercial tax levied on the raw material of

food processing industry; set-up in food parks shall be adjusted (set off) against the commercial tax of the finished goods.

With a view to encouraging food processing industry, reimbursement of up to Rs. 1 lakh or 10 per cent of actual expenditure made for obtaining quality certification and research work would be given. Food processing industry, which is in the small scale category, would also be eligible for marketing grant. Efforts for brand building of food processing industry in the small-scale sector would also be encouraged. For this purpose, reimbursement for establishing stalls in national level/state level, exhibition/seminars or giving advertisements would be made, on the basis of actual expenditure. In the first year Rs. 75 thousand, in the second year Rs. 50 thousand, and in the third year Rs. 25 thousand could be reimbursed.

14. The new policy contains special packages for textile, medicinal and herbal industries and automobile component industry.

15. Special packages for reviving the small scale, large and medium scale sick/closed units and for restarting by a new entrepreneur have been provided in the New Industrial Policy.

16. Partial reimbursement of expenditure: Incurred for project report, ISO 9000, quality certification patent.

17. Land at concessional rate for warehousing would be provided.

18. Encouragement for the development of industrial parks by private sector: All assistance would be provided including subsidy up to Rs. 1.00 crore.

13. TRIFAC—An Empowered Single Window

The Madhya Pradesh Trade & Investment Facilitation Corporation Limited (TRIFAC), a government undertaking, was recently created to provide single window facilitation for investments in Madhya Pradesh. TRIFAC is an empowered single window secretariat for mega projects with investment of over Rs. 25 crore; also for thrust sector projects of over 10 crore. For any project in these categories, TRIFAC pilots the case in the apex level committee headed by the chief minister where a customised economic assistance package is sanctioned besides in-principle clearances and registration for land, pollution control, commercial tax, power, water, building plans and industrial health and safety.

TRIFAC is also the secretariat for the state level investment promotion empowered committee chaired by the Minister of Commerce, Industry and Employment for projects with investment in the range of Rs. 3 to 25 crore. In-principle clearances are given of the basis of one's composite application for land, water, power, building plans, industrial safety and factories act. Final clearances follow within prescribed time limits failing which the state level committee at the instance of TRIFAC issues the final sanctions. TRIFAC has also the government mandate for initiating issues pertaining to rationalisation of state taxes and policy changes.

13.1 Conclusion

- The Indian Investment Centre (IIC), a government organisation responsible for investment promotion, identifies optical fibres, automobiles, soyabean processing, cement, fertilisers, paper and pulps, tyre and tubes, gases, jelly filled telephone cables and electric goods as the major industries in the state of Madhya Pradesh.
- Because of its pre-eminent position in certain crops including soyabean and gram with a share of about 62 per cent and 42 per cent production in the country, the state has identified food processing and agro-based industries as part of its priority sector, along with few others.
- The industrial panorama seems to be quite encouraging and reflects the emergence of considerable potential for further growth in the industrial sector of the state. Madhya Pradesh today boasts of India's first green field special economic zone with comprehensive policy, attractive packages and an ambitious plan.
- The economic development policy for Madhya Pradesh should focus on industrial development for higher economic growth. Industrialisation can be catalysed through connecting industry to quality infrastructure, superior skills and knowledge, energised government institutions and a liberal network of suppliers and markets.
- The role of government will be on the one hand to put in place both directly and through partnerships an infrastructure that attracts industries and two, to facilitate flow of information and assist entrepreneurs in

investment decisions. To make the state further an attractive destination for industrial investments, de-bureaucratisation of procedures should be simultaneously undertaken.

- It is equally important for industrial resurgence in the development of competitive industry clusters complete with soft industry-specific infrastructure and services. Keeping this objective in mind, the government should promote and nurture vibrant industry clusters across the state to achieve equitable growth along with global competitiveness.
- There has been some growth of the industrial sector, but this sector is not strong in the state contributing only 8 per cent to employment of the state workforce and 27 per cent to state GDP. The rate of annual industrial growth in the recent past has varied from 4 per cent to 6 per cent. In the short to medium term, the state needs to concentrate on industrial development as a source for value generation along with agriculture.
- The established industries in the state are facing a number of constraining factors. These factors on the one hand are a bottleneck for existing industries, but in some ways are also impediments for new investments.
- The image of Madhya Pradesh is of a primarily agrarian state, which is industrially backward and poor. This image coupled with the fact that there is no proper getaway[3] in Madhya Pradesh has put the state on a back foot in attracting business investments.
- There is a low level of awareness of the industrial potential in Madhya Pradesh among the investor community outside the state. Awareness of industrial development in the state is restricted to a few mineral based industries like cement, steel, aluminium and PSUs like BHEL, Ordinance factories at Jabalpur, Nepa Mills and Central Note Press at Dewas.

14. Road Ahead

Given the rate of growth of other sectors, it is imperative that in the coming years, there is a speeded-up industrialisation in the state. This can take three separate but inter-linked routes:

- revival or boost to existing industries;
- bringing in fresh investments into the state in key sectors;
- focus in promoting industries in consonance with local potential on a region to region basis.

- Government resource constraints make it imperative to shift to non-incentive (fiscal) based investment targeting and offering good quality infrastructure and an environment conducive to growth as a stimulus for investment attraction. This requires identifying and prioritising private investment along with vibrant industry and geographic clusters that offer the highest potential for industry. Model investment destinations like Hyderabad and Bangalore for IT and electronics, Ahmedabad for chemicals, pharmaceuticals and plastics, Pune and Gurgaon for auto etc., need to be evolved to give a strong signal to investors.
- Power supply is generally inadequate and inconsistent for industrial purposes in all parts of the state. Besides affecting the performance of industry in general, this problem assumes critical proportions for units, which are engaged in the production of high technology products. The constrained financial condition of MPEB and the transfer of large power generation capacity to Chhattisgarh create supply-side constraints in the industrial power sector. The new captive power policy of the state may however, help somewhat in this direction.
- As Madhya Pradesh is a land-locked state, industry suffers from lack of a seaport and other forms of connectivity. Physical connectivity in the form of roads and rail links needs to be improved for the inward and outward movement of raw materials and finished goods. The lack of sufficient cold chains, logistics infrastructure and air cargo facilities is a deterrent for the state in leveraging its central position within the Indian subcontinent and therefore, evolving as a hub for movement/distribution of goods.

3. By getaway, we refer to a city or a destination in Madhya Pradesh which attracts people to it and irrespective of the state is a preferred destination for people to settle in and want to live in. The role of Hyderabad and Bangalore cities in the development push to the state of Andhra Pradesh and Karnataka has been crucial and Madhya Pradesh has no such getaway into the state. Places like Gwalior, Indore and Bhopal, are far from being as attractive cities to live in as are the cities of Hyderabad and Bangalore.

- Inadequate development and operation and maintenance (O&M) of industry growth centres and industrial estates and the multiplicity of administration is a strong concern area for existing industry. Industrial areas lack specialised infrastructure like CETP, warehousing, training centres, testing laboratories etc.
- Knowledge-intensive industries such as pharmaceuticals, biotechnology, IT, hardware and software, etc., have not clustered in Madhya Pradesh in large numbers. Given that Madhya Pradesh has high quality urban clusters in the form of Bhopal, Indore and Gwalior, where real estate is available at low costs and is supported by a strong presence of educational facilities, there is an enormous potential for developing these industries. The "trickle-down effect" of these industries can assist the state economy in increased wealth creation and better quality of life for its people.
- Access to quality infrastructure is critical for industry to develop and flourish in Madhya Pradesh. Air linkage, road linkage, logistic facilities would be the few critical facilities at the doorstep of industry the state must provide to transform itself into a vibrant industrial economy.

Hard infrastructure: Adequate and high quality power, efficient logistics and warehousing, a well-developed road network, as well as other infrastructure facilities such as telecommunication, industrial parks, industrial water supply and sewerage.

Soft infrastructure: Development of shared facilities to promote vibrant industry clusters—testing centres, labs, CETPs, solid waste disposal, signal transfer point (STPs), tool rooms etc.

- Madhya Pradesh's strengths in its industry sector are its extensive land area, abundant agricultural and mineral resources and the availability of a large workforce. More than 70 per cent of the population lives in rural areas and is engaged in activities like agriculture and trading. To ensure broad-based socio-economic growth, it is important to concentrate on employment generation as an objective for industrialisation as opposed to pure investment attraction.
- As a long-term strategy, the state has to move away from providing incentives, to providing high quality infrastructure as a platform to attract investments. However, it is not practical for the state to offer high-end infrastructure at all locations and to all types of industries. Hence, the state should aim to identify and develop specific industry clusters in each geographic region as preferred destinations for investment. The strategy would enable focused growth with balanced regional development. These clusters or islands of competencies will showcase Madhya Pradesh as an attractive investment destination and provide the basis for further investment flows into the state.
- To address the mismatches between the new environmental realities and organisational role definitions and structures, the state should endeavour to realign institutions by adopting the principle of retaining monopoly roles within the government domain, while progressively divesting functions that are today in the realm of competitive commercial activity. There needs to be decentralisation at all levels of the government through greater participation from industry in governance and decision-making.
- Vibrant urban locations act as getaways in a state. To develop a quality city takes a long process and cities will only be built and emerge out of their strengths. For Madhya Pradesh, there is a tremendous opportunity to develop its two major cities, Indore and Bhopal into such getaways.

ANNEXURE 13.A

TABLE 13.A-1

Number of Factories, Per cent Share in All-India and Rankings among 19 States

States & All India	*1998-99*	*1999-2000*	*2000-01*	*2001-02*	*2002-03*	*2003-04*	*2004-05*
				Number of Factories			
Chhattisgarh	1259	1380	1275	1277	1253	1295	1343
Gujarat	15455	14710	14090	13950	13180	12795	13603
Madhya Pradesh	3216	3269	3221	3019	2995	2982	3028
Maharashtra	19390	19009	18528	17853	17570	17474	18912
Rajasthan	4778	5063	5112	5279	5409	5452	5740
Uttar Pradesh	10508	10303	9635	9157	8980	9237	9582
All-India	131706	131558	131268	128549	127957	129074	136353
				% Share in Number of Factories			
Chhattisgarh	0.96	1.05	0.97	0.99	0.98	1.00	0.98
Gujarat	11.73	11.18	10.73	10.85	10.30	9.91	9.98
Madhya Pradesh	2.44	2.48	2.45	2.35	2.34	2.31	2.22
Maharashtra	14.72	14.45	14.11	13.89	13.73	13.54	13.87
Rajasthan	3.63	3.85	3.89	4.11	4.23	4.22	4.21
Uttar Pradesh	7.98	7.83	7.34	7.12	7.02	7.16	7.03
				Rankings among 19 States, Number of Factories			
Chhattisgarh	17	17	17	17	17	17	17
Gujarat	3	3	3	3	4	4	4
Madhya Pradesh	12	12	12	12	12	12	12
Maharashtra	2	2	2	2	2	2	2
Rajasthan	9	9	9	9	9	10	9
Uttar Pradesh	5	5	5	5	5	5	5

Source: Annual Survey of Industries, NSSO, Ministry of Statistics, GoI for various years.

TABLE 13.A-2

Fixed Capital, Per cent Share in All-India and Rankings among 19 States

States & All-India	*1998-99*	*1999-2000*	*2000-01*	*2001-02*	*2002-03*	*2003-04*	*2004-05*
				Fixed Capital			
Chhattisgarh	637127	896413	660150	1187970	728551	848485	1227351
Gujarat	6947655	6660127	7208836	8707855	8235801	8578858	8711140
Madhya Pradesh	1751592	1673054	1408361	1333010	1389786	1385356	1746384
Maharashtra	5683728	7041232	6753151	6897502	7697089	8347229	9616976
Rajasthan	1143079	1994473	1367300	1421395	1355028	1401177	1476796
Uttar Pradesh	5142156	3772531	3477513	3021410	2847631	2992605	3152999
All-India	39000000	40186473	39960422	43196013	44475938	47333140	51306925
				% Share in Fixed Capital			
Chhattisgarh	1.63	2.23	1.65	2.75	1.64	1.79	2.39
Gujarat	17.76	16.57	18.04	20.16	18.52	18.12	16.98
Madhya Pradesh	4.48	4.16	3.52	3.09	3.12	2.93	3.40
Maharashtra	14.53	17.52	16.90	15.97	17.31	17.64	18.74
Rajasthan	2.92	4.96	3.42	3.29	3.05	2.96	2.88
Uttar Pradesh	13.15	9.39	8.70	6.99	6.40	6.32	6.15
				Rankings among 19 States, Fixed Capital			
Chhattisgarh	14	14	15	12	14	14	13
Gujarat	1	2	1	1	1	1	2
Madhya Pradesh	7	9	9	11	10	12	8
Maharashtra	2	1	2	2	2	2	1
Rajasthan	9	7	11	10	11	11	12
Uttar Pradesh	3	3	4	5	6	6	6

Source: Annual Survey of Industries, NSSO, Ministry of Statistics, GoI for various years.

TABLE 13.A-3

Productive Capital, Per cent Share in All-India and Rankings among 19 States

States & All India	*1998-99*	*1999-2000*	*2001-02*	*2002-03*	*2003-04*	*2004-05*
			Productive Capital			
Chhattisgarh	922036	1110158	284720	832846	1050405	1545319
Gujarat	8504993	8147235	10350259	9993803	54141	10902027
Madhya Pradesh	2115878	2305726	1737556	1662883	926105	2398024
Maharashtra	7770599	8972612	8415882	9037913	1762808	12038206
Rajasthan	1515320	2002665	1786177	1725923	1692272	2038611
Uttar Pradesh	5889584	4619314	3806465	3752097	3821330	4357510
All-India	50000000	50564909	53236598	54488048	59256241	67312322
			% Share in Productive Capital			
Chhattisgarh	1.87	2.20	0.53	1.53	1.77	2.30
Gujarat	17.22	16.11	19.44	18.34	0.09	16.20
Madhya Pradesh	4.28	4.56	3.26	3.05	1.56	3.56
Maharashtra	15.73	17.74	15.81	16.59	2.97	17.88
Rajasthan	3.07	3.96	3.36	3.17	2.86	3.03
Uttar Pradesh	11.92	9.14	7.15	6.89	6.45	6.47
			Rankings among 19 States, Productive Capital			
Chhattisgarh	14	13	18	15	13	14
Gujarat	1	2	1	1	19	2
Madhya Pradesh	7	7	10	11	14	9
Maharashtra	2	1	2	2	9	1
Rajasthan	10	8	9	9	11	11
Uttar Pradesh	3	4	4	6	6	6

Source: Annual Survey of Industries, NSSO, Ministry of Statistics, GoI for various years.

TABLE 13.A-4

Working Capital, Per cent Share in All-India and Rankings among 19 States

States & All-India	*1998-99*	*1999-2000*	*2000-01*	*2001-02*	*2002-03*	*2003-04*	*2004-05*
				Working Capital			
Chhattisgarh	284909	213745	160861	321868	104295	201921	317968
Gujarat	1557338	1487109	1532832	1642404	1758001	1867760	2190887
Madhya Pradesh	364286	632672	381713	404546	273097	377452	651640
Maharashtra	2086871	1931380	1778137	1518379	1340825	1822206	2421230
Rajasthan	372241	8193	404601	364781	370895	427196	561815
Uttar Pradesh	747428	846783	721168	785055	904466	828725	1204511
All-India	10000000	10378436	10520839	10040585	10012110	11923101	16005396
				% Share in Working Capital			
Chhattisgarh	2.77	2.06	1.53	3.21	1.04	1.69	1.99
Gujarat	15.16	14.33	14.57	16.36	17.56	15.67	13.69
Maharashtra	20.31	18.61	16.90	15.12	13.39	15.28	15.13
Rajasthan	3.62	0.08	3.85	3.63	3.70	3.58	3.51
Uttar Pradesh	7.27	8.16	6.85	7.82	9.03	6.95	7.53
				Rankings among 19 States, Working Capital			
Chhattisgarh	11	12	14	11	18	12	14
Gujarat	2	2	2	1	1	1	2
Madhya Pradesh	10	5	10	8	10	10	9
Maharashtra	1	1	1	2	2	2	1
Rajasthan	9	19	9	10	9	9	12
Uttar Pradesh	4	4	4	4	3	4	4

Source: Annual Survey of Industries, NSSO, Ministry of Statistics, GoI for various years.

TABLE 13.A-5

Invested Capital, Per cent Share in All-India and Rankings among 19 States

States & All-India	*1998-99*	*1999-2000*	*2000-01*	*2001-02*	*2002-03*	*2003-04*	*2004-05*
			Invested Capital				
Chhattisgarh	943451	1163096	905285	1646474	953582	1189674	1603833
Gujarat	8761928	8580412	9300141	11106001	10956152	11502721	12327519
Madhya Pradesh	2230263	2369511	1973342	1881102	1947125	2044016	2445338
Maharashtra	8618508	10469124	10363120	10508270	11891264	12401930	14368582
Rajasthan	1583978	2467886	1855306	1894140	1839425	1954894	2119235
Uttar Pradesh	6457333	5085709	4901000	4423859	4399806	4761440	5160776
All-India	54000000	56663430	57179940	60591285	63747308	67959853	75941770
			% Share in Invested Capital				
Chhattisgarh	1.76	2.05	1.58	2.72	1.50	1.75	2.11
Gujarat	16.31	15.14	16.26	18.33	17.19	16.93	16.23
Madhya Pradesh	4.15	4.18	3.45	3.10	3.05	3.01	3.22
Maharashtra	16.05	18.48	18.12	17.34	18.65	18.25	18.92
Rajasthan	2.95	4.36	3.24	3.13	2.89	2.88	2.79
Uttar Pradesh	12.02	8.98	8.57	7.30	6.90	7.01	6.80
			Rankings among 19 states, Invested Capital				
Chhattisgarh	15	14	15	12	15	14	14
Gujarat	1	2	2	1	2	2	2
Madhya Pradesh	7	9	10	11	9	9	9
Maharashtra	2	1	1	2	1	1	1
Rajasthan	11	7	11	10	12	12	10
Uttar Pradesh	3	4	4	4	6	5	6

Source: Annual Survey of Industries, NSSO, Ministry of Statistics, GoI for various years.

TABLE 13.A-6

Outstanding Loan, Per cent Share in All-India and Rankings among 19 States

States & All-India	*1998-99*	*1999-2000*	*2000-01*	*2001-02*	*2002-03*	*2003-04*	*2004-05*
			Outstanding Loan				
Chhattisgarh	459160	621240	250778	477217	263627	558483	675597
Gujarat	3892512	3975601	3854819	3632505	3348721	3924424	5485171
Madhya Pradesh	824015	938606	982595	802989	717995	885236	999619
Maharashtra	4035253	4799885	4736931	4922425	5562200	5631397	5941697
Rajasthan	747850	1000979	979632	910885	987212	943327	977662
Uttar Pradesh	2132235	1966618	1941344	1988711	1689801	1847593	1997825
All-India	23000000	25378161	25795392	26921926	26339233	28977564	33463375
			% Share in Outstanding Loan				
Chhattisgarh	2.01	2.45	0.97	1.77	1.00	1.93	2.02
Gujarat	17.06	15.67	14.94	13.49	12.71	13.54	16.39
Madhya Pradesh	3.61	3.70	3.81	2.98	2.73	3.05	2.99
Maharashtra	17.68	18.91	18.36	18.28	21.12	19.43	17.76
Rajasthan	3.28	3.94	3.80	3.38	3.75	3.26	2.92
Uttar Pradesh	9.34	7.75	7.53	7.39	6.42	6.38	5.97
			Rankings among 19 States, Outstanding Loan				
Chhattisgarh	13	11	17	15	16	14	14
Gujarat	2	2	2	2	2	2	2
Madhya Pradesh	9	9	9	10	9	11	8
Maharashtra	1	1	1	1	1	1	1
Rajasthan	10	8	10	9	8	9	10
Uttar Pradesh	4	4	4	6	7	7	7

Source: Annual Survey of Industries, NSSO, Ministry of Statistics, GoI for various years.

TABLE 13.A-7

Number of Workers, Per cent Share in All-India and Rankings among 19 States

States & All-India	*1998-99*	*1999-2000*	*2000-01*	*2001-02*	*2002-03*	*2003-04*	*2004-05*
				Number of Workers			
Chhattisgarh	73614	79421	65894	64311	63771	71604	77910
Gujarat	607763	613409	553704	521528	528217	538080	606847
Madhya Pradesh	212283	195912	191131	158230	156565	160976	163843
Maharashtra	813900	854349	817305	816501	829305	773976	814599
Rajasthan	175255	176941	175566	178521	190971	191589	207625
Uttar Pradesh	455816	428913	401674	382821	409116	439267	453007
All-India	6364464	6280659	6135236	5957848	6161493	6086908	6599298
				% Share in Number of Workers			
Chhattisgarh	1.16	1.26	1.07	1.08	1.03	1.18	1.18
Gujarat	9.55	9.77	9.02	8.75	8.57	8.84	9.20
Madhya Pradesh	3.34	3.12	3.12	2.66	2.54	2.64	2.48
Maharashtra	12.79	13.60	13.32	13.70	13.46	12.72	12.34
Rajasthan	2.75	2.82	2.86	3.00	3.10	3.15	3.15
Uttar Pradesh	7.16	6.83	6.55	6.43	6.64	7.22	6.86
				Rankings among 19 States, Number of Workers			
Chhattisgarh	16	16	16	16	16	16	16
Gujarat	4	4	4	4	4	4	4
Madhya Pradesh	11	11	11	12	12	12	12
Maharashtra	2	2	2	2	3	2	2
Rajasthan	12	12	12	11	11	11	11
Uttar Pradesh	6	6	6	6	6	5	5

Source: Annual Survey of Industries, NSSO, Ministry of Statistics, GoI for various years.

TABLE 13.A-8

Total Employees, Per cent Share in All-India and Rankings among 19 States

States & All India	*1998-99*	*1999-2000*	*2000-01*	*2001-02*	*2002-03*	*2003-04*	*2004-05*
				Total Employees			
Chhattisgarh	98284	101632	96389	93777	93794	99764	106409
Gujarat	815986	822884	752013	712804	717055	729310	808618
Madhya Pradesh	301438	267685	253444	209035	208874	214140	216563
Maharashtra	1393688	1217260	1172782	1162542	1170461	1114070	1162346
Rajasthan	237521	234651	232177	231875	244265	245274	268437
Uttar Pradesh	621155	571719	539737	513190	542160	569603	587702
All-India	8588581	8172836	7987743	7750366	7935948	7870081	8453624
				% Share in Total Employees			
Chhattisgarh	1.14	1.24	1.21	1.21	1.18	1.27	1.26
Gujarat	9.50	10.07	9.41	9.20	9.04	9.27	9.57
Madhya Pradesh	3.51	3.28	3.17	2.70	2.63	2.72	2.56
Maharashtra	16.23	14.89	14.68	15.00	14.75	14.16	13.75
Rajasthan	2.77	2.87	2.91	2.99	3.08	3.12	3.18
Uttar Pradesh	7.23	7.00	6.76	6.62	6.83	7.24	6.95
				Rankings among 19 States, Total Employees			
Chhattisgarh	16	16	16	16	16	16	16
Gujarat	4	4	4	4	4	4	4
Madhya Pradesh	10	11	11	12	12	12	12
Maharashtra	1	1	1	1	1	2	2
Rajasthan	12	12	12	11	11	11	11
Uttar Pradesh	6	6	6	6	5	5	5

Source: Annual Survey of Industries, NSSO, Ministry of Statistics, GoI for various years.

TABLE 13.A-9

Value of Output, Per cent Share in All-India and Rankings among 19 States

States & All-India	*1998-99*	*1999-2000*	*2000-01*	*2001-02*	*2002-03*	*2003-04*	*2004-05*
				Value of Output			
Chhattisgarh	1211850	1295791	1274307	1258175	1449707	2041254	2780028
Gujarat	11000000	11855115	12797728	14755010	18269979	20733426	26074860
Madhya Pradesh	2858558	4408900	3671234	3822625	3805750	4274433	4696851
Maharashtra	16000000	18133252	18497146	18122281	21759551	23829332	35887957
Rajasthan	2382042	2995996	3078418	3122742	3311696	3763555	4488205
Uttar Pradesh	5811990	6104692	6485418	6703704	8052063	9340067	10913874
All-India	78000000	89793835	92690185	96245663	113056111	128738002	167256142
				% Share in Value of Output			
Chhattisgarh	1.55	1.44	1.37	1.31	1.28	1.59	1.66
Gujarat	14.44	13.20	13.81	15.33	16.16	16.11	15.59
Madhya Pradesh	3.65	4.91	3.96	3.97	3.37	3.32	2.81
Maharashtra	20.56	20.19	19.96	18.83	19.25	18.51	21.46
Rajasthan	3.04	3.34	3.32	3.24	2.93	2.92	2.68
Uttar Pradesh	7.42	6.80	7.00	6.97	7.12	7.26	6.53
				Rankings among 19 States, Value of Output			
Chhattisgarh	14	14	15	15	15	14	14
Gujarat	2	2	2	2	2	2	2
Madhya Pradesh	10	7	9	9	10	10	10
Maharashtra	1	1	1	1	1	1	1
Rajasthan	11	11	11	11	11	11	11
Uttar Pradesh	4	4	4	4	5	4	4

Source: Annual Survey of Industries, NSSO, Ministry of Statistics, GoI for various years.

TABLE 13.A-10

Net Value Added, Per cent Share in All-India and Rankings among 19 States

States & All-India	*1998-99*	*1999-2000*	*2000-01*	*2001-02*	*2002-03*	*2003-04*	*2004-05*
				Net Value Added			
Chhattisgarh	319464	236161	249277	237192	349830	534594	870540
Gujarat	1889640	1927579	1685587	1688617	2288943	2886545	3601558
Madhya Pradesh	444016	563712	620834	595683	526046	528689	555351
Maharashtra	3130018	3458772	3126098	2939166	3491887	4190975	5130921
Rajasthan	357157	531474	525802	482328	477799	517323	658264
Uttar Pradesh	1046697	1022958	957702	1000649	1136484	1264899	1429776
All-India	15000000	15497442	14362141	14430212	17234004	20293276	25990686
				% Share in Net Value Added			
Chhattisgarh	2.20	1.52	1.74	1.64	2.03	2.63	3.35
Gujarat	12.99	12.44	11.74	11.70	13.28	14.22	13.86
Madhya Pradesh	3.05	3.64	4.32	4.13	3.05	2.61	2.14
Maharashtra	21.52	22.32	21.77	20.37	20.26	20.65	19.74
Rajasthan	2.46	3.43	3.66	3.34	2.77	2.55	2.53
Uttar Pradesh	7.20	6.60	6.67	6.93	6.59	6.23	5.50
				Rankings among 19 States, Net Value Added			
Chhattisgarh	14	15	14	14	14	10	10
Gujarat	2	2	2	2	2	2	2
Madhya Pradesh	11	10	7	9	11	12	14
Maharashtra	1	1	1	1	1	1	1
Rajasthan	13	12	10	11	12	13	11
Uttar Pradesh	4	4	4	5	6	6	7

Source: Annual Survey of Industries, NSSO, Ministry of Statistics, GoI for various years.

TABLE 13.A-11

Net Income, Per cent Share in All-India and Rankings among 19 States

States & All-India	*1998-99*	*1999-2000*	*2000-01*	*2001-02*	*2002-03*	*2003-04*	*2004-05*
				Net Income			
Chhattisgarh	226834	172307	175673	158799	279363	465794	817728
Gujarat	1240351	1257864	996640	973125	1757074	2406624	3145898
Madhya Pradesh	287149	380368	460638	451670	395470	401306	443656
Maharashtra	2260998	2417416	2171431	2004138	2629246	3375039	4365703
Rajasthan	215303	290453	350016	293132	316901	395892	545065
Uttar Pradesh	634660	651708	612608	702154	836780	1019043	1203034
All-India	10000000	10656621	9755619	9833306	13019466	16479964	22291481
				% Share in Net Income			
Chhattisgarh	2.23	1.62	1.80	1.61	2.15	2.83	3.67
Gujarat	12.20	11.80	10.22	9.90	13.50	14.60	14.11
Madhya Pradesh	2.82	3.57	4.72	4.59	3.04	2.44	1.99
Orissa	0.96	1.44	1.16	0.92	1.19	1.24	2.26
Rajasthan	2.12	2.73	3.59	2.98	2.43	2.40	2.45
Uttar Pradesh	6.24	6.12	6.28	7.14	6.43	6.18	5.40
				Rankings among 19 States, Net Income			
Chhattisgarh	13	14	14	14	14	10	10
Gujarat	2	2	3	3	2	2	2
Madhya Pradesh	12	10	7	8	11	12	14
Maharashtra	1	1	1	1	1	1	1
Rajasthan	14	12	10	11	12	13	11
Uttar Pradesh	6	4	4	4	4	6	7

Source: Annual Survey of Industries, NSSO, Ministry of Statistics, GoI for various years.

TABLE 13.A-12

Net Fixed Capital Formation, Per cent Share in All-India and Rankings among 19 States

States & All-India	*1998-99*	*1999-2000*	*2000-01*	*2001-02*	*2002-03*	*2003-04*	*2004-05*
				Net Fixed Capital Formation			
Chhattisgarh	19704	-61176	15916	458005	-1195	90530	322217
Gujarat	756984	399305	-74801	2101512	-184507	-58993	-2506
Madhya Pradesh	120617	48950	44668	-50661	-32305	6846	125753
Maharashtra	379241	297714	212029	41107	66163	593337	462632
Rajasthan	84888	10470	383	-9496	-18776	20669	72475
Uttar Pradesh	553904	86333	24489	93669	12972	196268	174295
All-India	4080495	1507954	1215034	3122442	541866	1271031	2553722
				% Share in Net Fixed Capital Formation			
Chhattisgarh	0.48	-4.06	1.31	14.67	-0.22	7.12	12.62
Gujarat	18.55	26.48	-6.16	67.30	-34.05	-4.64	-0.10
Madhya Pradesh	2.96	3.25	3.68	-1.62	-5.96	0.54	4.92
Maharashtra	9.29	19.74	17.45	1.32	12.21	46.68	18.12
Rajasthan	2.08	0.69	0.03	-0.30	-3.47	1.63	2.84
Uttar Pradesh	13.57	5.73	2.02	3.00	2.39	15.44	6.83
				Rankings among 19 States, Net Fixed Capital Formation			
Chhattisgarh	15	16	12	2	14	4	3
Gujarat	2	1	19	1	19	18	18
Madhya Pradesh	8	8	7	19	16	11	7
Maharashtra	4	3	1	8	6	1	1
Rajasthan	10	12	16	18	15	8	10
Uttar Pradesh	3	7	8	4	9	3	5

Source: Annual Survey of Industries, NSSO, Ministry of Statistics, GoI for various years.

TABLE 13.A-13

Gross Fixed Capital Formation, Per cent Share in All-India and Rankings among 19 States

States & All-India	*1998-99*	*1999-2000*	*2000-01*	*2001-02*	*2002-03*	*2003-04*	*2004-05*
			Gross Fixed Capital Formation				
Chhattisgarh	73360	10393	69035	517569	59782	158478	400580
Gujarat	1218714	1010059	538819	2872066	640038	746684	858338
Madhya Pradesh	245826	185479	165570	90231	103682	138241	263717
Maharashtra	879121	940797	854596	713269	784866	1352757	1370863
Rajasthan	179798	160093	121036	122601	112573	168149	220383
Uttar Pradesh	815327	354122	307076	362851	296900	496002	513637
All-India	6907081	4867882	4687927	7015145	4745424	5753380	7525046
			% Share in Gross Fixed Capital Formation				
Chhattisgarh	1.06	0.21	1.47	7.38	1.26	2.75	5.32
Gujarat	17.64	20.75	11.49	40.94	13.49	12.98	11.41
Madhya Pradesh	3.56	3.81	3.53	1.29	2.18	2.40	3.50
Maharashtra	12.73	19.33	18.23	10.17	16.54	23.51	18.22
Rajasthan	2.60	3.29	2.58	1.75	2.37	2.92	2.93
Uttar Pradesh	11.80	7.27	6.55	5.17	6.26	8.62	6.83
			Rankings among 19 States, Gross Fixed Capital Formation				
Chhattisgarh	15	16	15	3	16	9	7
Gujarat	1	1	3	1	3	3	3
Madhya Pradesh	9	8	10	15	13	10	9
Maharashtra	3	2	1	2	1	1	1
Rajasthan	10	9	12	12	12	8	12
Uttar Pradesh	4	5	6	6	6	4	5

Source: Annual Survey of Industries, NSSO, Ministry of Statistics, GoI for various years.

TABLE 13.A-14

Gross Capital Formation, Per cent Share in All-India and Rankings among 19 States

States & All-India	*1998-99*	*1999-2000*	*2000-01*	*2001-02*	*2002-03*	*2003-04*	*2004-05*
			Gross Capital Formation				
Chhattisgarh	71852	-40489	82422	691270	22498	268386	381339
Gujarat	1255330	1196476	730236	3204294	958004	938212	1402195
Madhya Pradesh	241300	243984	191941	74334	138690	230637	294443
Maharashtra	959324	1385763	1231978	633520	1301251	1478573	1817705
Rajasthan	191156	206412	155597	117403	133323	229071	294346
Uttar Pradesh	840979	472320	484910	443841	389955	742034	776545
All-India	7217800	6466535	6141480	7387299	6397638	7418713	11007290
			% Share in Gross Capital Formation				
Chhattisgarh	1.00	-0.63	1.34	9.36	0.35	3.62	3.46
Gujarat	17.39	18.50	11.89	43.38	14.97	12.65	12.74
Madhya Pradesh	3.34	3.77	3.13	1.01	2.17	3.11	2.67
Maharashtra	13.29	21.43	20.06	8.58	20.34	19.93	16.51
Rajasthan	2.65	3.19	2.53	1.59	2.08	3.09	2.67
Uttar Pradesh	11.65	7.30	7.90	6.01	6.10	10.00	7.05
			Rankings among 19 States, Gross Capital Formation				
Chhattisgarh	15	17	15	2	18	8	9
Gujarat	1	2	2	1	2	3	3
Madhya Pradesh	9	8	11	15	12	9	11
Maharashtra	3	1	1	3	1	1	1
Rajasthan	10	9	12	11	13	10	12
Uttar Pradesh	4	5	4	5	5	4	5

Source: Annual Survey of Industries, NSSO, Ministry of Statistics, GoI for various years.

TABLE 13.A-15

Profits, Per cent Share in All-India and Rankings among 19 States

States & All-India	*1998-99*	*1999-2000*	*2000-01*	*2001-02*	*2002-03*	*2003-04*	*2004-05*
				Profits			
Chhattisgarh	94085	58498	48101	25675	129968	281410	653797
Gujarat	741254	650316	412624	368841	1119278	1711617	2345939
Madhya Pradesh	129945	183076	248574	268235	215095	208680	233028
Maharashtra	1055438	1122234	858838	633070	1198408	1865556	2734891
Rajasthan	77637	136021	191411	135219	146771	216723	341957
Uttar Pradesh	230956	265782	236043	326993	409972	574080	709537
All-India	4730623	4733475	3569880	3488385	6185254	9234531	14460199
				% Share in Profits			
Chhattisgarh	1.99	1.24	1.35	0.74	2.10	3.05	4.52
Gujarat	15.67	13.74	11.56	10.57	18.10	18.53	16.22
Madhya Pradesh	2.75	3.87	6.96	7.69	3.48	2.26	1.61
Maharashtra	22.31	23.71	24.06	18.15	19.38	20.20	18.91
Rajasthan	1.64	2.87	5.36	3.88	2.37	2.35	2.36
Uttar Pradesh	4.88	5.61	6.61	9.37	6.63	6.22	4.91
				Rankings among 19 States, Profits			
Chhattisgarh	13	14	13	13	13	9	8
Gujarat	2	2	3	2	2	2	2
Madhya Pradesh	10	9	4	5	9	12	14
Maharashtra	1	1	1	1	1	1	1
Rajasthan	14	11	6	10	12	11	11
Uttar Pradesh	6	5	5	4	3	4	7

Source: Annual Survey of Industries, NSSO, Ministry of Statistics, GoI for various years.

ANNEXURE 13.B

TABLE 13.B-1
Output per Worker

States & All-India	*1998-99*	*1999-2000*	*2000-01*	*2001-02*	*2002-03*	*2003-04*	*2004-05*
All-India	12.31	14.30	15.11	16.15	18.35	21.15	25.34
Chhattisgarh	16.46	16.32	19.34	19.56	22.73	28.51	35.68
Gujarat	18.62	19.33	23.11	28.29	34.59	38.53	42.97
Madhya Pradesh	13.47	22.50	19.21	24.16	24.31	26.55	28.67
Maharashtra	19.80	21.22	22.63	22.20	26.24	30.79	44.06
Rajasthan	13.59	16.93	17.53	17.49	17.34	19.64	21.62
Uttar Pradesh	12.75	14.23	16.15	17.51	19.68	21.26	24.09
			Rankings among 19 States, Output per Worker				
Chhattisgarh	4	7	5	6	6	4	3
Gujarat	2	4	1	1	1	1	2
Madhya Pradesh	7	1	6	2	3	5	5
Maharashtra	1	2	2	4	2	3	1
Rajasthan	6	6	7	9	12	11	13
Uttar Pradesh	8	9	9	8	9	9	10

Source: Annual Survey of Industries, NSSO, Ministry of Statistics, GoI for various years.

TABLE 13.B-2
Value Added per Worker

States & All-India	*1998-99*	*1999-2000*	*2000-01*	*2001-02*	*2002-03*	*2003-04*	*2004-05*
All-India	2.29	2.47	2.34	2.42	2.80	3.33	3.94
Chhattisgarh	4.34	2.97	3.78	3.69	5.49	7.47	11.17
Gujarat	3.11	3.14	3.04	3.24	4.33	5.36	5.93
Madhya Pradesh	2.09	2.88	3.25	3.76	3.36	3.28	3.39
Maharashtra	3.85	4.05	3.82	3.60	4.21	5.41	6.30
Rajasthan	2.04	3.00	2.99	2.70	2.50	2.70	3.17
Uttar Pradesh	2.30	2.39	2.38	2.61	2.78	2.88	3.16
			Rankings among 19 States, Value Added per Worker				
Chhattisgarh	2	7	3	3	3	1	2
Gujarat	5	4	6	5	5	6	5
Madhya Pradesh	9	8	5	2	8	10	11
Maharashtra	3	2	2	4	6	5	4
Rajasthan	10	6	8	9	13	13	12
Uttar Pradesh	6	10	10	11	12	12	13

Source: Annual Survey of Industries, NSSO, Ministry of Statistics, GoI for various years.

TABLE 13.B-3

Workers per Factory

States & All-India	*1998-99*	*1999-2000*	*2000-01*	*2001-02*	*2002-03*	*2003-04*	*2004-05*
All-India	48.32	47.74	46.74	46.35	48.15	47.16	48.40
Chhattisgarh	58.47	57.55	51.68	50.36	50.89	55.29	58.01
Gujarat	39.32	41.70	39.30	37.39	40.08	42.05	44.61
Madhya Pradesh	66.01	59.93	59.34	52.41	52.28	53.98	54.11
Maharashtra	41.98	44.94	44.11	45.73	47.20	44.29	43.07
Rajasthan	36.68	34.95	34.34	33.82	35.31	35.14	36.17
Uttar Pradesh	43.38	41.63	41.69	41.81	45.56	47.56	47.28
Rankings among 19 States, Workers per Factory							
Chhattisgarh	8	8	9	10	8	5	6
Gujarat	16	15	15	17	15	15	15
Madhya Pradesh	5	5	5	8	7	8	8
Maharashtra	15	12	13	13	12	14	16
Rajasthan	17	19	18	19	18	18	18
Uttar Pradesh	14	16	14	14	14	12	13

Source: Annual Survey of Industries, NSSO, Ministry of Statistics, GoI for various years.

TABLE 13.B-4

Fixed Capital per Factory

States & All-India	*1998-99*	*1999-2000*	*2000-01*	*2001-02*	*2002-03*	*2003-04*	*2004-05*
All-India	296.99	305.47	304.42	336.03	347.59	366.71	376.28
Chhattisgarh	506.06	649.57	517.76	930.28	581.45	655.20	913.89
Gujarat	449.54	452.76	511.63	624.22	624.87	670.49	640.38
Madhya Pradesh	544.65	511.79	437.24	441.54	464.04	464.57	576.75
Maharashtra	293.13	370.42	364.48	386.35	438.08	477.69	508.51
Rajasthan	239.24	393.93	267.47	269.25	250.51	257.00	257.28
Uttar Pradesh	489.36	366.16	360.93	329.96	317.11	323.98	329.05
Rankings among 19 States, Fixed Capital per Factory							
Chhattisgarh	5	2	4	2	5	5	3
Gujarat	8	6	5	5	4	4	5
Madhya Pradesh	4	5	6	7	7	8	6
Maharashtra	10	9	9	9	8	7	7
Rajasthan	11	7	13	13	14	14	14
Uttar Pradesh	7	10	10	10	12	12	13

Source: Annual Survey of Industries, NSSO, Ministry of Statistics, GoI for various years.

TABLE 13.B-5

Fixed Capital per Worker

States & All-India	*1998-99*	*1999-2000*	*2000-01*	*2001-02*	*2002-03*	*2003-04*	*2004-05*
All-India	6.15	6.40	6.51	7.25	7.22	7.78	7.77
Chhattisgarh	8.65	11.29	10.02	18.47	11.42	11.85	15.75
Gujarat	11.43	10.86	13.02	16.70	15.59	15.94	14.35
Madhya Pradesh	8.25	8.54	7.37	8.42	8.88	8.61	10.66
Maharashtra	6.98	8.24	8.26	8.45	9.28	10.78	11.81
Rajasthan	6.52	11.27	7.79	7.96	7.10	7.31	7.11
Uttar Pradesh	11.28	8.80	8.66	7.89	6.96	6.81	6.96
Rankings among 19 States, Fixed Capital per Worker							
Chhattisgarh	7	1	5	1	5	5	2
Gujarat	1	3	1	2	1	3	3
Madhya Pradesh	8	8	9	8	8	8	7
Maharashtra	9	9	7	7	6	6	6
Rajasthan	10	2	8	9	11	10	10
Uttar Pradesh	3	6	6	10	12	12	11

Source: Annual Survey of Industries, NSSO, Ministry of Statistics, GoI for various years.

TABLE 13.B-6

Value Added to Output

States & All-India	1998-99	1999-2000	2000-01	2001-02	2002-03	2003-04	2004-05
All-India	0.19	0.17	0.15	0.15	0.15	0.16	0.16
Chhattisgarh	0.26	0.18	0.20	0.19	0.24	0.26	0.31
Gujarat	0.17	0.16	0.13	0.11	0.13	0.14	0.14
Madhya Pradesh	0.16	0.13	0.17	0.16	0.14	0.12	0.12
Maharashtra	0.19	0.19	0.17	0.16	0.16	0.18	0.14
Rajasthan	0.15	0.18	0.17	0.15	0.14	0.14	0.15
Uttar Pradesh	0.18	0.17	0.15	0.15	0.14	0.14	0.13
Rankings among 19 States, Value Added to Output							
Chhattisgarh	2	7	4	2	2	2	2
Gujarat	13	13	16	18	18	13	13
Madhya Pradesh	18	19	8	8	15	17	16
Maharashtra	7	6	9	5	8	6	12
Rajasthan	19	8	7	10	11	14	10
Uttar Pradesh	10	9	11	11	12	15	15

Source: Annual Survey of Industries, NSSO, Ministry of Statistics, GoI for various years.

TABLE 13.B-7

Capital-Output Ratio

States & All-India	1998-99	1999-2000	2000-01	2001-02	2002-03	2003-04	2004-05
All-India	0.50	0.45	0.43	0.45	0.39	0.37	0.31
Chhattisgarh	0.53	0.69	0.52	0.94	0.50	0.42	0.44
Gujarat	0.61	0.56	0.56	0.59	0.45	0.41	0.33
Madhya Pradesh	0.61	0.38	0.38	0.35	0.37	0.32	0.37
Maharashtra	0.35	0.39	0.37	0.38	0.35	0.35	0.27
Rajasthan	0.48	0.67	0.44	0.46	0.41	0.37	0.33
Uttar Pradesh	0.88	0.62	0.54	0.45	0.35	0.32	0.29
Rankings among 19 States, Capital-Output Ratio							
Chhattisgarh	8	2	8	1	6	6	3
Gujarat	6	8	5	5	8	8	9
Madhya Pradesh	7	14	13	15	13	14	5
Maharashtra	13	13	14	12	14	12	15
Rajasthan	11	3	9	9	9	10	10
Uttar Pradesh	2	6	6	10	15	15	13

Source: Annual Survey of Industries, NSSO, Ministry of Statistics, GoI for various years.

TABLE 13.B-8

Outstanding Loan per Factory

States & All-India	1998-99	1999-2000	2000-01	2001-02	2002-03	2003-04	2004-05
All-India	173.27	192.90	196.51	209.43	205.84	224.50	245.42
Chhattisgarh	364.70	450.17	196.69	373.70	210.40	431.26	503.05
Gujarat	251.86	270.27	273.59	260.39	254.08	306.72	403.23
Madhya Pradesh	256.22	287.12	305.06	265.98	239.73	296.86	330.13
Maharashtra	208.11	252.51	255.66	275.72	316.57	322.27	314.18
Rajasthan	156.52	197.70	191.63	172.55	182.51	173.02	170.32
Uttar Pradesh	202.92	190.88	201.49	217.18	188.17	200.02	208.50
Rankings among 19 States, Outstanding Loan per Factory							
Chhattisgarh	2	2	12	4	9	4	4
Gujarat	5	7	6	9	7	8	6
Madhya Pradesh	4	4	4	8	8	9	7
Maharashtra	9	8	8	7	4	7	9
Rajasthan	12	10	13	13	12	13	13
Uttar Pradesh	10	12	11	12	11	11	11

Source: Annual Survey of Industries, NSSO, Ministry of Statistics, GoI for various years.

TABLE 13.B-9

Profit per Factory

States & All-India	*1998-99*	*1999-2000*	*2000-01*	*2001-02*	*2002-03*	*2003-04*	*2004-05*
All-India	35.92	35.98	27.20	27.14	48.34	71.54	106.05
Chhattisgarh	74.73	42.39	37.73	20.11	103.73	217.31	486.82
Gujarat	47.96	44.21	29.28	26.44	84.92	133.77	172.46
Madhya Pradesh	40.41	56.00	77.17	88.85	71.82	69.98	76.96
Maharashtra	54.43	59.04	46.35	35.46	68.21	106.76	144.61
Rajasthan	16.25	26.87	37.44	25.61	27.13	39.75	59.57
Uttar Pradesh	21.98	25.80	24.50	35.71	45.65	62.15	74.05
			Rankings among 19 States, Profit Per Factory				
Chhattisgarh	3	8	4	10	4	2	2
Gujarat	6	7	8	7	5	5	5
Madhya Pradesh	9	6	2	2	7	10	11
Maharashtra	5	4	3	5	8	6	9
Rajasthan	14	13	5	9	13	12	13
Uttar Pradesh	12	14	10	4	11	11	12

Source: Annual Survey of Industries, NSSO, Ministry of Statistics, GoI for various years.

TABLE 13.B-10

Net Income per Factory

States & All-India	*1998-99*	*1999-2000*	*2000-01*	*2001-02*	*2002-03*	*2003-04*	*2004-05*
All-India	77.20	81.00	74.32	76.49	101.75	127.68	163.48
Chhattisgarh	180.17	124.86	137.78	124.35	222.96	359.69	608.88
Gujarat	80.26	85.51	70.73	69.76	133.31	188.09	231.27
Madhya Pradesh	89.29	116.36	143.01	149.61	132.04	134.58	146.52
Maharashtra	116.61	127.17	117.20	112.26	149.64	193.15	230.84
Rajasthan	45.06	57.37	68.47	55.53	58.59	72.61	94.96
Uttar Pradesh	60.40	63.25	63.58	76.68	93.18	110.32	125.55
			Rankings among 19 States, Net Income per Factory				
Chhattisgarh	2	4	4	3	2	2	2
Gujarat	9	9	9	10	8	7	6
Madhya Pradesh	7	5	3	2	9	10	11
Maharashtra	4	3	5	6	6	6	7
Rajasthan	16	14	11	13	16	15	14
Uttar Pradesh	13	11	13	9	11	12	13

Source: Annual Survey of Industries, NSSO, Ministry of Statistics, GoI for various years.

References

Census of India (2001). *Census of India 2001 Primary Abstract-Madhya Pradesh*. Director of Census Operation, Bhopal, Madhya Pradesh.

GoI (2004). *Administrative Report 2003-04*. Department of Civil Aviation, Government of India, New Delhi, India.

———. (2006). *Report of National Commission on Macroeconomics and Health, Government of India 2005*. Government of India. New Delhi, India.

———. (2007). *Eleventh Five Year Plan 2007-12*. Planning Commission of India, Government of India, New Delhi, India.

———. (2008). *Administrative Report 2007*. Central Electricity Authority, Government of India, New Delhi, India.

———. (2008). *Study on Elected Women Representatives (EWRs) in Gram Panchayats*, 2007-08. Ministry of Panchayati Raj, Government of India, New Delhi, India.

———. (2009). *Economic Survey 2008-09*. Ministry of Finance, Government of India. New Delhi, India.

GoMP (2004). *Administrative Report 2003-04*. Home Department, Government of Madhya Pradesh, Bhopal, Madhya Pradesh.

———. (2005). *Economic Survey 2004-05*. Directorate of Economics and Statistics Department, Government of Madhya Pradesh, Bhopal, Madhya Pradesh.

———. (2006). *Economic Survey 2005-06*. Directorate of Economics and Statistics Department, Government of Madhya Pradesh, Bhopal, Madhya Pradesh.

———. (2006). Administrative Report 2005-06. Directorate of Horticulture, Government of Madhya Pradesh, Bhopal, Madhya Pradesh.

———. (2007). Estimates *of State Domestic Product of Madhya Pradesh 1999-00 to 2006-07*. Directorate of Economics & Statistics, Government of Madhya Pradesh. Bhopal, Madhya Pradesh.

———. (2007). *Economic Survey 2006-07*. Directorate of Economics and Statistics Department, Government of Madhya Pradesh, Bhopal, Madhya Pradesh.

———. (2007). *Compendium of Agriculture Statistics of Madhya Pradesh 2006-07*. Government of Madhya Pradesh, Bhopal, Madhya Pradesh.

———. (2007). *Administrative Report 2006-07*. Water Resource Department, Government of Madhya Pradesh, Bhopal, Madhya Pradesh.

———. (2007). *Administrative Report 2006-07*. Department of Rural Industries, Government of Madhya Pradesh, Bhopal, Madhya Pradesh.

———. (2007). *Administrative Report 2006-07*. Handicraft and Handloom Development Corporation, Government of Madhya Pradesh, Bhopal, Madhya Pradesh.

———. (2007). *Compendium of Agriculture Statistics 2006-07*. Government of Madhya Pradesh, Bhopal, Madhya Pradesh.

———. (2008). *Administrative Report 2007-08*. Department of School Education, Government of Madhya Pradesh, Bhopal, Madhya Pradesh.

———. (2008). *Administrative Report 2007-08*. Department of Technical Education and Training, Government of Madhya Pradesh, Bhopal, Madhya Pradesh.

———. (2008). *Administrative Report 2007-08*. Tourism Development Corporation, Government of Madhya Pradesh, Bhopal, Madhya Pradesh.

———. (2008). *Annual Administrative Report 2007-08*. Public Works Department, Government of Madhya Pradesh, Bhopal, Madhya Pradesh.

———. (2008). *Economic Survey 2007-08*. Directorate of Economics and Statistics Department, Government of Madhya Pradesh, Bhopal, Madhya Pradesh.

———. (2009). *Economic Survey 2008-09*. Directorate of Economics and Statistics Department, Government of Madhya Pradesh, Bhopal, Madhya Pradesh.

———. (2008). *Administrative Report 2007*. Department of Health & Family Welfare, Government of Madhya Pradesh, Bhopal, Madhya Pradesh.

———. (2009). *State Budget 2009-10*. Finance Department, Government of Madhya Pradesh, Bhopal, Madhya Pradesh.

International Institute for Population Sciences (2001). *National Family Health Survey (NFHS-3) India 1998-99*. International Institute for Population Sciences, Mumbai.

———. (2007). *National Family Health Survey (NFHS-3) India 2005-06*. International Institute for Population Sciences, Mumbai.

Kaufmann Daniel, Kraay Aart and Mastruzzi Massimo (2010). *Governance Matters VIII: Aggregate and Individual Governance Indicators 1996-2008*. World Bank.

Reserve Bank of India (2009). *State Finances A Study of Budgets of 2008-09*. Reserve Bank of India, Mumbai.